D0138895

Research
in Education

FIFTH EDITION

Research
in Education

A Conceptual Introduction

JAMES H. McMILLAN
Virginia Commonwealth University

SALLY SCHUMACHER
Virginia Commonwealth University

Longman

New York   Boston   San Francisco
London   Toronto   Sydney   Tokyo   Singapore   Madrid
Mexico City   Munich   Paris   Cape Town   Hong Kong   Montreal

Publisher: Priscilla McGeehon
Acquisitions Editor: Amy M. Cronin
Marketing Manager: Marilyn Borysek
Supplements Editor: Jennifer Ackerman
Production Manager: Joseph Vella
Project Coordination, Text Design, Electronic Page Makeup, and Art Studio:
    Thompson Steele, Inc.
Cover Design Manager: Nancy Danahy
Cover Designer: Neil Flewellyn
Senior Manufacturing Buyer: Dennis J. Para
Printer and Binder: R. R. Donnelley & Sons, Inc.—Harrisonburg
Cover Printer: Coral Graphics Services.

Library of Congress Cataloging-in-Publication Data

McMillan, James H.
    Research in education : a conceptual introduction / James H. McMillan, Sally
Schumacher.--5th ed.
        p. cm.
    Includes bibliographical references and indexes
    ISBN 0-321-08087-4
        1. Education--Research. 2. Education--Research--Evaluation. 3. Educational statistics.
    I. Schumacher, Sally. II. Title
    LB1028 .M365 2001
    370'.7'2--dc21
                                                                            00-032711

Copyright © 2001 by Addison Wesley Longman, Inc.

All rights reserved. No part of this publication may be reproduced, stored in a
retrieval system, or transmitted, in any form or by any means, electronic,
mechanical, photocopying, recording, or otherwise, without the prior written
permission of the publisher. Printed in the United States.

Please visit our website at http://www.awl.com/mcmillan

ISBN: 0-321-08087-4

2345678910—DOH—03020100

Brief Contents

Detailed Contents   vii

Preface   xix

PART I
Fundamental Principles of Educational Research   1

CHAPTER 1
Introduction to the Field of Educational Research   2

CHAPTER 2
**Modes of Inquiry, Data Collection Techniques,
and Research Reports**   29

CHAPTER 3
Research Problems: Statements, Questions, and Hypotheses   74

CHAPTER 4
Literature Review   107

CHAPTER 5
Educational Research on the Internet   145

PART II
Quantitative Research Designs and Methods   163

CHAPTER 6
Introduction to Designing Quantitative Research   164

CHAPTER 7
Descriptive Statistics   204

CHAPTER 8
Quantitative Data Collection Techniques   237

CHAPTER 9
Nonexperimental Research Designs and Surveys   282

CHAPTER 10
Experimental and Single-Subject Research Designs   319

CHAPTER 11
Inferential Statistics   358

PART III
Qualitative Research Designs and Methods   393

CHAPTER 12
Introduction to Designing Qualitative Research   394

CHAPTER 13
Qualitative Strategies   427

CHAPTER 14
Qualitative Data Analysis   460

PART IV
Analytical Research   497

CHAPTER 15
Concept Analysis and Historical Research   498

PART V
Evaluation and Policy Research
Designs and Methods   525

CHAPTER 16
Evaluation Research and Policy Analysis   526

Answers to Self-Instructional Review Exercises   560

APPENDIX A
Guidelines for Research Proposals   573

APPENDIX B
Glossary   584

APPENDIX C
**Calculations for Selected Descriptive
  and Inferential Statistics**   604

References   625
Author Index   641
Subject Index   645

Detailed Contents

Preface   xix

PART I
Fundamental Principles of Educational Research   1

CHAPTER 1
Introduction to the Field of Educational Research   2

Key Terms   3

Educational Research in the Twenty-First Century   3

Importance of Educational Research   5
Development of Knowledge to Improve Educational
   Practices   6
Research as Scientific and Disciplined Inquiry   7
Scientific Inquiry   8
Research Defined   9
Educational Research as Disciplined Inquiry   10

The Characteristics of Educational Research   11

The Research Process   13

Quantitative and Qualitative Research Approaches   14

The Functions of Research   17

Basic Research   18
Applied Research   19
Evaluation Research   20

Education as a Field of Inquiry and Practice   21

Interdisciplinary Field of Inquiry   21
Limitations of Educational Research   22
The Relevance of Educational Research   24

Summary   25

Self-Instructional Review Exercises   27

CHAPTER 2
**Modes of Inquiry, Data Collection Techniques,
and Research Reports**   **29**

  Key Terms   30

  Modes of Inquiry   30

  Quantitative Modes of Inquiry   31

  Experimental Modes of Inquiry   32
  Nonexperimental Modes of Inquiry   33

  Qualitative Modes of Inquiry   35

  Interactive Inquiry   35
  Noninteractive Inquiry   38

  Data Collection Techniques   39

  Quantitative Techniques   40
  Qualitative Techniques   41

  How to Read Research   43

  How to Read Quantitative Research: A Nonexperimental Example   43
  Guidelines for Evaluating Quantitative Research   53
  How to Read Qualitative Research: An Ethnographic Example   55
  Guidelines for Evaluating Qualitative Research   69

  Summary   70

  Self-Instructional Review Exercises   71

CHAPTER 3
**Research Problems: Statements, Questions,
and Hypotheses**   **74**

  Key Terms   75

  The Nature of Research Problems   75

  Sources of Problems   77
  Formal Problem Statements   78

  Problem Formulation in Quantitative Research   80

  The Deductive Logic of Constructs, Variables, and
     Operational Definitions   81
  Problem Formulation   84
  Specific Research Questions   86
  Research Hypotheses   88

  Problem Formulation in Qualitative Research   90

  The Inductive Logic of Qualitative Field Records,
     Descriptions and Abstractions   91
  Problem Reformulations   94
  Statements of Qualitative Research Purposes and Questions   95

  The Significance of Problem Selection   99

Standards of Adequacy for Problem Statements   101

Summary   102

Self-Instructional Review Exercises   104

CHAPTER 4
Literature Review   **107**

Key Terms   108

Functions of a Review of Related Literature   108

Purposes of a Literature Review   109
Reviewing the Literature   110

Sources for a Literature Review   112

Sources for Reviews of Secondary Literature   113
Sources for Primary Literature   115

Steps for Conducting a Computer Search   119

Abstracting and Organizing the References   130

Presentation of the Literature Review in Quantitative Research   132

Organization of the Literature Review   132
Criticism of the Literature   132

Literature Reviews in Qualitative Research   134

Preliminary Literature Review   134
Continuous Review and Criticism of the Literature   136
Alternative Presentations of Literature   136

Meta-Analysis Literature Reviews   137

The Research Process   137
A Developing Methodology   139

Standards of Adequacy   139

Summary   140

Self-Instructional Review Exercises   141

CHAPTER 5
Educational Research on the Internet   **145**

Key Terms   146

What Is the Internet?   146

Strengths and Weaknesses of the Internet for Educational Research   146

An Internet Research Strategy   148

Choosing the Right Internet Search Tool   148
Beyond Web Pages—Scholarly Communication   152
Known Locations   153

Educational Web Sites   153

Datasets   155

Evaluating and Citing Sources on the Internet   155

Evaluating Internet Resources   155
Citing Internet Resources   158

Putting It All Together: An Internet Search   158

Summary   159

Self-Instructional Review Exercises   160

PART II
Quantitative Research Designs and Methods   **163**

CHAPTER 6
Introduction to Designing Quantitative Research   **164**

Key Terms   165

The Purpose of Research Design   166

Sources of Variability   166
Design Validity   167

Subjects: Populations and Samples   169

What Is a Population?   169
Probability Sampling   170
Nonprobability Sampling   173
Sample Size   177

Data Collection Techniques   180

Test Validity   181
Test Reliability   181
Sources for Locating and Evaluating Existing
    Instruments   183
Developing Instruments   185

Procedures   186

Internal Validity of Design   186

History   186
Selection   187
Statistical Regression   188
Pretesting   189
Instrumentation   189
Subject Attrition   190
Maturation   190
Diffusion of Treatment   190

Experimenter Effects   191
Treatment Replications   191
Subject Effects   192
Statistical Conclusion   192

External Validity of Design   193

Population External Validity   193
Ecological External Validity   193

Ethical and Legal Considerations   195

Ethics of Research   196
Legal Constraints   199

Summary   200

Self-Instructional Review Exercises   201

CHAPTER 7
Descriptive Statistics   **204**

Key Terms   205

Introduction to Descriptive Statistics   205

Types of Statistics   206
Scales of Measurement   207

Graphic Portrayals of Data   210

Frequency Distribution: A Picture of a Group   210
Histograms and Bar Graphs   211
Frequency Polygons   212

Measures of Central Tendency   214

The Mean   215
The Median   216
The Mode   217
Relationships among Measures of Central Tendency   218

Measures of Variability   219

The Range   220
Standard Deviation   221
Box-and-Whisker Plot   224
Standard Scores   225

Measures of Relationship   228

Scatterplot   228
Correlation Coefficient   230

Summary   233

Self-Instructional Review Exercises   234

CHAPTER 8
Quantitative Data Collection Techniques   **237**

Key Terms   238

Fundamentals of Quantitative Measurement:
   Technical Adequacy   239

Validity   239
Reliability   244

Paper-and-Pencil Tests   250

Standardized Tests   250
Norm- and Criterion-Referenced Interpretation   251
Aptitude Tests   252
Achievement Tests   254
Alternative Assessments   254

Personality, Attitude, Value, and Interest Inventories   256

Questionnaires   257

Justification   258
Defining Objectives   258
Writing Questions and Statements   258
Types of Items   260
Item Format   265
General Format   266
Pilot Testing   267

Interview Schedules   267

Preparing the Interview   268
During the Interview   270

Observation Schedules   271

Justification   273
Defining Observational Units   274
Recording Observations   274
Training Observers   275

Unobtrusive Measures   275

Summary   277

Self-Instructional Review Exercises   278

CHAPTER 9
Nonexperimental Research Designs and Surveys   **282**

Key Terms   283

Descriptive Research   283

Relationships in Nonexperimental Research   286

Comparative Research   287

Correlational Research   291

Bivariate Correlational Studies   291
Prediction Studies   292
Interpreting Correlational Research   296

Survey Research   304

Ex Post Facto Research   310

Characteristics of *Ex Post Facto* Research   310
Conducting *Ex Post Facto* Research   311

Standards of Adequacy   313

Summary   315

Self-Instructional Review Exercises   316

CHAPTER 10
Experimental and Single-Subject Research Designs   **319**

Key Terms   320

An Introduction to Experimental Research   320

Characteristics of Experimental Research   321
Strengths and Limitations of Experimental Research   323
Planning Experimental Research   324

Internal Validity of Experiments   326

External Validity of Experiments   327

Pre-Experimental Designs   329

Notation   329
One-Group Posttest-Only Design   330
One-Group Pretest–Posttest Design   330
Nonequivalent Groups Posttest-Only   333

True Experimental Designs   335

Pretest–Posttest Control Group Design   335
Posttest-Only Control Group Design   339

Quasi-Experimental Designs   342

Nonequivalent Groups Pretest–Posttest Design   342
Time-Series Designs   344

Single-Subject Designs   348

A–B Designs   349
A–B–A Designs   350
Multiple-Baseline Designs   352

Standards of Adequacy   353

Summary   355

Self-Instructional Review Exercises   355

CHAPTER 11
Inferential Statistics   **358**

Key Terms   359

The Logic of Inferential Statistics   359

Probability   360
Error in Sampling and Measurement   360

Null Hypothesis   363

Level of Significance   364

Errors in Hypothesis Testing   365
Interpreting Level of Significance   365

Comparing Two Means: The *t*-Test   368

Comparing Two or More Means: Analysis of Variance   373

One-Way Analysis of Variance   373
Post Hoc and Planned Comparison Procedures   374
Factorial Analysis of Variance   376
Analysis of Covariance   380

Nonparametric Tests   382

Multivariate Analyses   384

Summary   389

Self-Instructional Review Exercises   390

PART III
Qualitative Research Designs and Methods   **393**

CHAPTER 12
Introduction to Designing Qualitative Research   **394**

Key Terms   395

Purposes, Research Questions, and Case Study Design   395

Research Approach and Orientation   395
Purpose and Research Questions   397
Case Study Design   398
Significance and Justification   399

Purposeful Sampling   400

Site Selection   401
Comprehensive Sampling   401
Maximum Variation Sampling   402
Network Sampling   403
Sampling by Type of Case   403
Sample Size   404

Phases of Data Collection and Analysis Strategies   405

Validity of Qualitative Designs   407

Qualitative Design Validity   407
Strategies to Enhance Validity   407

Disciplined Subjectivity in Qualitative Research   411

Interpersonal Subjectivity   411
Strategies to Enhance Reflexivity   412

Critical Reflexivity   414

Extension of Qualitative Findings   414

Issues of Authenticity and Usefulness   414
Design Components to Generate Extension of Findings   415

Research Ethics: Roles and Reciprocity   420

Ethical Dilemmas in Fieldwork   420
Research Ethics in Fieldwork   421

Standards of Adequacy   422

Summary   423

Self-Instructional Review Exercises   424

CHAPTER 13
Qualitative Strategies   **427**

Key Terms   428

Multimethod Strategies   428

Foreshadowed Problems and Reformulations   429

Entry into the Field   431

Site Selection and Mapping the Field   432
Selection of Interviewees   433
Research Role   435

Participant Observation   437

In-Depth Interviews   443

Documents and Artifact Collection   451

Types of Artifacts   451
Analysis and Interpretation of Artifact Collections   453

Field Observations and Supplementary Techniques   454

Field Observation   454
Supplementary Techniques   454

Standards of Adequacy for Qualitative Strategies   456

Summary   457

Self-Instructional Review Exercises   457

CHAPTER 14

Qualitative Data Analysis   **460**

   Key Terms   461

   Inductive Analysis: An Overview   462

   Discovery Analysis in the Field   465

    Discovery Analysis   465
    Interim Analysis   466

   Coding Topics and Categories   466

    Developing an Organizing System from Data   468
    Developing Topics as Categories   473
    Predetermined Categories   473
    Emic and Etic Categories   474

   Patterns   476

    The Process of Pattern-Seeking   476
    Techniques of Pattern-Seeking   477
    Evaluating Discrepant or Negative Evidence   478
    Ordering Categories for Patterns   479
    Plausibility of Explanations   480

   Manual and Computer Techniques in Data Management   482

    Developing a Data Filing System   482
    Manual Data Management   483
    Using Computer Programs   484

   Variations in Narrative Structure and Representation   487

    Audience and Authorial Presence   487
    Framing the Narrative and Participants' Language   488
    Narrative Structures and Visual Representations   489

   Summary   493

   Self-Instructional Review Exercises   494

PART IV

Analytical Research   **497**

CHAPTER 15

Concept Analysis and Historical Research   **498**

   Key Terms   499

   General Characteristics of Analytical Research   499

    Topics of Analysis   500
    Types of Sources   502
    The Search for Evidence   503

Analytical Generalizations and Interpretations   504
Approaches to Analytical Research   505

Analysis of Educational Concepts   506

Analysis of Educational Historial and Policy Events   507

The Topic and Problem Statement   508
Location and Criticism of Sources   508
Facts, Generalizations, and Interpretations   515

Analytical Research in Perspective   517

Credibility Standards for Historical Studies   519

Summary   521

Self-Instructional Review Exercises   522

PART V
Evaluation and Policy Research Designs and Methods   **525**

CHAPTER 16
Evaluation Research and Policy Analysis   **526**

Key Terms   527

Purposes and Definition of Evaluation Research   528

Purposes and Roles of Evaluation   528
Evaluation Research Defined   528
Formative and Summative Evaluation   529
Standards for Judging the Quality of Evaluation Research   530

Selected Approaches to Evaluation   531

Objectives-Oriented Evaluation   533
Decision-Oriented Evaluation   536
Naturalistic/Participant Evaluation   538

Mixed Methods Forms   541

Mixed Methods Types and Purposes   542
Mixed Methods Forms   543
Issues in Mixed Methods Studies   544

Policy Analysis   545

Characteristics of Policy Analysis   546
Policy Analysis Methods   547
Cost Analysis   548

**Educational Evaluation and Policy Analysis: Potential Benefits
    and Limitations**   551

Credibility of Evaluation and Policy Proposals and Reports   553

Standards for Evaluation and Policy Research Proposals   553
Credibilty of Evaluation and Policy Reports   554

Summary   555

Self-Instructional Review Exercises   555

Answers to Self-Instructional Review Exercises   **560**

APPENDIX A
Guidelines for Research Proposals   **573**

APPENDIX B
Glossary   **584**

APPENDIX C
**Calculations for Selected Descriptive
  and Inferential Statistics**   **604**

References   **625**
Author Index   **641**
Subject Index   **645**

Preface

The increasing use of research as a basis for knowledge about education and for influencing decisions, programs, and policy requires educators to possess research skills. To assist students in attaining skills in reading, conducting, and understanding research, *Research in Education,* Fifth Edition, presents a comprehensive, yet relatively nontechnical, introduction to the principles, concepts, and methods currently used in educational research.

Students enrolled in their first educational research course typically have two instructional needs. Some plan to do additional work in statistics, research design, qualitative methodologies, or evaluation. In addition to mastering the fundamental principles of research, these students also need to develop both an awareness of the breadth of educational research and a broad conceptual base for understanding more technical and advanced aspects of research. Other students, whose immediate career goals lie more in educational practice than in conducting research, need an emphasis on key research terms, practice in reading studies critically, a knowledge of the way design and procedures may affect empirical findings, and an understanding of applied and evaluation research. *Research in Education* is designed to meet both of these instructional needs.

RATIONALE

Educational research has become more diverse during the past few decades. It is now well established that both quantitative and qualitative inquiry modes contribute significantly to our knowledge of education. We have maintained our *balanced* treatment of both approaches in research. Our experience has been that by presenting both quantitative and qualitative research and changing one's "lenses" when viewing education, students gain a deeper understanding, knowledge, and appreciation for each tradition in educational research.

In this edition, we extend our dual emphasis by illustrating the diversity within qualitative research as we had previously done in quantitative research. We introduce five selected interactive research traditions whose characteristics are discussed within topics of the qualitative chapters. Qualitative inquiry now is parallel to our past treatment of quantitative research.

We choose to emphasize the distinctions between the two approaches. Students first need to understand the logic of each approach before moving to more advanced designs that integrate quantitative and qualitative methods. In the last chapter, Evaluation and Policy Research, we introduce mixed methods designs and issues. Evaluation and policy research are often more pragmatic than basic or applied research.

ORGANIZATION OF THE FIFTH EDITION

Those of you who are familiar with the fourth edition will note that we have retained the basic organization of the book with some modifications. We added a chapter for educational research on the Internet, organized qualitative research chapters in line with current conceptualizations, and treated proposal development as a brief appendix.

You will also observe that there is more revision, expansion, and reorganization of some topics with some additions of entirely new topics. These revisions were prompted by the encouragement of our colleagues to keep the book length reasonable and to continue in the direction in which we began in 1984.

We have divided the fifth edition into five parts. In Part I, "Fundamental Principles of Educational Research," we present separate, but parallel, discussions of quantitative and qualitative approaches. In Part II, "Quantitative Research Designs and Methods," and Part III, "Qualitative Research Designs and Methods," each approach is discussed more specifically. Part IV "Analytical Research," focuses on noninteractive qualitative research. Part V, "Evaluation and Policy Research Designs and Methods," presents the application of quantitative and qualitative methods in evaluation research and policy analysis.

Part I defines research as scientific and disciplined inquiry designed to produce knowledge and to improve educational practices. We briefly introduce quantitative and qualitative research and delineate the functions of basic, applied, and evaluation research. Two variations of evaluation research are action research and policy analysis. We present an overview of research designs, techniques, and formats. Selection, formulation, and statements of both quantitative and qualitative problems are discussed and illustrated. The literature review chapter includes updated techniques for computer searches and guidelines for writing literature reviews in quantitative and qualitative research. The Internet chapter introduces essential skills for using the vast resources of the World Wide Web for educational research. Specific Internet Web sites that focus on educational research are identified and reviewed.

Part II introduces quantitative designs by presenting fundamental principles of sampling, measurement, and internal and external validity. The section on sampling in Chapter 6 has been extensively revised. Descriptive statistics are presented to provide a foundation for understanding the more detailed coverage of measurement. Chapter 9 covers nonexperimental designs; it is followed by a chapter on experimental and single-subject designs. We have retained our nontechnical introduction to inferential statistics. Computational methods are reserved for Appendix C.

Part III begins with an introduction to designing qualitative research, which emphasizes research questions and significance, design, purposeful sampling and strategies to enhance validity, usefulness, reflexivity, and fieldwork ethics. Chapter 13, "Qualitative Strategies," includes entry into the field, participant-observation, in-depth interviews, and supplementary techniques. Qualitative data analysis presents coding, categorizing, and pattern-seeking strategies with a current discussion of qualitative data analysis (QDA) programs and narrative structures.

In Part IV, analytical research of the past or recent events, includes concept analysis and historical. We emphasize the search and criticism of sources.

Part V returns to a more general discussion with educational evaluation research and policy analysis. An overview of three approaches to evaluation is followed by a discussion of mixed methods purposes, forms and issues. Policy analysis presents an overview of research methods and cost analysis.

INSTRUCTIONAL AIDS

In each chapter we have retained a number of instructional aids to assist students: a concept map at the beginning of each chapter, a list of key terms, sample self- instructional test items and application problems, and criteria for evaluating studies conducted by different methodologies. We believe the instructor, rather than the book, should determine the course objectives and level of student competency. The book has been organized so that the instructor can emphasize general knowledge, certain methodologies, or specific skills, such as making an annotated bibliography on a topic, writing a critical literature review, developing a preliminary proposal with a problem statement and design, or conducting a small-scale study. We have used numerous approaches to meet different student and programmatic needs.

A major instructional aid of this book is the use of excerpts from published studies in all chapters except Chapters 1 and 16. Excerpts were chosen to represent different disciplines and to be applicable to the practices in a variety of education areas, such as administration, supervision, instruction, special education, early childhood, counseling, adult education, and programs in noneducational agencies. Most excerpts have been updated for this edition. The excerpts are especially helpful in introducing students gradually to the style and format of published articles.

SUPPLEMENTS

New for the fifth edition is a book Web site (http://www.awl.com/mcmillan) that can be accessed by students and instructors to provide additional supplemental help in understanding the content, with links to additional resources. A CD-ROM is available, containing the *Instructor's Manual* with course objectives, alternative course organizations, teaching techniques, and test items for each chapter, along with PowerPoint slides.

ACKNOWLEDGMENTS

Because this book resulted from a merging of our specializations as researchers and professors, there is no senior author; each author contributed equally to the book. Many people contributed to this endeavor. We gratefully acknowledge the support of our colleagues, mentors, and friends who are too numerous to name. We especially thank our master-degree and doctoral candidates, who challenged us to be more explicit, and the reviewers whose ideas, criticisms, and suggestions helped shape the book. The reviewers for the first edition were H. Parker Blount, Georgia State University; Alice Boberg, University of Calgary; David J. Cowden, Western Michigan University; Jane A. Goldman, University of Connecticut; Harry Hsu, University of Pittsburgh; Sylvia T. Johnson, Howard University; Stephen Olejnick, University of Florida; and Robert J. Yonker, Bowling Green State University. The reviewers for the second edition were Gerald W. Bracey, Cherry Creek Schools, Colorado; Jane A. Goldman, University of Connecticut; Harry Hsu, University of Pittsburgh; and Herman W. Meyers, University of Vermont. The reviewers for the third edition were Jane A. Goldman, University of Connecticut; Laura Goodwin, University of Colorado at Denver; James McNamara, Texas A & M University; Bud Meyers, University of Vermont; Anton Netusil, Iowa State University; Ellen Weissinger, University of Nebraska; and Wen-Ke Wang, National Changhua Normal University in Taiwan. Reviewers for the fourth edition included Laura Goodwin, University of Colorado at Denver; Judith A. Kennison, Ithaca College; Anton Netusil, Iowa State University; and Ellen Weissinger, University of Nebraska.

For the fifth edition reviewers included David Anderson, Salisbury State University; Shann Ferch, Gorzaga University; Brian Hinrichs, Illinois State University; Daniel Robinson, University of Louisville; David Tan, University of Oklahoma; James Webb, Kent State University.

Although some of the topic reorganization of this edition is relatively new, we hope that it facilitates teaching and learning. We appreciate comments and suggestions from colleagues and students as we gather material for the fifth edition. Feel free to contact either one of us by e-mail (jmcmillan@edunet.soe.vcu.edu or sschumacher@edunet.soe.vcu.edu).

We especially appreciate the continued guidance and support of our editor, Amy Cronin. We also appreciate the special assistance of Art Pomponio, Tom Kulesa, and Cori Gabbard, all from Longman, during the revision and production phases. Finally, our families, Mrs. F. X. Schumacher, Donald F. X. and Marcia Schumacher, and Janice McMillan have provided continued encouragement for this exciting, if at times difficult undertaking.

James H. McMillan
Sally Schumacher

Research
in Education

Fundamental Principles of Educational Research

What is research? Educators unfamiliar with scientific methods frequently ask this question. They may also ask: Why is research considered more useful in making decisions than experience or the advice of others? How does research influence educational practices? What kinds of studies are done in education? Is there a systematic way to understand a research article?

Chapters 1 and 2 answer these questions by providing an introduction to the field of educational research, an overview of modes of inquiry and data collection techniques, and the format of quantitative and qualitative research journal articles. This introduction will familiarize you with basic terminology and fundamental concepts of research. All research begins with a problem statement and usually involves a literature review. Chapter 3 will help you recognize, state, and evaluate a research problem. How is a problem stated in order to be useful in planning a study? What should a problem statement convey to a reader? How are problem statements evaluated? Chapter 4 shows how related literature is used to enhance a study. Why is a literature review important? What are the sources for a literature review? How does one conduct a manual or a computer search of the literature? How is a literature review evaluated? Chapter 5 introduces the Internet and shows how the vast resources of the Internet can be used in many ways to enhance educational research. How is the Internet organized? How are directories and search engines used? What are some useful Web sites?

Together, these five chapters present basic principles of research that are necessary for a student to understand when conducting, reading, and analyzing different types of research and methodologies. Subsequent parts will discuss in greater detail the designs and procedures for specific methodologies.

Introduction to the Field of Educational Research

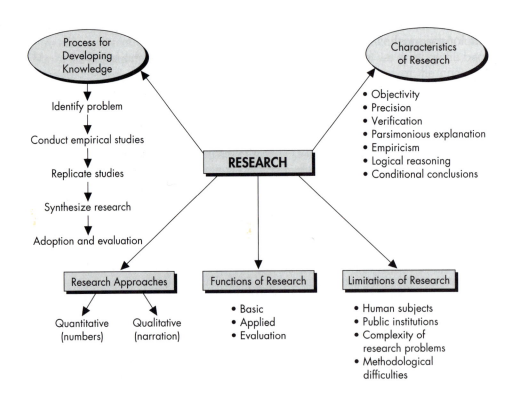

KEY TERMS

replication	empirical
research synthesis	data
science	deductive reasoning
theory	inductive reasoning
scientific inquiry	quantitative research
scientific method	qualitative research
research	generalizability
research methods	basic research
disciplined inquiry	applied research
objectivity	evaluation research
verification	action research
explanation	policy analysis

Educational research has gradually affected most of our ideas about educa-tion and the practices we use to achieve our objectives in education. Yet many excellent teachers and administrators know little about educational research and assume that research has had no effect on their daily activities. Practitioners may also assume that research cannot be useful in program devel-opment and in policy formulation.

This chapter introduces the reader to the field of educational research by describing the development of knowledge to improve educational practices. Educational research is scientific and disciplined inquiry using quantitative and qualitative approaches. Educators and others use basic, applied, and evaluation research for different purposes. Some contributions and limitations of educa-tional research are described. Most important, we introduce the language and the logic of research used in reading and conducting studies.

Educational Research in the Twenty-First Century

Some headlines in the *Education Week*, a widely read newspaper, illustrate the variety of topics recently investigated.

- "Study Links High School Courses with College Success" (6/2/99, p. 5).
- "Researchers Find Teacher Tests Short on Covering College Content" (6/2/99, p. 5).
- "More Teachers and Students Say Violence in Schools is Declining" (6/2/99, p. 8).
- "Study Highlights Benefits, Shortcomings of Magnet Programs" (6/9/99, p. 7).
- "Study: Effects of Child Care Linger in Early Grades" (6/16/99, p. 3).

- "Study Finds Mismatch Between California Standards and Assessments" (6/23/99, p. 10).
- "Finding School's Danger Zones" (6/23/99, p. 38).
- "Study: Voucher Parents Satisfied with Schools" (6/23/99, p. 11).

Recent articles in journals also illustrate the variety of topics studied.

- "Why aren't more African Americans going to college?" by M. Carnoy, *Journal of Blacks in Higher Education.*
- "Researching 'my people,' researching myself: Fragments of a reflexive tale," by L. N. Chaudhry, *Qualitative Studies in Education.*
- "The beginning science teacher: Classroom narratives of convictions and constraints," by N. Brickhous and G. M. Bodner, *Journal of Research in Science Teaching.*
- "Shared governance principals: The inner experience," by J. Blase and J. Blase, *NASSP Bulletin.*
- "Inhibitors in implementing a problem-solving approach to teaching elementary science: Case study of a teacher in change," by M. L. Martens, *Social Science and Mathematics.*
- "'Hey, those shoes are out of uniform:' African American girls in an elite high school and the importance of habitus," by E. M. Horvat and A. L. Antonio, *Anthropology & Education Quarterly.*
- "Alternatives to traditional instruction: Using games and simulations to increase student learning and motivation," by D. L. Garard, et al., *Communication Research Reports.*
- "Middle school programmatic practices and student satisfaction with school," by J. Gulino and J. S. Valentin, *NASSP Bulletin.*
- "Supply and demand of minority teachers in Texas: Problems and prospects," by S. N. Kirby, et al., *Education Evaluation and Policy Analysis.*
- "School counselor's perceptions of the usefulness of standardized tests, frequency of their use, and assessment training needs," by F. G. Giordano, et al., *The School Counselor.*
- "Impact of class size on instructional strategies and the use of time in high school mathematics and science courses," by J. K. Rice, *Educational Evaluation and Policy Analysis.*
- "We'll never turn back: Adult education and the struggle for citizenship in Mississippi's Freedom Summer," by J. R. Rachal, *American Educational Research Journal.*
- "Teachers embracing the magic: How do effective teachers make use of their intuitive knowledge?" by D. M. Maxwell, *The Journal of the Association of Teacher Educators.*
- "Research translated into practices for increasing student involvement in transition-related activities," by J. P. Lehmann, et al., *Career Development for Exceptional Individuals.*
- "'Playing between classes': America's troubles with class, race, and gender in a black high school and community," by L. H. Cousins, *Anthropology and Education.*

- "Who will lead? The top 10 factors that influence teachers moving into administration," by V. Cooley and J. Shen, *NASSP Bulletin.*
- "Stress and coping: A qualitative study of 4th and 5th graders," by J. L. Romano, *Elementary School Guidance and Counseling.*
- "The behavioral effects of variations in class size: The case of math teachers," by J. R. Betts and J. L. Shkolnik, *Educational Evaluation and Policy Analysis.*

Further, three national groups have issued reports that suggest priorities for what educational research should focus on in the twenty-first century. A well-known educational researcher with more than 30 years in the field, L. B. Resnick, stated "there is more interest in research knowledge in education than I think I can remember at any time in my career. There is almost a bandwagon now where everybody is . . . [asking] . . . 'Is it research-based? What is the research evidence?'" (Viadero, 1999, p.1).

Importance of Educational Research

Why has educational research become a valuable source of information to a number of diverse groups? We suggest some reasons for this interest and scrutiny of educational research.

First, *educators are constantly trying to understand educational processes and must make professional decisions.* These professional decisions have immediate and long-range effects on others: students, teachers, parents, and, ultimately, our communities and nation. How do educators acquire an understanding to make decisions? Most of us tend to rely on several sources, including personal experience, expert opinion, tradition, intuition, common sense, and beliefs about what is right or wrong. Each of these sources is legitimate in some situations and yet, in other situations, each source may be inadequate as the only basis for making decisions.

Second, *noneducational policy groups, such as state and federal legislatures and courts, have increasingly mandated changes in education.* How do policy groups acquire their views of education and obtain their information about schools and instruction? Most policy-makers prefer to have research-based information relevant to the specific policy issue. Many state legislatures mandate state education departments to conduct studies on state educational policies. Both federal and state departments of education also commission funded studies. Researchers are increasingly being asked to work on complex problems in highly politicized environments.

Third, *concerned public, professional, and private groups and foundations have increased their research activities.* Professional educational associations, teacher labor unions, Parent Teacher Associations, and foundations such as the National Science Foundation have conducted or commissioned studies on topics of special concern to the organization.

Fourth, *reviews of prior research have interpreted accumulated empirical evidence.* For example, studies on retention indicate that retaining a child in a grade serves few educational purposes. Other research reviews have addressed such topics as thinking aloud and reading comprehension; hypermedia and learner comprehension, control, and style; why parents become involved in their children's education; parameters of affirmative action in education; teacher efficacy; the effects of single-sex and co-educational schooling on social, emotional, and academic development; and teacher occupational stress, burnout, and health. Other research reviews identify areas of needed research.

Fifth, *educational research is readily available.* Research about educational practices is found in professional and research journals, funding agencies' published reports, books, library databases, newspapers, television, and the Internet. Although the quality of the research may vary with the specific source, educational research is very accessible.

Sixth, *many educators who are not full-time researchers read research and conduct studies.* This research assists educators in planning new programs, improving educational practices, assessing learning, and allocating resources to changing needs in their own settings.

Increasingly, reliable information has become a necessity in a complex technical society. Research provides valid information and knowledge about education in order to make informed decisions. In situations where diverse views exist, a well-done study brings a rational perspective to the discussion arenas and to policy making tables. The research process suggests principles to guide educators in wise decision making.

Because research systematically describes or measures phenomena, it is a better source of knowledge than one's own experience, beliefs, tradition, or intuition alone. Some studies are abstract and provide general information about common educational practices and policies. This type of research influences the way one thinks about education. Some studies provide detailed information about a specific practice at a particular site, such as a school, a classroom, or a program. This type of research can be used immediately in planning, developing, or improving a specific practice.

Development of Knowledge to Improve Educational Practices

The impact of educational research on schools and policymakers seeking to improve educational practices may be seen as a process (Walberg, 1986). Figure 1.1 shows the five phases of the process of developing educational knowledge to improve practices. These phases are (1) identification of research problems, (2) empirical studies, (3) replications, (4) research synthesis and reviews, and (5) practitioner adoption and evaluation.

Research problems (Phase 1) begin with an identification of valued outcomes. Practical fields, like education, are concerned with valued outcomes such as learning. Research questions and problems come from the following sources: common observation, practical wisdom, policy controversies, prior research, and new methodological techniques applied in the study of education. Researchers conduct empirical studies (Phase 2), and then they attempt research

FIGURE 1.1　Development of Knowledge to Improve Educational Practice

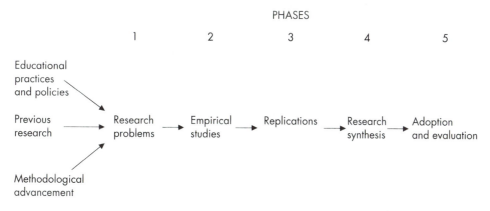

replication[1] (Phase 3) with different subjects and in a variety of settings and circumstances. Exact replication studies by subsequent investigators, although often attempted and highly desired, are rare in education. **Research synthesis** and reviews (Phase 4) systematically evaluate and statistically or narratively summarize comparable studies. Such an analysis helps to organize and make sense of the overall findings of prior research. Thus, the preponderance of evidence from many careful studies, rather than a few exact replications of the original research, builds a research-based knowledge in education. Practitioners and policymakers can reasonably accept the implications of research findings that are consistent, "that are effective considering total costs, and that are without harmful side effects" (Walberg, 1986, p. 215). Continuing local evaluation (Phase 5) is still needed.

Research as Scientific and Disciplined Inquiry

Research is a relatively new activity in the history of education, just as the concept of free public schools for all children is relatively recent in the history of humanity. In the early centuries, before reading and writing were common, individuals developed knowledge of the world around them by two means. One way was through personal experiences and observations of others' experiences. They then passed their knowledge to the next generation in the form of storytelling. They conveyed their collective wisdom as a series of detailed descriptions of individuals and events in particular situations and contexts. No one expected these stories to predict one's future actions, because actions depended on perceptions and feelings about a situation. Life was tenuous and hazardous in those times. Stories, however, provided an understanding, a repertoire of

---

[1]Boldfaced terms are key terms and are defined in the glossary.

wisdom from which a person could *extrapolate* or *extend* known experience into an unknown area so as to arrive at a useful conjecture or image of the future.

Knowledge was also developed in another manner: human activities that were measured with numbers. The early units of measure and scales had very practical purposes: to measure in a consistent, reliable manner the length of a day, the distance one walked, or the amount of space in an area. By having the same units of measure stand for the same meaning, one did not need to know the descriptive contextual details of the measured activity. A mile was a mile whether it was on flat soft sand or on rocky terrain. A foot was twelve inches whether it measured the height of a person, the length of an animal's skin, or the interior of a hut. If these measurements were reliable, one could measure segments of natural laws that caused events to be orderly and predictable.

Different kinds of knowledge are needed about education, and many types of research are conducted in education to develop this knowledge. Educational research has been called scientific inquiry and disciplined inquiry (social science). Both views are included in our definition of research and the characteristics of research in education.

Scientific Inquiry

The ultimate aim of **science** is the generation and verification of theory. A **theory** predicts and explains natural phenomena. Instead of explaining each and every separate behavior of adolescents, for example, the scientist seeks general explanations that link together different behaviors. Similarly, instead of trying to explain adolescents' methods of solving mathematical problems, the scientist seeks general explanations of all kinds of problem-solving.

A noted scholar, Fred N. Kerlinger (1986), defines *theory* as a set of interrelated constructs and propositions that specify relations among variables to explain and predict phenomena. This definition indicates three things about a general theory. First, a theory is a set of propositions consisting of defined constructs. Second, a theory states the interrelations among a set of variables. Third, a theory explains phenomena. By explaining which variables relate to which other variables and how they relate, a scientist can predict from certain variables to certain other variables. If one can predict from variable A (test anxiety, for example) to variable B (test performance), then one can deduce the possibility of "control" through intervention with, say, instruction on test-taking skills.

Much valuable social science research is not specifically theory-oriented. Instead, this research concentrates on the shorter-range goals of finding specific relations. The most useful and valued relations, however, are those that are most generalized, those that are tied to other relations of a theory. Specific relations (such as test anxiety relating to test performance), although interesting and important, are less widely applicable than if one found the relations in a "network of interrelated variables that are parts of a theory" (Kerlinger, 1986, p. 10). Modest, limited, and specific aims are good, but theory formulation and verification are better because they are more general and explanatory.

Theory generation and verification are central to scientific inquiry. A theory, to be useful in the development of scientific knowledge, must meet certain criteria. First, a theory should provide a simple explanation of the observed relations relevant to a particular problem. Second, a theory should be consistent with both the observed relations and an already established body of knowledge. A theoretical statement is the most efficient and probable account of the evidence accumulated through prior research. Third, a theory is considered a tentative explanation and should provide means for verification and revision. Fourth, a theory should stimulate further research in areas that need investigation. Careful analysis of a theory and its empirical support can suggest relations to be studied in subsequent research.

A scientist values the empirical approach for "its manner of exposing to falsification, in every conceivable way, the system to be tested" (Popper, 1959, p. 42). The purpose is not to promote false knowledge, but to select that which is most accurate and reliable by subjecting competing theories to empirical testing. Scientific inquiry thus contrasts sharply to other ways of arriving at valid and trustworthy knowledge.

Scientific inquiry is the search for knowledge by using recognized methods in data collection, analysis, and interpretation. The term *scientific* refers to an approach and is not synonymous with science. Science is a body of established knowledge, whereas "scientific" refers to the way the knowledge was generated. The scientific method is usually a sequential research process. The typical steps in the **scientific method** are

1. Define a problem.
2. State the hypothesis to be tested.
3. Collect and analyze data.
4. Interpret the results and draw conclusions about the problem.

Scientific inquiry is simply an approach to developing valid and trustworthy knowledge.

Research Defined

Briefly defined, **research** is a systematic process of collecting and logically analyzing information (data) for some purpose. This definition is general because many methods are available to investigate a problem or question. Educational research is not limited to the approaches used in the physical and natural sciences, nor should the word "research" be used indiscriminately to describe what is actually casual observation and speculation. **Research methods (sometimes called "methodology") are the ways one collects and analyzes data.** These methods have been developed for acquiring knowledge by reliable and valid procedures. Data collection may be done with measurement techniques, extensive interviews and observations, or a collection of documents.

Research methodology is systematic and purposeful. Procedures are not haphazard activities; they are planned to yield data on a particular research problem. In a broader context, methodology refers to a design whereby the researcher selects data collection and analysis procedures to investigate a specific research problem. It is possible to have a design that provides no valid or reliable data on the problem, but the deliberate choice of a design increases the likelihood that the data will yield information on the research question.

Educational Research as Disciplined Inquiry

When we speak of research in education, we refer to a family of methods that share the characteristics of disciplined inquiry. **Disciplined inquiry**, unlike opinion and belief, "is conducted and reported in such a way that the argument can be examined painstakingly. The report does not depend for its appeal on the eloquence of the writer or any surface plausibility" (Cronbach & Suppes, 1969, p. 15). "Disciplined" does not refer to ritualization and narrow forms of investigation, nor does it necessarily refer to following well-established, formal procedures. Some of the most excellent inquiry is speculative in its initial stages, trying out combinations of ideas and procedures or restlessly casting about for ideas. Cronbach and Suppes (1969, pp. 15–16) further suggest:

> *Whatever the character of a study, if it is disciplined, the investigator has anticipated the traditional questions that are pertinent. He institutes control at each step of information collection and reasoning to avoid the sources of error to which these questions refer. If the errors cannot be eliminated, he takes them into account by discussing the margin for error in his conclusions. Thus, the report of a disciplined inquiry has a texture that displays the raw materials entering the argument and the logical processes by which they were compressed and rearranged to make the conclusion credible.*

L. S. Shulman (1981) notes several reasons why educational researchers debate about appropriate research methods to study education. First, educational inquiry demands the selection of a particular set of measured observations or facts from infinite possibilities. After all, educational institutions and practices are abundant in American society. Just as in a court of law, legal adversaries may disagree profoundly about the relevance of a piece of evidence or the correctness of the verdict drawn from reasoning with the evidence, so it is in a disciplined inquiry in education. There is often a lack of consensus about the data or evidence and/or the chains of reasoning.

Second, disciplined inquiry refers not only to a systematic investigation but also to the disciplines themselves. Disciplines such as psychology, sociology, history, political science, anthropology, and others serve as sources for principles of research and for the canons of evidence (data) used by the investigator. Research principles are somewhat different in each of the disciplines.

Third, the major reason why research methodology is an exciting area in education is that education is not itself a science or a discipline. Education is a field of inquiry where the phenomena, events, people, processes, and institutions constitute the raw materials for inquiries of many kinds. The perspectives and research methods of many disciplines can be brought to bear on the questions arising from education and inherent in education.

The Characteristics of Educational Research

The following characteristics are common to many types of research conducted in education: objective, precise, verifiable, explanatory, empirical, logical and conditional. Taken together, these characteristics describe the nature of research (Table 1.1).

1. *Objectivity* Objectivity is both a procedure and a characteristic. To the lay person, objectivity means unbiased, open-minded, not subjective. As a procedure, **objectivity** refers to data collection and analysis procedures from which a reasonable interpretation can be made. Objectivity refers to the quality of the data produced by procedures which either control for bias or take into account subjectivity.

2. *Precision* Research uses a technical language. Technical research language is employed not to confuse the reader but to convey exact meanings. Expressions such as *validity* and *reliability* in measurement, *research design, random sample,* and *statistical significance* convey technical procedures. Other phrases such as *constant comparison* and *reflexivity* refer to strategies in qualitative inquiry. Precise language describes the study accurately so that the study may be replicated or extended and the results may be used correctly.

3. *Verification* To develop knowledge, a single study attempts to be designed and presented in such a manner to allow **verification**—the results can

TABLE 1.1

Characteristics of Educational Research

Characteristics	Quantitative	Qualitative
Objectivity	Explicit description of data collection and analysis procedures	Explicit description of data collection and analysis procedures
Precision	Measurement and statistics	Detailed description of phenomenon
Verification	Results replicated by others	Extension of understandings by others
Parsimonious explanation	Least complicated explanation preferred	Summary generalizations
Empiricism	Numerical data	Sources, evidence
Logical reasoning	Primarily deductive	Primarily inductive
Conditional conclusions	Statements of statistical probability	Tentative summary interpretations

be confirmed or revised in subsequent research. Results are verified in different ways, depending on the purpose of the original study. If the research tests a theory, then further testing with other groups or in other settings could confirm or revise the theory.

Most qualitative studies, however, provide descriptive interpretations about the selected situation or "case." These interpretations are extended, but not replicated, in subsequent research of other similar situations for revision. Qualitative research is not verified in the same manner as quantitative research.

The characteristic of verification or extension also refers to sharing the results of the study. Research is a social enterprise, and its information is presented to the professional community for public scrutiny. Through this process of progressive discussion, researchers develop a body of knowledge and identify new research questions.

4. *Parsimonious explanation* Research attempts to explain relationships among phenomena and to reduce the **explanation** to simple statements. The theory "frustration leads to aggression" is an explanation that predicts, and it can be tested for verification. The summary generalization "Teacher learning and curriculum change cannot be isolated from the social situations in which the curriculum is implemented" (Tobin & LaMaster, 1995) is an explanation that can be investigated further. The ultimate aim of research is thus to reduce complex realities to simple explanations.[2]

5. *Empiricism* Research is characterized by a strong empirical attitude and approach. The word *empirical* has lay and technical meanings. The lay meaning of *empirical* is that which is guided by practical experience, not by research. This pragmatic perspective states that if it works, it is right; regardless of the reasons, it must be right because it works. To the researcher, **empirical** means guided by evidence obtained from systematic research methods rather than by opinions or authorities. Generally, an empirical attitude requires a temporary suspension of personal experience and beliefs. Critical elements in research are evidence and logical interpretations based on the evidence.

To a researcher, evidence is **data**, that is, results obtained from research from which interpretations or conclusions are drawn. In a general sense, the terms *data, sources,* and *evidence* are used synonymously, meaning information obtained by research methods. Test scores and computer printouts, field notes and interview records, artifacts and historical documents are all called data.

6. *Logical reasoning* All research requires logical reasoning. Reasoning is a thinking process, using prescribed rules of logic, in which one proceeds from a general statement to the specific conclusion (deduction) or, the reverse, from specific statements to a summary generalization (induction).

In **deductive reasoning**, if the premises are correct, then the conclusion is automatically correct. Totally "new" conclusions cannot occur because the

---

[2]Qualitative researchers debate whether the explanations are propositions, assertions, naturalistic/summary generalizations, or conclusions. See Stake (1995), Lincoln & Guba (1985), and LeCompte & Preissle (1993).

premises are not challenged empirically. Deductive logic, however, can identify new relationships within existing knowledge.

In **inductive reasoning**, a researcher reaches a conclusion by observing particular cases (individuals, situations, events) and forming summary general-izations. The conclusions are thus limited to the particular cases observed. Nei-ther system of logical reasoning is totally satisfactory, but when both are integrated into a research process, they make a single study more effective.

7. *Conditional conclusions* One misconception of research is that the results are absolute and that conclusions are true beyond a shadow of a doubt. This is incorrect. As noted by a leading educational researcher, "Behavioral sci-ence and research does not offer certainty. (Neither does natural science!) It does not even offer relative certainty. All it offers is probabilistic knowledge. If A is done, then B will probably occur" (Kerlinger, 1979, p. 28). One way of defining research might be to say that it is a method of reducing uncertainty. The social sciences have more uncertainty than the physical sciences.

Drawing conditional conclusions is central to research. All scientific and applied disciplines contain restricted interpretations. Both quantitative and qualitative research statements have an implicit or explicit conditional conclu-sions. Researchers thus often write that their results "tend to indicate" or "are suggestive."

The Research Process

The research process typically involves several phases. These phases are not always sequential nor are they an orderly step-by-step process. Research is more an interactive process between the researcher and the logic of the problem, design, and interpretations. Below is a summary of the process with variations noted (Figure 1.2).

1. *Select a general problem*. The problem defines the area of education in which research will be conducted, such as instruction, administration, adult education, or special education.

2. *Review the literature on the problem*. The most important literature is prior research and theory, but other literature may be useful. In some studies, an exhaustive literature review is done before one collects data. In other stud-ies, the literature review is tentative and preliminary before data collection and then expanded as data are collected.

3. *Decide the specific research problem, question, or hypothesis*. This requires the investigator to select whether a quantitative or qualitative mode of inquiry is appropriate for the research problem. If a qualitative approach is selected, the research problem or questions are a preliminary guide and will become more specific as the research progresses.

4. *Determine the design and methodology*. The researcher decides from whom data will be collected, how the subjects are selected, and how data will be collected.

FIGURE 1.2   The Research Process

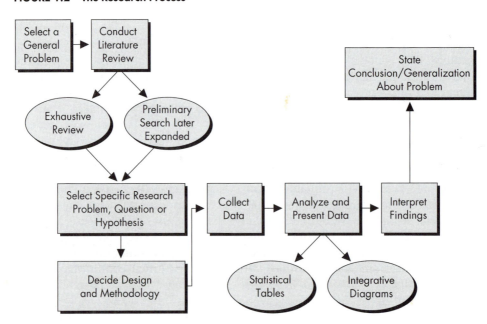

5. *Collect data.* Ethical and legal concerns regarding data collection and analysis must also be resolved.

6. *Analyze data and present the results.* Usually summary visual representations are used such as statistical tables or integrative diagrams.

7. *Interpret the findings and state conclusions or summary generalizations regarding the problem.* Decisions about the reporting format appropriate for the purpose of the study and the intended audiences or readers are made. The research process may be relatively short or it may take several years or longer.

The inquiry process is essentially one of reflective inquiry. Each decision made by the researcher is reported explicitly, often with a rationale for the choice. It is an exciting intellectual process with different skills used in the various phases.

Quantitative and Qualitative Research Approaches

The terms "quantitative" and "qualitative" are used frequently to identify different modes of inquiry or approaches to research. We introduce the terms on two levels of discourse. At one level, quantitative and qualitative[3] refer to distinc-

---

[3]Qualitative research is also called "interpretative" research, referring to the study of the immediate and local meanings of persons' social actions (Erickson, 1986).

TABLE 1.2

Quantitative and Qualitative Research Approaches

Orientation	Quantitative	Qualitative
Assumptions about the world	A single reality, i.e., measured by an instrument	Multiple realities, e.g., interviews of principal, teachers and students about a social situation
Research purpose	Establish relationships between measured variables	Understanding a social situation from participants' perspectives
Research methods and process	Procedures (sequential steps) are established before study begins	Flexible, changing strategies; design emerges as data are collected
Prototypical study (clearest example)	Experimental design to reduce error and bias	Ethnography using "disciplined subjectivity"
Researcher role	Detached with use of instrument	Prepared person becomes immersed in social situation
Importance of context	Goal of universal context-free generalizations	Goal of detailed context-bound generalizations

tions about the nature of knowledge: how one understands the world and the ultimate purpose of the research. On another level of discourse, the terms refer to research methods—how data are collected and analyzed—and the type of generalizations and representations derived from the data.

Both quantitative and qualitative research studies are conducted in education. The most obvious distinction to a reader between quantitative and qualitative research is the form of data presentation. **Quantitative research** presents statistical results represented with numbers; **qualitative research** presents data as a narration with words. The distinctions, however, go beyond the form of data presentation (Denzin & Lincoln, Eds., 1994).[4] Purists suggest that quantitative and qualitative research methods are based on different assumptions about the world, the research purpose, research methods, prototypical studies, the researcher role, and the importance of context in the study (see Table 1.2).

1. *Assumptions about the world* Quantitative research is usually based on some form of "logical positivism," which assumes there are stable, social facts with a *single reality,* separated from the feelings and beliefs of individuals. Qualitative research is based more on "constructionism", which assumes *multiple realities* are socially constructed through individual and collective perceptions or views of the same situation.

2. *Research purpose* Quantitative research seeks to establish relationships and explain *causes* of changes in measured social facts. Qualitative research is more concerned with *understanding* the social phenomenon from

---

[4]See N. K. Denzin & Y. S. Lincoln (Eds.) (1994). *Handbook of qualitative research.* Our future citations will be to the 1998 paperback reprints of the 1994 *Handbook,* called *The landscape of qualitative rsearch, Strategies of qualitative inquiry,* and *Collecting and interpreting qualitative materials.*

the participants' perspectives. This occurs through the researcher's participation to some degree in the life of those persons while in a research role.

3. *Research methods and process* In quantitative studies there is an established set of procedures and steps that guide the researcher. In qualitative studies, there is greater flexibility in both the strategies and the research process. Typically, a qualitative researcher uses an *emergent design* and revises decisions about the data collection strategies during the study. In contrast, quantitative researchers choose methods as part of a *preestablished design* before data collection.

4. *Prototypical studies* The quantitative researcher employs *experimental* or *correlational* designs to reduce error, bias, and extraneous variables. The prototypical qualitative study of ongoing events is an *ethnography,* which helps readers understand the multiple perspectives of the situation by the persons studied. Whereas quantitative research seeks to control for bias through design, qualitative research seeks to take into account subjectivity in data analysis and interpretation.

5. *Researcher role* The ideal quantitative researcher is *detached* from the study to avoid bias. Qualitative researchers become *immersed* in the situation and the phenomenon being studied. For example, qualitative researchers assume interactive social roles in which they record observations and interviews with participants in a range of contexts. Qualitative scholars emphasize the importance of data collected by a skilled, prepared *person* in contrast to an *instrument.* Qualitative research is noted for "disciplined subjectivity" (Erickson, 1973) and "reflexivity" (Mason, 1996), that is, critical self-examination of the researcher's role throughout the entire research process.[5]

6. *Importance of the context in the study* Most quantitative research attempts to establish *universal context-free generalizations.* The qualitative researcher believes that human actions are strongly influenced by the settings in which they occur. Further, as Wilson (1977) states, "those who work within this tradition [qualitative] assert that the social scientist cannot understand human behavior without understanding the framework within which the subjects interpret their thoughts, feelings, and actions" (p. 249). This framework or context is noted by the qualitative researcher during data collection and analysis. Qualitative research develops *context-bound generalizations.*

Many of these distinctions between quantitative and qualitative research are not absolute when one conducts research or reads a completed study. Experienced researchers can and do combine both quantitative and qualitative research methods in a single study in order to investigate a particular research problem (see Chapter 16). However, combining both approaches in a single study is more difficult than it may appear (Tashakkori & Teddlie, 1998). The distinctions, however, are useful devices in an introduction to research for describing and understanding research methods, a goal of this textbook. These distinctions are

---

[5]Sometimes called "insertion of self" in the text to distinguish from data collected from participants. See M. Fine (1998).

further introduced in Chapter 2 and explained in detail in Part II, Quantitative Research Designs and Methods, and Part III, Qualitative Research Designs and Methods.

The Functions of Research   AKIP

[handwritten: Avanza conocimiento y Mejora practica   ACMP]

Research advances knowledge and improves practice. This simple statement raises many questions. What does it mean to advance knowledge—that is, to develop a scientific body of knowledge? How can scientific knowledge, often characterized as impractical, improve educational practice? These questions are not new to researchers, readers, or users of research. They are perhaps more relevant and pressing today because of the increased use of research results. Some misconceptions of the functions of research have led to unwarranted criticism of research efforts and scientific knowledge.

Consider some of the possible uses of research in educational situations. Suppose a needs assessment study found that many students in a school were reading below grade level and a few students were achieving high scores on a standardized test. Should this school use its limited resources for a gifted program or for a remedial program? Suppose an administrator reads that underachieving children who received "massive rewards" scored higher in mathematics than the control group. Does this mean that the administrator should ask the teacher to use a positive reinforcement program with each underachieving child? Suppose a guidance counselor reads a scientific study verifying the theory that frustration leads to aggression. Does this theory suggest an explanation as to why a high school student who lost a part-time job, scored poorly on college entrance exams, was removed from the track team for academic ineligibility, and was sent to the office for fighting? Does this theory, verified by one study, tell his counselor what to do in this situation?

A useful way to understand how research advances knowledge and improves practice is to examine the functions or usage of different types of research. We classify the functions of research as *basic, applied,* and *evaluation.* Basic research is sometimes called *pure* or *fundamental* research. The differences between basic, applied, and evaluation research are essentially in the functions, especially the degree to which they facilitate decision making.[6]

The distinctions between basic, applied, and evaluation research are in the research topic, purpose, level of discourse and generalizability of explanations, and intended use of the study (Table 1.3). **Generalizability** is the extent to which the findings of one study can be used as knowledge about other populations and situations—that is, to predict. Understanding the functions of basic, applied, and evaluation research aids in conducting, reading, and using research. Most studies are designed and judged adequate as one type of research

---

[6]The authors recognize that the distinctions between basic, applied, and evaluation research as presented here are probably oversimplified and overemphasized for illustrative purposes.

TABLE 1.3

Functions of Types of Research

	Basic	Applied	Evaluation
Topic of Research	1. Physical, behavioral, and social sciences	1. Applied field: medicine, engineering, education	1. Practice at given site(s)
Purpose	1. To test theories, scientific laws, basic principles	1. Test the usefulness of scientific theories within a given field	1. Assess the merit of specific practice
	2. Determine empirical relationships among phenomena and analytical generalizations	2. Determine empirical relationships and analytical generalizations within a given field	2. Assess the worth of a specific practice
Level of Discourse/ Generalizability	1. Abstract, general	1. General, related to a given field	1. Concrete, specific to a particular practice
			2. Apply to specific practice at given site(s)
Intended Use	1. Add to scientific knowledge of basic laws and principles	1. Add to research-based knowledge in a given field	1. Add to research-based knowledge about a specific practice
	2. Advance further inquiry and methodology	2. Advance research and methodology in a given field	2. Advance research and methodology of a specific practice
			3. Aid in decision making at given site(s)

and less adequate as other types of research. Rarely is a single study equally adequate as all these types.

First, we need to define *field, discipline,* and *science. Field,* in this discussion, is an area of research, knowledge, and practice that is more than a single academic discipline, as is medicine or education. "Discipline" refers to a method of organizing academic knowledge. Disciplines are usually classified as the physical, behavioral and social sciences. Although scholars and scientists debate whether a particular discipline is a science, they generally agree it is the research topic that distinguishes physical, behavioral, and social sciences.

Basic Research

Basic research is research done to test theory with little or no thought of applications of the research results to practical problems. Basic research, which is concerned exclusively with knowing, explaining, and predicting natural and social phenomena, starts with a theory, a basic principle, or a generalization. A theory may or may not have empirical support. When a theory has considerable empirical support, it is called a scientific law. A scientific law such as gravity is generalizable—that is, it explains many individual cases.

Abstractness is necessary for any theory in basic research. For example, the abstract statement "reinforcement leads to retention of learning" is valuable because it covers many manifestations of reinforcement and retention. Abstractness, part of the power of science, is always remote from everyday concerns and warm human relations.

Basic research is not designed to solve social problems. The scientist is preoccupied with developing knowledge and is not required to spell out the practical implications of a study. Both goals usually cannot be done within a single study. However, basic research influences social practices only after a considerable time. This is because new knowledge challenges fixed sets of beliefs and dogma. Basic research influences indirectly the ways people think and perceive, an impact that may or may not lead to action.

Thus, the purpose of basic research is first to add to our knowledge of basic principles and scientific laws and second to advance scientific inquiry and methodology. Scientists may test organizational theories in educational settings to develop theories of educational administration; or they may test theories of learning, cognitive development, creativity, and others in instructional programs.

Applied Research

Applied research is conducted in a field of common practice and is concerned with the application and development of research-based knowledge about that practice. Medicine, engineering, social work, and education are applied fields that use scientific knowledge but are not themselves science. Applied research (as opposed to basic research) produces knowledge relevant to providing a solution (generalizable) to a *general* problem. In other words, applied studies focus on research problems common to a given field.

Applied research tests the usefulness of scientific theories and determines empirical and analytical relationships within a given field. A scientist, for example, might investigate human intelligence in many situations, including schooling. An educational researcher might determine the relationship of intelligence to achievement or analyze federal policy on the instructional use of certain books. Implications of such studies are stated in general terms and not as specific recommendations for immediate action.

Applied research, like basic research, is abstract and general, using the language common to those in the field. Many educational studies on achievement, teaching, learning, exceptional children, and the like use terms that have a special meaning within the profession. The generalizability of applied research is usually limited to the delineated field. Educational research thus focuses on knowledge about *educational* theories and practices rather than on *universal* knowledge.

Applied research adds to the research-based knowledge in the given field. The effects of applied research are felt indirectly over time. When a series of

studies is published and critiqued for a considerable time, this knowledge influences the way practitioners think and perceive a common problem. Applied
studies stimulate further research, suggest new theories of practice, and can
stimulate methodological development. An example is the development of more
appropriate statistics to study phenomena that relate to school achievement.

Evaluation Research

Evaluation research focuses on a particular practice at a given site(s). The practice may be a program, a product, or a process, but the site is crucial. **Evaluation
research** assesses the *merit* and *worth* of a particular practice in terms of the values operating at the site(s). Evaluation determines whether the practice
works—that is, does it do what is intended at the site? Evaluation also determines whether the practice is worth the costs of development, implementation,
or widespread adoption. Costs may be those of materials, space, staff development, teacher morale, and/or community support.

Formal evaluation can be conducted by a researcher in a given field or by a
practitioner at the site. Evaluation research usually requires specialized training
in several methodologies and disciplines as well as skills in interpersonal relations and communication. Many comprehensive evaluations contain both
quantitative and qualitative data from a series of studies conducted at different
implementation phases of the practice.

An evaluation study is communicated in concrete language specific to the
practice and meaningful to the participants. Because evaluation aids in immediate decision making, the findings usually have limited generalizability. Both
applied and evaluation research may study practices common to many education settings, but the evaluation focuses first on the concerns and issues related
to the practice at a given site.

Evaluation research can add to our knowledge about a specific practice and
can stimulate further research and methodological development to study practices. A series of evaluation studies on the particular practice at diverse sites,
such as Title IV (Head Start) classrooms, or on organization change processes
can add to the existing knowledge in the applied field.

Variations of Evaluation Research   Variations of evaluation research include
action research and policy studies. **Action research** involves teachers using
research methods to study classroom problems. A teacher conducts the study or
has an important role in the research process. Because the focus is on a solution
to a local problem in a local site, rigorous research control is not essential. A
more recent variation is collaborative action research (Oja & Smulyan, 1989;
Stinger, 1996). In collaborative action research, practitioners conduct the
inquiry with the help of a consultant. Collaborative action research usually
focuses on both the processes and the outcomes of a change strategy, such as a
staff development program.

Policy analysis evaluates government policies to provide policymakers
with practical recommendations. Policy research focuses on present or past

policies of schools and districts and of local, state, and federal governments. Policy analysis (1) investigates policy formulation, especially deciding which educational issues to address; (2) examines implementation of programs to carry out policies; and (3) determines policy effectiveness and/or efficiency. Many studies investigate several policy alternatives within the existing economic and political realities of the users.

To summarize, basic, applied, and evaluation research differ primarily because of different purposes, questions of investigation, and intended uses. Neither basic nor applied research is designed to produce direct solutions to a specific problem at a given site. Both types of research can influence indirectly, after a considerable time, the way scientists, researchers, and practitioners think about and perceive their respective problems. Evaluation research assesses the merit and worth of a particular practice at a given site (or sites). Unlike basic and applied research, evaluation studies provide information for immediate use as policies and practices are developed, implemented, and institutionalized.[7] All three types of research are valued for knowledge development.

Remember also, the *function* (purpose) of the research and the *quality* of the research are two separate dimensions of inquiry. Researchers use the same kinds of designs and methods for these different types of research. The criteria for determining the quality of a study is related to design and procedures. There can be poorly designed basic research and excellent applied studies. Small-scale action research and policy analysis can be well designed; large-scale evaluation studies may provide questionable information because of procedural difficulties.

Education as a Field of Inquiry and Practice

Education is an area of interdisciplinary research which provides descriptions, explanations, predictions, and evaluations of educational practices. Educational practice centers on instruction and learning and includes practices that influence instruction, such as curriculum development, innovations, administration, staff development, and policies. Research-based knowledge reflects this duality of education as a field of both inquiry and practice.

Interdisciplinary Field of Inquiry

Education, an interdisciplinary field of inquiry, has borrowed concepts and theories from psychology, sociology, anthropology, political science, economics, and other disciplines. Theories using concepts such as role, norm, status, power, authority, cost effectiveness, self-concept, human development, culture, and the like have been tested in educational practices, and new educational concepts have emerged. When economic analysis was applied to education, for

---

[7]See Cousins & Leithwood (1986) for factors that influence evaluation utilization from a review of empirical studies on this issue.

example, the concept of profit was modified to cost-benefit, implying that not all educational outcomes could be stated as monetary values.

Educational research has also borrowed methodologies developed originally in the social sciences. Psychology, especially measurement, has traditionally dominated educational research and continues to exert a strong influence. Researchers also value other methodologies such as sociological survey research, anthropological participant observation, historical research, and political analysis. Some of these approaches are applied directly to education, while other approaches are modified to investigate an educational problem. Such modifications, however, can rarely violate those disciplines from which the methods were drawn.

The use of different concepts and methodologies from various disciplines enriches and extends research-based knowledge in education. Researchers can study almost any single topic with a variety of methods. The topic of science education can, for example, be studied by a survey of curriculum needs at a site, an experiment comparing student achievement with different instruction, an observation study of classroom interaction, a historical study of science textbooks, or an ethnographic study of the instructional processes in specific science classrooms. Each of these approaches adds to our knowledge about science education.

In an interdisciplinary field, all research methodologies are valued for their potential usefulness in developing knowledge. Some researchers may feel that one methodology is better than another, but this is misleading because each methodology has its own limitations. Different methodologies and designs provide different kinds of knowledge about educational practices and in some studies provide complementary methods to investigate a research question (Jaeger, 1988).

Limitations of Educational Research

Researchers have been concerned about the quality of educational research since the 1930s (Daniel, 1999). Education is often compared to the medical field and the role of scientific studies in health policy and medical practice. Education scholars contend that the two fields and their research constraints are not analogous. Besides a number of institutional and methodological constraints, cost is a "major concern in a field [education] that is widely considered to be underfunded" (Viadero, 1999b, p. 34; see Biddle, 1996).

Knowledge acquired through research is limited by the nature of both educational practice and research. Educational research is constrained by ethical and legal considerations in conducting research on human beings, the public nature of education, the complexity of educational practices, and methodological limitations. Each of these four constraints ultimately influences our knowledge about education (Figure 1.3).

1. *Human subjects* Educational research focuses primarily on human beings. The researcher is ethically responsible for protecting the rights and wel-

FIGURE 1.3   Limitations of Educational Research

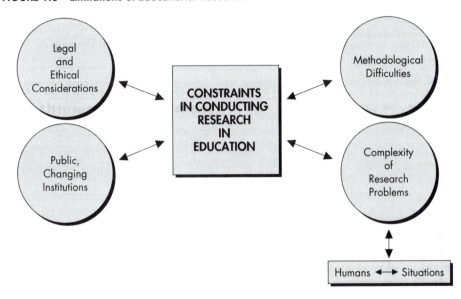

fare of the subjects while conducting a study. Researchers must protect subjects from physical and mental discomfort, harm, and danger. Most studies require informed consent from the subjects, parents, or institution, and there are laws to protect the confidentiality of the data and the privacy of the individual.[8] Researchers have followed many of these ethical principles informally for years. These principles often impose limitations on the kinds of studies that can be conducted in valid ways in education. Physical and mental discomfort of subjects may affect the length of testing periods, the replication of studies, the types of treatments, and ultimately the research questions investigated.

   2. *Public institution* Education is a public enterprise influenced by the external environment. Although many practices seem to undergo no drastic change, the institutions themselves change. An elementary school can change its entire faculty and school population every six years. The community surrounding a school can change drastically when industry or an ethnic group establishes itself in the area. Legislative mandates and judicial orders have changed the structure of schools and added or deleted programs. Because schools exist for educational purposes, not for research purposes, studies cannot unduly interfere with educational processes. Longitudinal and replication studies on a changing clientele and institution are difficult to conduct. It is often said that we do not ultimately know the effects of schooling because these effects may occur years later outside of the educational setting.

---

[8]The laws, passed in 1974, are the Family Education Rights and Privacy Act, the National Research Act, and the Privacy Act. Although there is consensus about the intent of these laws, the interpretation of the regulations varies. A researcher abides by the procedures of the agency for which data is collected.

The public nature of education also influences the kinds of research questions investigated. Most studies make the subjects and other groups aware of the research topic. Some topics may be too controversial for a conservative community or too divisive for a staff. Some studies are not conducted because of possible subsequent reactions that may be detrimental to maintaining an educational organization.

3. *Complexity of research problems* A third constraint in educational research is the complexity of the research problems. The people involved—students, teachers, administrators, parents, the collective community—are complex human beings, and they actively select the elements to which they respond. Furthermore, different individuals process ideas differently. Educational research has demonstrated the complexities of individual differences. The educational researcher thus deals simultaneously with many variables, often ambiguous ones, in a single study.

In addition, most social scientists believe that individuals cannot be studied meaningfully by ignoring the context of real life. Behavior is determined by both individual and situational characteristics, and to study individuals without regard to situations is incomplete. Thus, educational researchers must contend not only with individual differences among people but must also consider a myriad of situational elements.

4. *Methodological difficulties* A fourth constraint in educational research is methodological difficulties. Educational research measures complex human characteristics, thinking, and problem-solving skills. The measurement of achievement, intelligence, leadership styles, group interaction, or readiness skills involves conceptual definitions and issues of validity. Some educational research has been possible only as valid and reliable instruments have been developed. Other difficulties are the inappropriate use of methodology and reporting practices (Daniel, 1999; Thompson, 1996).

Qualitative research also has methodological difficulties, especially those inherent in employing multi-method strategies, addressing the reflexive research role, and making explicit data analysis techniques. Qualitative research is sometimes criticized from the conventional viewpoint for the lack of reliable and generalizable findings, but case studies provide context-bound generalizations for future research (Peshkin, 1993).

The Relevance of Educational Research

Despite these difficulties, educational research has made considerable gains in knowledge. Some areas of educational research have a long tradition of resolving methodological problems. Methodologies, employed more recently in education, are producing accumulated knowledge. The importance of educational research is demonstrated in part by the increase in the number of educational research journals and published studies in professional journals. Our society and educational leaders have used research increasingly to aid in policy and decision making.

In a technological society, valid information is necessary for educational decisions. Research-based information is more likely to define the problem carefully and to reflect the complexity of educational processes. If one plans to improve education, the first step is to have valid information and knowledge about education.

Research influences the roles of educators and their institutions in many ways. Educators are frequently unaware that they have used the results of educational research or have performed some part of a research process in their professional lives. The activities enumerated below illustrate the more common uses of educational research in educational programs and institutions. It is not an exhaustive list.

1. Acquire a new or different perspective about education or an educational process that generates ideas on how to approach a practical problem.
2. Use research results to aid in policy making and decision making and to justify decisions between alternatives.
3. Recognize a much-heralded "innovation" as similar to that which was done twenty or forty years ago.
4. Adopt programs identified from a research literature review that have a greater likelihood of producing desirable effects.
5. Determine the next step of program development from a formal local evaluation report.
6. Read published research studies critically.
7. Separate educational claims by authorities and position papers of organized groups from those based on research.
8. Identify an instructional or educational need systematically rather than intuitively.
9. Test an assumption or a hypothesis deduced from a theory or a claim to provide more reliable knowledge and implications for educational practice.
10. Intelligently interpret standardized test results of students in a program.
11. Administer standardized group or individual tests in such a manner as to increase the validity and reliability of the data.
12. Respond to requests to participate in a research project.

With a conceptual understanding of research, practitioners can read, conduct small-scale studies, and take an active role in research projects. With further training and experience, practitioners can design and conduct studies for the advancement of knowledge and the improvement of educational practice.

Summary

This chapter has discussed the development of educational knowledge, scientific and disciplined inquiry, characteristics of research in education, and the functions of basic, applied, and evaluation research, and it has described education as a field of interdisciplinary inquiry and practice. The major ideas in the chapter are summarized below.

1. Research provides a better source for knowledge and decision making than personal experience, beliefs, tradition, or intuition alone.
2. The process of developing reliable educational knowledge involves identification of research problems, empirical studies, replications, research synthesis, and practitioner adoption and evaluation.
3. Science aims at the generation and verification of theory: a set of interrelated propositions that specifies relations among variables to explain and predict phenomena.
4. A theory should provide a simple explanation of observed relations, account for accumulated evidence, provide for verification, and stimulate further research.
5. Educational research is disciplined inquiry in which different disciplines - provide different principles of research by which to collect and reason from data.
6. Research is a systematic process of collecting and logically analyzing data for some purpose.
7. Characteristics of research in education are objective, precise, verifiable, explanatory, empirical, logical, and conditional.
8. Quantitative and qualitative research, both of which are conducted in education, differ in the assumptions about the world, research purpose, research methods and process, prototypical studies, researcher role, and the importance of the context in the study.
9. Basic research tests theories and explains empirical and analytical relations in physical, behavioral, and social sciences.
10. Applied research tests the usefulness of scientific theories in an applied field and investigates relationships and analytical generalizations common to the given profession.
11. Neither basic nor applied research is designed to provide direct solutions to a specific problem at a given site. Both basic and applied research can influence indirectly, after considerable time, the way scientists, researchers, and practitioners think about and perceive their respective problems.
12. Evaluation research assesses the merit and worth of a particular practice at a given site or sites against one or more scales of values. Variations include action research and policy analysis.
13. The quality of a study depends on the design and methods, not the type of research, such as basic, applied, or evaluation.
14. Education is an interdisciplinary field of inquiry—that is, researchers borrow concepts, theories, and methodologies from disciplines and apply these to education.
15. Educational knowledge is constrained by ethical and legal considerations, the public nature of education, the complexity of educational practices, and methodological limitations.

Self-Instructional Review Exercises

Sample answers are in the back of the book.

Test Items

1. Knowledge based on systematic collection and analysis of data is
   a. a belief.
   b. research.
   c. personal experience.
   d. tradition.
2. A theory, generated and verified by research, is useful because it
   a. provides a simple explanation of observed relations.
   b. accounts for accumulated evidence.
   c. is general enough to cover many individual cases and manifestations.
   d. All of the above are correct.
3. Research
   a. is the use of systematic, explicit methods and logical reasoning that can be examined critically.
   b. is limited to measurement and statistical approaches.
   c. depends on the researcher's personal characteristics.
   d. is characterized as being unquestionable or absolute, beyond a shadow of a doubt.
4. Quantitative and qualitative research are similar in
   a. the researcher role.
   b. the prototypical studies.
   c. assumptions about the world.
   d. empirical data emphases.

Statements 5 through 7 are functions of different types of research. Match each of the functions with the type of research.

   a. Basic research
   b. Applied research
   c. Evaluation research
   d. Action research
5. tests theories and explains relations in physical, behavioral and social sciences.
6. assesses the merit and worth of a particular practice at a given site.
7. tests the usefulness of scientific theories in a given field.
8. The most general abstract knowledge is derived from
   a. evaluation research on a practice.
   b. applied research in a given field.
   c. basic research in a physical, behavioral, or social science.
   d. educational research.

9. An explanation—that is, a statement of relations of some particular though broad phenomenon—is *not*
   a. theory.
   b. a scientific law.
   c. an analytical generalization.
   d. an expert's opinion.
10. Educational research is *not* limited by
   a. ethical and legal constraints in conducting research.
   b. dependence on one methodology.
   c. methodological difficulties.
   d. complexities of practices of human subjects.

Application Problems

The following are examples of research results. How could these results be used? Choose one of the following responses and illustrate it. There is not a single correct answer. For feedback, you can compare your answers with the sample answers in the back of the book.

   a. to influence the way the reader thinks or perceives a problem
   b. to generate decision making that leads to action
   c. to generate a new research question or problem
1. A teacher reads a research study reporting that children from broken homes are more likely to exhibit deviant behavior in schools than are children from intact homes.
2. A study reports that a test measuring reading comprehension in grades 1 through 4 has been validated on students in grades 1 and 2 but not grades 3 and 4.
3. An educational historian notes that a well-known study of the organization of public schools from 1900 to 1950 stops short of the 1954 Supreme Court ruling on "separate but equal."
4. A principal reads a survey of the parents of his school pupils suggesting that these parents do not understand the new report card and grading system.
5. A curriculum developer field-tests a pilot module of a strategy to help adult basic education teachers teach a reading strategy. The results of a representative sample of the teachers in the state suggest that the module be revised to include a rationale for the strategy, a clear specification of the type of student who would benefit from the strategy, and alternative techniques to respond to student difficulties.
6. Previous research indicates that school systems have been tightly structured organizations with hierarchical authority. A professor of school administration recalls that several superintendents and principals have seen many elements of autonomous behavior by principals and teachers at the school level even though no empirical studies have reported this.

CHAPTER 2

Modes of Inquiry, Data Collection Techniques, and Research Reports

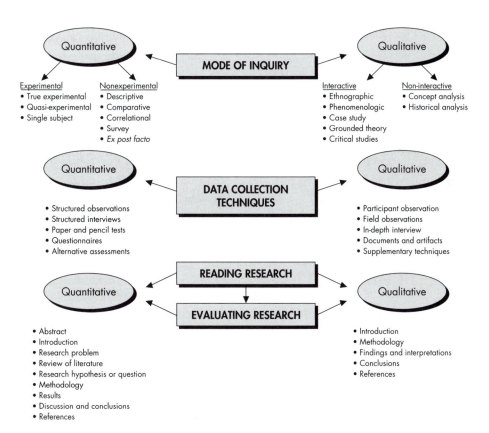

Quantitative

Experimental
• True experimental
• Quasi-experimental
• Single subject

Nonexperimental
• Descriptive
• Comparative
• Correlational
• Survey
• Ex post facto

MODE OF INQUIRY

Qualitative

Interactive
• Ethnographic
• Phenomenologic
• Case study
• Grounded theory
• Critical studies

Non-interactive
• Concept analysis
• Historical analysis

Quantitative

DATA COLLECTION TECHNIQUES

Qualitative

• Structured observations
• Structured interviews
• Paper and pencil tests
• Questionnaires
• Alternative assessments

• Participant observation
• Field observations
• In-depth interview
• Documents and artifacts
• Supplementary techniques

READING RESEARCH

EVALUATING RESEARCH

Quantitative

Qualitative

• Abstract
• Introduction
• Research problem
• Review of literature
• Research hypothesis or question
• Methodology
• Results
• Discussion and conclusions
• References

• Introduction
• Methodology
• Findings and interpretations
• Conclusions
• References

KEY TERMS

mode of inquiry
research design
experimental
true experimental
random assignment
quasi-experimental
single-subject
nonexperimental
descriptive
cormparative
correlational research
correlation
survey research
ex post facto
qualitative inquiry
ethnography
phenomenological study

case study
grounded theory
critical studies
analytical research
concept analysis
historical analysis
structured observations
structured interview
questionnaires
paper and pencil tests
alternative assessments
participant observation
field observation
in-depth interview
documents
artifacts
supplementary techniques

This chapter completes our overview of the field of educational research. Its goals are to introduce terminology related to the way research is designed and data are gathered, and to acquaint you with the organization of published research reports. We will cover each of the modes of inquiry and techniques in greater detail in later chapters. Our experience in teaching research is that it is best to become acquainted with these terms and concepts as early as possible. As they are reviewed in the context of actual studies and explained in greater detail, you will gain more complete understanding and increased retention.

Modes of Inquiry

We have examined how research can be viewed as scientific inquiry and disciplined inquiry, that approaches to research can be primarily quantitative or qualitative, and that research can be categorized as basic, applied, or evaluation. Another way to think about research is based on the *mode of inquiry* of the study. A **mode of inquiry** is a collection of eclectic research practices based on a general set of assumptions and involves methodological preferences, philosophical and ideological beliefs, research questions, and feasibility issues. Other authors may call these modes of inquiry *research traditions*.

A mode of inquiry informs the more specific *research design*. A **research design** describes the procedures for conducting the study, including when, from whom, and under what conditions the data will be obtained. In other words, design indicates how the research is set up, what happens to the subjects and what methods of data collection are used.

The purpose of a research design is to provide, within an appropriate mode of inquiry, the most valid, accurate answers possible to research questions. Since there are many types of research questions and many types of designs, it is important to match the design with the question. Research design is a very important part of an investigation, since certain limitations and cautions in interpreting the results are related to each design, and also because the research design determines how the data should be analyzed.

To help you understand modes of inquiry better we have classified them first into two major types: *quantitative* and *qualitative*. Two major categories of quantitative modes of inquiry (experimental and nonexperimental) and two categories of qualitative modes of inquiry (interactive and noninteractive) are included. We will introduce the most common designs in each of these categories, and we will discuss them in greater detail in later chapters.

Table 2.1 lists the major modes of inquiry. Each type communicates something different about the nature of the study. It should be noted that these categories are independent of the classification of research as scientific or disciplined inquiry or as basic, applied, or evaluation; that is, for example, basic research can be experimental or nonexperimental, and applied research can be single-subject or correlational.

Quantitative Modes of Inquiry

Quantitative modes of inquiry were initially developed from research in agriculture and the hard sciences. These fields of study adopted a positivist philosophy of knowing that emphasized objectivity and quantification of phenomena. As a result, the research designs maximize objectivity by using numbers, statistics, structure, and experimenter control.

TABLE 2.1

Modes of Inquiry

Quantitative		Qualitative	
Experimental	**Nonexperimental**	**Interactive**	**Noninteractive**
True experimental	Descriptive	Ethnographic	Concept analysis
Quasi-experimental	Comparative	Phenomenologic	Historical analysis
Single-subject	Correlational	Case study	
	Survey[a]	Grounded theory	
	Ex post facto	Critical studies	

[a]Surveys are classified here as a research design. Surveys are also classified as a type of data collection technique.

Experimental Modes of Inquiry

In an **experimental** mode of inquiry the researcher manipulates what the subjects will experience. In other words, the investigator has some control over what will happen to the subjects by systematically imposing or withholding specified conditions. The researcher then makes comparisons between subjects who have had and others who have not had the imposed conditions or between subjects who have experienced different conditions. Experimental modes of inquiry also have a particular purpose in mind: to investigate cause-and-effect relationships between manipulated conditions and measured outcomes.

Experimental modes of inquiry are characterized primarily by many different types of experimental research designs. Here we will describe the three most common types. Chapter 10 will present these designs, and others, in greater detail.

True Experimental The unique characteristic of a **true experimental** mode of inquiry is a design in which there is random assignment of subjects to different groups. With **random assignment**, every subject used in the study has an equal chance of being in each group. This procedure, when carried out with a large enough sample, helps ensure that there are no major differences between subjects in each group before experimental treatment begins. This enables the researcher to conclude that the results are not due to differences in the subjects before receiving each treatment or while subjects experience the treatment.

The physical and biological sciences frequently use true experimental designs because they provide the most powerful approach for determining the effect of one factor on another. In these disciplines it is also relatively easy to meet the conditions of random assignment and manipulation. If a group of farmers wants to determine which of two fertilizers causes the best growth, they can divide large plots of land into smaller sections and randomly give some sections fertilizer A and the others fertilizer B. As long as the same amount of rain and sun and the same insect problems and other factors affect each section—which would probably be the case—the farmers can determine which fertilizer is best. In the social sciences, however, and especially in education, it is often difficult to meet these conditions. True experiments are especially difficult to employ in applied research, in which researchers minimize changes to naturally occurring conditions.

Quasi-experimental A **quasi-experimental** mode of inquiry approximates the true experimental type. The purpose of the method is the same—to determine cause and effect—and there is direct manipulation of conditions. However, there is no random assignment of subjects. A common situation for implementing quasi-experimental research involves several classes or schools that can be used to determine the effect of curricular materials or teaching methods. The classes are "intact," already organized for an instructional purpose. The classes are not assigned randomly and have different teachers. It is possible, however, to give an experimental treatment to some of the classes and treat other classes as controls.

Single-Subject Research in education has been influenced heavily by a tradition in which groups of subjects, rather than individuals, are studied. The reason for studying groups is that intra-individual differences and measurement error can be assessed by using an average score for the whole group. In many situations, however, it is impossible or inconvenient to study entire groups of subjects. Furthermore, the researcher may be interested in one or two subjects, not large groups of subjects. **Single-subject** modes of inquiry offer an alternative by specifying methods that can be used with a single individual or just a few subjects and still allow reasonable cause-and-effect conclusions.

Similar to quasi-experimental research, there is direct manipulation but no random assignment. Suppose, for example, you are interested in the effectiveness of a new behavior modification program on controlling unruly behavior. There are three students in your class with whom you want to try the program, so a group design is inappropriate. Conceptualizing the problem as a single-subject design, you would first record the behavior of one of the students to assure yourself that the behavior is stable and consistent before implementing the new program. You then continue recording behavior after the new program has been implemented. If you see a change in behavior that coincides with the implementation of the new method, and other causes cannot be identified, you may be able to infer that the new program caused the change in behavior.

Nonexperimental Modes of Inquiry

Nonexperimental modes of inquiry describe something that has occurred or examine relationships between things without any direct manipulation of conditions that are experienced. There are five types of nonexperimental modes of inquiry: descriptive, comparative, correlational, survey, and *ex post facto*.

Descriptive Research using a **descriptive** mode of inquiry simply describes an existing phenomenon by using numbers to characterize individuals or a group. It assesses the nature of existing conditions. The purpose of most descriptive research is limited to characterizing something as it is. The following questions could be answered by means of descriptive designs: How many times during a school day does Ms. Jones use negative reinforcement with her pupils? What are the pupils' attitudes toward school discipline? What is the self-concept of the school's fourth graders? What is the reading achievement level of students in the school?

Comparative In a **comparative** mode of inquiry the researcher investigates whether there are differences between two or more groups on the phenomena being studied. Like descriptive inquiry modes, there is no manipulation or direct control of conditions experienced, but the comparative approach takes descriptive studies a step further. For example, rather than simply describing pupil attitudes toward discipline, a comparative study could investigate whether attitudes differed by grade level or gender. Another example would be to compare the grades of athletes and nonathletes. Often comparative modes of inquiry are used to study relationships between different phenomena, for example, the relationship between participation in athletics and grade point average.

Correlational **Correlational research** is concerned with assessing relationships between two or more phenomena. This type of study usually involves a statistical measure of the degree of relationship, called **correlation**. The relationship measured is a statement about the degree of association between the variables of interest. A *positive correlation* means that high values of one variable are associated with high values of a second variable. The relationship between height and weight, between IQ scores and achievement test scores, and between self-concept and grades are examples of positive correlation. A *negative correlation* or relationship means that high values of one variable are associated with low values of a second variable. Examples of negative correlations include those between exercise and heart failure, between successful test performance and feelings of incompetence, and between absence from school and school achievement.

Survey In **survey research** the investigator selects a sample of subjects and administers a questionnaire or conducts interviews to collect data. Surveys are used frequently in educational research to describe attitudes, beliefs, opinions, and other types of information. Usually the research is designed so that information about a large number of people (the population) can be inferred from the responses obtained from a smaller group of subjects (the sample). Surveys are used for a wide variety of purposes. They can describe the frequency of demographic characteristics or traits held, explore relationships between different factors, or delineate the reasons for particular practices. A specified sequence of steps is followed in survey research, as detailed in Chapter 9.

Ex Post Facto An *ex post facto* mode of inquiry is used to explore possible causal relationships among variables that cannot be manipulated by the researcher. The investigator designs the study to compare two or more samples that are comparable except for a specified factor. The possible causes are studied after they have occurred. Rather than manipulating what *will* happen to subjects, as in experimental designs, the research focuses on what has happened differently for comparable groups of subjects, then explores whether the subjects in each group are different in some way. For example, an important question concerning day care for children is the relative effect the type of day care program may have on school readiness. Some day care programs are more "academic" than others. Since it would be very difficult to manipulate experimentally the type of day care a child attends, an *ex post facto* mode of inquiry would be appropriate. The investigator would identify two groups of children who have similar backgrounds but who have attended different types of day care. The subjects would be given a school readiness test to see whether those who attended a highly academically oriented day care facility differ from children who attended a less academically oriented day care facility.

Qualitative Modes of Inquiry

Qualitative modes of inquiry can be classified as interactive or noninteractive. These qualitative modes of inquiry are important because each has a prominent history in one of the disciplines and has generated journals, books, and distinctive methodologies that characterize its approach. As a group, these qualitative modes of inquiry are reported frequently in journals; espouse rigorous and systematic methodologies; and illustrate diversity in research design, researcher role, and data gathering techniques. Other approaches and variants within these selected approaches exist but their discussion is beyond the scope of this book.[1]

Interactive Inquiry

Interactive **qualitative inquiry** is an in-depth study using face-to-face techniques to collect data from people in their natural settings. The researcher interprets phenomena in terms of the meanings people bring to them. Qualitative researchers build a complex, holistic picture with detailed descriptions of informants' perspectives. Some qualitative researchers openly discuss the values that shape the narrative. Interactive researchers describe the context of the study, illustrate different perspectives of the phenomena, and continually revise questions from their experience in the field.

The five interactive modes of inquiry in Table 2.1 are ethnographic (anthropology and sociology), phenomenologic (psychology and philosophy), case study (human and social science and applied areas such as evaluation), grounded theory (sociology), and critical studies (several disciplines). These inquiry modes can be organized by (a) a focus on *individual lived experience* as seen in phenomenology, case study, grounded theory, and some critical studies and (b) a focus on *society and culture* as defined by ethnography and some critical studies. Further, each inquiry mode is supported by either traditional or more contemporary critical and postmodern assumptions. "Traditional" qualitative research assumes (a) society is an orderly structure and (b) the researcher learns from participants by maintaining a relatively neutral stance.

Ethnography An **ethnography** is a description and interpretation of a cultural or social group or system. Although there is considerable disagreement about the meaning of the term "culture," the focus is on learned patterns of actions,

---

[1]For example, see N. Denzin & Y. Lincoln (Eds.) (2000) *Handbook of Qualitative Research* and others. We treat constructivism and naturalistic inquiry as foundational to most interactive qualitative research.

language, beliefs, rituals, and ways of life. As a process, ethnography involves prolonged field work, typically employing observation and casual interviews with participants of a shared group activity and collecting group artifacts. A documentary style is employed, focusing on the mundane details of everyday life and revealing the observation skills of the inquirer. The informants' point of view is painstakingly produced through extensive, closely edited quotations to convey that what is presented is not the fieldworker's view but authentic and representative remarks of the participants. The final product is a comprehensive, holistic narrative description and interpretation which integrates all aspects of group life and illustrates its complexity.

There are several variants of ethnography. Whereas many anthropologists employ participant observation in ethnographic studies of a culture, educational researchers utilize the technique to produce micro-ethnographies (Erickson, 1973; LeCompte & Preissle, 1993; Wolcott, 1995). A micro-ethnography is a participant observation study of one aspect of a cultural component (education) such as participants in an educational activity, i.e. an urban classroom or principals in an innovative program. If the study is an exhaustive examination of a very specific activity, or of a very small unit in an organization or of everyday practical reasoning and ordinary conversation, it is an ethnometholology (Schwandt, 1997).

Phenomenology Phenomenology is both a philosophy of science and a mode of inquiry. A **phenomenological study** describes the meanings of a lived experience. The researcher "brackets" or puts aside all prejudgments and collects data on how individuals make sense out of a particular experience or situation. The aim of phenomenology is to transform lived experience into a description of "its essence—in such a way that the effect of the text is at once a reflexive reliving and reflective appropriation of something meaningful" (Van Manen, 1990, p.36). The typical technique is long interviews between the informants and researcher directed toward understanding informants' perspectives on their everyday lived experience with the phenomenon (Moustakas, 1994; Seidman, 1998). The study enables readers to feel that they understand more fully the concept relating to the particular experience such as acquiring a physical handicap as young adult or a child living through his parents' separation and divorce.

Case Study Whereas some classify "the case" as an object of study (Stake, 1995), and others consider it a methodology (Yin, 1994), a **case study** examines a "bounded system" or a case over time in detail, employing multiple sources of data found in the setting. The case may be a program, an event, an activity, or a set of individuals bounded in time and place. The researcher defines the case and its boundary. Cases are not chosen for representativeness; a case can be selected because of its uniqueness or the case may be used to illustrate an issue (Stake, 1995). The focus may be one entity (within-site study) or several entities (multi-site study). However, the more cases of individual sites added, the less depth of analysis of any single site. The study provides a detailed description of the case, an analysis of the themes or issues, and the researcher's interpretations or assertions about the case. These interpretations may be called "lessons learned" (Guba and Lincoln, 1989).

Grounded Theory Although the hallmark of qualitative research is detailed description and analysis of phenomena, **grounded theory** goes beyond the description to develop "dense" (detailed) concepts or conditional propositional statements that relate to a particular phenomenon (Glaser & Strauss, 1967; Strauss & Corbin, 1998). The term "grounded theory" is often used in a non-specific way to refer to any approach to forming theoretical ideas that somehow begins with data. But grounded theory methodology is a rigorous set of procedures for producing substantive theory. Using a constant comparative method, the data analysis simultaneously employs techniques of induction, deduction, and verification. The researcher collects primarily interview data, making multiple visits to the field. The initial data collection is done to gain a variety of perspectives on the phenomena; then, the inquirer uses constant comparison to analyze across categories of information. Data are collected until the categories of information are "saturated." At this point, the researcher selects the central phenomenon, develops a "story line," and suggests a conditional matrix that specifies the social and historical conditions and consequences influencing the phenomenon.

Some researchers consider grounded theory to be a form of modified analytical induction in that the initial theory is developed early as a "working hypothesis" and then "tested" out on different cases to develop the properties forming the conditional propositions. For each return visit, the data collection is more limited to the particular dimension of the category of information. Modified analytical induction is often done in multi-site studies employing participant observation (Bodgan & Biklen, 1998).

Critical Studies This mode of inquiry draws from critical theory, feminist theory, race theory, and postmodern perspectives, which assume that knowledge is subjective.[2] These researchers also view society as essentially structured by class and status, as well as by race, ethnicity, gender, and sexual orientation. Thus, a patriarchal society maintains the oppression of marginalized groups (Lather, 1991). Critical researchers are suspicious of most modes of inquiry for ignoring the power relations implicit in the data collection techniques and for excluding other ways of knowing (Marshall & Rossman, 1999). Whereas feminist and ethnic research focus on gender and race as the "problem" of a study, postmodernism and critical theory tend to focus more on society and social institutions. Much of the critique of traditional qualitative research is located in narrative analysis, action research, critical ethnography, participatory action research, and feminist research.

---

[2]Critical studies, as a group, employ a variety of methodologies including quantitative and interactive and noninteractive qualitative modes of inquiry (Harding, 1987).

Critical studies begin with a commitment to expose social manipulation and oppression and to change oppressive social structures. They often have explicit emancipatory goals either through sustained critique or through direct advocacy and action taken by the researcher or the participants. A researcher may identify his or her gender, race, age, ethnicity, social status, and political positions to inform the reader that the interpretations are not value-free (Carspecken, 1996; Rossman & Rallis, 1998).

Two clarifications are necessary. First, these modes of inquiry are not necessarily discrete modes even though each has distinguishable methodological implications. The inquiry modes differ in their objectives, the importance of theory, the originating discipline, primary data collection technique, researcher role, and the narrative format of the report. Because some overlap exists among these selected four "traditional" qualitative traditions, the predominate mode of inquiry for the study is stated. For example, both ethnography of a cultural system and case study of a bounded system typically investigate systems. However, an ethnography (except micro-ethnography) examines a cultural system; a case study focuses on smaller units such as an event or activity and explores a range of topics not limited to cultural behavior, rituals, or beliefs (Creswell, 1998). Thus a study of a single classroom (micro-ethnography) might be approached as a case study or as an ethnographic study within one component of a culture (education). An entirely different examination of a single classroom would be a critical study.

Second, we use the term *case study design* to refer to a single "case," studied in depth, in contrast to experimental and nonexperimental designs in which groups are compared through statistical analysis. In qualitative design, a "case" is the single entity or phenomenon examined in depth. This could be an individual, one group of students, a school, a program, or a concept. Case study design is applicable to all traditional and nontraditional interactive and noninteractive qualitative research. Case study *design*, then, is not the same as case study *inquiry mode*.

Noninteractive Inquiry

Noninteractive modes of inquiry, termed **analytical research**, investigate historical concepts and events through an analysis of documents. The researcher identifies, studies, and then synthesizes the data to provide an understanding of the concept or a past event that may or may not have been directly observable. Authenticated documents are the major source of data. The researcher interprets "facts" to provide explanations of the past and clarifies the collective educational meanings that may be underlying current practices and issues.

Examples of analytical research include concept analysis and historical analysis. **Concept analysis** is the study of educational concepts such as "cooperative learning," "ability grouping," or "leadership" to describe the different meanings and appropriate use of the concept. **Historical analysis** involves a systematic collection and criticism of documents that describe past events. Educational historians study past educational programs, practices, institutions, persons, policies, and movements. These are usually interpreted in the context of historical economic, social, military, technological, and political trends. The analysis examines causes and the subsequent events, often relating the past to current events.

Data Collection Techniques

Another way to classify research is to examine the technique used in the study to collect the data. That is, how did the researcher obtain the data? Like mode of inquiry, the techniques can be classified as either quantitative or qualitative, as indicated in Table 2.2. One fundamental difference is that quantitative approaches use numbers to describe phenomena, while qualitative techniques use narrative descriptions. (Some studies that use qualitative data collection techniques, however, use numbers to summarize the findings.) While most of the techniques can be used with any modes of inquiry, more specific research design is closely related to technique. Virtually all experimental designs use quantitative techniques, and most case study designs use qualitative techniques. Below you will find an introduction to each technique. More detail is given in later chapters.

TABLE 2.2

Techniques to Collect Data

	Quantitative	**Qualitative**
Types	Structured observations Standardized interviews Paper and pencil tests Questionnaires Alternative assessments	Participant observation Field observations In-depth interview Documents and artifacts Supplementary techniques
Characteristics	Instrument used in data collection Data appear as numbers A *priori* decision in data presentation Data take one form—response as determined by instrument Data are tabulated and described statistically Meaning is derived from statistical procedures employed	Data collected without an instrument Data appear as words Not *a priori* decision on data presentation; depends on data collected Data may take many forms—field notes, documents, interview notes, tape recordings, artifacts Tabulation limited to help identify patterns; used to support qualitative meanings Meaning is derived from qualitative strategies employed

Quantitative Techniques

Quantitative research techniques emphasize *a priori* categories to collect data in the form of numbers. The goal is to provide statistical descriptions, relationships, and explanations. Quantitative techniques are used with experimental, descriptive, and correlational designs as a way to summarize a large number of observations and to indicate numerically the amount of error in collecting and reporting the data.

Structured Observations All research requires some kind of observation about people, things, or processes. What we are concerned with in **structured observations**, however, is a particular kind of data-gathering, one in which the researcher directly observes, visually and auditorily, some phenomenon, and then systematically records the resulting observations. The observer has predetermined specific categories of behavior that will be recorded; what he or she will observe is determined before the research is conducted. Usually, behavioral units are identified and a systematic process of recording is used to check or count specific behaviors. For example, the observer may record how many times students ask questions, the type of question asked, or how long the teacher took to respond to each question.

Structured Interviews In an interview there is direct verbal interaction between the interviewer and the subject. A **structured interview** is an oral, in-person administration of a standard set of questions that is prepared in advance. The questions are usually selected-response or semistructured. When asked a selected-response question, the subject selects the response from alternatives provided by the interviewer. Semistructured questions are phrased to allow unique responses for each subject. Regardless of the type of question, the responses are coded, tabulated, and summarized numerically.

Questionnaires Questionnaires encompass a variety of instruments in which the subject responds to written questions to elicit reactions, beliefs, and attitudes. The researcher chooses or constructs a set of appropriate questions and asks the subjects to answer them, usually in a form that asks the subject to check the response (e.g., yes, no, maybe). This is a very common technique for collecting data in educational research, and most survey research uses questionnaires. Questionnaires are not necessarily easier than other techniques and should be employed carefully.

Paper and Pencil Tests In a **paper and pencil test** the respondent is asked a series of questions that are objectively scored. Typical items formats include multiple-choice, matching, true-false, and completion. The resulting test scores are used as data. Because these types of tests are well established and have strong technical qualities, they are often used in educational research as a measure of student performance. However, as we will see in later chapters, caution is needed when using these types of measures.

Alternative Assessment Alternative assessments are measures of performance that require demonstration of a skill or proficiency by having the respondent create, produce, or do something. One type of alternative assessment is performance-based, such as a making a speech, writing a paper, making a musical presentation, demonstrations, athletic performance, and other projects. Portfolios constitute another type of alternative assessment. Many alternative assessments are *authentic,* reflecting real-life problems and contexts. While alternative assessments have become popular in recent years, as a technique to use in research these approaches are fraught with technical difficulties. This is primarily because of the subjective nature of the scoring of the performance or product.

Qualitative Techniques

As indicated earlier, qualitative techniques collect data primarily in the form of words rather than numbers. The study provides a detailed narrative description, analysis, and interpretation of phenomena. Most interactive qualitative researchers employ several techniques in a study but usually select one as the central method. To some extent participant observation, observation, and interviewing are a part of all interactive research. Other strategies are used to supplement or to increase the credibility of the findings. Noninteractive research primarily depends on documents. Qualitative techniques provide verbal descriptions to portray the richness and complexity of events that occur in natural settings from the participants' perspectives. Once collected, the data are analyzed inductively to generate findings.

Participant Observation Participant observation is an interactive technique of "participating" to some degree in naturally occurring situations over an extended time and writing extensive field notes to describe what occurs. The researcher does not collect data to answer a specific hypothesis; rather the explanations are inductively derived from the field notes. Since the context of the observations is important, the researcher is careful to document his or her role in the situation and what effect that may have on the findings. Most field workers remain a respectful distance from the informants—cultivating empathy but not sympathy, rapport but not friendship, familiarity but never "going native" (Schwandt, 1997). However, other researchers, because they spend a considerable time at the setting, also learn from their own experience in the setting. These personal reflections are integrated into the emerging analysis of the social group of interest. Collaborative and participatory research introduce the notion of active participation by the researcher and sharing the research role with the participants. In each variation of participant observation, the research role is established at the beginning of the study and then monitored with documentation.

Field Observation A technique fundamental to most qualitative research is field observation—direct, eyewitness accounts of everyday social action and settings taking the form of field notes. Qualitative **field observations** are detailed descriptions of events, people, actions, and objects in settings. Field observation is used in interactive data collection, such as participant observation and in-depth interviewing. In the former, the researcher relies on careful observation as he or she initially explores several areas of interest at a site, selecting those to study in detail, and searching for patterns of behavior and relationships. In the later, the researcher notes the nonverbal body language and facial expressions of the interviewee to help interpret the verbal data.

In-Depth Interviews An **in-depth interview** is often characterized as a conversation with a goal. The researcher may use a general interview guide or protocol but not a set of specific questions worded precisely the same for every interview. Rather, there are a few general questions, with considerable latitude to pursue a wide range of topics. The interviewee can shape the content of the interview by focusing on topics of importance or interest. In fact, the researcher usually encourages the person to talk in detail about areas of interest. In-depth interviews typically last an hour or more. Often the researcher will tape the interviews and transcribe the tapes to analyze common themes from descriptions of experiences.

Documents and Artifacts **Documents** are records of past events that are written or printed; they may be anecdotal notes, letters, diaries, and documents. Official documents include internal papers, communications to various publics, student and personnel files, program descriptions, and institutional statistical data. In interactive data collection techniques, the researcher finds these documents at the site or a participant offers to share these personal records with researcher. Documents may also provide background information on the topic.

Documents are the most important data source in concept analysis and historical studies. Documents are usually catalogued and preserved in archives, manuscript collection repositories, or libraries. These collections are scattered throughout the United States. Because collections house original documents, the papers are not allowed to leave the archive. The documents must first be located by the historian, who uses indexes to archives, and then permission must be obtained to work with the original texts. Rigorous techniques of criticism are applied to documents to ascertain authenticity. Other documents may be in private collections saved by individuals or family members; these must be located and the same methodological procedures applied.

Artifacts are material objects and symbols of a current or past event, group, person, or organization. These objects are tangible entities that reveal social processes, meanings, and values. Examples of symbols are logos and mascots of schools and teams; some examples of objects are diplomas, award plaques, and student products such as art work, papers, posters. The qualitative researcher is less interested in the artifact itself and more interested in the meanings assigned to the artifact and the social processes that produced the artifact.

Supplementary Techniques Qualitative researchers employ a variety of supplementary techniques to provide credible findings. **Supplementary techniques** are approaches selected to help interpret, elaborate, or corroborate data obtained from participant observation, in-depth interview, documents, and artifacts. Although each of these techniques is a completely separate method, they are often incorporated into qualitative research. Examples of supplementary techniques include visual techniques, film ethnography, and the use of videos, films, and photographs to capture the daily life of a group under study. Kinesics is the study of body movements and nonverbal communication. The analysis of interpersonal symbolic use of space is proxemics. A focus group is a group interview of eight to fifteen selected individuals who share certain characteristics relevant to the study's purpose. Surveys may be a participant-constructed instrument or the researcher's confirmation survey of the emerging findings.

How to Read Research

Research is reported in a variety of ways, most commonly as a published article or as a paper delivered at a conference. The purpose of the report is to indicate clearly what the researcher has done, why it was done, and what it means. To do this effectively, researchers use a more or less standard format. This format is similar to the process of conceptualizing and conducting the research. Since the process of doing research is different for quantitative compared with qualitative approaches, there are differences in the reporting formats used for each approach. We will review the basic formats for reporting research for each approach separately.

In reading research it is important to judge the overall credibility of the study. This judgment is based on an evaluation of each of the major sections of the report. Each part of the report contributes to the overall credibility of the study. Thus, following a description of the format of each type of research we introduce guidelines that are useful in evaluating each section of the report.

How to Read Quantitative Research: A Nonexperimental Example

Although there is no universally accepted format for reporting quantitative research, most studies adhere to the sequence of scientific inquiry. There is variation in the terms used, but the components indicated below are included in most studies:

1. Abstract
2. Introduction

3. Statement of research problem
4. Review of literature
5. Statement of research hypotheses or questions
6. Methodology
   a. subjects
   b. instruments
   c. procedure
7. Results
8. Discussion, implications, conclusions
9. References

In writing a research report, the writer begins with the introduction and continues sequentially to the conclusion. In planning to conduct research, the researchers begin by formulating a research problem. Excerpt 2.1 illustrates the above components in a quantitative research article.

Abstract The *abstract* is a paragraph that summarizes the journal article. It follows the authors' names and is usually italicized or printed in type that is smaller than the type in the article itself. Most abstracts contain a statement of the purpose of the study, a brief description of the subjects and what they did during the study, and a summary of important results. The abstract is useful because it provides a quick overview of the research, and after studying it, the reader usually will know whether to read the entire article.

Introduction The introduction is typically limited to the first paragraph or two of the article. The purpose of the introduction is to put the study in context. This is often accomplished by quoting previous research in the general topic, citing leading researchers in the area, or developing the historical context of the study. The introduction acts as a lead-in to a statement of the more specific purpose of the study. In Excerpt 2.1 the introduction includes the first and second paragraphs.

Research Problem The first step in planning a quantitative study is to formulate a research problem. The *research problem* is a clear and succinct statement that indicates the purpose of the study. Researchers begin with a general idea of what they intend to study, such as the relationship of self-concept to achievement, and then they refine this general goal to a concise sentence that indicates more specifically what is being investigated. For example, what is the relationship between fourth graders' self-concept of ability in mathematics and their achievement in math as indicated by standardized test scores?

The statement of the research problem can be found in one of several locations in articles. It can be the last sentence of the introduction, or it may follow the review of literature and come just before the methods section. In our illustrative article, the problem is stated in the first paragraph.

EXCERPT 2.1

EXAMPLE OF A QUANTITATIVE RESEARCH REPORT

THE RELATIONSHIP BETWEEN LOCUS OF CONTROL AND ACADEMIC LEVEL AND SEX OF SECONDARY SCHOOL STUDENTS

Marvin W. Boss, *University of Ottawa*
and Maurice C. Taylor, *Algonquin College*

The relationships among locus of control, academic program, and sex of grade 9 secondary school students were investigated. Two hundred sixty-seven high school students from advanced, general, and basic level programs were administered the modified forms of the Nowicki-Strickland Locus of Control Scale for Children and the Intellectual Achievement Responsibility Questionnaire. As hypothesized, students in the advanced level program were more internally controlled than either general or basic level students. As well, advanced level students were more internally responsible for their intellectual–academic failures than general level students. Sex differences as they relate to specific expectancies in intellectual achievement situations are also discussed.

The purpose of this study was to determine whether academic level and sex of grade 9 secondary school students are related to generalized expectancies for locus of control of reinforcements. In addition the relationship of academic level and sex to specific expectancies in intellectual achievement situations was explored.

Locus of control is defined (Rotter, 1966) as a generalized expectancy of the extent to which a person perceives that events in one's life are consequences of one's behavior. People, described as "internal," believe that they exercise more control over events and outcomes affecting them. In contrast, "externals" tend to believe that they have little control over what happens to them. These expectancies are perceived to be the result of many past experiences.

Lefcourt (1980) suggests that some expectancies are very general, relating to most life events; other expectancies are quite specific and are related to very specific life events. Most instruments used to measure locus of control provide measures of a generalized expectancy. The Intellectual Achievement Responsibility Questionnaire (IARQ) (Crandall, Katkovsky, & Crandall, 1965) does provide a measure of specific expectancies of responsibility for academic success and failure. The scale gives a score for internalized success (I+) and one for internalized failure (I−).

In a literature review of the relationship between locus of control (generalized and specific expectancies) and achievement, Bar-Tal and Bar-Zohar (1977) stated that 31 of 36 studies reviewed indicated a significant relationship between locus of control and academic achievement with internals having higher achievement than externals. McGhee and Crandall (1968) investigated specific expectancies and reported I+ as a predictor of male achievement and I− as a predictor of female achievement.

Nowicki and Strickland (1973) found that particularly for males an internal score on the Nowicki-Strickland Scale is related to academic competence and to social maturity and appears to be a correlate of independent, striving, and self-motivated behaviors.

Dweck and Licht (1980) maintain that girls and boys have different characteristic ways of coping with positive and negative outcomes. The two sexes interpret their successes and failures differently and have different views of the implications for their abilities. They differ in the persistence of their attempts to solve a difficult problem, in the quality of their performance after failure, and in their task choices after they encounter difficulty.

Lochel (1983) reviewed sex differences in achievement. She suggests that females are more inclined to take responsibility for failure. She views females as lacking in confidence in their abilities and not being prepared to cope with failure.

As Parsons (1981) has recently pointed out, the conclusion that males tend to attribute their failures to external or unstable causes while females tend to attribute their failures to internal causes appears to be an oversimplification. In a review of the attributional literature she cites several examples. Using the IARQ, Dweck and Reppucci (1973) reported no sex difference in general internality for failure but found boys to be slightly more likely to attribute their failures to lack of effort than girls. In contrast, Crandall et al. (1965) found girls to be more internal for their failures; Beck (1977) found no sex differences in either internality or lack of effort attributions; Diener and Dweck (1978) did not report a significant sex difference on either lack of effort or internality for failure; and Nicholls (1975) found no main effect for sex difference in attributions of failure due to lack of effort. Similarly, inconsistent patterns emerge for the measures of attributions of failure to external causes (Dweck and Reppucci, 1973; Nicholls, 1975; Parsons, 1978).

Ontario secondary school students take courses at one of three levels: advanced, general, and basic. Advanced level students are expected to continue their education at a university. General level students are prepared to continue education by taking technical or professional courses related to specific occupations or they may not continue studies. Basic level students follow vocational courses at high school and are generally not considered to be capable of succeeding at the general or advanced levels.

Students enrolling in basic level vocational programs are directed to these programs by elementary school staff. Typically, these students have a record of low achievement and many have specific learning problems. They have likely received special help throughout their elementary school experience.

Students with the advice of both elementary and secondary school staff choose to study either general or advanced level academic courses (biology, chemistry, English, geography, history, mathematics, physics). In making this choice past achievement is more likely a greater determinant than aptitude. However, both achievement and aptitude would undoubtedly be lower for general level students.

Because of these past experiences which cause students to select or to be counseled into specific levels, it was hypothesized that advanced level students would be most internal and basic level students least internal for both generalized and specific locus of control measures.

On the basis of the literature reviewed, it was also hypothesized that females would take more responsibility for failure than males.

Method

Research Subjects The research subjects were 267 grade 9 students from three secondary schools located in an affluent suburban community. One of the schools was a vocational school serving students from the entire district and included basic level students only. The other two schools (academic) had students at general and advanced levels and were considered to have students representative of those within the district. If students were taking two or more academic courses at the general level, they were classified as general.

Measuring Instruments The Nowicki-Strickland Locus of Control Scale for Children (NS) was used to measure generalized expectancies and the IARQ was used to measure specific expectancies (I+ and I−). Because of limited testing time a 21-item version of the NS (Nowicki & Strickland, 1973) for grades 7–12 and a 20-item version of the IARQ (Crandall, 1968) for grades 6–12 were used. Crandall (1968) reported correlations of .89 for I+ and .88 for I− between the short form (grades 6–12) and the long form of the IARQ.

Data Collection The measuring instruments were administered to students in grade 9 English classes by their teachers during a regular class period. Prior to test administration, a researcher met with the teachers or vice-principal to review administration procedures. Testing at two schools (the vocational school and one of the academic schools) was completed in December 1985. Data were collected from the other academic school in April 1986.[1]

Results

Reliabilities of the three measures were estimated using the α coefficient. They were .70 for the NS, .43 for I+, and .46 for I−. The reliabilities for I+ and I− were quite low; this could have increased the probability of type II error when data were analyzed.

Prior to testing the hypotheses, analyses of variance were used to test for differences between the two academic schools. No significant differences were found between schools.

---

[1]Originally, data were collected from a second academic school in December 1985. However, data were discarded, because uniform administration procedures were not followed. Thus, a replacement school was included.

To determine whether differences were as hypothesized, analyses of variance were used with level and sex as independent variables and NS, I+, and I− scores as dependent variables. Results are shown in Table 1.

Since sample sizes were not equal an unweighted means analysis was used.

TABLE 1   Results of Analyses of Variance with Level and Sex as Independent Variables and NS, I+, and I− Scores as Dependent Variables

Dependent Variable	Source	SS	DF	MS	F
NS	Level	212.45	2	106.23	8.11*
	Sex	27.12	1	27.12	2.07
	Interaction	14.49	2	7.25	.55
	Error	2999.67	229	13.10	
I+	Level	6.21	2	3.10	.97
	Sex	5.41	1	5.41	1.69
	Interaction	6.79	2	3.40	1.06
	Error	732.11	229	3.20	
I−	Level	27.74	2	13.88	3.78*
	Sex	6.77	1	6.77	1.85
	Interaction	5.07	2	2.54	.69
	Error	840.17	229	3.67	

*Significant at .05 level.

TABLE 2   Means and Standard Deviations by Level and Sex for the NS, I+, and I− Scores

	MALE			FEMALE			TOTAL	
	N	M	SD	N	M	SD	N	M
Nowicki-Strickland								
Basic	30	9.97	3.09	15	10.33	3.18	45	10.09
General	50	8.76	3.28	33	9.21	4.21	83	8.94
Advanced	65	6.86	3.50	42	8.31	3.82	107	7.43
Total	145	8.16		90	8.98			
I+								
Basic	30	6.67	1.58	15	7.27	2.40	45	6.87
General	50	6.30	1.94	33	6.85	1.55	83	6.52
Advanced	65	6.97	1.69	42	6.83	1.72	107	6.92
Total	145	6.68		90	6.91			
I−								
Basic	30	6.53	2.09	15	6.00	2.54	45	6.36
General	50	6.00	1.94	33	5.42	2.23	83	5.80
Advanced	65	6.36	1.64	42	5.80	1.63	107	6.51
Total	145	6.35		90	6.03			

Since sample sizes were not equal, an unweighted means analysis was used. Significant differences were found only for level on both the Nowicki-Strickland and I−. Post hoc, the Tukey-Kramer modification of Tukey's WSD procedure was used to determine which groups differed significantly. For the NS, advanced level students were significantly more internal than either general or basic level students (see Table 2 for means). These results were as expected. For I−, advanced level students were significantly more internal than general level students; basic level students did not differ significantly from either advanced or general level students.

Sex differences were not found for any of the dependent variables. It had been predicted that females would have I− scores higher than those of males. Although not significant, the opposite was found. Males had an I− mean higher than that of females. Their mean for I+ was lower than that of females. To further investigate, a difference score, I+ minus I−, was used as a dependent variable. A significant sex difference was found. For males, the difference between I+ and I−scores was less (*M* = .32) than that for females (*M* = .88). To further explore, correlated *t* tests were used to determine whether males or females scored significantly higher on I+ as compared to I−. Females did score significantly higher on I+ than on I− (*t* = 3.35); there was no significant difference for males (*t* = 1.68). The results for sex were not consistent with what had been suggested in the literature. In examining the means for sex by groups it would appear that the sex differences are attributable to basic and general level students. At the advanced level the mean differences between I+ and I− were .46 for males and .31 for females, while at the general level differences were .26 for males and 1.43 for females; at the basic level males differed by .14 and females by 1.27. Thus for basic and general levels, females scored substantially more internal for academic success than for academic failure. It would be of interest to explore these relationships in future studies.

Discussion

The results suggest that the generalized expectancy of reinforcement is related to level of academic program of Ontario grade 9 secondary school students. The student in the advanced level program is more internally controlled than either the general or basic level student. It is assumed that advanced level students achieve more than general level and basic level students. Although the relationship between locus of control and academic achievement has been found before, its occurrence in the present study further emphasizes the importance of a generalized expectancy of reinforcement in determining academic performance. The results of this investigation support the belief that the more internal the individual's orientation, the higher the individual's achievement.

The specific expectancies were also found to be related to the type of academic program of secondary school students. Advanced level students were more internally responsible for their intellectual-academic failures than general level students. Surprisingly, neither general nor advanced level students were more internally responsible for their intellectual-academic failures than the basic level students. It may well be that students in vocational schools function better as a separate student body rather than in an integrative stream. Students in a vocational school may have a culture and a set of beliefs about responsibility for academic failures slightly different than what they would have in an academic school. Isolated from the advanced and general level students, the basic level student may feel more accepted and more likely to persist in the face of temporary failure. General level students educated in the same environment as the advanced level students undoubt- edly receive messages from the environment which suggest that they are not as capable of determining their own reinforcements. As suggested above, this may also be a function of performing at lower levels throughout elementary school. In a further investigation with the three groups of students, the relationships of responsi- bility for intellectual-academic successes and failures to various personal factors and to different classroom instructional methods may be considered.

The results of the study also raise the issue of attribution retraining for low achievement students. As Dweck and Licht (1980) point out, the cognitions of mas- tery-oriented students (a motivational orientation) reflect their tendency to look toward the future, to emphasize the positive, and to invest their energies in actively pursuing solution-relevant strategies (p. 201). Given this, does it not seem like a rea- sonable strategy to teach helpless students to attribute their failures to variable fac- tors such as personal effort? According to Dweck and Licht (1980) it would appear to be necessary to rid seriously helpless individuals of their maladaptive attributions by such a direct method before they can effectively employ the more adaptive self- instructions and self-monitoring of the mastery-oriented student.

This study also supports the notion that although locus of control seems related to academic level its relationship to sex is not consistent. The hypothesis regarding sex was not supported. However, females were more apt to take responsibility for success and less apt to accept responsibility for failure. The differences between I+ and I− scores showed that males ($M = .33$) had a difference significantly smaller than that of females ($M = .88$). In addition, females were significantly more internal for success than for failure. These differences seemed to be a result of a rather large difference between I+ and I− for basic and general level female students. These results are in contrast to those of Lochel (1983) who suggested that females are more inclined to take responsibility for failure than for success. Could it be that basic and general level female students have a greater need to take responsibility for suc- cess and to deny responsibility for failure than advanced level students? Because of social behavior, low achieving boys tend to receive much negative reinforcement. In addition, they receive negative reinforcement for academic behaviors. Thus, they may not be as threatened by taking responsibility for failures since they may not dif- ferentiate between negative reinforcements for social behaviors and those for acad- emic achievement.

The sex differences found in this study are interesting; however, it is recom- mended that additional research be completed to explore these relationships.

References

Bar-Tal, D., & Bar-Zohar, Y. (1977). The relationship between perception of locus of control and acade- mic achievement. *Contemporary Educational Psychology, 2,* 181–199.

Beck, J. (1977). Locus of control, task experiences and children's performance following failure. *Journal of Educational Psychology,* **71,** 207–210.

Crandall, V. C. (1968). *Refinement of the IARQ scale.* (NIMH Progress Report, Grant No. MH–022 38, pp. 60–67).

Crandall, V. C., Katkovsky, W., & Crandall, V. J. (1965). Children's beliefs in their own control of rein-forcement in intellectual-academic achievement situations. *Child Development,* **36,** 91–109.

Diener, C., & Dweck, C. (1978). An analysis of learned helplessness. *Journal of Personality and Social Psychology,* **36,** 451–462.

Dweck, C., & Licht, B. (1980). Learned helplessness and intellectual achievement. In J. Garber & M. E. P. Seligman (Eds.), *Human helplessness: Theory and applications* (pp. 197–221). New York: Academic Press.

Dweck, C., & Reppucci, N. (1973). Learned helplessness and reinforcement responsibility in children. *Journal of Personality and Social Psychology,* **25,** 109–116.

Lefcourt, H. M. (1980). Personality and locus of control. In J. Garber & M. E. P. Seligman (Eds.), *Human helplessness: Theory and applications* (pp. 245–259). New York: Academic Press.

Lochel, E. (1983). Sex differences in achievement motivation. In J. Jaspars, F. D. Finchman, & M. Hewstone (Eds.), *Attribution theory and research: Conceptual, developmental and social dimensions* (pp. 193–220). London: Academic Press.

McGhee, M. G., & Crandall, V. C. (1968). Beliefs in internal-external control of reinforcements and academic performance. *Child Development,* **39,** 91–102.

Nicholls, J. (1975). Causal attributions and other achievement-related cognitions. *Journal of Personality and Social Psychology,* **31,** 379–389.

Nowicki, S., & Strickland, B. (1973). A locus of control scale for children. *Journal of Consulting and Clinical Psychology,* **40,** 148–154.

Parsons, J. (1978). *Cognitive mediation of the effects of evaluative feedback on children's affect and expectancy for success.* Symposium paper presented at the annual meeting of the American Educational Research Association, Toronto.

Parsons, J. C. (1981). *Attributions, learned helplessness and sex differences in achievement.* Paper presented at the annual meeting for the American Educational Research Association, Los Angeles.

Rotter, J. B. (1966). Generalized expectancies for internal locus of control of reinforcement. *Psychological Monographs,* **80** (1, Whole No. 60).

Source: Boss, M. W., & Taylor, M. C. (1989). The relationship between locus of control and academic level and sex of secondary students, *Contemporary Educational Psychology,* 14, 315–322.

Review of Literature After researchers formulate a research problem they conduct a search for studies that are related to the problem. The review summarizes and analyzes previous research and shows how the present study is related to this literature. The length of the review can vary, but it should be selective and should concentrate on the way the present study will contribute to existing knowledge. As in the example, it should be long enough to demonstrate to the reader that the researcher has a sound understanding of the relationship between what has been done and what will be done. There is usually no separate heading to identify the review of literature, but it is always located before the methods section.

Research Hypothesis or Question Following the literature review researchers state the hypothesis, hypotheses, or question(s). Based on information from the review, researchers write a *hypothesis* that indicates what they predict will happen in the study. Hypotheses can be tested empirically, and they provide focus for the research. For some research it is inappropriate to make a prediction of results, and in some studies a research question rather than a hypothesis is indicated. Whether it is a question or a hypothesis, the sentence should contain objectively defined terms and state relationships in a clear, concise manner, as do the hypotheses in our example (last two sentences before the methods section).

Methodology In the methods or *methodology* section, the researcher indicates the research design, subjects, instruments, and procedures used in the study. Ideally, this section contains enough information to enable other researchers to replicate the study. There is usually a subheading for each part of the methods section.

In the *subjects* subsection (sometimes referred to as the *sample participants* or *data source*), the researcher describes the characteristics of the individuals from whom information is gathered. There is an indication of the number of subjects and the way they were selected for the study.

The *instruments* subsection describes the techniques used to gather information. There should be an indication of the validity and reliability of the results for each measuring device to show that the techniques are appropriate for the study. Sometimes examples of items are included to help the reader understand the nature of the instrument.

The *procedure* or data collection subsection is used to explain how the study was conducted. The authors describe when the information was collected, where, and by whom. They describe what was done to the subjects and the manner in which the data were collected. It is important to provide a full description of the procedures. There needs to be sufficient information so that the reader would know how to proceed in replicating the study. The procedures may also affect the ways subjects respond. Readers thus need to examine the procedures carefully in interpreting the results.

Results A summary of the analyses of the data collected is reported in the *results* or *findings* section. This section may appear confusing to the beginning researcher because statistical language, symbols, and conventions are used in presenting the results. The results are usually indicated in tables and graphs within the text of the article. The results should be presented objectively without interpretation or discussion, summarizing what was found. (Sometimes interpretation will follow the results in this section.) Since the results section contains crucial information in the article, the reader must be able to understand and evaluate the material. This is important in order to avoid uncritical acceptance of the conclusions. At this point do not be concerned with understanding the statistics presented in our example.

Discussion, Implications, and Conclusions In this section the researchers indicate how the results are related to the research problem or hypothesis. It is a non-technical interpretation of whether the results support a hypothesis or answer a research question. If the study is exploratory or contains unexpected findings, the researchers explain why they believe they obtained these results. The explanation should include an analysis of any deficiencies in the methodology utilized and an indication of other research that may explain why certain results were obtained. This section is also used to indicate implications of the study for future research and practical applications and to give overall conclusions. This section is identified by several different labels. The most common words are *discussion, conclusion,* or *summary.*

References *References* and reference notes that are cited in the article follow the discussion. The style of the notation will vary. The journal in which our model article is published uses 1974 APA (American Psychological Association) format, which has since been revised.

Guidelines for Evaluating Quantitative Research

There is no agreed-upon method or approach in reading research articles. Some readers begin with the conclusion, and others follow the written sequence. Our experience suggests that a reader should begin with the abstract, then scan the introduction, research problem, and conclusion sections. If, after reading these sections, the reader is still interested in the article, he or she should start at the beginning and read the entire article more carefully. Whenever reading research, one should keep in mind the practical or meaningful significance of the study. Research is significant if there are no serious weaknesses in the design and the differences obtained between groups or individuals or relationships reported are large enough to suggest changes in theory or practice.

Other questions should be kept in mind in reading research. While you need to become acquainted with these considerations now, a full understanding and application of the questions is expected only after further study of each topic. The following questions, organized according to each major section of a research article, constitute a guideline for evaluating quantitative investigations.[3]

Research Problem

1. How clearly and succinctly is the problem stated?
2. Is it sufficiently delimited to be amenable to investigation? At the same time, does it have sufficient practical or theoretical value to warrant study?
3. Possibly with the exception of some descriptive research, is it stated in such a way that it expresses the relationship of two or more variables?
4. Does it have a rationale? Has the problem been studied before? If so, should this problem be studied again? Is the study likely to provide additional knowledge?
5. Will the findings give rise to further hypotheses, thereby increasing the probability of adding to existing knowledge?

---

[3]Adapted from *Educational Research: Readings in Focus,* Second Edition, by Irvin J. Lehmann and William A. Mehrens. Copyright © 1979 by Holt, Rinehart and Winston, Inc., reprinted by permission of the publisher.

Review of Literature

1. How adequately has the literature been surveyed?
2. Does the review present pertinent material, or is it just filler?
3. Does the review critically evaluate previous findings and studies, or is it only a summary of what is known without pointing out any possible deficiencies or alternative explanations?
4. Does the review support the need for studying the problem?
5. Does the review establish a theoretical framework for the problem?
6. Does the review relate previous studies to the research problem?

Hypotheses or Questions

1. Are any assumptions advanced with respect to the hypotheses or questions? If so, are they explicit (they should be), or are they implicit?
2. Are hypotheses consistent with theory and known facts? Are they testable? Do they provide a suggested answer to the problem?
3. Are all terms adequately defined in operational fashion?

Methodology

1. Are the procedures, design, and instruments employed to gather the data described with sufficient clarity to permit another researcher to replicate the study?
2. Is the population described fully? Did the researcher use the total population, or was there a sample used? If a sample is used, is it representative of the population from which it was selected?
3. Is evidence presented about validity and reliability score?
4. Was a pretest used? Was there a pilot study? If so, why? What were the results? Was the problem or question or procedure changed as a result of the pretest or pilot study, and if so, was this modification justifiable or desirable?
5. Are there any obvious weaknesses in the overall design of the study?

Results

1. Are statistical techniques needed to analyze the data? If so, were the most appropriate and meaningful statistical techniques employed?
2. Have the results been presented adequately?

Discussion, Implications, Conclusions

1. Are the conclusions and generalizations consistent with the findings? What are the implications of the findings? Has the researcher overgeneralized the findings?
2. Does the researcher discuss the limitations of the study?
3. Are there any extraneous factors that might have affected the findings? Have they been considered by the researchers?

4. Are the conclusions presented consistent with theory or known facts?
5. Have the conclusions (both those relevant to the original hypothesis and any serendipitous findings) been presented adequately and discussed?

How to Read Qualitative Research: An Ethnographic Example

There is greater diversity in the formats used to report qualitative research than in the formats typical of quantitative studies. This is because of the many types of qualitative studies, and the fact that until recently not much educational qualitative research has been reported. While there is not a single mode for representing qualitative research, many of the published reports will have the major sections presented below. In contrast to quantitative studies, however, these sections may not be identified clearly or are identified by descriptive terms related to the topic. See Excerpt 2.2 for an example of a qualitative research report.

Introduction The introduction provides a general background of the study, indicating the potential importance of the research. It summarizes the general intentions of the investigator, along with a general statement of the research problem or purpose. For a journal article, usually only one of many research foci are reported. The introduction includes a preliminary literature review to present possible conceptual frameworks that will be useful in understanding the data and results. The review justifies the need for a descriptive case study. The introduction may also indicate the structure of the rest of the report.

Methodology The methodology section describes the design of the study, including the selection and description of the site, the role of the researcher, initial entry for observation, the time and length of the study, the number of participants and how they were selected, and data collection and analysis strategies. This information is needed to evaluate the soundness of the procedures. The amount of detail contained in this section will vary, depending on the type of research report. In relatively short published articles the methodology may be part of the introduction.

Findings and Interpretations In this section the researcher presents the data that were gathered, usually in the form of lengthy narratives, and analyzes the data. This should be done in sufficient detail to allow the reader to judge the accuracy of the analysis. The data are used to illustrate and substantiate the researcher's interpretations. Analysis is often intermixed with presentation of data. The data are often in the form of quotes by participants. It is important to indicate the purpose of data analysis and to describe what has been learned by synthesizing the information. Because the presentation is in narrative form, frequently there are a number of descriptive subtitles connoting different findings.

EXCERPT 2.2

EXAMPLE OF A QUALITATIVE RESEARCH REPORT

CAN ELEMENTARY SCHOOLTEACHING BE A CAREER? A SEARCH FOR NEW WAYS OF UNDERSTANDING WOMEN'S WORK

Sari Knopp Biklen, *Syracuse University*

INTRODUCTION

Is the prevailing notion of career sufficient? To examine this question, we first look at how literature and society construct meaning for the concept of career. We then compare this perspective with those of a particular group, women who teach elementary school. We show, through the informants' life stories, how the traditional external concept is inadequate to organize these women's lives. Finally, we suggest what elements a revised concept of career must include.[1]

Recent work in both education and gender scholarship make this a particularly appropriate time to examine these concerns. Scholarly as well as federal concern with the quality of education has marshalled national attention to schools and particularly to teachers.[2] Little of this focus on teachers, however, has revealed how gender issues intersect with educational concerns.[3] Since elementary schoolteaching is considered an occupation for women, this omission is stunning.

Demographic analysts suggest that expanding opportunities for women have contributed to the drain of bright women from the field.[4] The public wonders whether the lack of upwardly mobile applicants to teach creates a mediocre teaching force. Concomitantly, public disdain exists for those who want to spend the day with young children. Policy-makers turn their attention, therefore, to figuring out how to attract bright, creative recruits into teaching, certainly an important problem.

Careers: Traditional Definitions

In spite of changes in the work force, the opening of fields that were previously more resistant to women, and the addition of women in professional and upper management positions, the structure of career is based on the ways in which men have been able to live their lives, free from primary responsibility for the family. One begins work, that is, after college or graduate school, or advanced medical or scientific training, and works continually, moving upward in graduated stages. From this perspective, a career is "a pre-established total pattern of organized professional activity, with upward movement through recognized preparatory stages, and advancement based on merit and bearing honor."[5] This view emphasizes the coherence of the career and the goal orientation of the career occupant.[6] One can therefore study the structure of individual careers, such as the medical, the legal, and the academic.[7]

Two elements are paramount. First is upward movement.[8] This view presents careers as trajectories, measurable in the public sphere. The professional career is defined by the nature of participation in the wage-labor system and by the status that accrues from that participation.[9] Looked at in this way, teaching is at least a "semi-professional," at best a fringe profession.[10]

The second element is career commitment. By commitment is meant dedication to one's work. Personal or family life is supposed to be fit around the demands of work. Career commitment has two major aspects, both of which relate to time. The first aspect is long-term commitment. Here, career commitment refers to the decision to undertake a career in the first place. Hence, if a woman decides to become a teacher rather than a principal, she is said to have lowered her career commitment.[11] Associated with this aspect of career commitment is the question of the length of time a woman expects to work. Mason measured teachers' career commitment, for example, by asking them where they planned to be in five years.[12]

The second aspect of career commitment relates to the short-term use of time for work. One common yardstick for differentiating occupations from professional careers, for example, is the career's tendency to spill over the 9-to-5 time slot. Doctors are a case in point:

> *Central to the status of a profession is a field's ability to induce members to do their job no matter how long it takes and no matter what other demands are made on their lives. These requirements are stringent in medicine, where lives may be at stake in the physician's decision about how high a priority should be given to finishing a job.*[13]

Our notion of the professional career includes a heavy work load and a large time commitment.[14] Women in professional careers must accept this view in order to succeed: "To the extent that male work values dominate, women who wish to succeed must accept male definitions and expectations about work commitments."[15] The implications of this view for women are direct. For women to put career commitment over family commitments, to set their professional priorities straight, so to speak, they must act against social norms.[16]

Two key elements of the external understanding of the career, then, are upward movements and career commitment.[17] We will examine the work perspectives of a group of elementary schoolteachers to depict an alternative view. First, however, we examine literature on teachers' work lives.

Teachers and Careers

Teaching has been described both as "careerless"[18] and as an occupation of "lateral careers."[19] Movement between schools can signify a lateral career change. Teachers may, for example, consider a transfer to a school in a higher socioeconomic neighborhood a promotion. The label of "careerless" refers to the structure of the teaching occupation; namely, to the impossibility of promotion within teaching. Advancement means becoming an administrator and leaving teaching. Additionally, teaching is structured to accommodate the in-and-out patterns of women's employment; that is, "To persist in teaching is, in a sense, to be 'passed over' for higher position or marriage."[20] In this view, a lifetime commitment to teaching evidences failure rather than success.

Elementary schoolteachers' low career commitment has been widely noted and correlated primarily with gender.[21] This literature reflects a notion that normative expectations about women's roles carry over into the occupational setting. Teaching becomes an extension of the female role.

More recent research on women and work, undertaken from the new scholarship-on-women perspective, has questioned this approach,[22] suggesting that the ways in which we have examined women's working lives has been inadequate and misleading because it is based on stereotypical assumptions about women.[23] In this view, we are hindered in thinking clearly about the work women do because of our immersion in a sociology of occupations which takes the lives of men as the norm.[24]

Scholars working from this perspective have looked at the issue of work commitment somewhat differently. They have examined factors in the workplace which may account for women's differing experience.[25] They have argued that power rather than gender influences behavior,[26] and discussed work commitment in a different frame.[27] They have criticized the models sociologists have brought to the study of men's and women's work.[28] Some have analyzed media advice to working women.[29] This study can be seen in this context of the new scholarship on women.

METHODOLOGY

Methods and Participants

The issues discussed in this paper are part of a larger study that focused on how a group of elementary schoolteachers looked upon their work, what they valued and criticized about their occupation, and how they negotiated their work interests with sex role and family expectations.[30] The investigator relied upon the qualitative methods of participant observation and in-depth interviewing.[31] The inductive nature of these methodological approaches and the emphasis on participant perspectives causes researchers in this mode to search for the ways that those being studied make sense out of their experiences. Qualitative researchers assume that people act on the basis of their interpretations of experience. Hence, they are interested in what subjects experience and how they interpret these experiences.[32]

Observations and interviews were conducted in schools over an eight-month period in one primary setting and a subsidiary one. Both schools were located in a middle-sized city in the American Northeast. The primary setting, Vista City Elementary,[33] had a student population of 800, and an outstanding academic reputation. When the local newspaper published achievement test results each spring, Vista City Elementary always boasted the highest scores. The data reported in this paper come from this primary setting.

All but two of the classroom teachers at Vista City were women. They ranged in age from their mid-twenties to their late fifties. They were single, married, and divorced. Most of the single women had worked continuously at teaching, though two had tried other kinds of jobs for a short period, hoping for more recognition. Those who were married had families and children who were important in their lives. Among the married women, as well, there was some variety in their long-term patterns. Some of the married teachers had husbands who wanted traditional families and had conservative values about women's roles. Some of the older teachers had conservative fathers who had forbidden them as young adults to enter the labor market. Still others had taken only six weeks out for the births of their children, or had stayed home for a few years before returning to work. In one case, a teacher never finished her undergraduate education until her children went to school.

There was a range of interest and involvement in women's issues as well. Two of the teachers were active in the local National Organization for Women. Others expressed some interest in factors that facilitated women's working or that promoted women's advancement. None of the single women who were interviewed expressed any interest in women's issues; although some of the married women did, they assumed primary responsibility for the home as well as their classrooms. They could not be described as rebels against social norms.

Characterized as their lives were by "interrupted careers" and by deference to their husband's social values, it is difficult to understand how one could argue that these women had a sense of their work as teaching careers. Yet, I will suggest that the traditional way of evaluating career or work commitment—as continuous upward movement through occupational stages—fails to do justice to the views of these women. In this next section, we move to the internalized structuring of career as we examine how the teachers described their work.

Teachers Describe Their Work

During the first several months of interviewing and observing, teachers would often say, in response to a question asking them to describe their work experiences, "I have always worked." In the early stages of my research, I would then form a mental picture of a person who had worked continuously in a full-time position and had a career goal clearly in sight. I would settle back in my seat waiting to hear the details, thinking to myself, "I'm on to something. This certainly contradicts what I've read about women's in-and-out employment patterns." As the women described their work histories to me, however, they almost always described a discontinuous pattern of childraising, part-time work, and finally, full-time re-entry into the employment market. Most surprisingly, they would end their stories reiterating that they had always worked.

Kate Bridges was one of the teachers who described herself as having always worked, but who portrayed her actual work history in this discontinuous pattern. She described her feelings about her occupation: "I have felt passionately about teaching for 20 years." She may have felt passionately about it but she had not, exactly, been teaching for 20 years.

She recalled "teaching fairly consistently since 1960–61," but she was "in and out" with babies. "I'd come home for a year and I'd say: 'Mother in the home forever.' And then all of a sudden I was back teaching again." She had a variety of teaching assignments:

> I started out in the public schools in San Francisco, I taught there for two
> years in an inner-city kind of school and I loved that. And then when the

babies came along I was looking for part-time work and I worked with disturbed kids. It seemed ideal because I had a friend with children the same ages and we were both teachers. We decided to start a nursery school and then she got pregnant again and left it to me. And I had it for two years and just loved it. There it was, my own school.

She moved to Chicago in connection with her husband's work and taught teachers part-time in a college education department. At that point, her teaching had "gotten increasingly almost full-time and you know any part-time job is a full-time-and-a-half one anyway." Her last move was to Vista City, again for her husband's work. She stayed "mostly" at home for about seven years, though she had worked part-time at a drug rehabilitation center developing its educational program. Then she felt she must return to teaching. She got a full-time teaching position at an elementary school. She described her determination at that time: "I'm going to start my teaching career and if I don't accept this job now, God knows if I will ever get my foot in the door."[34] As the above comment indicates, Kate formally acknowledged that the beginning of her teaching career started when she began to teach full-time in an elementary school. Her conflicts arose from her perception, however, that she had been interested in, involved with, and thinking about teaching for 20 years. As she saw it, she had remained committed to teaching because of her internal occupational consistency. She had always thought of herself as a teacher.

Kate had worked hard for 20 years, and some of this work involved teaching children in schools. She had not always been able, then, to translate her passion for teaching into an occupational reality. While she always considered herself a teacher, she had not always physically engaged in full-time teaching. And this is the crux of the issue. As Kate and her colleagues saw it, bearing and caring for children of one's own did not necessarily reflect upon one's career commitment.

Again, these teachers were not women who would violate acceptable social norms. They were in the mainstream. At the same time, however, they valued their work identities as teachers and did not want to have to choose between work and family. The career pattern Kate reveals is one defined by internal consistency about one's occupation rather than continuing external employment.[35]

Teachers and Their Husbands

Husbands had a major impact on the ways in which married teachers made decisions about work. Some women, like Kate, spoke to their husbands directly about their occupational intentions. Other women had husbands who resisted their wives' occupational interest. The cases of three women whose desire to work full-time outside the home compelled them to develop strategies to overcome their husbands' resistance reveal the tactics they developed to enable them to return to the labor market. Their situations are valuable to study because on the surface these women appear the most complacent with women's roles.

Sylvia Richardson, in her fifties, had taught seventh graders for five years prior to taking a nine-year hiatus to raise her children, "and wait until my youngest was solidly in school." She had since been teaching for nine years. Her husband had not wanted her to return to work because he liked having her at home. "We're not for this women's lib thing," she said. As her urge to return to the classroom strengthened, she decided that, to gain flexibility, she would become a substitute teacher. At this time, one of her old teaching friends gave her a little advice: "Listen," said the friend, "Don't go and sub in the seventh grade because the kids are really different from when you were there." Sylvia decided that, "If seventh and eighth graders were really violent, and if it was going to be just a terribly difficult situation for me every day, then I'd better pick a group that wasn't going to be this demanding." Then her husband would not be able to say to her, "We don't need this aggravation. Come on home." What enabled her to change from subbing, which her husband did not classify as a full-time position, to full-time teaching, was her availability. As she began subbing every day, her husband finally relented on the full-time teaching position. "At least we'll know where to find you," he told her.

Sylvia Richardson employed a strategy in order to re-enter teaching. She chose a grade level that would be less "difficult" than junior high so that she could leave her work problems behind her when she came home. Sylvia represents an interesting example of how women may strategize to accomplish their goals when they do not want to challenge social norms.

While Sylvia used every opportunity to dissociate herself from feminism, she shared, at the same time, feminist appraisals of the damage to self-esteem that may be the toll of full-time housework. As she put it, "It's really hard for someone to just stay home and take care of a child and do all the housework because you feel terrible about yourself. But, on the other hand, the family needs attending to."[36] While the strategy that Sylvia Richardson chose seemed to have reaped benefits for her, the costs others had to pay were higher.

Take the case of Jessica Bonwit. She had also stopped working in schools when her three children were born, though she ran a family day-care program during this period. But, "something went click after six years," and she knew that she had to get back to teaching in a school. Her husband, however, did not share in the work. Jessica promised her husband that his life would not alter as far as his home commitments were concerned. As she said, "He didn't mind so much when I went back to work, because his life didn't change at all from before I was working to when I went back to work, but he also knew that I had a real professional interest in teaching and also that I was really happy doing it."[37]

Jessica's price for full-time work was to carry both home and school responsibilities. She resented her husband's selfishness: "I love my husband, but sometimes I don't like him very much." Her teaching was so important to her that, at least for the time, she was willing to carry this burden. The impact of her choice will only emerge in the future.

Carrie Amundsen had never worked before she had children, but, like the other two women, she, too, had to develop a strategy in order to join the work force as a full-time employee. Although Carrie was in her fifties, she had only been teaching for 10 years. Her husband had never wanted her to work. In fact, she confided, she almost did not marry him because of his views on working women. She referred to him as "the original male chauvinist pig." She had to find a way to ease herself into the work market. She said, "Here's how I did it."

"Actually," she began, "I wasn't even planning to go back to work, I had never gotten my bachelor's degree, so I went and took a course in math at the university." She reportedly had no goal in mind except "enrichment," but she had "loved" the course and "ended up taking some more courses." When she had taken as much math as she could, she "somehow made some connections" between her own children's experiences in school learning how to read and the special struggles some other children had. Further, there were particular reasons for these struggles. Her interest sparked. When she finished her undergraduate degree, she got a master's degree in special education.

By this time, she had gained experience in schools and wanted to put it to good use. In the city where she lived, a specialist in her area was starting a program and asked her if she would work in it. She told him, "My husband will never let me work full-time." Her future employer responded, "Let me worry about your husband." So she and the faculty member "worked out a deal" where she would say to her husband that she would just try it out for one year. "It worked," and she "loved" teaching. At the end of that year she "weaseled" her way into first one year and then another.

These three teachers chose tactics to maneuver their way into teaching without having to do an ideological battle with their husbands or to rebel against social norms. On their own time tables they translated their mental commitment into occupational reality. While away from their positions in institutions of schooling, the women often ran home day-care centers, they stayed in touch with their colleagues and discussed classroom life, they planned to return to work, and they sometimes strategized to overcome their husbands' resistance to their working.

Externally, then, the lives of these women represent the interrupted career pattern. Internally, however, they thought of themselves as teachers, whether or not they were in the job market, and they made choices that kept them close to children or to educational concerns. While they did not, in some ways, challenge the boundaries of their lives, they exhibited a coherence in their attitude toward their work.

External Structure and Internal Concepts

Clearly, this is a different way of thinking about coherence in one's working life. We have been accustomed to thinking about coherence in work life in terms of continual upward movement. These women, on the other hand, said, through their lives, that they wanted to have children and family life as well as be teachers. They questioned why breaks for child-rearing were equated with lack of job commitment when they had always thought of themselves as teachers. The external structure and their internal conceptualization conflicted.

Career commitment is, as we have said, however, inseparable from upward mobility in the traditional concept of career. Again, many of the teachers studied brought a different perspective to these issues. As we have seen, the teachers focused on children and this focus determined to a large part their work orientation.

The most committed teachers at Vista City Elementary School brought a high level of idealism to their work. These expectations caused them to work hard to accomplish their goals. It contributed to their reputations as excellent teachers. At the same time, the work setting brought frustrations because it did not match their conceptions of how they wanted to work. Some of these teachers focused more determinedly on their classroom work, isolating them from other adults in the building. Not all teachers reflected this pattern, however, for some brought their idealism to other aspects of the job, such as committee work. In neither case, however, did teachers' high commitment or idealism further their careers. Few opportunities for advancement are available. The structure of the occupation was determined. Idealism caused teachers to focus on the quality of work and work setting.

Since administrative opportunities are limited, few teachers face the situation of deciding what to do when opportunity knocks. Those who are faced with such a decision, however, reveal the idealism about teaching that other teachers often exhibited in their daily work. When Barbara Timmitts was first offered the position of instructional specialist, for example, she turned it down. She felt that she had not taught long enough to do the job well. She took it the second time it was offered, not because she was certain that she would do excellently at it, but because she wanted the job and was fearful it would not be offered a third time.

If we examine how Barbara Timmitts thinks about her job offer, we notice that her major concern was whether or not she would perform well, rather than how the position might serve her career advancement. It is this kind of work orientation that I define as idealistic, because it reflects a person's ideal concept of how a job ought to be done. The teachers focused on the content of the occupation, rather than on their work as a link to other occupational choices. Quality of performance overrode career value. These teachers often thought of how they served the occupation rather than of how the occupation could serve them.

Christine Bart did not have an administrative position. Although she chaired the first-grade team, she received no extra remuneration for it. Like Barbara, however, she played a strong role among teachers both at the school and on district-wide committees. Like Barbara, her sense of idealism shaped the commitments she undertook. When I asked Christine about her leadership goals, she said that she thought she would not be interested in being a school principal. From her view, principals seemed powerless. Caught between parents' demands and central administration regulations, their hands were tied.

Bart was not sure that what administrators do is effective. She shared the view of many teachers at Vista City—that one cannot be effective or productive as an administrator and that those positions waste valuable talent. She saw Barbara Timmitts as a case in point: "My priority is in here with these kids. You look at someone like Barbara Timmitts. Barbara Timmitts is about the best teacher in this school and she was promoted to pushing a cart around the halls. She walks around with requisition slips and a pencil in her hand. Now what is that?" Children are the core of the work.

Amelia Dickenson had directed the gifted program before she was transferred out of the administrative position back into the classroom. When I asked her what it was like being back in the classroom full-time, she replied, "It's really great; I just love it! You really feel like you're accomplishing something."[38]

Teachers' commitment to their work and their attempt to execute their jobs close to their ideal conception of it, were revealed in daily work as well. While teachers often complained about the small number of breaks they had during the day, many teachers gave up their breaks in service to their teaching. Roberta Blake, for example, said that she had no free periods during the day, not even lunch. She explained that she believes in mainstreaming, so instead of having her class of special education students go out in a group to "the specials" (art, music, and gym), she sends them out a few at a time with different typical classes. Her beliefs, then, cause more work for her. As she put it, "After all, that's why this class is here—to be mainstreamed."

Kate Bridges rarely went to the teachers' room to eat her lunch. It was not just that the smoke bothered her. She decided, rather, that returning papers to her pupils in the afternoon, that they completed in the morning, improved educational results. "I have so many papers that have accumulated over the morning. Why not correct a paper and give instant feedback? If you could pass back the paper and have the kids working on it as soon as they return from lunch—I mean, the mileage on it is infinitely more. It is taking it out of your skin, though. So I'm sitting here eating a sandwich and correcting these papers and I also know it's better education (and I'm not having to correct that set of papers at night)." Kate saw her choice as a "tradeoff," however, because remaining in her room isolated her from collegial relationships.

The sixth grade team also gave up the opportunity to take a break during the day. They had asked the administration to schedule all their students' "specials" at 8:15 (school started at 8 o'clock) so that they could spend the rest of the day with their students. Because their students "switched" classes for different subjects, team members said that they did not have "a lot of time with the students." Apparently they wanted as much time with their students as they could get.

Sandra Miller gave up her lunchtimes and every afternoon for a month to do her "levels testing" because she wanted to give the tests to her pupils in the way she thought students ought to be tested—"when there was nobody else around." That way she would also not have to cut her reading groups to give the tests.

At Vista City Elementary, these "breaks" amounted to little time. Teachers got three "free" periods a week while their students went to art, music, or gym classes. From the perspective of these teachers, the day was not structured so as to maximize the education of their students. Teachers reported that they felt able to reach their goals only when they sacrificed some of their own planning time. This sacrifice did not mean that teachers wanted to be without breaks, but in the balance of things, they preferred to create optimal teaching conditions.

Sacrificing time was not the only way in which teachers attempted to live closely to their ideal of good teaching. Their idealism was expressed in many other ways. One teacher had taken a tutoring job the previous summer because she wanted the particular experience she would gain, even though the pay was terrible. She summed up her views with, "And I really learned a lot." Jessica Bonwit turned down a teaching assignment, when she came back from teaching after time home with her children, because it was not close enough to her minimum requirements for a good teaching situation. She did not mean a situation that would be easy for her, she said, but one that would enable her to work at even a near distance to her image of a good educational situation.

A teaching assistant gave up the tenure she had gained in the district because the special child with whom she worked was being transferred to another district. She had not wanted the child to be transferred because it was the middle of the year. Her attempts to postpone the move until the next year had been unsuccessful. She could have remained in the district while the child got a new aide in the new district, but she could not face jeopardizing all the progress her student had made that year. It was most important to her to finish the work she had begun. Even though the school to which she was going had no program for the child, she was determined to continue to make mainstreaming a successful experience for him: "We're going to make this work. Even if they don't have a program there, we'll make it successful. No matter what, we will make a good program for Jacob there."

These teachers focused their energies on the content of the work, not on its use to them for upward mobility. Hence, their major frustrations came, not when their hopes for advancement were crushed, but rather when they were forced to make compromises which they felt endangered their educational vision.[39]

The Vista City teachers carried their occupational ideals into the workplace. These ideals centered on the content of the work rather than on its career-ladder potential. This idealism is symbolized, perhaps, by the language one teacher used to describe her first teaching position: It was a "marriage" between her and the children; it is this kind of relationship that many teachers sought.

The teachers' idealism about their work also affected their aspirations about how worthwhile it would be to be an administrator. The teachers at Vista City Elementary were particularly critical of those in the central offices, whether of the personnel who planned the staff development sessions or of the special education administration, who were criticized for being out of touch with the school staffs and incapable of handling difficult problems. From the perspective of these teachers, it was usually mediocre teachers who became principals and central office staff. Since the hassles and demands were also great there, they could see little reason to hanker after these positions.

They did have goals—of being what they called "great teachers." A great teacher had a school or district-wide reputation for excellence. Style did not determine one's reputation. Some were more or less strict, more or less interested in, say, learning centers. They were the teachers whose classes the parents hoped their children would be placed in because in these classes most children learned, were stimulated, and were happy.

Those with reputations as great teachers were able to wield more power and strengthen their autonomy. These were great benefits. Formally, for example, they were elected to faculty council and nominated to serve on district-wide committees. Informally, the principal solicited their views and gave them greater leeway to organize their classrooms and curricula. But foremost stood the reputation and the personal satisfaction it generated. As the teachers saw it, to be a great teacher meant "something." They were not sure that being a great administrator carried an equivalent weight.

CONCLUSION

The perspectives that Vista City teachers brought to their work reveal the inadequacy of current conceptualizations of career. To substantively include women, the concept of career must describe the patterns of women's lives as well as those of men's. To do this, data must be generated from both women's as well as men's experiences, not from the lives of men applied to women. As the study of these teachers' lives suggest, we cannot have a career model which describes only those women who combine great ambition with a willingness to challenge social norms.

To revise our conceptualization, we need to approach the working lives of women freed from the confines of the concept of the male career. As the life stories presented here suggest, parent roles must be conceptualized as compatible, not competitive, with work roles. Parenting is not the opposite of career commitment. Or, to put it another way, when women choose to bear and nurture children, they do not thus signify a lack of career commitment. If we need to account for why some women hesitate to leave their children, we might rather consider the structural effects of the social neglect of child care options and the stigma accorded to day-care.

A revised concept of career must reflect an alternative concept of success, one that does not equate success in life with success at work. Critics of current perspectives in the sociology of occupations have rightly noted that employing a gender model for women (in which work and family concerns are discussed) and a job model for men (in which only issues from the work setting are relevant) leads to social inequity.[40] If careers are essentially masculine, then women who have children may never be taken seriously in their work. We must hold varied models rather than a narrowly defined concept of career paths in mind. That we think of the bearing and nurturing of children as a detour reveals the limitations of the concept's applicability to contemporary society. Even women in higher status professions than teaching, who slow down the pace of their careers to have children, are considered to take their work "less seriously" than those whose careers are not interrupted. The term "career interruption" suggests deviance from the ideal pattern which is molded around "the clockwork of male careers."[41] In this view, women occupy career niches but do not shape career paths. A generic career model must, at its base, account for the lives of both men and women equally well.

NOTES

[1]Earlier versions of this paper were presented at the 10th Research on Women and Education Conference. CSU/Long Beach, California, November 1984, and at the A.E.R.A. annual meeting, Chicago, April 1985. The research reported here was conducted under a grant from the National Institute of Education. The views expressed here, however, are my own. I would like to thank Sally Gregory Kohlstedt, Douglas Biklen, Charol Shakeshaft and the anonymous reviewers at *Issues in Education* for their helpful comments on earlier drafts.

[2]*See*, for example, The National Commission on Excellence in Education, *A Nation At Risk: The Imperative for Educational Reform* (Washington: U.S. Department of Education, 1983); Ernest Boyer, *High School: A Report on Secondary Education in America* (Princeton, NJ: Carnegie Foundation for the Advancement of Teaching, 1983); and John Goodlad, *A Place Called School: Prospects for the Future* (New York: McGraw-Hill, 1983).

[3]Mary Kay Tetreault and Patricia Schmuck, "Equity As An Elective: An Analysis of Selected Educational Reform Reports and Issues of Gender," *Issues in Education* 3 (1985): 45–67.

[4]Philip Schlecty and V. Vance, "Recruitment, Selection and Retention: The Shape of the Teaching Force" (Paper delivered at invitational conference "Research on Teaching: Implications for Practice," Warrentown, VA, February 1982).

[5]Burton Bledstein, *The Culture of Professionalism* (New York: Norton, 1976), 172. See, also, Harold Walensky, "The Professionalization of Everyone," *American Journal of Sociology* 70 (1964): 137–158.

[6]An alternative use of the concept has been the employment of career to describe change in people's lives. In this use it refers to the various positions, stages, and ways of thinking people pass through in

the course of their lives. It emphasizes the participant's perspectives on life. *See* Everett Hughes, "Institutional Office and the Person," *American Journal of Sociology* 43 (1937): 404–413.

[7]Oswald Hall, "Stages of A Medical Career," *American Journal of Sociology* 26(1948): 524–538; Dan Lortie, "Laymen to Lawmen: Law Schools, Careers and Professional Socialization," *Harvard Educational Review* 29 (1959): 352–369; and L. Wilson, *The Academic Man* (New York: Oxford University Press, 1942).

[8]Dan Lortie, *School-teacher* (Chicago: University of Chicago, 1975).

[9]*See,* for example, M. Blaxall and B. Reagan, eds., *Women and the Workplace: The Implications of Occupational Segregation,* special issue of *SIGNS* 1, pt. 2 (1976); and M. S. Larson, *The Rise of Professionalism* (Berkeley: University of California, 1977).

[10]Amitai Etzioni, ed., *The Semi-Professions and Their Organization* (New York: Free Press, 1969); and Blanche Geer, "Teaching," *International Encyclopedia of the Social Sciences* 15 (1968): 560–565.

[11]*See* Veronica Nieva and Barbara Gulick, *Women and Work* (New York: Praeger, 1981).

[12]W. S. Mason, *The Beginning Teacher: Status and Career Orientations* (Washington DC: Government Printing Office, 1961).

[13]B. G. Bourne and N. J. Wilker, "Commitment and the Cultural Mandate: Women in Medicine," in *Women and Work,* eds. Rachel Kahn-Hut, Arlene Kaplan Daniels and Richard Colvard (New York: Oxford University Press, 1982): 111–122.

[14]Mary Frank Fox and Sharlene Hesse-Biber, *Women at Work* (Palo Alto, CA: Mayfield, 1984).

[15]Kahn-Hut, Daniels and Colvard, *Women and Work,* 2.

[16]Rose Coser and Gerald Rokoff, "Women in the Occupational World: Social Disruption and Conflict," *Social Problems* 18 (1970): 534–554.

[17]It is important to remember that these are not rigid categories. The movement upward, for example, is not the same for all professions. Think of doctors, who once having achieved their professional status and position, practice in the same town for the rest of their lives. They may do emergency room work to break the routine or expand their practices, but if they are not connected with a university hospital, becoming a department chair is not a career goal. And, while some university professors would want to advance to a deanship, others consider the scholar's role at odds with the administrator's, and would not more deign to take the position than they would to write for *Parade.*

[18]Lortie, *School-teacher.*

[19]Howard S. Becker, "The Career of the Chicago Public School Teacher," *American Journal of Sociology* 57 (1952).

[20]Lortie, *School-teacher,* 89.

[21]*See* W. S. Mason, R. J. Dressel, and R. K. Bain, "Sex Role and the Career Orientations of Beginning Teachers," *Harvard Educational Reviews* 29 (1959): 370–383; Robert Dreeben, *The Nature of Teaching* (Glenview, IL: Scott, Foresman, 1970); Blanche Geer, "Occupational Commitment and The Teaching Profession," *The School Review* 74 (1966); Oswald Hall, "The Social Structure of the Teaching Profession," in *Struggle for Power in Education,* eds. F. W. Lutz and J. J. Azzarelli (New York: Center for Applied Research in Education, 1966), 35–48; Dan Lortie, *School-teacher;* J. D. Grambs, "The Roles of the Teacher," in *The Teacher's Role in American Society,* ed. T. Stiles, 14th Yearbook of the John Dewey Society, New York; R. L. Simpson and I. H. Simpson, "Women and Bureaucracy in the Semi-Professions," in *The Semi-Professions and Their Organization,* 196–255; and M. G. Sobel, "Commitment to Work," in *Working Mothers,* eds. L. W. Hoffman and F. I. Nye (San Francisco: Jossey-Bass, 1975): 63–80.

[22]Sari Knopp Biklen and Charol Shakeshaft, "The New Scholarship on Women," in *Handbook for Achieving Sex Equity in Schools,* ed. Susan Klein (Baltimore: Johns Hopkins Press, 1985), and Catharine Stimpson, "The New Scholarship about Women: The State of the Art," *Annals of Scholarship* 2 (1980): 2–14.

[23]*See* Kahn-Hut, Daniels, and Colvard, *Women and Work;* Cynthia F. Epstein, " Sex Role Stereotyping, Occupations and Social Exchange," *Women's Studies* 3 (1976): 185–194; Rosabeth M. Kanter, "The Impact of Hierarchical Structures on the Work Behavior of Women and Men," *Social Problems* 23 (1976): 415–430; Judith Long Laws, " Work Aspirations of Women: False Leads and New Starts," *Signs* 1:3, pt. 2 (1976): 33–49; and Coser and Rokoff, "Women in the Occupational World."

[24]*See* Joan Acker, "Issues in the Sociological Study of Women's Work," in *Women Working,* eds. A. H. Stromberg and S. Harkness (Palo Alto, CA: Mayfield, 1978): 134–161. More studies are appearing which examine how women in teaching construct experience. *See,* for example, Dee Spencer-Hall, *Teachers as Persons: Case Studies of the Lives of Women Teachers* (Final report to N.I.E., July 1982); Margaret Nelson, "From the One-Room Schoolhouse to the Graded School: Teaching in Vermont, 1910–1950," *Frontiers* 7 (1983): 14–20; Richard Quantz, "Teachers as Women: An Ethnohistory of the 1930s" (Paper delivered at the annual meeting of the American Educational Research Association, New York, March 1982); Polly Kaufman, *Women Teachers on the Frontier*

(New Haven, CT: Yale University Press, 1984); Boston Women Teachers Group, "A Study of the Effect of Teaching on Teachers" (Paper delivered at the American Educational Research Association's annual meeting, Boston, 1980); and Michael Apple, "Work, Gender and Teaching," *Teachers College Record* 84 (1983): 611–628.

[25]Judith Agassi, "The Quality of Women's Working Life," in *The Quality of Working Life,* eds. L. Davis and A. Cherns, vol. 1 (New York: New York Free Press, 1975), 280–298; Sobel, " Commitment to Work"; Fox and Hess-Biber, "Women at Work," and Nieva and Gulick, "Women at Work."

[26]Kanter, "The Impact of Hierarchical Structures."

[27]*See,* for example, Constantina Safilios-Rothschild, "Towards the Conceptualization and Measurement of Work Commitment," *Human Relations* 24 (1971): 489–493, and Sobel, "Commitment to Work."

[28]R. L. Feldberg and E. R. Glenn, "Male and Female: Job Versus Gender Models in the Sociology of Work," *Social Problems* (1979): 524–538.

[29]Nona Glazer, "Overworking the Working Woman: The Double Day in a Mass Magazine," *Women's Studies International Quarterly* 3 (1980): 79–93.

[30]Sari Knopp Biklen, *Teaching as an Occupation for Women: A Case Study on an Elementary School* (Final Report to N.I.E. under Grant no. NIE-G–81–007).

[31]Robert Bogdan and Sari Knopp Biklen, *Qualitative Research for Education* (Boston: Allyn and Bacon, 1982). *See,* also, Judith P. Goetz and Margaret Lecompte, *Ethnography and Qualitative Design in Educational Research* (Orlando, FL: Academic Press, 1984).

[32]Ibid.

[33]The names of the schools and the teachers have been changed to protect their promised anonymity.

[34]To accept this position, she had to refuse to go with her husband to Europe on his sabbatical. This caused some temporary marital discord.

[35]Kate's pattern was reflected in the lives of other married teachers at Vista City Elementary. Jessica Bonwit, for example, left full-time teaching for a six-year period while her three children were very young. During this period, however, she did not stop working. She started a home day-care program for six to eight children. Christine Bart described her work history as "continuous" though "not always in permanent jobs."

[36]I suggest that this example is typical of many teachers' solutions to problems. They often sought the individual resolution rather than a change in the status quo.

[37]Perhaps, Jessica was prepared in some way for a marriage of this type. Her own upbringing did not emphasize her worth in a world of men: *I was raised in an Italian family where the boys were valued much more highly than the girls. So with my brother, they always listened to him with both ears. But, with me, they only listened with one ear. It was like, "What were you saying?" So, I got in the habit of talking things over with myself.*

[38]Even the principal explained her reluctance to consider applying for a superintendency on this basis. It would take her too far away from her children.

[39]At the same time, teachers who were untenured were fearful about the insecurity of their positions. As untenured, Jessica Bonwit said on the last day of school when she was unsure whether she would be able to return the following year, "The job status situation is so disheartening for me. I just think it is devastating to teachers not to know where they are going to be next year. It's a terrible way to treat us." The occupational structure was disheartening.

[40]Feldberg and Glenn, "Male and Female."

[41]Arlie Hochschild, "Inside the Clockwork of Male Careers," in *Women and the Power to Change,* ed. Florence Howe (New York: McGraw-Hill, 1971): 47–80.

Source: "Can Elementary Schoolteaching Be a Career? A Search for New Ways of Understanding Women's Work" by Sari Knopp Biklen, *Issues in Education,* Vol. III, No. 3, Winter 1985. Copyright © 1985 by the American Educational Research Association. Reprinted by permission.

Conclusions The conclusion usually includes a restatement of the initial focus of the study and how the data results and analyses impinge on that focus. Implications of the results can be elaborated, as well as implications for further research.

Guidelines for Evaluating Qualitative Research

To understand qualitative research it is necessary to carefully read the entire report. This is how you are able to identify with the investigators and understand how they have come to their conclusions. The process by which this occurs is important, and to understand this process it is necessary to read from beginning to end. As with quantitative studies, there are certain questions that should be asked about the report to judge its quality.

Introduction

1. Is the focus, purpose, or topic of the study stated clearly?
2. Are there situations or problems that lead to the focus of the study? Is there a rationale for the study? Is it clear that the study is important?
3. Is there background research and theory to help refine the research questions?
4. Does the introduction contain an overview of the design?
5. Is the literature review pertinent to the focus of the research? Is the literature analyzed as well as described?

Methodology

1. Are the particular sites described to identify their uniqueness or typicality?
2. How was initial entry into the field established?
3. How was the researcher's presence in the field explained to others? What was the role of the researcher?
4. Who was observed? How long were they observed? How much time was spent collecting data?
5. Does the researcher report any limitations to access of pertinent data?
6. Are the data representative of naturally occurring behavior?
7. Are limitations of the design acknowledged?

Findings and Interpretations

1. Are the perspectives of the different participants clearly presented? Are participants' words or comments quoted?
2. Is contextual information for participants' statements provided?
3. Are multiple perspectives presented?
4. Are the results well documented? Are assertions and interpretations illustrated by results?
5. Is it clear what the researchers believe the data indicated? Are personal beliefs kept separate from the data?
6. Are the interpretations reasonable? Were researcher preconceptions and biases acknowledged?

Conclusions

1. Are the conclusions logically consistent with the findings?
2. Are limitations of the research design and focus indicated?
3. Are implications of the findings indicated?

Summary

This chapter has provided an overview of common terminology of types of research with reference to their mode of inquiry, the techniques used to collect data, and the standard format of published articles. The major points in this chapter are as follows:

1. Mode of inquiry is the general approach and methodological preference used in the study.
2. Research design is the general plan of the study, including when, from whom, and how data are collected.
3. In experimental research the investigator studies cause-and-effect relationships by manipulating a factor and seeing how that factor relates to the outcome of the study.
4. True experimental research is characterized by random assignment of subjects to groups, control over factors that might disrupt the study, and decisions as to which treatment is given to each group.
5. Quasi-experimental research investigates causation without random assignment and complete control.
6. Single-subject research investigates the causal relationship between a factor and the behavior of a single individual.
7. "Nonexperimental" is a generic term that refers to research in which there is no direct control over causation. Nonexperimental modes of inquiry can be classified as descriptive, comparative, correlational, survey or *ex post facto*.
8. Techniques to gather information include quantitative and qualitative approaches. Quantitative techniques, like questionnaires and tests, use numbers as data, while qualitative techniques, like ethnography, use narrative descriptions.
9. Interactive qualitative modes of inquiry use face-to-face data collection to construct in-depth understandings of informants' perspectives.
10. An ethnography is a detailed description and interpretation of a culture or system.
11. A phenomenological study describes the meanings of a lived experience from the perspective of the informants.
12. A case study investigates a single bounded system over time, using multiple sources of data.
13. Grounded theory is used to develop detailed concepts or propositions about a particular phenomena.
14. Critical studies emphasize the subjectivity of knowledge and contemporary perspectives of critical, feminist, and postmodern theory.

15. Noninteractive qualitative modes of inquiry, or analytic research, investigates concepts and events through document analysis.
16. The format of quantitative studies follows a well-established sequence with similar sections. In qualitative studies the format will vary but will usually include an introduction and literature review, methodology, findings and interpretation, and conclusions.

Self-Instructional Review Exercises

Sample answers are in the back of the book.

Test Items

1. True experimental research contains all of the following characteristics *except*
    a. a control or comparison group.
    b. random assignment of subjects.
    c. intensive interviews with subjects.
    d. manipulation of subjects.
2. Quasi-experimental designs differ from true experimental designs in
    a. degree of control.
    b. use of comparison or control group.
    c. random assignment.
    d. Both a and c are correct.
3. In nonexperimental research the investigator can do all of the following *except*
    a. make inferences from a sample to a population.
    b. describe existing conditions.
    c. establish cause-and-effect relationships.
    d. predict one phenomenon from another.
4. An ethnographic study can be classified as
    a. phenomenological.
    b. noninteractive.
    c. interactive.
    d. grounded theory.
5. In correlational research the investigator is studying
    a. the existing conditions in a descriptive manner.
    b. cause-and-effect relationships.
    c. the same event at two points in time.
    d. the degree of relationship between two phenomena.
6. Structured observations are in the same category as
    a. applied research.
    b. descriptive research.
    c. evaluation research.
    d. none of the above.

7. Qualitative data collection techniques are distinguished from quantitative techniques by
    a. the research design used.
    b. the function of the research.
    c. using words rather than numbers.
    d. providing more meaningful results.
8. Phenomenologic research is often characterized by
    a. intense interviews.
    b. copious field notes.
    c. clearly defined hypotheses.
    d. unobtrusive observations.
9. The abstract of an article contains
    a. a full description of the subjects.
    b. recommendations for further study.
    c. the purpose of the study.
    d. Both a and c are correct.
10. The methodology section of a quantitative research article contains
    a. subjects, materials, instruments.
    b. participants, instruments, procedure.
    c. subjects, instruments, data analyses.
    d. participants, subjects, procedures.
11. The hypotheses in quantitative research should follow the
    a. research problem.
    b. review of literature.
    c. introduction.
    d. abstract.
12. The purpose of the methodology section of qualitative studies is to
    a. provide a general background for the study.
    b. summarize the design of the study.
    c. show how researcher interpretations will be made.
    d. present the focus of the study.

Application Problems

1. Classify each study described below with respect to its research design: experimental, nonexperimental, quantitative, or qualitative. More than one type may be appropriate.
    a. a pilot investigation of the validity of the Back Stroke Test to identify problem swimmers
    b. a comparison of the effect of two reading programs on fourth-grade classes in Kalamazoo
    c. an investigation of the structure of attitudes of college students
    d. the effect of extrinsic rewards on the motivation of randomly assigned children to play groups
    e. a survey of principals' attitudes toward collective bargaining
    f. a study of the relative effectiveness of different counseling techniques used by counselors over the past five years

g. an investigation of the difference in attendance between two high schools with different leadership styles

h. a posttest-only study of the effect of humorously written review sentences on comprehension for two groups of children

i. a study of the meaning of merit pay to teachers

2. Read a quantitative research article and identify the sentences that correspond to the standard sections named below.
   a. abstract
   b. introduction
   c. statement of research problem
   d. review of literature
   e. statement of research hypotheses
   f. subjects
   g. instruments
   h. procedures
   i. results
   j. discussion, implications, conclusions

3. Read a qualitative research article and identify the major sections:
   a. introduction
   b. methodology
   c. results and interpretations
   d. conclusions

4. Describe the research in problems 2 and 3 with respect to mode of inquiry and technique for collecting data.

CHAPTER 3

Research Problems: Statements, Questions, and Hypotheses

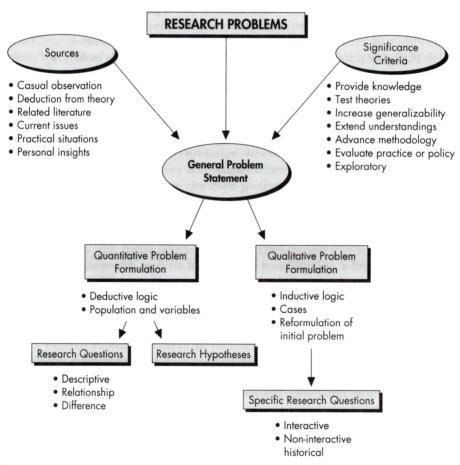

K E Y   T E R M S

research problem
quantitative:
   construct
   variable
   categorical variable
   continuous or measured
     variable
   dependent variable
   independent variable
   manipulated or experimental
     variable
   predictor variable
   criterion variable
   operational definition
   research hypothesis

qualitative:
   case
   qualitative field records
   narrative descriptions
   synthesized abstractions
    foreshadowed problems
significance of the problem

This chapter presents what is perhaps the most difficult aspect of research: formulating a clear, concise, and manageable research problem. The research problem statement is crucial because it communicates to others the focus and importance of the problem, the educational context and scope, and the framework for reporting the results. To state a formal research problem requires considerable preliminary work and the selection of appropriate deductive or inductive logic.

This chapter also discusses common sources used to generate research problems and criteria for the significance of research problems. Quantitative problem formulations use deductive reasoning to select the constructs, variables, and instruments. Qualitative problems require inductive reasoning. Qualitative problems are reformulated as the researcher builds from observations of social situations of current or past events of a selected case and later relates them to broader phenomena. We also cite criteria for judging the adequacy of the problem statement.

The Nature of Research Problems

Researchers can ask many questions about educational theories and practices. Consider the following range of questions:

> What is the present status of a group's opinions or performance?
> What are the effects of a specific practice, innovation, or policy?

How do past historical events, court rulings, or policies influence current educational issues?

How does Mrs. Kay teach biology to lower-achieving students?

What are the theoretical assumptions that guide daily practices and long-range planning?

Why is Ellen quiet during small group reading and disruptive when students choose their learning centers and their activities?

What is the best way to conduct one's work?

Questions such as these constitute the initial step in research.

Some questions, although important to an individual or a group, may not connote research problems as stated. The noun *problem* has conventional and technical meanings. In the conventional sense, a problem is a set of conditions needing discussion, a decision, a solution, or information. A **research problem** implies the possibility of empirical investigation—that is, of data collection and analysis.

Explanations of how to do something, vague propositions, and value questions are not research problems *per se*. Questions like, "How can we achieve equal opportunity?" or "How can we prevent student dropout?" are how-to questions. Such propositions as "Democratic institutions are a natural manifestation of the American culture" are too vague or broad to be researchable. Value questions ask which of two or more things is good or bad, desirable or undesirable, better or worse, should or should not be done. Value questions, as stated, cannot be investigated empirically. Although how-to questions, vague propositions, and value questions are meaningful to administrators, parents, teachers, philosophers, and political leaders, these questions, as stated, are beyond research. In the process of asking such questions, however, a researchable problem may emerge.

A research problem, in contrast with a practical problem, is formally stated to indicate a need for empirical investigation. Quantitative research problems may be phrased as questions or hypotheses. Let us look at some examples. "What are the attitudes of the parents toward a school's student retention policy?" "Is there a difference in Levinson's adult development periods between age cohorts of male and female graduate students?" "There is a positive relationship between preschool attendance and social maturity in elementary students—that is, A relates to B." "Do academic aptitude, self-concept, and level of aspiration influence academic achievement—that is, do A, B, and C relate to D?" Each of these statements implies data collection and analysis.

Qualitative research problems are phrased as research statements or questions, but *never* as hypotheses. A research hypothesis implies deductive reasoning; qualitative research uses primarily inductive reasoning to suggest an understanding of a particular situation or historical period. Qualitative problems usually are phrased more broadly than quantitative problems by using terms such as *how, what,* and *why*. Qualitative problems state the situation or context in such a way as to limit the problem. A qualitative problem might be a study of one specific situation, a person, one state, or a historical period. Some examples of qualitative research questions are "How does Mrs. Jackson, an elementary teacher, assist Jim, a student teacher, during his student teaching?" or "What does being a 'single parent' mean to Mr. Strong who has two young children to rear—how does being a single parent affect his parenting role and other aspects of his life?"

Qualitative studies also examine the past through historical or legal documents. These research questions are typically phrased in the past tense. For example, "When and why were teachers first required to be certified by the state of Vermont, how have the requirements for teacher certification changed since then, and why were these changes made?" Qualitative research problems may be phrased as research statements such as "The purpose of this study is to examine and analyze the legal grounds upheld by federal and state courts in cases involving student disruption from 1952 to 1999 to provide a judicial definition of the term 'student disruption.'"

Sources of Problems

Problems are identified initially as general topics. After much preliminary work, the general topic is focused as a specific research problem. Where does one begin to find even general topics? The most common sources are casual observations, deductions from theory, review of the literature, current social issues, practical situations, and personal experiences and insights. We'll examine the kinds of studies these sources might suggest.

Casual Observations Casual observations are rich sources of questions and hunches. Decisions are frequently based on the probable effects of practices on pupils, staff, or the community without empirical data. Research questions can be suggested by observations of certain relationships for which no satisfactory explanation exists, routine ways of doing things that are based on authority or tradition lacking research evidence, or innovations and technological changes that need long-term confirmation. Such studies may solve a practical problem, propose a new theory, or identify variables not yet in the literature.

Deductions from Theory Deductions from theory can suggest research problems. Theories are general principles whose applicability to specific educational problems are unknown until tested empirically. The validity and scope of a variety of theories might be tested under educational conditions. Such studies could verify the usefulness of a theory for explaining educational occurrences.

Related Literature Related literature may suggest a need to replicate a study with or without variation. Repeating a study may increase the generalizability and validity of the previous findings. In many instances, it is impossible to randomize the subjects, which limits the *generalizability* of the findings. As experiments are repeated at different times and in different settings, with similar results, however, researchers can have more confidence in the findings. Citing related literature enables qualitative studies to *extend the empirical understandings* to other situations.

Current Social and Political Issues Current social and political issues in American society often result in educational research. The women's movement raised questions about sex equity in general and gender stereotyping of educational materials and practices. The civil rights movement led to research on the education of minority children and the effects of desegregation on racial attitudes, race relations, self-concept, achievement, and the like. Recent immigration policies suggested research questions of multiculturalism in education.

Practical Situations Because information is needed by decision-makers at a given site, practical situations may suggest evaluation and policy studies. Although a research problem is not stated as a value question, the information it engenders is used to make value-based decisions. Questions for such research may focus on educational needs; information for program planning, development, and implementation; or the effectiveness of a practice.

Personal Experience and Insights Personal experience and insights may suggest research problems that should be examined more in depth through qualitative methodologies. For example, a teacher who has worked with exceptional children can recognize more readily the meanings in a situation involving exceptional children than an ethnographer who has had no prior contact with exceptional children. A historian who has served as a department chairperson could more easily empathize with a historical figure who was the president of a university. The ability to empathize and to recognize the subtle meanings in a situation is important in most qualitative research.

Formal Problem Statements

Researchers use formal problem statements to guide their research. The statements introduce the reader to the importance of the problem, place the problem in an educational context, and provide the framework for reporting the results. The problem statement orients the reader to the significance of the study and the research questions or hypotheses to follow.

The Focus, Educational Context, and Significance of the Problem In any well-written problem statement, the reader is not kept in suspense but is told directly and immediately the general focus, educational context, and significance of the problem. For example, the reader is told in the first paragraphs of "Who will lead? The top 10 factors that influence teachers moving into administration" (Cooley & Shen, 1999) about the expected shortage in the number of school administrators and teacher reluctance to enter administration. The study was conducted to identify factors that influenced teachers' decision to apply for an administration position. (See Excerpt 3.1).

EXCERPT 3.1

PROBLEM STATEMENT: FRAMEWORK

Who will lead the schools during the 21st century? Approximately 60 percent of the principals currently holding administrative posts reach retirement age by next year [2000] (Parkay and Currie, 1992). The problem is exacerbated by the declining number of teachers seeking administrator certification and the fact that many who are studying for the degree do not plan to seek an administrative position after completing degree requirements (Jordon, 1994). . . .Teacher reluctance to enter administration coupled with the number of administrator retirements present a significant challenge to boards, superintendents, and communities. . . .

To help find a solution to this problem, a study was conducted of 189 master's students enrolled in a midwestern university's educational leadership program. Students completed a survey identifying factors that influenced their decision to apply for an administrative position. . . .

The top 10 factors that influence teachers applying for administrative position suggest a complex list of "wants and needs" for this new generation of school leaders. The factors listed in Table 1 have implications for retaining and recruiting school leaders.

Source: From Cooley, V. & Shen, J. (April, 1999). Who will lead? The top 10 factors that influence teachers moving into administration (p. 75). *NASSP Bulletin, 83* (606), 75-80.

A different focus, educational context, and significance of the problem are stated in "The High School as a Social Service Agency: Historical Perspectives on Current Policy Issues". "The purpose of this essay is to examine historically the expansion of social services to youth through American public secondary education....[to] shed light on the difficult choices policy-makers face today" (Tyack, 1979, p. 45). Within the first two paragraphs of the study the reader is told that the educational context is American public secondary education; that the concept examined is social services expansion; that the study is historical, encompassing the years 1890 to 1975; and that an understanding of the reasons such programs were added in the first place may help policymakers decide which educational functions and services to cut for balanced budgets.

A Framework for Results and Conclusions The problem statement also provides the framework for reporting the conclusions. Unlike the research design, in which researchers state what methods they will use to complete the study, the problem statement merely indicates what is probably necessary to conduct the study and explains that the findings will present this information. Excerpt 3.1 exemplifies the framework for the findings of a study. Ten factors that teachers consider in applying for administrative positions were reported and discussed with implications for recruiting and retaining a new generation of school leaders.

Qualitative problem statements also provide the framework for reporting the findings and interpretations. For example, in a recent study, the problem was to report the "findings on the perception of poor single mothers regarding the helpfulness of their support systems in enabling them to work" (Wijnberg & Weinger, 1998). The findings were organized as early dreams and their retrieval, perceived network support and resources, coping styles, and social support when ill.

The introductory paragraphs of a study are difficult to write: they must convey much information succinctly. Researchers frequently rewrite the paragraphs as they formulate the significance of the study and research questions. They may even write the final version of the paragraphs after the study is completed. Researchers, however, begin with an initial problem statement to guide their activities.

Problem Formulation in Quantitative Research

Asking questions about a topic related to education is the starting point for defining a research problem, but educational research topics are not problem statements *per se*. A problem statement is more specific than a topic and limits the scope of the research problem.

A researcher starts with a general topic and narrows the topic to a problem. For example, the topic of educational policymaking might focus on school board policies. This is still a broad topic and may be narrowed to certain policies, such as fiscal, student, or personnel. The topic can be focused even more: Is the researcher interested in the antecedents to policies, the process of policymaking, or the consequences of policies? Is it the effects of policies, and if so, effects on whom? From one general topic, a number of questions could thus be generated: What influences school board formulations of policies? What was the intent of the teacher evaluation policy and how were the procedures implemented? What effect does teacher evaluation have on teachers' morale? What effect does teacher evaluation have on administrators' attitudes and behavior? What are the opinions of administrators, parents, and teachers toward our present teacher evaluation policy? How frequently in the past five years has the teacher evaluation policy in a school system led to changed teacher behavior, nonrenewal of contract, denial of tenure, or proceedings resulting in a court case?

Suppose the topic of interest were instruction. Again, a researcher could ask similar questions: What kind of instruction? Is the focus on antecedents, the process, or the consequences? Is the focus on specific ages, or students with certain characteristics? A topic such as the use of hand calculators in mathematics instruction might generate the question, "Is there a difference among comparable students in the use of hand calculators in mathematics computation?" Notice that the question fails to specify how frequently hand calculators are used, how mathematics computation is determined, or which students are similar. This problem would be more precise if it were stated: "Among comparable fourth-grade students, is there a difference in the mathematics computation scores of the SRA Achievement Test between students who had used hand calculators in mathematics for a semester and those who had not?"

To make the study manageable, researchers narrow their topics to a particular problem. If a problem is too general the results are difficult to interpret. Several activities can help focus a topic as a problem. Reading secondary literature may clarify the problem and narrow it to possible questions and variables. Talking with those who might use the study can clarify their needs and questions. Brainstorming with others who have research training, experience, or specialized knowledge of the problem area is beneficial. Ultimately, the researcher has to make decisions about the selection of variables, the population, and the *logic for the problem*. Initial problem statements are usually reworked and reworded many times as each word is scrutinized for the exact meaning and the logical reasoning to be employed in the research. The deductive logic of quantitative problems is illustrated in Figure 3.1. We explain each term and its various meanings in the next section.

The Deductive Logic of Constructs, Variables, and Operational Definitions

To formulate a problem, the researcher begins with an abstract construct and then determines whether the selected variables are logically deduced from the construct. The next step is to select the observations reasoned to relate to the variables by deduction. The observations are then operationally defined by a researcher-chosen instrument to measure the phenomenon. The three-step deductive reasoning from abstract constructs to less abstract variables to a set of

FIGURE 3.1   Deductive Logic in Quantitative Research: Constructs, Variables, and Observations

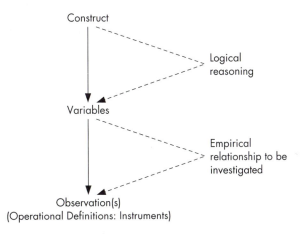

observations is schematically represented in Figure 3.1 and is explained in more detail below. Note that the direction of the arrows is from top to bottom, to illustrate deductive reasoning. In other words, the researcher must make several decisions to propose a predetermined design *before* data are collected.

Constructs In research, higher-level, abstract concepts are called **constructs.** Constructs express the idea behind a set of particulars. A construct is often derived from a theory. The construct *anxiety,* for example, is derived from personality theory. A **construct** is a complex abstraction that is not directly observable. Examples of constructs are motivation, intelligence, thinking, anxiety, aggression, self-concept, achievement, and aptitude. What is observable is the behavior or response presumed to be a consequence of the hypothesized construct. Another way to define a construct is to say that we create constructs by combining concepts in meaningful patterns. Such concepts as visual perception, sight-sound discrimination, audio acuity, and left-to-right orientation are meaningfully combined to suggest the construct of *reading readiness.* The construct *creativity* is generally recognized to consist of flexibility, originality, elaboration, and other concepts. Constructs change their meaning or are discarded as theories are developed or empirical evidence is accumulated.

Because constructs are intangible entities and not directly observable, researchers use indicators as a way of measuring or classifying most of the particulars of the construct. These indicators are called *variables.* As noted above, there may be more than one variable for a construct and more than one type of observation for a variable. The researcher deductively chooses the most valid indicators.

Variables A **variable** is an event, category, behavior, or attribute that expresses a construct and has different values, depending on how it is used in a particular study. There are several types of variables. A variable used to separate subjects, objects, or entities into two or more categories is a **categorical variable.** The simplest type of categorical variable has only two classes; it is a dichotomous variable. Male–female, married–single, and pass–fail are dichotomous variables. Categorical variables can have more than two classes, such as income level, educational level, nationality, or religious affiliation. A **continuous** or **measured variable** is one in which the property or attribute of an object, subject, or entity is measured numerically and can assume an infinite number of values within a range. Weight, height, and age are common examples of continuous variables. In education, typical measured variables are achievement, verbal ability, aptitude, attitudes, and specific skills.

Quantitative research typically involves relationships of categorical and measured variables. Some variables are antecedents to other variables. Researchers may know this from previous studies, or they may hypothesize from a theory that one variable is an antecedent to another. They may, for example, say that academic achievement is preceded by intelligence. It is assumed that to achieve in school, a child needs to have some degree of intelligence. The variable *intelligence* is an antecedent to the variable *achievement.* To some extent, achievement is a consequence of intelligence; it is dependent on an individual's degree of intelligence. The variable that is a consequence of some phenomenon is the focus of the study; it is usually a measured variable. The antecedent variable may be either categorical or measured. Each variable should be a separate and distinct phenomenon. Educational research investigates many factors as variables: classroom variables such as teaching styles, interaction patterns, cognitive level of questions; environmental variables such as parental educational level, social class, family structure; and personal variables such as age, gender, intelligence, motivation, or self-concept.

In experimental research, we often call the variable that is the consequence of or is dependent on antecedent variables the **dependent variable.** A variable that is antecedent to or precedes the dependent variable is called the **independent, manipulated,** or **experimental variable,** that is, the variable that is manipulated or changed by the researcher to investigate the effect on a dependent variable. The effect of the manipulation is observed on the dependent variable. It is called a dependent variable because its value depends on and varies with the value of the independent variable. Suppose a researcher wanted to see the effect of the timing of a review on social studies achievement. The research manipulates the timing of the review—immediate and delayed—and then measures the effects on social studies achievement. After the relationship has been established empirically, the researcher can predict from the independent variable to the dependent variable.

In nonexperimental research such as descriptive, correlational, and survey studies, the variables are *not* directly or actively manipulated by the researcher. In descriptive research and some survey research, there may be only one variable of interest. Studies that describe the reading achievement level of second graders or surveys of parental attitudes toward a school policy contain only one variable of interest.

In some correlational research, the antecedent variable is called the **predictor variable** and the predicted variable is the **criterion variable.** In a study that examines the relationship of scores on the Scholastic Assessment Test to success in college, the predictor variable is the SAT scores and the criterion variable is college success. In other correlation studies, there is no obvious antecedent variable. An example is a study of the relationship between self-concept and achievement. The researcher is not interested in which variable precedes the other, but, instead, is interested in the strength and direction of the relationship between the variables. Some researchers will use the terms *independent* and *dependent* variable with correlational and other nonexperimental research when it is clear that one variable precedes or is antecedent to the other variable, or that categories are created to allow comparisons.

A variable may be independent in one study and dependent in another; a variable also may be a predictor or a criterion variable. Whether the variable functions as an independent or dependent variable, as a predictor or a criterion variable, or as the only variable in a study depends on the purpose, logic, and design of the study. The problem statement is phrased to indicate how the variables will function in the proposed study.

Observations: Operational Definitions   *Observation(s)* in Figure 3.1 refers to the data collection method, which the researcher deductively reasons is related to the variable of interest. In quantitative research, *observation* usually refers to an instrument that can measure a variable.

Each variable in a quantitative study must be defined operationally and subsequently categorized, measured, or manipulated. There are two kinds of definitions: constitutive and operational. A constitutive definition, similar to that found in a dictionary, defines a term by using other terms. A dictionary may define *anxiety* as "apprehension or vague fear" or *intelligence* as "mental acuity" and "the ability to think abstractly." These definitions are insufficient for researchers. Notice that for *intelligence* common synonyms are part of the constitutive definition. Researchers use operational definitions. An **operational definition** assigns meaning to a variable by specifying the activities or operations necessary to measure, categorize, or manipulate the variable. Operational definitions tell the researcher and reader what is necessary for answering the question or testing the hypothesis.

To use an extreme example, the hypothesis "Intelligence relates positively to achievement" can be defined operationally by specifying how the researcher will measure the two variables. The variable "intelligence" is measured by the scores on X intelligence test, or, stated another way, intelligence is what X intelligence test measures in the study. Achievement may be defined operationally by citing a standardized test, a teacher-made achievement test, grades, or other assessment methods. Variables frequently can be defined operationally in several ways, and some operations may be more valid for a research problem than others. The operational definition for a variable is often not as valid as a researcher desires. To conduct research, however, one must define each variable operationally.

Specific research questions and hypotheses may operationalize the variables. For example, the hypothesis "There is a positive relationship between self-esteem and creativity" may be stated operationally by saying: "There is a positive relationship between the scores on the Coopersmith Self-Esteem Scale and the scores on the Torrance Test of Creative Thinking." Such a statement indicates that the researcher has chosen these particular operational procedures.

Problem Formulation

A useful procedure for transforming a general topic or question into a manageable problem is to identify the population, the variables, and the logic of the problem. Suppose a supervisor is interested in different ways to organize a program for elementary students found to be talented and gifted and to learn its effect on student creativity. Talented and gifted programs have been organized in several ways: as special programs in which students remain together for a comprehensive program; as pullout programs in which students attend regular classes except for two hours' daily instruction by selected teachers; and as enrichment programs in which students complete enrichment activities as an extension of their regular instruction. The question becomes: "Is there a difference in creativity (the dependent variable) between talented and gifted elementary students (the population) who participate in a special program, a pullout program, or an enrichment program (three levels of one independent variable)?" This question is narrowed to the degree that it identifies the population and the two variables. The logic of the question is clear because the relationship between the independent and dependent variables can be identified.

Suppose a question is phrased: "Does mainstreaming do any good?" As phrased, the question has neither a population nor variables. A researcher might decide that the real interest lies in changes in the attitudes of nonhandicapped children toward handicapped children. Attitude becomes the dependent variable, and nonhandicapped children is a partial identification of the population. The researcher decides that probably the age group most likely to experience a change in attitudes is high school students rather than younger children, who may be just forming attitudes. High school students constitute the designated population. The researcher decides, furthermore, that "mainstreaming" is too vague, and the independent variable should be six weeks' participation in a mainstreamed class. Now the research problem is phrased: "Is there a difference between high school students' (the population) attitudes toward handicapped students (the dependent variable) who participated in a six weeks' mainstreamed class and the attitude of those who did not (the independent variable)?" Notice that the question fails to mention change, the primary focus of the study. The question is thus rephrased: "Is there a difference between the pre- and post-attitudes toward handicapped students (dependent variable) between high school students (the population) who participated in a six weeks' mainstreamed class and those who did not (the independent variable)?" Now the question is focused and the logic of the problem explicit.

Some problems have a defined population and variables, but one cannot distinguish the independent from the dependent variable. If a researcher is interested in self-esteem and academic achievement, which is the dependent variable? Is the problem investigating whether achievement relates to positive self-esteem (the dependent variable) or is the problem whether self-esteem relates positively to achievement (the dependent variable)? The difficulty here lies in the nature of the variables. In these problems, categorical and measured variables are used, but not manipulated or experimental variables. The problem can be phrased: "Among sixth-grade students, is there a difference between students with low self-esteem and those with high self-esteem and their academic achievement?" The population is sixth-grade students, and the variables are self-esteem and academic achievement. Neither variable is manipulated, since the subjects already have these attributes—that is, self-esteem and achievement. Neither variable is labeled as independent or dependent because one cannot determine which is antecedent to the other.

By identifying the major construct, variables, and population, the researcher clarifies the focus and logic of a problem. This process is not easy and, as mentioned previously, it is not done without preliminary work. Reading literature, brainstorming with others, and talking with experienced researchers can help in stating a problem. With the idea now clearly in mind, the researcher can write a formal problem statement. A formal problem statement may be phrased as statements of research purpose, as specific research questions, or as research hypotheses, depending on the purpose of the study and the selected design. Each of these ways of stating specific research problems is explained below.

Specific Research Questions

In quantitative studies the research problem may be stated in question form. The question format is often preferred because it is simple and direct. Psychologically, it orients the researcher to the immediate task: to develop a design to answer the question. Research questions may be descriptive questions, relationship questions, or difference questions. Each type of question implies a different design (see Figure 3.2).

FIGURE 3.2   Logic of Quantitative Problem Statements and Specific Research Questions

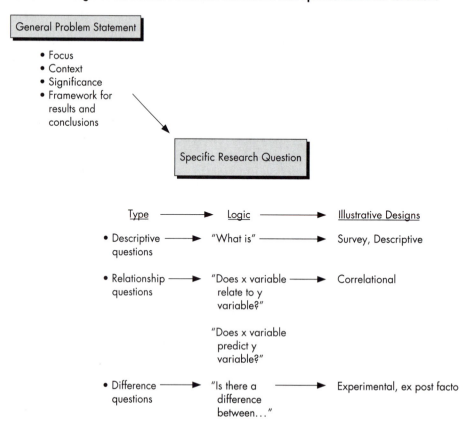

Descriptive Research Questions Descriptive research questions typically ask "what is" and imply survey and descriptive research designs. These terms, however, are not always used in the wording of the research questions. For example, a research question may be "What is the achievement level of our fourth-grade students on the Iowa Test of Basic Skills?" Survey research often investigates the perceptions of groups concerned with a practice, such as "What are the administrators' opinions of a program?" "What are the attitudes of our students toward the mainstreamed children?" "Which of the alternative bus routes do our pupils' parents prefer?" or "What does the staff perceive as our most important instructional needs?"

Relationship Questions Relationship questions ask, "What is the relationship between two or more variables?" and imply a correlational design. This does not mean that the exact words "What is the relationship between variable A and variable B?" always appear in the statement. As an example, "Does self-concept relate to achievement?" asks a question about the relationship between one variable (self-concept) and another variable (achievement). Studies that determine the best predictors for a variable, such as predictors of college success, imply relationship questions between the possible predictor variables like high school grade point average and class rank, recommendations, and participation in extracurricular activities and the dependent variable, college success. Excerpt 3.2 illustrates a problem statement that implies a relationship question between selected long-range predictors and children's social adjustment. The problem statement suggests the design for the study.

Difference Questions Difference questions typically ask "Is there a difference between two groups, two or more treatments or two data sets (measurements)?" They are used when the study compares two or more observations. Stating the question as "Is there a difference?" rather than "Is there a relationship?" between two or more observations clarifies the underlying logic of the study. Questions such as "Is there a difference between pretest and posttest

---

EXCERPT 3.2

RELATIONSHIP QUESTIONS

The objectives of the present inquiry were: (a) to identify long-range correlates or predictors of social adjustment and (b) to determine the multiple correlation between a best set of these correlates or predictors and the social adjustment of children after 6 or 9 years had elapsed. The subjects were children who were first evaluated in third or sixth grade and for whom social adjustment was assessed 6 or 9 years later.

Source: From Feldhusen, J. F., Roeser, T. D., & Thurston, J. R. (1977), Prediction of social adjustment over a period of 6 or 9 years, *Journal of Special Education, 11* (1), 31.

scores?" are more useful than those phrased "Is there a relationship between pretest and posttest scores?"

Experimental and *ex post facto* designs employ difference questions. Excerpt 3.3 illustrates research questions which require comparisons of two treatments (traditional instruction with game/simulation instruction) on three different dependent variables.

If researchers firmly believe that in addition to predicting a difference between two or more observations, they can predict the direction in which the difference lies, then the direction is stated in the research question. The question "Is there a difference in pretest and posttest scores?" may thus be stated: "Is there greater mastery of reading comprehension on the posttest than on the pretest?"

Research questions are not statistical questions stated for data analysis. Statistical questions may be phrased: "Is there a statistically significant difference between A and B observations?" or "Is there a statistically significant relationship between A variable and B variable?" Statistical questions are stated in the methodology section of a study. Research questions are stated in the introduction of a study and suggest the design.

Research Hypotheses

A **research hypothesis** is a tentative statement of the expected relationship between two or more variables. The statement describes, in other words, the predicted results. Problem statements and research hypotheses are similar in substance, except that research hypotheses are declarative statements, more specific than problem statements, clearly testable, and indicative of the expected results. For the research problem, "Is there a relationship between review and retention?" the research hypothesis might be: "There is a positive relationship between review and retention." Empirical testing is feasible to the extent that each variable can be manipulated, categorized, or measured. If a

---

EXCERPT 3.3

DIFFERENCE QUESTIONS

RQ 1: Are there significant differences in student affective learning between traditional classroom instruction and instruction through a game/simulation?

RQ 2: Are there significant differences in student cognitive learning between traditional classroom instruction and instruction through a game/simulation?

RQ 3: Are there significant differences in student state motivation between traditional classroom instruction and instruction through a game/simulation?

Source: From Garard, D. L., Hunt, S. K., Lippert, L., & Paynton, S.T. (1998). Alternative to traditional instruction: Using games and simulation to increase student learning and motivation (p. 38). *Communication Research Reports, 15* (1), 36–44.

variable cannot be manipulated, categorized, or measured, there is no quantitative method of analysis for testing the hypothesis.

Three examples of research hypotheses are "The greater the perceived differences between adults as learners and adolescents as learners, the greater the differences in teaching behaviors"; "Low reading students in a remedial reading course will achieve higher reading comprehension than comparable students in an English literature course"; and "Democratic leadership style produces greater faculty satisfaction than authoritarian leadership style." Although the word *relationship* is not used in every hypothesis, relation expressions such as *will achieve, produces, is a function of,* and *effects* connect the variables.

A hypothesis implies an if-then logic. Most hypotheses can be put into an if-then form to indicate the relationship between variables. In each of the three examples above, the hypothesis has an independent and a dependent variable: If perceived differences, then greater differences in teaching behavior; if a remedial course, then higher reading comprehension; and if democratic leadership style, then faculty satisfaction. The logic is similar for hypotheses with more than two variables.

A hypothesis is a conjectural explanation of phenomena that is accepted or rejected by empirical evidence. In the above examples, the perceived difference between adults as learners and pre-adults as learners explains the differences in teaching behaviors; a remedial reading course explains higher achievement; and democratic leadership style accounts for faculty satisfaction.

Hypotheses are especially important in correlational and experimental research that investigate relations between variables. To be useful in research, a hypothesis should meet several standards:

1. *The hypothesis should state the expected relationship or difference between two or more variables.* A statement such as "if teacher feedback, then student science achievement" implies a relationship but it is not a hypothesis. The directional hypothesis might state: "Teacher feedback will relate positively to student science achievement" or "There is a positive relationship between teacher feedback and student science achievement."

In experimental research in which a treatment is administered to one group of subjects but not to another group, researchers should hypothesize directional differences. For example: "Fifth-grade students who receive microcomputer-assisted instruction will have higher math achievement than comparable students who did not receive microcomputer-assisted instruction."

2. *A hypothesis should be testable.* A testable hypothesis is verifiable; one can draw conclusions from empirical observations that indicate whether the relationship is supported or not supported. The researcher can determine whether the hypothesized consequences did or did not occur. To be testable, a hypothesis must include related variables that can be measured or categorized by some objective procedure. For example, because one can classify first-grade students as having attended preschool or not, a hypothesis might state: "Children who attend preschool will have higher scores on a scale of social

maturity than children who do not attend preschool." If a variable cannot be measured or categorized, there is no method to make the necessary statistical comparisons.

3. *A hypothesis should offer a tentative explanation based on theory or previous research.* A well-grounded hypothesis indicates there is sufficient research or theory for considering the hypothesis important enough to test. A research hypothesis usually is stated after a literature review; the researcher has knowledge of the previous work. A hypothesis generally does not disagree with the preponderance of prior evidence, but, if tested, it could extend our knowledge of the research problem. If the hypothesis is theoretically grounded in social science, it is possible for the results of the study to contribute to the theory under examination. In many areas of education, however, there is little conclusive evidence, and only some educational research can serve as a basis for the research hypothesis.

4. *A hypothesis should be concise and lucid.* A hypothesis in its simplest form should have logical coherence and a clear order of arrangement. Brief statements aid both the reader and the researcher in interpreting the results. A general rule is to state only one relationship per hypothesis. Although a researcher may have one general broad hypothesis, it is better to rephrase the broad statement into more specific hypotheses for clarity.

Problem Formulation in Qualitative Research

Problem formulation in qualitative research begins with selecting a general topic and a mode of inquiry (interactive or noninteractive). The topic and methodology are *interrelated* and are selected almost simultaneously rather than in separate research steps. For example, an early research decision is whether to examine ongoing or past events. A study of current phenomena requires the researcher to have access to a site or a group of people who have some shared social experience, such as working in the same school system, participating in a special project or a class, and the like. A study of past events requires archival collections of primary documents that are available and accessible to the researcher. These considerations begin to shape and influence the selection of a general topic.

Qualitative researchers begin by narrowing a general topic to a more definitive topic. Suppose one is interested in the teaching of reading and writing. There are several theoretical orientations to literacy, such as decoding, skills, and whole language. The researcher is interested in the whole language approach and his or her personal observations and experience suggest that a *whole language* classroom operates differently from the *phonics* or *skills* classroom. For example, there would be no spelling books, no sets of reading texts with controlled readability, and no writing assignments. Instead, children's writing would be integrated in a children's literature reading program with "whole meaningful texts" as instructional materials rather than "isolated words, sounds, or vocabulary-controlled 'stories' " (Edelsky, Draper, & Smith, 1983, p. 259). The researcher begins to wonder, "How does a teacher get children to read and to write regularly to meet expectations in this unusual situation?"

As another example, suppose a researcher noticed that testing in the public schools had increased in the last decade, and she or he had heard criticism that teachers, administrators, and counselors use testing to segregate children and promote social control through "tracking" and ability grouping. The researcher, however, is interested in whether the past can provide an understanding of how testing was used originally: in the past, were tests accepted as a scientific vehicle for separating students by intelligence or were tests found to be unreliable measures for Mexican and black children? The broad topic of testing in public schools is now a more definitive topic of intelligence testing and its measurement properties when applied to the public schools for grouping or "tracking" children.

Most qualitative research interests come from personal experiences and a long interest in a topic developed from opportunities from current biography and personal history. These opportunities give the researcher physical and/or psychological access to present or past social settings (Riemer, 1977). Such access becomes the starting point for meaningful qualitative research only when it is accompanied by some degree of interest or concern. Examples of current biography are a job, a change in an intimate relationship, or an enjoyed activity. Personal history refers to some prior experience, such as a researcher developing an interest in how working married professional women manage their changing lives because of changes in her own life. In other words, research problems lie in many personal situations and experiences and general reading, which need only to be recognized as potential research problems. Further thinking, puzzling, and awareness of qualitative research traditions enable a researcher to select the logic for the problem.

The Inductive Logic of Qualitative Field Records, Descriptions, and Abstractions

Qualitative research, in contrast to quantitative research, employs primarily *inductive reasoning*. The "problem" is most clearly stated after much data collection and preliminary analysis. The researcher obtains many field records of a present or past situation, which form detailed descriptions of people's perceptions and social realities, and then generates from these descriptions synthesized abstractions to explain the phenomenon. Inductive reasoning allows one to *explore* and *discover* with an emerging research design rather than to test deductions from theories in a predetermined design. The research problem is typically reformulated during data collection so that the data closely represent the reality of the shared social experiences.

Problem formulation begins with the selection of a particular case for an in-depth study. The inductive process is schematically represented in Figure 3.3.

FIGURE 3.3   Inductive Logic in Qualitative Research: Observations, Descriptions, and Concepts

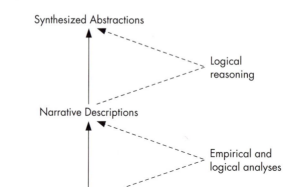

Notice that the direction of the arrows is from the bottom to the top, to illustrate inductive reasoning. We explain each term in Figure 3.3, beginning with qualitative field records of a selected case.

Qualitative Field Records: A Case   Researchers select a specific case for in-depth study. A case is a particular situation chosen by the researcher in which some phenomenon will be described by participants' perceptions. The researcher also selects a primary qualitative methodology (participant-observation, in-depth interview, or analysis of documents). For example, in a study of "Hookin' 'Em In at the Start of School in 'Whole Language' Classroom" (Edelsky, Draper, & Smith, 1983), the case selected was that of a sixth-grade classroom whose teacher who had a *whole language* view of literacy. The case chosen for a study of the origins of the high school extracurriculum was that of Chicago, 1880 to 1915 (Gutowski, 1988), to be examined from historical documents of the Chicago school system, school newspapers, student annuals and club productions, journals of the times, and the *Chicago Tribune*. The selected case limits the research problem to a particular context—in our examples, one sixth-grade classroom or one school system in the 1930s, or high school extracurricular in one school system from 1880 to 1915.

Researchers select a particular case, rather than variables, through which they they gain an understanding of a broader phenomenon. The broader phenomenon in each of the examples cited above was the teaching of reading and writing and the high school extracurricular program.

Qualitative field records (data), obtained over a lengthy time, are recorded as participant observation field notes, in-depth interviews, or researcher notes of historical documents. Each field note, transcript, or historical document note contains the date of occurrence and the context, such as the social scene, situation, and participants. Initial field data may lead to the collection of data from other people, sites, and archive collections as the researcher discovers more aspects about the selected case. In other words, "case" does not refer to one person, one archival collection, or one locale but the *social situation* examined. Data collection strategies are adjusted to obtain a holistic view of the phenomena and then to study certain aspects in depth. In Excerpt 3.4 the selected case was one group of women teachers in a particular locale, Hamilton, Ohio. The researcher chose to study a phenomenon in depth with a case study design rather than an experimental or nonexperimental design.

Narrative Descriptions Researchers use the data to construct **narrative descriptions**, detailed narrations of people, incidents, and processes. The entire descriptive narration is completed after data collection because of the discovery-orientation of the research. To inductively generate a descriptive narration, certain kinds of data must be in the field notes, transcripts, or notes of historical/legal documents.

Descriptive narrations, sometimes called "rich" or "thick" description told in "loving detail," contain at least four elements: people, incidents, participants' language, and participants "meanings." (1)Participants are described as individuals who have different personal histories and display different physical, emotional, and intellectual characteristics in various situations. (2)Incidents form a narration about the social scenes, similar to telling a story. (3) Descriptions emphasize the participants' language, not that of the researcher or of social

---

EXCERPT 3.4

SELECTED CASE FOR IN-DEPTH INTERVIEWS

If unionization failed, it is because real people made choices concerning their own very personal worlds. Attention to the larger forces of history provide a framework of understanding, but without a depiction of the finer detail of the participants' subjective realities, we fail fully to understand the dynamics of history . . . [which] . . . often involved real women living in their own subjective, but equally real, worlds.

This paper is an oral history. Its goal is to describe the shared subjective reality of one group of women teachers during the 1930s and to compare that reality with some assumptions historians make about unionization. Based primarily on oral interviews and influenced by ethnohistory, the paper presents a group definition of schools and life in a small midwestern city during the Great Depression. As such it brings an anthropological perspective to historical study. By attempting to discover the cultural definitions of participants in an historical situation, it investigates the subjective side of history. This paper is less interested in portraying the way things really were than in exploring the way participants perceived them to be. As a case study, it lays no claim to a generalizable truth.

Source: From "The Complex Visions of Female Teachers and the Failure of Unionization in the 1930s: An Oral History" by Richard A. Quantz, *History of Education Quarterly.* Vol. 25, No. 4, 1985. Reprinted by permission of the author.

science. Participants' names for incidents, locations, objects, special events, and processes are noted. Language refers to many forms of communication such as verbal and nonverbal expression, drawings, cartoons, symbols, and the like. (4)Descriptions emphasize participant "meanings." Participant ``meanings" are people's views of reality or how they perceive their world. Participant meanings are conveyed when a person states "why" or "because" an event happened.

Synthesized Abstractions Researchers inductively generate abstractions from the data. **Synthesized abstractions** are summary generalizations and explanations of the major research findings of a study. These synthesized abstractions may take different formats such as a list of narrative themes, "lessons learned," the essence of a shared experience, a delineated concept, assertions, or propositional statements. The researcher constructs a picture that takes shape as he or she collects data and examines the parts. The subtle meanings of the phenomenon can be understood more clearly by the readers. For example, a study explained the meanings of teacher unionization failure with teachers' descriptions of their relationship to schools. Teachers described this relationship in terms of "four metaphors: the subordinate authority figure, the school as family, the natural female avocation, and the dual-self" (Quantz, 1985, p. 442). Only one teacher did not use one of these metaphors.

Problem Reformulations

Qualitative research problems are reformulated several times *after* the researcher has begun data collection. The research problem is stated initially in planning for the study, reformulated during beginning data collection, and reformulated again as necessary throughout data collection. The continuing reformulation of the research problem reflects an emergent design. Reformulations of a research problem relate to changing data collection strategies to acquire the "totality" of the phenomena and then to studying some aspect in greater depth. The specific research problem then evolves and is condensed toward the end of data collection. The condensed version of the research problem in most publications is often not the exact same problem statement that initiated the research.

Foreshadowed Problems Qualitative researchers begin with **foreshadowed problems,** anticipated research problems that will be reformulated during data collection (Malinowski, 1922). The statement of foreshadowed problems depends to some extent on prior knowledge of the events and processes at a site, of the people to be interviewed, or archival collection documents. Thus, foreshadowed problems are not directly derived from an exhaustive literature review, but rather from initial researcher experiences gained from planning the study. A preliminary literature review, however, aids the researcher in the phrasing of foreshadowed problems.

Foreshadowed problems are usually phrased as broad, general questions. Questions focus on the "what," "how," and "why" of the situation. The "what" refers to who, when, where, and which social scenes occur. The "how" refers to processes to be examined and what influenced these processes. The "why" refers to participant "meanings," their explanations for the incidents and social scenes observed. Each of these questions are deliberately broad for the logic of discovery and an emergent design.

Foreshadowed problems are reformulated frequently during the early phases of data collection. Ethnographers may switch from observations to interviewing; interviewers may adjust the questions to illicit descriptions of topics not originally planned; historical researchers often scan documents to decide what is important to glean from the written records.

An ethnographic study of a *whole language* classroom illustrates this process (see Excerpt 3.5). The foreshadowed problem based on preliminary knowledge was "How does this teacher get children to meet her unusual expectations? ...What are the norms here for reading and writing? How does the teacher get students to expect to write? How are certain procedures established (e.g., journal and book writing)? What student-teacher relationships are in evidence?" (Edelsky, Draper, & Smith, 1983, pp. 261–262). Although the researchers expected to see a gradual change, it was evident that students were already becoming what the teacher desired during the first school day. The researchers changed their plans and interviewed children on the second school day. This led to a reformulation of the problem: "What is happening here?" The final reformulation and condensed problem statement became "how it [how teachers get classroom life to become what they want it to be] happens in a classroom with an effective teacher who has a whole language view of literacy" (Edelsky, Draper, & Smith, 1983, p. 260).

Condensed Problem Statement   Condensed problem statements may be written any time during or after data collection. The condensed problem statement is usually the selected major research question that focuses the entire report. The title, literature review, and discussion often use abstract terms of qualitative scholars; however, the research problem may or may not be phrased in descriptive terms. For example, in "Individualism and Community: Ritual Discourse in a Parochial High School," the research problem is "Such continuing ties [to St. Anne's School] are not formed only of good intentions; they must be reaffirmed through repeated concrete experiences that are deemed 'good' and 'worthwhile.' What brought about attachment to St. Anne's when the school restricted students' freedom of movement through a closed campus, restricted their choice of courses, and added financial burdens to many students' families?" (Lesko, 1986, p. 26). The title "Individualism and Community..." refers to concepts found in anthropology and sociology.

Statements of Qualitative Research Purposes and Questions

Qualitative studies contain statements of research purposes and questions that imply the inductive logic for the problem. The statement of research purpose is the final condensed version of the initial problem statement. Specific research

EXCERPT 3.5

PROBLEM REFORMULATIONS
AND EMERGENT DESIGN

What confronted the sixth-grade students in our research, however, were the expectations of one of a small minority of teachers who work from a *whole language* view of literacy. Karen Smith (hereafter referred to as KS), the sixth-grade teacher and one of the authors, used no workbooks or skillsheets. . . .

Final condensed problem statement

The phenomenon we were attempting to explore was how, at the beginning of the year, teachers "coerce" children . . . so that classroom life becomes what they want it to be. However, we were interested in more than just how that happens in any classroom, but how it happens in a classroom with an effective teacher who has a *whole language* view of literacy. . . .

Data collection strategies

Our main data collection was through participant observation of teacher–student interaction all day every day for the first two weeks of school and then three days per week for the next three weeks. Video and audio tape recordings, made periodically, were used to confirm and modify the focus for further observations. We made field notes during classroom observations and videotape viewings. Students were interviewed during the first and third weeks. We also interviewed KS prior to the beginning of school and during the fourth week. We returned in December and again in January to verify if the kinds of interaction observed in September were still occurring.

Preliminary knowledge from planning the research

No researcher looks at everything. Decisions about what to look at are based, in part, on the researchers' prior knowledge. In addition to knowledge of research findings, we began with considerable prior knowledge of this teacher. Both the data collection and analysis were informed by this prior knowledge; one cannot unknow what one knows.

Foreshadowed problems

We began with the question: How does this teacher get children to meet her unusual expectations? Our initial observations were guided by an assortment of questions: What are the norms here for reading and writing? How does the teacher get students to expect to write? How are certain procedures established (e.g., journal and book writing)? What student–teacher relationships are in evidence?

We expected to see gradual change occurring over the first few weeks of school, with some students wavering in accepting KS's uncommon demands, some adapting to the new concept of school and literacy almost immediately, and others taking considerable time to adjust. However, during the first day of school it was evident that the students already were becoming what the teacher wanted them to be. By that afternoon, they were cleaning up without being asked, helping one another, and taking responsibility for making decisions and completing assignments. Here were children in a relatively new environment almost immediately performing like "natives."

Initial expectations and first day of data collection

Quickly we realized that we had made an erroneous assumption regarding gradual adaptation. Our original plan had called for student interviews following the first week of school, but these indications that our object of interest was rushing by prompted us to interview some children on the second day of school. These students had recognized that this class was different; they reported the absence of traditional classroom skills practices, spelling books, sets of textbooks, and subject designation. But they were unable to verbalize what KS expected or how they knew what to do. . . .

Changed data collection strategies and data summary

After the second day of school we began looking for unstated rules (tacit understandings) as explanations for how the students knew when to do exactly as the teacher said and when to follow the general idea of her statement and act prudently. To our original question (How does this teacher, with her theory of literacy, get students to meet her demands?), we now had added a second: What's happening here? The process of addressing (juggling) both questions was cyclical, requiring a shifting focus from broad to narrow and back again. In viewing the videotapes, it was evident that addressing both questions was necessary to account for what we were observing: a teacher who managed to get things going her way very quickly, but who certainly did not match the description of an effective teacher at the beginning of the year, as found in the literature on effective schools.

First reformulation of research problem

Source: From "Hookin' 'Em In at the Start of School in a 'Whole Language' Classroom" by Carole Edelsky, Kelly Draper, and Karen Smith. Reproduced by permission of the American Anthropological Association from *Anthropology & Education Quarterly* 14:4, 1983. Not for further reproduction.

questions may be stated or implied. Statements of purpose imply the chosen qualitative mode of inquiry: forms of interactive or noninteractive research.

Ethnographic Problem Statements and Questions Qualitative research traditions of ethnography, phenomenology, case study, grounded theory, and critical study focus on current phenomena for which data can be obtained through interacting with the participants in a selected social situation. Excerpt 3.6 illustrates an ethnographic problem statement and research questions for a study of sibling acceptance of a youth with severe disabilities. The logic of the problem statement implies the research design.

Historical Problem Statements and Questions Historical research problems focus on past events and require access to documents in historical archives. Research problems are often generated when archival documents are made available to scholars. Excerpt 3.7 illustrates a historical study that focused on a 1939 published doctoral dissertation by Horace Mann Bond, who became an administrator, teacher, and president of several black universities during his lifetime. The Bond Papers archive provided the documents to examine briefly "the personal and historiographical circumstances surrounding the book's publication" (Urban, 1987, p. 365). The logic of the statement of purpose implies five research questions that focused on Bond's personal circumstances, historiographical circumstances, Reconstruction history, educational history, and black history.

EXCERPT 3.6

ETHNOGRAPHIC PROBLEM STATEMENT AND RESEARCH QUESTIONS

Social relationships for people with disabilities have been a central concern of the field for many years. So too have sibling relationships. This article brings together data on both types of relationships, in an attempt to extend our understanding of what is needed to support relationships between youth with significant disabilities and their peers without disabilities. Specifically, we will report the findings of a case study of the sibling relationships of Raul, a young man with Down syndrome. . . .

We focused on the following questions:

1. What are the predominant types of interactions between the siblings and Raul?
2. How does Raul participate in these interactions?
3. How do the observed sibling interactions compare to findings about Raul's interactions with nondisabled peers at school?
4. What lessons can we learn from these sibling relationships about facilitating inclusion for a student with disability?

Source: From Harry, B., Day, M., & Quist, F., (1998). "He Can't Really Play": An ethnographic study of sibling acceptance and interaction (pp. 289, 291). *JASH: Journal of the Association for Persons with Severe Handicaps, 23* (4) 289–299.

EXCERPT 3.7

HISTORICAL PROBLEM STATEMENT AND RESEARCH QUESTIONS

The recent opening of the Horace Mann Bond Papers to scholars, along with publication of an article on Bond's early career which used those papers, should spark renewed interest in the work of this noted teacher, scholar, and educational administrator. . . . He wrote noted critiques of the mental testing movement at several stages of his long career, did historical research for the plaintiffs in the *Brown v. Topeka* school desegregation suit, and traveled extensively to Africa and studied its civilizations in the later stages of his career.[1]

One of Bond's greatest contributions to scholarship is the topic of this essay: his doctoral dissertation which was published in 1939 under the title *Negro Education in Alabama: A Study in Cotton and Steel.* The merits of Bond's book were noted almost immediately after its publication. . . .

The continuing importance of Bond's work is demonstrated by numerous citations of it in recent and contemporary works in history, educational history, and black history. . . . This essay . . . looks briefly at the personal and historiographical circumstances surrounding the book's publication. Then it discusses the content of the work in relation to subsequent historical studies in Reconstruction history and educational history. Finally, it attempts to place the book in the larger stream of work in black history.

Source: From "Horace Mann Bond's *Negro education in Alabama*" by Wayne J. Urban, *History of Education Quarterly,* Vol. 27, No. 3, Fall 1987. Reprinted by permission of Wayne J. Urban.

The Significance of Problem Selection

The **significance of the problem** is the rationale for a study. It tells the reader why the study is important and indicates the reasons for the researcher's choice of a particular problem. Because research requires knowledge, skills, planning, time, and fiscal resources, the problem to be investigated should be important. In other words, the study should have a potential payoff.

A research problem is significant when it is related to developing educational theory, knowledge, or practice. The significance of a study increases when there are several reasons for the inquiry. The significance may be based on one or more of the following criteria: whether it provides knowledge about an enduring practice, tests a theory, is generalizable, extends our understanding of a broader phenomenon, advances methodology, is related to a current issue, evaluates a specific practice at a given site, or is an exploratory study.

1. *Knowledge of an Enduring Practice* The study may provide knowledge about an enduring educational practice. Previous research on the practice may

have been done, but this particular research problem has not been investigated. The practice being studied is common to many schools but is not necessarily found in every school. The study adds knowledge about an enduring common practice.

2. *Theory Testing* The study may test an existing theory with a verification design. The focus may be on social science theories of child or adult development, organizational development, conflict, or the like. Educational theories may focus on curricula, instructional models, staff development learning styles, teaching strategies, or the like. By testing a theory in different situations or on different populations, the researcher may modify or verify it.

3. *Generalizability* The study may be designed for the results to be generalizable to different populations or practices. A study may replicate or include other variables not investigated in previous research. The proposed design may call for using a different population than the original research to enhance generalizability.

4. *Extensions of Understanding* Many qualitative studies conducted in the phenomenological tradition provide an extension of understanding rather than generalizability. By describing a selected case of a social situation in detail, these studies give an understanding of the phenomena observed. An understanding of the phenomena provides an image or a configuration of reasonable expectations that might be useful in similar situations.

5. *Methodological Advancement* The study may increase the validity and reliability of an instrument or use a methodology different from that of previous studies. Much of the research on educational measurement investigates questions related to assessment, such as testing procedures, the order of the items on an instrument, the item format or response set, or the information processes of the respondent. Other studies may develop a statistical or methodological technique and elaborate its usefulness for research.

6. *Current Issues* The study may focus on a social issue of immediate concern. As mentioned previously, such organized political movements as women's rights and civil rights generated educational research. Public recognition of social problems has frequently led to an assessment of their educational effects. The increasing phenomenon of single-parent families, for example, raised questions about the impact of single parenting on student self-concept and achievement. Studies on the effects of extensive television watching on students and the use of calculators and microcomputers in educational programs originated from social concerns about a highly technological society.

7. *Evaluation of a Specific Practice or Policy at a Given Site* The study may evaluate a specific practice or policy for decision-makers at a given site or for external groups. As noted in Chapter 1, evaluation research determines merit: Does the practice work, and how can it be improved at the site? It also determines the worth of a practice: Is the practice effective? Is it worth the costs? Do we want to expand its usage? Does it meet our needs? Similar questions are addressed in policy studies. Such research supplies information for immediate use in site decision making, which may be at the local, state, or

national level. While the study is not concerned initially with generalizability or theory development, it may have implications for developing such knowledge.

8. *Exploratory Research* Exploratory research is usually conducted in new areas of inquiry. Such studies may be quantitative or qualitative. For example, a study might field test a particular testing format to determine whether it can be used by sixth-grade students and whether it discriminates against any particular student group. Qualitative exploratory studies often examine phenomena that have not been studied previously. Most of the excerpts of qualitative research in this chapter are illustrations of exploratory research. Some exploratory studies develop theory.

Standards of Adequacy for Problem Statements

Research problems are critically evaluated on the three elements discussed in this chapter: the statement of the general research problem, the significance of the problem, and the specific research purpose, question, or hypothesis. In addition other criteria may be applied.

General Research Problem

The following questions appraise the general statement of the problem:

1. Does the statement of the general research problem imply the possibility of empirical investigation?
2. Does the problem statement restrict the scope of the study?
3. Does the problem statement give the educational context in which the problem lies?

Significance of Problem

Readers assess the significance of the problem in terms of one or more of the following criteria:

- develops knowledge of an enduring practice
- develops theory
- generalizable—that is, expands knowledge or theory
- provides extension of understandings
- advances methodology
- is related to a current social or political issue
- evaluates a specific practice or policy at a given site
- is exploratory research

Specific Research Question or Hypothesis

Different criteria are applied in the evaluation of quantitative and qualitative research questions.

Quantitative

1. Does the specific research purpose, question, or hypothesis state concisely what is to be determined?
2. Does the level of specificity indicate that the question or hypothesis is researchable? Or do the variables seem amenable to operational definitions?
3. Is the deductive logic of a research question or hypothesis precise? Are the independent and dependent variables identified?
4. Does the research question or hypothesis indicate the framework for reporting the results?

Qualitative

1. Do the research questions, foreshadowed problems, or condensed problem statement indicate the particular case of some phenomena to be examined?
2. Is the qualitative methodology appropriate for the description of present or past events?
3. Is the inductive logic of the research reasonably explicit?
4. Does the research purpose indicate the framework for reporting the findings?

Other Criteria for Standards of Adequacy

Before conducting a study, the researcher, a possible funding agency, review committees, and other groups also evaluate the problem according to additional criteria. These criteria concern the ability of the researcher to conduct the study and the feasibility and ethics of the research design. Typical questions asked are these:

1. Is the problem one in which the researcher has a vital interest and a topic in which the researcher has both knowledge and experience?
2. Are the problem and the design feasible in terms of measurement, access to the case, sample, or population, permission to use documented data, time frame for completion, financial resources, and the like?
3. Does the researcher have the skills to conduct the proposed research and to analyze and interpret the results?
4. Does the proposed research ensure the protection of human subjects from physical or mental discomfort or harm? Is the right of informed consent of subjects provided? Will ethical research practices be followed?

Summary

The following statements summarize the major aspects of research problem statements, problem formulation in quantitative and qualitative research, significance of a problem, and standards of adequacy for a problem statement.

1. A research problem implies the possibility of empirical investigation.
2. Sources for research problems are casual observations, theory, literature, current issues, practical situations, and personal insights.
3. A research problem statement specifies the focus, educational context, importance, and the framework for reporting the findings.
4. In quantitative research, deductive logic is employed in selecting the construct, variables, and operational definitions.
5. A construct is a complex abstraction that is not directly observable.
6. A variable is an event, category, behavior, or attribute that expresses a construct and has different values, depending on how it is used in a particular study.
7. Variables may be categorical or continuous. A variable may be a dependent, independent, manipulated, experimental, predictor, or criterion variable in different designs.
8. An operational definition assigns meaning to a variable by specifying the activities or operations necessary to measure, categorize, or manipulate the variable.
9. To formulate a quantitative problem, a researcher decides the variables, the population, and the deductive logic of the design.
10. Specific quantitative research questions may be descriptive questions, relationship questions, difference questions, or a hypothesis.
11. A research hypothesis should state the expected relationship or difference between two or more variables, be testable, and offer a tentative explanation based on theory or previous research.
12. In qualitative research the general topic, the case, and the methodology are interrelated and selected interactively rather than in separate research steps.
13. A case is a particular situation selected by the researcher in which some phenomenon will be described by participants' meanings of events and processes.
14. A qualitative study employs inductive logic to use field records to form a descriptive narration and to develop abstractions from that narration.
15. Qualitative field records, obtained over a lengthy time, are recorded as participant-observation notes, transcripts of in-depth interviews, or the researcher's notes of historical documents.
16. Qualitative descriptions are detailed narrations of people, incidents, and processes that emphasize participants' meanings.
17. Qualitative research problems are reformulated several times during data collection, while quantitative research problems are stated before data collection.
18. A research problem is significant if it provides knowledge about an enduring practice, tests theory, increases generalizability or extends empirical understandings, advances methodology, focuses on a current issue, evaluates a specific practice or policy, or is an exploratory study.
19. Problem statements are judged by criteria for statement of a research problem, the problem significance, the specific research questions or hypotheses, and the appropriate logic and feasibility.

Self-Instructional Review Exercises

Sample answers are in the back of the book.

Test Items

1. Which of the following statements is phrased as a research problem? The purpose of this study is to determine
   a. whether the promotion policy should be changed.
   b. the truth of the proposition that American education has encouraged a social class system in the United States.
   c. how students can overcome test anxiety.
   d. whether there is a difference in the mean gain scores in reading achievement between comparable students taught word attack skills and those taught comprehension skills.

2. The statement of the research problem provides
   a. the educational context of the study.
   b. the framework for reporting the results.
   c. the importance of the study.
   d. All of the above are correct.

3. Quantitative problem formulation requires
   a. the use of deductive logic for the problem.
   b. selection of a construct, variables, and operational definitions.
   c. selection of a population and/or sample.
   d. All of the above are correct.

4. Quantitative research questions may be phrased to indicate
   a. a descriptive study of the current status of a group.
   b. a relationship study predicting the influence of one variable on another variable.
   c. a comparative study between two or more data sets.
   d. All of the above are correct.

5. Which is an *incorrect* statement regarding a research hypothesis? A research hypothesis
   a. is supported or not supported.
   b. relates variables that can be measured, manipulated, or categorized.
   c. is more specific than the problem statement.
   d. is the same as a statistical hypothesis.

6. Which of the following is *not* an operational definition?
   a. ratings of art drawings by three professors of art education
   b. IOWA Tests of Basic Skills
   c. divergent thinking of problem-solving skills
   d. classification of students in a graduate research course by whether or not they have had a statistical course

7. Which of the following criteria for a good research hypothesis is violated most in the following hypothesis: Students in an exploratory vocational educational

program will make more contributions to society than those not enrolled in the program.

  a. A hypothesis is concise.
  b. A hypothesis is worthy of testing.
  c. A hypothesis can be stated operationally.
  d. A hypothesis is logically precise.

  8. Qualitative problem formulation requires
  a. selection of a case and a particular methodology.
  b. use of inductive logic to build from qualitative field records a descriptive narration.
  c. physical and/or psychological access to social situations in the past or present.
  d. All of the above are correct.

  9. A case in qualitative research refers to
  a. one person for an in-depth study.
  b. one archival collection or legal library.
  c. a particular situation selected by the researcher through which an understanding of some broader phenomena might be acquired.
  d. a variable.

  10. Qualitative problems
  a. are reformulated several times after data collection has begun.
  b. are usually stated as broad foreshadowed problems that will be condensed later.
  c. focus on "what," "who," "how," and "why" of social situations.
  d. All of the above are correct.

  11. Which does *not* suggest significance for a research problem?
  a. evaluation of a specific practice or policy at a given site
  b. expansion of generalizability of prior research or extension of understandings in exploratory research
  c. a focus that is unrelated to prior research or broader phenomena
  d. a current issue

Application Problems

Answer the questions for each problem.

  1. The following are examples of research topics. Indicate the decisions necessary in order to conduct the study, and restate each as a useful research question.
  a. effects of different ways of learning social studies
  b. effects of cooperative versus competitive instruction on attitudes toward learning
  c. opinions of parents toward education
  d. family characteristics and school attendance
  e. validity of WISC for school performance

  2. Write a directional hypothesis for the following problem statement, and identify the type of variables in the hypothesis. "Low-achieving students frequently

respond positively to behavior modification programs. Is there any relationship between the type of reward (tangible or intangible) and the amount of learning?"

3. State a hypothesis based on each of the research questions listed below:
   a. What is the effect of individualized and structured social studies on high school students?
   b. Is there any difference in students' engagement in tasks when a teacher uses a positive introduction and when a teacher uses a neutral introduction to tasks?
   c. Does nonpromotion of elementary pupils improve their social adjustment?
   d. Do teachers' perceptions of job stress differ among teachers of mildly retarded, moderately retarded, and nonretarded children?

4. State the most likely independent and dependent variables for each research title listed below or state that no variables are identified.
   a. "Liberal Grading Improves Faculty Evaluations"
   b. "Classroom Behavior in Elementary School Children: Perceptions of Principals"
   c. "Relationship of Teacher Cognitive Styles to Pupils' Academic Achievement Gains"
   d. "Ideas of Early Sex Education Movements in America, 1890–1920"
   e. "Reducing Inter-Sentence Interference via Contextual Aids"
   f. "Effect of Two School-Based Intervention Programs on Depressive Symptoms of Preadolescents"

5. Which research titles listed above also clearly identify the subjects?

6. In the following qualitative problem statements, identify the case to be studied.
   a. This study describes and analyzes how women faculty members at an urban university perceive their professional and personal lives and how they integrate their lives.
   b. School board records of a suburban school system were analyzed for the ideologies articulated by various school board members to legitimize system-wide curriculum policies from 1950 to 1980.
   c. The research problem is to describe how Miss Sue, a first-year elementary school teacher, learns a professional role with students, faculty, administrators, and parents, and how she develops "meaning" for teacher professionalism.
   d. The research problem is to describe and analyze a faculty social system in the implementation of an innovative middle school program to propose grounded theory.

CHAPTER 4

Literature
Review

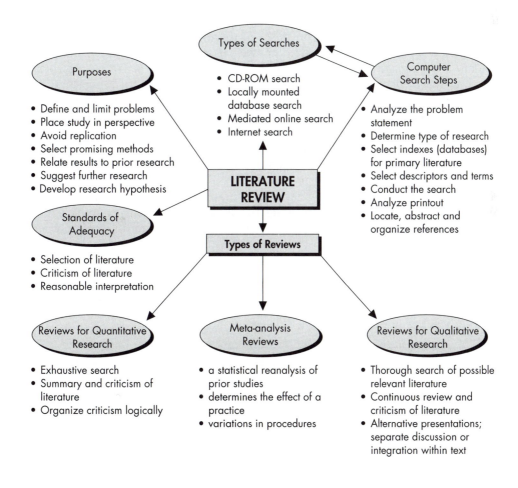

Types of Searches

- CD-ROM search
- Locally mounted database search
- Mediated online search
- Internet search

Purposes

- Define and limit problems
- Place study in perspective
- Avoid replication
- Select promising methods
- Relate results to prior research
- Suggest further research
- Develop research hypothesis

Computer Search Steps

- Analyze the problem statement
- Determine type of research
- Select indexes (databases) for primary literature
- Select descriptors and terms
- Conduct the search
- Analyze printout
- Locate, abstract and organize references

LITERATURE REVIEW

Standards of Adequacy

- Selection of literature
- Criticism of literature
- Reasonable interpretation

Types of Reviews

Reviews for Quantitative Research

- Exhaustive search
- Summary and criticism of literature
- Organize criticism logically

Meta-analysis Reviews

- a statistical reanalysis of prior studies
- determines the effect of a practice
- variations in procedures

Reviews for Qualitative Research

- Thorough search of possible relevant literature
- Continuous review and criticism of literature
- Alternative presentations; separate discussion or integration within text

KEY TERMS

literature review

electronic resources

related literature

secondary literature

primary literature

ERIC

ERIC Digest

report literature

preliminary search

exhaustive search

database

thesaurus

meta-analysis

Literature reviews, if conducted carefully and presented well, add much to an understanding of the selected problem and help place the results of a study in a historical perspective. Without reviews of the literature, it would be difficult to build a body of accepted knowledge on an educational topic.

This chapter explains the purposes of the literature review, and the steps to locate, search, and criticize the literature. It also describes sources for secondary and primary literature. Most literature reviews are a narrative interpretative criticism of the existing research. A literature review for a quantitative study follows specific guidelines in the presentation and criticism of the literature to provide an understanding of the existing knowledge of the problem and a rationale for the research questions. Qualitative researchers present literature discussions and integrate criticism of the literature into the text of a study. Later in the chapter we discuss meta-analysis, a literature review that summarizes statistically the results of prior research. Finally, we suggest some standards of adequacy for evaluating narrative literature reviews. Because use of the Internet is now essential in reviewing the literature, we will examine some Internet resources in this chapter. Chapter 5 reviews additional Internet resources.

Functions of a Review of Related Literature

An interpretative review of the literature is exactly that—a summary and synthesis of relevant literature on a research problem. A **literature review** is usually a critique of the status of knowledge of a carefully defined topic. The literature review enables a reader to gain further insights from the study.

Literature for a review includes many types of sources: professional journals, reports, scholarly books and monographs, government documents, dissertations, and electronic resources. **Electronic resources** are literature "published" on the Internet, a global network of computer databases. Some refereed journals and conference proceedings are "published" only electronically. Literature may include empirical research, theoretical discussions, reviews of the status of knowledge, philosophical papers, and methodological treatises.

Related literature is that which is directly relevant to the problem, such as previous research investigating the same variables or a similar question, references to the theory and the empirical testing of the theory, and studies of similar practices. Thoroughly researched topics in education usually have sufficient studies pertinent to the research topic. New or little-researched topics usually require a review of any literature related in some essential way to the problem to provide a conceptual framework or rationale for the study. Related literature may be found outside the original field or context of the research problem.

Purposes of a Literature Review

A review of the literature serves several purposes in research. Knowledge from the literature is used in stating the significance of the problem, developing the research design, relating the results of the study to previous knowledge, and suggesting further research. A review of the literature enables you to do the following:

1. *Define and limit the problem.* Most studies that add to educational knowledge investigate only one aspect of the larger topic. The researcher initially becomes familiar with the major works in that topic and the possible breadth of the topic. The research problem is eventually limited to a subtopic within a larger body of previous theory, knowledge, or practice and stated in the appropriate terms. Thus, the review of literature is used to refine an initial general idea or problem into one that is more specific.

2. *Place the study in a historical perspective.* To add to the knowledge in any subfield, researchers analyze the way their studies will relate to existing knowledge. A researcher may thus state that the research of A, B, and C has added a certain amount to knowledge; the work of D and E has further added to our knowledge; and this study extends our knowledge by investigating the stated question.

3. *Avoid unintentional and unnecessary replication.* A thorough search of the literature enables the researcher to avoid unintentional or unneeded replication. The researcher, however, may deliberately replicate a study for verification. A research topic that has been investigated with similar methods that failed to produce significant results indicates a need to revise the problem or the research design. Evaluation studies may seem to duplicate prior research, but this duplication is necessary if the study is designed for site specific decision-making.

4. *Select promising methods and measures.* As researchers sort out the knowledge on a subject, they assess the research methods that have established that knowledge. Previous investigations provide a rationale and insight for the research design. Analysis of measures, sampling, and methods of prior research

may lead to a more sophisticated design, the selection of a different instrument, a more appropriate data analysis procedure, or an improved methodology for studying the problem.

5. *Relate the findings to previous knowledge and suggest further research.* The results of a study are contrasted to those of previous research in order to state how the study adds new knowledge. If the study yields nonsignificant results, the researcher's insights may relate to the research problem or to the design. Most researchers suggest directions for further research based on insights gained from conducting the study within the context of the literature review.

6. *Develop research hypotheses.* In some quantitative studies the researchers use the literature to justify the formulation of specific research hypotheses. Previous studies may suggest a certain result, and the hypotheses should be consistent with these studies. Sometimes researchers use theories rather than empirical studies to justify research hypotheses.

Reviewing the Literature

A review of the literature is usually carried out in sequential steps. Researchers often return to a prior step, however, as they gain understanding of the topic or if the problem is restated. Steps in reviewing the literature include the following:

1. *Analyze the problem statement.* The problem statement contains concepts or variables that indicate the topic for the literature search (e.g., mildly retarded children, reading instruction, or administrator evaluation).

2. *Search and read secondary literature.* Reading several secondary sources provides a brief overview of the topic and helps a researcher define the problem in more precise terms.

3. *Select the appropriate index for a reference service or database.* For most problems, a researcher selects more than one index or database to locate the most important primary literature. The number of databases used depends on the purpose and scope of the review.

4. *Transform the problem statement into search language.* The concepts or variables are cross-referenced manually with a thesaurus or index for a specific database to identify the *descriptors*, or terms, in order to locate the desired literature. Descriptors, or terms, constitute the search language.

5. *Conduct a manual and/or computer search.* Reviewers use combinations of the selected terms with logical connectors such as *and*, *or*, and *not* in the search. The search is often limited by years to be searched or by document type. Reviewers then print a bibliography of the most relevant literature.

6. *Read the pertinent primary literature.* A reviewer writes a brief analysis of each primary source that is relevant to the problem on note cards that contain the bibliographic citation.

7. *Organize notes.* Empirical studies may be classified several ways: by the variables, by the population, historically, by similar results, or by methodology. The reviewer then organizes the note cards by ideas.

8. *Write the review.* The review cites only studies, theories, and practices relevant to the problem statement, and it will differ somewhat with the type of study, such as basic, applied, or evaluation research, hypothesis-testing or exploratory research, or quantitative or qualitative studies.

We have listed important sources for review of the secondary and primary literature for an educational problem in Tables 4.1 and 4.2 (reviews of secondary literature in Table 4.1 and for indexes of primary literature in Table 4.2). Computer search techniques are described later in the chapter..

TABLE 4.1

Selected Sources for Reviews of Secondary Literature

General references

Review of Educational Research (1931–present, journal)

Review of Research in Education (1973–present, annual)

Educational Psychology Review

Yearbook of the National Society for the Study of Education (1902–present, annual)

Encyclopedia of Educational Research, 6th ed. (1992)

Books in Print

Specialized references

Handbook of Educational Psychology (1996)

Handbook of Qualitative Research in Education (2000)

Handbook of Reading Research (1990)

Handbook of Research on Curriculum (1992)

Handbook of Research on Educational Administration (1999)

Handbook of Research on Mathematics Teaching and Learning (1992)

Handbook of Research on Music Teaching and Learning (1992)

Handbook of Research on School Supervision (1998)

Handbook of Research on Social Studies Teaching and Learning (1991)

Handbook of Research on Teacher Education (1996)

Handbook of Research on Teaching, 3rd ed. (1986)

Handbook of Research on Teaching the English Language Arts (1991)

Handbook of Research on the Education of Young Children (1993)

Handbook of Schooling in Urban America (1993)

Handbook of Research on Science Teaching and Learning (1994)

Handbook of Special Education: Research and Practice (1988)

Handbook of Sport Psychology (1992)

Yearbook of Adult and Continuing Education (1976–present)

Yearbook of Special Education (1976–present)

The Second Handbook on Parent Education (1988)

International Handbook of Bilingualism and Bilingual Education (1988)

International Handbook of Early Childhood Education (1994)

International Handbook of Women's Education (1989)

TABLE 4.2

Selected Indexes for Primary Literature

Educational journals	*Current Index to Journals in Education* (1969–present)
Report literature	*Resources in Education* (1969–present)
General and educational periodicals, yearbooks, and monographs	*Educational Index* (1929–present)
Selected abstracts and indexes in specialized areas	*Psychological Abstracts* (PsycINFO) (1927–present) *Sociological Abstracts* (1954–present) *Child Development Abstracts and Bibliography* (1927–present) *Exceptional Child Education Resources* (1969–present) *Research Related to Children* (1950–present) *Resources in Vocational Education* (1967–present) *Business Education Index* (1940–present) *Completed Research in Health, Physical Education, and Recreation, Including International Sources* (1959–present) *Physical Education Index* (1978–present) *State Education Journal Index* (1963–present) *Educational Administration Abstracts* (1966–present)
Government documents	*Monthly Catalogue of U.S. Government Publications* (1895–present) *Digest of Educational Statistics* (1962–present) *American Statistics Index* (1973–present)
Dissertations and theses	*Dissertation Abstracts International* (1938–present) *Comprehensive Dissertation Index* (1861–present)
Citation indexes	*Science Citation Index* (1961–present) *Social Science Citation Index* (1973–present)
Research in progress or recently completed	Smithsonian Science Information Exchange (1973–present)

Sources for a Literature Review

Although a review emphasizes primary literature, secondary literature is also useful. **Secondary literature** reviews prior research and synthesizes theoretical and empirical studies. Secondary literature provides a quick overview of research developments on the topic. These sources eliminate much technical information about each original study but cite extensive references. Examples of secondary literature are monographs, articles in encyclopedias, and journals that contain reviews of research. Secondary literature may be a book that combines many primary sources into a single unifying framework.

   Primary literature is the original research studies or writings by a theorist or researcher. Primary literature contains the full text of a research report or a theory and thus is more detailed and technical. Examples of primary literature are empirical studies published in journals or placed in databases, research reports, scholarly monographs, and dissertations.

Primary literature and secondary literature provide different information. A secondary source gives an overview of the field, a general knowledge of what has been done on the topic, and a context for placing current primary sources into a framework. The essence of a review, however, is the primary literature. Primary sources provide detailed information of current research, theories, and methodologies used to investigate the problem.

Three formats may be used to access sources for a literature review: (1) print, such as a published index or the catalog; (2) microtext, such as microfilm and microfiche; and (3) electronic databases or resources such as the Internet and CD-ROMs. Reference librarians can provide information regarding which formats access which types of sources in a particular library. Furthermore, libraries use different software programs to access the literature and usually provide orientation sessions to help library users. Before a literature review is conducted, a reference librarian or search analyst should be consulted.

Sources for Reviews of Secondary Literature

Recognized authorities write reviews of original studies when sufficient work has been done to enable a critical assessment of the status of knowledge. The topics for a review are usually selected by a committee of researchers and scholars who are aware of current issues and research. Because continued work on a topic may not warrant a thorough review for several years, some reviews, although seemingly dated, provide useful information. We will describe the usefulness of the secondary sources listed in Table 4.1.

Quarterly and Annual Reviews General references provide reviews of prior research on topics selected from the entire field of education. Quarterly or annually published reviews such as the *Review of Educational Research*, *Review of Research in Education*, and *Educational Psychology Review* provide detailed syntheses on a narrow topic and exhaustive bibliographies. Usually the author develops a conceptual framework, which serves as the criteria for selecting the reviewed studies.

Professional Books Professional books, including some textbooks, give a detailed analysis of a broad field from a particular perspective. These books are written for other professionals and students. The subject index of *Books in Print* cites all currently published books. This index is readily available on-line at most libraries.

Encyclopedias Short authoritative summaries of a topic in an encyclopedia are helpful in the early stages of a review. The *Encyclopedia of Educational Research* (6th ed.), with 257 articles and extensive bibliographies, represents a comprehensive analysis of 16 fields of educational research. Other encyclopedias, many of which are more specialized, include *Encyclopedia of Educational Evaluation*, *Encyclopedia of Early Childhood Education*, *Encyclopedia of Special*

Education, Encyclopedia of School Administration and Supervision, International Encyclopedia of Teaching and Teacher Education, and *International Encyclopedia of Education.*

Specialized Handbooks and Yearbooks Handbooks and yearbooks that specialize in an area of practice and research are similar to encyclopedias, with several exceptions. Authoritative chapters in a specialized handbook or yearbook are usually more comprehensive, longer, but more narrowly focused than those in encyclopedias. If a handbook or yearbook exists on the topic you wish to review, this would be a better place to find an overview of the specialized field of education. One good example is the *Annual Review of Research for School Leaders.* Another example is the *NSSE Yearbooks.* The *NSSE Yearbooks* present a general overview by recognized authorities on selected topics. Because each annual volume comprises two books, each about a different educational topic, an entire book provides a comprehensive perspective on a topic.

Other Specialized References Other handbooks and encyclopedias, primarily from social science disciplines, may serve as secondary sources for literature reviews. Specialized references, for example, are available in anthropology, social psychology, aging, applied psychology, child psychology, developmental psychology, adolescent children, nonverbal behavior research, small group research, organization management, political science, and public administration.

ERIC Resources The **ERIC** system (Educational Resources Information Center) contains several indexes and sources for both primary and secondary literature. For secondary sources, ERIC offers three very helpful services. One of these is **ERIC Digests.** The Digests are short reports that synthesize research and ideas about contemporary educational issues. There are over 1,600 Digests in the ERIC Digest database. They are accessed through computer searches by key terms once you have gained access to the database. Another helpful ERIC resource is access to 16 subject-specific Clearinghouse sites on the Internet. Each Clearinghouse database contains a wealth of information, resources, literature, and links to additional sites. The Clearinghouses are summarized in the next chapter. Third, ERIC has a service called AskERIC that allows you to send a personalized request to an ERIC Network Information Specialist in the appropriate area. The Specialist will respond within 48 hours with ERIC database searches, ERIC Digests, and other Internet resources. Finally, general ERIC searches can be limited so that only literature reviews, bibliographies, and digests are reported. You can do this by selecting these terms from the pulldown menu following the "Limited to" category (as explained on page 129 and shown in Figure 4.8).

Searching for Secondary Sources Most libraries have computerized catalogs of their books which will allow you to conduct different types of searches. Not only can you search by author or title, you can also search by additional commands that allow you to target a specific topic or field of study. The most commonly used commands are *subject* and *keyword* used with logical connectors such as *and, or*, and *not*.

Keyword searching with connectors will result in a precise retrieval. Keyword searches are used when you have incomplete information about an author or title, and subject headings are too broad. If the keywords *cooperative learning* and *achievement* are connected with "and," the search is narrowed to records that contain both of these terms. "Not" also narrows the search by including records with one term but not ones that follow the connector (e.g., "cooperative learning not achievement" excludes records that contain the term "achievement" even if "cooperative learning" is in the record). If the "or" connector is used, the search is broadened to records that have either term.

Another approach to identify secondary sources is to use one of the databases that can be accessed through *FirstSearch*, a search engine on the World Wide Web. *FirstSearch* allows you to search *Education Abstracts Information*, a database that contains English-language periodicals and yearbooks. Subjects include administration, teaching methods and curriculum, literacy, government funding, and more (*Education Abstracts* can also be accessed through other databases, or directly at <u>http://www.hwwlison.com/databases/edicat</u>).

Each library will have somewhat different searching procedures for their catalogs. Thus, although the basics are very similar for all libraries, you will need to become acquainted with specific searching procedures in the library in which you are working.

Sources for Primary Literature

Primary literature includes empirical studies, research reports, government documents, and scholarly monographs. Indexes identify primary literature published or on microtext. An index gives the location of the source, and an abstract helps the reviewer decide which sources are relevant. Selected sources for a review of primary literature are listed in Table 4.2. Many of these are available on the World Wide Web.

Current Index to Journals in Education (CIJE) Since 1969, *CIJE* has been published monthly and cumulated semiannually by ERIC. It provides abstracts from over 780 educational journals and periodicals. It is the most thorough indexing and abstracting service for educational periodicals, but it also includes educationally relevant articles published in such periodicals as the *Personnel Journal, Journal of Family Counseling*, and *Urban Affairs Quarterly*.

Resources in Education (RIE) *RIE*, a monthly and cumulative semiannual publication furnished since 1969 by ERIC, indexes and abstracts more than 1000 documents per issue. The Educational Resources Information Center was initiated by the U.S. Office of Education to provide a retrieval system of current research findings to teachers, administrators, researchers, and the public. ERIC consists of a central office and sixteen clearinghouses. Each clearinghouse catalogs, abstracts, and indexes documents in its subject. In addition, each clearinghouse publishes its own newsletters, bibliographies, and interpretive studies. Names of some of the clearinghouses are Elementary and Early Childhood Education, Counseling and Personnel Service, Educational Management, Handicapped and Gifted Children, Reading and Communication Skills, and Urban Education.

RIE reviews what it calls **report literature**—documents other than journals. This includes speeches and presentations made at professional meetings, monographs, final reports of federally funded research, state education department documents, final reports of school district projects, and the like. Most of these reports are not published in full text in periodicals, but their research findings may be summarized a few years after the report is completed. Other reference services generally do not abstract report literature. Before 1966, therefore, report literature was not retrievable: it was not preserved or indexed. Most documents indexed in the *RIE* are in the ERIC Document Microfiche Collection. Universities, state departments of education, and many public school systems own the microfiche collection. For many educational problems, a search through *CIJE* and *RIE* is adequate for locating most recent relevant sources.

Educational Index The *Educational Index* primarily references educational periodicals, yearbooks, and monographs printed in English. It is published for ten months a year and indexes more than 300 journals related to education. *CIJE* is the preferred reference because it includes both an indexing system and an annotation of educational periodical literature. If an exhaustive search is required, the *Educational Index* is useful because it provides coverage from 1929. Most reviewers use *CIJE* from 1969 to date and, for enduring topics, the *Educational Index*.

PsycINFO PsycINFO is a department of the American Psychological Association (APA) that develops and maintains APA's comprehensive electronic resources. It covers all types of scholarly documents, including journal articles, books, book chapters, technical reports, and dissertations. Retrospective coverage of literature is available as far back as 1887. The database is updated monthly. PsycLIT is a CD-ROM database derived from PsycINFO, and is available by institutional subscription.

Selected Abstracts and Indexes in Subjects Related to Education The sources discussed above have very broad coverage for most educational research problems. Several abstracts and indexes have more narrow coverage by focusing on a single subject related to education. If a research problem is limited to a specific topic, a thorough search would include the more specialized reference.

Psychological Abstracts, published in print format monthly by the American Psycholog-ical Association since 1927, indexes and abstracts more than 950 journals, technical reports, monographs, and other scientific documents in psychology and related disciplines. *Psychological Abstracts* usually provides more thorough coverage than *CIJE* in educational problems related to psychological topics, such as human development, counseling, exceptional children, attitudes, or learning.

Sociological Abstracts, which is similar to *Psychological Abstracts,* has been published five times a year since 1954. Because the subject index uses single terms, the reviewer must check the abstract in order to determine the article's relevance.

Child Development Abstracts and Bibliography cites articles from several disciplines and applied fields, including education. Since 1927 this quarterly publication has included an author index, a subject index, and abstracts.

Exceptional Child Education Resources (ECER), published since 1969, uses a format similar to that of *CIJE.* Of the 200 journals covered here, many are not listed in *CIJE.*

Research Related to Children, a series of bulletins published by the ERIC Clearinghouse on Elementary and Early Childhood Education since 1950, provides descriptions of research in process as well as recently completed research. Each bulletin contains subject, investigator, and institutional indexes along with project descriptions.

Resources in Vocational Education, formerly *Abstracts of Instructional and Research Materials in Vocational and Technical Education (AIM/ARM)* has been published six times a year since 1967. It provides subject and author indexes, projects in progress, and summaries of research, instructional materials, and curriculum projects.

Business Education Index, published annually since 1940, is a combined subject–author index. It covers articles from about 40 periodicals.

Completed Research in Health, Physical Education and Recreation Including International Sources, published since 1959, covers the research and articles from 168 periodicals and includes theses and dissertations. It is the best abstracting service in physical education and provides a detailed subject index.

The *Physical Education Index* (1978—present), published quarterly, provides a subject index on educational topics and specific sports. It also indexes sports medicine.

State Education Journal Index, published twice a year since 1963, is a subject and bibliographic index on articles in about 100 state education journals. These journals cover a broad range of topics and are useful primarily for such state educational issues as federal aid, collective bargaining, and teacher certification.

Educational Administration Abstracts, published since 1966, abstracts articles from about 100 journals. The reference classifies abstracts into forty-two subjects and provides an author and journal index but not a subject index.[1]

Government Documents Indexes The *Monthly Catalogue of United States Government Publications* indexes books, pamphlets, maps, and periodicals of all

---

[1]References for measurement are cited in Chapter 5.

types—over 15,000 per year. Congressional, departmental, and bureau publications are organized alphabetically by department and bureau with monthly and cumulative author, title, and subject indexes and series/report numbers. Two indexes to educational statistics compiled by the federal government are the *Digest of Educational Statistics* and the *American Statistics Index.* The *Digest of Educational Statistics,* published annually by the National Center for Education Statistics, contains demographic statistics and some longitudinal analyses providing statistics on enrollment, organizational patterns, staffing, student retention rates, educational finances, and educational achievement at all levels of education and in federally funded programs. The *American Statistics Index,* published monthly as an annual index and abstract service, cites publications of departments or agencies other than the Department of Education. For example, information on vocational education, employment and specialized training programs, welfare recipients with children in school, and drug abuse may be collected by the Departments of Agriculture, Commerce, Health and Welfare, and Justice.

Dissertations and Theses Because most dissertations and theses are original unpublished research, the *Dissertation Abstracts International* and *Comprehensive Dissertation Index* are used to locate relevant studies. The *Comprehensive Dissertation Index* provides a subject and author index for every dissertation and thesis for an advanced degree in education accepted by U.S. and Canadian universities. *Dissertation Abstracts International* abstracts dissertations accepted by more than 375 institutions in the United States and Canada. Presently, Section A abstracts dissertations in the humanities and social sciences, including education, and Section B abstracts dissertations in engineering and the sciences, including psychology.

Citation Indexes Citation indexes enable a researcher to determine the impact of a key study or theory on the works of other scholars and researchers. This is particularly important if the first work was controversial, began a subfield, or initiated a series of studies. The *Science Citation Index (SCI)* and *Social Science Citation Index (SSCI)* provide the bibliographic information for all the references that cited the earlier work. SCI indexes citations in science, medicine, agriculture, technology, and the behavioral sciences, including psychology. *SSCI* indexes citations in social, behavioral, and related sciences, including education and psychology.

Smithsonian Science Information Exchange (SSIE, 1973–present) The SSIE is a clearinghouse for work in progress. Because there is a time lag between the completion of a study and its publication, the SSIE enables a reviewer to locate research in progress or research recently completed but not yet in the literature. All fields of the social, behavioral, biological, and medical sciences and the summaries of about 80 percent of federally funded research are indexed and abstracted. To use this service, a reviewer must either request the information through a computer search or write Smithsonian Science Information Exchange, Suite 300, 1730 M Street, N.W., Washington, DC 20036.

Steps for Conducting a Computer Search

Computer searches require reviewers to analyze the problem, determine the type of search, select the indexes (databases), and conduct the search. Most universities now have databases that are accessed through computer hardware in the library. Each library then selects a software searching program to access the database. Although there are common searching strategies, the specific techniques for searching index databases may be unique to an individual library. By using library-mounted databases, the reviewer can search by computer independently, without the cost of searching remotely located databases. Sometimes library-mounted databases can also be accessed from a home or office computer.

Most academic libraries have ERIC and PsycINFO on computers, as well as other indexes and databases. A reference librarian can inform you of the databases locally mounted and how to access them. You can also access many databases through the Internet from any location.

A typical literature search encompasses the past ten years; however, some exhaustive searches encompass more than ten years. Specialized indexes and abstract services, in addition to the more general indexes, may be necessary to locate primary literature.

Specific terms and directions given to a computer will differ with each database. Most computer searches require the following: the search topic, the keywords with synonyms and related terms, the years to be searched, and the language selection (English only, or any other language). Additional directions or commands may be added for the search depending on the scope (broad or narrow). Remember, while there are certain searching functions that are done by most library software, such as by author, keyword, subject, and title, there are numerous methods and specific commands that are unique to each library in conducting the search. Figure 4.1 describes the literature search process.

1. *Analyze the Research Problem* The researcher states the problem specifically and analyzes it. For example, the question "What are the effects of high school remedial mathematics programs on student computational skills?" describes the research problem in a few words and focuses the search on the terms *remedial mathematics program*, *high school*, and *computational skills*. A problem stated as "What are the effects of remedial programs on achievement?" is too imprecise to describe the problem. Reading secondary sources can help focus and narrow the research problem. Many secondary sources may be located through computer searches of either the catalogue or specialized indexes.

FIGURE 4.1   Literature Search Process

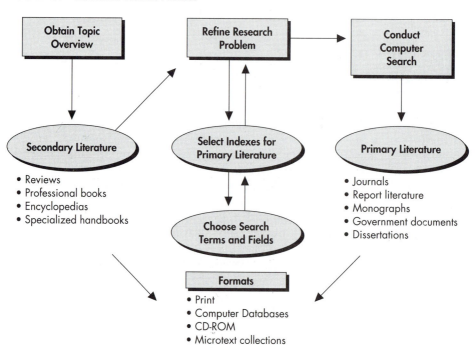

2. *Determine the Type of Search*   Searches are made for several reasons: as a preliminary search to select a research problem; as an exhaustive review for a thesis, dissertation, or major research study; and as an update for a previous literature review. A **preliminary search** to refine a research problem usually needs only about ten of the most recent references from one or two reference services. Because the problem is not yet narrowed, the researcher uses broad descriptors and few combinations. The broad scope is limited by the number of years searched and number of databases. An **exhaustive search** of the literature is done for a narrowly focused problem for ten or more years and may search in more databases. For example, the search for "teacher attitudes toward merit pay" is limited to three concepts: *teachers*, *attitudes*, and *merit pay*. An exhaustive search will require a computer search. The scope of the search may be narrowed by the type of teacher, specific aspects of merit pay, publication type, or educational level of the merit pay system. A search also may be used to update a literature review prepared by the reviewer or one found in a secondary source. Updating a literature review is done by selecting the descriptors used in the initial search and requesting the citations that have been recorded since the first search.

3. *Select the Indexes for Primary Literature*   The problem is transformed into search terms, which conceptually relate to the variables and the population for the study. The reviewer selects the index to obtain the words to use in the

search. Although you may think that a variable has a common definition, the index will define your variable the way the database does. If your definition of a variable—for example, *role*—does not match that of the index, you will not locate primary literature by using the term *role* in the search.

Reviewers first select the index that should contain the most relevant citations and then use other indexes if necessary. Most literature for a research problem on computer-assisted instruction may be found in *CIJE* and *RIE*. If the problem is the effects of computer-assisted instruction on the cognitive processes of children, *Psychological Abstracts* may be useful. If the problem is the administration of computer-assisted instruction, then *Educational Administration Abstracts* will be useful. A research problem on teacher evaluation may be found in *CIJE*, *RIE*, *Educational Administration Abstracts*, and *State Education Journal Index* (see Table 4.3).

By selecting the index, the reviewer is choosing the database, and, consequently, the sources to be searched. Although there is much overlap between some databases, some sources will be unique to each. In addition, different indexes provide additional aids to the reviewer, such as annotations, abstracts, or different "searchable fields" to refine a search. We will use the ERIC database in our example, which is indexed by *CIJE* and *RIE*.

The *CIJE* contains a Subject Index, an Author Index, and a Main Entry Section. The EJ numbers locate the reference in the Main Entry Section, which

TABLE 4.3

Selected Indexes, Abstracts, and Databases*

ERIC (1966–present)
Exceptional Children Educational Resources (1966–present)
PsycINFO [Psychological Abstracts] (1887–present)
Books in Print (1979–present)
Social SCISEARCH and Backfiles [Social Science Citation Indexes] (1972–present)
GPO Monthly Catalogue [Monthly Catalogue of U.S.Government Documents] (1976–present)
Public Affairs Information Service [PAIS] 1972–present)
Legal Resources Index [LAWS] (1980–present)
Sociological Abstracts (1963–present)
Family Resources [NCFR] (1970–present)
Ageline [AARP] (1978–present)
National Rehabilitation Information Center [NRIC] (1950–present)
National Institute of Mental Health Database [MCMH] (1969–present)
Resources in Vocational Education (1978–present)
Sport Database (1949–present)
Bilingual Education Database (1978–present)
Dissertation Abstracts On-line (1861–present)
National Newspaper Index (1979–present)

*The dates given are for the Bibliographic Retrieval Service (BRS). Most services offer the same years for the database; however, DIALOG offers Books in Print from 1900 to the present.

FIGURE 4.2   CIJE Main Entry Section

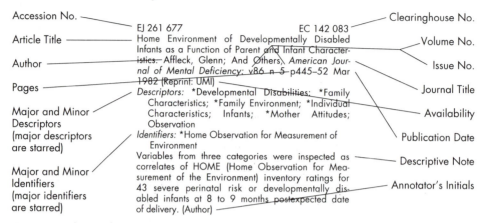

Source: Sample entry from *Current Index to Journals in Education.*

provides the full bibliographic citation, major and minor descriptors for the citation, and an annotation. An annotation is a brief (usually one sentence) summary of the article rather than a 100- or 200-word abstract. Figure 4.2 is an example of a Main Entry Section of *CIJE.*

RIE provides several indexes (subject, author, institution, and publication type) to the abstracts called Document Resume. Using any of these indexes, a reviewer obtains an ED number to locate the reference in the Document Resume section. Each entry in the Document Resume section contains the complete reference, an abstract, and other useful information. Figure 4.3 illustrates an *RIE* Document Resume. If the document is important to the researcher's problem, the reviewer uses the ED number to locate the document in an ERIC Document Microfiche Collection.

An abstract provides more detail than an annotation or a citation. As a rule, abstracts provide enough information to indicate which literature is related to the problem.

4. *Select the Descriptors and Terms* Descriptors and terms are chosen from the *Thesaurus of ERIC Descriptors* or the *Thesaurus of Psychological Index Terms* for PsycINFO. A **thesaurus** is a publication that lists and cross-references descriptors and terms used in an index for a database such as ERIC. Figure 4.4 is a sample entry from the *Thesaurus of ERIC Descriptors.*

Notice in Figure 4.4 that the descriptor *computers* has 2680 citations in CIJE (journals) and 2492 citations in RIE (report literature). During the computer search, the possible number of citations you can search will be updated from the last issue of the *Thesaurus.* The Scope Note defines the word computers in the index for the ERIC database. By using one of the NT terms you will obtain more on target citations than if you were to use the BT term *electronic equipment.* Thus, you need to select for each important word in your research problem those terms in the *Thesaurus* that most closely relate to your meaning

FIGURE 4.3   RIE Document Resume

ERIC Accession Number—
Identification number sequentially assigned to documents as they are processed.

Author(s)

Title

Institution.
(Organization where document originated.)

Date Published
Contract or Grant Number

Language of Document—
documents written entirely in English are not designated, although "English" is carried in their computerized records.

Publication Type— broad categories indicating the form or organization of the document, as contrasted to its subject matter. The category name is followed by the category code.

ERIC Document Reproduction Service (EDRS) Availability—
"MF" means microfiche; "PC" means reproduced paper copy. When described as "Document Not Available from EDRS," alternate sources are cited above. Prices are subject to change; for latest price code schedule see section on "How to Order ERIC Documents," in the most recent issue of RIE.

ED 654 321   CE 123 456
Butler, Kathleen   Smith, B. James
Career Planning for Women.
Central Univ., Chicago, IL.
Spons Agency — Office of Educational Research
   and Improvement (ED), Washington, DC.
Report No. — ISBN-0-3333-5568-1; OERI-91-34
Pub Date — 1992-05-00
Contract — RI900000
Note — 30p.; An abridged version of this report
was presented at the National Conference on
Educational Opportunities for Women (9th,
   Chicago, IL, May 14-16, 1992)
Available from — Campus Bookstore, 123
   College Avenue, Chicago, IL 60690 ($5.95).
Language — English, Spanish
Journal Cit — Women Today; v13 n3 p1-14 Jan
1992
PubType— Reports— Descriptive
(141)—Tests/Questionnaires (160)
EDRS Price—MF01/PC02 Plus Postage.
Descriptors — Career Guidance, *Career
   Planning, *Demand Occupations,
*Employed
Women, *Employment Opportunities,
Females,
   Labor Force, Labor Market,
Postsecondary
   Education
Identifiers — Consortium of States, *National
   Occupational Competency Testing Institute
   Women's opportunities for employment will be
directly related to their level of skill and
experience and also to the labor market demands
through the remainder of the decade. The number
of workers needed for all major occupational
categories is expected to increase by about one-
fifth between 1990 and 1999, but the growth
rate will vary by occupational group. Professional
and technical workers are expected to have the
highest predicted rate (39 percent), clerical
workers (26 percent), sales workers (24 percent),
craft workers and supervisors (20 percent),
managers and administrators (15 percent), and
operatives (11 percent). This publication contains
a brief discussion and employment information (in
English and Spanish) concerning occupations for
professional and technical workers, managers
and administrators, skilled trades, sales workers,
clerical workers, and service workers. In order for
women to take advantage of increased labor
market demands, employer attitudes toward
working women need to change and women
must: (1) receive better career planning and
counseling, (2) change their career aspirations,
and (3) fully utilize the sources of legal protection
and assistance that are available to them.
(Contains 45 references.) (SB)

Clearinghouse Accession Number

Sponsoring Agency— agency responsible for initiating, funding, and managing the research project.

Report Number—assigned by originator.

Descriptive Note (pagination first).

Alternate source for obtaining document

Journal Citation

Descriptors—subject terms found in the *Thesaurus of ERIC Descriptors* that characterize substantive content. Only the major terms (preceded by an asterisk) are printed in the Subject Index.

Identifiers—additional identifying terms not found in the *Thesaurus*. Only the major terms (preceded by an asterisk) are printed in the Subject Index.

Informative Abstract

Abstractor's Initials

Source: Sample entry from Resources in Education, 1982, 17(5), 201.

FIGURE 4.4 ERIC Descriptors and Terms

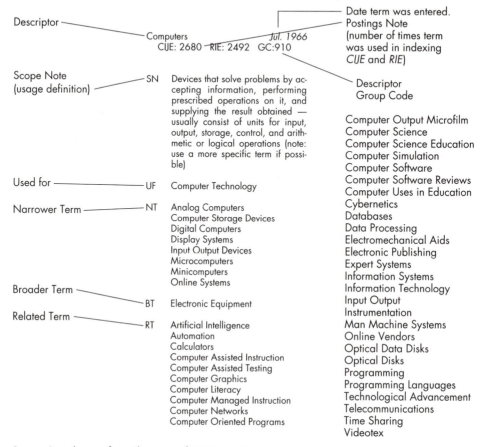

Source: Sample entry from *Thesaurus of ERIC Descriptors.*

for the word. The ERIC *Thesaurus* is available in print and in commercial Web versions of ERIC, such as FirstSearch.

 5. *Conduct the Computer Search* Directing a computer search takes planning if you want to identify the most relevant literature efficiently. First, obtain from the *Thesaurus* the selected descriptors, narrow terms, and related terms that you plan to use in the search. Then, determine the order (most important to least important) in which the descriptors with logical connectors *or* and *and* are entered into the computer. Once into the database, follow your initial plan, revise it when insufficient citations are found, and print or make a disk copy of the citations immediately.

 Let us take a hypothetical example to demonstrate the logic of a computer search. For example, a search of *"teaching styles and elementary"* would have fewer "hits" than using only *"teaching styles"* (*teaching styles* by itself would

FIGURE 4.5 Combining Descriptors

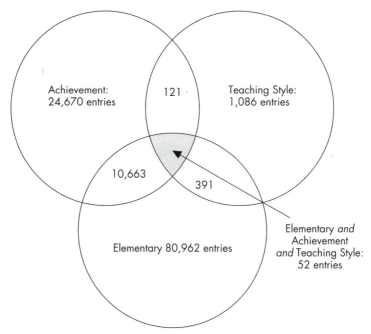

include elementary, middle, and high schools, and colleges and universities). If a third descriptor, *achievement,* is added, the search is further refined. This process of narrowing the search is illustrated in Figure 4.5. (The numbers of entries were retrieved in May, 1998, and are those entered between 1989 and 1998.) You can use either sets (preferred) or boolean logic (or, and) to construct a query. Put parentheses around sets, quotations around phrases, and commas between terms. A space is an implied "and." For example, a search constructed as *(self-concept, self esteem) college* will find references to self-concept or self-esteem and college.

A computer search plan (see Figure 4.6) lists in order of importance the selected descriptors for each concept and then directs the search with appropriate search language. The *or* connectors increase the number of citations for a broad search, whereas the *and* connectors reduce the number of citations for a narrow search because all descriptors must be present in each citation. The first search is with combinations of descriptors that precisely fit the problem. The results will show how much work has been done on the topic and whether there is sufficient literature on target. If there is insufficient literature, more searches are necessary to obtain the relevant literature.

Search 1 will locate only citations with all four descriptors. The search will produce fewer references, but they will be on target. Search 2 broadens the search by omitting one descriptor, school level. Search 3 searches for references with terms 1 or 4 (reading comprehension and reading skills) and either of

FIGURE 4.6   Computer Search Plan

Purpose: _preliminary search: Teaching methods_
for reading comprehension for bilingual
students in the primary grades.

Database to Be Searched:
ERIC

ERIC DESCRIPTORS:

1. _reading comprehension_
2. _reading difficulty_
3. _reading_
4. _reading skills_
5. _remedial reading_

6. _reading instruction_
7. _reading program_
8. _bilingual students_
9. _second language students_
10. _teaching methods_

11. _teaching procedures_
12. _teaching techniques_
13. _primary grades_
14. _elementary grades_
15. _____

SEARCH 1   _1 and 10 and 8 and 13_

- -

SEARCH 2   _1 and 10 and 8_

- -

SEARCH 3   _(1 or 4) and (10 or 11 or 12) and 8 and 13_

- -

SEARCH 4   _(1 or 4) and (10 or 11 or 12) and (8 or 9) and 13_

- -

SEARCH 5   _(1 or 2 or 3 or 4) and (6 or 10 or 11 or 12) and (8 or 9)_

- -

SEARCH 6   _(1 or 2 or 3 or 4) and (6 or 10 or 11 or 12) and (8 or 9) and (13 or 14)_

three descriptors for teaching methods, but it limits the search to bilingual students and primary grades. Search 5 broadens the search again. Search 6 produces the largest number of citations because all terms related to the four major concepts are used. Because of the ERIC indexing procedures, both narrow and related terms must be used for an exhaustive search.

To refine the search, you can ask for only the most recent references, use only major descriptors, or use nonsubject descriptors. Each ERIC citation is assigned up to six major descriptors to cover its main focus. Minor descriptors are used to indicate less important aspects of the topic or nonsubject features such as educational level or research methods. Limiting the search to only minor descriptors, some of which are optional classifications, will severely limit the number of citations. Because not all citations may have been assigned the type of minor descriptor, such as research method, some relevant literature may be omitted. Publication type, however, is assigned to every document in the ERIC database.

While all search software contains similar logic and "fields" for conducting the search, each library chooses its search software from several vendors. Thus, it is best to consult with a reference librarian for the particular software used and for the commands available.

Mediated on-line searches are used when the reviewer found insufficient literature by searching the library-mounted databases and now needs to search distant index databases. A mediated on-line search is one conducted by a search analyst who "dials out" via computer to remotely located databases. For educational research, the DIALOG and BRS databases contain most of the indexes. A search analyst usually conducts the search, because the costs are based on how long a searcher is connected to the database and how many citations are printed.

To minimize the time on-line, it is important to work with the search analyst to select the appropriate descriptors before going on-line. Usually a sample of titles retrieved is reviewed to be sure that the selected descriptors are locating the relevant literature. Remember, printing the results of the search adds to the costs. The computer can print or copy to a diskette the results of the search.

Internet searches enable you to search distant library catalogues, government agency documents, electronic journals, and other resources. Now that ERIC is available through the Internet, most searches will use one of the four access points found in the Internet version of ERIC. The four access points for ERIC are summarized in Figure 4.7. You can use any of these four points to search the ERIC database, but each has particular strengths and weaknesses. For example, using the ERIC Document Reproduction Service limits the search to *RIE* documents and ERIC Digests. Since most beginning searches of the literature depend heavily on published articles, it is preferable to search using one of the other three access points. One very nice feature of the ERIC Clearinghouse on Information & Technology is that it tells you immediately the number of "hits" identified in your search. If you find you have 10,000 hits you know the search is much too general and that additional focus is needed. With all four of these access points you will search the database by entering appropriate terms as directed by the computer prompt. While each access point uses a different search engine to conduct the inquiry, with unique commands and conventions to delimit the scope of a search, a similar logic and approach is used in all four. We will look at one of the access points as an illustration, the ERIC Clearinghouse on Assessment and Evaluation (ERIC/AE).

You will note in Figure 4.8 that below the "search" prompt there are a number of options you can choose for focusing your search. *These are very important and need to be attended to **before** submitting your search.* The default option for Database is "On-Demand." This means that the search will include only a subset of full RIE documents that can be downloaded if the host (library)

FIGURE 4.7   ERIC Access Points

Access Point	ERIC Clearinghouse on Information and Technology http://ericir.syr.edu/Eric/	ERIC Document Reproduction Service http://www.edrs.com/	ERIC Clearinghouse on Assessment and Evaluation http://ericae.net/research.htm	ERIC Clearinghouse on Assessment and Evaluation http://ericae.net/scripts/ewiz/amain2.asp
Available Information	**ERIC Database (1966–)** • Journal Abstracts *(CIJE)* • Document Abstracts *(RIE)* • ERIC Digests (Full Text)	**ERIC Database (1966–)** • Document Abstracts *(RIE)* • ERIC Digests (Abstracts)	**ERIC Database (1966–)** • Journal Abstracts *(CIJE)* • Document Abstracts *(RIE)* • ERIC Digests (Full Text)	**ERIC Database (1966–)** • Journal Abstracts *(CIJE)* • Document Abstracts *(RIE)* • ERIC Digests (Full Text) *Thesaurus of ERIC Descriptors*
Searchable Fields	• keyword* • descriptor • identifier • ERIC number • title • author • publication type • publication date	• keyword* • descriptor • identifier • title • ERIC Clearinghouse • ERIC number • author • publication type • publication date • abstract • institution	• keyword* *a word (or words) appearing anywhere in the document	• descriptor
Search Engine	**PL Web** • provides relevance ranking • supports field and crossfield searching	**EDRS** • provides online full-text document order and delivery service • supports field and crossfield searching	**Webinator** • allows natural language queries • provides "more like this" searching • provides relevance ranking • allows online ordering of ED's	**Search Wizard** • interactively develops search strategies • interactively identifies correct descriptors • saves up to five search strategies • provides prepackaged, "hot topic" searches • allows online ordering of ED's
Search Operators	• proximity • wildcards • stemming • Boolean • synonyms • concepts • field restricted • exact match	• proximity • wildcards • stemming • synonyms • field restricted • Boolean	• word forms • proximity • sets • Boolean • special pattern matchers	• sets • wild cards

FIGURE 4.8   Sample ERIC Webpage to Initiate Search

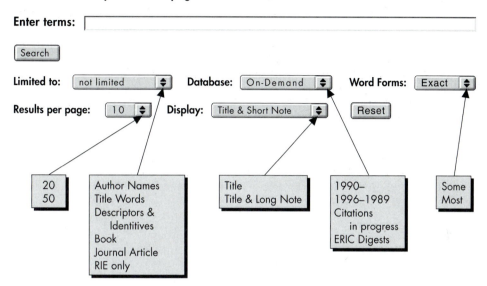

is what is called an E* subscribe customer. Individuals can pay by credit card if the host is not an E* subscriber. To access all CIJE and RIE documents since 1990, you need to pull down the menu and click 1990–. Since each entry is cataloged in a number of ways, the "Limited to" option allows you to focus on a particular characteristic, such as author names, titles, bibliography, book, journal articles, ERIC Digests, and so on. For example, for initial searches it is usually wise to limit your search to journal articles. This would be done by accessing the pull down menu next to the "Limited to" box and selecting "Journal Articles." This will focus the search so that only journal articles (CIJE) will be included. Once the sources are displayed they can be reviewed in greater detail by clicking on the title to reveal the full abstract and bibliographic information. Another helpful way to limit initial searches is to select the term "descriptors." For more advanced searching try the ERIC Clearinghouse on Information & Technology or the ERIC Search Wizard. The Search Wizard provides access to the ERIC *Thesaurus*.

6. *Analyze the Printout* Many libraries provide the option of copying the search results to a computer printer or to a diskette. In addition, the library may have a software program that transforms an ERIC database list of citations into a reference list using APA style or *The Chicago Manual of Style* format.

The printout of a computer search can provide three levels of information with each reference, depending on the option selected by the reviewer. The first option provides the title and accession number (the EJ and/or ED number). The second option includes the complete bibliographic citation, the EJ and/or ED number and the descriptors for each reference. The third option includes all of the above plus the abstract; it is the most useful in selecting sources.

Reviewers then read the abstracts for each reference on the printout in order to determine the relevance of the citation to the problem. Most reviewers code or rank order each citation by degree of potential usefulness. A typical code might be 3 to indicate *on target and most important,* 2 to indicate *related literature and may be useful,* and 1 to indicate *irrelevant and unnecessary.*

7. ***Locate the References*** The majority of references will probably be in professional journals, although for some topics monographs, dissertations, and reports may be relevant. To locate references, one should spend time learning how a library is organized—which references are in bound volumes, on microfiche or microfilm, or in special collections—and the procedure for obtaining these within the library. Reviewers frequently obtain photocopies of important references that may need rechecking.

References not available locally may be obtained through interlibrary loan or by obtaining a photocopy from another library. Some databases services, such as *Psychological Abstracts,* provide the author's address. Using a directory of membership for the American Psychological Association and the American Educational Research Association, one can get the address and write the author for a reprint of an article or paper.

You may also want to use an article reproduction service (UnCover by CARL: http://uncweb.carl.org; UMI—University Microforms International: http://www. lib.umi.com/infostore/; and ISI—Institute for Scientific Information: http:// www.isinet.com).

Abstracting and Organizing the References

The reviewer now reads, abstracts, and classifies each source, reading the most relevant and recent literature first. These articles and reports are more likely to benefit from previous research and literature reviews. From this reading the reviewer can gain a reasonable understanding of the problem and decide on a method of classifying the references.

1. *Abstracting the literature.* Abstracting an article or report on an index card, usually a four- by six-inch size, requires several steps. The abstract or summary is read first to determine whether it contains any information that justifies reading the entire article or report. If the source is sufficiently related to the problem, then it is skimmed for the main points, and the pertinent sections are selected for more careful reading for the purpose of abstracting. The exact bibliographic citation is recorded on the index card if that has not already been done. If the final review must follow a particular bibliographic style, the reference is recorded in that form. If not, the American Psychological Association style is frequently used.

As noted in Chapter 2, most research articles and reports follow a standard format that reduces the reading time and facilitates note-taking: abstract; introduction with the problem statement, significance, and a brief literature review; specific research statement, question, or hypothesis; research procedures; results; and summary with discussion or implications. This format is generally followed in abstracting information on note cards.

Some journal articles are less than six pages long and can be read quickly. Research reports, dissertations, and monographs are usually much longer. For lengthy references, the reviewer skims the entire source and reads only the parts relevant to the problem.

Because one cannot tell which references are the most important for the writing of a literature review until after all sources are read, note-taking is kept very brief. If the notes prove insufficient for the literature review, the reviewer can reread the source. Phrases and abbreviations are used, although crucial points may be quoted, with the page numbers on which they were found. All basic aspects, however—the problem, procedures, findings, and implications—are noted. In addition, reviewers write their critical assessment of the study and its relationship to the problem. Any promising research techniques or limitations of the study are noted. The reviewer's comments are important for generating ideas for criticism of the literature in the review.

Sources that present a theory, describe a program, or summarize opinions and recommendations are abstracted in a different manner. Only the main propositions of the theory, the unique aspects of the program, or the major position of opinion articles are noted. Quotations are very selective and are taken more for illustrative purposes than for documentation. A literature review consists not of a series of quotes but of the reviewer's synthesis and interpretation of the existing knowledge of the problem.

2. *Organizing the references.* Finally, the reviewer develops a *classification system* appropriate for the way the literature provides insights about the problem and for the rationale of the study. The classification system for each literature review differs with the significance of the problem and the reviewer's criticism of the literature. For example, a study that investigates the effects of desegregation might categorize the sources by different effects studied: student achievement, student self-concept, student racial attitudes, school–community relations, teacher–administrator relations, and the like. If the study uses a design or methodology different from that of prior research on the same problem, the references might be categorized by research procedures. If the study asks a question different from the one asked by previous research, the studies might be categorized by research questions. Opinions and theories should have categories distinct from those of empirical studies. Once the classification system is developed, each note card is coded, usually in the upper right-hand corner.

Classifying the references is the first step in organizing the review. The amount of research in any category can be determined quickly. Comparisons and contrasts in methodologies or findings can be synthesized by grouping similar studies. Usually the classification system becomes the subtopics in the written literature review.

Presentation of the Literature Review in Quantitative Research

Searching the literature provides the researcher with much information, not all of which is written in the literature review. Only articles and studies relevant to the study are cited. The literature review demonstrates that the researcher has an understanding of the topic and knowledge of the recent developments in the field. The review should clearly indicate how the selected literature relates to the objectives of the study. The problem statement precedes the literature review, and the more specific research question or hypothesis follows the review. The significance of the study may precede or follow the review.

Organization of the Literature Review

A literature review is often organized by three sections: introduction, critical review, and summary. The introduction states the purpose or scope of the review. The purpose may be a preliminary review in order to state a problem or develop a proposal, or it may be an exhaustive review in order to analyze and critique the research-based knowledge of the topic.

The essence of the review is criticism of the literature. The reviewer must organize the literature review logically as it relates to the selection and significance of the problem. Summarizing one study after another does not make for an informative literature review. Studies are classified, compared, and contrasted in terms of the way they contribute or fail to contribute to knowledge, including criticism of designs and methodologies used to obtain that knowledge.

The summary of the literature review states the status of knowledge on the topic, identifies gaps in it, and relates the review to the present study. The gaps in knowledge may be due to methodological difficulties, a lack of studies on the problem, or inconclusive results from prior research. The summary provides the rationale for the specific research statement, question, or hypothesis.

Criticism of the Literature

Criticism in a literature review serves to illuminate, to discuss both the strengths and limitations of the knowledge of the problem. The criticism of the literature may be organized several ways: (a) historically, by dates of publication; (b) by variables or treatments; (c) by research designs and methods; (d) by the most general literature (least related) and ending with the most closely related references; or (e) by a combination of all of these.

Studies that are better designed than previous research emphasize *methodological* criticisms of that research. In Excerpt 4.1, the experimenters investigated the effects of grades on students' study behavior, attendance, and course evaluations. The literature review notes that the "literally hundreds" of studies on this topic have identified the "biasing" influence of student rating of instruc-

EXCERPT 4.1

LITERATURE REVIEW: METHODOLOGICAL CRITICISM

Beginning with Remmers' pioneering work (e.g., Remmers, 1930; Remmers, Hadley, & Long, 1932), the factors affecting students' ratings of instruction have been the subject of literally hundreds of research investigations. One important focus of much of this research has been the identification of "biasing" influences on student objectivity—that is, variables which alter students' ratings of presumably unrelated aspects of the instructional process (e.g., evaluations of textbook clarity affected by sex of the instructor). Perhaps the area receiving the most attention in this regard has been the relationship between students' grades and their ratings of the quality of instruction. Yet Feldman's (1976) recent extensive review of the literature offers only inconclusive support for the role of grades as a source of student bias:

> Currently available evidence cannot be taken as definitely establishing a bias in teacher evaluation due to the grades students receive . . . but neither is it presently possible to rule out such bias. (p. 69)

One recurring difficulty in establishing the grade-evaluation relationship has been the correlation nature of most previous research. For example, it frequently has been reported that students receiving higher grades evaluate the quality of instruction more favorably than those receiving lower grades (e.g., Doyle & Whitely, 1974; Gessner, 1973; Kennedy, 1975). Although suggestive, such data do not clearly establish that the receipt of the grade had any effect on the student's evaluation of the course instruction. A plausible alternative hypothesis would be that the amount of effort expended for a particular course, or even the student's previous abilities or aptitude in the area, influence their perceptions of the quality of instruction (as well as, of course, their grade). This problem has been addressed previously (e.g., Costin, Greenough, & Menges, 1971), but it never has been adequately resolved.

Source: From Vasta, R., & Sarmiento, R. F. (1979). Liberal grading improves evaluations but not performance. *Journal of Educational Psychology, 71*(2), 207.

tion, especially on grading. The criticism rests on the correlational nature of most previous research, which led to inconclusive findings. The literature review thus states a rationale for a design in a natural setting that maintains experimental control sufficient to examine grade effects independent of subject variables, such as student study habits, aptitude, and perceptions of the quality of instruction.

A literature review may also be organized by the *variables* or *experimental treatments* in the study. The hypothesis, for example, in H. G. Smith, "Investigation of Several Techniques for Reviewing Audio-Tutorial Instruction" (1979) was that students using an audio-tutorial review retained more than students using only a study guide. Subjects were randomly assigned to one of four groups: review with study guide only, review with summary audiotape, review with compressed speech audiotape, and no review. The literature review first summarized the research, which indicated that forgetting increases with time and that reviewing previously learned material enhances the ability to recall. The study thus has three review groups and one group with no review. Research on the nature of the review suggested that reading (group one) and listening to a summary (group two) enhanced recall. Finally, while no studies of the use of accelerated speech in reviewing material were found, there was extensive literature suggesting that accelerated speech recording increased original learning (group three). The literature review from both on-target and related literature provided an empirical rationale for the design and for the research hypotheses.

For each topic or idea introduced in the review, the researcher explains how it relates to the study. The writer cannot assume that readers will make the connection. If a particular study does not relate to his or her investigation, then it's not really needed. It may be interesting information, but it fails to further the understanding of the topic or provide a rationale for the study.

Literature Reviews in Qualitative Research

Qualitative researchers conduct preliminary literature reviews to propose a study. Unlike in many quantitative studies, these researchers locate and criticize most of the literature for the study during data collection and analysis. They do a continuing literature review because the exact research focus and questions evolve as the research progresses. Thus, by the completion of a study, these researchers have done an extensive literature review. The approach to reviewing the literature merely reflects the discovery orientation and inductive approach typical of qualitative research.

Preliminary Literature Review

The preliminary literature review represents possible conceptual frameworks for phrasing foreshadowed problems. The literature review frequently cites broad areas of scholarly thinking, such as sociological, psychological, anthropological, and political, with representative scholars, and it illustrates why certain concepts may become relevant in data collection and analysis. The preliminary literature review makes explicit the initial frameworks the researcher begins with to focus the observations and interviewing.

Literature reviews differ in qualitative research with a phenomenological purpose, which is to describe and analyze naturalistic social scenes or a process without suggesting grounded theory. Reviews in these studies justify the need for an in-depth descriptive study using a qualitative approach. For example, prior research was conducted with quantitative procedures and did not examine the phenomena in descriptive depth as a human collective process or event. Or, prior qualitative research, for example, studied secondary classes but ele-

EXCERPT 4.2

AN ETHNOGRAPHIC LITERATURE REVIEW

If one wishes to understand the term *holy water,* one should not study the properties of the water, but rather the assumptions and beliefs of the people who use it. That is, holy water derives its meaning from those who attribute a special essence to it (Szasz, 1974).

Similarly, the meaning of the term *mental retardation* depends on those who use it to describe the cognitive states of other people. As some have argued, mental retardation is a social construction or a concept that exists in the minds of the "judges" rather than in the minds of the "judged" (Blatt, 1970; Braginsky and Braginsky, 1971; Dexter, 1964; Hurley, 1969; Mercer, 1973). A mentally retarded person is one who has been labeled as such according to rather arbitrarily created and applied criteria.

Retardate and other such clinical labels suggest generalizations about the nature of men and women to whom that term has been applied (Goffman, 1963). We assume that the mentally retarded possess common characteristics that allow them to be unambiguously distinguished from all others. We explain their behavior by special theories. It is as though humanity can be divided into two groups, the "normal" and the "retarded."

To be labeled retarded is to have a wide range of imperfections imputed to you. One imperfection is the inability to analyze your life and your current situation. Another is the inability to express yourself—to know and say who you are and what you wish to become.

Source: From "The Judged, Not the Judges: An Insider's View of Mental Retardation" by Robert Bogdan and Steven Taylor, *American Psychologist,* January 1976. Copyright © 1976 by the American Psychological Association. Reprinted by permission of the publisher and authors.

mentary classes had not yet been examined. Frequently, as in Excerpt 4.2, there are unique or unusual events that have not been studied systematically at all. Excerpt 4.2 is an insider's view, which provides an understanding of mental retardation. The researchers point out that the meaning of the term *mental retardation* depends on those who use the term. The literature review suggests that the social construction of the term *mental retardation*, originally a clinical label, has other connotations. The researchers used ethnographic interviews of a 26-year-old man who had been labeled "retarded" by his family, teachers, professionals, and a state institution for the retarded. The person's words reveal how his understanding of himself and his situation differed from that of others who labeled him. Hence, mental retardation, as a concept, is more than a clinical label.

Historical and legal researchers also conduct preliminary literature reviews. The researcher contrasts the proposed focus and questions with prior research to justify a need for the study. Historians frequently contrast their work with prior research by citing access to "new" documents or archives made available only to the historian or to the scholarly community. The literature review may also cite current policies and the need to examine the past for an understanding of current debates. Legal researchers often trace a legal principle as it is applied to new areas of educational law. The principle of liability, for example, may have been investigated in private organizations and certain areas of public school law but not in school athletics.

Continuous Review and Criticism of the Literature

Qualitative researchers continue to read broadly in the literature as they collect data. The literature does *not* provide the ethnographer with preconceived ideas, but it enables the researcher to understand the social scenes observed. Relevant literature may provide analogies to the observed social scenes, a scholarly language to synthesize descriptions, or general analytical schemes to analyze data. The literature helps the ethnographer to look at social scenes from many general perspectives and to understand the complexities to illuminate more subtle meanings.

The historian also reads broadly to acquire the necessary historical context of the era studied. The historical context includes general knowledge of social customs, institutions, political movements (international, national, and regional), education, recreation, economic cycles, technological changes, and the like. Knowledge of the general historical context of the event, person (biography), or institution examined allows the historian to understand and interpret the past event or people from the participants' perspectives rather than the historian's modern perspective.

Alternative Presentations of Literature

Literature in qualitative studies is presented as (a) separate discussions and (b) integration within the text. Prior research is presented as a separate discussion in the introduction to illustrate the importance of the study in extending our knowledge, and possibly to relate the topic to current discussions or policies (see Excerpt 4.2). A more detailed discussion is presented in the concluding interpretations of the study. Seldom is an entire section of a journal article or an entire chapter of a report called a Literature Review because the traditional format of qualitative research is that of a narrative. Some journals impose this format on articles because of the typical readers. A comparison of Excerpts 2.5 and 2.8 illustrates some of these distinctions.

Most of the literature is integrated in the text with explanatory footnotes. One can see how the use of explanatory footnotes differs in Excerpts 2.5 and 2.6. The typical style manual used by historians, legal researchers, and many ethnographers allows for explanatory footnotes rather than just text citations. Thus, the qualitative researcher can cite, extend, or contrast each fact and interpretation with the exact document or reference. The footnotes and the bibliography, which includes background reading for ethnographic and historical context, reflect the extensive literature review for a qualitative study.

Meta-Analysis Literature Reviews

Unlike a narrative criticism of the literature, **meta-analysis** is a review procedure that uses statistical techniques to summarize the results of prior independently conducted studies. It is sometimes referred to as a *rigorous research review*, a *systematic research synthesis*, an *integrative research review*, or simply meta-analysis.

Statisticians have long noted that in many applied fields, the treatment effects are small and therefore difficult to detect in a single study. A natural question is whether the aggregate of studies might not have statistical and practical significance even though no single study does. Thus, meta-analysis determines the size of the effect of educational practices investigated in a number of individual studies.

A key concept in any synthesis is *pattern*. The distinction between primary analysis and meta-analysis may be analogous to the distinction between taking observations at ground level and taking observations from the air. As one rises in an airplane, the precision achieved at ground level lessens and is replaced by a greater recognition of patterns. Thus, the pattern of skyscrapers that is indiscernible when driving into a large city becomes more evident from a higher-elevation vantage point (Hedges & Olkin, 1986). Second, the conclusions based on a meta-analysis can be stronger than those of the component studies because pooling of data generally increases statistical power of the *effect size*.[2]

The Research Process

The steps to conduct integrative research reviews are similar to the tasks of original research. Cooper (1998) characterized rigorous research synthesis as five phases: problem formulation, data collection, data evaluation, analysis and interpretation, and public presentation. Each phase of the review involves methodological issues and requires subjective decisions that can lead to procedural variations which can profoundly affect the outcome of the review. Obviously, the validity of the conclusions of research or research reviews depends on the decisions made in each phase. Each of these phases will be summarized below from the viewpoint of helping you to evaluate a research synthesis.

1. *Problem Formulation* To formulate a research synthesis problem, the reviewer decides what questions or hypotheses to address and what evidence should be included in the review. Meta-analysis procedures are primarily used

---

[2]Effect size (ES) in principle is the difference on a criterion measure between an experimental and a control group divided by the control group's standard deviation.

to integrate research results and are seldom applied to theoretical or method-ological literature.

2. ***Data Collection*** This phase involves the specification of procedures to be used in finding relevant reviews. Whereas the primary researcher samples individuals, the reviewer, in a sense, retrieves researchers. In reality, reviewers are not trying to draw representative samples of studies from the literature, but they are attempting to retrieve an *entire population* of studies. This goal is rarely achieved, but it is more feasible in a review than in primary research. The inves-tigator hopes the review will cover "all previous research" on the problem.

To minimize bias in data collection, a reviewer should use more than one major database, informal communications, and the bibliographies of past researchers or reviews. Reviewers should be explicit about how studies were gathered, providing information on sources, years, and keywords used in the search, and they should present whatever indices of potential retrieval bias is known to them. Characteristics of individuals used in the separate studies should be summarized.

3. ***Data Evaluation*** The data evaluation phase involves specifications about decisions concerning evidence that will be included in the review. Both primary researchers and research reviewers examine their data sets for extreme values, errors in recording, and other unreliable measurements. In addition, the research reviewer should discard data because of questionable research design validity. In other words, the reviewer makes either a discrete decision—whether to include or exclude the data in the review—or a continuous decision—whether to weigh studies dependent on their relative degree of trustworthiness. Most social scientists agree that methodological quality should be the primary criterion for inclusion.

4. ***Data Analysis and Interpretation*** In contrast to primary study review-ers, meta-analysis reviewers interpret data using rules of inference that build on standard statistical techniques. Analysis and interpretation methods are fre-quently idiosyncratic to the particular reviewer. This leads to criticisms of sub-jectivity and a concern that a variety of methods have been introduced into the reviewing process. Further, quantitative reviewing is based on certain premises. The basic premise is that a series of studies was selected that address an identi-cal conceptual hypothesis.

Methods for data analysis range from simple vote counting methods to sophisticated statistical techniques to obtain indices of the effect size. Either the results or the raw data of each component study can be integrated. Reviewers should be careful to distinguish between study- and review-generated evidence.

5. ***Public Presentation*** The presentation of a meta-analysis involves deci-sions about what information should be included in the final report. Two pri-mary threats to validity are the omission of details on how the review was conducted and the omission of evidence about variables and moderators of rela-tions that other inquirers may find (or will be) important to the hypothesis. Slavin (1984) suggests that the effect size for each study be included and the coding of studies on various criteria should be presented.

A Developing Methodology

Researchers criticize both meta-analysis and narrative reviews. Narrative reviews can be susceptible to the reviewer's biases in deciding which studies are sufficiently "methodologically adequate" to be included. Criticisms of meta-analysis have centered on the issue of "combining apples and oranges." Critics suggest that by combining the results of different studies, especially different types of designs, concepts, and their operations, one runs the risk of producing results that make neither conceptual nor statistical sense. Researchers continue to differ on whether meta-analyses should be conducted only for studies selected as "the best evidence" (Slavin, 1986) or should include all studies, regardless of research design (Joyce, 1987). Further, because of methodological variations, the conclusions of a series of meta-analyses on the same topic, such as the effects of teacher questioning levels on student achievement, can be quite different.[3] Because there is nothing inherent in the procedures that makes misleading conclusions either inevitable or impossible, there is a growing consensus that meta-analysis can be a useful tool in research reviews, *if properly used.*

An inherent danger is that meta-analysis may discourage further research in the synthesized area. For example, in the area of mainstreaming, only a few studies have used random assignment to special or regular classes. It would be tragic if the publication of a meta-analysis on this topic ended this line of inquiry. Meta-analysis should be recognized as a legitimate supplement to narrative interpretive reviews, rather than as a replacement.

Standards of Adequacy

A narrative literature review is judged adequate by three criteria: its selection of the sources, its criticism of the literature, and its summary and overall interpretation of the literature on the problem. Below are questions that aid a reader in determining the quality of the literature review.

Selection of the Literature

1. Is the purpose of the review (preliminary or exhaustive) indicated?
2. Are the parameters of the review reasonable?
   a. Why were certain bodies of literature included in the search and others excluded from it?
   b. Which years were included in the search?
3. Is primary literature emphasized in the review and secondary literature, if cited, used selectively?

---

[3]G. E. Samson, B. Strykowski, T. Weinstein, & H. J. Walberg (1987), The effects of teacher questioning levels on student achievement: A quantitative synthesis, *Journal of Educational Research, 80*(5), 290–295.

4. Are recent developments in the problem emphasized in the review?
5. Is the literature selected relevant to the problem?
6. Are complete bibliographic data provided for each reference?

Criticism of the Literature

1. Is the review organized by topics or ideas, not by author or date?
2. Is the review organized logically?
3. Are major studies or theories discussed in detail and minor studies with similar limitations or results discussed as a group?
4. Is there adequate criticism of the design and methodology of important studies so that the reader can draw his or her own conclusions?
5. Are studies compared and contrasted and conflicting or inconclusive results noted?
6. Is the relevance of each reference to the problem explicit?

Summary and Interpretation

1. Does the summary provide an overall interpretation and understanding of our knowledge of the problem?
2. Do the implications provide theoretical or empirical justification for the specific research questions or hypotheses to follow?
3. Do the methodological implications provide a rationale for the design to follow?

A literature review is judged adequate in the context of the proposal or the completed study. The problem, the significance of the study, and the specific research question or hypothesis influence the type of literature review. A literature review is not judged by its length nor by the number of references included. The quality of the literature review is evaluated according to whether it furthers the understanding of the status of knowledge of the problem and provides a rationale for the study.

Summary

The following statements summarize the reasons for conducting a literature review, the process of reviewing the literature, and the literature reviews in quantitative research, qualitative studies, and meta-analysis.

1. Literature includes theoretical discussions, reviews of the status of knowledge by authorities, philosophical papers, descriptions and evaluations of current practices, and empirical research.
2. Literature for a review is taken from journals, reports, monographs, government documents, dissertations, and electronic resources.
3. Reviewing the literature enables the researcher to define and limit the problems, place the study in historical and relationship perspective, avoid unnecessary replication, select promising methods and measures, relate the findings to previous knowledge, suggest further research, and suggest research hypotheses.

4. The selected literature should be relevant to the problem, either on target or related.

5. Primary literature is valued more highly in a review; secondary literature, however, provides useful information to get started.

6. The process of reviewing the literature is as follows: analyze the problem statement, read secondary sources, select the appropriate indexes, transform the problem into search language, conduct a computer search, read pertinent primary sources, organize notes, and write the review.

7. Secondary literature is a synthesis of the original work and usually consists of articles in general and specialized educational journals, annuals, yearbooks, handbooks, encyclopedias, or books.

8. Primary literature is the original empirical studies or writings by a researcher, which is found by using indexes to journals, educational documents, government documents, and dissertations.

9. Steps in conducting a search are to analyze the research problem, determine the type of search, select the indexes (databases), select the descriptors and terms, conduct the search, code the bibliography or printout for relevant sources, and locate the references.

10. Computer searches for the literature include library mounted databases, CD-ROMs, Internet, or a mediated on-line search of remotely located databases.

11. The reviewer reads each source that is most likely to be relevant, abstracts and makes commentary notes, and organizes the notes into a classification system.

12. In quantitative research, the literature review is organized logically by ideas and provides an understanding of our knowledge of the problem and a rationale for the research question or hypothesis.

13. Criticism of the literature indicates the strengths and limitations of our knowledge in terms of lack of studies on the problem, inconclusive results from studies on the same problem, or methodological difficulties.

14. In qualitative research, preliminary literature reviews suggest the need for the study, but the search for and criticism of the literature are continuous during data collection and analysis. Literature is presented in introductory discussions and integrated in the text with extensive explanatory footnotes.

15. Meta-analysis is a research procedure that uses statistical techniques to summarize the results of prior independently conducted studies.

Self-Instructional Review Exercises

Sample answers are in the back of the book.

Test Items

1. Which of the following is the major advantage of conducting a literature review?
   a. encourages unnecessary duplication of research
   b. identifies variables and promising instruments

   c. places a study in a historical and associational perspective

   d. provides the research design

2. The literature review should be based as much as possible on which sources?

   a. preliminary

   b. secondary

   c. primary

   d. abstracts

3–8 Match the following descriptor statement with its source.

3. subsequent citations of a study	a. *Current Index to Journals in*
4. articles in educational research	*Education* and professional
journals	b. *Resources in Education*
5. report literature in the ERIC system	c. Citation indexes
6. statistical data of government agencies	d. encyclopedias, handbooks,
7. status of knowledge on selected topics	annuals
8. research in progress	e. none of the above

9. Which is the major method for locating literature?

   a. one's personal library or journal

   b. databases

   c. tracking research cited in relevant literature (ancestry approach)

   d. attendance at professional meetings

10. Which of the following is the most useful in determining whether a reference will probably be relevant to the problem?

   a. descriptor

   b. annotation

   c. abstract

   d. database

11. An exhaustive search is done for which of the following purposes?

   a. for a major study

   b. to define and limit a problem

   c. to develop a proposal

   d. to make a minor educational decision

12. A computer search is time efficient if the reviewer:

   a. has analyzed the problem statement.

   b. knows the databases, years, and descriptors for a search.

   c. can selectively limit the search.

   d. has decided the purpose of the literature search.

   e. All of the above are correct.

13–16. Match items 13 through 16 with the step in a computer search.

13. self-concept, self-esteem, remedial education, remedial program, elementary school children	a. define research problem b. state specific purpose of computer search
14. *CIJE, Exceptional Child Education Abstracts,* and *Psychological Abstracts*	c. select database(s) d. select descriptors

15. review relevant research articles for the past ten years
16. academic self-concept of elementary students in remedial programs

17. The literature review section in a completed quantitative study should *not* do which of the following?
    a. include all the references read by the reviewer
    b. provide criticism of the designs and methodologies used to develop knowledge of the problem
    c. show an understanding of the status of knowledge of the problem
    d. form an empirical or theoretical rationale, or both, for the research question or hypothesis
18. Meta-analytical literature reviews
    a. are narrative criticisms of prior research.
    b. can be applied in every literature review.
    c. statistically analyze the results of prior selected research to produce the effect size of a treatment.
    d. require few researcher decisions in the review process.

Application Problems

1. A supervisor wants to locate mathematics curriculum guidelines and evaluation studies of mathematics programs formulated under Title I of the elementary and Secondary Education Act and those most recently done through Chapter I (in the current terminology). Which database and type of computer search would be most efficient?
2. Below is a problem statement and descriptors for each concept. The descriptors are listed in order of importance to a literature search.

   How do teacher questioning techniques affect fourth-grade students' learning in social studies?
   a. questioning techniques
   b. questioning
   c. questioning behavior
   d. questions
   e. achievement
   f. skills
   g. recall
   h. social studies
   i. history
   j. upper elementary
   k. elementary education

   (a.) Direct a narrow computer search to obtain pertinent literature using *and* to join the descriptors from a through k that most closely match the research question.
   (b.) Direct a more thorough computer search using *or* to join the different key terms for the same concept, and *and* to connect the descriptors a through k.

3. A reviewer has classified his or her relevant sources in the following manner:
   a. evaluations of behavior modification programs: effects on instructional approach, teacher questioning style
   b. descriptions of behavior modification programs and management implications
   c. evaluations of behavior modification programs and management implications
   d. theories of stimulus–response learning
   e. studies of operant conditioning on animals

   Organize these in order for a literature review on the problem of "evaluation of instruction, student behavior, and learning in a behavior modification program."

CHAPTER 5

Educational Research on the Internet

James Ghaphery
Suzanne Nash

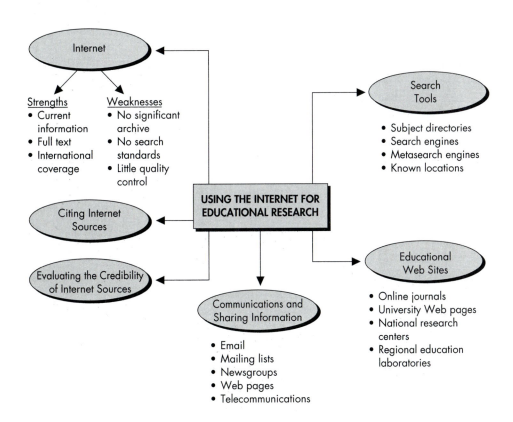

K E Y   T E R M S

Internet

ERIC

controlled vocabulary

subject directories

search engines

hyperlink

metasearch engines

retrieval algorithms

newsgroups

mailing list

real time

datasets

The information in this chapter, like the Internet, is a work in progress. No matter how quickly these words are rushed to press, Web addresses change, new Web sites emerge, and search engines surface. It is also safe to say that the technology behind the Internet will continue to change the ways in which information is organized and presented. With that in mind, we will focus on those strategies and concepts for Internet research that should stand the test of time.

What Is the Internet?

The **Internet** is a series of interconnected computers that are able to talk to each other by virtue of a shared language or "protocol." The Internet includes email, ftp, telnet and the World Wide Web. While the Internet was developed by the United States Department of Defense in the late 1960s, the first web pages didn't appear until the early 1990's. Today there are more than 800 million web pages. Buried within these, you will find lists of jokes, family reunion pictures, plenty of advertisements, and a wealth of information for the educational researcher.

Strengths and Weaknesses of the Internet for Educational Research

Since the Internet encompasses a worldwide network of interconnected computers, the amount of information that you have at your fingertips is truly unprecedented. The challenge is to find *quality* information. A careful consideration of the Internet's strengths and weaknesses will help you determine when and how to search the Internet for a specific topic. The Internet is particularly good at delivering current and targeted information about a specific topic. On the other hand, the Internet does not serve as an exhaustive source for educational research. It is not organized with the educational researcher in mind and generally has not been reviewed for accuracy or quality.

A comparison with the **ERIC** database, as illustrated in Table 5.1, illustrates both the strengths and limitations of Internet research. With the ERIC

TABLE 5.1

Comparison of ERIC and Internet Sources

Source	Strengths	Weaknesses
ERIC	Controlled vocabulary 30+ year archive Reviewed for quality	International coverage Abstracts instead of full text of journal articles Currency of information
Internet	Current information Full text on-line journal articles International coverage	No significant archive No search standards No quality control

database, you can search through the contents of more than 800 education journals dating back to 1966, all at the same time. In comparison, when searching the Internet for education journals, you must find out which journals have Web sites and then browse through their archives, usually one journal at a time. Further, most on-line journals do not have an archive beyond the past 5 years.

Every item in the ERIC database has been assigned a series of subject headings. The consistency and quality of these subject headings allows you to retrieve specific information from the database. The Internet does not have such a system of **controlled vocabulary**. There is no thesaurus to consult to find out what the best search terms are. For example, if you were looking for educational research about teenagers, would the best search term be teens, adolescents, or high school and middle school students?

Everything that you find in ERIC has been through some type of review process. Many journals in ERIC have an editorial staff of experts who judge the quality of all of the submissions. This does not mean that everything in ERIC should be accepted as without fault, but it is certainly better reviewed than the Internet. Anyone (from a teenager to a respected scholar) can publish a Web page. While there is an appealing democratic beauty to the Internet, it is crucial to evaluate the quality of Internet sources.

Even though ERIC offers a more comprehensive, better organized, and peer reviewed set of information about educational research, the Internet does have its own advantages. If a journal has an on-line version, you will be able to browse the most recent literature that might take many months to appear in ERIC. Abstracts are the norm for entries in ERIC, whereas on-line journals will often contain the full text of each article. While ERIC covers educational research and issues in the United States very well, the Internet offers a wider access to educational research from other countries. You will also find other useful information on the Internet beyond journal articles and research reports, such as statistics, email links to experts, governmental information, data sets, and discussion forums.

Fortunately, you are not limited in your research to either the Internet or journal indexes like ERIC. In framing your research question, think about the type of information that each might offer. This in turn will help with your searches in each source. For example, you would certainly want to know what the research on your topic has been for the past ten years as well as in the past months. By combining the Internet with the research tools that were presented in Chapter 4, you can capture a well-rounded and diverse portrait of the research literature in the area being investigated.

An Internet Research Strategy

The research strategies discussed in Chapter 4 are also relevant to Internet research. Before you start typing words into the first search engine that comes along, it is very important to have a focused search strategy with a number of key terms and subject headings. Based on that search strategy, you must choose from an assortment of secondary finding tools including *subject directories* and *search engines*. Once you have identified appropriate Internet search tools, pay attention to the various search options that each one offers, and construct your computer search accordingly. Finally, evaluate the sources that you find for their quality and relevance to your research question.

Choosing the Right Internet Search Tool

Each Internet search company (like Yahoo! or AltaVista) compiles their own database of Internet sites. When you "search the Internet," you are really searching these databases. That is, your search does not go out onto the Web and look at every page in existence. In choosing an Internet search tool, it is important to determine the quality, content, organization and scope of the data behind the scenes. The three primary types of Internet search utilities are *subject directories, search engines,* and *metasearch engines* (See Table 5.2 for selected examples of each). Understanding the differences between these will improve your Internet searching considerably.

Subject Directories Internet **subject directories** are the "yellow pages" of the Internet, where you are able to browse through lists of Internet resources by topic. Typically, each topic is located within a hierarchy of subjects. For example, in a subject directory there may be a choice for "Education," then numerous choices under that subject like "Universities, K–12, Government, History, etc." Examples of subject directories include Yahoo!, WWW Virtual Library, and the Librarians' Index.

The advantage of subject directories is that the content has been reviewed and organized by a human! Subject directories rely on teams of editors who have knowledge of specific disciplines. Thus, under each category you will find a high degree of relevance and quality. Subject directories are often the quickest way to assemble a manageable list of Internet resources for a topic. Here are some research questions that would be especially good for a subject directory:

TABLE 5.2

Internet Search Tools

Subject Directories

Argus Clearinghouse	http://www.clearinghouse.net
Education Internet Guide	http://www.library.usyd.edu.au/Guides/
Britannica Internet Guide	http://www.britannica.com
Librarian's Index	http://www.lii.org
Open Directory	http://www.dmoz.org
WWW Virtual Library	http://www.vlib.org
Yahoo!	http://www.yahoo.com

Search Engines

Alta Vista	http://www.altavista.com
Excite	http://www.excite.com
Fast	http://www.alltheweb.com
Google	http://www.google.com
HotBot	http://www.hotbot.com
Northern Light	http://www.northernlight.com

Metasearch Engines

Dogpile	http://www.dogpile.com
MetaCrawler	http://www.metacrawler.com
SavvySearch	http://www.savvysearch.com

- Where can I find a list of educational associations?
- Where can I find the Web addresses to the department of education from each state?
- Where can I find a listing of on-line education journals?

Although subject directories are especially well organized, their size is much smaller than the average search engine. For example, Yahoo!, one of the largest subject directories, indexes approximately 1.2 million Web pages, compared to the more than 300 million pages included in the Fast search engine. Some subject directories have partnered with search engines in order to increase their coverage. For example, if you use the search box in Yahoo!, there will be options to run the same search in any number of search engines. By clicking over to a search engine from Yahoo!, you will search a bigger set of data but will not have the advantage of Yahoo!'s organization. Often the best search strategy in a subject directory is to avoid the search box and use the categories. The search function of a subject directory is most useful when you are not sure what category to choose for a particular subject. For example, in Yahoo! it is somewhat difficult to find Montessori education, especially if you choose the education category "K–12." If you search Yahoo! for "Montesorri education" you will find that it is listed in the education category of "Theory and Methods."

Search Engines Search engines are large searchable databases of Web pages. Whereas subject directories are assembled and organized by human editors, search engines are compiled in an automated fashion. Each search engine uses a "spider" or "robot" that trolls through the Web from **hyperlink** to hyperlink, capturing information from each page that it visits. Therefore, the content of each search engine is dependent on the characteristics of its spider:

- How many pages has it visited?
- How often does it visit each page?
- When it visits, how much of the web page does it record?

A recent study in the journal *Nature* (Lawrence and Giles, 1999) concludes that search engines have plenty of room for improvement. There are an estimated 800 million Web pages available to search spiders. Yet, less than 20 percent of these pages appear in even the largest search engines. In terms of "freshness," the addition of new pages or modifications can take several months. Especially interesting is that there is not a consistent amount of overlap between search engines. *This means that the Internet researcher is wise to try searches in several search engines.* The authors of the *Nature* study also consider the effect of "spidering the Web" to create a search engine database. They suggest that this practice gives greater weight to popular sites (which have many links pointing to them) and dilutes the presence of the scholarly information available on the Web.

Despite the limitations of search engines, they do index hundreds of millions of Web pages. Search engines offer a quick way to search for specific words that may appear in Web pages. Here are some research questions that would be especially appropriate for a search engine:

- Are there any Web pages that cover standardized testing in the state of California?
- Are there any Web pages that deal with John Dewey's *Democracy in Education?*
- Are there any Web pages with a biography of Paulo Freire?

In searching through a large set of data like a search engine, there are a number of strategies to keep in mind. The concepts discussed in Chapter 4 about computer searching, such as logical connectors, apply to Internet searches as well. Note that in all of the examples above, you would want to combine two or more concepts for an effective search. Your Internet searching can be more effective by paying attention to search language, special search features, and the most relevant search results.

Metasearch Engines A metasearch engine submits your search to multiple search engines at the same time. Examples of metasearch engines include Dogpile and Metacrawler. Metasearch engines can be especially useful since studies have shown that each search engine includes pages that others do not.

On the other hand, no single metasearch engine includes all of the major search engines. Also, you cannot take advantage of the specific search language or features that are native to each search engine. For this reason, it is best to use search engines for your complex Internet searching, and rely on metasearch engines for searches that are very simple, like one or two words (especially if those words are uniquely spelled). With metasearch engines it is especially important to pay attention to relevancy, since you have less control over how each search engine interprets your metasearch query. Examples of good questions for a metasearch engine are:

- Are there any Web pages that mention the Australian Ngarkat Conservation Park?
- Are there any Web pages that mention Jonathan Kozol?

Consult these sites for the latest information about Internet search directories, search engines, and metasearch engines:

- Search Engine Showdown. (http://www.notess.com/search/)

  From subject directories to metasearch engines: reviews, statistics, and search tips for the Internet researcher.

- Search Engine Watch. (http://www.searchenginewatch.com/)

  Includes search tips as well as ratings of the major search engines.

Search Language There is no standard search language that is valid across all search engines. Some search engines understand logical connectors like "and" whereas others insist that you use a "+" before each word if you wish to limit your results to combined terms. Despite the lack of standards, there are several features that are common to most search engines. For example, even though some engines use "and" while others look for "+", the feature of combining more than one idea into a single search is available in most search engines. One of the best places to find out about each engine's search language is their on-line help page. It is even advisable for seasoned Internet searchers to revisit the help pages of their favorite search engine periodically.

Special Search Features and Relevancy Search engines continue to make advancements in the area of special search features. You will find these on the "advanced search" option within most search engines. Special search features help you construct very complex searches through the selection of various options from a menu. Special search features include the ability to limit your search by language, date, location, and media (such as audio or images). For example, by using HotBot's advanced search menu it is possible to access images of robots that are located only on pages hosted by the Massachusetts Institute of Technology.

In addition to search options, you should also be familiar with the **retrieval algorithms** of various search engines. *Retrieval algorithms* determine both how many pages each search retrieves as well as how the results of each search are ordered. The search algorithm is a mathematical formula that determines how many times and where your search terms appear in each document. For example if you were searching for "Max Apple," the Web pages that appear at the top of your search results should be the most relevant. Perhaps these pages had both words "Max Apple" as part of their title, whereas the Web pages that appear at the very end of your search results might simply have the word "apple" somewhere in their text. If your results start to look less and less relevant, don't keep looking through the same list, move on to a new search or a new search engine.

Beyond Web Pages—Scholarly Communication

Perhaps the most revolutionary aspect of the Internet is its ability to connect people with shared interests. This is especially powerful in highly technical and specific areas of study where geographical boundaries might otherwise hinder communication between a limited number of experts. For example, it might be hard to find a group of scholars in any one location who were all interested in the sociology of education. Through the Internet, however, such groups are able to form and discuss various issues specific to their field of study. Through the use of email, mailing lists, newsgroups, and conferencing, educational researchers are able to access the "braintrust" of their peers and need not feel isolated by location.

Email Email can be an especially valuable tool in conducting research. The speed and ease of email communication allows you find resources and experts. Through email it is possible to easily contact researchers, librarians or institutions in order to get guidance on a specific research question. Email is also an excellent way to collaborate with colleagues on works in progress by sharing ideas, drafts, and files.

Newsgroups and Mailing Lists On the Internet there are literally thousands of **newsgroups** and **mailing lists** covering every conceivable interest. For example, there is a mailing list called arlist-l that is solely dedicated to the discussion of action research. Most Internet browsers, such as Netscape and Microsoft Internet Explorer, include a *news reader* which allows you to read and post messages about various subjects to a newsgroup. A mailing list is similar to a newsgroup, except that the messages are transmitted as email and are therefore available only to individuals who have subscribed to the mailing list. The ERIC Educational Listserv Archive (http://www.askeric.org/Virtual/Listserv_Archives/) provides an excellent menu of high-quality educational mailing lists as well as a searchable archive of previous discussions. Another good resource for mailing lists is the Listz directory (http://www.liszt.com/select/Education) offering a collection of the addresses to more than 100 lists in the field of education.

Conferencing and Telecommunications One of the fastest growing aspects of conducting business, either in the business world or at universities, is through Internet telecommunications and collaboration. Examples include chatting, video and audio conferencing, on-line data collection and networked, shared folders in virtual offices or workspaces on the Web. Free or fairly inexpensive software is available to help academics and researchers communicate in **real time** through these convenient and timesaving resources (real time is immediate communication). New technology is being developed daily as the need arises and the benefits and savings of its use for educational research is still being explored.

Known Locations

A final method of Internet research is to go directly to Internet sites that are known for their quality and authority. This is certainly important given the amount of time that it takes for fresh information to appear in subject directories and search engines. For example, if you didn't visit the Web site of your favorite on-line journal you would miss out on the articles from the current issue.

A good starting point for Internet research is your library's Web page. Many college and university libraries have developed research guides for various disciplines including education. If you want to explore research guides from other libraries, a comprehensive international listing of library Web pages can be found at Libweb (http://sunsite.berkeley.edu/Libweb).

Educational agencies are often represented within international, federal, state, and local governmental Web pages and offer access to a number of resources. Government Web sites are especially rich in statistical data and reports. Other sources for known locations include national associations and organizations, nonprofit organizations, newspapers, and on-line journals. In the following pages we will highlight a number of Web sites that exemplify the type of quality that you should demand from Internet resources. Perhaps you will even add some of them to your own list of known locations for scholarly research.

Educational Web Sites

This section briefly introduces and reviews several categories of Web sites to show the kind of information included at those sites. The categories and specific sites selected for inclusion in Table 5.3 are examples only, since there are literally thousands from which to choose. The criteria for selection of both categories and sites focuses on their relevancy and ability to answer this question for an educational researcher, " Where might I find . . . ?"

There are also Web sites that contain multiple and diverse sources of information such as full-text journal articles, abstracts, archives, book reviews, indexes and datafiles. ERIC is the best known of this type of educational

TABLE 5.3

Educational Web Sites

Categories and Examples	Web Address	Relevant Information and Services Available
On-line Journals, Journal Reviews, and Abstracts[a]		
Education Policy Analysis Archives	http://olam.ed.asu.edu/epaa/	Full text of all EPAA articles; abstracts; submission of articles
Chronicle of Higher Education	http://thisweek.chronicle.com/	Major links include *Today's News, Information Technology,* and *This Weeks Chronicle*
Technological Horizons in Education (T. H. E.)	http://www.thejournal.com/	On-line access to current and back journal issues (full articles and editorials); representative of more narrow field of interest
Statistics and General Information[b]		
U.S. Department of Education	http://www.ed.gov	Current news and headlines about initiatives and the departments' priorities and objectives; valuable statistical information (National Center for Education Statistics)
The Qualitative Report	http://www.nova.edu/ssss/QR/	Research papers, abstracts, and proposals pertaining to qualitative research
Organizations and University Web Pages[c]		
Arizona State University Book Review	http://www.ed.asu.edu/edrev/	Review articles of recently published educational books indexed by topic, book author, title, author of the review, and publish date
American Education Research Association	http://www.aera.net	Encourages scholarly inquiry related to education and promotes the dissemination and practical application of research results
Scholarly Articles and Conference Papers[d]		
Cognitive Sciences Eprint Archives (Cogprints)	http://cogprints.soton.ac.uk/	Free access to scholarly papers providing current international information on the hottest topics in the cognitive sciences
Multi-Purpose Web Sites[e]		
Educational Resources Information Center (ERIC)	http://ericir.syr.edu/Eric/	Indexes of educational literature at sixteen subject-specific Clearinghouse locations
National Research Centers and Regional Education Laboratories[f]		
Center for Research on Education, Diversity, and Excellence (CREDE)	http://www.cal.org/crede/	One of five national institutes established by the U.S. Department of Education; provides links to current projects
Office of Educational Research and Improvement (OERI)	http://www.ed.gov/offices/OERI/	One of ten regional libraries whose mission is to link knowledge from research with the wisdom from practice in order to improve teaching and learning

[a]Current and back issues of journals in both full text and abstract format are available in increasing numbers on the Internet.

[b]General information usually includes information about budgets and legislation that affects education and provides links to other departmental offices and contacts.

[c]National associations and universities have Web sites that provide primary information for research.

[d]Newer trend with limited number of Web sites available

[e]More diversified sites offering multiple sources of information are common on the World Wide Web.

[f]These sites are designed to address nationally significant problems and issues in education and support university-based national educational research.

research site. The Eric Clearinghouses are accessible on the Internet. Each has it's own Web site, with many links to related sites (see Table 5.4).

Datasets

One of the most useful features of the Internet is the availability of very large sets of data that have been collected. These **datasets** are ideal for conducting replication studies and other investigations without collecting original data. The best resource to use when searching for these datasets is the Inter-university Consortium for Political and Social Research (ICPSR). The ICPSR has 350+ member institutions in 16 countries and represents the largest archive of its type in the United States. Membership can greatly facilitate the researcher's access to these quantitative social science datasets. Some of the key datasets, accessible through ICPSR, include the U. S. Census data, General Social Survey, National Election Studies, news polls, and various other national and state datafiles. Anyone can search terms at the ICPSR Web site. Member university students can also download datasets including their appropriate documentation in the form of codebooks with the assistance of their official university representative. The address for the ICPSR is http://www.icpsr.umich.edu.

For those who are not members of the ICPSR, Table 5.5 contains some of the best sources for available secondary datasets and their Web addresses. Many of these datafiles can be downloaded in multiple formats allowing you to analyze them through different statistical packages such as SPSS or SAS.

These lists and examples are just a few of the many available datafile resources available to you on the Internet. Visiting these Web sites should lead you to others, and this journey in cyberspace may convince you that the information you need for that thesis or class project has already been collected by experts who are willing to organize and share their findings with others in the educational community.

Evaluating and Citing Sources on the Internet

Evaluating Internet Resources

Many Internet sites contain materials that are not of sufficient quality to be used for educational research. You can evaluate Internet material by asking the following questions:

- Who is the author or publisher of the information?
- What is the author's reputation and qualifications in the subject covered?

TABLE 5.4

ERIC Clearinghouse

ERIC Clearinghouses	Address	Description
Clearinghouse on Adult, Career, and Vocational Education	http://ericacve.org/	Provides comprehensive information, publications and services in adult and continuing education
ERIC Clearinghouse on Assessment and Evaluation	http://ericae.net/	Provides balanced information concerning educational assessment and resources to encourage responsible test use
ERIC Clearinghouse for Community Colleges	http://www.gseis.ucla.edu/ERIC/eric.html	Coordinates searches on community-college related topics
ERIC Clearinghouse on Counseling and Student Services	http://www.uncg.edu/edu/ericcass/	School counseling, school social work and school psychology
ERIC Clearinghouse on Disabilities and Gifted Education	http://ericec.org/	Focuses on the professional literature, information, and resources relating to persons of all ages who have disabilities and/or who are gifted
ERIC Clearinghouse on Educational Management	http://eric.uoregon.edu	Database information related to educational management and related topics
ERIC Clearinghouse on Elementary and Early Childhood Education	http://ericeece.org/	Information on the development, education, and care of children
ERIC Clearinghouse on Higher Education	http://www.eriche.org/	Broad range of topics and issues pertaining to all types of higher education
ERIC Clearinghouse on Information and Technology	http://ericir.syr.edu/ithome/	Information on educational technology and library/information science at all academic levels
ERIC Clearinghouse on Languages and Linguistics	http://www.cal.org/ericcll	Information on current developments and research of several language and linguistic areas
ERIC Clearinghouse on Reading, English and Communication	http://www.indiana.edu/~eric_rec	Provides materials, services and coursework to those interested in the language arts
ERIC Clearinghouse on Rural Education and Small Schools	http://www.ael.org/eric/	Access to resources about rural education
ERIC Clearinghouse on Science, Mathematics, and Environmental Education	http://www.ericse.org	Retrieves and disseminates information related to science, mathematics, and environmental education
ERIC Clearinghouse on Social Studies/Social Science Education	http://www.indiana.edu/~ssdc/eric_chess.htm	Monitors issues about the teaching of history, geography, civics, economics, and related subjects
ERIC Clearinghouse on Teaching and Teacher Education	http://www.ericsp.org	Information on teaching, teacher education, and health, recreation and dance
ERIC Clearinghouse on Urban Education	http://eric-web.tc.columbia.edu/	Monitors curriculum and instruction of students of diverse racial, ethnic, and social class in urban and suburban schools

TABLE 5.5

Internet Datasets

Site	Address	Description
Statistical Abstract of the United States	http://www.census.gov/stat_abstract	Includes data from private as well as government sources
Fedstats	http://www.fedstats.gov	Contains data from 14 federal agencies
American Demographics	http://www.demographics.com	
American National Election Studies	http://www.umich.edu/~nes	Data about U.S. politics and political candidates and office holders
Eurostat	http://europa.eu.int/comm/eurostat/	European statistics
National Denter for Education Statistics	http://nces.ed.gov/	U.S. Department of Education providing multiple sources of educational research collections
UNESCO	http://unescostat.unesco.org	Wide range of international educational statistics maintained in the UNESCO database

- Is the information objective or is there a noticeable bias?
- Are the facts or statistics verifiable?
- Is there a bibliography?
- Is the information current?

The final key to evaluating any type of research is to carefully read and analyze the content. It is also helpful to find a variety of sources so that you can compare and contrast in order to get a fully informed view of any subject. More information about evaluating sources on the Internet can be found at *Evaluating Web Sites for Educational Uses: Bibliography and Checklist* (http://www.unc.edu/cit/guides/irg-49.html).

EXCERPT 5.1

EVALUATING INTERNET RESEARCH

One of my seventh graders was so excited when he got his first computer that he spent much of his time on it. His love of technology led him to the Internet, and he soon built his own Web site. His site is now among the millions of sites on the Internet, and if you search for a site on computer repair and network consultation, you may have to wait for his services—because he needs to be home in time for dinner.

Source: From Caruso, C. (1997), Before you cite a site. *Educational Leadership, 55*(3), p. 24.

Citing Internet Sources

As with all other research, it is important to document your sources so that other researchers can visit the same sites you have found. One of the unique things about documenting Internet sites is that the addresses can often change. For this reason, most citation formats encourage you to list the date that you accessed the site. Most educational research is documented in APA format. You can find the APA's official guideline for citing electronic sources in the APA Style Manual and on the APA Web page (http://www.apa.org/journals/webref.html). The following is an example of an APA Citation of an on-line journal article:

> Jacobson, J. W., Mulick, J. A., & Schwartz, A. A. (1995). A history of facilitated communication: Science, pseudoscience, and antiscience: Science working group on facilitated communication. *American Psychologist, 50,* 750–765. Retrieved January 25, 1996 from the World Wide Web: http://www.apa.org/journals/jacobson.html

Putting It All Together: An Internet Search

To illustrate a search on the Internet, consider a topic such as "charter schools." When we searched "charter schools and research" on a large search engine, the richest information came from links within the documents we retrieved. For example, one of the best results was a review of research from 1996. While this was dated by Internet standards, the site contains links back to the home source of the Center for Education Reform, where there was an assortment of current information about charter school research. Likewise, search results also included a listserv message about charter schools, which identifies the existence of a charter school electronic mailing list (and its searchable archive). An advanced search in another search engine to just government Web sites retrieved 43 results, including links to the Department of Education research and federal legislation.

By repeating the search in a subject directory, the Charter School Research Project was found, which in turn led to a current bibliography with links to charter school research. The subject directory also provided good lists of links to charter schools and charter school organizations. Using known locations, the Department of Education Web site and FedStats were searched. These searches led us to even more material, including 1,022 entries from the Department of Education (such as a Presidential radio address from the previous month) and 42 statistical reports through FedStats (from sources such as the National Center for Educational Statistics and the Office of Management and Budget).

In reviewing these results, each search led to unique material. Further, by following links, we found other sites that were not included in any of our original results. This illustrates the importance of searching across a variety of

FIGURE 5.1 Example of an Internet Search

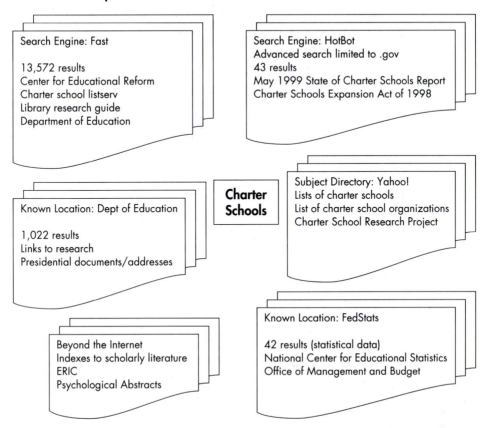

Search Engine: Fast

13,572 results
Center for Educational Reform
Charter school listserv
Library research guide
Department of Education

Search Engine: HotBot
Advanced search limited to .gov
43 results
May 1999 State of Charter Schools Report
Charter Schools Expansion Act of 1998

Known Location: Dept of Education

1,022 results
Links to research
Presidential documents/addresses

Charter Schools

Subject Directory: Yahoo!
Lists of charter schools
List of charter school organizations
Charter School Research Project

Beyond the Internet
Indexes to scholarly literature
ERIC
Psychological Abstracts

Known Location: FedStats

42 results (statistical data)
National Center for Educational Statistics
Office of Management and Budget

sources. The final step would be to evaluate the quality of each site. Here, too, a variety of sources and a handful of ERIC searches could help you compare and contrast the research on "charter schools." Figure 5.1 shows different results depending on the search strategy.

Summary

The following statements summarize the major aspects of educational research on the Internet:

1. The Internet is a series of interconnected computers that contain a wealth of information for the educational researcher.
2. The strengths of using the Internet for educational research include access to full text documents, the most current research, discussion forums, and information from around the world.

3. The Internet does not contain controlled vocabulary, consistent quality, or a significant archive for educational research.
4. The three primary types of Internet search tools are subject directories, search engines, and metasearch engines.
5. Subject directories contain lists of Web sites organized by topic.
6. Search engines are large searchable databases of Web sites.
7. Metasearch engines simultaneously query multiple search engines.
8. Each search tool has its own search features and strengths.
9. Scholars and researchers are able to share information over the Internet through the use of email, mailing lists, newsgroups, and conferencing.
10. Accessing known locations on the Internet such as associations, newspapers, on-line journals, government pages, and statistical sites can lead the researcher to high quality information.
11. Finding datasets on the Internet is a good way to find existing statistical data and build upon past studies.
12. National research centers and regional educational laboratories sponsored by the US Department of Education are excellent resources for combining educational research with practice.
13. Since just about anyone can post a Web page, it is especially important to evaluate the quality of the information you find on the Internet.
14. No single search tool includes everything that is available on the Internet.
15. It is best to try searches across a number of different search tools and known locations.

Self-Instructional Review Exercises

Sample answers are in the back of the book.

Test Items

1. What is the best search tool to use for locating specific words that appear on the Web pages?
   a. subject directories.
   b. search engines.
   c. listservs.
   d. Internet browser.
2. Datasets/datafiles are a good source to locate what kind of research material?
   a. qualitative data.
   b. book reviews.
   c. quantitative data.
   d. full text journal articles.
3. Two examples of metasearch engines are
   a. Alta Vista and Excite.
   b. Yahoo and Lycos.
   c. Dogpile and Metacrawler.
   d. HotBot and Metacrawler.

4. A weakness of using the Internet for educational research includes which of the following?
   a. delivering current and niche information
   b. providing readily available government information
   c. providing sites for downloading datasets/datafiles
   d. serving as an exhaustive source for educational research

5. Compared with searching ERIC, searching the Internet
   a. provides more up-to-date information.
   b. provides a higher quality of information.
   c. is more efficient.
   d. provides greater access to help.

6. The major advantage of using a subject directory rather than a search engine is that
   a. literature reviews have already been completed.
   b. there is a more comprehensive listing of Web sites.
   c. category placement depends on a review of what is in each Web site.
   d. large categories are subdivided as needed to facilitate the search.

7. Yahoo! Is an example of a
   a. Web site.
   b. hyperlink.
   c. search engine.
   d. subject directory.

8. Which of the following should be accessed to monitor current trends and recent research in a specific field of study?
   a. search engines
   b. subject directories
   c. university Web pages
   d. mailing lists and newsgroups

9. Which of the following is most likely to have the most current information on a subject?
   a. ERIC database
   b. subject directory
   c. regional laboratories
   d. on-line journal

10. What information would *not* be easily located at the national Department of Education?
   a. budget information
   b. Web sites for other departmental offices and contacts
   c. educational statistics
   d. full text on-line journal articles

Application Questions

1. A school administrator needs to locate samples of Internet policies and guidelines for the state of Georgia. Which Internet search tools and searches would find the most relevant information? In addition, list at least two known locations that might help with this research.

2. Would you trust this Web site? How would you verify that it is legitimate?
   Feline Reactions to Bearded Men
   http://www.uofl.edu/infoliteracy/feline.htm
   Author's credentials: Catherine Maloney, Fairfield University,
   Fairfield,Connecticut
   Abstract: Cats were exposed to photographs of bearded men. The beards
   were of various sizes, shapes, and styles. The cats' responses were
   recorded and analyzed.
   Research Methodology: While each cat was viewing the photographs, it
   was held by a laboratory assistant. To ensure that the cats were not influenced by stroking or other unconscious cues from the assistant, the assistant was anesthetized prior to each session.
   Entry from bibliography: Boone, Patrick, "Cat reactions to clean-shaven
   men," in *Western Musicology Journal,* March/April 1958, vol. 11, no. 2,
   pp. 4–21.
3. Visit the US Department of Education's Web site (http://www.ed.gov) and
   locate at least one set of on-line statistics about education. Write a brief annotation of the data including title, the Internet address, summary, and one
   statistic.

PART II

Quantitative Research Designs and Methods

Part II presents the designs and methods of quantitative research. We begin by presenting fundamental principles of sampling, measurement, and research design. Next, we review descriptive statistical concepts and procedures that are essential to understanding quantitative studies. We also review in some detail score validity and reliability, sources to use to evaluate instruments, and different ways of collecting quantitative data. These principles are useful in answering questions such as these: How can researchers summarize large amounts of data? Why is variability of results important? How can relationships be measured? What are the types of evidence researchers use to make valid inferences from subjects' responses? How do researchers establish reliability? What are the advantages and disadvantages of questionnaires compared with interviews? How are questionnaires designed? How is observational research or survey research conducted? The next two chapters summarize the essentials of quantitative research designs. Chapter 9 considers descriptive, comparative, correlational, predictive, and *ex post facto* designs, and Chapter 10 covers experimental and single-subject designs. The last chapter in this part is a conceptual introduction to inferential statistics. The intent is to provide an understanding of the logic of probability as applied to testing hypotheses and questions. Basic terminology and statistical procedures are presented to enable a reader to interpret the results sections of quantitative research and a researcher to select appropriate statistical procedures, based on the design of the study.

Introduction to Designing Quantitative Research

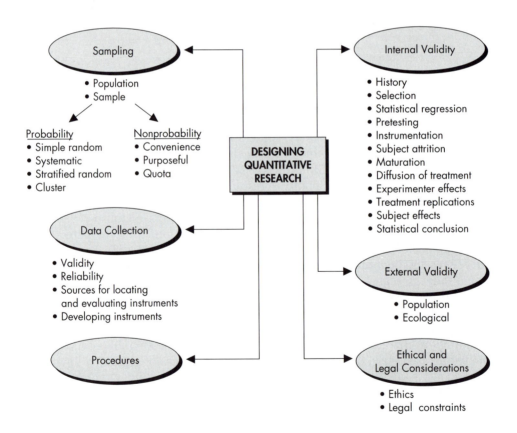

KEY TERMS

research design
credibility
variability
sources of variability
validity
internal validity
external validity
plausible rival hypotheses
subjects
sample
population
probability sampling
random sampling
simple random sampling
systematic sampling
stratified random sampling
proportional sampling
nonproportional sampling
cluster sampling
nonprobability sampling
convenience sample
purposeful sampling
quota sampling
test validity
test reliability
history
selection

statistical regression
pretesting
instrumentation
subject attrition
maturation
diffusion of treatment
experimenter effects
treatment replications
subject effects
demand characteristics
population external validity
ecological external validity
Hawthorne effect
construct validity
informed consent

Designing quantitative research involves choosing subjects, data collection techniques (such as questionnaires, observations, or interviews), procedures for gathering the data and procedures for implementing treatments. Together, these components constitute the methods part of the study. The essential elements of designing quantitative research will be discussed in this chapter, with an emphasis on important principles for conceptualizing and planning a study. We will discuss each of these components, with attention to principles in each component that enhance the quality of the research. We also discuss important ethical and legal considerations in planning and conducting research.

The Purpose of Research Design

Research design[1] refers to a plan for selecting subjects, research sites, and data collection procedures to answer the research question(s). The design shows which individuals will be studied, and when, where, and under which circumstances they will be studied. The goal of a sound research design is to provide results that are judged to be *credible*. **Credibility** refers to the extent to which the results approximate reality and are judged to be trustworthy and reasonable. Credibility is enhanced when the research design takes into account potential sources of error that may undermine the quality of the research and may distort the findings. The goal of a good research design, then, is to provide a credible answer to a question, and error reduces the credibility of the results. By carefully designing the study the researcher can eliminate or at least reduce sources of error. Not every potential source of error can be controlled completely in research, but there are principles for planning research to minimize such influences.

Sources of Variability

One of the important principles of quantitative research is to consider different *sources of variability*. **Variability** refers to how much observations of something take on different values. For example, we know that our mood varies day to day, just as we know that a student's academic performance will not be the same each time he or she completes a test.

From the standpoint of design, it is important to recognize and control three **sources of variability**: systematic, error, and extraneous. Systematic variance is related to the variables that are being investigated. What you want is a design that will maximize this kind of variation. For instance, when studying the relationship between engaged time and achievement, you would want to design the research so that the two variables of interest, engagement and achievement, both have high variability. If, say, all the students got the same or very similar achievement scores, then you would not be able to demonstrate the relationship.

Similarly, in an experiment, you want to maximize the variance of the dependent variable when comparing the groups. This is often accomplished by making sure that the treatments in the study will potentially produce quite different results. For example, systematic variance is likely to be greater in a study comparing individualized instruction with small group discussion than comparing two kinds of small group discussion formats.

---

[1]The term *research design* is often used to refer to specific types of designs, called "pre-experimental," "experimental," and "quasi-experimental" designs by Campbell and Stanley (1963). This book's emphasis is on relating the fundamentals of error control to all aspects of collecting information, including but not limited to the designs of Campbell and Stanley. The principles discussed are important for nonexperimental research as well as for studies that infer causal relationships.

Error variance is something to be minimized. It includes sampling and measurement error, and other kinds of random events that make it difficult to show relationships. Extraneous variance needs to be controlled. This kind of variability affects relationships directly, rather than in a random fashion. For instance, in examining the relationship between test scores and class size, socioeconomic status of the students would be a variable that would need to be controlled. That is, you would get a better estimate of the relationship if the effect socioeconomic status, which is related to achievement, is removed statistically.

Design Validity

In the context of research design, the term **validity** means the degree to which scientific explanations of phenomena match the realities of the world. Validity refers to the truth or falsity of propositions generated by research. Explanations about observed phenomena approximate what is reality or truth, and the degree to which the explanations are accurate comprises the validity of the research. There are two types of design validity in quantitative research. **Internal validity** expresses the extent to which extraneous variables have been controlled or accounted for. **External validity** refers to the generalizability of the results, the extent to which the results and conclusions can be generalized to other people and settings. In some studies, such as most applied research, there is a clear intent to generalize to other people and other settings, while in other studies generalization beyond the people, time, and context of the research is not intended or possible. Both internal and external validity are important concepts to understand in designing research, and we will examine each in greater depth.

In designing or reading quantitative research it is necessary to consider who will be assessed (subjects), what they will be assessed by (instruments), how they will be assessed (procedures for data collection), and, for experimental designs, how experimental treatments are administered. Then it is important to ask: Is there anything that occurred or was done that could provide an explanation of the results by means of a rival hypothesis? "Rival" is used in the sense that it is in addition to the stated hypothesis or intent of the research. (A rival hypothesis to the study of whether smoking causes lung cancer, for example, is that diet may contribute to the cause of lung cancer.) This question represents the search for extraneous variability. Campbell and Stanley (1963) refer to such explanations as **plausible rival hypotheses**. The search for plausible rival hypotheses is essential to ensure the quality of the research. Consider, for example, the questions below. Each addresses a possible source of error that could lead to a plausible rival hypothesis that might explain results.

1. Does the researcher have an existing bias about the subjects or about the topic researched?
2. Are the subjects aware that they are being studied?
3. Are the subjects responding honestly?

4. Did both groups receive the treatments as described?
5. Does the sex of the interviewer make a difference?
6. Did very many subjects drop out before the end of the study?
7. Did the time of day the research was done affect the results?

Several techniques are used to reduce extraneous variance in quantitative research, including randomization of subjects, holding conditions or factors constant, building conditions or factors into the design as independent variables, and making statistical adjustments (Wiersma, 2000). Randomization is desirable either in selecting subjects from a larger population or in assigning subjects to groups to investigate the effect of one variable on another. Random selection, which is discussed in greater detail later in the next section, allows the researcher to generalize the results beyond the immediate group studied. Random assignment helps control error associated with characteristics of subjects in different groups.

If the researcher believes that the conditions of data collection might affect the results, the study can be designed to ensure that all conditions are as similar as possible. For example, in an observational study of the relationship between teacher behavior and student attention to the material, the time of day the observer records data and the subject matter of the lesson (mornings versus afternoons, or math versus history) could make a difference in student attention. One way to control this potential source of error is to make sure that all the observations are done at the same time of day during lessons on the same topic. In this example, the researcher could also control these potential influences by making them independent variables. This could be achieved by assigning observers to each subject of interest and having each topic observed in both the morning and the afternoon. Now the researcher can assess the effect of time of day and subject rather than simply controlling for it.

In quantitative studies control of possible extraneous variables is essential, although educational research rarely exhibits the degree of control evident in studies of physical phenomena or psychology. Thus, the researcher must search constantly for factors (extraneous variables) that might influence the results or conclusions of the study. For quantitative research the concept of internal validity describes the efficacy with which extraneous variables have been controlled. The concern is with the way the procedures, sampling of subjects, and instruments affect the extent to which extraneous variables are present to complicate the interpretation of the findings. A study high or strong in internal validity successfully controls all or most extraneous variables so that the researcher can be confident that, for instance, X caused changes in Y. Studies low or weak in internal validity are difficult to interpret since it is impossible to tell whether the results were due to the independent variable or to some extraneous variable that was uncontrolled or unaccounted for. It is important for researchers to be aware of common factors that may be extraneous and to conceptualize and read research with these factors in mind. Since complete control of extraneous variables in educational research is difficult, if not impossible, all relevant threats to internal validity that cannot be prevented should be accounted for in interpreting the results.

Subjects: Populations and Samples

One of the first steps in designing quantitative research is to choose the subjects. **Subjects** (abbreviated as *S*) are the individuals who participate in the study; it is from them that data are collected. In an experiment, for instance, each person who is given a treatment and whose response is measured is a subject. In nonexperimental studies, individuals whose present or past behavior is used as data are considered subjects. For example, a researcher might use 1995 tenth-grade test scores; each tenth grader who provided scores would be considered a subject.

As a group, subjects are usually referred to as a **sample**. The sample can be selected from a larger group of persons, identified as the population, or it can simply refer to the group of subjects from whom data are collected (even though the subjects are not selected from the population). The nature of the sampling procedure used in a particular study is usually described by one or more adjectives, such as *random* sampling, *convenience* sampling, or *stratified* sampling. This tells you about the technique used to form the sample. We will consider two major categories of different sampling techniques: probability and nonprobability. First, though, some further discussion of *population* is needed.

What Is a Population?

A **population** is a group of elements or cases, whether individuals, objects, or events, that conform to specific criteria and to which we intend to generalize the results of the research. This group is also referred to as the *target population* or *universe*. The target population is often different from the list of elements from which the sample is actually selected, which is termed the *survey population* or *sampling frame*. For example, in a study of beginning teachers, the target population may be first-year teachers across the United States, in all types of schools. The survey population may be a list of first-year teachers from 24 states. Thus, although the intent of the research is to generalize to all beginning teachers, the sampling frame places some limitations on such generalizations.

It is important for researchers to carefully and completely define both the target population and the sampling frame. This begins with the research problem and review of literature, through which a population is described conceptually or in broad terms. A more specific definition is then needed, based on demographic characteristics such as age, gender, location, grade level, position, and time of year. These characteristics are sometimes referred to as *delimiting variables*. For example, in a study of rural first grade minority students, there are four delimiting variables: rural, students, first grade, and minority. A complete description is then included in the subjects section of the report.

Probability Sampling[2]

In **probability sampling** subjects are drawn from a larger population in such a way that the probability of selecting each member of the population is known, though probabilities are not necessarily equal. This type of sampling is conducted to efficiently provide estimates of what is true for a population from a smaller group of subjects (sample). That is, what is described in a sample will also be true, with some degree of error, of the population. When probability sampling is done correctly, a very small percentage of the population can be selected. This saves time and money without sacrificing accuracy. In fact, in most social science and educational research it is both impractical and unnecessary to measure all elements of the population of interest.

Several methods of probability sampling can be used to draw representative, or *unbiased,* samples from a population. Each method involves some type of **random sampling**, in which each member of the population as a whole, or of subgroups of the population, has the same chance of being selected as other members in the same group. Bias is avoided with random sampling because there is a high probability that all the population characteristics will be represented in the sample. If you don't follow the correct procedures, though, what may seem to be random sampling actually produces a biased sample (biased in the sense that certain population characteristics are over- or under-represented). For example, you may think that you can obtain a "random" sample of college students by standing by a busy corner and selecting every third or fourth student. However, you may not be able to keep an accurate count, and you may inadvertently select more males or females, or older or younger students. Such a procedure would result in a biased sample.

While there are several probability sampling procedures, we will discuss the four most common ones used in educational research: simple random sampling, systematic sampling, stratified sampling, and cluster sampling.

Simple Random Sampling In **simple random sampling**, subjects are selected from the population so that all members of the population have the same probability of being chosen. This method is often used when the population is small. For example, a common type of simple random sampling is drawing names out of a hat.

With a large population it is necessary to use a more precise procedure. One such procedure is to use a table of random numbers, which is a set of randomly assorted digits. (A table of random numbers is illustrated in Appendix B.) Suppose, for example, that a researcher had a population of 100 third graders and wanted to select 20 by simple random sampling. First, each third grader in the population is assigned a number from 001 to 100 (it could be 00 to 99). Second, the researcher randomly selects a starting point in a table of ran-

---

[2]See R. M. Jaeger (1984), *Sampling in education and the social sciences,* New York: Longman, Inc., and G. T. Henry (1990), *Practical sampling,* Newbury Park, CA: Sage, for a more detailed discussion of how to select probability samples.

dom numbers. Then he or she reads all three-digit numbers, moving either across rows or down columns. The researcher follows the three-digit rows or columns while selecting twenty three-digit numbers between 000 and 100. Table 6.1 contains an example of simple random sampling. Five of the twenty subjects chosen to be included in the sample are circled, beginning with the top left and moving down each column.

A more efficient and increasingly popular way to draw a simple random sample is through an appropriate computer software program. This is especially easy and effective if the sampling frame is in an electronic format.

Systematic Sampling In **systematic sampling** every *n*th element is selected from a list of all elements in the population, beginning with a randomly selected element. Suppose there is a need to draw a 10 percent sample from a population of 100. A number from one to ten is randomly selected as the starting point. If 5 is selected, every tenth name on the list will be selected: 5, 15, 25, 35, and so on. This approach can be used only when the researcher has a sequential list of all the subjects in the population, but it is easier than simple random sampling because not every member of the population needs to be numbered.

There is a possible weakness in systematic sampling if the list of cases in the population is arranged in a systematic pattern that is related to what is being investigated. For example, suppose you are sampling teachers from many schools and the list obtained from each school is rank ordered in terms of length of service. If this cyclical pattern (referred to as *periodicity*) is related to every *n*th subject, the sample would systematically exclude teachers with certain ages and not represent the population. Alphabetical lists do not usually create periodicity and are suitable for choosing subjects systematically.

TABLE 6.1

Randomly Assorted Digits

46614	20002	17918
16249	05217	54102
91530	62481	05374
62800	62660	20186
10089	96488	59058
47361	73443	11859
45690	71058	53634
50423	53342	71710
89292	32114	83942
23410	41943	33278
59844	81871	18710
98795	87894	00510
86085	03164	26333
37390	60137	93842
28420	10704	89412

An advantage to systematic sampling is that if the population is rank ordered on a variable that is related to the dependent variable, this ordering has the effect of stratifying and making sure that the sample is represented by each level of that variable. For instance, if the population list is ordered by aptitude test scores (highest scores first, followed by lower scores), when you then select every *n*th subject you are assured that all levels of aptitude will be represented in the sample. Systematic sampling is illustrated in Excerpt 6.1. In this study the first of three samples, practicing teachers, is selected randomly "from a list." Contrast this with the next two samples, which are not randomly selected.

Stratified Random Sampling A common variation of simple random sampling is called **stratified random sampling**. In this procedure, the population is divided into subgroups, or strata, on the basis of a variable chosen by the researcher, such as gender, age, or level of education. Once the population has been divided, samples are drawn randomly from each subgroup. The number of subjects drawn is either *proportional* or *nonproportional*. **Proportional sampling** is based on the percentage of subjects in the population that is present in each stratum. Thus, if 40 percent of the subjects in the population are represented in the first stratum, then 40 percent of the final sample should be from that stratum. In **nonproportional** (or disproportionate) **sampling**, the researcher selects the same number of subjects to be in each stratum of the sample. Whether proportional or nonproportional, stratified random sampling is often more efficient than simple random sampling because a smaller number of subjects will need to be used. Dividing the population into subgroups also allows the researcher to compare subgroup results.

EXCERPT 6.1

SYSTEMATIC AND CONVENIENCE SAMPLING

Three samples were drawn from this study. They were samples of (a) practicing teachers, (b) college sophomores beginning a teacher education program, and (c) college seniors completing a teacher education program (but prior to student teaching). For the first sample, survey forms were mailed in a rural western state to 700 teachers randomly selected from the State Department of Education list of all licensed educators.

The second sample was a convenience sample of three sections of an educational foundations class typically taken by college sophomores who have just enrolled in a teacher education program.

The third sample was also a convenience sample of four sections of a tests and measurement class taken by college seniors.

Source: From Green, K. E. (1992). Differing opinions on testing between preservice and inservice teachers. *Journal of Educational Research, 86,* 37–42. Reprinted by permission.

EXCERPT 6.2

STRATIFIED RANDOM SAMPLING

PARTICIPANTS

Thirty-six female elementary school teachers were randomly selected from a volunteer pool in a southern school district. The sample consisted of 18 second-grade teachers and 18 fifth-grade teachers and was restricted to female teachers, since there were few male teachers in the school district at the primary level. Based on the EFT* scores, 9 teachers at each grade level were randomly selected from those who were field independent, and 9 others were selected from those who were field dependent. There were 12 students (6 males and 6 females) who were selected randomly from each teacher's classroom for purposes of testing. The second-grade children ranged in age from 7 years to 7 years 11 months, whereas the fifth-grade children ranged in age from 10 years to 10 years 11 months.

*EFT refers to the Embedded Figures Test.

Source: From Saracho, O. N., & Dayton, C. M. (1980). Relationship of teachers' cognitive styles to pupils' academic achievement gains, *Journal of Educational Psychology, 72,* 544–549.

In Excerpt 6.2, for example, the researchers have stratified the teacher population on the basis of grade level and scores on the EFT (Embedded Figures Test) and the student population by classroom. The sampling is diagramed in Figure 6.1. To ensure that the final sample has a sufficient number of subjects in each group, nonproportional sampling is used.

Cluster Sampling Cluster sampling is similar to stratified random sampling in that groups of individuals are identified from the population and subjects are drawn from these groups. In **cluster sampling**, however, the researcher identifies convenient, naturally occurring group units, such as neighborhoods, schools, districts, or regions, not individual subjects, and then randomly selects some of these units for the study. Once the units have been selected, individuals are selected from each one. Cluster sampling thus involves two stages, and because only the clusters have to be chosen in the first stage the researcher is saved the cost of individual selection from the full population. Cluster sampling usually results in a less representative sample of the population than either simple or stratified random sampling, and it is used most often in cases when it is infeasible or impractical to obtain a list of all members of the population.

Nonprobability Sampling

In many educational studies, particularly experimental and quasi-experimental investigations, probability samples are not required or appropriate, or it may be impossible or unfeasible to select subjects from a larger group. Rather,

FIGURE 6.1   Stratified Random Selection Of Subjects For Saracho And Dayton Study

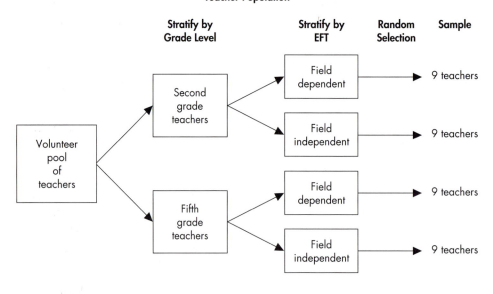

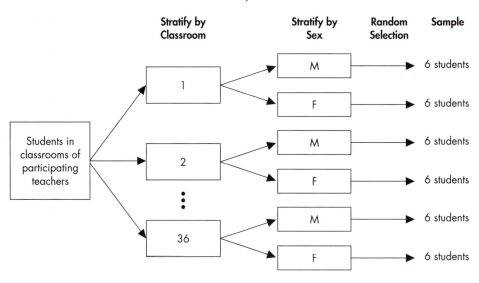

nonprobability sampling is used. In fact this form of sampling is the most common type in educational research. Nonprobability sampling does not include any type of random sampling. Rather, the researcher uses subjects who happen to be accessible or who may represent certain types of characteristics. For example, this could be a class of students or group gathered for a meeting.

Many circumstances bring people together in situations that are efficiently and inexpensively tapped for research. We will consider three types of nonprobability sampling: convenience sampling, purposeful sampling, and quota sampling. Additional nonprobability sampling techniques are covered in Chapter 12 for qualitative designs.

Convenience Sampling A **convenience sample** is a group of subjects selected on the basis of being accessible or expedient. It is convenient to use the group as subjects. This could, for example, be a university class of a professor who is doing research on college student learning styles, classrooms of teachers enrolled in a graduate class, school principals who participate in a workshop or conference, people who decide to go to the mall on Saturday, or people who respond to an advertisement for subjects (see Excerpt 6.1). While this type of sample makes it easier to conduct the research, there are two important limitations. First, there is no precise way of generalizing from the sample to any type of population. This means that the generalizability of the findings will be limited to the characteristics of the subjects. This does not mean that the findings are not useful; it simply means that caution is needed in generalizing. Often researchers will describe convenient samples carefully to show that although they were not able to employ random selection, the characteristics of the subjects match those of the population or a substantial portion of the population.

Although we need to be very wary of convenience samples, often they provide the only possibility for research. Also, the primary purpose of the research may not be to generalize but to better understand relationships that may exist. In this case it may not be necessary to use probability sampling. Suppose a researcher is studying the relationship between creativity and intelligence, and the only possible sample consists of children in an elementary school in his town. The study is completed, and the results indicate a moderate relationship: children who are more intelligent tend to be more creative. Because there is no probability sampling, should we ignore the findings or suggest that the results are not credible or useful? That decision seems overly harsh. It is more reasonable to interpret the results as valid for children similar to those studied. If the school serves a low socioeconomic area, the results will not be as useful as they would be if the school represented all socioeconomic areas. The decision is not to dismiss the findings, but to limit them to the type of subjects in the sample. As more and more research accumulates with different convenient samples, the overall credibility of the results is enhanced.

Purposeful Sampling In **purposeful sampling** (sometimes called *purposive, judgment*, or *judgmental sampling*) the researcher selects particular elements from the population that will be representative or informative about the topic of interest. On the basis of the researcher's knowledge of the population, a judgment is made about which subjects should be selected to provide the best information to address the purpose of the research. For example, in research on effective teaching, it may be most informative to observe expert or master teachers rather than a sample of all teachers. To study school effectiveness it may be most informative to interview key personnel rather than a random sample of the staff.

As we will see in Chapter 12, there are several types of purposeful sampling procedures for qualitative investigations. In quantitative studies the emphasis is more on relying on the judgment of the researcher to select a sample that is representative of the population. That is, the emphasis tends to be on representativeness, while qualitative researchers are more interested in selecting cases that are "information rich." Excerpt 6.3 is an example of using a purposeful sampling procedure in a quantitative study.

Quota Sampling Quota sampling is used when the researcher is unable to take a probability sample but is still able to select subjects on the basis of characteristics of the population. Certain "quotas" are established so that the sample represents the population according to these characteristics. Different composite profiles of major groups in the population are identified, and then subjects are selected, nonrandomly, to represent each group. For example, it is typical to establish quotas for such characteristics as gender, race, age, grade level, position, and geographic location. The advantage of this type of sampling is that it is more representative of the population than a purposeful or convenience sample will be, but there is still great reliance on the judgment of the researcher to select the subjects.

There are two major limitations with nonprobability sampling. First, the sample is not representative of a larger population, so generalizing is more restricted. The generalizability of the findings will be limited to the characteristics of the subjects. This does not suggest that the findings are not useful; it simply means that greater caution is necessary in generalizing the results. Often researchers will describe the subjects carefully to show that although they were not selected randomly from a larger population, the characteristics of the subjects appear representative of much of the population.

A second limitation is that a nonprobability sample may be biased. This is particularly true for *volunteer samples,* in which subjects volunteer to participate in the research. Studies indicate that volunteers differ from nonvolunteers

---

EXCERPT 6.3

PURPOSEFUL SAMPLING

Data for the study were collected in 16 high schools in California and Michigan. The 16 schools were chosen purposefully to guarantee diversity in secondary-school teaching contexts in terms of state policies, district resources, school organization, and student composition.

Source: From Raudenbush, S. W., Rowan, B., & Cheong, Y. F. (1993). Higher order instructional goals in secondary schools: Class, teacher, and school influences. *American Educational Research Journal, 30,* 523–553.

in important ways. Rosenthal and Rosnow (1975) conclude that, in general, volunteers tend to be better educated, of higher social class, more intelligent, more sociable, more unconventional, less authoritarian, less conforming, more altruistic, and more extroverted than nonvolunteers. These characteristics could obviously affect the results to lead to conclusions that would be different if a probability sample was used. For example, suppose a researcher wanted to survey students on their attitudes toward the college they attended. Letters are sent to the graduated class of 500; 25 agree to come back to campus for interviews. Is it reasonable to conclude that the attitudes of these 25 volunteer students are representative of the class?

In deciding on a sampling procedure it is helpful to keep in mind the strengths and weaknesses of the different procedures, as summarized in Table 6.2. The final choice of procedure will depend on your purpose, availability of subjects, and your financial resources.

Sample Size

The number of subjects in a study is called the *sample size,* represented by the letter *n*. The researcher must determine the size of the sample that will provide sufficient data to answer the research question. The general rule in determining sample size is to obtain a sufficient number to provide a credible result. In situations in which a random sample is selected, a sample size that is only a small percentage of the population can approximate the characteristics of the population satisfactorily. Rowntree (1941) illustrates this point in a study of the percentage of income that was spent on rent by five categories of working-class families in England. Data were collected for the entire population and compared with the data that would have been reported by different sizes of random samples. As indicated in Table 6.3, there was little difference between a sample size of 2 percent (one in fifty) and 10 percent (one in ten).

The determination of sample size should take into consideration several factors—the type of research, research hypotheses, financial constraints, the importance of the results, the number of variables studied, the methods of data collection, and the degree of accuracy needed. The impact of these factors is summarized below:[3]

1. *The type of research.* Correlational research should have a minimum of thirty subjects, and in research comparing groups there should be at least fifteen subjects in each group (some highly controlled experiments will contain as few as eight to ten subjects in each group). In survey research studies there should be about one hundred subjects for each major subgroup that is analyzed and twenty to fifty subjects in minor subgroups.

---

[3]For a discussion of more systematic procedures for estimating the number of subjects needed, depending on the research design of the study, see H. C. Kraemer and S. Thielman (1987), *How many subjects? Statistical power analysis in research.* Newbury Park, CA: Sage, and Jaeger (1984).

TABLE 6.2

Strengths and Weaknesses of Sampling Methods

Sampling Method	Strength	Weakness
	Probability	
Simple random	Easy to understand Little knowledge of population needed Free of subject classification error Easy to analyze and interpret results	Requires numbering each element in the population Larger sampling error than in stratified sampling for same sample size
Systematic	Simplicity of drawing sample Easy to understand Free of subject classification error Easy to analyze and interprets results Subjects do not need to be numbered	Larger sampling error than in stratified sampling for same sample size Periodicity in list of population elements
Proportional stratified	Allows easy subgroup comparisons Usually more representative than simple random or systematic Fewer subjects needed if strata are related to the dependent variable Results represents population without weighting	Requires subgroup identification of each population element Requires knowledge of the proportion of each subgroup in the population May be costly and difficult to prepare lists of population elements in each subgroup
Nonproportional stratified	Allows easy subgroup comparisons Usually more representative than simple random or systematic Fewer subjects needed if strata are related to the dependent variable Assures adequate numbers of elements in each subgroup	Requires subgroup identification of each population element May be costly and difficult to prepare lists of population elements in each subgroup Requires weighting of subgroups to represent population
Cluster	Low cost Efficient with large populations Permits analysis of individual clusters	Less accurate than simple random, systematic, or stratified May be difficult to collect data from elements in a cluster Requires that each population element be assigned to only one cluster
	Nonprobability	
Convenience	Less costly and time-consuming Ease of administration Usually assures high participation rate Generalization possible to similar subjects	Difficult to generalize to other subjects Less representative of an identified population Results dependent on unique characteristics of the sample Greater likelihood of error due to experimenter or subject bias
Purposeful	Less costly and time-consuming Ease of administration Usually assures high participation rate Generalization possible to similar subjects Assures receipt of needed information	Difficult to generalize to other subjects Less representative of an identified population Results dependent on unique characteristics of the sample Greater likelihood of error due to experimenter or subject bias

(continued)

TABLE 6.2 (*continued*)

Sampling Method	Strength	Weakness
Quota	Less costly and time-consuming Ease of administration Usually assures high participation rate Generalization possible to similar subjects Tends to provide more representative samples than convenience or purposeful	Requires identification information on each subject Difficult to generalize to other subjects Less representative of an identified population Results dependent on unique characteristics of the sample Greater likelihood of error due to experimenter or subject bias More time-consuming than convenient or purposeful

2. *Research hypotheses.* If the researcher expects to find small differences or slight relationships, it is desirable to have as large a sample as possible. The effect of coaching courses on standardized test scores, for example, produces relatively small but perhaps important practical differences. This effect would be generally undetectable in studies with small numbers of subjects.

3. *Financial constraints.* Obviously, the cost of conducting a study will limit the number of subjects included in the sample. It is best to estimate these costs before beginning the study.

4. *Importance of results.* In exploratory research a smaller sample size is acceptable because the researcher is willing to tolerate a larger margin of error in the results. In research that will result in the placement of children in programs, or in the expenditure of a large amount of money, it is imperative for the researcher to attain a sample large enough to minimize error.

TABLE 6.3

Percentage of Income Spent on Rent

Income Class	Number of Families	Population Data	Sample Size			
			1 in 10	1 in 20	1 in 30	1 in 50
A	1748	26.5	26.6	25.9	28.3	27.1
B	2477	22.7	22.9	23.5	22.3	22.6
C	2514	19.8	18.1	17.2	17.2	18.0
D	1676	15.8	16.0	14.4	17.1	16.9
E	3740	11.3	11.0	10.1	11.2	11.5

Source: Rowntree, B. S. (1941). *Poverty and Progress: A Second Social Survey of York.* London: Longman, Green. Reprinted by permission of The Joseph Rowntree Charitable Trust.

5. *Number of variables studied.* A larger sample is needed for studies that have many independent or dependent variables, or for studies in which many uncontrollable variables are present.

6. *Methods of data collection.* If methods of collecting information are not highly accurate or consistent, a larger sample will be needed to offset the error inherent in the data collection.

7. *Accuracy needed.* The accuracy of the results (the degree of confidence that can be placed in a statement that the sample data are the same as for the population) is greater as the sample size increases. As the study by Rowntree demonstrates, however, a point of diminishing returns is reached as the sample size increases to a certain percentage of the population.

8. *Size of the population.* As the size of the population increases, the researcher can take a progressively smaller percentage of subjects from the population.

In educational research a major consideration with sample size is concluding that a study with a relatively small sample that found no difference or no relationship is true. For example, suppose that you are studying the relationship between personality type and effectiveness as a leader and, with only twenty-five subjects, find that there is no relationship. Is it reasonable to conclude that, in reality, there is no relationship? Probably not, since a significant reason for not finding a relationship is the small sample size. That is, with a larger sample size a relationship may be revealed. (On the other hand, it is possible to report a "significant" relationship in a study that has a very large number of subjects, even though the relationship is quite small. As we will see in later chapters, this "significant" relationship is often misinterpreted as an important or meaningful relationship.) When researchers want to be confident that a finding of no relationship or no difference accurately reflects reality, they design the research to ensure what is called adequate "power" in the analysis. A large sample size is the best method of enhancing power in a study.

Data Collection Techniques

Research involves gathering information about the variables in the study. The researcher chooses from a wide range of techniques and approaches for collecting data from the subjects. Each method has advantages and disadvantages, and the specific approach adopted should be the best method for answering the research question. Here are few common methods of gathering quantitative information:

1. Questionnaires
2. Structured interviews
3. Tests

4. Structured observations
5. Inventories
6. Rating scales
7. Unobtrusive measures

These methods will be discussed in greater detail in later chapters. At this point, however, it is important to understand two basic principles of measurement, test validity and reliability, that are common for all methods. Knowledge of these principles is used both to choose instruments and to evaluate the adequacy of data collection reported in research studies.

Test Validity

Test validity is the extent to which inferences and uses made on the basis of scores from an instrument are reasonable and appropriate. Validity is a judgment of the appropriateness of a measure for specific inferences, decisions, consequences or uses that result from the scores that are generated. In other words, validity is a situation-specific concept: validity is dependent on the purpose, population, and situational factors in which measurement takes place. The results of a test, questionnaire, or other measure can therefore be valid in one situation and invalid in another.

This definition has important implications for designing and evaluating research, since the findings are directly related to the measure selected. The investigator who is designing research should first clearly define the inferences, uses, or decisions that will be made from the results. Then an instrument should be selected that provides good evidence that making such inferences or decisions is valid.

Evidence for validity is reported in texts that summarize and critique measures, such as the *Mental Measurements Yearbooks*, in manuals that describe technical information about the measure, and in research articles in which the measure is used. In evaluating research the reader should look for statements that refer to validity and then evaluate the evidence provided in relation to the inference or decision made in the article. For instance, if normative data are to be used from a standardized instrument, the norms should have been generated from a population that is similar to the subjects in the study. In general, it is important to keep in mind that instruments are valid for some groups and in some situations, and invalid for other subjects or in other situations.

Test Reliability

Test reliability refers to the consistency of measurement, the extent to which the scores are similar over different forms of the same instrument or occasions of data collection. The goal of developing reliable measures is to minimize the influence on the scores of chance or other variables unrelated to the intent of the measure.

The specific methods for estimating and reporting reliability are very precise and are explained in detail in Chapter 8. Designers and readers of research should interpret reliability in much the same way as validity, looking for evidence that sufficient reliability of each score is documented. Also, many studies fail to support a hypothesis because there is significant error in measuring the variables (with more reliable measures the hypothesis might be supported).

In reading the instruments section of a study or in designing data collection, there are a few things to keep in mind:

1. Are the scores reliable for the subjects of the particular research?
2. Are the characteristics of the subjects used to establish validity and reliability similar to the characteristics of the subjects in the study? If not, is it reasonable to use the instruments?
3. Are the instruments used the best ones? Are there others that are more reliable and would provide more valid results?
4. Why did the researcher choose these instruments?
5. Are they instruments described well enough or referenced to allow another researcher to replicate the research?

Excerpt 6.4 is from the instruments section of a study. The extent of the description provided is about what is expected in reporting most types of research.

EXCERPT 6.4

INSTRUMENTS SECTION

FUTURE CAREER PREFERENCE.

Girls rated the probability of entering each of 19 potential job or career categories on a 7-point scale ranging from "very unlikely" to "very likely." Each category was presented with a label, followed by a brief description (e.g., food service, like waiter, waitress, cook, food preparation). The categories that involved science were (a) health paraprofessional, (b) health professional with a bachelor's degree, (c) science- or math-related professional with a bachelor's degree, (d) health professional with an advanced degree, and (e) science professional with an advanced degree. Examples and degree qualifications were given for each category. Ratings for all five categories were averaged to create a single score for a science career (alpha = .78); ratings for categories (b) and (d) were averaged to create a health professional score (alpha = .81); and ratings for categories (c) and (e) were averaged to create a physical science professional score (alpha = .77).

Source: From Jacobs, J. E., Finken, L. L., Griffin, N. L., & Wright, J. D. (1998). The career plans of science—talented rural adolescent girls. *American Educational Research Journal, 35* (4), 681–704.

Sources for Locating and Evaluating Existing Instruments

A general rule of advice in conducting research is to choose an instrument that has established the reliability and validity the researcher needs. Although reliability and validity are the most important considerations in selecting an instrument, there are other considerations such as purchasing costs, availability, simplicity of administration and scoring, copyright limitations, level of difficulty, and appropriateness of norms.

While it is often difficult to find an instrument that will meet all criteria a researcher might have, there are thousands of instruments that have been developed, and it is probable that one is available that can be used intact or modified to meet a specific purpose. The easiest way to locate existing instruments is to use sources that summarize information on several measures. The sources in the following list are widely used and accessible in most university libraries.

Tests in Print, published periodically by the Buros Institute (Volume V, 1998), provides a summary of tests reviewed in all preceding mental measurement yearbooks. (Earlier editions edited by Oscar Buros.)

Handbook of Research Design and Social Measurement, 5th edition (Miller, 1991): Reviews and critiques popular social science measures.

Index to Tests Used in Educational Dissertations (Fabiano, 1989): Describes tests and test populations used in dissertations from 1938 to 1980; keyed by title and selected descriptors.

Directory of Unpublished Experimental Mental Measures, Volume 6 (Goldman & Mitchell, 1995): Describes nearly 1700 experimental mental measures that are not commercially available. Includes references, source, and purpose on topics ranging from educational adjustment and motivation to personality and perception.

The ETS Test Collection: The Educational Testing Service (ETS) has developed several sources that describe more than 10,000 tests and instruments. The *Test Collection Bibliographies* cover published and unpublished measures in several areas, including achievement, attitudes and interests, personality, special populations, and vocation/occupation. Each of over 200 separate bibliographies describes instruments and appropriate uses and can be ordered from ETS. *Tests in Microfiche* lists unpublished research instruments, also in a wide variety of areas. *The ETS Test Collection Catalog* includes six volumes: *Volume 1: Achievement Tests and Measurement Devices* (1993), *Volume 2: Vocational Tests and Measurement Devices* (1995), *Volume 3: Tests for Special Populations* (1989), *Volume 4: Cognitive Aptitude and Intelligence Tests*

(1990), *Volume 5: Attitude Measures* (1991), and *Volume 6: Affective Measures and Personality Tests* (1992). Each volume contains full descriptions of the instruments, with author, title, and subject indexes. The ERIC Clearinghouse on Assessment and Evaluation is a host for the ETS test collection database (http://ericae.net/testcol.htm).

Tests: A Comprehensive Reference for Assessments in Psychology, Education, and Business, 4th ed. (Maddox, 1996): Provides a description of over 3100 published tests, including purpose, cost, scoring, and publisher.

Test Critiques, Vols. 1–10 (Keyser & Sweetland, 1984–1994): Gives in-depth evaluations for widely used, newly published, and recently revised instruments in psychology, education, and business. Contains "user-oriented" information, including practical applications and uses, as well as technical aspects and a critique by a measurement specialist. The companion, *Test Critiques Compendium,* reviews 60 major tests from *Test Critiques* in one volume.

Mental Measurements Yearbooks (MMY; Buros Institute of Mental Measures): Provides reviews of commercially available tests in several areas, including character and personality, achievement, and intelligence. References for most of the tests facilitate further research. The MMY have been published periodically for sixty years. The *Thirteenth MMY* was published in 1998. Future MMY editions may be published every two years with supplements released on alternate years. Thus, if a test had not been revised recently information could be obtained by consulting an earlier volume. It is also convenient to access the Buros Institute Web site (http://www.unl.edu/buros).

Tests and Measurements in Child Development: Handbook I and II (Johnson, 1976): Two volumes describe about 900 unpublished tests and instruments for children through age 18.

A Sourcebook of Mental Health Measures (Comrey, Backer, & Glaser, 1973): This reference describes about 1100 instruments related to mental health, including juvenile delinquency, personality, and alcoholism.

Measures for Psychological Assessment: A Guide to 3,000 Original Sources and Their Applications (Chun, Cobb, & French, 1974): A list of tests used in research reported in 26 different psychological journals.

Measures of Social Psychological Attitudes (Robinson & Shaver, 1973): Describes hundreds of attitude instruments used in psychological and sociological research.

Socioemotional Measures for Pre-School and Kindergarten Children: A Handbook (Walker, 1973): Describes instruments to measure attitudes, personality, self-concept, and social skills of young children.

Handbook for Measurement and Evaluation in Early Childhood Education (Goodwin & Driscoll, 1980): A comprehensive review of affective, cognitive, and psychomotor measures for young children.

Dictionary of Behavioral Assessment Techniques (Hersen & Bellack, 1988): Provides descriptions of approximately 300 instruments that assess psychological and behavioral traits.

Developing Instruments

Although many instruments are available, there are occasions when researchers have to develop their own measures. The most common situation that requires a "locally" developed measure is evaluation research for a specific setting. Unless the research will have an important direct impact on programs or individuals, it is unusual for the researcher to systematically establish reliability and validity (as summarized in Chapter 8) prior to conducting the study. A more common approach is to develop an instrument that seems reasonable and to gather pilot data on it to revise as needed. While it is probably not necessary to establish sophisticated estimates of reliability and validity, it is still possible for the instrument to be of such inferior quality that the results attained are uninterpretable. Thus, it is important for a researcher to follow a few basic steps if faced with the development of an instrument:

1. Become acquainted with common approaches to measure the trait or behavior of interest. There are many existing sources that summarize approaches for measuring such variables as achievement, attitudes, interests, personality, and self-concept.
2. Write out specific objectives for your instrument, with one objective for each trait or behavior of interest.
3. After reading about the area and conducting discussions with others about what approach would best measure the trait, brainstorm several items for each objective.
4. Ask professionals who are knowledgeable in the assessed area to review the items: Are they clear? Unbiased? Concise? Is the meaning the same for all readers?
5. Find a small sample of individuals that is similar to those who will be used in the actual study and administer the instrument to them. This could be referred to as a "pilot test" of the instrument. Check for clarity, ambiguity in sentences, time for completion, directions, and any problems that may have been experienced.
6. Check for an adequate distribution of scores for each item in the instrument. If all the responses to an item are the same, it is difficult to know whether the question is inadequate or whether the trait actually lacks variability. As long as the responses result in a spread of scores, the chances are good that the item is an adequate measure of the trait.
7. Revise, delete, and add items where necessary, depending on feedback from the sample subjects in the pilot test.

Procedures

In quantitative studies the researcher plans the procedures that will be used to collect data, and, in the case of experimental research, the nature and administration of the experimental treatment. The researcher decides where the data will be collected (such as in a school, city, or laboratory setting), when the data will be collected (time of day and year), how the data will be collected (by whom and in what form), and, if necessary, specifics of the experimental treatment. Any procedures used to control bias (such as counterbalancing the order of instruments to control subject fatigue or boredom or being sure observers are unaware of which group is receiving the treatment and which is the control) are planned and implemented as part of the procedures. In reporting the study the researcher should present the procedures in sufficient detail to permit another researcher to replicate the study.

Internal Validity of Design

Internal validity, which we have defined as the extent of control over extraneous variables, is strongest when the study's design (subjects, instruments, and procedures) effectively controls possible sources of error so that those sources are not reasonably related to the study's results. The sources of error for quantitative studies are thought of as "threats," because each source may invalidate the study's findings.

Several categories or types of threats to internal validity are pertinent to most quantitative studies. Each of these threats, as they are called, is described below with examples. These categories are taken from Campbell and Stanley (1963), Cook and Campbell (1979), and McMillan (2000). It is best to keep in mind that the names of these various threats to internal validity should not be interpreted literally. Often they have a broader meaning than the names may suggest at first. While some of the names are unique to this book, most were established many years ago by Campbell and Stanley (1963). Also, most of these threats were originally conceived for experimental research. While we believe most of the threats can relate to both experimental and nonexperimental designs, there are some that only make sense in the context of an experiment.

History

In the context of internal validity, **history** refers to extraneous incidents or events affecting the results that occur during the research. This is a threat to any research that is conducted across points in time, and it becomes more serious as the time between measures increases. If some event occurs during the study that is plausibly related to the dependent variable, it is difficult to know if the independent variable, the event, or a combination of the two produced the result. In this sense, the event is "confounded" with the independent variable; the two cannot be separated.

History can occur "within" the study as subjects are affected by something that happens during the treatment in an experiment, or "outside" of the research setting. For example, suppose a class is studying the Far East and the researchers are trying to determine what effect this unit has on multicultural attitudes. During the unit a major crisis occurs in China. If the students are affected by the crisis, which in turn influences the way they respond to a multicultural attitude questionnaire, this event constitutes a history threat to the internal validity of the study. History threats can also occur within a research setting. For example, a series of unexpected announcements that distracts a class receiving one method of instruction adversely affects the influence of the lesson. Students in this class might score lower than other classes, but the researcher does not know if this result is caused by the distraction or the method of instruction.

History also includes confounding variables that are associated with levels of the independent variable. For example, suppose an experiment compares two methods of instruction: one treatment is in the morning and the other is in the afternoon. Time of day would constitute a history threat associated with the level of the independent variable.

Selection

There are two types of selection threats to consider: those that occur in experiments and *ex post facto* designs, and threats related to sampling. In experiments groups of subjects are formed in order to study an independent variable of interest. If there is a systematic difference between the groups, however, it is possible that the results may be due to these existing differences. The threat of **selection** exists whenever groups of subjects cannot be assigned randomly, and although there are several approaches that help control this problem in cases where randomization is undesirable or impossible (matching, testing subjects more than once [repeated measures], adjusting posttest scores on the basis of initially measured group characteristics [analysis of covariance], and giving each group every treatment [counterbalancing]), the researcher should always be concerned with this important threat.

Consider, for example, a teacher who wants to investigate whether the mastery or inductive approach is best for teaching adjectives and adverbs. The teacher secures the cooperation of another class in order to conduct a study. The two teachers flip a coin to decide which will use the discovery approach and which will use the mastery approach. The teachers assess achievement by giving each group a pretest and a posttest to determine growth in knowledge. It happens, however, that the average IQ score of the mastery group is 115 and of the discovery group 95. Here selection is a major problem, since we would expect the higher IQ group to achieve more than the lower IQ group under almost any condition. If uncontrolled and unaccounted for in some way, then such a threat to internal validity could render the study useless. The teacher would falsely conclude that the mastery learning method is more effective when its apparent success is really due to initial differences in ability.

As discussed previously, selection is also related to the manner in which the researcher chooses a sample. As pointed out, a common problem in research is using volunteers for the sample. The volunteer group may be more motivated or motivated for special reasons; hence, they would respond differently to the treatment or questions from the way a nonvolunteer group would respond.

Statistical Regression

Statistical regression refers to the tendency of subjects who score very high or low on a pretest to score closer to the mean ("regress" to the mean) on the posttest, regardless of the effects of the treatment. All our measures have some degree of error, and statistical regression occurs because of changes in error from the pretest to the posttest. Scores on a posttest will be different from the pretest for students on the basis of mathematical probability alone because of this error. For groups of students who score either very high or very low on a pretest, this error works to change the scores on the posttest so that they are closer to the mean of the posttest than they were to the mean of the pretest.

To illustrate this concept, think of Figure 6.2 as representing the same test taken twice by two groups of students in a class in which the average score is 100. The average score for the Superstars on the first test was 150 whereas the

FIGURE 6.2   Illustration of Statistical Regression

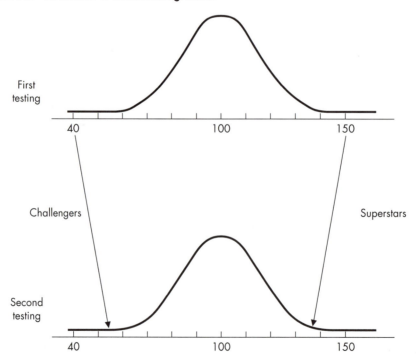

score for the Challengers was 40. On the second test we would expect the average score for the Superstars to be lower and the Challengers' score to be higher, even if their true ability or knowledge remains the same.

Regression is a problem whenever the researcher purposely chooses groups on the basis of extremely high or low scores. A school district may, for example, want to implement a special program to improve the self-concept of children who score low on a self-concept inventory. An assessment of the impact of the program could examine self-concept scores after the program (in a posttest), but the researcher would have to keep in mind that even if there is no program effect whatsoever, the initially low scores (on a pretest) would improve to some degree because of statistical regression. Similarly, it is usually difficult to find positive changes in programs for gifted children since, because of regression, posttest scores will tend to be slightly lower on average.

Pretesting

Whenever research utilizes a pretest (some form of measurement that precedes a treatment or experience), it is possible that the test itself will have an impact on the subjects. Just taking a pretest could provide the subject with motivation or practice on the type of questions asked, or familiarize the subject with the material tested. This kind of **pretesting** effect is found in experiments measuring achievement over a short time and in research on attitudes or values when a single group is given a pretest and a posttest. If an attitude questionnaire is used as a pretest, simply reading the questions might stimulate the subject to think about the topic and even change attitudes. A researcher might, for instance, be interested in evaluating the effect of a series of films on changes in students' attitudes toward physically handicapped children. The researcher gives a pretest, shows the films, then gives a posttest to find out whether changes have occurred. Any observed changes, however, might be caused by the pretest. The items in the questionnaire could have been enough to change the attitudes. Pretesting is not a threat for nonexperimental designs.

Instrumentation

A threat to internal validity that is related to testing is called instrumentation. **Instrumentation** refers to the way changes in the instruments or persons used to collect data might affect the results. This threat is particularly serious in observational research, when the observers may become fatigued or bored or change in some other way so as to affect the recording of data. A good example of how instrumentation could affect results occurs when scores from the same standardized test are used to track achievement across several years. If there has been a renorming of the test, and a new form, it is problematic to compare results from the old test with those from the new one. The 1995 renorming and other changes in the SAT is a good illustration of how this can lead to errors in interpretation, since the meaning of the same score, for example, 500, is different in the new form. Testing is a change in the subject resulting from taking the test, while instrumentation is a recorded change in the results from inadequacies of the testing.

Subject Attrition

Subject attrition (also called *subject mortality*) occurs in a study when subjects systematically drop out or are lost during the investigation. This is a threat to many longitudinal studies that last over several weeks or months. For example, a study of the effect of a program to assist low-achieving ninth graders con-ducted between the ninth and the twelfth grades would have apparent success if the lowest-achieving students dropped out of school before twelfth grade and were not even included in the posttest analyses. For most nonexperimental and short-duration research, attrition is not a threat unless the treatment is espe-cially demanding and systematically causes low-performing subjects to drop out. In studies that have differential loss of subjects from different groups because of selection bias or the nature of the treatments, mortality is a serious threat to internal validity. Mortality is essentially the same problem as selection, but it happens after the study is already set up and under way.

Maturation

Maturation refers to changes in the subjects of a study over time that affect the dependent variable. Subjects develop and change as a part of growing older, and in interpreting research that occurs over an extended time, such changes should be considered. Some changes, such as getting hungry, tired, bored, or discouraged, can occur in a relatively short time and are also considered matu-rational threats to internal validity. Suppose a researcher is investigating the attitudes of fourth graders toward reading, mathematics, and science. The researcher has developed an instrument and gives it to all subjects in the same order. It takes the subjects a half hour to finish the reading instrument and another half hour to complete the mathematics questions. How will they respond to the science instrument? They will probably be tired, bored, and inat-tentive, and maturation would thus be a major problem in using their responses to the science items as an indication of their attitude toward science. Other examples are students who become more knowledgeable because of experience, or first graders who learn to dribble a basketball not because of an effective teacher but because they are maturing physically.

Diffusion of Treatment

In experimental designs a treatment is given to one group, and the control or alternative condition group never comes in contact with the experimental treat-ment. If, for instance, a psychologist is studying cheating behavior and manipu-lates the incentive to cheat as the independent variable, one group might receive a high incentive for cheating and the other group a low incentive, but neither group would be aware of the treatment the other group was receiving. If, however, a teacher decided to test this notion with a class of students and told half the students they would receive a high incentive and the other half that they would, at the same time, receive a low incentive, then each group knows the conditions of the other. In such circumstances the treatments are diffused throughout all subjects. It is possible that both treatments could affect either group, resulting in **diffusion of treatment**. Diffusion also occurs if the effects of the treatment spread to subjects in a control or comparison group.

Experimenter Effects

Experimenter effects refer to both deliberate and unintentional influences that the researcher has on the subjects. This may be reflected in differential treatment of subjects, such as using a different voice tone, being more reassuring to one group than to others, reinforcing different behaviors, displaying different attitudes, selectively observing different subject responses, and any other demeanor that influences either the subjects' behavior or the evaluation of the behavior by the researcher. Experimenter effects also occur if the characteristics of the investigator or person collecting data, such as clothing, age, sex, educational level, and race affect subjects' responses. For example, if an experimenter is carrying out a study on the difference in behavior with students of so-called "master" teachers compared with behavior with students of so-called "novice" teachers, and if observers are used to record behavior with students of both types of teachers, it is important that the observers do not know which teachers have been classified as master or novice. If the observers were aware of which group the students were in (master or novice teacher) this knowledge may influence what the observers notice in the classrooms. In most research that involves the use of researchers as a part of the study it is best to keep them unaware of the specifics of the research. They need to have only enough information to carry out the research objectively and to collect the information.

Treatment Replications

In an experiment the treatment is supposed to be repeated so that each of the members of one group receive the same treatment separately and independently of the other members of the group. Thus, if the researcher is testing a new method of instruction with a class, there is really only one replication of the treatment; that is, the treatment is conducted once. Each class is like one subject, and hence several classes are needed to do the research properly. **Treatment replications** are a threat to internal validity to the extent that the reported number of subjects in the study is not the same as the number of independent replications of the treatment.

This threat is a particularly troublesome limitation for educational research because it is so difficult to use multiple groups of students. Often a study will compare two treatments, one given to one class, the other to a different class. While this type of design usually results in a technical sample size of two, rather than the number of students in the classes, the threat of treatment replications does not mean the results are uninterpretable. Rather, what needs to be recognized is that whatever the results, interpretations and conclusions should be made with great caution. Some experimental treatments are given to students as a group assignment but the actual treatment condition, such as a particular type of homework assignment, is individualized. In this circumstance, treatment replications is not a threat to internal validity.

Subject Effects

In ideal research the subjects behave and respond naturally and honestly. However, when people become involved in a study they often change their behavior simply because they understand they are "subjects," and sometimes these changes affect the results. **Subject effects** refer to subject changes in behavior, initiated by the subjects themselves, in response to the research situation. If subjects have some idea of the purpose of the study or the motivation for doing "well," they may alter their behavior to respond more favorably. Subjects will pick up cues from the setting and instructions, which will motivate them in specific ways. These cues are called **demand characteristics.** Subjects in most studies will also want to present themselves in the most positive manner. Thus, there may be positive self-presentation, social desirability, or a belief that certain responses are expected, which may affect the results. For instance, most people want to appear intelligent, competent, and emotionally stable, and they may resist treatments that they perceive as manipulating them in negative ways, or they may fake responses to appear more positive. Some subjects may increase positive or desirable behavior simply because they know they are receiving special treatment (this is termed the Hawthorne effect, considered by some researchers as a threat to external validity; see section on ecological external validity). Control group subjects may try harder because they see themselves in competition with a treatment group or may be motivated because they did *not* get the treatment (this may be termed the *John Henry* effect or *compensatory rivalry*). Other subjects, when they realize that they were not selected for what they believe is a preferred treatment, may become demotivated (*resentful demoralization*). Finally, many individuals will react positively, with increased motivation or participation, because they are doing something new and different (this is termed the *novelty effect*). As you can see, there are many possible subject effects.

Statistical Conclusion

In most educational research, statistics are used as a basis for making conclusions about presumed effects and relationships. There are several principles of statistics that, if violated, can affect the inferences made from results as well as subsequent conclusions of the research. Cook and Campbell (1979) list several threats in this category that are beyond the scope of this book. Researchers need to understand, however, that the use of impressive-sounding and impressive-looking statistics does not guarantee valid results. The best approach is to consult statisticians familiar with these threats.

External Validity of Design

External validity refers to the generalizability of the results. For quantitative designs there are two general categories of external validity that need to be considered when designing studies or in evaluating research findings: population external validity and ecological external validity.

Population External Validity

The subjects used in an investigation have certain characteristics and can be described with respect to such variables as age, race, sex, and ability. Strictly speaking, the results of a study can be generalized only to other people who have the same, or at least similar, characteristics as those used in the experiment. The extent to which the results can be generalized to other people is referred to as **population external validity**. Consider the prevailing situation in much psychological research. Because of time, money, and other constraints, psychologists often use college students as subjects in research. The results of such research, strictly speaking, are limited in generalizability to other similar college students. In other words, what might be true for certain college students may not be true for sixth-grade students. Similarly, research conducted with elementary students should not be generalized to secondary students, nor males generalized to females, nor Hispanics generalized to Blacks, and so forth. A treatment might be effective with one type of student and be ineffective with another. If subjects are volunteers for research, the findings may be limited to characteristics of the volunteers.

Ecological External Validity

Ecological external validity refers to the conditions of the research and the extent to which generalizing the results is limited to similar conditions. The conditions of the research include such factors as the nature of the independent and dependent variables, physical surroundings, time of day or year, pretest or posttest sensitization, and effects caused by the presence of an experimenter or treatment. Included in these factors is the well-known **Hawthorne effect**: the tendency for people to act differently simply because they realize they are subjects in research. (It is called the Hawthorne effect because the original study was conducted at the Western Electric Hawthorne Plant in Chicago. Although some research has questioned the validity of the original study, the label *Hawthorne effect* endures.) Much as with subject effects threats, subjects become anxious, fake responses in order to look good, or react in many other ways because of their knowledge of aspects of the research.

It should be noted that many of the factors that limit generalizability may also act as extraneous variables (threats to internal validity) and affect the dependent variable. Often such factors are said to be *confounded* with the treatment or study. For example, if a study shows a change in a morning class that received one method of instruction and no change in an afternoon class that received a different method, time of day is an extraneous variable that could affect the dependent variable, and it is confounded with the effectiveness of the treatment. It may be that similar results will be obtained—that is, generalized—to other morning classes. In this instance, generalizability is limited by the ecological factor time of day, but time of day is also a threat to internal validity. Similarly, if one teacher is implementing curriculum X and a different teacher is implementing curriculum Y, teacher is confounded with curriculum treatments and would be considered an extraneous variable because it is not possible to separate the effect of the teacher from the curriculum. The generalizability of the results must include the teachers as well as the curricula. As previously noted, the Hawthorne effect is an example of a factor that can affect both internal and external validity.

Consider once again the psychologist in a university setting. Psychological experiments are often conducted in a small room in which the subject is alone. This procedure is desirable for controlling threats to internal validity, but it tends to restrict the degree of possible generalization, since the way subjects respond in an artificial setting may not be the same as in naturally occurring conditions.

A special type of limitation to generalizability is the extent to which a treatment is a representative instance of the underlying construct that is hypothesized to exist. This type of external validity is termed by Cook and Campbell (1979) **construct validity**. It refers to the adequacy with which we understand and communicate the complexity of the so-called treatment package, particularly the components of it that will allow the observed effect to be replicated as another test of the underlying construct. A specific behavior modification program, for example, might be employed as a method of using a principle of behaviorism (shaping, intermittent reinforcement, satiation, and so on), but for purposes of generalization, the consumer must analyze the adequacy with which the construct is represented by the program and whether there are peculiarities in the treatment that would make replication difficult. This problem occurs extensively in research that investigates the impact of a new curriculum or set of materials. The results may be impressive, but unless there is evidence that a generalizable construct has been used, and that the treatment is clear and easily understood, the external validity will be limited.

Another variation of external validity is to be careful not to conclude that what may be true for an entire group of subjects is also true for subgroups of subjects. For example, if research with a large high school shows a positive relationship between amount of time spent with homework and achievement for all students, it doesn't necessarily follow that this same relationship holds for high-ability students or low-ability students, or that it is just as true for sophomores as for seniors. This is called generalizing *across* a population and can lead to erroneous interpretations.

EXCERPT 6.5

EXTERNAL VALIDITY

DISCUSSION

Since only one teacher and the students from one classroom participated, and since the study focused only on language arts curriculum, the results of this study have to be accepted tentatively until replications are conducted. The congruence of the results with existing theory and previous research does provide some corroboration of their validity. . . .

While the results of this study and the previous research indicate a pragmatic superiority of cooperative over competitive and individualized learning structures, it does not follow that all individualization or competition should be dropped. What is needed is a series of studies which demonstrate the specific conditions under which each type of learning structure is effective and useful in achieving desired educational outcomes.

Source: From Johnson, D. T., Johnson R. T., Johnson, J., & Anderson, D. (1976). Effects of cooperative versus individualized instruction on student prosocial behavior, attitudes toward learning, and achievement, *Journal of Educational Psychology, 68,* 446–452.

It is possible to be so strict with respect to external validity that practically all research is useful only in specific cases. While it is necessary to consider the external validity of studies, we need to be reasonable, not strict, in interpreting the results. It is common, for example, for researchers to cite, in the discussion or conclusion sections of the article, the limitations of generalizing their results. Excerpt 6.5 is a good example of researchers addressing the problem of external validity by limiting the generalization that should be made.

Ethical and Legal Considerations[4]

Since most educational research deals with human beings, it is necessary to understand the ethical and legal responsibilities of conducting research. Often researchers face situations in which the potential costs of using questionable

---

[4]A more detailed analysis of ethical and legal considerations is summarized in P. Reynolds (1982). *Ethics and Social Research.* Englewood Cliffs, NJ: Prentice-Hall; Homan, R. (1991). *The Ethics of Social Research.* London: Longman; American Psychological Association (2000). *The Ethics of Research with Human Participants.* Washington, DC: American Psychological Association; Howe, K. R., & Moses, M. S. (1999). *Ethics in Educational Research.* In *Review of Research in Education,* A. Iran-Nejad and P. D. Pearson (ed.). Washington, DC: American Educational Research Association and in guidelines published by the American Educational Research Association.

methods must be balanced by the benefits of conducting the study. Questionable methods come about because of the nature of the research questions and methodology designed to provide valid results. The costs include injury or psychological difficulties, such as anxiety, shame, loss of self-esteem, and affronts to human dignity, or they may involve legal infringement on human rights. Such costs, if a potential result of the research, must be weighed against benefits for the research participants like increased self-understanding, satisfaction in helping, and knowledge of research methods, as well as more obvious benefits to theory and knowledge of human behavior.

It is ultimately the responsibility of each researcher to weigh these considerations and make the best professional judgment possible. To do this, it is necessary for the researcher to be fully aware of ethical and legal principles that should be addressed. We present these principles with discussion of implications.

Ethics of Research

Ethics generally are considered to deal with beliefs about what is right or wrong, proper or improper, good or bad. Naturally, there is some degree of disagreement about how to define what is ethically correct in research. But it is a very important question, one of increasing concern for private citizens, researchers, and legislators. Many professional and governmental groups have studied ethical issues in depth and have published guidelines for planning and conducting research in such a way as to protect the rights and welfare of the subjects. Most relevant for educational research are ethical principles published by the American Educational Research Association. Another useful source is the American Psychological Association.[5] The principles of most concern to educators are discussed here.

1. The primary investigator of a study is responsible for the ethical standards to which the study adheres.

2. The investigator should inform the subjects of all aspects of the research that might influence willingness to participate and answer all inquiries of subjects on features that may have adverse effects or consequences.

3. The investigator should be as open and honest with the subjects as possible. This usually involves a full disclosure of the purpose of the research, but there are circumstances in which either withholding information about the

---

[5]American Educational Research Association (1992), Ethical standards of the American Educational Research Association, *Educational Researcher, 21,* 23–26; American Psychological Association (1992), Ethical principles of psychologists and code of conduct. *American Psychologist, 47,* special insert, *Ethical principles in the conduct of research with human participants* (1982). Washington, DC: American Psychological Association.

research or deceiving the subjects may be justified. Withholding information means that the participants are informed about only part of the purpose of the research. This may be done in studies where full disclosure would seriously affect the validity of the results. For example, in research on students' racial attitudes, it may be sufficient to inform students that the research is investigating attitudes toward others.

A more volatile issue involves research in which, to put it bluntly, the researcher deliberately lies to the subjects. A good example is the classic study on teacher expectations by Rosenthal and Jacobson (1968). The researchers informed the teachers that certain students had been identified as "bloomers" on a test designed to predict intellectual gain. In fact, the "test" was a measure of intelligence, and the students were identified at random. In this design it was necessary to tell the teachers an untruth. Is such deception justified? After all, in this case the students would only benefit from the misinformation, and the results did have very important implications.

From one perspective, the deception may be justified on the basis of the contribution of the findings. On the other hand, it is an affront to human dignity and self-respect and may encourage mistrust and cynicism toward researchers. It seems to us that deception should be used only in cases where (1) the significance of the potential results is greater than the detrimental effects of lying; (2) deception is the only valid way to carry out the study; and (3) appropriate debriefing, in which the researcher informs the participants of the nature of and reason for the deception following the completion of the study, is used. Deception does not mean that the subjects should not have a choice whether to participate at all in the study.

4. Subjects must be protected from physical and mental discomfort, harm, and danger. If any of these risks is possible, the researcher must inform the subjects of these risks.

5. Most studies require the investigator to secure informed consent from the subjects before they participate in the research. **Informed consent** is achieved by providing subjects with an explanation of the research, an opportunity to terminate their participation at any time with no penalty, and full disclosure of any risks associated with the study. Consent is usually obtained by asking subjects (or parents of minors) to sign a form that indicates understanding of the research and consent to participate. Almost all data-gathering in public schools that requires student participation beyond normal testing requires parental as well as school district and principal permission.

Informed consent implies that the subjects have a choice about whether to participate. Yet there are many circumstances when it seems acceptable that the subjects never know that they have been participants. Sometimes it is impractical or impossible to locate subjects; sometimes knowledge of participation may invalidate the results. Some educational research is quite unobtrusive and has no risks for the subjects (such as the use of test data of students over the past ten years in order to chart achievement trends). Still, the researcher infringes on what many believe is the ethical right of participants to make their own decision about participation. In general, the more the research inconveniences subjects or creates the potential for harm, the more severe the ethical question in using them as subjects without their consent.

Certainly people should never be coerced into participating. Coercion is enacted in different degrees. At one extreme, teachers can insist that their students participate, or employers can "strongly suggest" that their employees cooperate as subjects. Less obvious subtle persuasion is exerted by convincing subjects that they are "benefiting" science, a program, or an institution. The researcher may indicate freedom of choice to participate or not participate, but the implicit message "you're letting us down if you don't participate," may also be clear, resulting in partial coercion. In other cases, subjects are simply bribed. Where does freedom of choice end and coercion begin? It is often difficult to know, but it is the responsibility of the researcher to be aware of the power of subtle coercion and to clearly maintain the freedom of the potential participant to decide whether or not to be a subject in the research. Whenever possible, participation should be voluntary, and invasion of privacy should be minimized.

6. Information obtained about the subjects must be held confidential unless otherwise agreed on, in advance, through informed consent (see section on legal constraints). This means that no one has access to individual data or the names of the participants except the researcher(s) and that the subjects know before they participate who will see the data. Confidentiality is ensured by making certain that the data cannot be linked to individual subjects by name. This can be accomplished in several ways, including (1) collecting the data anonymously; (2) using a system to link names to data that can be destroyed; (3) using a third party to link names to data and then giving the results to the researcher without the names; (4) asking subjects to use aliases or numbers; and (5) reporting only group, not individual, results. Boruch and Cecil (1979) provide details of many different procedures for ensuring confidentiality.

7. For research conducted through an institution, such as a university or school system, approval for conducting the research should be obtained from the institution before any data are collected.

8. The investigator has a responsibility to consider potential misinterpretations and misuses of the research and should make every effort to communicate results so that misunderstanding is minimized.

9. The investigator has the responsibility of recognizing when potential benefits have been withheld from a control group. In such situations, the significance of the potential findings should be greater than the potential harm to some subjects. For example, a new program that purports to enhance achievement of learning disabled children may be withheld from some learning disabled children in the belief that an experiment is necessary to document the effectiveness of the program. In the process the controls who may have benefited are denied participation in the program.

10. The investigator should provide subjects with the opportunity to receive the results of the study in which they are participating.

Some research, such as studies of the effects of drugs, obviously has potential danger that must be considered carefully by the investigator. Much educational research may not seem to involve any ethical problems, but the investigator's view may be biased, and it is best to be conservative and seek the advice and approval of others. Most universities and funding agencies have committees for the review of research in order to help ensure ethical safeguards. One of the continuing difficulties faced by educational researchers is securing cooperation from administrators, teachers, and parents. This difficulty is lessened by researchers who are aware of ethical principles and adhere to them.

There is also an interesting, if not frustrating, interaction between being ethical, on the one hand, and designing the research to provide the best, most objective data, on the other. It is relatively easy, for example, to observe behavior unobtrusively, and the subjects might never know they were in an experiment. As we have previously noted, the Hawthorne effect can reduce the validity of the study. To maximize both internal and external validity, therefore, it seems best for the the subjects to be unaware that they are being studied. Suppose, for instance, a researcher planted a confederate in a class in order to record unobtrusively the attending behavior of college students. Does the researcher have an obligation to tell the students that their behavior is being recorded? If the students are aware of being observed, will this awareness change their behavior and invalidate the results? Such situations present ethical dilemmas, and the researcher must weigh the criteria listed above in order to determine the best course of action.

Legal Constraints

Most of the legal constraints placed on researchers since 1974 have focused on protecting the rights and the welfare of the subjects. These requirements are generally consistent with the ethical principles summarized above, and are in a constant state of reinterpretation and change by the courts.

The Family Educational Rights and Privacy Act of 1974, known as the Buckley Amendment, allows individuals to gain access to information pertaining to them, such as test scores, teacher comments, and recommendations. The act also provides that written permission of consent is legally necessary with data that identifies students by name. The consent must indicate the information that will be disclosed, the purpose of the disclosure, and to whom it will be disclosed. Exceptions to this requirement are granted for research using school records in which the results are of "legitimate educational interest," and when only group data are reported. It should be noted that data gathered in a study can usually be subpoenaed by the courts, even if confidentiality has been promised to the participants by the researcher.

The National Research Act of 1974 requires review of proposed research by an appropriate group in an institution (school division or university) to protect the rights and welfare of the subjects. While most research involving human subjects must be reviewed by such a group, there are some exceptions, such as research using test data that result from normal testing programs, or analyzing existing public data, records or documents without identifying individuals (see the January 26, 1981, *Federal Register,* published by the Department of Health and Human Services, for a complete listing of exemptions). It is advisable to have an authorized group, rather than an individual, review the research prior to conducting the study.

Summary

This chapter introduced the fundamental characteristics of designing quantitative research. We focused particular attention on selecting subjects and instruments and on variables that should be considered in designing and interpreting the research.

1. Research design refers to the way a study is planned and conducted.
2. The purpose of a good research design is to enhance the credibility of the results by taking into account three sources of variability: systematic, error, and extraneous.
3. Internally valid research controls potential sources of bias or error.
4. External validity refers to the generalizability of the results.
5. Randomization, holding factors constant, and statistical adjustments can be employed in quantitative studies to mitigate plausible rival hypotheses.
6. Probability sampling is used to be able to generalize to a larger population.
7. Probability sampling is done through simple random sampling, systematic sampling, stratified random sampling, and cluster sampling.
8. Nonprobability sampling includes purposeful, convenience, and quota types. While available and easily obtained, the use of such samples limits generalizability.
9. The size of the sample should be as large as possible without reaching a point at which additional subjects contribute little or no new information.
10. In order to have acceptable reliability and validity for the subjects used in the study, instruments should be chosen carefully. Validity is an estimate of the appropriateness of the use of scores and reliability is an indication of the consistency of the assessment.
11. Researchers should try to locate existing instruments before developing their own.
12. Threats to the internal validity of quantitative studies include selection, history, statistical regression, pretesting, instrumentation, subject attrition, maturation, diffusion of treatment, experimenter effects, treatment replications, subject effects, and statistical conclusion.
13. Threats to the external validity of quantitative studies are classified as population characteristics or ecological conditions.
14. The procedures section of a study should show how the information was collected in detail sufficient to allow other researchers to replicate or extend the study.

15. Researchers should be aware of ethical responsibilities and legal constraints that accompany the gathering and reporting of information.

Self-Instructional Review Exercises

Sample answers are in the back of the book.

Test Items

1. The purpose of research design is to
   a. select the instruments for a study.
   b. provide a valid, credible answer to a problem.
   c. determine the best type of statistical analysis.
   d. balance internal and external validity.
2. Bias in research
   a. answers research questions.
   b. provides control of extraneous variables.
   c. is error that affects the results.
   d. is always controlled.
3. Control of extraneous sources of error in quantitative research is provided by
   a. randomization of subjects.
   b. holding conditions constant.
   c. using factors as independent variables.
   d. all of the above.
4. Internal validity in quantitative research design is an assessment of
   a. the control of extraneous variables.
   b. the generalizability of the results.
   c. how well a test measures what it was intended to measure.
   d. the accuracy of the test.
5. If an unplanned event occurs while an experiment is being conducted and affects the results, _____ is a threat to the interpretation of the results.
   a. maturation
   b. regression
   c. pretesting
   d. history
6. Researchers assign subjects to groups randomly primarily to control for
   a. selection.
   b. maturation.
   c. regression.
   d. subject attrition.
7. Diffusion of treatment results when
   a. treatments are given to all subjects.
   b. one group knows about and is influenced by treatments other groups are receiving.
   c. the researcher effectively pretests the treatment.
   d. one group resents another.

8. External validity for quantitative research refers to
   a. the generalizability of the results.
   b. how well the research was done.
   c. the characteristics of the subjects.
   d. the use of research results in only the setting in which the experiment was done.
9. A sample in quantitative research is all of the following *except* for
   a. the group selected by the researcher.
   b. the group of subjects studied.
   c. the group to whom the researcher intends to generalize results.
   d. the group selected from a population.
10. A random sample
    a. must be as large as possible.
    b. is one in which every subject has an equal chance of being selected.
    c. is the same as randomization.
    d. is both b and c.
11. Stratified random sampling
    a. uses existing physical conditions in order to form groups.
    b. takes random samples from each subgroup.
    c. is less efficient than simple random sampling.
    d. needs more subjects than simple random sampling.
12. The degree to which the scores from a test are meaningful and appropriate is called
    a. validity.
    b. reliability.
    c. accuracy.
    d. stability.
13. The reliability of a test is an estimate of
    a. consistency.
    b. generalizability.
    c. what kind of error exists in the test.
    d. Both a and c are correct.
14. In the procedures section of most quantitative studies, there is an indication of
    a. where, when, and how the data were collected.
    b. who participated in the study.
    c. how the data were analyzed.
    d. Both a and b are correct.
15. Probability samples are
    a. usually proportional.
    b. used primarily in experimental research.
    c. drawn from a larger population.
    d. about the same as volunteer samples.
16. Informed consent is
    a. required for all research.
    b. providing subjects with a choice to be involved in research.

c. the same as debriefing subjects.

d. a procedure to allow subjects to see the results of the study.

Application Problems

1. For each case described here, list potential threats to internal and external validity.

   a. Two researchers designed a study to investigate whether physical education performance is affected by being in a class with students of the same sex only or in a class with both sexes. A college instructor is found to cooperate with the researchers. Three sections of the same tennis class are offered, an all-male section, an all-female section, and a mixed section. The researchers control the instructor variable by using the same person as the instructor for each section, informing the instructor about the study and emphasizing to the instructor the need to keep instructional activities the same for each section. One section is offered in the morning, one at noon, and one in the afternoon. Students sign up for the course by using the same procedure as for all courses, though there is a footnote about the gender composition in the schedule of courses. A pretest is given to control for existing differences in the groups.

   b. In this study the effect of day care on children's prosocial behavior is examined. A group of volunteer parents agree to participate in the study (the investigators pay part of the day care fees). Children are assigned randomly from the pool of volunteers either to attend a day care of their choice or not to attend. Observers measure the degree of prosocial behavior before and after attending day care for nine months by observing the children on a playground.

   c. A superintendent wishes to get some idea of whether or not a bond issue will pass in a forthcoming election. Records listing real estate taxpayers are obtained from the county office. From this list a random sample of 10 percent of 3,000 persons is called by phone two weeks before election day and asked whether they intend to vote yes or no.

   d. The Green County School Board decided that it wanted a status assessment of the ninth graders' attitudes toward science. A questionnaire was designed and distributed in January to all ninth-grade science teachers. Each teacher was told to give the questionnaire within six weeks, calculate mean scores for each question, and return the questionnaires and results to the district office. The instructors were told to take only one class period for the questionnaires in order to minimize interference with the course. Sixty percent of the questionnaires were returned.

Descriptive Statistics

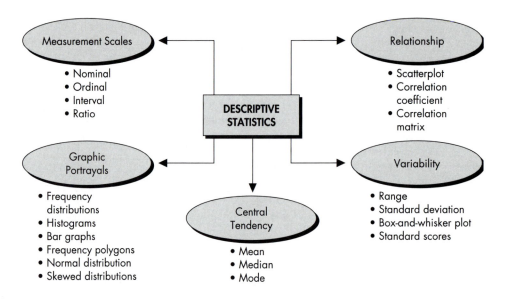

KEY TERMS

statistics

descriptive statistics

inferential statistics

measurement scales

nominal

ordinal

interval

ratio

frequency distribution

histogram

bar graph

frequency polygon

measures of central tendency

mean

median

mode

normal distribution

skewed

positively skewed

negatively skewed

measures of variability

range

standard deviation

percentile rank

variance

box-and-whisker plot

standard scores

z-score

scatterplot

positive relationship

negative relationship

correlation coefficient

intercorrelation matrix

This chapter explains some common statistical procedures that are used to describe instrument reliability and validity and to report data in a quantitative study. The procedures represent parsimonious ways to summarize and organize data that have been collected. The most frequently used descriptive statistical procedures (those that describe phenomena) are presented, including frequency distributions, measures of central tendency, measures of variability, and measures of relationship. The reasons for using each procedure are discussed, with examples from published articles to illustrate how results are reported.

Introduction to Descriptive Statistics

Quantitative research relies heavily on numbers in reporting results, sampling, and providing estimates of instrument reliability and validity. The numbers are usually accompanied by unrecognized strange words and even stranger symbols and are manipulated by something called *statistics*. Like magic, statistics lead to conclusions. Often, readers of research simply prefer to skip over anything related to statistics. In the words of a prominent specialist in educational measurement: "For most educators, mere contemplation of the term 'statistics' conjures up images akin to bubonic plague and the abolition of tenure" (Popham, 1981, p. 66).

Even though some statisticians may like the image just described, in truth the fundamental concepts and principles of statistics are readily comprehensible. Skill in mathematics is not a prerequisite to an understanding of statistics, and there is no need to memorize complex formulas. In fact, learning about statistics can be fun, especially considering the great new words learned that are perfect for impressing friends and family!

More seriously, there are important reasons for all educators to gain a functional command of statistical principles:

1. To understand and critique professional articles (for example, were appropriate statistical tools used?).
2. To improve evaluation of student learning.
3. To conduct, even in modest and informal ways, research studies (for example, how should the results be analyzed?).
4. To understand evaluations of programs, personnel, and policies.
5. To help become better equipped as a citizen and consumer, making decisions based on quantitative data or arguments.
6. To upgrade the education profession by providing standard skills to communicate, debate, and discuss research that has implications for educational practice.

Types of Statistics

Statistics are methods of organizing and analyzing quantitative data. These methods are tools designed to help the researcher organize and interpret numbers derived from measuring a trait or variable. The mere presence of statistical procedures does not ensure high quality in the research. While the contribution of some results does depend on applying the correct statistical procedure, the quality of the research depends most on proper conceptualization, design, subject selection, instruments, and procedures. Statistics is an international language that only manipulates numbers. Statistics and numbers do not interpret themselves, and the meaning of the statistics is derived from the research design. Of course, the improper use of statistics invalidates the research, but the interpretation of statistical results depends on carefully designing and conducting the study—that is, it depends heavily on producing high-quality quantitative data.

There are two broad categories of statistical techniques: descriptive and inferential. **Descriptive statistics** transform a set of numbers or observations into indices that describe or characterize the data. Descriptive statistics (sometimes referred to as *summary statistics*) are thus used to summarize, organize, and reduce large numbers of observations. Usually the reduction results in a few numbers, derived from mathematical formulas to represent all observations in each group of interest. Descriptive statistics portray and focus on *what is* with respect to the sample data, for example: "What is the average reading grade level of the fifth graders in the school?" "How many teachers found the in-service valuable?" "What percentage of students want to go to college?" and "What is the relationship between socioeconomic status of children and the effectiveness of token reinforcers?" The use of descriptive statistics is the most fundamental way to summarize data, and it is indispensable in interpreting the results of quantitative research.

Inferential statistics, on the other hand, are used to make inferences or predictions about the similarity of a sample to the population from which the sample is drawn. Since many research questions require the estimation of population characteristics from an available sample of subjects or behavior, inferential statistics are commonly used in reporting results. Chapter 11 discusses in greater detail the function and types of inferential statistics. Inferential statistics depend on descriptive statistics. Without a complete understanding of descriptive statistics, therefore, inferential statistics make very little sense. Figure 7.1 illustrates the relationship between descriptive and inferential statistics. It shows how a researcher would first take a sample from a population, use descriptive statistics to describe the sample, and then use inferential statistics to estimate the true value of the test score for the population.

There are many types of descriptive statistics that researchers may choose in characterizing a set of data. The choice usually depends on two factors: the type of measurement scale employed and the purpose of the research. The measurement scale is usually noted and, as indicated in the next section, there are descriptive statistical techniques that correspond to each scale. The purpose of the research, or research problem, actually depends on a knowledge of different statistical techniques, since each technique offers information for answering particular kinds of questions. Hence, each of the common descriptive techniques is presented here, with examples of the research problems it addresses.

Scales of Measurement

Measurement in education usually involves assigning numbers to things in order to differentiate one thing from another. Unlike measurement of physical phenomena, however, such as weight, density, or length, researchers can use numbers in different ways for investigating problems. These different ways are

FIGURE 7.1   Relationship of Descriptive to Inferential Statistics

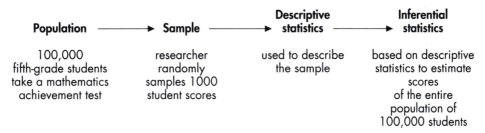

based on four properties of numbers. The four properties are these: numbers can be distinct from one another (for example, 10 is different from 13; 0 is different from -5); numbers are relative to one another (for example, 13 is larger than 10; -3 less than 0); numbers can be related to each other in identified units (for example, 10 is five units of 2 greater than 5); and numbers can be related proportionately (for example, 10 is twice as large as 5; 25 is to 5 as 30 is to 6). These properties, in turn, determine what psychometricians refer to as **measurement scales** or levels of measurement. There are four measurement scales: nominal, ordinal, interval, and ratio. These terms are often used to describe the nature of the measure, indicating, for example, that a "nominal measure" or "nominal measurement" was used.

Nominal   The first and most rudimentary level of measurement is called **nominal**, or *categorical*, or *classificatory*. The word *nominal* implies *name*, which describes what this scale accomplishes—a naming of mutually exclusive categories of people, events, or other phenomena. Common examples of nominal levels include classifying on the basis of eye color, gender, political party affiliation, and type of reading group. The groups are simply names to differentiate them, no order is implied (one group does not come before or after another), and there is no indication of the way the groups differ from each other. Often researchers assign numbers to the different groups (for example, yes = 1, no = 2, maybe = 3), but this is only for convenient coding of the groups in analyzing the data. Nominal data result in categorical variables and results are reported as frequencies in each category.

Ordinal   The second type of measurement scale is called **ordinal**, and, as the name implies, measurement of this type assumes that categories of the variable can theoretically be rank-ordered from highest to lowest. Each value can thus be related to others as being equal to, greater than, or less than. In other words, there is an inherent order to the categories. Examples of ordinal measurement include ranking class members by means of grade point average, ranking ideas from most important to least important, and use of percentile ranks on achievement tests.

Interval   Interval measures share characteristics of ordinal scales and, in addition, indicate equal intervals between each category. Interval scales give meaning to the difference between numbers by providing a constant unit of measurement. The difference or interval between 5 and 6, for example, is the same as the difference between 18 and 19. Percentile scores associated with the normal curve, for example, are not interval because the distance between percentile points varies depending on the percentiles compared. There is a greater difference between extreme percentiles (for example, 2nd and 3rd or 95th and 96th) than percentiles near the middle of the distribution. Examples of interval scales include Fahrenheit and Centigrade temperatures and most standardized achievement test scores.

Ratio **Ratio** scales represent the most refined type of measurement. Ratio scales are ordinal and interval, and in addition, the numbers can be compared by ratios: that is, a number can be compared meaningfully by saying it is twice or three times another number, or one-half or one-fourth of a number. Such observations as distance attained, strength expressed as weight lifted, or times in the mile run are ratio scale measurements. Most measurement in education, however, is not expressed as a ratio. Educators think in terms of less than or greater than, not multiples (for example, a student is more cooperative or less cooperative, not twice as cooperative or half as cooperative).

While it is not always easy to identify the scale of measurement of some variables, it is important to distinguish between nominal and "higher" levels. The use of many of the more common statistical procedures, such as the mean and variance, usually requires an interval or ratio scale of measurement, although an ordinal scale is often acceptable. The choice of other, more advanced statistical procedures depends on whether the data are nominal or in the higher levels. If, for example, a researcher wants to compare minority and nonminority students on the basis of their choices of careers, the data are nominal and certain statistical procedures would be appropriate for analyzing the data. If, on the other hand, these same students were being compared on achievement or attitudes toward school, a different set of statistical procedures would be appropriate because the scale of the achievement and attitude data is ordinal or interval. These differences will be discussed further in Chapter 11.

Figure 7.2 summarizes the characteristics and provides further examples of the four scales of measurement.

FIGURE 7.2 **Measurement Scales**

Scale	Scale Characteristics	Examples
RATIO	Numbers represent equal amounts from an absolute zero. Scores can be compared as ratios or percentages.	Age, dollars, time, speed, class size
INTERVAL	Equal differences between numbers represent equal differences in the variable or attribute being measured.	Year (A.D.), °F, °C
ORDINAL	Numbers represent rank order of the variable being measured.	Any ranked variable, percentile norms, social class
NOMINAL	Numbers distinguish among the categories. Numbers do not represent quantity or degree. Assignment of numbers to groups is arbitrary.	Sex, ethnicity, political party, personality type

Source: Glass, G. V., & Hopkins, K. D. (1996). *Statistical Methods in Education and Psychology.* (3rd Ed.) Needham Heights, MA: Allyn & Bacon.

Graphic Portrayals of Data

When data are collected the observations must be organized so that the researcher can easily and correctly interpret the results. This section presents three common methods to represent group data.

Frequency Distribution: A Picture of a Group

In most studies there are many different scores, and if these scores are arrayed (arranged) without regard to their values, as in Table 7.1, it is difficult to make sense out of the data. The simplest organization of the scores would be to list them from highest to lowest and create what is called a rank-order distribution. The rank-order distribution is transformed to a **frequency distribution** by indicating the number of times each score was attained, as indicated in Table 7.2.

It is also common to combine scores into class intervals and tally the number of scores in each interval, as indicated in Table 7.3. Intervals are especially useful for data in which few of the numbers are the same (such as ranking of states on median income). Since the grouped frequency distributions only indicate the total number of scores within each interval, a *stem-and-leaf* display is occasionally used to show the actual scores in the interval. The "stems" are the score intervals. They are typically listed vertically, and for each stem a row is included that shows the scores.

Frequency distributions are very useful for answering many important questions. They indicate quickly the most and least frequently occurring scores; the general shape of the distribution (for example, clusters of scores at certain places or scores spread out evenly) and whether any scores are isolated from the others.

TABLE 7.1

Unorganized Examination Scores of Fifty Students

47	37	41	50	45
39	49	44	43	40
42	43	42	46	40
44	45	47	45	45
36	45	46	48	44
42	48	40	43	37
46	45	45	44	42
43	43	42	43	41
44	45	42	44	36
44	38	44	46	42

TABLE 7.2

Frequency Distribution of Scores in Table 7.1

Scores in Rank Order	Tallies	Frequency (f)
50	1	1
49	1	1
48	11	2
47	11	2
46	1111	4
45	⅃⅂⅂⅂ 111	8
44	⅃⅂⅂⅂ 111	8
43	⅃⅂⅂⅂ 1	6
42	⅃⅂⅂⅂ 11	7
41	11	2
40	111	3
39	1	1
38	1	1
37	11	2
36	11	2
		n = 50

Histograms and Bar Graphs

Frequency data are often effectively displayed pictorially. One type of illustration uses columns in a two-dimensional graph to represent the frequency of occurrence of each score or interval. This way of presenting a frequency distribution is called a **histogram.** The data from Tables 7.1 and 7.2 are presented as a histogram in Figure 7.3. In this example, the vertical dimension on the graph

TABLE 7.3

Interval Frequency Distribution of Scores in Table 7.1

Class Interval	Frequency (f)
48–50	4
45–47	14
42–44	21
39–41	6
36–38	5
	n = 50

FIGURE 7.3   Histogram of Scores from Table 7.1

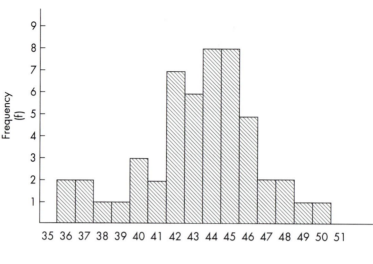

Scores

lists the frequencies of the scores, and the horizontal dimension rank-orders the scores from lowest to highest. The columns are drawn in the graph to correspond with the results. In similar fashion, Excerpt 7.1 shows how histograms can depict results in an article.

A **bar graph** looks very much like a histogram, with columns that present an image of the findings. In a bar graph, however, the ordering of the columns is arbitrary, whereas in a histogram there is an order from least to most. Bar graphs are used, then, with nominal variables such as gender, state, political party affiliation, and similar categorical variables that have no implied order. A bar graph is illustrated in Excerpt 7.2.

Histograms are effective because they provide an easily comprehended image of results. However, the image may be distorted by manipulating the spacing of numbers along the vertical dimension of the graph. The intervals between score frequencies can vary, and the size of the units that are used can be changed to give different images. For example, a crafty researcher can make a very small difference appear great by increasing the space between measurement units. Consider the two graphs in Figure 7.4. Each graph has summarized the same data, but the visual results are different.

Frequency Polygons

Another way to illustrate a frequency distribution is to use a **frequency polygon**. A frequency polygon is very similar to a bar graph except that single points rather than bars are graphed and these points are then connected by a line.

FIGURE 7.4   Graphs of Reading Scores of First, Second, and Third Graders

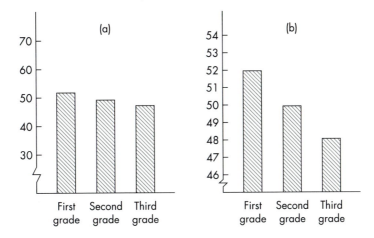

Figure 7.5 shows our example data in a frequency polygon. Notice that this representation is very similar to Figure 7.3.

Finally, it is also useful to represent the distribution graphically by curving the straight lines of a frequency polygon. The well-known normal curve, discussed later in this chapter, is an example of using this technique.

FIGURE 7.5   Frequency Polygon of Scores from Table 7.1

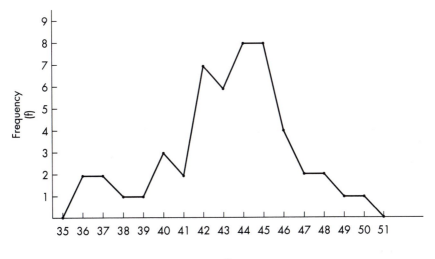

EXCERPT 7.1

HISTOGRAM

A histogram of the distribution of word recognition scores is presented in Figure 1. Subjects were divided into two groups. Those who learned the sounds in fewer than 10 trials are represented in white, those who took 10 or more trials, in black. From this figure, it is clear that there is very little overlap between the two groups of subjects. Those with large printed word repertoires learned the sounds easily. Those with small repertoires did not.

FIGURE 1   Distribution of good and poor sound learners on the printed-word identification task in Experiment 1.
(PA 5 paired-associate learning)

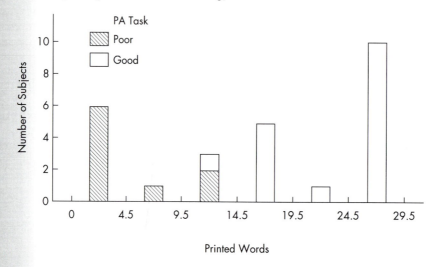

Source: From Ehri, L. C., & Wilce, L. S., "The mnemonic value of orthography among beginning readers," *Journal of Educational Psychology, 71*, 26–40. Copyright © 1979 by the American Psychological Association. Reprinted by permission of Linnea Carlson Ehri.

Measures of Central Tendency

For most sets of data it is useful to get some idea of the typical or average score or observation in addition to knowing the frequency distribution. While the word *average* has many connotations, in research only the mean refers to the average score. Two other indices, the median and the mode, also provide information about typical scores of a group. Together, these three indices are referred

EXCERPT 7.2

BAR GRAPH

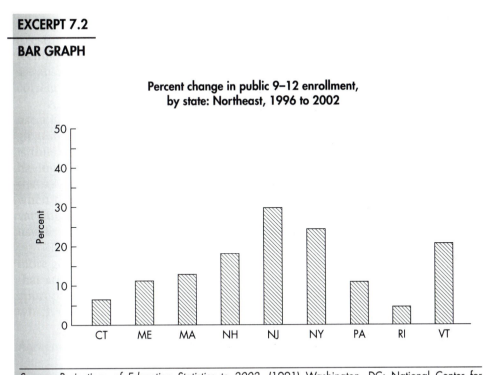

Percent change in public 9–12 enrollment, by state: Northeast, 1996 to 2002

Source: Projections of Education Statistics to 2002. (1991) Washington, DC: National Center for Education Statistics

to as **measures of central tendency.** Each provides a numerical index of the typical score of a distribution. (Calculations for these and other descriptive statistics can be found in Appendix B.)

The Mean

The **mean** (symbolized by $\overline{X}$ or M) is simply the arithmetic average of all the scores. It is calculated by summing all the scores and then dividing the sum by the number of scores. If, for example, we have a distribution of 5, 8, 9, and 2, the mean is 6 (5 + 8 + 9 + 2 = 24; 24 ÷ 4 = 6). The mean is the most frequently used measure of central tendency because every score is used in computing it. The weakness of the mean is that when a distribution contains extremely high or low scores, those very untypical of the rest of the distribution, the mean is pulled toward the extreme score. If, for example, a distribution contained scores of 4, 5, 7, and 40, the mean would be 14. Since in this case most of the scores are considerably lower than 14, the mean is somewhat misleading with respect to central tendency.

EXCERPT 7.3

THE MEAN

The means for the three testing periods are given in Table 3. They show a decrease in the number and percentage of cross-racial friendship choices in the control class from pre- to posttest and an increase over that period in the experimental class.

TABLE 3   Follow-up Sociometric Measures

| Measure | Mean Number of Friendship Choices | | | | | |
| | Control[a] | | | Experimental[b] | | |
	Pretest	Posttest	Follow-up	Pretest	Posttest	Follow-up
Within-race	5.95	6.37	7.35	4.00	3.77	4.00
Cross-race	2.65	1.58	.80	1.62	2.73	2.44
Percentage	30.8	19.9	9.8	28.8	37.2	37.9

[a]n = 20. [b]n = 16.

Source: From Slavin, R. E. (1979). Effects of biracial learning teams on cross-racial friendships. *Journal of Educational Psychology, 71.* Reprinted by permission of the author.

The mean is frequently reported in quantitative research reports and is essential to the interpretation of results in which groups are compared with each other. Excerpt 7.3 illustrates the use of means in an article.

The Median

The **median** is that point which divides a rank-ordered distribution into halves that have an equal number of scores. Fifty percent of the scores thus lie below the median and 50 percent of the scores above it. The median is unaffected by the actual values of the scores. This is an advantage when a distribution contains atypically large or small scores. For example, the median of the set of scores 10, 15, 16, 19, and 105 is 16, since half the scores are above 16 and half below. Sixteen would thus be a better indicator of central tendency than the mean, which is 33. If a distribution contains an even number of scores, the median is the midpoint between the two middle scores (for example, for the scores 2, 2, 4, 7, 8, and 12, the median is 5.5).

The median is used to describe data that may have extreme scores, such as income level in the United States. Medians also are often employed to divide one group of respondents into two groups of equal numbers. A researcher may, for example, get an indication of perceived degree of success from each respondent on a 7-point scale (extreme success = 7, extreme failure = 1). If the researcher wanted to divide the group of subjects into those with high and low

EXCERPT 7.4

THE MEDIAN

One trend in families that has clear implications for educational needs within urban communities is the decrease in financial resources that all families are now experiencing, with an even greater impact in ethnic minority urban families. The latest reported nationwide median income of white families was $18,370, for Hispanics $12,570, and for Blacks $10,880 (ACYF, 1980). While 16% of all children are below the poverty level, a Black child has a 4-times greater chance of being under this level, for 11% of whites and 42% of Blacks live in poverty (Edelman, 1980).

Single mothers had median incomes that were much lower than the total and that earned by two-parent families; Black mothers had a median income that was only 40% that of the two-parent families; Hispanics had 39%, and white mothers had 38% of the two-parent incomes. The lower proportion of white mothers is due to the fact that almost half of white mothers do not work, in spite of the marked increase of white urban employment (see Table 1).

TABLE 1   Median Income and Percentage of Ethnic Groups Unemployed and Below Poverty Line

Year		Black	Hispanic	White
1977	Husband, wife, family	13,832	13,432	18,756
	Single mothers	5,598	5,247	8,799
1978		10,880	12,570	18,370

Source: From McAdoo, H. P., (1981) Youth, school, and the family in transition, *Urban Education, 16,* 261–277. Copyright © 1981 by Urban Education. Reprinted by permission of Sage Publications, Inc.

self-perceptions of success, the median could be used. This procedure is called a *median-split technique*. Excerpt 7.4 shows how the median can be used in reporting research.

The Mode

The **mode** is simply the score that occurs most frequently in a distribution. The mode is a crude index of central tendency and is rarely used in educational research. It is useful only when there is an interest in knowing the most common score or observation or when the data are in nominal form. The word *mode* is used more frequently, perhaps, to describe a distribution by indicating that the distribution is bimodal (two modes) or trimodal (three modes). These terms are used even when, technically, there is only one mode but at least two scores that have definitely higher frequencies than the rest.

Relationships among Measures of Central Tendency

As long as a distribution of scores is relatively symmetrical, the mean, median, and mode will be about the same. In what is referred to as a **normal distribution**, these indices are exactly the same. The normal distribution (see Figure 7.11 on page 227) forms a bell-shaped symmetrical curve. The normal curve is the theoretical distribution that is used to transform data and calculate many statistics. While many educational variables—for example, large numbers of achievement scores—are normally distributed, the data from a single research study may be distributed unevenly; that is, the distributions are unsymmetrical, and the scores tend to bunch up at one end of the distribution or the other. Such distributions are called **skewed**, and with skewed distributions the choice of measure of central tendency becomes more important. Distributions are **positively skewed** if most of the scores are at the low end of the distribution with a few high scores, and **negatively skewed** if most scores are located at the high end. To remember the difference between positive and negative skew, think of the curved shape of the distribution forming an arrow or a pointer. If it forms an arrow that points in a positive or higher direction, the distribution is positively skewed, and if in a negative or lower direction, the distribution is negatively skewed. That is, using the median or mode as reference point, the mean is higher in a positively skewed distribution and lower in a negatively skewed distribution. Actually, you can think of the mean as being either positively or negatively skewed in relation to the median. In Figure 7.6 positively and negatively skewed distributions are illustrated with corresponding means, medians, and modes. Notice that the mean in each distribution is farther toward the tail of the distribution than the median or mode, and the mode is farthest from the tail.

To further illustrate this relationship, consider the following example. Suppose a teacher wants to report an average reading score for his class. He has a reading score for each of 20 students, ranging from 5 to 80. The distribution of scores is represented in Table 7.4.

FIGURE 7.6 Skewed Distributions

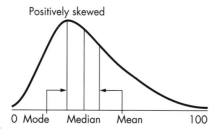
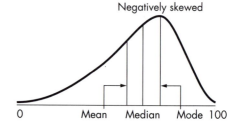

Positively skewed

0 Mode   Median   Mean   100

Negatively skewed

0   Mean   Median   Mode 100

TABLE 7.4

Frequency Distribution of Reading Scores

Scores	(f)
5	8
10	4
12	2
15	2
80	4
	n = 20

If the teacher reports the average as the mean, it would be 22.7. The median is 10, and the mode is 5. Which is correct? Because of a few students who scored very well (80) the distribution is positively skewed, and hence the median is probably the most accurate single indicator. In such cases, however, it is probably best to report the mean for the students who scored between 5 and 15 (8.4) and report the four high scores separately, or to report both the mean and the median. Since many distributions in education are at least somewhat skewed, it is often best to report both the mean and median.

Measures of Variability

Central tendency is only one index used to represent a group of scores. In order to provide a full description, a second statistical measure is also needed. This statistic is referred to as a measure of variability. **Measures of variability** show how spread out the distribution of scores is from the mean of the distribution, or how much, on the average, scores differ from the mean. Variability measures are also referred to in general terms as measures of *dispersion, scatter,* or *spread.*

The need for a measure of dispersion is illustrated in Figure 7.7. This figure shows how two classrooms with the same mean score can actually be very different. In class B the students are rather homogeneous, similar to each other, with few high- or low-achieving students. In class A, however, the teacher has a great range of achievement, a heterogeneous group of students whose scores spread from 55 to 100.

Or suppose a person is going to bet on Saturday's basketball game between the Bombers and the Dunkers. The sports section of the newspaper lacks the statistics on individual players, but the sports writer reports that both teams have approximately equal height: the average height is 6' 6 1/2" and 6' 7 1/2", respectively, for the Bombers and Dunkers. With only the mean to help decide,

FIGURE 7.7   Score Dispersion

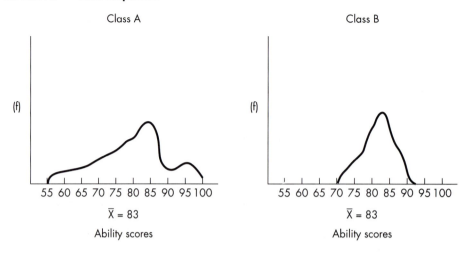

the bettor places a bet on the Dunkers. When the bettor sees the program with the heights of the players, he or she discovers a shortcoming of the mean.

Bombers	Dunkers
Leary, guard—6'0"	Regen, guard—6'5"
Burns, guard—6'3"	Lambiotte, guard—6'6"
Parker, forward—6'5"	Hambrick, forward—6'8"
Gallagher, forward—6'7"	Lang, forward—6'9"
Robinson, center—7'3"	Wergin, center—6'10"
$\bar{X}$ = 6'6½"	$\bar{X}$ = 6'7½"

As the Bombers' offense proceeds to take advantage of Robinson's height over Wergin's to score, the bettor realizes that the mean fails to tell about the characteristics of the distribution. The Dunkers have little variability, while the Bombers have high variability, and so the bettor loses the bet!

Variability, then, tells us about the difference between the scores of the distribution. While we can use such words as *high, low, great, little,* and *much* to describe the degree of variability, it is necessary to have more precise indices. Two common measures of variability are range and standard deviation.

The Range

The **range** is the most obvious measure of dispersion. It is simply the difference between the highest and lowest scores in the distribution. If, for example, the lowest of 30 scores on a test was 65 and the highest score 90, the range would be 25 (90 − 65 = 25). Since there are only two scores involved in calculating the range, it is very simple to obtain. However, it is also a very crude measure of dispersion, and can be misleading if there is an atypically high or low score. The range also fails to indicate anything about the variability of scores around the mean of the distribution. Sometimes researchers will use the *interquartile range,* which indicates the dispersion among the middle half of the scores.

Standard Deviation

The **standard deviation** is a numerical index that indicates the average variability of the scores. It tells us, in other words, about the distance, on the average, of the scores from the mean. A distribution that has a relatively heterogeneous set of scores that spread out widely from the mean (for example, Class A of Figure 7.7) will have a larger standard deviation than a homogeneous set of scores that cluster around the mean (Class B of Figure 7.7). The first step in calculating the standard deviation (abbreviated *SD, σ* [sigma], or *s*) is to find the distance between each score and the mean (see Figure 7.8), thus determining the amount that each score deviates, or differs, from the mean. In one sense, the standard deviation is simply the average of all the deviation scores, the average distance of the scores from the mean.

For any set of scores, then, a standard deviation can be computed that will be unique to the distribution and indicates the amount, on the average, that the set of scores deviates from the mean. (Appendix B reviews the steps for computing the standard deviation. The steps are not complex.) The most common convention in reporting the standard deviation is to indicate that one standard deviation is equal to some number (for example, *SD* = 15.0; σ = 3.40). One standard deviation added to and subtracted from the mean has a special meaning; it tells us about the distance that most, but not all, of the scores are from the mean. For example, 68 percent of the scores will fall within the first standard deviation with a normal distribution. This property of standard deviation is illustrated in Figure 7.9, where 1 *SD* = 5. Notice that on both sides of the mean (15) there is a line that designates −1 *SD* and +1 *SD*. The negative and positive directions from the mean are equivalent in score

FIGURE 7.8   Illustration of Distance of Each Score from the Mean

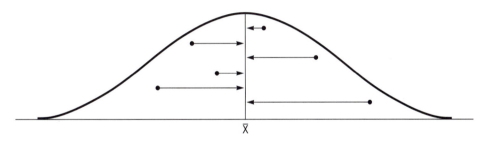

$\overline{X}$

FIGURE 7.9   Relation of Standard Deviation to Percentile Rank in a Normal Distribution

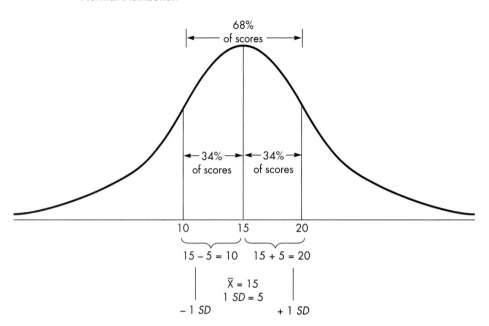

units (that is, both − and +1 *SD* = 5 units) and between −1 and +1 *SD* there are about 68 percent of the total number of scores in the distribution. If we assume that the distribution is normal, then 50 percent of the scores are above the mean and 50 percent below the mean. Now, since we know there is an equal number of scores on either side of the mean, we know that 34 percent of the scores must be between the mean and − or + 1 *SD*, and if 50 percent of the scores are below the mean and we add 34 percent by going up +1 *SD*, then we know that about 84 percent of the scores of the distribution are below +1 *SD*. Similarly, if we subtract 34 from 50, we know that 16 percent of the scores are below −1 *SD*.

When we indicate that a certain percentage of the scores is at or below a particular score, we are referring to the **percentile rank** of the score. If, for example, a score of 38 is at the 87th percentile, it means that 87 percent of the scores are the same as or lower than 38. In other words, only 12 percent of the scores are higher than 38. With normal distributions +1 *SD* is always at the 84th percentile, and −1 *SD* is at the 16th percentile.

The interpretation of 1 *SD* is always the same with regard to the percentage of scores within certain points of a normal distribution. Because the numerical units used to represent scores change, however, the standard deviation can equal 15 in one distribution and .32 in another distribution. Or, in a circumstance with the same numerical units but two different distributions,

FIGURE 7.10   Comparison of Distributions with Different Standard Deviations

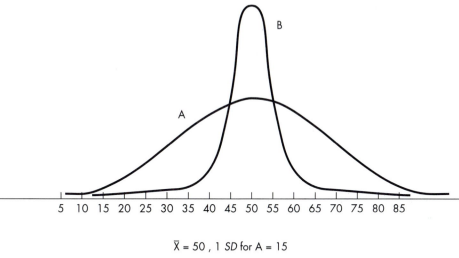

$$\bar{X} = 50 \, , \, 1 \; SD \text{ for A} = 15$$

$$\bar{X} = 50 \, , \, 1 \; SD \text{ for B} = 5$$

the standard deviations will be unique to each distribution. That is, one *SD* has a meaning that is constant for any distribution regardless of the actual value of 1 *SD* for each distribution. For example, in Figure 7.10 two distributions are illustrated. Distribution A has a large standard deviation, B a small one; a score of 65 in distribution A has the same percentile rank as 55 in distribution B.

Along with the mean, the standard deviation is an excellent way to indicate the nature of the distribution of a set of scores. Standard deviation is typically reported in research with the mean. A measure of dispersion related to the standard deviation is termed the **variance** of a distribution (noted by σ^2 or s^2; thus the standard deviation is equal to the square root of the variance). The term *variance,* however, is usually used as a general term in regard to dispersion (for example, in stating that the variance is large or small) and is rarely reported as a specific number to indicate variability.

In Excerpts 7.5 and 7.6 there are examples of the way standard deviation can be reported. Standard deviations are almost always reported along with means. In Excerpt 7.5, for each of several factors used in grading students, there is a mean and standard deviation for middle school teachers, a mean and standard deviation for high school teachers, and means and standard deviations for the total sample. Notice how the values of standard deviation range from .76 to 1.32, showing different degrees of variance. Means at the ends of the scale are associated with smaller standard deviations. In Likert-type scales such as this one, standard deviations about 1 are typical. In Excerpt 7.6, the standard deviations are in parentheses.

EXCERPT 7.5

STANDARD DEVIATION

TABLE 12   Means and Standard Deviations of Items of Factors Used in Grading Practices by Secondary Teachers[1]

Factors	Middle (N = 630)		High (N = 846)		Total (N = 1476)	
	Mean	SD	Mean	SD	Mean	SD
Disruptive student performance	1.5	.83	1.60	.91	1.56	.88
Improve since the beginning of the year	2.86	1.14	2.83	1.12	2.85	1.13
Student effort—how much the student tried to learn	3.31	1.13	3.16	1.10	3.23	1.11
Ability levels of the students	3.38	1.33	3.43	1.28	3.41	1.30
Work habits and neatness	2.80	1.07	2.68	1.06	2.73	1.07
Completion of homework (not graded)	3.02	1.06	2.95	1.12	2.98	1.10
Quality of completed homework (graded)	3.18	1.15	3.22	1.14	3.20	1.15
Academic performance as opposed to other factors	4.37	1.08	4.34	1.09	4.35	1.08
Performance compared to other students in the class	2.06	1.13	2.23	1.18	2.16	1.17
Performance compared to a set scale of percentage correct	4.44	1.24	4.45	1.31	4.43	1.29
Specific learning objectives mastered	4.38	.92	4.35	.91	4.37	.92
Degree to which the student pays attention and/or participages in class	3.12	1.11	3.20	1.12	3.17	1.12
Inclusion of 0s in determining final percentage correct	3.61	1.29	3.90	1.32	3.77	1.12
Extra credit for nonacademic performance	1.54	.86	1.49	.76	1.51	.80
Extra credit for academic performance	2.66	1.18	2.54	1.06	2.60	1.11

[1]A six point scale was used, where 1 = not at all and 6 = completely..

Source: McMillan, J. H., & Workman, D. (1998). Teachers' Classroom Assessment and Grading Practices. Richmond, VA: Metropolitan Educational Research Consortium and Virginia Commonwealth University.

Box-and-Whisker Plot

The **box-and-whisker plot** is used to give a picture or image of the variability. A "box" is formed for each variable. The size of this rectangular box is determined by the first and third quartiles of the distribution (25th to 75th percentile). The "whiskers" are lines drawn from the ends of the rectangle to the 10th and 90th

EXCERPT 7.6

STANDARD DEVIATION

Means and Standard Deviations for All Variables

Dependent Variables		
Any science career	4.40	(1.55)
Physical science professions[1]	4.24	(1.79)
Health science professions	4.56	(2.01)
Human services professions	4.22	(1.77)
Independent Variables		
Science GPA[2]	3.66	(.48)
Friends' support	5.69	(1.08)
Number of science/math activities[3]	1.73	(1.32)
Number of nonscience activities[4]	9.74	(3.67)
Mothers' perceptions of child's science ability	6.10	(1.05)
Mothers' valuing of science for females	4.57	(1.04)
Adolescents' interest in biology	5.10	(1.43)
Adolescent's interest in physical science	4.75	(1.40)

[1]Professional includes jobs requiring bachelor's degrees and advanced degrees. [2]Range = 1–4.
[3]Range = 0–5. [4]Range = 2–21.

Source: From Jacobs, J. E., Finken, L. L., Griffin, N. L., & Wright, J. D. (1998). The career plans of science-talented rural adolescent girls. *American Educational Research Journal, 35*(4), 681–704..

percentiles. Sometimes additional points are included to show extreme high or low scores. The box-and-whisker plot in Excerpt 7.7 shows how U.S. student achievement in mathematics compares with Japanese student achievement. Notice the wider variation of the achievement of U.S. students.

Standard Scores

You may have observed that it is cumbersome to analyze several distributions if the means and standard deviations are different for each distribution. To alleviate this problem and expedite interpretation, the raw score distributions are often converted to standard scores. **Standard scores** have constant normative or relative meaning. They are scores that are obtained from the mean and standard deviation of the raw score distribution.

Because, as we have seen, a normal distribution has certain properties that are useful for comparing a person's score with those of others, by converting to normalized standard scores the normal curve properties can be assumed. Thus, raw score distributions with different means and standard deviations that are difficult to compare can be transformed to the same standard scores

EXCERPT 7.7

BOX-AND-WHISKER PLOT

Given the differences in the patterns of coverage of algebra between these U.S. course types, what happens when U.S. achievement in algebra is disaggregated by course type? Figure 3 presents such a disaggregation for class-level posttest scores—extended to include the parallel posttest achievement for Japan—and shows a striking pattern.

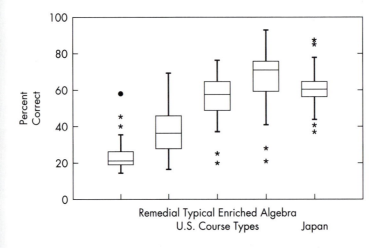

FIGURE 3. United States and Japan: Posttest achievement in population A algebra. (*Note:* In boxplots like those found in Figures 3, 4, and 5, the length of the box, the rectangle bounded by the "hinges," represents the proportion of the distribution that falls between the 25th and 75th percentiles. The line across the box represents the median. The length of the "whiskers" represents the min and the max or the adjacent outermost value,

$$1.5 = (pctile_{75} - pctile_{25}),$$

If this is less than the min and the max. The * and the ● represent extreme values.

Source: Westbury, I. (1992). Comparing American and Japanese achievement: Is the United States really a low achiever? *Educational Researcher, 21*(5), 18–24.

and compared easily. Since standard scores are linear transformations, it is conceivable that a small raw score difference is exaggerated when converted to standard scores. For example, the Scholastic Assessment Test has a standard score mean of 500 and standard deviation of 100, while the raw scores are much lower. Thus, a raw score difference of 2 or 3 questions may result in a standard score difference of 10 to 20 "points."

FIGURE 7.11   Normal Curve, Standard Deviations, Percentiles, and Selected Standard Scores

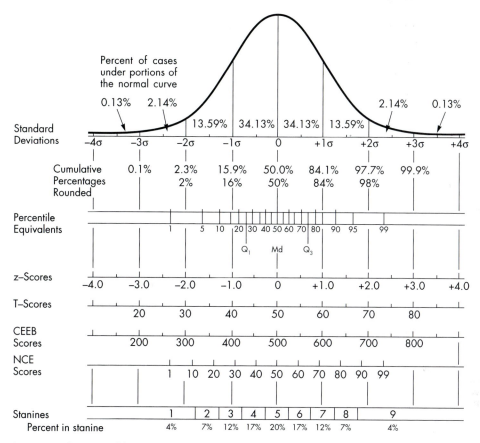

Source: Seashore, Harold G. (1980). Methods of expressing test scores, in *Test Service Notebook 148.* New York: The Psychological Corporation.

The **z-score** is the most basic standard score, with a mean of 0 and a standard deviation of 1. Thus, a z-score of +1 is at the 84th percentile for a normal distribution, −1 is at the 16th percentile, and −2 is at the 2nd percentile. Other standard scores are linear transformations from the z-score, with arbitrarily selected means and standard deviations. That is, it is possible to choose any mean and any standard deviation. Most IQ tests, for example, use 100 as the mean and 15 to 16 as the standard deviation. The resultant IQ score is a standard score (the ration IQ, mental age divided by chronological age × 100, is rarely used today). Figure 7.11 shows a normal distribution, standard deviations, percentiles, and some common standard scores.

Measures of Relationship

Up to this point we have been discussing descriptive statistics that are used to summarize or give a picture of groups on one variable at a time. There are, however, many questions of interest that are dependent on the way two or more variables are related to each other. Are brighter students more motivated? If we increase the frequency of reinforcement, will the reinforced or target behavior also increase? Is there a relationship between self-concept and achievement? If students exert more effort in studying, will they feel better about their achievement? In each instance, two variables are measured for each subject in the group.

Scatterplot

The most fundamental measure of relationship is called a *scatterplot* or *scatter diagram*. The **scatterplot** is a graphic representation of the relationship, achieved by forming a visual array of the intersection of each subject's scores on the two variables. As illustrated in Figure 7.12, one variable is rank-ordered on the horizontal axis (age, in this example) and the second variable is rank-ordered on the vertical axis (weight). Each subject's scores are indicated next to the graph in random order, and the intersections noted by the letter assigned each subject. Together, the intersections form a pattern that provides

FIGURE 7.12   Scatterplot

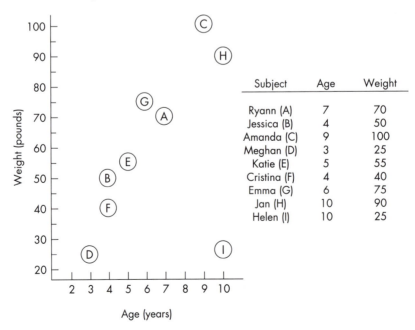

Subject	Age	Weight
Ryann (A)	7	70
Jessica (B)	4	50
Amanda (C)	9	100
Meghan (D)	3	25
Katie (E)	5	55
Cristina (F)	4	40
Emma (G)	6	75
Jan (H)	10	90
Helen (I)	10	25

a general indication of the nature of the relationship. Obviously, as children grow older their weight increases, and in such cases the relationship is said to be positive or direct. Thus, with a **positive relationship**, as the value of one variable increases, it is accompanied by increases in the second variable. Conversely, as the value of one variable decreases, the value of the other variable also decreases.

Scatterplots are useful in identifying scores that are very atypical (outliers) as compared with the overall pattern. For instance, in Figure 7.12, Helen was 10 years old and reported a weight of 25 pounds, which is quite different from what is represented in points A through H. In such cases the researcher might look for errors in scoring, measurement, or recording of data, since the scores represented by the outlier are unlikely. Scatter diagrams also provide a first hint about whether the relationship is linear or curvilinear (see Figure 7.13). (The

FIGURE 7.13 Scatterplots of Relationships

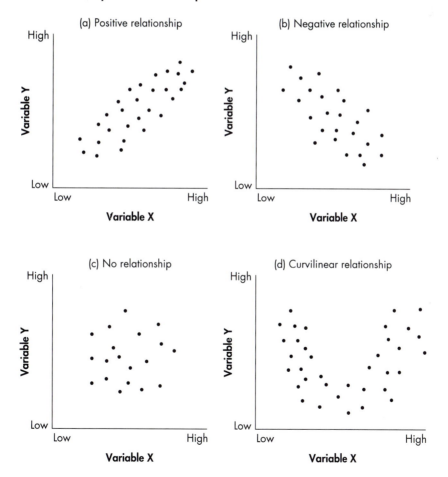

usual approach in graphing relationships is to use dots, not circles, within the graph at the intersections.)

Several different types of patterns can emerge in scatterplots. When one variable decreases as the other increases (for example, the number of miles on a tire and the depth of remaining tread), there is a **negative** or *inverse* **relationship**. If there is no pattern at all in the graph, there is no relationship. Figure 7.13 illustrates different scatter diagrams. Notice the curvilinear relationship in Figure 7.13(d). Curvilinear relationships are not uncommon but are usually detected only by plotting the scores. An example of a curvilinear relationship might be anxiety level and test performance. Performance could often be low during either high- or low-level anxiety and high for medium-level anxiety.

The direction of the pattern in the scatterplot, then, indicates whether there is a relationship and whether the relationship is positive, negative, or curvilinear. If a line is drawn through the plotted dots to minimize the distance of each dot to the line, then the degree of clustering around the line indicates the strength of the relationship. Plots that have mostly scattered dots have weak or low relationships, while dots clustered near the line indicate a strong or high relationship. The strength of the relationship is independent of its direction. Dots clustered so tightly as to form a straight line represent a perfect relationship (maximum strength). Correlations thus indicate three things: whether there is any relationship at all, the direction of the relationship, and the strength of the relationship.

Correlation Coefficient[1]

Even though scatterplots are indispensable tools for evaluating the relationship between two variables, researchers rarely report such graphs in published articles. The typical convention is to calculate a number to represent the relationship, called a **correlation coefficient**. There are many types of correlation coefficients, and the choice of the one to use is determined by the scale used in data collection and the research question. The interpretation of the number used, however, is basically the same. The number that represents the correlation can range from -1.00 to $+1.00$. A high positive value (for example, .85, .90, .90, .96) represents a high positive relationship; a low positive value (.15, .20, .08) a low positive relationship; a moderate negative value (for example, $-.40$, $-.37$, $-.52$) a moderate negative relationship, a value of 0 no relationship, and so on. Thus, the strength of the relationship becomes higher as the correlation approaches either $+1$ or -1 from zero. This is illustrated in Figure 7.14. Note that strength is independent of direction.

---

[1]This discussion is limited to simple correlation. More advanced correlational procedures, such as multiple correlation, partial correlation, discriminant function analysis, and canonical correlation, are based on these principles to examine the combined relationships of several variables.

FIGURE 7.14 **Relationship of Strength and Direction of Correlations**

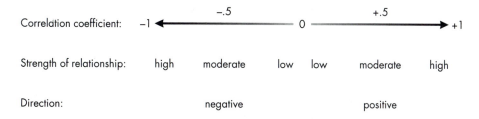

The most common correlation technique is the Pearson product-moment coefficient (represented by r), and the correlation is indicated by $r = .65, r = .78, r = .03$, and so on. (Notice that there is no plus sign before positive values, but there is a negative sign for negative values.) The product-moment correlation is used when both of the variables use continuous scales, such as scores from achievement tests, grade point average, self-concept inventories, and age. Since scores can also be reported as dichotomies, in several categories, or ranks, other correlation techniques, depending on the scale for the variables, are used to measure the relationship. Some of these techniques are summarized in Table 7.5.

Excerpts 7.8 and 7.9 show how to report correlational data. In Excerpt 7.7, there is a list of all correlations of interest in the study. In Excerpt 7.8 there is an **intercorrelation matrix**, in which many variables are correlated with each other. The numbers in a row on top of the table correspond to the variables listed vertically on the left. The correlation of teachers' disapproval and criticism with teachers' encouragement is $-.54$; the correlation of engagement with teachers' long-term expectations is .44.

In Chapter 9 we will discuss important principles of interpretation of correlation coefficients.

TABLE 7.5

Types of Correlation Coefficients

Type of Coefficient	Symbol	Types of Variables
Pearson product-moment	r	Both continuous
Spearman	r_s	Both rank-ordered
Biserial	r_b	One continuous, one an artificial dichotomy
Point-biserial	r_{pb}	One continuous, one a true dichotomy
Tetrachoric	r^t	Both artificial dichotomies
Phi coefficient	ϕ	Both true dichotomies
Contingency coefficients	C	Both 2 or more categories
Correlation ratio, eta	η	Both continuous (used with curvilinear relationships)

EXCERPT 7.8

PEARSON PRODUCT-MOMENT CORRELATION

Pearson product–moment correlations were computed between all demographic variables (i.e., percentage White; low income; attendance rate; percentage mobility; high school dropout rate; high school gradiation rate; average class size; average teacher experience in years; pupil–teacher ratio; average teacher salary; average per-pupil expenditure) and the achievement scores (i.e., scores in reading and mathematics). The 1994 correlations (see Table 2) were similar across grade levels and subject matter within the 1994 data.

To summarize, we detected statistically significant relationships (or associations) between the school demographic variables and the achievement scores. The strongest relationships occurred for the following variables;: low income, percentage White, high school graduation, and dropout rate. Moderate relationships existed for attendance, mobility, and high school pupil–teacher ratio. The weakest relationships occurred for average class size, elementary pupil–teacher ratio, teacher salary, teacher experience, and expenditure per pupil.

TABLE 2   Correlations of Attitude Measures with Achievement Scores

Variable	Grade 3		Grade 10	
	Reading	Mathematics	Reading	Mathematics
Percentage White	.78	.66	.75	.67
Low income	−.79	−.72	−.79	−.75
Attendance	.59	.53	.82	.72
Mobility	−.52	−.46	−.54	−.49
Dropout	—	—	−.69	−.61
High school graduation	—	—	.76	.69
Average class size, Grade 3	−.09**	−.06**	—	—
Average class size, high school	—	—	−.18	−.11**
Teacher experience	−.14	−.13	−.05	.00
Elementary pupil–teacher ratio	−.26	−.22	−.32	−.24
High school pupil–teacher ratio	—	—	−.32	−.24
Teacher salary	−.20	−.08	−.05	.07
Expenditure per pupil	−.31	−.19	.10*	−.01

Note: Grade 3, $n = 2{,}307$; Grade 10, $n = 644$. Correlations are statistically significant at the .001 level unless otherwise notes.

*$p < .05$. **$p < .01$.

Source: Sutton, A., & Soderstrom, I. (1999). Predicting elementary and secondary school achievement with school-related and demographic factors. *Journal of Educational Research, 92*(6), 330–338.

EXCERPT 7.9

CORRELATION MATRIX

Zero-order correlations among the motivational context variables and behavioral signs of alienation are depicted in Table 2. All correlations were in the expected direction. Students' disciplinary problems were most strongly related to their reports of teachers' disinterest and criticism and teacher expectations. The strongest relation to emerge was between students' perceptions of teacher's expectations and student engagement. Peers' academic aspirations and their perceptions of the economic limitations of education were related to both disciplinary problems and engagement.

TABLE 2   Zero-Order Correlations between Perceived Motivational Context Variables and Indexes of Alienation

Motivation Context Variables	1	2	3	4	5	6	7	8	9	10
1. Teachers' disapproval and criticism	—									
2. Teachers' encouragement	−.54***	—								
3. Teachers' long-term expectations	−.39***	.34***	—							
4. Peers' academic aspirations	−.21***	.13**	.36***	—						
5. Peers' resistance to school norms	.27***	−.09	−.22***	−.47***	—					
6. Peers' academic support	−.32***	.31***	.29***	.47***	−.44***	—				
7. Economic limitations of education	.38***	−.24***	−.35***	−.38***	.27***	−.25***	—			
8. Economic benefits of education	−.12*	.21***	.32***	.32***	−.12*	.21***	−.36***	—		
Indexes of alienation										
9. Discipline problems	−.35***	.15**	−.36***	−.26***	.17**	−.21***	.29***	−.11**	—	
10. Engagement	−.16**	.04	.44***	.27***	−.14**	.19***	−.22***	.11**	−.47***	—

*$p < .05$. **$p < .01$. ***$p < .001$.

Source: Murdock, T. B. (1999). The social context of risk: Status and motivational predictors of alienation in middle school. *Journal of Educational Psychology, 91*(1), 62–75.

Summary

This chapter has introduced fundamental principles of descriptive statistics. The statistical procedures are used in one way or another in nearly all quantitative research studies. The major points that are covered are summarized below.

1. Descriptive statistics are indices that summarize or characterize a large number of observations.
2. Measurement scales (nominal, ordinal, interval, and ratio) and the purpose of the research suggest the descriptive statistics that are appropriate.
3. Frequency distributions in the form of class intervals, histograms, frequency polygons, and stem-and-leaf displays provide an overview picture of all the data.
4. Measures of central tendency include the mean, median, and mode. Each measure provides a numerical index of the typical score in the distribution.

5. The mean is the best measure of central tendency for distributions that have no extremely high or low scores; the median is best for highly skewed data. Often, both the mean and the median should be reported.

6. Measures of variability indicate the spread of scores from the mean of the distribution.

7. Measures of variation include the range, standard deviation, and box-and-whisker plots.

8. Standard deviation is a measure of variability unique to each distribution that indicates, on the average, how much scores deviate from the mean.

9. Standard scores are converted raw score distributions with common units to indicate the mean and the standard deviation.

10. Scatterplots are used to indicate the general direction and strength of a relationship between two variables in one group or sample.

11. Correlation coefficients are numbers that represent the direction and strength of the relationship between two or more variables.

Self-Instructional Review Exercises

Sample answers are in the back of the book.

Test Items

1. Which of the following statements is true (more than one may be true) concerning descriptive statistics?
   a. Descriptive statistics are used to summarize data.
   b. Descriptive statistics are used to infer population characteristics from a sample.
   c. Descriptive statistics are not needed to interpret inferential statistics.
   d. Correlation coefficients are descriptive statistics.
   e. The choice of descriptive statistics depends on the purpose of the research and size of the sample.

2. Scales of measurement that provide categories without order are called
   a. interval.
   b. nonordinal.
   c. nominal.
   d. ratio.

3. Percentile scores are examples of a scale of measurement called
   a. nominal.
   b. interval.
   c. ordinal.
   d. ratio.

4. Frequency distributions are represented by all of the following *except*
   a. histograms.

    b. polygons.

    c. normal curve.

    d. rank-order grouping.

5. The _____ is the most widely used measure of central tendency.

    a. mean

    b. median

    c. standard deviation

    d. mode

6. Given the following scores: 4, 7, 7, 8, 10, 12, 12, 12, 18; the mean is _____ ; the median is _____ ; and the mode is _____ .

    a. 8, 12, 10

    b. 8, 10, 12

    c. 10, 10, 12

    d. 10, 10, 10

    e. 12, 12, 12

7. The average amount of dispersion of a set of scores around the mean is assessed numerically by the

    a. range.

    b. standard deviation.

    c. percentile ranks.

    d. median.

8. Plus one standard deviation is always at about the _____ percentile in a normal distribution.

    a. 60th

    b. 50th

    c. 90th

    d. 84th

9. Which of the following correlations shows the strongest relationship?

    a. .50

    b. −.75

    c. .67

    d. −.30

10. A good reason to graph correlations is to find

    a. curvilinear relationships.

    b. positive relationships.

    c. negative relationships.

    d. both a and b.

Application Problems

1. For each case below, choose the most appropriate statistical procedure.

    a. A teacher of a low reading group is interested in what the average score is for the group of 25 students.

    b. An administration wants to find out if there is a relationship between teacher absences and student achievement.

     c. A math teacher wants to know how many ability groups should be formed within a class of 30 students.

     d. A student teacher is interested in the number of students who rate his performance as good, excellent, average, or poor.

2. Identify the scale of measurement in each of the following:

     a. attitudes toward school.

     b. grouping students on the basis of hair color.

     c. asking judges to rank order students from most cooperative to least cooperative.

C H A P T E R   8

Quantitative Data Collection Techniques

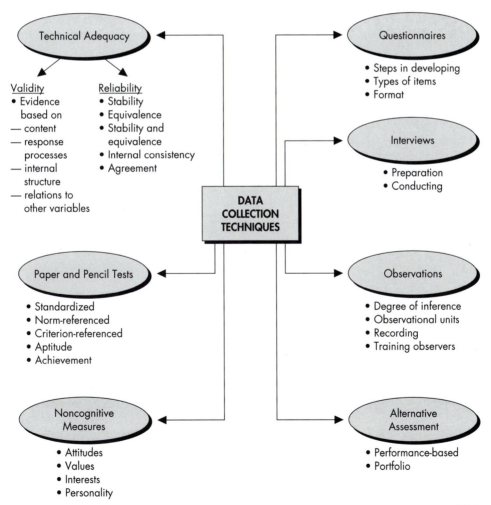

KEY TERMS

construct underrepresentation
construct irrelevant variance
evidence based on test content
evidence based on response
   pocesses
evidence based on internal
   structure
evidence based on relations
   to other variables
reliability
stability
equivalence
internal consistency
split-half
Kuder–Richardson
Cronbach Alpha
agreement
standardized tests
norm-referenced
criterion-referenced
aptitude test
achievement tests
alternative assesment
performance-based assessment
portfolio
noncognitive
social desirability

questionnaire
double-barrelled questions
closed form
open form
scale
Likert scale
semantic differential
checklist
contingency questions
structured questions
semistructured questions
unstructured questions
leading question
probing
complete observer
high inference
low inference
duration recording
frequency-count recording
interval recording
continuous observation
time sampling
nonreactive
unobtrusive measures

This chapter elaborates on principles of validity and reliability as important considerations of the quality of measures and presents the characteristics of five major techniques for gathering quantitative data: tests, questionnaires, interviews, observation, and unobtrusive measures. The advantages and disadvantages of each type are discussed in relation to the objectives of research problems and procedures employed with each technique. These techniques are used in different types of research, as defined by both purpose and research design. Once the purpose of the research and the constraints of the research situation are clear, a particular technique is chosen to fit the research design. No single technique is best, easiest, or most convenient.

Fundamentals of Quantitative Measurement: Technical Adequacy

Quantitative measurement uses some type of instrument or device to obtain numerical indices that correspond to characteristics of the subjects. The numerical values are then summarized and reported as the results of the study. Consequently, the results depend heavily on the quality of the measurement. If the measure is weak or biased, then so are the results. Conversely, strong measures increase confidence that the findings are accurate. It is imperative, then, to understand what makes measurement "strong" or "weak." Whether you need to choose instruments to conduct a study or to evaluate results, it is necessary to understand what affects the quality of the measure. In this section two technical concepts of measurement, validity and reliability, are discussed as important criteria for determining quality.

Validity

As indicated in Chapter 6, test validity is the extent to which inferences made on the basis of numerical scores are appropriate, meaningful, and useful. Validity is a judgment of the appropriateness of a measure for specific inferences or decisions that result from the scores generated. In other words, validity is a situation-specific concept: validity is assessed depending on the purpose, population, and environmental characteristics in which measurement takes place. A test result can therefore be valid in one situation and invalid in another. Consequently, in order to assure others that the procedures have validity in relation to the research problems, subjects, and setting of the study, it is incumbent on the investigator to describe validity in relation to the instruments used to collect data.

This conceptualization of test validity implies much more than simply determining whether a test "measures what it is supposed to measure." More recent definitions by measurement scholars, as well as what is stated in the *Standards for Educational and Psychological Testing* (1985; 2000), make it clear that it is an *inference*, *use*, or *consequence* that is valid or invalid, not a test. For example:

> *Validity refers to the appropriateness, meaningfulness, and usefulness of the specific inferences made from test scores (Standards, 1985 p. 9).*

> *Validity refers to the degree to which evidence and theory support the interpretations of test scores entailed by specific uses of tests. (Standards, 2000, p. 9)*

> *[Validity is] an integrated evaluative judgment of the degree to which empirical evidence and theoretical rationales support the adequacy and*

appropriateness of inferences and actions based on test scores or other modes of assessment (Messick, 1989, p. 13).

To assure validity, then, the researcher needs to identify assumptions or make arguments to justify an inference or use for a specific purpose, (e.g., concluding that students in one group have more knowledge or have a stronger self-concept than students in another group) and then collecting evidence to support these assumptions (Shepard, 1993). This emphasis is consistent with the idea that validity is a single, unitary concept that requires evidence for the specific use that is cited. It follows, then, that a test by itself is not valid or invalid because the same test can be used for different purposes. For example, a college entrance test may lead to valid inferences about a student's future performance as an undergraduate but to invalid inferences about the quality of the high school program.

Two kinds of inferences are typically used in educational research. The first is related to assessing achievement, which depends primarily on how well the content of a test or other assessment represents a larger domain of content or tasks. For this kind of inference, evidence based on the content of the assessment is needed to support inferences that are made. A second kind of inference, one that is even more common in educational research, is about traits or characteristics that are more abstract than clearly defined content. These traits or characteristics are often called *constructs,* and include, for example, intelligence, creativity, reading ability, attitudes, reasoning, and self-concept.

When inferences involve these constructs, it is important to have a clear theoretical conceptualization about what is being measured and evidence that there are no viable rival hypotheses to challenge the intended interpretation. Two types of rival hypotheses can be considered, *construct underrepresentation and construct irrelevant variance.* **Construct underrepresentation** occurs if the assessment fails to capture important aspects of the construct. For example, if a self-concept measure did not include items on social as well as academic areas, it would measure less than the proposed construct "self-concept." **Construct irrelevant variance** refers to the extent to which a measure includes material or factors that are extraneous to the intended construct. An example of this kind of factor would be measuring mathematical reasoning ability with story problems. Since reading comprehension is needed to understand the problems, this ability is important to success, as well as mathematical reasoning. Thus, the measure is influenced to some extent by factors that are not part of the construct.

Whether the inference involved in research is primarily content or construct, there are five major types of evidence that can be used to both support intended interpretations and eliminate any rival hypotheses about what is being measured: evidence based on content, on response processes, on internal structure, on relations to other variables, and on consequences. We will consider the first four, which have the greatest relevance for research.

Evidence Based on Test Content   In general, **evidence based on test content** demonstrates the extent to which the sample of items or questions in the instrument is representative of some appropriate universe or domain of content or tasks. This type of evidence is usually accumulated by having experts examine the contents of the instrument and indicate the degree to which they measure predetermined criteria or objectives. Experts are also used to judge the relative criticality, or importance, of various parts of the instrument. For example, to gather evidence for a test of knowledge for prospective teachers, it is necessary to have experts examine the items and judge their representativeness (e.g., is a question about Piaget representative of what needs to be known about child development?) and whether the percentage of the test devoted to different topics is appropriate (e.g., 20 percent of the test is on classroom management, but maybe it should be 40 percent). Evidence based on test content is essential for achievement tests. Also, the domain or universe that is represented should be appropriate to the intended use of the results.

Unfortunately, evidence based on test content for validity is often not reported in research articles, usually because there is no systematic effort to obtain such evidence for locally devised instruments. When standardized instruments are used it is important to refer to previous research, reviews of the instrument, or technical manuals.

Evidence based on content is similar to *face validity*, but face validity is a less systematic appraisal between the measure and the larger domain. Face validity is a judgment that the items appear to be relevant, while content validity evidence establishes the relationship empirically.

Evidence Based on Response Processes   Evidence based on response processes is focused on an analysis of performance strategies or responses to specific tasks, and whether these strategies and responses are consistent with what is intended to be measured. For example, if students are to be involved in mathematical reasoning, it would be possible to ask them about their thinking in relation to solving problems to assure that reasoning, and not rote application of an alogrithm, is used. Similarly, observers or judges can be asked to indicate criteria used for their judgments to be sure appropriate criteria are being applied.

Evidence Based on Internal Structure   The *internal structure* of an instrument refers to how items are related to each other and how different parts of a instrument are related. **Evidence based on internal structure** is provided when the relationships between items and parts of the instrument are empirically consistent with the theory or intended use of the scores. Thus, if a measure of self-concept posits several "types" of self-concept (e.g., academic, social, athletic), then the items measuring the academic component should be strongly related to each other and not as highly related to the other components.

Evidence Based on Relations to Other Variables   The most common way that validity of interpretations is established is by showing how scores from a given measure relate to similar as well as different traits. There are several ways this can be done. When scores from one instrument correlate highly with scores from another measure of the same trait, we have what is called *convergent* evidence. *Discriminant* evidence exists when the scores do not correlate highly with scores from an instrument that measures something different. Thus, we would expect that scores from a measure of self-concept would correlate highly with other measures of self concept and show less correlation to related but different traits such as anxiety and academic performance. In many research articles this type of evidence will be referred to as "construct validity."

Another approach to gathering **evidence based on relations to other variables** pertains to the extent to which the test scores or measures predict performance on a criterion measure (test-criterion relationships). Two approaches are used to obtain test-criterion evidence: predictive and concurrent. With predictive evidence, the criterion is measured at a time in the future, after the instrument has been administered. The evidence pertains to how well the earlier measure can predict the criterion behavior or performance. For instance, in gathering evidence on a new measure to select applicants for leadership positions, the scores on the instrument would be correlated with future leadership behavior. If persons who scored low on the test turned out to be poor leaders and those who scored high were good leaders, predictive test-criterion evidence would be obtained. With concurrent evidence, the instrument and the criterion are given at about the same time. Criterion-related evidence is often reported in research by indicating that a measure correlates with criteria that assess the same thing. For example, in Excerpt 8.1, from a published study on student prosocial behavior in the classroom, the researchers reported agreement between observers' and teachers' perceptions of prosocial behaviors.

Validity is clearly the single most important aspect of an instrument and the findings that result from the data. The quality of the evidence judged by the users of the findings varies a lot in educational research. If standardized tests are used there will be sophisticated evidence, while locally developed questionnaires may have little systematic evidence. In either case good researchers always ask: Are the inferences appropriate? What evidence supports my conclusion? The components of test validity are summarized in Table 8.1.

EXCERPT 8.1

VALIDITY EVIDENCE BASED ON RELATIONS TO OTHER VARIABLES

The teacher questionnaire measure of student cooperation showed a significant positive correlation . . . with the observation measure of Student Supportive and Friendly Behavior. . . . The questionnaire measure of student disruptiveness scorrelated negatively with observed Sport and Friendly Behavior . . . Student Harmony, . . . and Spontaneous Prosocial Behavior.

Source: Solomon, D., Watson, M. S., Delucchi, K. L., Schaps, E., & Battistich, V. (1988). Enhancing children's prosocial behavior in the classroom. *American Educational Research Journal, 25,* 536.

TABLE 8.1

Components of Test Validity

Component	Description	Procedure
Evidence based on content	Extent to which the items or factors represent a larger domain	Examine the relationship between content in the items and content in the domain.
Evidence based on response processes	Whether thinking and response processes are consistent with intended interpretation	Examine the respondent explanations and patterns of responses.
Evidence based on internal structure	Extent to which items measuring the same trait are related	Correlate items measuring the same trait.
Evidence based on relations to other variables	Whether the measure is related to similar or predicted variables and unrelated to different variables	Correlate the measure to other measures of the same trait and to measures of different traits.

Effect of Validity on Research Because validity implies proper interpretation and use of the information gathered through measurement, it is necessary for both consumers and investigators of the research to judge the degree of validity that is present, based on available evidence. In this sense, validity is a matter of degree and is not an all-or-nothing proposition. Investigators should show that for the specific inferences and conclusions made in their study there is evidence that validity exists. Consumers need to make the same decision based on their use of the results. Does this suggest that validity must be established for each research situation and possible use? Such a requirement would add a considerable amount of data collection and analysis to each study and is therefore impractical. In practice, it is necessary to generalize from other studies and research that interpretation and use are valid. That is one reason why already established instruments, for which some evidence on validity has probably accumulated, usually provide more credible measurement. On the other hand, it would be a mistake to assume that just because an instrument is established, its results are valid.

Locally devised instruments, with no history of use or reviews by others, need to be evaluated with more care. When researchers develop new instruments it is more important to gather appropriate evidence for validity and then report this evidence in the study.

Whether a locally prepared or established instrument is used, it is best to gather evidence for validity before the data for a study are collected. This is a major reason for a pilot test of the instrument and procedures for administering it. The research should be consistent with the use of the results. For example, if you will use the results to determine which students have mastered a body of knowledge, content-related evidence is necessary. If you are examining a theory related to the development of cognitive study, construct-related evidence is needed.

Reliability

Reliability refers to the consistency of measurement—the extent to which the results are similar over different forms of the same instrument or occasions of data collection. Another way to conceptualize reliability is to determine the extent to which measures are free from error. If an instrument has little error it is reliable, and if it has a great amount of error it is unreliable. We can measure error by estimating how consistently a trait is assessed.

Think for a minute about tests you have taken. Were the scores you received accurate, or was there some degree of "error" in the results? Were some results more accurate than others? In measuring human traits, whether achievement, attitude, personality, physical skill, or some other trait, you will almost never obtain a result that does not have some degree of error. Many factors contribute to the less than perfect nature of our measures. There may be ambiguous questions, the lighting may be poor, some subjects may be sick, guessing on an achievement test may be lucky or unlucky, observers may get tired, and so on. What this means is that even if a trait remained the same when two tests were given a week apart, the scores would not be exactly the same because of unavoidable error.

The obtained score may be thought of as having two components, a *true* or *universe score,* which represents the actual knowledge or skill level of the individual, and *error,* sources of variability unrelated to the intent of the instrument:

$$obtained\ score\ =\ true\ or\ universe\ score\ +\ error$$

Common sources of error are listed in Table 8.2. The objective in selecting or evaluating instruments, then, is to look for evidence that error has been controlled as much as possible.

TABLE 8.2

Sources of Measurement Error

Conditions of Test Administration and Construction	Conditions Associated with the Person Taking the Test
Changes in time limits	Reactions to specific items
Changes in directions	Health
Different scoring procedures	Motivation
Interrupted testing session	Mood
Race of test administrator	Fatigue
Time the test is taken	Luck
Sampling of items	Fluctuation in memory or attention
Ambiguity in wording	Attitudes
Misunderstood directions	Test-taking skills (test wiseness)
Effect of heat, light, ventilation in testing situation	Ability to comprehend instruction
Differences in observers	Anxiety

TABLE 8.3

Types of Reliability

Type	Description	Procedure	Common Examples[a]
Stability (test–retest)	Consistency of stable characteristics over time	Administer the same test to the same individuals over time.	Aptitude tests IQ tests
Equivalence	Comparability of two measures of the same trait given at about the same time	Administer different forms to the same individuals at about the same time.	Achievement tests
Equivalence and stability	Comparability of two measures of the same trait given over time	Administer different forms to the same individuals over time.	Assessments of changes over time Personality assessment
Internal consistency (split-half; K–R; Cronbach Alpha)	Comparability of halves of a measure to assess a single trait or dimension	Administer one test and correlate the items to each other.	Most measures except for speeded tests. Attitude questionnaires
Agreement	Consistency of ratings or observations	Two or more persons rate or observe.	Observations and interviews

[a]These examples are not meant to suggest that forms of reliability other than those indicated are inappropriate (for example, achievement tests also use test-retest reliability).

The actual amount of error variance in test scores, or the reliability, is determined empirically through several types of procedures.[1] Each type of reliability is related to the control of a particular kind of error, and is usually reported in the form of a reliability coefficient. The reliability coefficient is a correlation statistic comparing two sets of scores from the same individuals. The scale for a reliability coefficient is from .00 to .99. If the coefficient is high, for example .90, the scores have little error and are highly reliable. The opposite is true for the correlation near .20 or .35. An acceptable range of reliability for coefficients for most instruments is .70 to .90.

The five general types of reliability estimates are stability, equivalence, stability and equivalence, internal consistency, and agreement (Table 8.3).[2]

---

[1]Most of the procedures are based on the assumption that there will be a sufficient dispersion or spread in the scores to calculate correlation coefficients. Some types of tests (such as criterion-referenced) do not provide much score variability, and traditional correlational indicators of reliability may be inappropriate. For such tests, researchers examine percentages of test-takers who are classified in the same way after taking the test twice or after taking different forms of the same test, or the percentage of answers that are the same at different times, rather than the correlation coefficient. The presentation of reliability in this chapter will focus on traditional correlational procedures, since these are the ones you will encounter most frequently in the literature.

[2]According to the new *Standards for Educational and Psychological Testing* these traditional indices of reliability are special cases of a more general classification called *generalizability theory*. Generalizability theory has the ability to combine several sources of error into a single measure of variability. Though it is not reported frequently in the literature, it does provide a more accurate indication of the degree of error.

Stability A coefficient of **stability** is obtained by correlating scores from the same test on two different occasions of a group of individuals. If the responses of the individuals are consistent (that is, if those scoring high the first time also score high the second time, and so on) then the correlation coefficient, and the reliability, are high. This *test-retest* procedure assumes that the characteristic measured remains constant. Unstable traits, such as mood, should not be expected to yield high stability coefficients. Furthermore, stability usually means that there is a long enough time between measures (often several months) so that the consistency in scores is not influenced by a memory or practice effect. In general, as the time gap between measures increases, the correlation between the scores becomes lower.

Equivalence When two equivalent or parallel forms of the same instrument are administered to a group at about the same time, and the scores are related, the reliability that results is a coefficient of **equivalence**. Even though each form is made up of different items, the score received by an individual would be about the same on both forms. Equivalence is one type of reliability that can be established when the researcher has a relatively large number of items from which to construct equivalent forms. Alternative forms of a test are needed in order to test initially absent subjects who may learn about specific items from the first form or when an instructor has two or more sections of the same class meeting at different times.

Equivalence and Stability When a researcher needs to give a pretest and posttest to assess a change in behavior, a reliability coefficient of equivalence and stability should be established. In this procedure, reliability data are obtained by administering to the same group of individuals one form of an instrument at one time and a second form at a later date. If an instrument has this type of reliability, the researcher can be confident that a change of scores across time reflects an actual difference in the trait being measured. This is the most stringent type of reliability and it is especially useful for studies involving gain-scores or improvement.

Internal Consistency **Internal consistency** is the most common type of reliability since it can be estimated from giving one form of a test once. There are three common types of internal consistency: split-half, Kuder–Richardson, and the Cronbach Alpha method. In **split-half** reliability the items of a test that have been administered to a group are divided into comparable halves, and a correlation coefficient is calculated between the halves. If each student has about the same position in relation to the group on each half, then the correlation is high and the instrument has high reliability. Each test half should be of similar difficulty. This method provides a lower reliability than other methods, since the total number in the correlation equation contains only half the items (and we know that other things being equal, longer tests are more reliable than short tests). (The Spearman–Brown formula is used to increase split-half reliabilities to estimate what the correlation would be for a whole test.) Internal consistency techniques should not be used with speeded tests. This is because not all items are answered by all students, a factor that tends to increase spuriously the inter-correlation of the items.

A second method for investigating the extent of internal consistency is to use a **Kuder–Richardson** (K–R) formula in order to correlate all items on a single test with each other when each item is scored right or wrong. K–R reliability is thus determined from a single administration of an instrument, but without having to split the instrument into equivalent halves. This procedure assumes that all items in an instrument are equivalent to each other, and it is appropriate when the purpose of the test is to measure a single trait. If a test has items of varying difficulty or it measures more than one trait, the K–R estimate would usually be lower than the split-half reliabilities.

The **Cronbach Alpha** also assumes equivalence of all items. It is a much more general form of internal consistency than the K–R, and it is used for items that are not scored right or wrong. The Cronbach Alpha is generally the most appropriate type of reliability for survey research and other questionnaires in which there is a range of possible answers for each item.

Agreement The fifth type of reliability is expressed as a coefficient of **agreement**. This is established by determining the extent to which two or more persons agree about what they have seen, heard, or rated. That is, when two or more observers or raters independently observe or rate something, will they agree with each other about what was observed or rated? If they do, then there is some consistency in measurement. This type of reliability is commonly used for observational research and studies involving performance-based assessments in which professional judgments are made about student performance. It will be reported as *inter-rater* reliability or *scorer agreement* and will be expressed either as a correlation coefficient or as percentage of agreement. However, this type of analysis does not indicate anything about *consistency* of performance or behavior at different times (ironically, internal consistency estimates don't either). This means that it is one thing to obtain high inter-rater agreement, which is relatively easy to do, and quite another to obtain data that show that the behavior or trait is consistent over time.

We have summarized these five types of reliability estimates in Table 8.4 according to when different forms of an instrument are given.

Interpretation of Reliability Coefficients Several factors should be considered in interpreting reliability coefficients:

1. The more heterogeneous a group is on the trait that is measured, the higher the reliability.
2. The more items there are in an instrument, the higher the reliability.
3. The greater the range of scores, the higher the reliability.

TABLE 8.4

Procedures for Estimating Reliability[a]

	Time 1	Time 2
Stability	A	A
Equivalence	A B	
Stability and Equivalence	A	B
Internal Consistency	A	
Agreement	R1 R2	

[a]A and B refer to different forms of the same test; R1 and R2 refer to rater 1 and rater 2, though more than two raters or observers can be used with agreement.

Source: Adapted from McMillan, J. H. (2000), *Educational Research: Fundamentals for the Consumer* (3rd ed.), New York: Longman.

4. Achievement tests with a medium difficulty level will result in a higher reliability than either very hard or very easy tests.
5. Reliability, like validity, when based on a norming group, is demonstrated only for subjects whose characteristics are similar to those of the norming group.
6. The more that items discriminate between high and low achievers, the greater the reliability.

Researchers often ask how high a correlation should be for it to indicate satisfactory reliability. This question is not answered easily. It depends on the type of instrument (personality questionnaires generally have lower reliability than achievement tests), the purpose of the study (whether it is exploratory research or research that leads to important decisions), and whether groups or individuals are affected by the results (since action affecting individuals requires a higher correlation than action affecting groups). However, a good rule of thumb is to be wary of reliabilities below .70.

Effect of Reliability on Research As with validity, the reliability of scores should be established before the research is undertaken, and the type of reliability should be consistent with the use of the results. If you will use the results for prediction or selection into special programs, stability estimates of reliability are necessary. If you are interested in programs to change attitudes or values, equivalency estimates are needed. Reliability should also be established with individuals who are similar to the subjects in the research. If previous studies report good reliability with middle school students and you intend to use the results with elementary school students, the reliability may not be adequate. More commonly, reliability is reported with the students used in the study.

Failure to report reliability would be cause to interpret the results with caution, though there are some simple measures for which reliability coefficients are not needed (see below).

You will read some research in which reliability is not addressed, yet the results of the research show what are called "significant differences." This is an interesting situation in research because it is more difficult to find differences between groups with instruments that have resulted in scores that have low reliability. It is as if the differences were observed despite what may have been low reliability. Of course it is possible that the measurement was reliable, even though no reliability estimates were reported. This situation is likely to occur in research in which the subjects are responding to questions so straightforward and simple that reliability is "assumed." For example, in studies of students' perceptions of success or failure following performance on a test, the subjects may be asked to indicate on a scale from 1 to 10 (1 being a high degree of failure and 10 being a high degree of success) their feelings of success or failure. In much research the subjects report information such as age, sex, income, time spent studying, occupation, and other questions that are relatively simple. For these types of data, statistical estimates of reliability are generally not needed.

Reliability is a function of the nature of the trait being measured. Some variables, such as most measures of achievement, provide highly reliable scores, whereas scores from personality measures have lower reliabilities. Consequently, a reliability of .80 or above is generally expected for achievement variables, whereas estimates of .70 may be acceptable for measuring personality traits. By comparison, then, a personality instrument reporting a reliability coefficient of .90 would be judged to have excellent reliability, and an achievement test with a reliability of .70 may be seen as weak. We need a much stronger reliability if the results will be used to make decisions about individuals. Studies of groups can tolerate a lower reliability, sometimes as low as .50 in exploratory research. Measures of young children are usually less reliable than those of older subjects.

To enhance reliability, it is best to establish standard conditions of data collection. All subjects should be given the same directions, have the same time frame in which to answer questions at the same time during the day, and so on. Error is often increased if different persons administer the instruments. It is important to know whether there are any unusual circumstances during data collection, because these may affect reliability. The instrument needs to be appropriate in reading level and language to be reliable, and subjects must be properly motivated to answer the questions. In some research it is difficult to get subjects to be serious, for instance, when students are asked to take achievement tests that have no implications for them. Reliability can also suffer when subjects are asked to complete several instruments over a long time. Usually an hour is about all any of us can tolerate, and for younger children less than a half hour is the maximum. If several instruments are given at the same time, the order of their administration should not be the same for all subjects. Some subjects should answer one instrument first, and other subjects should answer the same instrument last. This is called *counterbalancing* the instruments. If several instruments are given and there is no counterbalancing, the results, especially for the instruments given at the end, should be viewed with caution.

Finally, reliability is a necessary condition for validity. That is, scores cannot be valid unless they are reliable. However, a reliable measure is not necessarily valid. For example, we can obtain a very reliable measure of the length of your big toe, but that would not be valid as an estimate of your intelligence!

The remainder of this chapter will consider methods of data collection that are commonly used in quantitative research. While the basic principles of validity and reliability apply to all five types of data collection, note that each data collection technique has unique characteristics that affect the way validity and reliability are established.

Paper-and-Pencil Tests

The term *paper-and-pencil test* means that a standard set of questions is presented to each subject in writing (on paper or computer) that requires completion of cognitive tasks. The responses or answers are summarized to obtain a numerical value that represents a characteristic of the subject. The cognitive task can focus on what the person knows (achievement), is able to learn (ability or aptitude), chooses or selects (interests, attitudes, or values), or is able to do (skills). Different types of tests, and their uses in research, are summarized briefly in this chapter, but it is important to stress that all tests measure current performance. Tests differ more in their use than in their development or actual test items, particularly when comparing achievement and aptitude tests. In fact, it would be more accurate to say that there are different types of inferences and uses; it is what you do with the test results that creates distinctions such as achievement and aptitude.

Standardized Tests

Standardized tests provide uniform procedures for administering and scoring the instrument. The same questions are asked each time the test is used, with a set of directions that specifies how the test should be administered. This would include information about qualifications of the person administering the test and conditions of administration, such as time allowed, materials that can be used by subjects, and whether questions about the test can be answered during testing. The scoring of responses is usually objective, and most, but not all, standardized tests have been given to a norming group. The norm group, as it is called, allows comparison of a score with the performance of a defined group of individuals. This provides important and valuable information, but the researcher should take care in interpreting norm-referenced scores (see section on Norm- and Criterion-Referenced Tests below).

Most standardized tests are prepared commercially by measurement experts. This generally means that there will be careful attention to the nature of the norms, reliability, and validity. This results in instruments that are objective and relatively uninfluenced or distorted by the person who administers the instrument. Because most standardized tests are prepared commercially, they are intended to be used in a wide variety of settings. Consequently, whatever is tested is typically defined in broad and general terms. This may mean that for some research purposes a standardized test may not be specific enough to provide a sensitive measure of the variable. For instance, if you were conducting a study to investigate the effect of general education at a university on students' knowledge in social science or humanities, a standardized test that you might use would be intended as a measure of social science and humanities outcomes at nearly *all* universities. This means that what is taught at one particular university may not be well represented on the test. This illustrates a trade-off in using standardized tests in research. On the one hand you have a carefully constructed instrument, with established reliability, directions, and scoring procedures. On the other hand, the test may not be focused directly on the variable of interest in the study, may have inappropriate norms, or may cost too much. The alternative is to develop your own instrument; it will measure the variable more directly, but it may have questionable technical qualities.

Norm- and Criterion-Referenced Interpretation

A major distinction between tests is whether they are norm- or criterion-referenced. The purpose of a **norm-referenced interpretation** is to show how individual scores compare with scores of a well-defined reference or norm group of individuals. The interpretation of results, then, depends entirely on how the subjects compare with others, with less emphasis on the absolute amount of knowledge or skill. That is, what matters most is the comparison group and the ability of the test or instrument to distinguish between individuals. The goal is to know whether, for example, the subjects know more or less than the norm group, and the score is often reported to indicate specifically where the subject "stands" in relation to others (such as the 67th percentile, or upper quartile).

Researchers need to keep two characteristics of norm-referenced interpretations in mind. First, because the purpose of the test is to differentiate between individuals, the best distribution of scores is one that shows a high variance. To achieve a high variability of scores, the items must discriminate between individuals. To accomplish this, the test items, particularly in standardized norm-referenced tests, are fairly difficult. It is not uncommon for students at the 50th or 60th percentile to answer slightly more than half the items correctly. Easy items, ones that almost everyone gets correct, are used sparingly (obviously, if all the items are easy, everyone gets a high score, and there is no differentiation between individuals). Thus, important content or skills may not be measured, which will affect the meaning you give to the results. On the positive side, the large variability helps in establishing relationships. The highest correlations are often found with two variables that have large variability.

Second, researchers should attend carefully to the characteristics of the norm or reference group. Perhaps you have had the same experience as we have, being enrolled in a class of bright, hard-working students with an instructor who graded by the curve. You could learn a lot but still get low marks. The interpretation of norm-referenced scores makes sense only when we understand what we are being compared against. Many standardized norm-referenced tests indicate that "national" norms are used. Despite the fact that the term "national" is subject to different interpretations, if you are studying gifted students and compare their scores with the national norm, the chances are good your students will all score very high and show little variability. This gives you what is called a *ceiling effect* and a restricted range, which in turn may lead to nonsignificant results.

In a **criterion-referenced** or **standards-based interpretation** an individual's score is interpreted by comparing the score with professionally judged standards of performance. The comparison is between the score and a criterion or standard rather than the scores of others. The result is usually expressed as the percentage of items answered correctly, or as pass–fail in the case of minimum competency testing. There is a focus on "what" the subjects are able to do, with a comparison of that with standards of proficiency. Most criterion-referenced tests result in a highly skewed distribution, which lessens variability. Despite this limitation, criterion-referenced tests are good to use for diagnosis and for categorizing subjects into pass–fail groups. A related type of test, domain-referenced, is used to show how much of a specifically defined larger "domain" of knowledge is demonstrated by those being tested. For example, if the domain is knowledge of addition with three-digit numbers, the test will sample this domain, and the researcher will make a professional judgment using the percentage of correctly answered items to judge the "mastery" of the domain.

Aptitude Tests

The purpose of an **aptitude test** is to predict future performance. The results are used to make a prediction about performance on some criterion (like grades, teaching effectiveness, certification, or test scores) prior to instruction, placement, or training. The term *aptitude* refers to the predictive use of the scores from a test, rather than the nature of the test items. Some terms, such as *intelligence* or *ability*, are used interchangeably with aptitude. Intelligence tests are used to provide a very general measure, usually reporting a global test score. Because they are general, intelligence tests are useful in predicting a wide variety of tasks. Intelligence is measured by an individual or group test. For most research, group tests of intelligence are adequate and cost much less than individual tests. Most group tests are designed so that researchers need training to administer and score them. Usually these tests produce three scores: a verbal

TABLE 8.5

Examples of Standardized Tests

Aptitude	Achievement
Group Intelligence or Ability	**Diagnostic**
Cognitive Abilities Test	Stanford Diagnostic Mathematics Test
Otis–Lennon School Ability Test	Woodcock Reading Mastery Test
Scholastic Assessment Test	Key Math Diagnostic Arithmetic Test
	California Diagnostic Reading Test
Individual Intelligence	**Criterion-referenced**
Stanford–Binet Intelligence Scale	Objectives-Referenced Bank of Items and Tests
Wechsler Scales	Skills Monitoring System
Kaufman Assessment Battery for Children	Writing Skills Test
McCarthy Scales of Children's Abilities	
Multifactor	**Specific Subjects**
Differential Aptitude Test	Metropolitan Readiness Tests
General Aptitude Test Battery	Gates–MacGinitie Reading Tests
Armed Services Vocational Aptitude Battery	Modern Math Understanding Test
Special	**Batteries**
Minnesota Clerical Test	Terra Nova Comprehensive Tests of Basic Skills
Law School Admissions Test	California Achievement Tests
Medical College Admission Test	Metropolitan Achievement Tests
Bennett Mechanical Comprehension Test	Iowa Test of Basic Skills
Torrance Test of Creative Thinking	Stanford Achievement Test Series
Watson–Glaser Critical Thinking Appraisal	

language score, a nonverbal or performance score, and a combined score. Since virtually all school children have taken group intelligence tests, the scores are available, with parental and/or school permission, for use in research. The scores are often used to adjust for ability differences in intact groups of subjects. Some of the common individual and group intelligence tests are listed in Table 8.5.

There are many measures that assess multiple aptitudes or specific kinds of aptitudes. Multifactor aptitude tests are used to provide separate scores for each skill or area assessed. Some would argue that this makes more sense than a single score because relative strengths and weaknesses can be identified. Multifactor aptitude tests have become increasingly popular in vocational and educational counseling. However, the usefulness of factor scores in research is more problematic. Because there may be just a few items that measure one factor, the reliability of the scores may be questionable. Total single scores, while more general, are often more stable and reliable. Special aptitude tests are good for research, since the focus is on an accurate indication of ability in one area. Table 8.5 contains examples of both multiple-aptitude and special aptitude tests.

Achievement Tests

It is not always evident how achievement tests differ from aptitude tests. Often very similar items are used for both types of tests. In general, however, **achievement tests** have a more restricted coverage, are more closely tied to school subjects, and measure more recent learning than aptitude tests. Also, of course, the purpose of achievement tests is to measure what has been learned rather than to predict future performance.

There are many standardized achievement tests. Some are diagnostic, which isolate specific areas of strength and weakness; some are concerned with measuring achievement in a single content area, while others (survey batteries) test different content areas; some are norm-referenced and others are criterion-referenced; some emphasize principles and skills rather than knowledge of specific facts. The choice of achievement test depends on the purpose of the research. If the research is concerned with achievement in a specific school subject, then it would be best to use a test that measures only that subject, rather than using a survey battery. If comparisons between several schools will be made, it is best to use norm-referenced tests.

It is very important to assess content validity with a standardized achievement test before using it in research. This is because the curriculum in some schools may be different from the content of standardized tests that are designed for use in most schools. The best way to assess evidence for content validity is to examine the items of the test and make professional judgments of the match between what the item tests and the curriculum. Finally, those choosing a test should consider the difficulty level of the test and the abilities of the students. The desired goal is to have a fairly normal distribution of test scores. If results are skewed by a test that is too easy for bright students or too difficult for slow students, it will be difficult to relate the scores to other variables (such as measuring gain in achievement over a year or more with gifted students). Table 8.5 contains examples of some standardized achievement tests.

Alternative Assessments

In contrast to traditional testing formats that rely on written, objective items, **alternative assessments** are designed to provide different ways of demonstrating student performance and achievement, often in "authentic" contexts. Primarily relying on having students construct responses, alternative assessments are being used with increasing frequency, even for statewide testing programs. While there are many kinds of alternative assessments, including demonstrations and exhibitions, we will consider the two you are most likely to encounter in research: performance-based and portfolio.

Performance-Based Assessments With **performance-based assessment** the emphasis is on measuring student proficiency on cognitive skills by directly observing how a student performs the skill, often in an authentic context. Contexts are "authentic" to the extent that they reflect what students will actually do with what they are learning. For example, asking students to complete an oral history project based on a synthesis of interviews and written sources, write letters of inquiry about a job, complete a music recital, or prepare a portfolio of artwork could be considered performance-based assessments.

Performance-based assessments have the advantage of providing a direct, holistic measure of thinking skills that are indirectly assessed in written tests. These assessments also provide a better measure of skill performance in contexts more like those students will encounter outside of school. Performance-based assessments are typically criterion-referenced, without the sometimes unrealistic, arbitrary time constraints of written tests. Also, performance-based assessments are closely tied to instruction. This means that research on the relationships of instructional practices to dependent variables measured by performance-based assessments will be very sensitive, unlike more general standardized tests. However, the major drawback of performance-based assessments is the dependence on subjective ratings or observations of teachers, which often results in low reliability. This is most likely a problem when there is reliance on a single rating or observation. In addition, performance-based assessments are time-consuming to develop, administer to students, and score. Typically, teachers evaluate students singly or in small groups. Thus, from a research perspective, while these assessments can be very helpful in providing a direct measure of skills, careful planning is necessary to be certain that sufficient resources are allocated to provide reliable results.

Portfolio Assessment A **portfolio** is a purposeful, systematic collection and evaluation of student works that document progress toward meeting learning objectives. Portfolios have been used for years in fields such as architecture, art, and journalism as the primary method of evaluating learning and accomplishment. In education, portfolios are being used with increasing frequency, especially with the assessment of reading and writing skills.

While portfolios have the advantage of providing many examples of student work over time, which can be used to evaluate growth or change, from a psychometric perspective the reliability is often weak. Scoring of portfolios is done subjectively according to scoring guidelines or rubrics, and it is difficult to obtain high inter-rater reliability. This may result from scoring criteria that are too general and inadequate training of raters, even in national or statewide programs. If classroom teachers are scoring locally developed portfolios, even more scoring error can be expected.

Finally, evidence for validity needs to be carefully considered since there is usually a desire to generalize from the examples to broader learning traits and objectives. For example, if judgments are being made about the ability of the student to communicate by writing, and the only types of writing in the portfolio are creative and expository, then the validity of the inference to writing more generally is weak (construct underrepresentation).

Personality, Attitude, Value, and Interest Inventories

Aptitude and achievement tests are types of cognitive measures. Affective, or **noncognitive**, instruments measure traits such as interests, attitudes, self-concept, values, personality, and beliefs. Most agree that these traits are important in school success, but measuring them accurately is more difficult than assessing cognitive traits or skills. First, noncognitive test results may be adversely affected by response set, which is the tendency of a subject's answer to be influenced by a general "set" when responding to items. There are several types of response sets, including responding with all positive or negative answers regardless of the content of the items; guessing; and sacrificing speed for accuracy. Response set is particularly prevalent with ambiguous items or items that use a continuum such as agree–disagree or favorable–unfavorable. Second, noncognitive items are susceptible to faking. While there are some techniques that help reduce faking, such as using forced choice questions, disguising the purpose of the test, and establishing a good rapport with subjects, faking is always conceivable. One of the most serious types of faking is **social desirability**, in which subjects answer items in order to appear most normal or most socially desirable rather than responding honestly. Third, the reliability of noncognitive tests is generally lower than that of cognitive tests. Fourth, in most noncognitive tests we are interested in evidence of construct validity, which is difficult to establish. Finally, noncognitive tests do not have "right" answers like cognitive tests. The results are usually interpreted by comparison with other individuals, so the nature of the comparison group is particularly important. Despite these limitations, noncognitive traits are used in research because they are an integral part of the learning process.

Personality tests include a wide range of checklists, projective tests, and general adjustment inventories. Most are self-report instruments containing a structured question–response format, and they require specialized training for interpretation. Because of psychometric weakness in most personality tests the results should be used for groups of subjects rather than individuals. See Table 8.6 for some examples of personality tests.

Attitude and interest inventories are used extensively in educational research. Most are self-report instruments and are subject to faking and response set. Interest inventories measure feelings and beliefs about activities in which an individual can engage. Attitude inventories measure feelings and beliefs about something other than an activity, such as an object, a group, or place. Both are concerned with likes and dislikes, preferences, and predisposi-

TABLE 8.6

Examples of Noncognitive Instruments

Personality	Attitude	Value	Interest
The Adjustment Inventory	Survey of Study Habits and Attitudes	Study of Values	Strong–Campbell Interest Inventory
Minnesota Multiphasic Personality Inventory	Survey of School Attitudes	Rokeach Value Survey	Minnesota Vocational Interest Inventory
California Psychological Inventory	Minnesota School Affect Assessment	Gordon's Survey of Values	Kuder Occupational Interest Survey
Personality Inventory for Children	Children's Scale of Social Attitudes	Work Values Inventory	Kuder General Interest Inventory
Omnibus Personality Inventory	Learning Environment Inventory		Vocational Preference Inventory
Rorschach Inkblot Test	Student Attitude Inventory		
Thematic Apperception Test	Revised Math Attitude Scale		
Tennessee Self-Concept Scale			
Piers–Harris Children's Self-Concept Scale			
Coopersmith Self-Esteem Inventory			

tions. A complete discussion of these types of inventories, is beyond the scope of this book, although we discuss questionnaires as one way to assess attitudes later in this chapter. Table 8.6 lists examples of attitude, interest, and value inventories.

Questionnaires

For many good reasons the questionnaire is the most widely used technique for obtaining information from subjects. A **questionnaire** is relatively economical, has the same questions for all subjects and can ensure anonymity. Questionnaires can use statements or questions, but in all cases the subject is responding to something written for specific purposes. In this section of the chapter, information about questionnaires is presented by following the sequence of steps researchers use in developing them. The steps are summarized in Figure 8.1.

FIGURE 8.1   Steps in developing a questionnaire

Justification

A questionnaire is one of many ways information can be obtained. The researcher who wants to use one should be sure that, given the constraints of the situation, there are no other more reliable and valid techniques that could be used. This decision is based on knowledge of the strengths and weaknesses of each technique (which is addressed later in the chapter by comparing several commonly used techniques). Researchers should give much thought to justification whenever they develop new questionnaires. In many cases existing instruments could be used or adapted for use instead of preparing a new one. If the researcher can locate an existing questionnaire, time and money will be saved and an instrument with established reliability and validity may be located.

Defining Objectives

The second step in using a questionnaire is to define and list the specific objectives that the information will achieve. The objectives are based on the research problems or questions, and they show how each piece of information will be used. They need not be strict behavioral objectives, but they must be specific enough to indicate how the responses from each item will meet the objectives. By defining objectives the researcher is specifying the information that is needed. Unfortunately, many researchers include questions that have not been thought through properly, and the results are never used. Time and energy are wasted, and interested audiences are disenchanted.

Writing Questions and Statements

Once the researcher has defined objectives and has ascertained that no existing instruments can be used, he or she begins the task of writing the questions or statements. It is best to write the items by objective and to be aware of the way the results will be analyzed once the data are collected. There are two general considerations in writing the items: comply with rules for writing most types of items, and decide which item format is best.

Babbie (1998) suggests the following guidelines for writing effective questions or statements:

1. *Make items clear.* An item achieves clarity when all respondents interpret it in the same way. Never assume that the respondent will read something into the item. Often the perspectives, words, or phrases that make perfect sense

to the researcher are unclear to the respondents. The item may also be too general, allowing different interpretations. The question, "What do you think about the new curriculum?" for example, would probably evoke counter questions: for example, "Which curriculum? What is meant by 'think about'?" Finally, vague and ambiguous words like *a few, sometimes,* and *usually* should be avoided, as should jargon or complex phrases.

2. *Avoid double-barrelled questions.* A question should be limited to a single idea or concept. **Double-barrelled questions** contain two or more ideas, and frequently the word *and* is used in the item. Double-barrelled questions and statements are undesirable because the respondent may, if given an opportunity, answer each part differently. If, for instance, a respondent is asked to agree or disagree with the statement, "School counselors spend too much time with recordkeeping and not enough time with counseling of personal problems," it would be possible to agree with the first part (too much recordkeeping) and disagree with the second idea (not enough time with counseling).

3. *Respondents must be competent to answer.* It is important that the respondents are able to provide reliable information. Some questions that ask teachers to recall specific incidents or reconstruct what they did several weeks earlier, for example, are subject to inaccuracy simply because the teachers cannot reliably remember the incidents. Similarly, it would be of little value to ask college professors who teach the historical foundations of education to judge the adequacy of a minimum competency test of reading readiness skills which prospective teachers should demonstrate knowledge of for certification. In many instances the subjects are unable to make a response they can be confident of, and in such circumstances it is best to provide in the response options something like *unsure* or *do not know* in order to give the subjects an opportunity to state their true feelings or beliefs.

4. *Questions should be relevant.* If subjects are asked to respond to questions that are unimportant to them or are about things they have not thought about or care little about, it is likely that the subjects will respond carelessly, and the results will be misleading. This may occur, for instance, when teachers are asked their preferences in standardized tests when they rarely if ever use the results of these tests in teaching. Their answers might be based on an expedient response rather than a careful consideration of the tests.

5. *Short, simple items are best.* Long and complicated items should be avoided because they are more difficult to understand, and respondents may be unwilling to try to understand them. Assume that respondents will read and answer items quickly, and that it is necessary to write items that are simple, easy to understand, and easy to respond to.

6. *Avoid negative items.* Negatively stated items should be avoided because they are easy to misinterpret. Subjects will unconsciously skip or overlook the negative word, so their answers will be the opposite of the intended. If researchers use negative items, they should boldface, underline, or capitalize the negative word (<u>not</u>, or NO).

7. *Avoid biased items or terms.* The way in which items are worded, or the inclusion of certain terms, may encourage particular responses more than oth-

ers. Such items are termed *biased* and, of course, should be avoided. There are many ways to bias an item. The identification of a well-known person or agency in the item can create bias. "Do you agree or disagree with the superintendent's recent proposal to...?" is likely to elicit a response based on an attitude toward the superintendent, not the proposal. Some items provide biased responses because of the social desirability of the answer. For example, if you ask teachers whether they ever ridicule their students, you can be fairly sure, even if the responses are anonymous, that the answer will be *no* because good teachers do not ridicule students. Student responses to the same question or observations of other teachers might provide different information.

Researchers may also give a hint of what response they are hoping for. This occurs if the respondents want to please the researcher and provide responses they think the researcher wants, or it may occur if the subjects know the consequences of the responses. It has been shown, for example, that student evaluations of college professors are more favorable if the professor tells the students before they fill out the forms that the results will have a direct bearing on their (the teachers') tenure and salary raises. The students presumably feel less negative because of the important consequences of the results. Finally, items are ambiguous if the respondent thinks: "Well, sometimes I feel this way, sometimes I feel that way," or "It depends on the situation." Many items fail to specify adequately the situational constraints that should be considered, leading to inaccurate responses. If asked, for instance, to agree or disagree with the statement "The discovery method of teaching is better than the lecture method," a teacher would likely respond, "It depends on the student."

Given these general guidelines, how do you know if the items are well written? One approach is to ask friends, colleagues, and experts to review the items and look for any problems. Beyond this subjective method, a good way to demonstrate empirically that items are unbiased, unambiguous, and clear is to construct two equivalent forms of each item and give the items to random groups. If the two groups' responses are nearly the same on each pair of items, then the items are probably good. If not, then the items need to be rewritten.

Types of Items

There are many ways in which a question or statement can be worded and several ways in which the response can be made. The type of item should be based on the advantages, uses, and limitations of these options. Below is a summary of the more common approaches to the way questions and statements may be asked and answered.

Open and Closed Form The first consideration is to decide whether the item will have a **closed form**, in which the subject chooses between predetermined responses, or an **open form**, in which the subjects write in any response they want. The choice of form to use depends on the objective of the item and the advantages and disadvantages of each type. Closed form items (also called *structured, selected response,* or *closed-ended*) are best for obtaining demographic information and data that can be categorized easily. Rather than asking "How many hours did you study for the test?" for example, a closed form question would provide categories of hours and ask the respondent to check the appropriate box, as indicated below:

Check the box that indicates the number of hours you spent studying for the test.

- ☐   0–2
- ☐   3–5
- ☐   6–8
- ☐   9–11
- ☐   12+

Obviously, it will be much easier to score a closed form item, and the subject can answer the items more quickly. It is therefore best to use closed form items with a large number of subjects or a large number of items. It is very time-consuming for the researcher to categorize several hundred open-ended responses, not to mention the subjectivity involved.

There are certain disadvantages to using structured items, however. With the question "How many hours did you study for the test?" for example, if every subject checks a response labeled *3 to 5 hours,* the researcher has lost accuracy and variability (no spread of responses across all response categories) with this factor. In other words, if categories are created that fail to allow the subjects to indicate their feelings or beliefs accurately, the item is not very useful. This occurs with some forced choice items. Another disadvantage is that a structured item cues the respondent with respect to possible answers. If asked, for example, "Why did you do so poorly on the test?" students might, if an open-ended format was used, list two or three factors that were relevant, things that they thought were important. A structured format could, however, list twenty-five factors and have the student check each one that was important (such as *I didn't study hard enough; I was sick; I was unlucky*); the student may check factors that would have been omitted in the open-ended mode. One approach to the case in which both the open and the closed form have advantages is to use open-ended questions first with a small group of subjects in order to generate salient factors, and then use closed-ended items, based on the open-ended responses, with a larger group. Open-ended items exert the least amount of control over the respondent and can capture idiosyncratic differences. If the purpose of the research is to generate specific individual responses, the open-ended format is best; if the purpose is to provide more general group responses, the closed form is best.

Scaled Items A **scale** is a series of gradations, levels, or values that describes various degrees of something. Scales are used extensively in questionnaires because they allow fairly accurate assessments of beliefs or opinions. This is because many of our beliefs and opinions are thought of in terms of gradations. We believe something very strongly or intently, or perhaps we have a positive or negative opinion of something.

The usual format of scaled items is a question or statement followed by a scale of potential responses. The subjects check the place on the scale that best reflects their beliefs or opinions about the statement. The most widely used example is the **Likert scale** (pronounced Lick-ert). A true Likert scale is one in which the stem includes a value or direction and the respondent indicates agreement or disagreement with the statement. Likert-type items use different response scales; the stem can be either neutral or directional. The following is an example of a true Likert scale:

Science is very important:

Strongly agree	Agree	Neither agree nor disagree (undecided or neutral)	Disagree	Strongly disagree

It should be pointed out that while the agree–disagree format is used widely, it can also be misleading. We might, for example, disagree with the statement, "Mrs. Jones is a good teacher" because she is an outstanding teacher.

Likert-type scales provide great flexibility since the descriptors on the scale can vary to fit the nature of the question or statement. Here are examples:

Science is:

Critical important	Very important	Important unimportant	Somewhat	Very

How often is your teacher well organized?

Always	Most of the time	Sometimes	Rarely	Never

How would you rate Cindy's performance?

Very poor	Poor	Fair	Good	Excellent

Indicate the extent to which your performance was a success or failure.

Extreme success	Success	OK	Failure	Extreme failure

Indicate how you feel about your performance:

Immense pride	Some pride	Neither pride nor shame	Some shame	Immense shame

Very happy	Somewhat nor happy	Neither sad sad	Somewhat	Very sad

Researchers sometimes wonder whether the undecided or neutral choice should be included in a true Likert scale. While both forms are used, it is generally better to include the middle category. If the neutral choice is not included and that is the way the respondent actually feels, then the respondent is forced either to make a choice that is incorrect or not to respond at all. The forced choice format may lead to some frustration by the respondent However, the argument for deleting the undecided or neutral choice has merit in instances in which the respondents have a tendency to cluster evidences in that middle category. When the questionnaire items have been written, they should be randomized within each separate section of the questionnaire.

A variation of the Likert scale is the **semantic differential**. This scale uses adjective pairs, with each adjective as an end anchor in a single continuum. On this scale there is no need for a series of descriptors; only one word or phrase is placed at either end. The scale is used to elicit descriptive reactions toward a concept or object. It is an easily constructed scale and can be completed quickly by respondents. The examples that follow illustrate typical uses.

Math

| Like | —— —— —— —— —— —— —— | Dislike |
| Tough | —— —— —— —— —— —— —— | Easy |

My teacher

Easy	—— —— —— —— —— —— ——	Hard
Unfair	—— —— —— —— —— —— ——	Fair
Enthusiastic	—— —— —— —— —— —— ——	Unenthusiastic
Boring	—— —— —— —— —— —— ——	Not boring

Excerpt 8.2 shows how a semantic differential is used to assess responses of students toward various aspects of school. In this instrument, affect is assessed by

EXCERPT 8.2

SEMANTIC DIFFERENTIAL SCALE

28 Famous plays

| important | ○ ○ ○ ○ ○ | unimportant |
| pleasant | ○ ○ ○ ○ ○ | unpleasant |

29 Art

| important | ○ ○ ○ ○ ○ | unimportant |
| pleasant | ○ ○ ○ ○ ○ | unpleasant |

39 Being liked by other students

| important | ○ ○ ○ ○ ○ | unimportant |
| pleasant | ○ ○ ○ ○ ○ | unpleasant |

40 Being liked by teachers

| important | ○ ○ ○ ○ ○ | unimportant |
| pleasant | ○ ○ ○ ○ ○ | unpleasant |

Source: From *Minnestoa School Attitude Survey* by Dr. Andrew Ahlgren. Copyright © 1983 Science Research Associates. Reprinted by permission of the publisher, CTB Macmillan/McGraw-Hill.

EXCERPT 8.3

SEMANTIC DIFFERENTIAL SCALE FOR YOUNG CHILDREN

Black in the nose of the face that shows how YOU feel about what is written in the box.

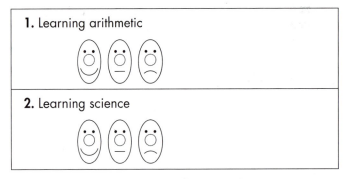

Source: From *Minnesota School Attitude* Survey by Dr. Andrew Ahlgren. Copyright © 1983 Science Research Associates. Reprinted by permission of the publisher, CTB Macmillan/McGraw-Hill.

the scale, anchored by the terms *pleasant–unpleasant,* while value of the activity is measured by *important–unimportant.* In Excerpt 8.3 another type of semantic differential is used, one that is obviously oriented toward younger children. The scale is limited but provides a range from *happy* to *sad.*

Ranked Items One problem with using a Likert scale or a semantic differential is that all the answers can be the same, making it difficult to differentiate between each item. If a Likert scale is used to investigate the importance of each of five ways of spending money by a university department, for instance, a respondent can mark *very important* for each one. The result would do little for the researcher's efforts to prioritize expenditure of funds. If, however, the respondents are asked to *rank-order* the five ways in sequential order from most to least important, then the researcher can gather more valuable information on ways to spend the money. A rank-order assessment of the above example might look like this:

Rank-order the following activities with respect to their importance as to ways our research fund should be allocated this year. Use 1 = most important, 2 = next most important, and so forth until 5 = least important.

_____ Annual colloquium   _____ Computer software

_____ Individual research projects   _____ Student assistantships

_____ Invited speakers

Checklist Items A checklist is simply a method of providing the respondent a number of options from which to choose. The item can require a choice of one of several alternatives (for instance, Check one: The biology topic I most enjoy is ___ ecology, ___ botany, ___ anatomy, ___ microbiology, or ___ genetics.); or respondents can check as many words as apply:

Check as many as apply. The more enjoyable topics in biology are

____ botany   ____ ecology

____ comparative anatomy   ____ microbiology

____ genetics   ____ zoology

Checklists can also be used in asking respondents to answer *yes* or *no* to a question, or to check the category to which they belong. For example:

Are you married? ____yes ____no

Check the appropriate category:

____ single   ____ separated

____ never married   ____ divorced

____ married   ____ widowed

Note that with categorical responses a respondent can be placed in one category and only one.

Item Format

There are several ways to present items and answers to items. The clearest approach is to write the item on one line and to place the response categories below, not next to, the item. It is also advisable to use boxes, brackets, or parentheses rather than a line to indicate where to place the check mark. For example:

Have you ever cheated?

    n   yes
    n   no

is better than

Have you ever cheated? ____ yes ____ no

With Likert and semantic differential scales the use of continuous lines or open blanks for check marks is not recommended, since the check mark is often entered between two options.

Sometimes when a researcher asks a series of questions, answering one question in a certain way directs the respondent to other questions. These are called **contingency questions** and are illustrated below:

Have you used the Mathematics Curriculum Guide?

    n yes
    n no

If yes: How often have you used the activities suggested?

- n   0–2 times
- n   3–5 times
- n   6–10 times
- n   more than 10 times

Did you attend the State Conference on Testing?

- n   yes (please answer questions 17–20)
- n   no (please skip to question 21)

If several questions will use the same response format, as is typical with Likert scale items, it is often desirable to construct a matrix of items and response categories. An example of a matrix is illustrated in Excerpt 8.4.

General Format

The general layout and organization of the questionnaire is very important. If it appears to be carelessly done or confusing, respondents are likely to set it aside and never respond. A well-done format and appearance provides a favorable first impression and will result in cooperation and serious, conscientious responses. The following rules should be adhered to carefully:

1. Carefully check grammar, spelling, punctuation, and other details.
2. Make sure printing is clear and easy to read.
3. Make instructions brief and easy to understand.

EXCERPT 8.4

QUESTION MATRIX

For questions 1–8 use the following response scale:

1	2	3	4	5	6
Not At All	Very Little	Some	Quite a Bit	Extensively	Completely

To what extent were final first semester grades of students in your class based on:

1. including 0s in the determination of final percentage correct if students failed to complete an assignment?   1 2 3 4 5 6
2. disruptive student behavior?   1 2 3 4 5 6
3. laudatory behavior of the student?   1 2 3 4 5 6
4. student attitudes toward learning?   1 2 3 4 5 6
5. improvement of performance since the beginning of the semester?   1 2 3 4 5 6
6. low student effort to learn?   1 2 3 4 5 6
7. high student effort to learn?   1 2 3 4 5 6
8. degree of effort of low-ability students?   1 2 3 4 5 6

4. Avoid cluttering the questionnaire by trying to squeeze many items onto each page.
5. Avoid abbreviated items.
6. Keep the questionnaire as short as possible.
7. Provide adequate space for answering open-ended questions.
8. Use a logical sequence, and group related items together.
9. Number the pages and items.
10. Use examples if the items may be difficult to understand.
11. Put important items near the beginning of a long questionnaire.
12. Be aware of the way the positioning and sequence of the questions may affect the responses.
13. Print response scales on each new page.

Pilot Testing

It is highly recommended that researchers conduct a pilot test of their questionnaires before using them in studies. It is best to locate a sample of subjects with characteristics similar to those that will be used in the study. While the size of the sample should be greater than twenty, it is better to have only ten subjects than to have no pilot test. The administration of the questionnaire should be about the same as that to be used in the study, and the pilot test respondents should be given space to write comments about individual items and the questionnaire as a whole. The researcher wants to know whether it takes too long to complete, whether the directions and items are clear, and so on. If there are enough pilot test subjects, an estimate of reliability may be calculated, and some indication will be given of whether there is sufficient variability in the answers to investigate various relationships. There are thus two steps in getting feedback about the questionnaire before it is used in the study: an informal critique of individual items as they are prepared and a pilot test of the full questionnaire.

Interview Schedules

Interviews in quantitative studies are essentially vocal questionnaires. The major steps in constructing an interview are the same as in preparing a questionnaire—justification, defining objectives, writing questions, deciding general and item format, and pretesting. The obvious difference is that the interview involves direct interaction between individuals, which has both advantages and disadvantages as compared with the questionnaire. The interview technique is flexible and adaptable. It can be used with many different problems and types of persons, such as those who are illiterate or too young to read and write, and responses can be probed, followed up, clarified, and elaborated to achieve specific accurate responses. Nonverbal as well as verbal behavior can be noted in face-to-face interviews, and the interviewer has an opportunity to motivate the respondent. Interviews result in a much higher response rate than questionnaires, especially for topics that concern personal qualities or negative feelings. For obtaining factual, less personal information, questionnaires are preferable.

The primary disadvantages of the interview are its potential for subjectivity and bias, its higher cost and time-consuming nature, and the lack of anonymity. Depending on the training and expertise of the interviewer, the respondent may be uncomfortable in the interview and unwilling to report true feelings; the interviewer may ask leading questions to support a particular point of view; or the interviewer's perceptions of what was said may be inaccurate. Because interviewing is labor-intensive it is costly and time-consuming (with the possible exception of telephone interviews), which usually translates to sampling fewer subjects than could be obtained with a questionnaire. Since interviews involve one person talking with another, anonymity is not possible. Confidentiality can be stressed, but there is always the potential for faking, or for being less than forthright and candid, because the subjects may believe that sharing certain information would not be in their best interest.

To mitigate potential bias, the interviewer should be thought of as a neutral medium through which information is exchanged. If this goal is attained, then the interviewer's presence will have no effect on the perceptions or answers of the respondent. In other words, if the interview is done correctly, it does not matter who the interviewer is; any number of different interviewers would obtain the same results. This aspect of interviewing is essentially one of reliability. If two or more interviewers agree on the way most of the responses to the questions should be classified, then the process is reliable, as assessed by inter-rater agreement. It is also possible to obtain a stability estimate of reliability by correlating the results of an original interview with results obtained a second time by the same interviewer. Another approach that can be used to increase the accuracy of the interview is to allow the respondent an opportunity to check the interviewer's perceptions. This can be accomplished if the interviewers write their perceptions of the answer to each question and send these written perceptions to the respondents. The respondents can then read the answers and make additions and corrections where appropriate. An additional advantage to this approach is that it helps build a positive relationship between the interviewer and respondent. This is helpful if the interviewer will be following up initial interviews or will be involved in a continuing evaluation or study.

Preparing the Interview

Once the researcher makes the decision to use an interview to collect data, an interview schedule is constructed. The schedule lists all the questions that will be asked, giving room for the interviewer to write answers. The questions are related directly to the objectives of the study and follow a given sequence that is adhered to in each interview. In most cases, the written questions are exactly what will be asked orally, with appropriate probing questions. The questions are usually in one of three forms: structured, semistructured, or unstructured. **Structured questions** (also called *limited response* or *selected response* questions) are followed by a set of choices, and the respondent selects one of the choices as the answer (for example, "Would you say the program has been highly effective, somewhat effective, or not at all effective?"). **Semistructured questions** have no choices from which the respondent selects an answer. Rather, the question is phrased to allow for individual responses. It is an open-ended question but is fairly specific in its intent (for example, "What has been the most beneficial aspect of your teacher training program?"). **Unstructured questions** allow the interviewer great latitude in asking broad questions in whatever order seems appropriate. In quantitative educational studies most interviews use a combination of structured and semistructured questions. This provides a high degree of objectivity and uniformity, yet allows for probing and clarification.

After the questions have been written, a pilot test is necessary as a check for bias in the procedures, the interviewer, or the questions. During the pilot test the procedures should be identical to those that will be implemented in the study. The interviewer should take special note of any cues suggesting that the respondent is uncomfortable or does not fully understand the questions. After the interview the respondent can evaluate the questions for intent, clarity, and so on. The pilot test provides a means of assessing the length of the interview and will give the researcher some idea of the ease with which the data can be summarized.

One potential problem that must be addressed before the actual study is conducted is the removal or rephrasing of leading questions. A **leading question** is worded so that the respondent is more aware of one answer than another, or contains information that may bias the response (as summarized earlier for questionnaire items). If, for example, the researcher asks: "Given the expense of adopting a new reading series, should we make the adoption this year?" the wording obviously makes it easy and desirable to answer *no*. Or consider the question: "Do you favor hot lunches in school?" It is more likely to elicit a *yes* than *no* response. As in the case of questionnaires, the best way to avoid leading questions in an interview is to solicit feedback from other experts and to pilot test the questions.

A final consideration in preparing the interview is to think about the way personal characteristics of the interviewer may influence the responses. Sax (1979, pp. 243–244) lists the following variables that have been shown to influence responses:

Variable	Effect on the Interview
1. Age of interviewer	a. Rapport is high for young interviewers and middle-aged respondents. Respondent's age is unimportant for older interviewers.
	b. The least inhibition in responding occurs with young persons of the same sex.
	c. Most inhibition in responding occurs with persons of same age but different sex.
	d. Interviewers between twenty-six and fifty years of age do a better job of interviewing than either younger or older interviewers.

(continued)

(continued)

2. College major	Interviewers trained in the behavioral sciences are rated as being more accurate than those in physical sciences; lowest rated are those who majored in fine arts, business, law, and the humanities.
3. Educational level	College graduates are rated higher than non–college-trained interviewers, but differences are slight.
4. Experience in interviewing	Interviewers' accuracy increases as their experience in interviewing increases.
5. Racial background	Responses of blacks differ depending on whether they are interviewed by whites or other blacks.
6. Religious background	Negative responses concerning Jews tend to be withheld if the interviewers introduce themselves by Jewish names.
7. Sex of interviewer	Males obtain fewer interview responses than do females.
8. Socioeconomic level	Middle-class interviewers report a greater degree of conservatism among working-class respondents than do working-class interviewers.

Many educational studies use naive or inexperienced interviewers. In this situation not only will the personal characteristics of the interviewer provide possible bias, but there is potential for error simply because the interviewer is unskilled at handling interviews. If novices are used, it is best to provide training and supervision. This can be expensive and time-consuming but will increase the validity and reliability of the study. For details on training interviewers, see Babbie (1998) and the *Interviewer's Manual* (1999).

During the Interview

Appearance is very important. It is best for the interviewer to dress according to existing norms or in a fashion similar to the respondents, and not in a way that may lead the respondent to think that the interviewer represents a particular point of view. The interviewer must be friendly, relaxed, and pleasant and should appear interested in the welfare of the respondents. To provide honest answers to questions, the respondent must feel comfortable with the interviewer. Appropriate appearance and demeanor provide a basis for establishing a comfortable relationship and rapport. The interviewer should spend a few minutes with small talk in order to establish a proper relationship.

Before asking specific questions the interviewer should briefly explain the purpose of the interview and ask whether the respondent has any questions or concerns. The questions are then addressed to the respondent in the exact words indicated on the interview schedule. Questions should not be rephrased.

The questions should be read without error or stumbling, in a natural, unforced manner. To accomplish this, the interviewer needs to be very familiar with the questions and should practice asking the questions aloud.

As the subject responds to the questions the interviewer needs to record the answers. The recording is usually done in one of two ways, by tape-recording or by means of written notes. Taped answers can be analyzed by several judges and used to estimate reliability. Tape-recording the answers is generally most useful with open-ended questions. A tape recorder will obviously collect the information more completely and objectively than notes, but the mere presence of a recorder may disrupt the interview and affect the responses, especially if personal questions are asked. If the questions are highly structured there is little need for recorded responses.

The most common method used to record responses is taking notes based on the answers. There are two extremes with note-taking. At one extreme the interviewer can try to write the exact response as it is given, and at the other the interviewer waits until the interview is over and then reconstructs the answer to each question. The problem with taking verbatim notes is that it takes much time during the interview; on the other hand information is lost when interviewers rely solely on their memories to write answers after the interview. Most interviewers compromise between these extremes and during the interview take abbreviated notes that can be expanded on after the interview is completed.

Probing for further clarification of an answer is a skill that, if misused, can lead to incomplete or inaccurate responses. The interviewer must allow sufficient time for the respondent to answer and should avoid anticipating and cuing a potential answer. Probes should also be neutral so as not to affect the nature of the response. If the initial question usually results in probing, then it is useful to list some probes next to the question. This allows time to develop the best probe and standardizes the probes for all interviews.

After all questions have been answered, the interviewer should thank the respondent and allow time for the respondent to make comments or suggestions regarding the topic of the questions or the interview in general. Since the respondent is taking time to cooperate, it is important to end the interview in a positive manner.

Excerpt 8.5 is taken from a study that used interviews as the technique to gather data. The excerpt is the material that was included in the methods section of the article under the subheadings Interviewers and Procedure. The purpose of the study was to assess the causal explanations children use to explain success and failure. The subjects were first, third, and fifth graders, and the second sentence of the excerpt shows that, to establish rapport, the interviewers spent time with the children before the interviews. The second paragraph of the excerpt shows how probes were made, and the Procedure section describes the setting of the interviews. The questions that the subjects responded to were semistructured. The children were to be told the story and then asked, "Why did he get a high grade?" or "Why did he do such a poor job?"

Observation Schedules

In a sense, all techniques of gathering data involve observation of some kind. As a general term, then, the word *observation* is used to describe the data that are collected, regardless of the technique employed in the study. Observational research methods also refer, however, to a more specific method of collecting information that is very different from interviews or questionnaires. As a

EXCERPT 8.5

INTERVIEWING

INTERVIEWERS

Four interviewers were used to collect the data: two male graduate students in psychology, one female graduate student in psychology, and one female with a Bachelor of Science in psychology. All interviewers were introduced to the children and spent time observing each of the six classrooms from which the subjects were taken.

Interviewers were trained in the use of the Elig-Frieze Coding Scheme (Elig & Frieze, 1975) (so that they could recognize responses that were of uncertain codability on one or more of the causal dimensions. When the child's response was unclear for coding purposes, the interviewer probed to clarify the exact meaning of the child's response. The first probe was always a simple repetition of the child's response, in the child's own words. In most cases this would cause the child to elaborate the initial response. However, if the child did not elaborate or if the elaboration still left a dimension uncertain, the interviewer would ask one of a set of prearranged questions. For example, the most common probe involved the clarification of the stability dimension, with a response such as "because he tried." If the repetition probe was ineffective, the interviewer would ask, "Did he always try or just try sometimes?" This always led to clarification. But overall, initial probes were needed in less than 5% of the responses. If during the coding of the transcribed interviews the judges believed that the interviewer's probing had biased the child's response, the judges were instructed to code only that part of the response that preceded that biasing intervention.

PROCEDURE

Interview schedules were determined in advance to incorporate the previously discussed design considerations. Arrangements were made with the school's administration to interview the children in vacant rooms near their classrooms and to audiotape all interviews. Each child was interviewed separately. Interviewers escorted the children from their classroom to the interviewing room. After a period of making the children as comfortable as possible by asking them about their families, what they had heard about the experiment, and by letting them listen to their voice on the tape recorder, the interview began. All interviews began with the interviewer reciting a common introduction.

> I am going to show you pictures that might be used in storybooks to help tell the stories. The stories will be about kids like you. And the stories will be about things that have probably happened to you or someone you know. What I am going to do is show you the pictures and tell you a little bit of the story. Because you know a lot about kids, I would like you to help me make the stories as true as possible.

Using a predetermined randomized order, the four stories with similar outcomes were presented to the child one at a time. Before telling the child the story, the interviewer handed the child a photograph representing the story. When interviewers thought that the child's response was of questionable codability, they probed. When interviewers were satisfied that they understood the child's response, they handed the child the next picture and the process continued. When all four stories were completed, children were escorted back to their classrooms by their interviewers.

Source: From Frieze, I. H., and Snyder, H. M. (1980). Children's beliefs about the causes of success and failure in school settings. *Journal of Educational Psychology, 72,* 186–196. Copyright © 1980 by the American Psychological Association. Reprinted by permission of the publisher and authors.

technique for gathering information, the observational method relies on a researcher's seeing and hearing things and recording these observations, rather than relying on subjects' self-report responses to questions or statements.

The role of the observer in most quantitative research is to remain detached from the group or process, and thus act as a **complete observer.** A researcher may, for example, want to study the adjustment of college freshmen to campus life by observing the behavior of freshmen in various settings as an outsider, not participating but simply recording information.

The role of observer also depends on the degree of inference or judgment that is required. At one extreme, the observer makes **high inference** observations, which require the observer to make judgments or inferences based on the observed behaviors. What is recorded with high inference observation is the judgment of the observer. For example, a high inference observation of a teacher would be a rating made by the principal on factors such as classroom management and enthusiasm. The principal would observe the class and make a rating of excellent, good, fair, or poor in each of the two areas. **Low inference** observation, on the other hand, requires the observer to record specific behaviors without making judgments in a more global sense. Thus, the principal might record the number of rebukes or cues used by the teacher as information that is used subsequently to judge classroom management. Low inference observation usually is more reliable, but many would argue that it is necessary to make judgments, based on the complexity and multitude of variables in a classroom, for valid observations. An in-between role for the observer is to make judgments (high inference) and then record the specific behaviors and context that led to the inference implied in the judgment.

Justification

The primary advantages of using observational methods are that the researcher does not need to worry about the limitations of self-report bias, social desirability, or response set, and the information is not limited to what can be recalled accurately by the subjects. Behavior can be recorded as it occurs naturally. This advantage is very important for research designed to study what occurs in real life as opposed to highly contrived or artificial settings. However, observational research is expensive and difficult to conduct reliably for complex behavior. It is relatively easy and straightforward to record simple behavior objectively, but most studies focus on more complex behavior that is difficult to define and assess through observation. There is also the problem of the way the observer affects the behavior of subjects by being present in the setting.

Defining Observational Units

The first step in developing an observational study is to define in precise terms what will be observed. Beginning with the research problem or question, the variables that need to be observed are ascertained. If the problem or question is general, such as "How long are students engaged academically?" then the researcher must narrow the purpose to obtain specific, measurable units that can be observed. Since it is impossible to observe everything that occurs, the researcher must decide on the variables or units of analysis that are most important and then define the behavior so that it can be recorded objectively.

Recording Observations

Once the researcher defines the behavior to be observed, the recording procedure is selected. There are five types: duration recording, frequency-count recording, interval recording, continuous observation, and time sampling.

Duration Recording In **duration recording** the observer indicates the length of time a particular kind of behavior lasts. Often a stop watch is used to keep track of the duration of the behavior. The researcher thus simply looks for a type of behavior (for example, *out of seat, talking to other students*) and records the length of time this type of behavior occurs within a given time span.

Frequency-Count Recording Frequency-count recording is used when the observer is interested only in the frequency with which the behavior occurs, not the length of time it persists. Generally, the observer has a list of several kinds of behavior that will be recorded and keeps a running tally to indicate how often each occurs. Obviously, this type of recording is best when the duration of the behavior is short (from one to five seconds).

Interval Recording In **interval recording** a single subject is observed for a given time (usually from ten seconds to one minute) and the behaviors that occur are recorded. The observer could indicate that each kind of behavior either does or does not occur, or he or she may record how many times it occurs within each interval.

Continuous Observation In **continuous observation** the observer provides a brief description of the behavior of the subject over an extended period. The description is written in chronological order and the observer must decide which kind of behavior is important.

Time Sampling In **time sampling** the observer selects, at random or on a fixed schedule, the time periods that will be used to observe particular kinds of behavior. This procedure is used in conjunction with each of the four previously mentioned procedures.

If possible, it is best to locate existing observational schedules that have been standardized to some degree. Virtually hundreds of schedules have been developed, and because they have been pilot tested and used in previous studies, they are more likely than new schedules to demonstrate good validity and reliability.

Training Observers

The most important limitation of complete observation is with the person who records what is seen and heard—the observer. The difficulty lies in obtaining observations that are objective, unbiased, and accurate in the sense that the observer has avoided influencing the behavior of the subjects. The objectivity of the observer depends to some degree on the specificity of the behavior. That is, a kind of behavior described as "teasing other students" is much less specific and subject to error in interpretation than something as specific and objective as "raises hand" or "leaves chair."

Bias is a factor in observational research to the extent that the idiosyncratic perceptions and interpretations of the observer, influenced by previous experiences, affect the recording of behavior. While it is next to impossible to eliminate bias, there is a need to control it. One way to control bias is by carefully choosing observers. Obviously it would be a bad idea to choose, as an observer of the effects of authentic assessment, an advocate of that kind of education, just as it would be unfair to choose a known opponent, since their preconceived notions could easily bias their observations. A second approach to controlling bias is to use carefully trained observers, comparing their observations with each other's in similar and different situations. Third, bias is mitigated by using two observers in each setting during the study. As long as the observers agree independently, there is less chance that bias is a confounding factor. A final type of bias that needs to be considered is contamination, which may occur if the observer is knowledgeable about the specifics of the study. In a study of the differences between so-called good and poor teachers, for example, if the observer knows before making the observations which teachers are supposedly good and which poor, this knowledge is likely to bias the observations. It is thus best for the observers to have little or no knowledge of the purpose of the study. Their job is to observe and record in an objective, detached manner.

Unobtrusive Measures

Questionnaires, interviews, and direct observation are intrusive or reactive in the sense that the participants realize they are being questioned or watched. A major difficulty with subjects' awareness that they are participants is that their behavior may be affected by this knowledge. A type of measurement that is considered to be **nonreactive**, in which subjects are asked or required to do nothing out of the ordinary, is called *unobtrusive*. **Unobtrusive measures** provide data that are uninfluenced by an awareness of the subjects that they are participants, or by an alteration in the natural course of events.

The major types of unobtrusive measures include physical traces, such as worn floors, books, or computers, documents, reports, letters, and observation in which the subject is unaware of being researched. See Webb, Campbell, Schwartz, and Sechrest (2000).

There are both strengths and weaknesses with each of the five major types of data collection techniques we have discussed in this chapter. These strengths and weaknesses are summarized in Table 8.7. Researchers need to consider

TABLE 8.7

Strengths and Weaknesses of Data Collection Techniques

Technique	Strengths	Weaknesses
Paper-and-Pencil Tests	Economical Standard questions Commercial tests strong in technical qualities Objective tests easy to score Standardized tests provide uniform procedures for all subjects and standard scores	Norms may be inappropriate Standardized tests may be too broad and general Standard scores may distort differences Standardized tests may give a false sense of validity Locally developed tasks often technically weak Test anxiety Restricted to subjects who can read
Alternative Assessment	Provides direct, holistic measure of skills Closely aligned to instruction Uses more authentic contexts	Subjective ratings result in low reliability Poor sampling of larger domain of skills Costly Time-consuming
Questionnaire	Economical Can be anonymous Standard questions and uniform procedures Usually easy to score Provides time for subjects to think about responses	Response rate of mailed questionnaires Inability to probe and clarify Scoring open-ended items Faking and social desirability Restricted to subjects who can read and write Biased or ambiguous items Response set
Interview	Flexible Adaptable Ability to probe and clarify Ability to include nonverbal behavior High response rate Used with nonreaders	Costly Time-consuming Interviewer bias Not anonymous Subject effects Effect of interviewer characteristics Requires training Leading questions
Observation	Captures natural behavior Mitigates social desirability, response set, and subject effects Relatively unobtrusive Reliable for low inference observations	Costly Time-consuming Effect of observer on subjects Observer bias Requires training Reliability difficult for complex behavior and high inference observations Inability to probe and clarify Usually not anonymous Interpretation of high inference observations

these in selecting appropriate methods of gathering information. What technique will provide the most reliable and valid measure of the trait? What technique is most feasible? How can potential weaknesses be mitigated?

Summary

This chapter has introduced several techniques that are commonly used to collect descriptive, quantitative data. These techniques are used in basic, applied, and evaluation research and can be used in experimental or nonexperimental research. The major points in the chapter are the following:

1. Evidence to establish valid inferences from test scores should be appropriate to the use of the results.
2. Evidence for validity is based on four components: content, response processes, internal structure, and relations to other variables.
3. There are five major types of reliability that are used to judge the consistency of scores: stability, equivalence, stability and equivalence, internal consistency, and agreement.
4. Standardized tests provide uniform procedures for administration and scoring.
5. Norm-referenced test results are based on comparing a score with the scores of a reference or norming group.
6. Criterion-referenced test results compare a score with an established standard of performance.
7. Aptitude tests predict behavior.
8. Achievement tests measure prior learning.
9. Alternative assessments, which include performance-based and portfolio assessments, provide a direct, constructed-response measure of skills.
10. Noncognitive instruments measure personality, attitudes, values, and interests.
11. Written questionnaires are economical, can ensure anonymity, and permit use of standardized questions.
12. Existing questionnaires probably have better reliability and validity than those developed by a researcher.
13. Items in a questionnaire should be based on specific objectives and be clear, relevant, short, and uncluttered. Biased items and terms should be avoided.
14. Items are in a closed or open format, depending on the objectives and nature of the information desired.
15. Scaled items, such as Likert and semantic differential items, use gradations of responses.
16. Questionnaires are economical and can be anonymous.
17. Interview schedules provide flexibility and the ability to probe and clarify responses; they note nonverbal as well as verbal behavior. They provide high response rates but are costly and more susceptible to bias.
18. Interview questions are either structured, semistructured, or unstructured. Each type has advantages and disadvantages.
19. Observational procedures can record naturally occurring behavior and avoid some of the disadvantages associated with questionnaires and interviews.

20. Establishing and maintaining reliability and validity in observational research is difficult.
21. Low inference observations stress objective recording of behavior, while high inference observations require greater subjective judgments of observers.
22. Recording procedures in direct observation include duration, frequency, interval, continuous, and time sampling.
23. Unobtrusive measures are nonreactive and can be used to collect data without disruption of a naturally occurring event.

Self-Instructional Review Exercises

Sample answers are in the back of the book.

Test Items

1. Evidence based on content is most appropriate for
   a. predictive tests.
   b. achievement tests.
   c. aptitude tests.
   d. Both b and c are correct.
2. Test criterion relationships differ from criterion-referenced tests in that
   a. criterion-referenced tests uses norm groups while test criterion relationships use criteria.
   b. criterion-related evidence is a type of reliability; criterion-referenced tests uses norm groups.
   c. test criterion relationship is for validity; criterion-referenced is for reliability.
   d. criterion-referenced tests use criteria; test criterion relationship is for validity.
3. Internal consistency estimates of reliability are widely used because
   a. only one form of a test is needed.
   b. the reliability coefficient is usually very high.
   c. it is the easiest to calculate.
   d. it is more accurate than stability and equivalence estimates.
4. Standardized tests are different from locally devised instruments in that standardized tests
   a. have norms as well as technical support.
   b. have greater flexibility.
   c. are more valid.
   d. have uniform administration and scoring procedures.
5. The purpose of an aptitude test is to
   a. measure intelligence.
   b. predict performance.
   c. measure multiple aspects of potential strengths.
   d. assess achievement.

6. Noncognitive inventories are generally
   a. susceptible to faking.
   b. high in reliability.
   c. high in validity.
   d. socially desirable.

7. Choose the correct sequence for developing a questionnaire.
   a. defining objectives, justification, writing items, pretesting
   b. pretesting, defining objectives, justification, writing items
   c. justification, pretesting, defining objectives, writing items
   d. justification, defining objectives, writing items, pretesting

8. All of the following should be adhered to in writing statements or questions *except* for
   a. avoiding biased items.
   b. avoiding negatively worded items.
   c. using double-barrelled questions.
   d. making items clear.
   e. making items short.

9. Social desirability is a form of
   a. bias.
   b. unreliability.
   c. situational constraint.
   d. Both a and c are correct.

10. The format of a questionnaire should
    a. use every available space on each page.
    b. use abbreviated items to save space.
    c. put important items first on long questionnaires.
    d. be as short as possible in number of pages.

11. Closed-form questions or statements are best used for
    a. easily categorized information.
    b. initial pilot studies.
    c. large-scale studies.
    d. Both a and c are correct.

12. Likert scale and semantic differential items are similar in that both
    a. use adjective opposites.
    b. are easy to construct.
    c. are difficult to score objectively.
    d. are scales.

13. Questionnaires need to be pilot tested because
    a. pretesting establishes reliability.
    b. insufficient variation in answers can be noted.
    c. trial data analyses can be noted.
    d. Both a and b are correct.

14. Semistructured questions in interviews are written in a format that allows
    a. free response to a limited question.
    b. forced choice response to a limited question.

c. free response to a broad question.

d. forced choice response to a broad question.

15. It is best for interviewers to adapt the specific wording of questions to the individual characteristics of the respondent. True or false?

a. true

b. false

16. Interviewers should always dress in a businesslike manner (for example, tie, suit, dress). True or false?

a. true

b. false

17. The most common approach to recording answers in an interview is

a. audiotape recorder.

b. videotape recorder.

c. writing verbatim responses.

d. writing notes.

18. The complete observer

a. tries to become a member of the group of subjects.

b. is unobtrusive.

c. is detached from the setting.

d. is completely informed as to the nature of the study.

19. Observation is most objective when the observer has to check appropriate boxes on a standard, easy to interpret form. True or false?

a. true

b. false

20. Observer bias can be controlled by all of the following except

a. choosing observers carefully.

b. informing the observer of the nature of the study.

c. carefully training observers.

d. using two or more observers in each situation.

21. Another word for *unobtrusive* measures would be

a. biased.

b. unreliable.

c. nonreactive.

d. unbiased.

Application Problems

1. For each of the following cases indicate whether the questionnaire, interview, or observation technique would be most appropriate, and justify your answer.

a. Reasons that 1,500 couples believe they have problems in their marriages

b. The attitudes of seventh-grade students toward mainstreamed children

c. Knowledge of parents regarding the curriculum in the school

d. Average age and experience of school principals

e. Effect of watching violent TV programs on aggressive behavior

f. College students' perceptions of the effectiveness of residence hall advisors

   g. Attitudes of preschool children toward their parents

   h. Attitudes of teachers toward competence-based instruction

2. Indicate what is wrong with the following questionnaire items:

   a. What do you think about open education?

   b. Rank the statements from most important to least important.

   c. Senior and junior high school teachers need more training in ways to motivate students.

| ——— | ——— | ——— | ——— |
| Strongly agree | Agree | Disagree | Strongly disagree |

   d. Mrs. Jones is a good teacher.

| ——— | ——— | ——— | ——— |
| Strongly agree | Agree | Disagree | Strongly disagree |

3. It is important for teachers to observe and record indications that their students are studying and trying to learn assigned material. If a third-grade teacher came to you and asked how such observations could be made with the least amount of disruption to the normal routine, what suggestions would you have?

CHAPTER 9

Nonexperimental Research Designs and Surveys

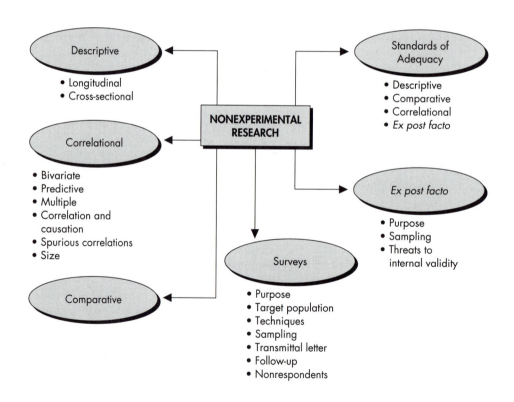

KEY TERMS

descriptive research

developmental studies

longitudinal

cross-sectional

comparative research

bivariate

prediction studies

predictor variable

criterion variable

multiple regression prediction
  equation

regression coefficient

beta weights

coefficient of multiple
  correlation

path analysis

spurious correlation

attenuation

restriction in range

coefficient of determination

survey research

ex post facto research

In Chapter 2 an important distinction was made between experimental and nonexperimental modes of inquiry. In this chapter we will consider four common types of nonexperimental designs in greater depth, along with survey research.

Descriptive Research

Descriptive research is concerned with the current or past status of something. This type of research simply describes achievement, attitudes, behaviors, or other characteristics of a group of subjects. A descriptive study asks *what is* or *what was*; it reports things the way they *are* or *were*. Descriptive research does not involve manipulation of independent variables.

Descriptive research provides very valuable data, particularly when first investigating an area. For example, there has been much research on the nature of classroom climate and its relationship to student attitudes and learning. A first step in this research was to describe adequately what is meant by "classroom climate." Climate surveys, which assess characteristics such as how students talk and act toward one another, how they feel about the teacher, and feelings of openness, acceptance, trust, and respect, are used to understand the atmosphere of the classroom. Once this descriptive understanding is achieved, various dimensions of climate can be related to student learning and teacher satisfaction, and ultimately climate can be controlled to examine causal relationships. For many teachers, simply describing the climate can be very useful in understanding the nature of their class. Or suppose you want to study the relationship between leadership styles of principals and teacher morale. Again, a first step is to describe principal leadership styles. The appropriate descriptive question might be: what are the leadership styles of principals? Here are some other descriptive research questions:

How much do college students exercise?

What are the attitudes of students toward mainstreamed children?

How often do students cheat?

What do teachers think about merit pay?

How do students spend their time during independent study?

What are the components of the gifted program?

Questions like these are very important because they provide the basis for asking additional questions. Once a phenomenon is described adequately, developmental, difference, and relationship questions can be addressed. **Developmental studies** investigate changes of subjects over time. The "same" group of subjects may be studied over some length of time (**longitudinal**) on factors such as cognitive, social–emotional or physical variables. For example, a longitudinal developmental study of adult development would begin by identifying a group of adults as subjects; measure dependent variables such as interests, goal satisfaction, friendship patterns, etc.; and then continue to measure these variables for the same subjects every five years. Actually, there are variations of longitudinal designs, depending on the subjects who are samples or are used to make up the "same" group. In a *trend* study a general population is studied over time, although the subjects are sampled from the population each year or other time of data collection. In a *cohort* longitudinal study the same population is studied over time, and in a *panel* study the same individuals are surveyed each time data are collected. Developmental studies can also be **cross-sectional**, in which different groups of subjects (for example, as in our study of adult 20-, 25-, 30-, 35-, 40-, and 45-year-old groups) are studied at the same time.

An obvious advantage of a panel study is that since the same group is studied over time, comparability of subjects is assured. Another advantage is that the subjects respond to present circumstances, attitudes, beliefs, etc., rather than trying to recollect the past. A disadvantage of trend studies is that the population of interest may change from one year to the next, which could affect the results. A good example of this is the trend analysis of SAT scores. While it is true that the average SAT score for all students taking the test has declined (until the renorming in 1995), this decline is more a function of who took the test than the performance of the students. As illustrated in Figures 9.1 and 9.2, the decline is really caused by more students who are less able taking the test. The actual finding, when SAT scores are analyzed for different levels of high school performers, is that the scores have remained relatively stable; they clearly do not show a decline.

A major disadvantage of longitudinal research is that it takes a long time to complete, and it involves significant commitments of the researcher's time, money, and resources. It is also difficult to keep track of subjects and maintain their cooperation for an extended period. Researchers involved in cross-sectional studies can study larger groups at less cost, all at the same time. Thus

FIGURE 9.1   Average SAT by High School Class Rank

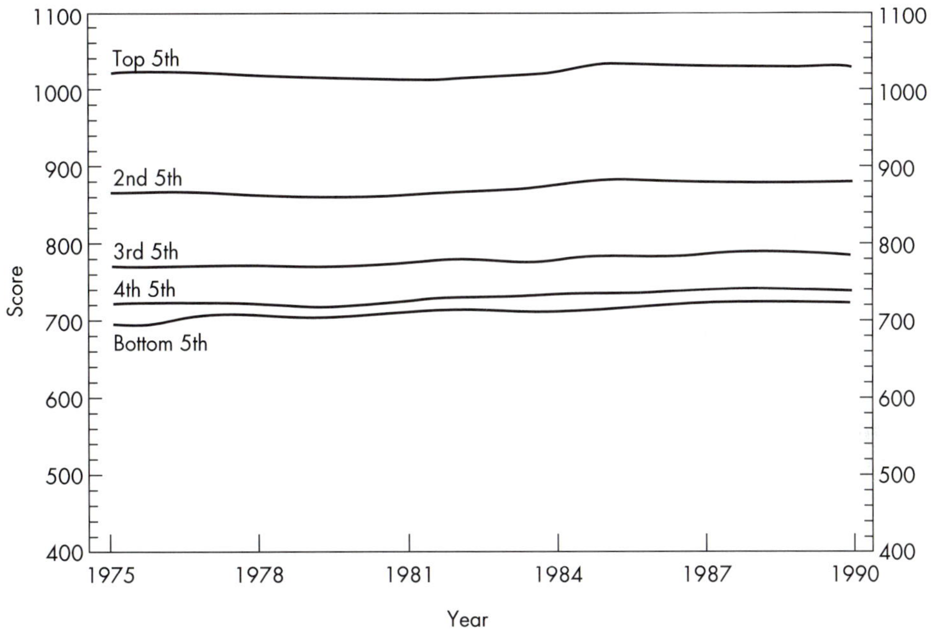

Source: Perspectives on Education in America (1991). Albuquerque, NM: Sandia National Laboratories.

they do not need to wait years to complete the research. The major disadvantage of cross-sectional research is that selection differences between the groups may bias the results.

An important limitation of descriptive studies is that relationship conclusions are not warranted. It is easy to make assumptions from simple descriptions about how two or more variables are related, but it will lead to spurious conclusions. For example, suppose a study describes the types of questions students and teachers ask in a classroom, and reports that teachers ask primarily "low-level" questions and students ask few if any questions at all. It would be tempting to conclude that there is a relationship between these phenomena, that is, a relationship between age or position and type of question asked. However, one cannot make such a conclusion unless students ask a certain type of question rather than no questions at all.

It is also important in descriptive research to pay close attention to the nature of the subjects and the instruments. You should know, for example, whether the sample is made up of volunteers and whether results could have been different if other subjects had been included. Data collection techniques need to address reliability and validity, and procedures for collection information should be specified. You need to indicate when the data were collected, by whom, and under what circumstances. For example, the description of a classroom may well differ, depending on whether the observer is a teacher, parent, or principal.

FIGURE 9.2   Percent of Students Taking SAT by Class Rank

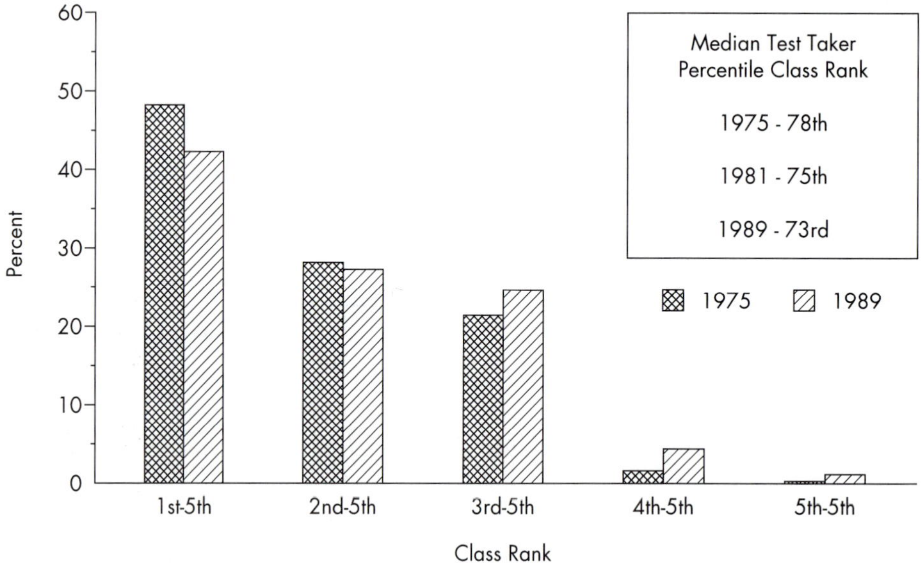

Source: *Perspectives on Education in America* (1991). Albuquerque, NM: Sandia National Laboratories.

Relationships in Nonexperimental Research

Before examining comparative and correlational studies, we must clarify the nature of *relationships among variables*. All quantitative research that is not simply descriptive is interested in relationships. A relationship, or association, is found when one variable varies systematically with another variable. This can be accomplished either by comparing different groups or with correlations.

A relationship established by comparing different groups is illustrated in Figure 9.3. Here the variables of interest are grade level and self-concept. There is a relationship between grade level and self-concept because there are progressively fewer students with a high self-concept as grade level increases. In this case the relationship is negative since as grade level increases, the number of high self-concept students decreases. This same research question could be examined by computing a correlation coefficient between grade level and self-concept score.

Relationships are important in our understanding of teaching and learning for several reasons. First, relationships allow us to make a preliminary identification of possible causes of important educational outcomes. Second, relationships help us identify variables that need further investigation. Third,

FIGURE 9.3   Relationship Between Grade Level and Self-Concept.

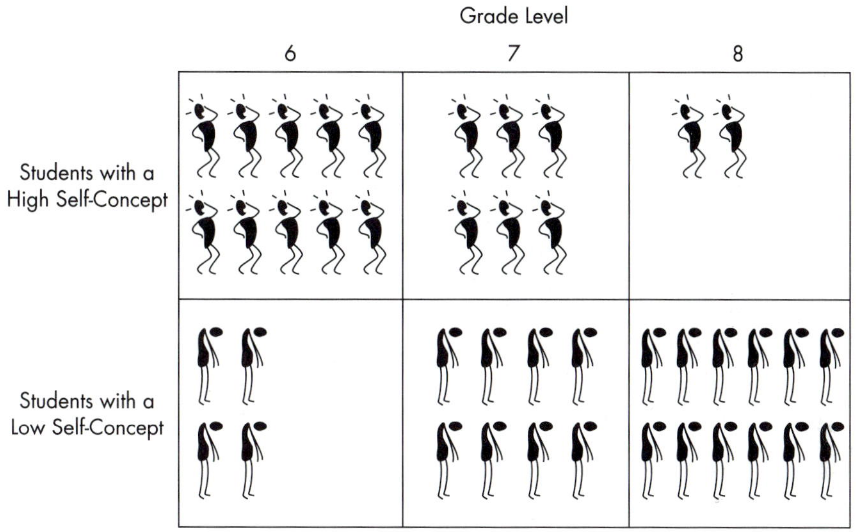

Grade Level

Source: From McMillan, J. H. (2000). *Educational Research: Fundamentals for the Consumer.* 3rd ed., New York: Longman, p. 180.

relationships allow us to predict one variable from another. As we will see later in this chapter, prediction is needed for a variety of purposes.

Comparative Research

The purpose of comparative studies is to investigate the relationship of one variable to another by simply examining whether the value of the dependent variable in one group is different from the value of the dependent variable in the other group. In other words, **comparative research** examines the differences between two or more groups on a variable.

Examples of difference questions are these:

Is there a difference in eighth-grade compared with ninth-grade attitudes toward school?

What is the difference between students attending private schools and students attending public schools?

How are new teachers different from experienced teachers?

Is there a difference between second-, third-, and fourth-grade self-concept scores?

In each case, the researcher makes a comparison based on descriptive data.

A simple example of comparative research is a study of the relationship between gender and school grades. A sample of female students' grades could be compared to the grades of a sample of male students. The results show how differences in one variable, gender, relate to differences on another variable, grades. If the results show that females have a higher grade point average (not surprising!), this indicates that there is a relationship between the two variables. Note, however, that this is not a *causal* relationship. While we can predict grades by knowing gender, we don't know why being male or female affects grades.

Another example is a study of the relationship between learning styles and achievement. Suppose there are four types or categories of learning styles and a measure of reading achievement. A sample of students representing each learning style can be obtained, and the average reading score for each group can be compared. If we find that some styles are associated with higher reading achievement there is a relationship, though, as in the example of gender and grades, it can not be concluded that the styles caused the achievement. This hypothetical study is diagramed in Figure 9.4.

A good example of published comparative research that investigated differences is a study of time allocated to instruction for elementary special education students (Ysseldyke, Thurlow, Christenson, & Weiss, 1987). This study was conducted because there was little indication from previous research how instructional time was allocated for handicapped students. There was also little evidence that showed whether instructional time allocation differed for differ-

FIGURE 9.4 Diagram of a Relationship Study Comparing Different Groups

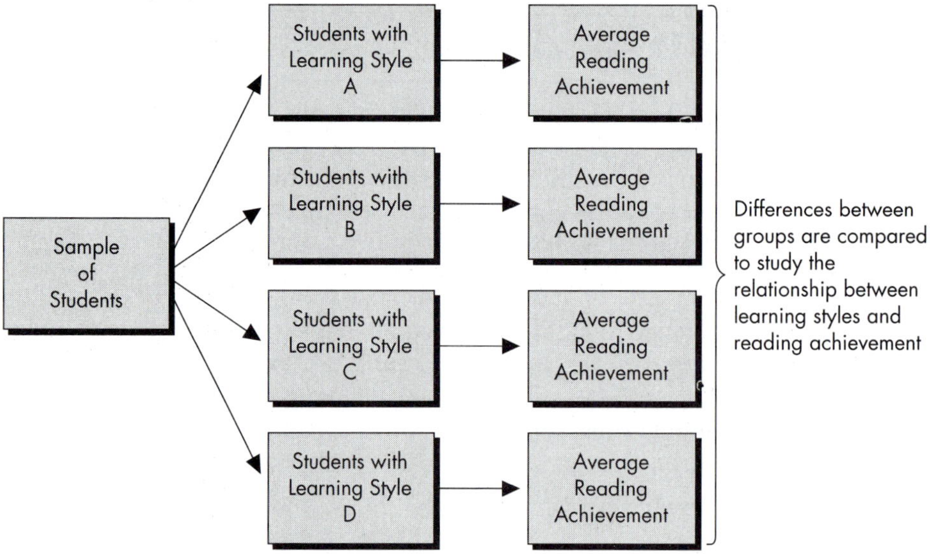

Source: From McMillan, J. H. (2000). *Educational Research: Fundamentals for the Consumer,* 3rd ed., New York: Longman, p. 181.

EXCERPT 9.1

DESCRIPTIVE RESEARCH COMPARING DIFFERENCES

To what extent are there differences in the amount of time allocated to instruction in specific subject matter areas for learning disabled, emotionally/behaviorally disturbed, educable mentally retarded, and nonhandicapped students?

Source: From Ysseldyke, J. E, Thurlow, M. L., Christenson, S. L., & Weiss, J. (1987). Time allocated to instruction of mentally retarded, learning disabled, emotionally disturbed, and nonhandicapped students. *The Journal of Special Education, 21,* 43–55.

ent categories of handicapped students. Thus, this study was comparative in the sense that it investigated differences between the handicapping conditions on time allocation. The research question from this study in Excerpt 9.1 illustrates comparative research.

An example of comparative research that investigates a relationship is illustrated in Excerpt 9.2. In this study the researchers surveyed teachers from public and Catholic private schools to investigate differences in organizational value orientation, teacher commitment, and job satisfaction. Thus, the question is: Is there a relationship (difference) between type of school (public or private) and value orientation, teacher commitment, and job satisfaction?

Excerpt 9.3 shows how the term *comparative* is used to describe the research.

Excerpt 9.4 is an example of how descriptive and comparative data are reported in journals. This study summarized children's responses to the question why they succeeded or failed in school. Essentially this is a description of children's responses. Since both success and failure conditions are used to generate the responses, the research also examines differences of success compared to failure conditions.

EXCERPT 9.2

DESCRIPTIVE RESEARCH INVESTIGATING RELATIONSHIPS

In this study, we investigate the relationship between organizational value orientation and two variables, organizational commitment and job satisfaction, among teachers from private and public schools. . . . results of this study suggested that (a) private schools exhibit a more normative orientation; and (b) schools with a more normative value orientation had significantly higher teacher organizational commitment and job satisfaction than did schools with a more utilitarian value orientation.

Source: From Reyes, P., & Pounder, D. G. (1993). Organizational orientation in public and private elementary schools. *Journal of Educational Research, 87,* 86–93.

EXCERPT 9.3

COMPARATIVE RESEARCH

The purpose was to identify variables that can promote effective science learning environments for all students. Specifically, comparisons were made between the perceptions of male and female students and of black and white students within the same classes. In addition, perceptions of the learning environment were compared for students in classes taught by male and female teachers as well as black and white teachers.

Source: Huffman, D., Lawrenz, F., & Minger, M. (1997). Within-class analysis of ninth-grade science students' perceptions of the learning environment. *Journal of Research in Science Teaching, 34,* 791–804.

EXCERPT 9.4

DESCRIPTIVE AND COMPARATIVE RESULTS

The data in Table I indicate that the children were able to identify the variables that affect their success and failure. Their initial attributions were primarily task attributions (46% to 58% said the words were easy). Their own effort was the next most common cause of their success (40% of the responses). When asked for a second response, the subjects evenly divided their answers among the four types of attributions. From the total responses, when they succeeded in reading a word, they were most likely to attribute their success to their effort (33%) or to task difficulty (37%). When they failed to read a word they were most likely to attribute their failure to task features (40%).

TABLE 1   Percentages of Children Who Named Various Attributes in Response to Why They Succeeded (S) or Failed (F)

	Question Condition					
	Initial[a]		Second[b]		Total	
Types of Attributions	S	F	S	F	S	F
Ability	.10	.02	.22	.05	.16	.03
Effort	.40	.12	.25	.15	.33	.14
Task Difficulty	.46	.58	.28	.22	.37	.40
Luck	.02	.15	.15	.20	.08	.18
Other[c]	.02	.12	.10	.38	.06	.25

[a]*Initial* includes those children who responded spontaneously and those who were given a choice of responses if they did not respond spontaneously.
[b]*Second* is a second attribution the children gave.
[c]Other is composed of "don't know's," "I guessed," and no response.
Note: N = 40.

Source: From Cauley, K. M., & Murray, F. B. (1982). Structure of Children's Reasoning About Attributes of School Success and Failure. *American Educational Research Journal, 19,* 473–480. Copyright © 1982, American Educational Research Association, Washington, DC. Reprinted by permission.

Like descriptive studies, comparative research needs to provide a clear description of subjects, instrumentation, and procedures. Also like descriptive research, causal conclusions can not be made. The best that can be concluded is that there is a difference or relationship. This principle is easily overlooked because some comparative studies seem to logically establish a causal connection between the independent and dependent variables. For example, suppose it is reported that students from private charter schools outperform students from public schools. It is tempting to conclude that the reason, or cause, of the difference is the nature of the school. However, there are many other possible explanations, such as differences in parental involvement, or socioeconomic status of the students.

Often comparative research results are presented in graphs. As pointed out in Chapter 7, sometimes a visual image does not match well with the actual data. When interpreting such graphs, be sure to examine the actual numbers or scales on which the graph is based and be alert to distortions.

Correlational Research

Chapter 7 described the correlation coefficient. In this chapter we use the basic idea of correlation as a way to conceptualize research problems. We first present simple relationship studies, then more complex multifactor prediction research, followed by cautions in interpreting correlations.

Bivariate Correlational Studies

In a bivariate correlational study, researchers obtain scores from two variables for each subject and then use the pairs of scores to calculate a correlation coefficient. The term **bivariate** or *zero-order* means that two variables are correlated. The variables are selected because theory, research, or experience suggest that they may be related. Then a sample is selected and data are collected from the sample. It is important in correlational studies that researchers select the subjects to provide a range of responses on the variables. If the subjects are homogeneous with respect to either variable, a relationship between the variables is unlikely. Similarly, it is important to select instruments that are reliable and will provide a range of responses. Various methods of instrumentation can be used, including tests, questionnaires, interviews, or observations. Regardless of the type of instrumentation it is best to conduct a pilot test or have previous data from similar subjects to ensure reliability and variability in responses. For instance, it is often difficult to relate student ratings of professors to other variables because of a ceiling effect in such ratings, which results in most professors being rated high. Similarly, norm-referenced achievement scores of gifted students are unlikely to correlate with other variables because the scores may have a restricted range (we will discuss restricted range in more detail later in the chapter).

In some relationship studies bivariate correlations of several variables may be reported. In fact, an advantage of correlational research is that it permits the simultaneous study of several variables. However, it is possible for some researchers, without reasonable justification, to measure a large number of variables to find some significant relationships. This is called the *shotgun* approach, and it is used inappropriately in the hope that some of the many correlations calculated will indicate significant relationships.

An example of how the results from a bivariate correlational study are presented is illustrated in Excerpt 9.5. In this study bivariate correlations were calculated to explore relationships between adolescents' and mothers' attitudes toward science, intrinsic value of science, peer support, available science activities, grades, science grade point average, and preference for future science careers.

Prediction Studies

There are many situations in education when we need to make predictions. Teachers predict student reactions in making certain assignments. Principals predict teacher behavior on the basis of the criteria used for evaluation of teacher effectiveness. Teachers counsel students to focus on particular majors on the basis of occupational interest or aptitude tests. Students are selected for special programs because teachers predict that they will do better than other students.

EXCERPT 9.5

PRESENTATION OF BIVARIATE CORRELATION RESULTS

Zero-Order Correlations between Perceived
Motivational Context Variables and Indexes of Alienation

Independent Variables	1	2	3	4	5	6	7	8	9
1. Science GPA	1.0								
2. Grade in school	.02	1.0							
3. Friends' support	.16	.05	1.0						
4. Number of science/math activities	.21*	−.15	.20*	1.0					
5. Number of nonscience activities	.21*	.02	.08	.23**	1.0				
6. Mothers' perceptions of child's science ability	.56**	−.05	.10	.17*	.07	1.0			
7. Mothers' valuing of science for females	.13	−.01	.09	.19*	.03	.30**	1.0		
8. Adolescents' interest in biology	.28**	.02	.19*	.36**	.14	.29**	.16	1.0	
9. Adolescents' interest in physical science	.29**	.08	.08	.29**	.23**	.39**	−.24**	.47**	.10

$*p < .05.$ $**p < .01.$

Source: Jacobs, J. E., Finken, L. L., Griffin, N. L., & Wright, J. D. (1998). The career plans of science-talented rural adolescent girls. *American Educational Research Journal, 35* (4), 681–704.

We conduct **prediction studies** to provide a more accurate estimation of prediction. Suppose you are the director of admissions at a small, selective college. A large number of students apply to the college each year, many more than can be admitted. How will you decide which students should be admitted? You could draw names from a hat randomly, but then some students will be admitted who may flunk out, while some well-qualified students will be rejected. You decide that it would be best if you could *predict,* on the basis of already established characteristics, which students are most likely to succeed. Since it seems reasonable that prior achievement will predict later achievement, you see whether there is a correlation between high school grade point average (GPA) (prior) and college GPA (later achievement). When you discover that these two variables correlate .70, then you have information that can be used to select students. Other things being equal, high school students with high GPAs are more likely to have high college GPAs than high school students with low GPAs.

In this case high school GPA is a **predictor variable**, and college GPA is a **criterion variable**. The predictor variable is determined *before* the criterion variable. Thus, in prediction studies, outcomes such as grade point average, dropouts, success as a leader or manager, effectiveness of a drug to cure a disease, and the like, are related to behaviors that occurred prior to the criterion. To do this, it is necessary to have data on the subjects that span some length of time. This can be done retrospectively through records on subjects, or it can be done longitudinally by first collecting predictor variable data, waiting an appropriate amount of time, and then collecting the criterion variable data. For example, suppose you need to select the best new teachers for a school division. Essentially you are predicting that the new teachers you choose will be effective. In your state all prospective teachers take the Teacher Examinations (TE), so you are able to study the predictive relationship of the TE to teacher effectiveness (measured by principal and supervisor evaluations). Once you have established the predictive power of the TE with one group of teachers, you would "test" the predictive relationship with another group of new teachers. In "testing" the prediction the researcher uses the values of the predictor variables from a new group of prospective teachers, in this example actual scores on the TE, and then weights each score by a factor calculated from the original prediction equation. This will indicate how well the researcher can expect the TE to predict teacher effectiveness. The "tested" relationship will be lower than the one originally used to establish a prediction equation.

Excerpt 9.6 provides a good example of predictive research. In this study student success in a gifted program was used as the criterion variable, and scores from the WISC-R, teachers' recommendations, grades, and achievement test scores were used as predictor variables. Notice that one group of students is used to establish the predictive relationship and another group of students is used to "test" it.

It may occur to you that by having several predictor variables you would be able to make a more accurate prediction. Suppose in our example of predicting

EXCERPT 9.6

PREDICTION RESEARCH

This study was conducted in two phases. The initial phase of the study involved 120 elementary school students aged 6 through 11 years. These students had different degrees of success in a gifted program. . . . The second phase of the investigation involved random selection of an additional 41 subjects from the same gifted program. . . . In phase two, an attempt was made, using the results of phase one data, to predict the students who were known to have been either marginally or highly successful in the program.

Source: From Lustberg, R. S., Motta, R., & Naccari, N. (1990). A model using the WISC-R to predict success in programs for gifted students. *Psychology in the Schools, 27*, 126–131.

effective teaching we also had information such as college GPA, references, results of an interview, and a statement by each applicant in addition to the TE scores. Each subject would receive a score for each variable (the references, results of the interview, and statement would be judged and scored according to a rating system). All of the predictor variables can be combined to form what is called a **multiple regression** prediction equation. This equation adds together the predictive power of several independent variables. Each predictor variable could be represented by X_1, X_2, X_3, etc., and the criterion variable by Y. Thus, in our example:

$$Y = x_1 + x_2 + x_3 + x_4 + x_5$$

where

$$Y = \text{teaching effectiveness}$$
$$x_1 = \text{TE score}$$
$$x_2 = \text{college GPA}$$
$$x_3 = \text{rating on references}$$
$$x_4 = \text{rating on interview}$$
$$x_5 = \text{rating on applicant's statement}$$

To obtain a predicted teacher effectiveness score, values on each of the five predictor variables would be placed in the equation and each would be weighted by a number, called a **regression coefficient**, to determine the contribution of each factor to predicting teacher effectiveness. Since the units of each predictor variable are different (ratings might range from 0 to 10, GPA from 0 to 4) the regression coefficients in the equation cannot be compared directly. To compare the predictive power of the variables, the regression coefficients are converted to **beta weights**, which can be compared directly. Thus, in our example the relative contribution of each variable can be compared. If the beta weight for TE is .32 and the beta weight for GPA is .48, then GPA is contributing more than the TE in predicting teaching effectiveness. The combined effect of the independent variables, in terms of predictive power, to the dependent variable is represented by R, the coefficient of multiple correlation. The **coefficient of multiple correlation** can be thought of as a simple correlation of all the independent variables together with the dependent variable.

When planning a predictive study, the researcher should keep in mind several factors that will affect the accuracy of the prediction. One is the reliability of the measurement of the predictor and criterion variables. More reliable measures will result in more accurate predictions. Another factor is the length of time between the predictor and criterion variables. In most cases, predictions involving short time spans (e.g., weeks or months) are more accurate than those in which there is a long time between the predictor and criterion variables (e.g., years). This is because of the general principle that the correlation between two variables decreases as the amount of time between them increases; also, with more time there is more opportunity for other variables to affect the criterion variable, which would lower the prediction. Finally, some criterion variables, such as success in college, leadership, and effective teaching, are more difficult to predict because they are influenced by so many factors. Relatively simple criterion variables, such as success on the next mathematics test or being admitted to at least one college, are much less difficult to predict.

It should be pointed out that multiple regression is a versatile data analysis procedure that is used for many different kinds of studies, not just prediction research. It can be used with comparative and even experimental studies, and with variables that are nominal, ordinal, or interval in nature. Usually multiple regression is used whenever researchers are interested in the relationship of several independent variables combined with a dependent variable. Multiple regression also allows researchers to "control" for selected variables to determine the relationship between the remaining independent variables and the dependent variable. For example, if a study is investigating the relationship between class size and achievement, a measure of socioeconomic status could be "entered" first in the regression so that it is "controlled," allowing a conclusion about the relationship without having to worry about socioeconomic status being confounded with class size (e.g., smaller classes have higher socioeconomic status students). It is as if variability in achievement due to socioeconomic status is removed, allowing the remaining variability in achievement to be related to class size. Excerpt 9.7 shows how student background variables are "controlled" in a study of the relationship between after-school activities and academic achievement.

Excerpt 9.8 provides an example of the use of multiple correlation. In this study teacher burnout was predicted by eleven independent variables. The table summarizes the predictive relationship of the eleven variables to three indices of teacher burnout: emotional exhaustion, depersonalization, and personal accomplishment. Of the eleven independent variables only those that were

EXCERPT 9.7

MULTIPLE REGRESSION ANALYSES TO "CONTROL" FOR SELECTED VARIABLES

Each regression used one of the three measures of achievement as the criterion variable. In all three analyses, five student background variables were entered simultaneously as the first group of variables predicting one of the achievement measures. The background variables were the students' gender, grade level, ethnicity, free-lunch eligibility, and whether or not an adult was home after school. As the second step of the hierarchical multiple regression analysis, all five after-school activity variables were added as a group to determine if they explained a significant amount of variability in the achievement measures beyond that explained by the background variables alone.

Source: Cooper, H., Valentine, J. C., & Nye, B. (1999). Relationships between five after-school activities and academic achievement. *Journal of Educational Psychology, 91* (2), 369-378.

entered first (sex and age) or added significantly to the overall relationship are included in the table. In multiple regressions some variables can be forced or entered into the equation first to control for certain factors, that is, to remove these factors as influences on the relationship. In this case the researchers wanted to control for the effect of sex and age to see how much other variables could predict.

Although the vast majority of correlational research is concerned only with relationships, some statistical techniques use multiple correlations to investigate cause-and-effect questions. One technique, **path analysis**, uses the correlations of several variables to study causal patterns. A causal "model" is established, based on theory, which shows by arrows the cause sequences that are anticipated. The correlations between the variables in the model provide empirical evidence of the proposed causal links. A relatively new technique, *structural equation modeling*, or *latent variable* or *trait causal modeling*, is more powerful than path analysis because the measures tend to be more reliable and the inferences more valid. LISREL is a common type of structural equation modeling. Although these techniques are useful for examining causal relationships, they are sophisticated statistically and are difficult to use. Also, they have the same fundamental limitations as all correlational data. Unmeasured variables related to both the independent and dependent variables are always a source of potential alternative causal explanations, and the direction is not always clear.

Interpreting Correlational Research

Correlation coefficients are widely used in research and appear to be simple, straightforward indices of relationship. There are, however, several limitations with the use of correlation that need to be understood fully. Most concern an

EXCERPT 9.8

MULTIPLE CORRELATION RESEARCH

Results presented in Table 2 support previous findings that various contributors to burnout have differing effects upon the aspects of emotional exhaustion, depersonalization, and personal accomplishment (Maslach & Jackson, 1981; Schwab & Iwanicki, 1982a). For example, after controlling for sex and age, Role Conflict explained the largest percentage of variance in emotional exhaustion and depersonalization (24% and 12% respectively) while Autonomy does so in personal accomplishment (12%). Five of the hypothesized predictors accounted for significant variance in emotional exhaustion, four in depersonalization and only two in personal accomplishment. The only predictor significantly related to all aspects was Colleague Social Support. As indicated by the beta weights, the relationships between the significant organizational conditions and the aspects of burnout were in the directions hypothesized and had been reported in previous research (Maslach & Jackson, 1981; Schwab & Iwanicki, 1982a).

TABLE 2 Stepwise Multiple Regression Analyses for the Relationship among Significant Organizational/Personal Variables and Three Aspects of Burnout When Controlling for Age and Sex (N = 339)

Step	Variable Entered	R	R^2	Increase R^2	Beta	For R^2 F**
Emotional Exhaustion						
1	Sex and age[a]	.120	.014	.014		NS[b]
2	Role conflict	.493	.243	.229	.48	35.17
3	Expectations	.537	.288	.059	.26	33.14
4	Colleague social support	.553	.306	.018	−.16	28.79
5	Contingent punishment	.562	.315	.009	.10	24.95
6	Role ambiguity	.570	.325	.010	−.13	22.27
Depersonalization						
1	Sex and age[a]	.285	.081	.081		14.56
2	Role conflict	.352	.124	.043	.21	15.50
3	Participation in decision making	.374	.140	.016	−.14	13.26
4	Contingent punishment	.393	.155	.015	.12	11.92
5	Colleague social support	.407	.166	.011	−.12	10.76
Personal Accomplishment						
1	Sex and age[a]	.192	.037	.037		6.33
2	Autonomy	.349	.122	.045	.29	15.14
3	Colleague social support	.366	.134	.012	.12	12.62

[a]The background variables of sex and age were forced into the Stepwise Analysis at Step One. The remaining variables were allowed to enter in a stepwise fashion.
[b]NS = not significant.
**p ≤ 0.01.

Source: From Schwab, R. L., Jackson, S. E., & Schuler, R. S. (1986). Educator burnout: Sources and consequences, *Educational Research Quarterly, 10*, (3). Copyright © 1986 by University of Southern California. Reprinted by permission.

overinterpretation—making too much of a measured relationship. In this section we present some important principles that will help you understand the meaning of results of correlational research.

Correlation and Causation You may be familiar with the well-known injunction "never infer causation from correlation." This is a principle that is virtually drilled into the minds of students, and for good reason, since it is probably the most violated principle of measures of relationship.

There are two reasons correlation does not infer causation: first, a relationship between X and Y may be high, but there is no way to know whether X causes Y or Y causes X; and second, there may be unmeasured variables that are affecting the relationship. With respect to the direction of possible causation, consider this example: A researcher finds a high positive correlation between self-concept and achievement. Does this mean that improving self-concept will cause an improvement in achievement? Perhaps, but it would be equally plausible for improved achievement to result in a higher self-concept. If we find that school dropout rates are negatively associated with teacher salaries, should we assume that higher teacher pay will cause fewer dropouts?

Unaccounted-for variables are also important to consider in interpreting correlations. Let us say that there is a positive relationship between attending church-related schools and honesty. Although the schools may help cause greater honesty, there are many other variables, such as family beliefs, parental attitudes, and methods of discipline, that would be more plausibly related in a causal way. Or what about the finding that schools that spend more per pupil have higher achievement? It would be a mistake to pump money into poor schools with the expectation that this will cause better achievement, because family background, an unmeasured variable, would more likely be a much larger factor in achievement than per pupil expenditure.

These two limitations seem straightforward enough, but correlations are still misinterpreted. Consider the *fact* that there is a strong positive relationship between body weight and reading achievement. Unbelievable? Examine the explanation that follows (adapted from Halperin, 1978).

1. Plot the body weight and scores of a group of first graders.

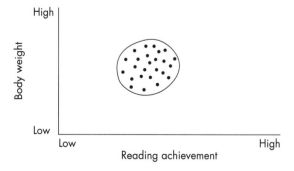

2. Next, add the scores of second graders:

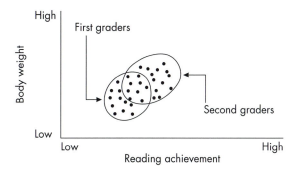

3. Finally, add the scores of pupils in grades three through six:

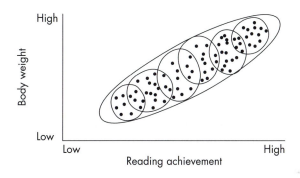

Voilà! We now have a positive relationship between body weight and reading achievement by stringing together a series of near-zero correlations. Why? Because a third variable that was not included, age, happens to be related to body weight, and, obviously, there is a positive relationship between age and reading achievement. If the reader believes that correlation did mean causation, then reading achievement could be improved by fattening up students! (Or improving reading achievement would lead to fatter students.)

Spurious Correlations When a correlation overrepresents or underrepresents the actual relationship it is called a **spurious correlation**. Spurious correlations that overestimate relationships are obtained if there is a common variable that is part of both the independent and the dependent variables. For example, if a researcher has pretest and posttest data and measures the relationship between posttest scores and the gain scores from pretest to posttest, the correlation would be spuriously high because the posttest score is included in both variables. Obviously, when something is correlated with itself the relationship will be very high. Similarly, if there is a third unmeasured variable that is common to both variables, as with our example of reading achievement and body weight, the correlation will be spuriously high. Such a result would occur when height is correlated with weight, since a third factor, age, is common to both.

Correlations obtained from two measures that are imperfectly reliable will result in coefficients lower than the true relationship between the measures. This lowering of the coefficient is referred to as **attenuation**, and occasionally researchers will compute a correction for attenuation to estimate what the correlation might have been if the measures were more reliable. A researcher will use this correlation most commonly with pilot studies in which the measures used have low reliability.

Another situation in which the correlation coefficient is lower than the actual relationship is a case in which the range of scores on one of the variables is confined to a representation of only a part of the total distribution of that variable. This problem is called **restriction in range**, and it results in a lowering of the correlation. Suppose, for example, a researcher wants to investigate the relationship between aptitude test scores and achievement of students in a program for the gifted. Figure 9.5 shows why the researcher would probably find only a small positive relationship between these two variables. Note that the figure illustrates the hypothetical aptitude and achievement scores for all students (A and B), along with the sample of students in the gifted program (B).

In this case the range of aptitude scores is thus limited, or "restricted", to a small part of the total range of aptitude scores. If the full range of scores is utilized, then the correlation is highly positive. Restriction in range in part explains the usually modest relationship between college admissions tests and achievement in college—the range is restricted to students who have high test scores on the admissions tests. Under certain conditions a correction for restriction in range can be applied in these cases in order to indicate what the correlation might have been if a large sample had been available.

Another situation that can lead to spurious correlations is one in which the sampling procedures result in a more heterogeneous or more homogeneous sample than is actually present in the population. This sampling bias would

FIGURE 9.5   Restriction of Range

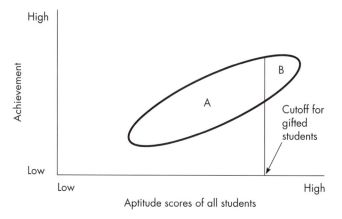

lead to either a high spurious correlation, if the sample is more heterogeneous, or a low spurious correlation for a sample more homogeneous. For example, if a researcher investigating the relationship between effective teaching behavior and student achievement for all students oversampled high achievers, resulting in a more homogeneous group than the population, the correlation would be spuriously low. If, however, the population had mostly gifted students but the procedures undersampled these gifted students, then the correlation would be spuriously high.

Finally, spurious correlations may be reported if "outlier" data are included in the calculations. The concept of outlier was introduced in Chapter 7 in relation to the need to create scatterplots of relationship data. Figure 9.6 shows two scatterplots to illustrate the effect an outlier can have on either increasing or decreasing the correlation coefficient so that the correlation misrepresents the data. Correlations have been calculated both with and without the outliers. As you can see, the difference in results obtained is dramatic.

Size of Correlation Coefficients It has already been pointed out in Chapter 7 that correlations such as .86, .95, and −.89 are high; .43, −.35, and .57 are moderate; and .07, −.01, and .12 are small, but these words only hint at the magnitude of the relationship. Because correlation coefficients are expressed as decimals, it is easy to confuse the decimal with percentages. The coefficient is a mathematical way of expressing the degree to which there is covariance between the variables, not an indication of the degree to which the variables share common properties or characteristics. To obtain an estimate of the proportion of the variance that the two measures share or have in common, the coefficient must be squared. A correlation of .40, squared, for example, indicates that the variables have 16 percent of their variance in common. In other words, 84 percent is left unexplained or unpredicted by the .40 correlation. Even for some high correlations, such as .70 and .80, the square of the correlations thus results in a moderate degree of common variance (49 and 64 percent, respectively, out of a total of 100 percent, which would be a perfect relationship). The index that results from squaring the correlation is called the **coefficient of determination.**

Another consideration with respect to the size of correlations is that many correlations are termed "significant" even though they may be quite low (such as .15, .08). Researchers use the word *significant* in the context of correlations to indicate that the coefficient is *statistically* different from zero (no relationship) at a specified level of confidence (Chapter 11 discusses *statistical significance* and *level of confidence* in greater detail). If a study has a very large number of subjects (more than 1,000), then small correlations can be "significant," but only in a statistical sense. We know that a simple correlation of .30, if significant, accounts for only 9 percent of the common variance, so that our interpretation needs to reflect the 91 percent of the variance that is unaccounted for. For research in which prediction is the primary goal, such low correlations, even though statistically significant, are of little practical significance. Generally, in studies investigating relationships only, correlations as low as .30 or .40 are useful, but in

FIGURE 9.6   The Effect of Outliers on Correlation Coefficients

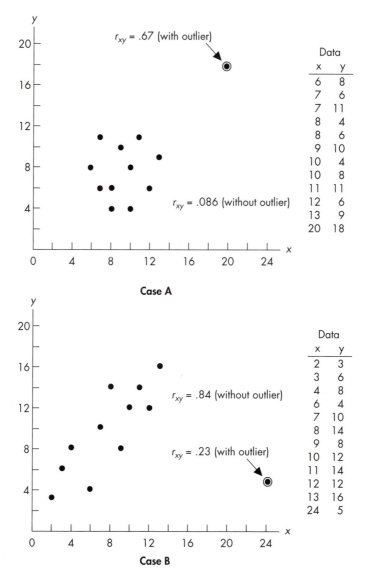

Case A

Case B

Source: Stevens, J. (1996). *Applied Multivariate Statistics for the Social Sciences,* 3rd ed., Mahwah, NJ: Lawrence Erlbaum Associates, p. 16.

prediction studies or estimates of reliability and validity, higher correlations are needed. In educational research, if a very high correlation is reported, such as 1.00, .99, or .98, then the reader should suspect spurious results caused by methodological, design, or calculation inadequacies. As a final illustration of the power of correlations, inspect the scatterplots in Figure 9.7. These figures show what actual correlations look like when graphed. Take the score of 5.5 on the

FIGURE 9.7   Scatterplots Indicating Correlations of Various Sizes (N = 50)

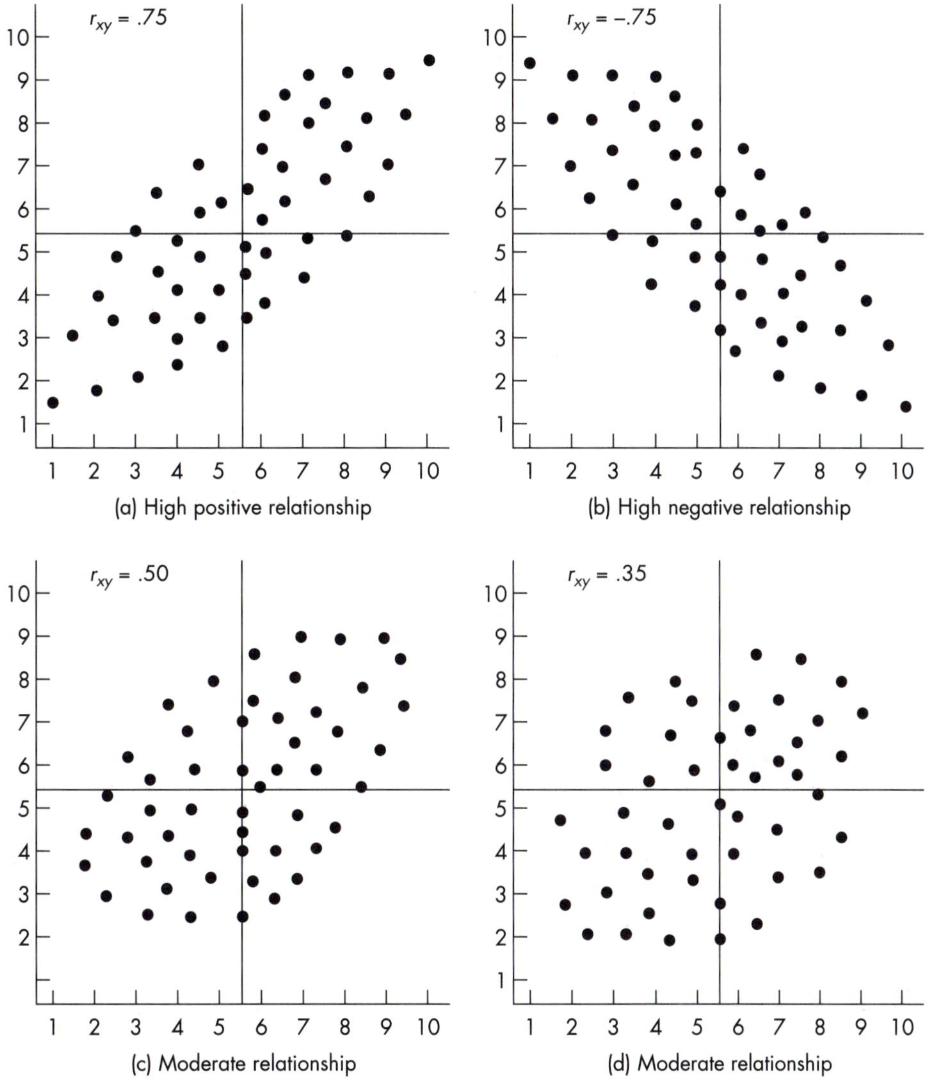

(a) High positive relationship
(b) High negative relationship
(c) Moderate relationship
(d) Moderate relationship

Source: Mehrens, W. A., and Lehmann, I. J. (1987). *Using Standardized Tests in Education,* 4th ed., White Plains, NY: Longman, p. 49.

horizontal axis in Figure 9.7 and look at the large range of scores it predicts. For scatterplot (a), which is a "high" correlation of .75, predicted scores range from 3 to 8. This isn't nearly as precise, then, as .75 might imply.

Finally, with respect to interpretation, the usefulness of correlations varies, depending on whether the investigation is focusing on groups or on individuals. Generally, a much larger correlation is needed for use with individuals than groups. For correlations below about .35, only a small relationship is shown;

this is of value in some exploratory research, but has little value in predictions concerning individuals or groups. In the middle range, from .35 to .75, crude group predictions can be made, and if several moderate correlations can be combined they can be used with individual predictions. Above .75 both individual and group predictions are useful with a single measure of correlation.

Survey Research

In **survey research** the investigator selects a sample of respondents and administers a questionnaire or conducts interviews to collect information on variables of interest. The data that are gathered are used to describe characteristics of a certain population. Surveys are used to learn about people's attitudes, beliefs, values, demographics, behavior, opinions, habits, desires, ideas, and other types of information. They are used frequently in business, politics, government, sociology, public health, psychology, and education because accurate information can be obtained for large numbers of people with a small sample.

Most surveys describe the incidence, frequency, and distribution of the characteristics of an identified population. In addition to being descriptive, surveys can also be used to explore relationships between variables, or in an explanatory way. Examples of topics in each of the three categories are given below.

Descriptive

What is the average length of time teachers use to prepare lessons?

Describe the science attitudes of fourth-grade students.

What are the most popular counseling techniques used by high school counselors?

What do principals think about mainstreaming emotionally disturbed children?

Exploring a Relationship

Do teachers who favor tenure try innovations less often than teachers who disapprove of tenure?

Is there a relationship between teacher attitudes toward discipline and student satisfaction with the class?

Do marital couples who blame each other for marital problems have more conflict than spouses who blame themselves?

In an Explanatory Way

Why do some principals send regular letters to parents and other principals rarely send letters?

What is the reason some integrated schools are truly integrated while others remain segregated?

Why are the students in one school achieving better than similar students in another school?

Survey research is very popular in education, just as it is in sociology and political science. There are three primary reasons for this popularity: versatility, efficiency, and generalizability (Schutt, 1996). Surveys are versatile because they can be used to investigate almost any problem or question. Many doctoral dissertations use surveys; state departments of education use surveys to determine levels of knowledge and to ascertain needs in order to plan programs; schools use surveys to evaluate aspects of the curriculum or administrative procedures; governmental agencies use surveys to form public policy; colleges of education use surveys to evaluate their courses and programs. Much of the use of surveys is for practical purposes and could be classified as evaluation or action research, although surveys are also used for basic and applied research.

Surveys are popular because credible information can be collected at a relatively low cost, especially written surveys that are mailed or otherwise distributed and collected (e.g., the Internet is now very economical for doing surveys, but often the response rates are not very good). On a comparative basis, for every one dollar spent on a mailed survey, five dollars are needed for telephone interviews, and ten dollars for personal interviews. In America, the efficiency of the postal service and nearly ubiquitous phone service to households helps enormously in contacting individuals quickly at a low cost. Surveys are also efficient because data on many variables can be gathered without substantial increases in time or cost.

The most important reason for the popularity of surveys is that small samples can be selected from a larger population in ways that permit generalizations to the population. In fact, surveys are often the only means of being able to obtain a representative description of traits, beliefs, attitudes, and other characteristics of the population. Surveys also allow for generalizability across the population, in which subgroups or different contexts can be compared.

Because surveys are used so frequently and are adaptable to a wide range of uses, some people develop the mistaken opinion that surveys are easy to conduct. Surveys involve much more than simply mailing a set of questions to a group of subjects, however. Without careful development of questions, sampling procedures, and overall survey design, it is unlikely that survey research methods will provide credible results. It is thus necessary to employ correct sampling procedures and to design the data collection techniques carefully in order to ensure reliability and validity.

In conducting survey research, it is helpful to follow a sequence of steps. The sequence is outlined below.

1. *Define purpose and objectives.* The first step is to define the purpose and objectives of the research. This should include a general statement and specific objectives that define in detail the information that needs to be collected. The objectives should be as clear-cut and unambiguous as possible. This is not always as easy as it sounds. An objective such as "The purpose of this research is to determine the values of college students" is actually quite vague. What is meant by "values"? Which college students are included? Another way

to evaluate the objectives is to ask whether there are specific uses for the results. Often data are collected with the idea that either "it would be nice to know" or "let's see what the results are and then decide how to use the data." Either notion is a weak reason to collect data. The researcher needs to know before the data are collected exactly how the results will be used. Careful consideration of objectives also helps in determining what to emphasize and what to treat in a more cursory way.

2. *Select resources and target population.* It is necessary to make decisions about the total amount of time, money, and personnel available before designing the specific methodology to gather the data. A locally developed questionnaire might be best, for example, but financial constraints may make it necessary to use an instrument that has established reliability and validity. The amount of money available will also affect the size of the sample that can be drawn. The objectives of the study may also need to be modified to reflect the financial constraints. It is better to do a small study well than a large study poorly.

It is also important to define the population or target group to which the researcher intends to generalize. The definition is a list of characteristics or boundaries to clarify external validity and specify the group from which the data are collected. The definition should consider principles of research design and practicality. If the population is too broad, such as "all teachers," or "all students," then it will be difficult and expensive to obtain a representative sample. If the population is too narrow, such as "male special education teachers with between five and ten years teaching experience," then the external validity of the study is weak.

3. *Choose and develop techniques for gathering data.* The questionnaire, telephone interview, and personal interview, reviewed in Chapter 8, are the most frequently used techniques for collecting data. When used in a survey, the techniques must be standardized so that information from each respondent is gathered in the same manner.

4. *Instructions.* It is important to develop clear instructions for the respondent, whether orally reviewed by phone or in person, or read on a written survey. There can be no ambiguity about how, where, and when participants will respond. For example, does the respondent check a box, circle the correct answer, or make checks on a continuum? If there is a separate answer sheet (which generally is not recommended; if you intend to use a scantron form it is best to have the questions printed right on the form), be clear about "bubbling," using a pencil if needed (some scantron forms only need a darkened area, not necessarily in pencil), and administer in person rather than mail the survey. Instructions should also clearly indicate how the participant should return the questionnaire. You can point this out in the letter of transmittal, at the beginning of the survey, or at the end of the survey. The best policy is to have the instructions for completing and returning the survey on the survey itself.

5. *Sampling.* The basic principles of sampling were presented in Chapter 6. Most surveys use probability sampling in order to ensure adequate representation of the population. The random sampling is often stratified on some vari-

ables, such as sex, grade level, ability level, and socioeconomic status.

6. *Letter of transmittal.* In the case of mailed questionnaires the nature of the cover letter, or letter of transmittal, is crucial in determining the percentage of subjects who return completed forms. The letter should be brief and should establish the credibility of the researcher and the study. This is accomplished by including the following: the names and identifications of the investigators; the purpose and intention of the study without complete details; the importance of the study for the respondent and profession; the importance of the respondent for the study; the protection afforded the respondent by keeping the identities of the respondents confidential; a time limit for returning a written survey that is neither too long nor too short (usually a week or less); endorsements for the study by recognized institutions or groups; a brief description of the questionnaire and procedure; mention of an opportunity to obtain results; a request for cooperation and honesty; and thanks to the respondent. Naturally, if the letter is neat, professional in appearance, and without grammatical or spelling errors, the respondent will be more likely to cooperate. It is best if the letter establishes that the research is being conducted by an organization that is recognized by the respondent as credible. If possible, letters of transmittal should be personalized. Excerpt 9.9 contains a sample letter illustrating these points.

7. *Pilot test.* It is critical to pilot test both the instructions and the survey before distributing to the identified sample. This pilot should be done with respondents similar to those in the sample. Generally the pilot can be successful in identifying needed changes if as few as ten individuals are willing to complete it and provide suggestions to improve clarity and format. The pilot test also gives you an estimate of the amount of time it will take to complete the survey. Finally, the pilot test provides an initial idea of the pattern of responses that are likely, and whether revisions need to be made to avoid ceiling or floor effects. Occasionally, an initial informal pilot test is conducted, followed by a more formal pilot test with a larger sample.

8. *Follow-up.* The initial mailing of the letter of transmittal, questionnaire, and stamped return-addressed envelope will usually result in a response rate of from 40 to 60 percent—that is, 40 to 60 percent of the sample will typically return the questionnaires. This rate is higher for short questionnaires of obvious importance and lower for long questionnaires on obscure a highly personal topic. The standard procedure for follow-up is to first send a reminder postcard about ten days to two weeks after receipt of the initial mailing. For nonrespondents, a follow-up letter is sent about three to four weeks after the initial mailing, which includes another copy of the survey. If the return rate is still low and resources permit, a certified letter with yet another copy of the survey is sent six to eight weeks after the initial mailing. In the case of surveys that have assured anonymity, it is impossible to know who has or has not returned the questionnaire. In this case researchers can use one of several procedures: They can send a follow-up letter or postcard to everyone, indicating that those who did return the questionnaire may ignore the follow-up; the researcher can code the questionnaires without the knowledge of the subjects in order to identify respon-

EXCERPT 9.9

LETTER OF TRANSMITTAL

Dear Parent Association Executive Board Member,

Importance of respondent

> Your position in education is an important one.
> Your concern for your children and their school is demonstrated by the position that you hold in the Parent Association. As an executive board member you are a key person in many ways. You listen to the parents and speak for them. You listen and speak to the principal and work with him or her. You are an important link between school and community. Your decisions have great importance for your children and their school.

Importance of study

> The elementary principal's position is also important. You are well aware of the serious responsibilities that he or she has. His or her decisions affect your children daily, and may very well affect them for the rest of their lives.

Identify investigator; purpose of study; importance of respondent

> I am doing a doctoral study at St. John's University, New York City, that is concerned with Parent Association executive board members and elementary principals. As an executive board member, you, and your executive role, are of particular interest to this study.
> This is a nationwide study. You, and all of the participants, have been randomly selected. Permission has been secured from the superintendent to request your cooperation.

Request cooperation

> We share a common interest and concern for the problems under investigation. It is on this basis of a common goal of increased knowledge about education that I am requesting your cooperation in filling out the enclosed questionnaire.

Description of questionnaire

> The questionnaire contains three parts. The first two parts are concerned with your perceptions of the principal and the third part requests personal information about you.

Endorsement of study

> The questionnaire has been carefully studied and evaluated by professionals and Parent Association executive board members.
> The executive board members were asked to complete the questionnaire. They unanimously reported that it took no more than twenty minutes to fill it out.

Protection afforded respondent

> You need not sign the questionnaire and you are assured that your response will remain anonymous and confidential. Your participation is, of course, voluntary.

Description of procedure (time limit)

> Please answer all of the questions and return the completed questionnaire to me in the enclosed envelope as soon as possible.

Opportunity to obtain results

> If you wish a summary of the study, please check the appropriate box at the end of the questionnaire and send your name and address on the enclosed postal card.

Thank respondent

> Thank you for your cooperation.

Yours truly,

Stanley Cogan
Assistant Principal
New York City Public Schools

Source: From "The relationship of the social class and personal characteristics of parent association executive board members to the role expectations and personal characteristics which they advocate in the selection of elementary principals in selected American cities," doctoral dissertation by Stanley Cogan. Reprinted by permission of Stanley Cogan.

dents; or the subjects can send a separate postcard when they return the questionnaire. The postcard follow-up usually brings 10 to 30 percent more returns, and a second follow-up will add another 10 to 20 percent to the return rate. If the researchers can obtain a total return rate of 70 percent or better, they are doing very well.

9. *Nonrespondents.* In most survey studies there will be a percentage of subjects who fail to return the completed questionnaire. These subjects are called *nonrespondents*, and the researcher may need to make additional efforts to check whether the inclusion of these subjects would have altered the results. For most mail surveys with a large sample (e.g., 200 or more), the nonrespondents will probably not affect the results in an appreciable way if the return rate is at least 70 percent. If the results are to be used for important decisions, or if the nature of the questions might cause a certain type of subject not to respond, then the nonrespondents should be checked. The suggested approach for investigating the possibility of a biased group of respondents is to somehow obtain a random sample of the nonrespondents. If possible, these individuals are interviewed and their responses are compared with those of the subjects who completed written questionnaires. If the responses are the same, then the researcher is safe in concluding that the obtained written questionnaires represent an unbiased sample. If it is impossible to interview the randomly selected nonrespondents, the next best procedure is to compare them with the subjects who did respond with respect to demographic characteristics. If either the responses or the demographic characteristics of the nonrespondents are different, then this difference should be noted in discussing and interpreting the results of the study. Special attention should be focused on studies with a relatively low rate of return (lower than 70 percent) and without an analysis of the way nonrespondents may have changed the results. Research has demonstrated that the response rate to mailed surveys can be substantially increased by the use of monetary gratuities (Hopkins & Gullickson, 1992). A $1.00 gratuity may increase response rate by an average of 20 percent.

Before leaving the topic of surveys, we once again want to emphasize that survey research is not simple to prepare and conduct. There are many factors related to item format, positioning of questions, wording, sampling, and other variables that need to be considered. For an excellent review of these problems, see Schuman and Presser (1996), and for additional information on developing and conducting surveys, see *The Survey Kit*.[1]

Because most surveys use closed-form items that are computer analyzed, it is essential for researchers to consult with experts who can assist in properly designing the survey for easy and accurate data entry. Such experts are also very helpful in reviewing wording, directions, layout, and other technical aspects of the survey.

---

[1]*The Survey Kit* is a series of volumes published by Sage Publications, Inc., that covers question development, conducting surveys, data analysis, and reporting.

Ex Post Facto Research

In descriptive and correlational designs it is almost always the case that causal relationships are not studied. However there are certain nonexperimental designs that are used to investigate causal relationships. One of these is termed *ex post facto*. In these studies the purpose of the research is to examine how an identified independent variable effects the dependent variable, but the circumstances of conducting the research do not allow for an experimental design. Consider the following list of research questions. In each case the implied cause-and-effect relationship rules out experimental manipulation of the independent variable.

> What is the effect of attendance at day care on the social skills of children?
>
> What is the effect of single parenting on achievement?
>
> Do teachers who graduate from liberal arts colleges have greater longevity in the teaching field than teachers who graduate from colleges of education?
>
> What is the relationship between participation in extracurricular activities and self-concept?

Characteristics of *Ex Post Facto* Research

It is simply impossible, unethical, or infeasible to manipulate variables such as single or couple parenting, day care attendance, or choice of college by students, as well as many other variables such as race, socioeconomic status, and personality. A researcher would probably have some difficulty assigning children on a random basis to either attend or not attend day care!

Although it is desirable to study cause-and-effect relationships in such situations, the circumstances of the research are such that manipulation of the independent variable cannot be carried out. The type of design most frequently used in these situations is called *ex post facto,* or causal-comparative. The purpose of *ex post facto* research is to investigate whether one or more preexisting conditions have possibly caused subsequent differences in the groups of subjects. In other words, the researcher identifies conditions that have already occurred (*ex post facto* is Latin for *after the fact*) and then collects data to investigate the relationship of these varying conditions to subsequent behavior. In *ex post facto* research the investigator attempts to determine whether differences between groups (the independent variable) have resulted in an observed difference on the dependent variable.

Ex post facto designs are easily confused with experimental designs because they both have a similar purpose (to determine cause–effect relationships), group comparisons, and the use of similar statistical analyses and vocabulary in describing the results. In experimental and quasi-experimental studies, however, the researcher deliberately controls the effect of some condition by manipulation of the independent variable, while in *ex post facto* research there is no manipulation of conditions because the presumed cause has already occurred before the study is initiated. In *ex post facto* designs, therefore, there is usually a treatment and a control group—a factor that can further confuse the research with experimental approaches.

   Ex post facto designs are also confused with comparative and correlational research, because all three involve no manipulation and there are similar limitations in interpreting the results. *Ex post facto* designs, however, attempt to identify causal relationships, while comparative and correlational research generally does not.

Conducting *Ex Post Facto* Research

Although in *ex post facto* research the independent variable cannot be manipulated and random assignment of subjects to groups is impossible, there are several procedures that are used in planning *ex post facto* research that enhance control and limit plausible rival hypotheses. The first step is to formulate a research problem that includes possible causes of the dependent variable. The choice of possible causes is based on previous research and on the researcher's interpretation of observations of the phenomena being studied. Suppose, for example, the researcher wants to investigate the effect of class size on achievement, and it is impossible to assign students randomly to different size classes to conduct a true experiment. The researcher's interest may be based on correlational research that shows a negative relationship between class size and achievement, and observations that students in smaller classes seem to do better. The research problem, then, is this: What is the effect of class size on achievement?

   A second step is to identify plausible rival hypotheses that might explain the relationship. The researcher might, for instance, list as possible causes of better achievement in smaller classes several factors such as the following: smaller classes have better teachers; students with higher ability are in smaller classes; students with stronger motivation are in smaller classes; more students from high socioeconomic backgrounds attend smaller classes than do students from low socioeconomic backgrounds; and perhaps teachers of smaller classes use a different type of instruction than those of larger classes use. Each of these factors might be related to the reason students in smaller classes achieve more than students in large classes.

   The third step is to find and select the groups that will be compared. In our example of class size and achievement, the researcher will first need to define operationally *large* and *small* class size as well as *achievement*. A *small* class could have fewer than fifteen students and a *large* class more than twenty-five. *Achievement* could be defined as the gain in knowledge of the students while in the class. The researcher also needs to identify grade levels and locations. Suppose in this case the researcher is interested in elementary grade levels and the accessible population is a single school district. Once the variables are defined, groups must be selected that are as homogeneous as possible in the characteristics that constitute rival hypotheses and that are different with respect to the independent variable. In our example, then, the researcher selects groups that differ with respect to class size but that are similar in such factors as ability, socioeconomic background, teaching methods, quality of teachers, and student motivation. Matching is a good approach to forming groups that will be as homogeneous as possible in factors affecting the dependent variable. For example, in our study of class size, the researcher could match and select students on the basis of initial ability so that only students with about the same level of ability are included in the analysis, even though other students are contained in the classes.

The fourth step is to collect and analyze data on the subjects, including data on factors that may constitute rival hypotheses. Since *ex post facto* research is after the fact, most data that are needed have already been collected, and only the data from appropriate sources need to be gathered. Data analysis is very similar to procedures used for experimental and quasi-experimental studies in that groups are compared on the variables of interest. In our proposed study of class size, for example, all achievement scores in the small classes would be averaged and compared with the average achievement in large classes. Data from the extraneous variables are also compared and incorporated into the statistical analyses to help make judgments about plausible rival hypotheses.

It must be stressed, in interpreting the results of *ex post facto* research, that cause-and-effect statements can be made only cautiously. In our example of large and small classes, if a difference in achievement is found between the groups, then the researcher can conclude that there is a relationship between class size and achievement. The results do not mean, unequivocally, that being in either small or large classes had a causative effect on achievement. There may be a cause-and-effect relationship, but this depends on the researcher's ability to select comparison groups homogeneous on all important variables except being in small or large classes, and by the confidence with which other plausible rival hypotheses can be ruled out. If, for example, it turned out that all the small classes came from one school and large classes from another, then policies or procedures unique to the schools and unrelated to class size (such as stress on basic skill attainment or a special training program for teachers) may constitute plausible rival hypotheses.

A good example of *ex post facto* research is a study investigating the effect of same-age and mixed-age preschool classrooms on play. As pointed out in Excerpt 9.10, modes of play and social interaction of children in four same-age classrooms were compared with those of children in two mixed-age classrooms. Notice that the researchers summarize in the second paragraph of the excerpt how the same-age and mixed-age classrooms were comparable with respect to physical layout, materials, teacher–child ratio, socioeconomic factors of the children, and the amount of time the children had been in the classroom. Presumably these characteristics were identified before data were collected to

EXCERPT 9.10

EX POST FACTO RESEARCH

METHOD

Subjects   The social-cognitive modes of play and peers' responses to them were observed in two classrooms of 3-year-olds (N = 40), two classrooms of 4-year-olds (N = 32), and two mixed-age classrooms of 3- and 4-year-olds (N = 36). The classrooms were considered mixed-age if at least 40% of the children were 3-year-olds and at least 40% of the children were 4-year-olds. Children considered 3-year-olds ranged from 2 years, 9 months to 3 years, 8 months, and 4-year-olds ranged from 3 years, 9 months to 4 years, 8 months at the beginning of the study. To assure equal opportunities for same-sex and cross-sex activities, classrooms were selected in which at least 40% of the children were boys and at least 40% were girls. These criteria for classifying classrooms as mixed-age were similar to those of previous research (e.g., Goldman, 1981; Roopnarine, 1984). These criteria were used because we wanted to study similar age groups of children in order to make comparisons with the findings of previous studies (e.g., Goldman's).

All classrooms assumed a child-centered orientation and were comparable in terms of physical layout, play and instructional materials, and teacher–child ratio (1:9). The children were from middle-income backgrounds as assessed by the Hollingshead Four Factor Index of Social Position (Hollingshead, undated). Preliminary analyses revealed no significant differences in sociodemographic factors between children in same-age and mixed-age classrooms. In addition, children in both classroom arrangements were enrolled for approximately the same length of time in the mixed-age classrooms prior to observations (same-age classrooms $\bar{x}$ = 6 months; mixed-age classrooms $\bar{x}$ = 5 months).

Source: From "Social-Cognitive Play Patterns in Same-Age and Mixed-Age Preschool Classrooms" by N. S. Mounts and J. L. Roopnarine, *American Educational Research Journal, 24,* 463–476. Copyright © 1987 American Educational Research Association, Washington, DC. Reprinted by permission.

rule out these plausible rival hypotheses. Of course there may be other differences between the groups besides the same-age/mixed-age variable that could affect the results. For instance, a difference in instructors could affect play and social interaction.

Standards of Adequacy

In judging the adequacy of the descriptive, comparative correlational, survey, and *ex post facto* research it will be helpful to keep the following questions in mind. The questions are organized to focus your attention on the most important criteria in designing and evaluating these types of research.

Descriptive Research

1. Is the research problem clearly descriptive in nature?
2. Is there a clear description of the sample, population, and procedures for sampling?
3. Will the sample provide biased or distorted results?
4. Are scores resulting from the instrumentation reliable and valid?
5. Do graphic presentations of the results distort the findings?
6. Are inappropriate relationship or causal conclusions made on the basis of descriptive results?
7. If cross-sectional, do subject differences affect the results?
8. If longitudinal, is loss of subjects a limitation?
9. Are differences between groups used to identify possible relationships?

Comparative Research

1. Does the research problem clearly indicate that relationships will be investigated by comparing differences between groups?
2. Is the description of subjects, sampling, and instrumentation clear?
3. Do sampling procedures bias the results?
4. Is there sufficient evidence for reliability and validity?
5. Are inappropriate causal inferences made?

Correlational Research

1. Does the research problem clearly indicate that relationships will be investigated?
2. Is there a clear description of the sampling? Will the sample provide sufficient variability of responses to obtain a correlation?
3. Are scores resulting from instrumentation valid and reliable?
4. Is there a restricted range on the scores?
5. Are there any factors that might contribute to spurious correlations?
6. Is a shotgun approach used in the study?
7. Are inappropriate causal inferences made from the results?
8. How large is the sample? Could sample size affect the "significance" of the results?
9. Is the correlation coefficient confused with the coefficient of determination?
10. If predictions are made, are they based on a different sample?
11. Is the size of the correlation large enough for the conclusions?

Survey Research

1. Are the objectives and purposes of the survey clear?
2. Is it likely that the target population and sampling procedure will provide a credible answer to the research question(s)?
3. Is the instrument clearly designed and worded? Has it been pilot tested? Is it appropriate for the characteristics of the sample?

4. Is there assurance of confidentiality of responses? If not, is this likely to affect the results?
5. Does the letter of transmittal establish the credibility of the research? Is there any chance that what is said in the letter will bias the responses?
6. What is the return rate? If low or borderline, has there been any follow-up with nonrespondents?
7. Do the conclusions reflect return rate and other possible limitations?

Ex Post Facto **Research**

1. Was the primary purpose of the study to investigate cause-and-effect relationships?
2. Have the presumed cause-and-effect conditions already occurred?
3. Was there manipulation of the independent variable?
4. Were groups being compared already different with respect to the independent variable?
5. Were potential extraneous variables recognized and considered as plausible rival hypotheses?
6. Were causal statements regarding the results made tenuously?
7. Were threats to external validity addressed in the conclusions?

Summary

This chapter has provided a review of descriptive, correlational, survey, and *ex post facto* research, stressing design principles that affect the quality of the research. The main points in the chapter are:

1. Descriptive research is concerned with current or past status of something.
2. Developmental studies investigate changes of subjects over time and are longitudinal or cross-sectional.
3. Comparative relationship studies examine differences between groups.
4. Correlational relationship studies use at least two scores that are obtained from each subject.
5. Comparative and correlational studies should clearly define sampling, instrumentation, and procedures for gathering data.
6. The selection of subjects and instruments in correlational research should ensure a range of responses on each variable.
7. In predictive research the criterion variable is predicted by a prior behavior as measured by the independent variable.
8. Multiple correlation allows several independent variables to combine in relating to the dependent or criterion variable.
9. Correlation should never infer causation because of third nonmeasured variables and the inability to assess causal direction between the two variables.
10. Spurious correlations overrepresent or underrepresent the actual relationship between two variables.

11. The coefficient of determination is the square of the correlation coefficient, and it estimates the variance that is shared by the variables.

12. Correlation coefficients should be interpreted carefully when they are statistically significant with low relationships and a large number of subjects.

13. Decisions for individuals require higher correlations than do decisions for groups.

14. Survey research uses questionnaires or interviews to describe characteristics of populations.

15. Surveys are used for descriptive, relationship, or explanatory purposes.

16. The nature of the letter of transmittal in mail surveys is crucial to obtaining an acceptable response rate of 60 percent or greater.

17. *Ex post facto* designs are used to study potential causal relationships after a presumed cause has occurred.

18. In *ex post facto* research subjects are selected on the basis of the groups they were in at one time; there is probably no random assignment of subjects to different groups; and there is no active manipulation of the independent variable.

Self-Instructional Review Exercises

Sample answers are in the back of the book.

Test Items

1. Descriptive research investigates
   a. difference and causal questions.
   b. dependent variables like achievement.
   c. the current state of affairs.
   d. cause-and-effect relationships.

2. Longitudinal studies investigate
   a. different subjects over time.
   b. cross-sectional relationships.
   c. different subjects at the same time.
   d. the "same" subjects over time.

3. Restricted range and homogeneous samples are especially troublesome for
   a. shotgun studies.
   b. relationship studies.
   c. descriptive studies.
   d. longitudinal studies.

4. In a prediction study the measurement of the independent variable
   a. occurs before the measure of the dependent variable.
   b. occurs at the same time as the dependent variable.
   c. should be made directly by the research.
   d. occurs after the measure of the dependent variable.

5. Multiple correlation studies
   a. compare beta weights to regression coefficients.
   b. use many independent variables.
   c. use many dependent variables.
   d. compare *R* with beta weights.
6. Correlations are spurious if they
   a. are too high.
   b. are interpreted incorrectly.
   c. are too low.
   d. overestimate or underestimate the true relationship.
7. Correlations should not be used to infer causation because
   a. only two variables are studied.
   b. they are not well controlled.
   c. of third unmeasured variables.
   d. only inferential statistics can be used to infer causation.
8. Survey research employs the following techniques:
   a. interviews.
   b. observation.
   c. questionnaires.
   d. Both a and c are correct.
   e. All of the above are correct.
9. Surveys can be used for each of the following purposes *except*
   a. causal.
   b. relationship.
   c. explanatory.
   d. descriptive.
10. Which sequence describes the correct order of steps to be taken in conducting survey research?
   a. define purpose, identify techniques, identify population, sample, mail, follow-up.
   b. define purpose, sample, identify techniques, mail, follow-up.
   c. define purpose, identify population, sample, identify techniques, mail, follow-up.
   d. define purpose, identify population, identify techniques, sample, mail, follow-up.
11. Two characteristics of *ex post facto* research are
   a. randomization and comparison groups.
   b. nonmanipulation and nonrandomization.
   c. nonrandomization and manipulation of the independent variable.
   d. nonmanipulation and randomization.
12. The selection of appropriate comparison groups is crucial in *ex post facto* research because
   a. the groups must be equal in all respects except the independent variable.
   b. the groups must be about the same with respect to the dependent variable.

    c. otherwise the groups would not be comparable.

    d. if the groups are incorrectly chosen, rival hypotheses may be more plausible.

Application Problems

1. In a study of motivation and learning a teacher employed the following research strategy: Students were asked what teaching strategies were most motivating. The teacher then looked back at her test scores to investigate whether the test scores were higher for the more motivating sessions compared with the less motivating sessions. The teacher found that, indeed, student achievement rose as the teacher used more and more motivating techniques. From this result she decided to use the more motivating techniques all the time. Was her decision to use more motivating techniques correct? Why or why not?

2. Indicate from the description below whether the research is descriptive, comparative, correlational, predictive, or *ex post facto*.

    a. A researcher finds that there is a positive relationship between grades and attendance.

    b. A researcher finds that students who are more lonely have more permissive parents than students who are less lonely.

    c. The dean of the school of education uses SAT scores to identify students who may have trouble with National Teacher Examinations.

    d. Children in supportive, loving homes have a higher self-concept than children in rejecting homes.

    e. The majority of faculty at U.S.A. university favor abolishing tenure.

    f. Researchers find that graduate students who attended a small college have stronger writing skills than students from a large university.

CHAPTER 10

Experimental and Single-Subject Research Designs

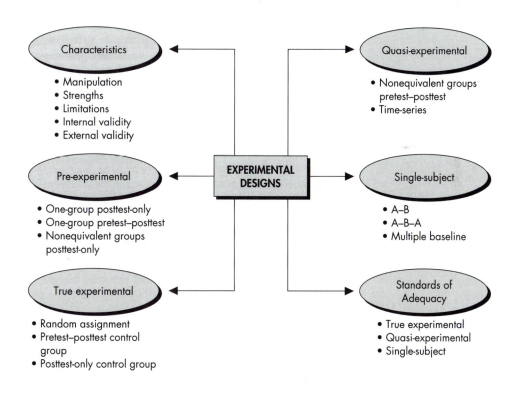

KEY TERMS

true experimental
assigned variables
attribute variables
experimental or treatment
  group
control or comparison group
pre-experimental designs
one-group posttest-only design
one-group pretest–posttest
  design
pretest–posttest design
nonequivalent groups
  posttest-only design
true experimental designs
pretest–posttest control group
  design

posttest-only control group
  design
quasi-experimental designs
nonequivalent groups
  pretest–posttest design
time-series design
single group interrupted time-
  series design
control group interrupted time-
  series design
single-subject designs
baseline
A–B design
A–B–A design
reversal or withdrawal design
multiple-baseline designs

In Chapter 2 the concepts experiment and experimental modes of inquiry were introduced. In this chapter we consider the conduct of experiments in greater detail. We focus on four major categories of experimental designs that are used to make causal inferences about the relationship between independent and dependent variables: pre-experimental, true experimental, quasi-experimental, and single-subject.

We summarize the purpose, strengths, and limitations of experimental research in general as well as more specific designs. Throughout, we stress the point that in any study in which causation is inferred, the investigator must rule out plausible rival hypotheses that may explain the results. Standards of adequacy for evaluating the designs are summarized at the end of the chapter.

An Introduction to Experimental Research

The term *experiment*, like many other terms, can have different meanings. Defined in a general way, experiments are simply a way of learning something by varying some condition and observing the effect on something else. In other words, we change something and watch for the effect. As humans, we use natural experiments constantly to learn—young children experiment with a host of tactics to see which one will affect Mom or Dad most; teachers try a new approach to discipline to see whether it works; and students vary study techniques to see which ones seem to result in the best grades. This simple trial-and-error behavior is an attempt to show causation, which is the primary purpose of an experiment. The difference between these experiments and highly sophisticated experiments conducted by laboratory scientists is the extent to which the experimenter can be certain that the varied conditions caused the observed effect. It is the interpretation of causation, then, that is a key element in experimental research.

Characteristics of Experimental Research

Traditionally defined experimental research has six distinguishing characteristics: statistical equivalence of subjects in different groups, usually achieved by random assignment of subjects; comparison of two or more groups or sets of conditions; direct manipulation of at least one independent variable; measurement of each dependent variable; use of inferential statistics; and a design that provides the potential for maximum control of extraneous variables. These characteristics are usually present in physical and biological science experimental research, but as we noted in Chapter 2, such conditions can rarely be achieved completely in educational research. This does not, however, diminish the importance of the experimental method for education. Much research in education approximates most of these characteristics, and we need to understand the way different methods of conducting research that investigates causal relationships affect the interpretation of the results. This is what Campbell and Stanley (1963) had in mind in writing their classic and influential chapter "Experimental and Quasi-Experimental Designs for Education." The following quotation leaves little doubt about their perspective at that time:

> *This chapter is committed to the experiment: as the only means for settling disputes regarding educational practice, as the only way of verifying educational improvements, and as the only way of establishing a cumulative tradition in which improvements can be introduced without the danger of a faddish discard of old wisdom in favor of inferior novelties (Campbell & Stanley, 1963, p. 2).*

We need to distinguish, then, between what can be labeled pure or **true experimental** research, in which the above six characteristics are completely present, and the experimental method of research more broadly, in which the characteristics are partially present. In this chapter, since we are concerned with research in education, we interpret experimental in its more general context.

The first characteristic of experimental research, achieving statistical equivalence of subjects in different groups, is necessary so that many important possible threats to internal validity are not factors in interpreting the results. In other words, the researcher wants to make the groups being compared to have the same traits and characteristics so that any differences in their performance cannot be attributed to differences in the groups or experiences they have during the experiment. Random assignment of subjects is the method used most often to achieve statistical equivalence of the groups. Other methods, such as matching subjects or groups or using subjects as their own controls, are also used for this purpose.

The second characteristic suggests that at least two groups or conditions need to be compared. An experiment cannot be conducted with one group of subjects in one condition at one time. The intent of an experiment is to compare the effect of one condition on one group with the effect of a different condition on a second group, or to compare the effect of different conditions on the same group. At least two groups or conditions are necessary to make such comparisons.

Direct manipulation of independent variables is perhaps the most distinct feature of experimental research. *Manipulation* in this sense means that the researcher decides upon and controls the specific treatment or condition for each group of subjects. The independent variable is manipulated in that different values or conditions (levels) of the independent variable are assigned to groups by the experimenter. If the conditions cannot be assigned as needed by the researcher, then the study is not an experiment. Suppose, for example, a research team is interested in investigating whether the order of difficulty of items in a test makes a difference in student achievement. The study might have one independent variable, order of items, with two levels, items ordered from easiest to most difficult, and items ordered from most difficult to easiest. These are the conditions that are manipulated by the researchers, who would probably divide a class into two groups, randomly, and give all students in each group one of two types of item order. It should be pointed out that there are many variables in education that can never be manipulated, such as age, weight, gender, and socioeconomic status. These variables are called **assigned** or **attribute variables** because they cannot be manipulated. Although assigned variables can be included in experimental research, there must be at least one manipulated variable for the research to be classified as an experiment.

The fourth characteristic of experimental research, measurement of dependent variables, means that experimental research is concerned with things that can be assigned a numerical value. If the outcome of the study cannot be measured and quantified in some way, then the research cannot be experimental.

Another characteristic that involves numbers is the use of inferential statistics. Inferential statistics are used to make probability statements about the results. This is important for two reasons. Because measurement is imperfect in education, and because we often want to generalize the results to similar groups or to the population of subjects, inferential statistics allow us to make such generalizations. (See Chapter 11 for details concerning inferential statistics.)

The final characteristic of experimental research is perhaps most important from a generic point of view because the principle of control of extraneous variables is not unique to experimental research. What is unique to experimental research is that there is a determined effort to make sure no extraneous variables that could be controlled provide plausible rival hypotheses to explain the results. We control extraneous variables either by making sure that these variables have no effect on the dependent variable, or by keeping the effect of the extraneous variable the same for all groups. This chapter places considerable emphasis on this characteristic of experimental research. Also, many of the principles of control of extraneous variables apply to *ex post facto* designs as well.

Strengths and Limitations of Experimental Research

The experimental method is clearly the best approach for determining the causal effect of an isolated, single variable on something. This is primarily because of the potential for a high degree of control of extraneous variables and the power of manipulation of variables. The careful control that characterizes good experimental research becomes a liability for the field of education, however. Control is most easily achieved with research on humans only in restrictive and artificial settings. This is a weakness in education for two reasons. Humans react to artificially restricted, manipulated conditions differently from the way they react to naturally occurring conditions, and if the research is conducted under artificial conditions, then the generalizability of the results (external validity) is severely limited.

Here is an example of this dilemma. The problem to be investigated is whether an individualized approach or a cooperative group discussion is the best method for teaching science concepts to fourth graders. The objective is to find the method of teaching that gives the best results in achievement. An experimental approach is selected because the problem is clearly one of causation, and presumably the method of instruction—the independent variable—could be manipulated easily. To maximize control of extraneous variables the experiment might be arranged as follows: At the beginning of one school day all fourth graders report to a special room, where they are randomly divided into individualized and cooperative groups. To remove any effect the present teachers might have, graduate assistants from the universities act as the teachers. To remove any effect of different rooms, each group of students is taken to similar rooms in different locations. To control possible distractions, these rooms have no windows. To ensure that directions are uniform, the teachers read from specially prepared scripts. The science material that is selected has been carefully screened so that it will be new information for all students. After studying the material for an hour, the students are tested on the concepts. The test format, length of time to complete questions, and other procedures are the same for both groups. The results compare the achievement of the groups, and since the design has controlled for most extraneous variables, this difference can be attributed to the independent variable, method of instruction.

What do we do with this knowledge? Because one approach seemed best in this experiment, does it mean that Mr. Jones, in his class, with his style of teaching, in his room, with students that may have particular learning strengths and weaknesses, should use the supposedly proven method? Perhaps, but the difficulty that is illustrated is one of generalizability, a common problem for experiments that are able to exhibit tight control over extraneous variables— that is, internal validity. On the other hand, if we want to maximize external validity, then we need to design the experiment right in Mr. Jones's class, as well as in the classes of other teachers, and somehow design the study to control as many variables as possible without disrupting the natural environment of the class. The researcher would need to select the variables most likely to affect achievement, such as aptitude, time of day, and composition of groups, and control these as well as possible. This approach makes it more difficult to show that one or the other method of teaching is more effective, but the results are more generalizable to normal classrooms. The real challenge is in designing the procedures so that the results obtained can be reasonably generalized to other people and environments—that is, balancing internal and external validity in a design. This task is difficult but not impossible, and one of the objectives of this chapter is to introduce various designs and procedures that allow reasonable cause-and-effect conclusions to be made in the context of natural settings.

We hope the use of the word *reasonable* is not confusing. The simple fact is that we approximate pure experimental design as well as we can because such designs convincingly determine causation. In the final analysis, however, since we are working with human beings in complex situations, we must almost always use professional judgment, or reason, in making conclusions on the basis of observed results. Knowledge of the designs covered in this chapter and threats to internal and external validity help us use this judgment.

Finally, before the designs are introduced, it should be pointed out that experimental research is not appropriate for all educational research; it is appropriate only for some investigations seeking knowledge about cause-and-effect relationships. The experimental method would be inappropriate for many educational problems, such as descriptive studies (for example, "What is the attitude or level of achievement?") or studies of relationship (for example, "Is there a relationship between age and self-concept?"). In some situations a qualitative approach would be more valid for explaining events, and in evaluation studies, experiments are frequently used with other approaches to investigate questions about a single practice.

Planning Experimental Research

While the sequence of steps in experimental research is basically the same as in other types of research, certain procedures and characteristics of planning are unique to the experimental design.

The first step is to define a research problem, search the literature, and state clear research hypotheses. It is essential that experimental research be guided by research hypotheses that state the expected results. The actual results will either support or fail to support the research hypotheses.

Second, the researcher selects subjects from a defined population, and, depending on the specific design used, usually "assigns" subjects to different groups. A simple experimental study involves two groups, one called the **experimental** or **treatment group** and the other referred to as the **control** or **comparison group**. Each group is then assigned one level of the independent variable. Technically, a control group receives no treatment at all (for example, when comparing people who smoke with people who do not), but in most educational research it is unproductive to compare one group receiving a treatment with another group receiving nothing. It would be like comparing children who received extra individual tutoring with children who did not, and then concluding on the basis of the results that children need individual tutoring. It is also unrealistic in school settings to expect that a group will be doing nothing while another group receives a special treatment. For these reasons, it is more accurate to conceive of the two groups in experimental research as the treatment and comparison groups, or as one group that receives method A and another group that receives method B, rather than as an experimental and a control group.

In assigning the treatments, as indicated by levels of the independent variable, the researcher determines the nature of the value, forms, or conditions each group receives. This could be a simple assignment, such as lecture versus discussion, loud reprimands versus soft reprimands, or an autocratic versus a participatory leadership style; or there could be more than two levels, with varying degrees of the condition in each level of the independent variable. For example, if a researcher were interested in the effect of different types of teacher feedback on student attitudes, then feedback, the independent variable, could be represented in four levels: grade only, grade plus one word only, grade plus one sentence, and grade plus three sentences. Hence, the researcher would "form" four levels by randomly assigning subjects into four groups. The researcher would arrange appropriate control so that any difference in attitude could be explained as caused by different types of feedback, or so that no difference in attitude would indicate no causative relationship between these types of feedback and attitudes.

One of the difficulties in planning experimental research is knowing that the treatments will be strong enough—that is, if the treatment condition is providing feedback to students, will the feedback make enough of an impact to affect student attitudes? Would feedback given over several consecutive days make a difference? Maybe the feedback has to be given for a month or more. In other words, either the treatment should be tested in advance to ensure that it is powerful enough to make an impact, or sufficient time should be allocated to give the treatment a chance to work. This can be an especially difficult problem in much educational research because there are many influences such as achievement, attitudes, motivation, and self-concept that may affect dependent variables, and it is hard to single out a specific independent variable that will have a meaningful, unique effect, given all other influences. Finally, experimental treatments are sometimes insufficiently distinct from treatments given comparison groups for a statistical difference to be possible. In a study of different counseling techniques, for example, if the only difference between the experimental and control conditions was the distance the counselor sat from the clients (say, four feet or six feet), it is unlikely, given all the other influences, that a researcher will obtain a difference in results.

Once treatment conditions have been established, it is necessary to specify the design that will be employed. This chapter summarizes most of the basic designs used in experimental educational research. The designs include the procedures for subject assignment, the number of groups, and when treatments are given to each group. The primary concern of the researcher in choosing a design is to maximize internal validity, a concept that is reviewed in the next section.

Internal Validity of Experiments

Chapter 6 discussed the concept of internal validity. The internal validity of a study is a judgment that is made concerning the confidence with which plausible rival hypotheses can be ruled out as explanations for the results. It involves a deductive process in which the investigators must systematically examine how each of the threats to internal validity, which constitute rival alternative hypotheses, may have influenced the results. If all the threats can be reasonably eliminated, then the researcher can be confident that an observed relationship is causal, and that the difference in treatment conditions caused the obtained results. Internal validity is rarely an all-or-none decision. Rather, it is assessed as a matter of degree, depending on the plausibility of the explanation. As will be pointed out, some designs are relatively strong with respect to internal validity because most rival hypotheses can be ruled out confidently, while other designs that lend themselves to a host of plausible rival explanations are weak in internal validity. It cannot be stressed too much that in the final analysis, researchers must be their own best critics and carefully examine all threats that can be imagined. It is important, then, for consumers of research, as well as for those conducting research, to be aware of the common threats to internal validity and of the best ways to control them.

A useful way to think about threats to internal validity is to distinguish what is *possible* from something that is *plausible*. A possible threat is clearly not controlled by the design, but to be considered seriously, the possible threat needs to be plausible in two respects. First, the factor needs to be something that potentially affects the dependent variable. For example, there can be differences between compared groups in the color of their eyes, but that is not likely to be related to the dependent variable! Second, the factor needs to be systematically related to one group. That is, it needs to affect one group more than the other group. If a factor affects both groups equally, then generally it is not a threat to internal validity.

The threats to internal validity discussed in Chapter 6 are summarized in Table 10.1 in order to help you commit each factor to memory. They will be discussed again in the context of each of the designs summarized in the next four

TABLE 10.1

Summary of Threats to Internal Validity

Threat	Description
History	Unplanned or extraneous events that occur during the research and affect the results
Selection	Differences between the subjects in the groups may result in outcomes that are different because of group composition
Statistical regression	Scores of groups of subjects taking on values closer to the mean due to respondents' being identified on the basis of extremely high or low scores
Pretesting	Occurs when the act of taking a test or responding to a questionnaire prior to the treatment affects the subjects
Instrumentation	Differences in results due to unreliability, changes in the measuring instrument, or in observers
Subject attrition	Occurs because of systematic loss of subjects
Maturation	Occurs when an effect is due to maturational or other natural changes in the subjects (for example, being older, wiser, stronger, tired)
Diffusion of treatment	Occurs when subjects in one group learn about treatments or conditions for different groups
Experimenter effects	Deliberate or unintended effects of the researcher on subject responses
Treatment replications	Number of replications of the treatment is different from the number of subjects
Subject effects	Changes in behavior in response to being a subject or to being in an experiment
Statistical conclusion	Violation of assumptions or misuse of statistical tests

sections of the chapter, both in the text and in Tables 10.3 to 10.5, which provide overviews of the threats that are controlled by each design.

External Validity of Experiments

External validity is the extent to which the results of an experiment can be generalized to people and environmental conditions outside the context of the experiment. That is, if the same treatment or experimental conditions were replicated with different subjects, in a different setting, would the results be the same? In other words, what are the characteristics of subjects and environmental conditions for which we can expect the same results? We conclude that an experiment has strong external validity if the generalizability is relatively extensive, and has weak external validity if we are unable to generalize very much beyond the actual experiment. Table 10.2 summarizes the sources of threats to external validity (see Chapter 6 for a review of threats to external validity).

It is difficult to view external validity in the same way we view internal validity because most experiments are not designed specifically to control threats to external validity. Researchers consciously control some threats to internal validity by using a particular design, but most threats to external validity are a consideration regardless of the design. In only a few designs can it be

TABLE 10.2

Summary of Threats to External Validity

Threat	Description
Population	
Selection of subjects	Generalization is limited to the subjects in the sample if subjects are not selected randomly from an identified population.
Characteristics of subjects	Generalization is limited to the characteristics of the sample or population (for example, socioeconomic status, age, location, ability, race).
Subject-treatment interaction	Generalization may be limited because of the interaction between the subjects and treatment (that is, the effect of the treatment is unique to the subjects).
Ecological	
Description of variables	Generalization is limited to the operational definitions of the independent and dependent variables.
Multiple-treatment interference	In experiments in which subjects receive more than one treatment, generalizability is limited to similar multiple treatment situations because of the effect of the first treatment on subsequent treatments.
Setting-treatment interaction	Generalization is limited to the setting in which the study is conducted (for example, room, time of day, others present, other surroundings).
Time of measurement—treatment interaction	Results may be limited to the time frame in which they were obtained. Treatments causing immediate effects may not have lasting effects.
Pretest–posttest sensitization	The pretest or posttest may interact with the treatment so that similar results are obtained only when the testing conditions are present.
Novelty or disruption effect	Subjects may respond differently because of a change in routine, and generalization may be limited to situations that involve similar novelty or disruption (for example, an initially effective treatment may become ineffective in time as novelty wears off).

concluded that sources of external validity are controlled. Under the ecological category, for example, such threats as description of variables, novelty effect, setting–treatment interaction, and time of measurement treatment interaction, are not controlled with any particular experimental design. These threats are more a function of procedures and definitions than of design, and in most studies the reader decides whether any of the threats are reasonable.

Two of the ecological threats, multiple treatment interference and pretest–posttest sensitization, are present only in particular designs. Multiple treatment interference is a consideration only if more than one treatment is applied in succession. Pretest sensitization is a serious threat when investigating personality, values, attitudes, or opinions, since taking the pretest may sensitize the subject to the treatment. For example, if a study investigating the effect of a workshop on attitudes toward the use of computers in education gave a pretest measure of attitudes, the pretest itself might affect subsequent attitudes regardless of or in interaction with the workshop. Pretest–treatment interaction is minimized in studies conducted over a relatively long time, such as several weeks or months, and in studies of small children. Posttest sensitization occurs only if the posttest sensitizes the subject to the treatment and affects the results in a way that would not have occurred without the posttest.

Educational researchers are often confronted with the difficult dilemma that as internal validity is maximized, external validity may be sacrificed. High internal validity requires strict control of all sources of confounding variables, a type of control that may mean conducting the study under laboratory-like conditions. The more the environment is controlled, however, the less generalizable the results are to other settings. This is a constant dilemma for educators because research that cannot be used with other populations in other settings contributes little to educational practice, but there must be sufficient control for making reasonable causal conclusions. Without internal validity, of course, external validity is a moot question. Most research strives to balance the threats of internal and external validity by using sufficient rigor to make the results scientifically defensible and by conducting the study under conditions that permit generalization to other situations. One good approach to solving the dilemma is to replicate tightly controlled studies with different populations in different settings.

Pre-experimental Designs

The three designs summarized in this section are termed **pre-experimental designs** because they are without two or more of the six characteristics of experimental research listed earlier. As a consequence, few threats to internal validity are controlled. This does not mean that these designs are always uninterpretable, nor does it mean that the designs should not be used. There are certain cases in which the threats can be ruled out on the basis of accepted theory, common sense, or other data. Because they fail to rule out most rival hypotheses, however, it is difficult to make reasonable causal inferences from these designs alone. They are best used, perhaps, as a way of generating ideas that can be tested more systematically.

Notation

In presenting the designs in this chapter we will use a notational system to provide information for understanding the designs. The notational system is unique, though similar to the basic notational system used by Campbell and Stanley (1963) and Cook and Campbell (1979). Our notational system is as follows:

R	random assignment
O	observation, a measure that records observations of a pretest or posttest
X	treatment conditions (subscripts 1 through n indicate different treatments)
A, B, C, D, E, F	groups of subjects, or, for single-subject designs, baseline or treatment conditions

One-Group Posttest-Only Design

In the **one-group posttest-only design** the researcher gives a treatment and then makes an observation, as is represented in the following diagram, where A is the treatment group, X is the treatment, and O is the posttest.

One-Group Posttest-Only Design

Group	Treatment	Posttest
A	X	O

Time

While not all threats to internal validity are applicable to this design, because there is no pretest and no comparison with other treatments, only tentative causal conclusions can, at best, be made. Without a pretest, for example, it is difficult to conclude that behavior has changed at all (such as when testing a method of teaching math to students who know the answers to the final exam before receiving any instruction). Without a comparison or control group it is also difficult to know whether other factors occurring at the same time as the treatment were causally related to the dependent variable. Even though only five of the threats to internal validity are relevant to this design, the above weaknesses are so severe that the results of research based on this design alone are usually uninterpretable (see Table 10.3). The only situation in which this design is reasonable is when the researcher can be fairly certain of the level of knowledge, attitude, or skill of the subjects before the treatment and can be fairly sure that history is not a threat. For example, let's say an instructor in research methods wants to conduct a study of how much students have learned about statistical regression from his or her class. It seems reasonable to conclude that they did not know much about regression before the course began, and that it is unlikely that they will learn about it in other ways—like during party conversations! Consequently, the one-group posttest-only design may provide valid results.

This design should not be confused with what is termed a "case study design." Case study designs, as we have used the term, are qualitative investigations of one person, group, event, or setting over a single time period. These studies conduct detailed examinations of complex phenomena (see Chapter 12 for further information).

One-Group Pretest–Posttest Design

This common design is distinguished from the one-group posttest-only design by a single difference—the addition of an observation that occurs before the treatment condition is experienced (pretest).

In the **one-group pretest–posttest design** a single group of subjects is given a pretest (O), then the treatment (X), and then the posttest (O). The

TABLE 10.3

Threats to Internal Validity of Pre-experimental Designs

Design	History	Selection	Statistical Regression	Pretesting	Instrumentation	Subject Attrition	Maturation	Diffusion of Treatment	Experimenter Effects	Treatment Replications	Subject Effects	Statistical Conclusion
1. One-group posttest only	−	−	?	NA	?	?	−	NA	?	?	?	NA
2. One-group pretest–posttest	−	?	?	−	?	?	−	NA	?	?	?	?
3. Non-equivalent groups posttest only	?	−	?	NA	?	?	?	?	?	?	?	?

Note: In this table, and in Tables 10.4 and 10.5, a minus sign means a definite weakness, a plus sign means that the factor is controlled, a question mark means a possible source of invalidity, and NA indicates that the threat is not applicable to this design (and is also, then, not a factor).

pretest and posttest are the same, just given at different times. The result that is examined is a change from pretest to posttest. (This design is popularized as the so-called **pretest–posttest design**.) While the researcher can at least obtain a measure of change with this design, there are still many plausible rival hypotheses that are applicable.

One-Group Pretest–Posttest Design

Group	Pretest	Treatment	Posttest
A	O	X	O

Time

Consider this example. A university professor has received a grant to conduct inservice workshops for teachers on the topic of mainstreaming. One objective of the program is to improve the attitudes of the teachers toward mainstreaming children with disabilities. To assess this objective the professor selects a pretest–posttest design, administering an attitude "pretest" survey to the teachers before the workshop, then giving the same survey again after the workshop (posttest). Suppose the posttest scores are higher than the pretest scores. Can the researcher conclude that the cause of the change in scores is the workshop? Perhaps, but there are several threats to internal validity that are plausible, and until these threats can be ruled out, the researcher cannot assume that attendance at the workshop was the cause of the change.

The most serious threat is history. Because there is no control or comparison group, the researcher cannot be sure that other events occurring between the pretest and posttest did not cause the change in attitude. Some of these events might occur within the context of the workshop (a teacher gives a moving testimonial about exceptional children in a setting unrelated to the workshop); or they might occur outside the context of the workshop (during the workshop an article about mainstreaming appears in the school paper). Events like these are uncontrolled and may affect the results. It is necessary for the researcher, then, to make a case either that such effects are implausible or that if they are plausible, they did not occur. Data are sometimes used as evidence to rule out some threats, but in many cases it is simply common sense, theory, or experience that is used. However argued, if a plausible threat cannot be ruled out, then the researcher must admit that the effect of the workshop on changing attitudes cannot be determined exactly.

Selection is not a threat to internal validity for this design because only one group is used, but the characteristics of the subjects may well interact with a treatment and affect the external validity of the results.

Statistical regression could be a problem with this design if the subjects are selected on the basis of extremely high or low scores. In our example with the workshop, for instance, suppose the principal of the school wanted only those teachers with the least favorable attitudes to attend. The pretest scores would then be very low and, because of regression, would be higher on the posttest regardless of the effect of the workshop.

Pretesting is often a threat to research carried out with this design, especially in research on attitudes, because simply taking the pretest can alter the attitudes. The content of the questionnaire might sensitize the subjects to specific problems or might raise the general awareness level of the subjects and cause them to think more about the topic. Instrumentation can also be a threat. If, for example, teachers take the pretest on Friday afternoon and the posttest the next Wednesday morning the responses could be different simply because of the general attitudes that are likely to prevail at each of these times of the day and week.

Subject attrition can be a problem if, between the pretest and posttest, subjects are lost because of particular reasons. If all the teachers in a school begin a workshop, for example, and those with the most negative attitude toward mainstreaming drop out because they do not want to learn more about it, then the measured attitudes of the remaining subjects will be high. Consider another example. To assess the effect of a schoolwide effort to expand favorable attitudes toward learning, students are pretested as sophomores and posttested as seniors. A plausible argument—at least one that would need to be ruled out—is that improvement in attitudes is demonstrated because the students who have the most negative attitudes as sophomores never make it to be seniors; they drop out. Attrition is especially a problem in cases with transient populations, with a long-term experiment, or with longitudinal research.

Maturation is a threat to internal validity of research based on this design when the dependent variable is unstable because of maturational changes. This threat is more serious as the time between the pretest and posttest increases. Suppose, for instance, a researcher is investigating self-concept of middle school students. If the time between the pretest and posttest is relatively short (two or three weeks), then maturation is probably not a threat; but if there is a year between the pretest and posttest, changes in self-concept would probably occur regardless of the treatment, because of maturation. Maturation includes such threats as being more tired, bored, or hungry at the time of test-taking, and these factors might be a problem in some pretest–posttest designs. In the example of the workshop on mainstreaming it is unlikely that maturation is a serious threat, and it would probably be reasonable to rule out these threats as plausible rival hypotheses.

Since there is only one treatment in this design, diffusion of treatment is not applicable. Treatment replications may be a threat, depending on the manner in which the treatment is administered. Experimenter effects, subject effects, and statistical conclusion threats are possible in any experiment, and these would need to be examined.

From the above discussion it should be obvious that there are many uncontrolled threats to the internal validity of one-group pretest–posttest designs. Consequently, this design should be used only under certain conditions that minimize the plausibility of the threats (e.g., use reliable instruments and short pretest-posttest time intervals), and when it is impossible to use other designs that will control some of these threats.

Nonequivalent Groups Posttest-Only

This design is similar to the one-group posttest-only design. The difference is that in a **nonequivalent groups posttest-only design** a comparison or control group that receives no treatment or a different treatment is added to the one-group posttest-only design. The design is diagrammed below.

Nonequivalent Groups Posttest-Only Design

Group	Treatment	Posttest
A	⟶ X ⟶	O
B	⟶	O

Time

This design is used frequently after a treatment has been implemented. The procedure is to give the treatment to one group and then assess the dependent variable (via the posttest), and give only the posttest to another group at the same time the posttest is administered to the first group. The term *nonequivalent groups* is used as the name for the design because selection is the most serious threat to the internal validity of the results. Notice that there is no random assignment of subjects to each group. Differences in the groups of subjects may therefore account for any differences in the results of the posttests. The more different the groups are, the more plausible selection becomes as a reason for the results. Suppose, for example, the professor conducting the mainstreaming workshop wanted to get a comparison group and located a school willing to help. Even if the posttest scores of the treatment group were better than the scores of the comparison group, it is untenable to conclude that the better scores were due to the workshop. It may be that the teachers in the treatment school had more favorable attitudes to begin with, and that the workshop had little effect on the attitudes of teachers there.

There are also other, less serious threats to the internal validity of research based on this design. These threats occur when the basic design includes alternate treatments, as indicated below.

**Nonequivalent Groups Alternate
Treatment Posttest-Only Design**

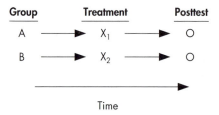

Group	Treatment	Posttest
A	X_1	O
B	X_2	O

Time

This design is used when a researcher wants to compare two or more treatments but cannot give a pretest or randomize the assignment of subjects to each group. In this case internal, or within-group, history is a threat, since what might occur within each group, unrelated to the treatments, could affect the posttest. External history is not usually a threat, unless selection differences expose subjects outside the context of the study to different conditions that affect the results. Regression may be a threat even though only one observation is made. Pretesting is not a threat because there is no pretest, but instrumentation could be a threat if there are differences in the way the posttest assessments are made for each group (such as an observer's being more alert for one group than the other). Attrition is a threat because subject loss, due either to the initial characteristics of the subjects (selection) or to different treatments, may cause certain subjects to drop out. Maturation may also be a threat, depending on selection characteristics. If the subjects in each group are aware of the treatment given the other group, it is possible for diffusion of treatment to be a threat. Experimenter effects, subject effects, treatment replications, and statistical conclusion threats are also possible.

The nonequivalent groups posttest-only design is relatively weak for testing causation. If the design is used, a researcher should make every effort to get comparable groups in order to decrease the selection threat.

The possible sources of invalidity for research carried out by the three pre-experimental designs are summarized in Table 10.3. Since different designs control different factors and also have unique weaknesses, the researcher chooses the best design on the basis of the research conditions. If, for example, the researcher can reasonably argue that two groups are about the same with respect to important variables (socioeconomic status, achievement, age, experience, motivation, and so on), then the strongest design would be the posttest-only with nonequivalent groups. In any event, all these designs are relatively weak for use in testing causal relationships, and usually with sufficient foresight they can be modified slightly to permit more reasonable causal inferences.

True Experimental Designs[1]

This section presents two designs that have been called **true experimental designs**. Both include procedures for ruling out intersubject differences through randomization of subjects to groups, and both include manipulation of the treatment variable. These designs represent what historically has been called experimental in the biological and physical sciences.

Pretest–Posttest Control Group Design

The **pretest–posttest control group design** is an extension of the one-group pretest–posttest design in two ways: a second group is added, called the control or comparison group; and subjects are assigned randomly to each group. This design is represented below. Group A is the experimental group.

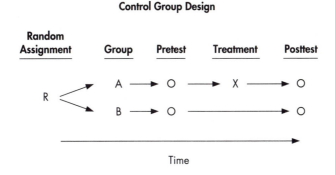

**Pretest–Posttest
Control Group Design**

The first step is random assignment of the subjects to the experimental group and the control group. In studies with a relatively small number of

---

[1]A third experimental design that is often presented is the Solomon four-group design.

subjects, it is usually best to rank-order the subjects on achievement, attitudes, or other factors that may be related to the dependent variable. Then, in the case of a two-group design, pairs of subjects are formed; the researcher randomly assigns one subject from each pair to the experimental group and the other subject to the control group. Another procedure is to match subjects on the basis of a variable and then randomly assign members of each matched pair to experimental and control groups. However implemented, the purpose of random assignment is to enable the researcher to reasonably rule out any differences between the groups that could account for differences found in the results. With a small group of subjects it is thus less likely that the groups will be the same. If only ten subjects are randomly assigned to two groups, for example, there is a good chance that even though the assignment is random, there will be important differences between the groups. If two hundred subjects are randomly assigned, however, there is a very small chance that the groups will differ. Generally, educational researchers like to have at least fifteen subjects in each group in order to assume statistical equivalence, and they have more confidence in the results if there are twenty to thirty subjects in each group.

The second step is to pretest each group on the dependent variable (in some designs the pretest is given first, followed by random assignment). The third step is to administer the treatment condition to the experimental group but not to the control group, keeping all other conditions the same for both groups so that the only difference is the manipulation of the independent variable. Each group is then posttested on the dependent variable.

In the diagrammed control group design there is no treatment at all for the control group. As indicated previously, it is more common, and usually more desirable, to have comparison rather than control groups. A comparison design uses two or more variations of the independent variable and can use two or more groups. Suppose, for example, a teacher wants to compare three methods of teaching spelling. The teacher randomly assigns each student in the class to one of three groups, administers a pretest, tries the different methods, and gives a posttest. The design would look like this:

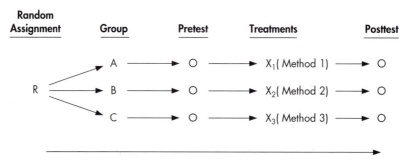

Pretest–Posttest Comparison Group Design

It would also be possible to combine several different treatments with a control group, as shown below.

Pretest–Posttest Control/Comparison Group Design

The pretest–posttest control group design controls four sources of threats to internal validity, as indicated in Table 10.4. Threats related to history are generally controlled insofar as events that are external to the study affect all groups equally. The reason for the question mark in the category, however, is that it is always possible that unique events may occur within each group to affect the results. Selection and maturation are controlled because of the random

TABLE 10.4

Threats to Internal Validity of True Experimental Designs

Design	History	Selection	Statistical Regression	Pretesting	Instrumentation	Subject Attrition	Maturation	Diffusion of Treatment	Experimenter Effects	Treatment Replications	Subject Effects	Statistical Conclusion
Pretest–posttest control group	?	+	+	+	?	?	+	?	?	?	?	?
Posttest-only control group	?	+	NA	NA	?	?	+	?	?	?	?	?

Note: In this table, and in Tables 10.4 and 10.5, a minus sign means a definite weakness, a plus sign means that the factor is controlled, a question mark means a possible source of invalidity, and NA indicates that the threat is not applicable to this design (and is also, then, not a factor).

assignment of subjects. Statistical regression and pretesting are controlled, since any effect of these factors is equal for all groups. Instrumentation is not a problem when the same standardized self-report procedures are used, but studies that use observers or raters must be careful to avoid observer or rater bias (knowing which students are receiving which treatments, or different observers or raters are used for each group). Subject attrition is not usually a threat unless a particular treatment causes systematic subject dropout.

Diffusion of treatments may be a source of invalidity in experiments in which subjects in one group, because of close physical proximity or communication with subjects in another group, learn about information or treatments not intended for them. Because the conditions that were intended for one group, then, are transmitted to other groups, the effect of the treatment is dispersed and cannot be assessed reasonably. For example, if a researcher compares two methods of instruction, such as cooperative group instruction and individualized instruction, and conducts the experiment within a single fourth-grade class by randomly assigning half the class to each method, it is likely that students in one group will know what is occurring in the other group. If the students in the individualized group feel left out, or believe they have a less interesting assignment, they may be resentful and may not perform as well as possible. Diffusion might also occur if students in the cooperative group learn to help others and then assist students in the individualized group.

Experimenter effects is another threat that may be a problem, depending on the procedures of the study. If the individuals who are responsible for implementing the treatments are aware of the purpose and hypotheses of the study, they may act differently toward each group and affect the results. If a teacher is involved in a study to investigate the effect of differential amounts of praise on behavior (more praise, better behavior), and understands what the hypothesized result should be, then the teacher may act more positively toward the students receiving more praise (be closer physically, give more eye contact, offer less criticism) and thus contaminate the intended effect of amount of praise.

Similarly, subject effects could be important if subjects in different groups respond differently because of their treatment, for example, subjects who know they are in the "control" group may try harder than they otherwise would, or they may be demotivated because they were not selected for the "special" treatment, or those in the "special" treatment may feel an obligation to try harder or give "better" responses. Treatment replications may be a threat, depending on how the treatments were administered, and statistical conclusion is always a possibility.

Excerpt 10.1 illustrates a pretest–posttest control group design. In this study the investigators administered the same instrument as the pretest and posttest. To ensure equal representation of subjects with different pretest scores in each group, the pretest scores were rank-ordered by score levels, and subjects were randomly assigned from each level to experimental or control groups. The steps in the research, then, are modified somewhat since randomization occurred after the pretest, not before. The design used in Excerpt 10.1 is represented below.

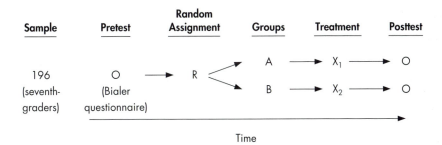

Posttest-Only Control Group Design

The purpose of random assignment, as indicated previously, is to equalize the experimental and control groups before introducing the independent variable. If the groups are equalized through randomization, is it necessary to give a pretest? While there are certain cases in which it is best to use a pretest with random assignment, if the groups have at least fifteen subjects each, the pretest may not be necessary—that is, it is not essential to have a pretest in order to conduct a true experimental study. The **posttest-only control group design** is exactly the same as the pretest–posttest control group design except that there is no pretest on the dependent variable. The posttest-only control group design is represented as follows:

Posttest-Only Control Group Design

Random Assignment	Groups	Treatments	Posttest
R	A	X	O
	B		O

Time

This basic design can be expanded to include several treatments:

R	A	X_1	O
	B	X_2	O
	C	X_3	O

The posttest-only control group design is used when it is unfeasible or inconvenient to give a pretest and in situations in which the pretest might have an effect on the treatment. There are four disadvantages to using a posttest-only

EXCERPT 10.1

PRETEST–POSTTEST CONTROL GROUP DESIGN

The purpose of the present study was to extend the research reported above by considering the effect of individually administered evaluative teacher comments over a period of time on the perception of control among inner-city junior high school students. Limitations of the above studies associated with the use of intact groups were avoided by randomly forming the experimental and control groups. Moreover, the treatments were designed to represent naturalistic interventions to an on-going instructional program rather than a "one-shot" treatment representing rather questionable educational practice.

METHOD

All 196 pupils were administered the Bialer questionnaire during their regularly scheduled science class. Bialer (1) designed this locus of control scale for use with children. It contains 23 items of the type: "Do you believe a kid can be whatever he wants to be?" to which the child expresses agreement or disagreement with each statement by circling the word yes or no. There are eighteen statements for which a "yes" is scored as an internal response and five items for which "no" is scored as an internal response. The total score is the sum of the number of internal responses marked. The standard directions were used with the exception that the second author read the directions and each item aloud to the students as they read it silently. The directions as well as a complete listing of the items are presented by Lefcourt (6) with only a few exemplar items appearing in the Bialer article cited above. However, neither source presents data regarding the reliability of the scale. The answers were recorded directly on the questionnaire form and were later key-punched for the computer analyses. The pretest questionnaires were arranged by score levels, and within score levels, subjects were assigned at random to either the experimental or control groups.

Five major-subject teachers including the second author cooperated in administering the treatment conditions to the 196 pupils. Each teacher was supplied with the names of students in each treatment condition. The teachers were directed to provide written comments of an encouraging, personalized nature on all papers and tests submitted by all pupils in the experimental groups. The cooperating teachers were given these guidelines: "Comments are to be positive statements regardless of the grade, readily visible to the receiver and contain the pronoun 'you' whenever possible, such as 'you are showing improvement.'" The teachers were directed to write no comments on papers or tests returned to pupils in the control group except for the customary check-mark or grade. Treatment conditions were imposed for a period of six weeks, at which time, the Bialer locus of control instrument was re-administered.

Source: From Cross, L. H. & Cross, G. M. (1981). Teachers evaluative comments and pupil perception of control. *Journal of Experimental Education, 49,* 68–71. Reprinted with permission of the Helen Dwight Reid Educational Foundation. Published by Heldref Publications, 4000 Albemarle St., N.W., Washington, DC 20016. Copyright © 1981.

rather than a pretest–posttest design: (1) if there is any chance that randomization has not controlled for initial group differences, the lack of a pretest makes it difficult either to check whether differences exist or control statistically those differences that may be found; (2) the researcher is unable to form subgroups on the basis of the pretest for investigating effects of the treatment on different subgroups; (3) the researcher is unable to determine whether differential attrition has occurred; and (4) the statistical analysis is less precise and less likely to show a difference between the experimental and control groups as in the pretest-posttest design. If the following conditions exist, the pretest–posttest design may thus be preferable:

1. There are subtle, small differences between treatment conditions.
2. Differential mortality is possible.
3. Subgroup analysis is desirable.
4. Anonymity is unnecessary.
5. Pretesting is a normal part of the subjects' routine.

The advantages of the posttest-only design are that it allows experimental evidence when it is impossible to give a pretest, it avoids the reactive effect of pretesting, and its use makes ensuring anonymity easier. This design is especially good, then, for attitude research for two reasons: the use of an attitude questionnaire as the pretest may well affect the treatment, and attitudes are generally reported more honestly if anonymity can be ensured.

The posttest-only control group design controls for almost the same sources of invalidity as the pretest–posttest control group design. Table 10.4 summarizes the sources of invalidity.

In Excerpt 10.2 a posttest-only design is used to investigate the effect of several sentence-combining revision strategies on writing skill, self-motivation, and intrinsic interest in writing. There were six experimental conditions and a control group.

EXCERPT 10.2

POSTTEST-ONLY CONTROL GROUP DESIGN

We randomly assigned the 84 participants to one of six experimental conditions or a practice-only control group, with 12 girls in each group. The experimental conditions were based on the three types of goal setting (process goal, outcome goal, and shifting process-outcome goal), and two variations in self-recording (present or absent). . . . As a check for effectiveness of random assignment, we compared the NEDT English usage of girls in the six experimental groups at baseline and found no significant differences . . . all girls were posttested in order for attributions, self-efficacy, writing skill, self-reaction, and intrinsic interest. The experimenter began and terminated each section of the study and recorded the posttest scores.

Source: Zimmerman, B. J., & Kitsantas, A. (1999). Acquiring writing revision skill: shifting from process to outcome self-regulatory goals. *Journal of Educational Psychology, 91*(2), 244–245.

Occasionally, a contingency arises in which the researcher needs to rule out the effect of the pretest on the treatment. The design used for this purpose is a combination of the posttest-only control group and pretest–posttest control group design, and is called the *Solomon four-group design*. Although this design controls for the effects of mortality and pretest-treatment interactions, the design is difficult to carry out in education because it requires twice as many subjects and groups as in other designs.

Quasi-Experimental Designs

True experimental designs provide the strongest, most convincing arguments of the causal effect of the independent variable because they control for the most sources of internal invalidity. There are, however, many circumstances in educational research for which, while causal inference is desired, it is unfeasible to design true experiments, or in which the need for strong external validity is greater. The most common reasons that true experimental designs cannot be employed are that random assignment of subjects to experimental and control groups is impossible and that a control or comparison group is unavailable, inconvenient, or too expensive. Fortunately, there are several good designs that can be used under either of these circumstances. They are termed **quasi-experimental designs** because, while not true experiments, they provide reasonable control over most sources of invalidity and they are usually stronger than the pre-experimental designs. Although there are many quasi-experimental designs (Cook & Campbell, 1979), we will discuss only the most common ones.

Nonequivalent Groups Pretest–Posttest Design

This design is very prevalent and useful in education, since it is often impossible to randomly assign subjects. The researcher uses intact, already established groups of subjects, gives a pretest, administers the treatment condition to one group, and gives the posttest. The only difference between this design, then, and the pretest–posttest control group design, is in the lack of random assignment of subjects. The design is represented below:

Nonequivalent Groups Pretest–Posttest Design

Group	Pretest	Treatment	Posttest
A	O	X	O
B	O		O

Time

As shown in Table 10.5 (p. 347), the most serious threat to the internal validity of research conducted with this design is selection; that is, because the groups may differ in characteristics that affect the dependent variable, the researcher must address selection and provide reasonable arguments that this threat is not a plausible rival hypothesis. Suppose a researcher is interested in studying the effect of three different methods of changing the attitudes of student teachers toward computer-assisted instruction. The researcher has three classes of student teachers to work with, and it is impossible to assign students randomly within each class to each of the three methods. The researcher therefore uses each class intact and gives each class a different treatment. The design would be as follows:

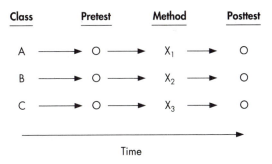

Class	Pretest	Method	Posttest
A	O	X_1	O
B	O	X_2	O
C	O	X_3	O

Time

The interpretation of the results will depend largely on whether the groups differed on some characteristic that might reasonably be related to the independent variable. This decision is made by comparing the three groups on such characteristics as gender, time the groups meet, size of groups, achievement, aptitude, socioeconomic status, major, and pretest scores. If, for instance, class A comprises all elementary majors and classes B and C secondary majors, and the results showed that class A gained more than B and C, the gain may be attributable to the values and backgrounds of elementary majors compared with those of secondary majors. On the other hand, if the classes are about the same in most characteristics, then it would be reasonable to assume that selection differences probably would not account for the results. Consequently, if the researcher knows in advance that randomization is impossible, the groups should be selected to be as similar as possible. The pretest scores and other measures on the groups are then used to adjust the groups statistically on the factor that is measured. Another approach to controlling selection, when intact groups such as classrooms must be used, is to use a large number of groups and then randomly assign entire groups to either control or treatment conditions. This procedure then changes the study to a true experimental design. This is, in fact, the preferred approach when diffusion of treatment or local history threats are viable.

The threats of maturation and statistical regression are the only other differences between this design and the pretest–posttest control group design. Regression is a problem if one of the groups happens to have extremely high or low scores. For example, if a study to assess the impact of a program on gifted children selected gifted children who score low and normal children who score high as comparison groups, then statistical regression will make the results look like a difference in posttest scores when nothing has actually changed. Maturation effects (growing more experienced, tired, bored, and so on) will depend on the specific differences in characteristics between the groups.

In Excerpt 10.3, a nonequivalent group's pretest-posttest quasi-experimental design is employed by using students in intact classes as subjects. Notice how even though there is random assignment of classes, the researchers properly indicate that this is not a true experimental design because students were not randomly assigned to classes. The study has a single independent variable with two levels, and measures of achievement and attitude as dependent variables.

Time-Series Designs

In the one-group pretest–posttest design a single group of subjects receives one pretest and one posttest. If the group is repeatedly measured before and after the treatment, rather than once before and once after, a different design, called "time series," is created. **Time-series designs** are especially useful when there are continuous naturally occurring observations of the dependent variable over time and there is a sudden or distinct treatment during the observations. These designs offer significant improvement over the pretest-posttest design because with a series of preobservations and postobservations, patterns of stability and change can be assessed more accurately. There are many different types of time-series designs (Cook & Campbell, 1979); we will discuss the most common ones.

Single Group Interrupted Time-Series Design This design requires one group and multiple observations or assessments before and after the treatment. The observations before the treatment can be thought of as repeated pretests, those after the treatment as repeated posttests. The design can be diagrammed as follows:

EXCERPT 10.3

QUASI-EXPERIMENTAL PRETEST–POSTTEST COMPARISON GROUP DESIGN

A nonequivalent control group quasi-experimental design (Campbell & Stanley, 1966) involving 16 intact classes was adopted. Random assignment of students to new classes is not likely in Taiwan's educational system; intact class set was the unit of the experimental design. Eight intact classes (n = 319) were randomly assigned to the inquiry-group instruction; eight classes (n = 293) were assigned randomly to the traditional lecture group. The participants in both groups were tested and surveyed before and after the 4-week intervention.

Source: Chang, C., & Mao, S. (1999). Comparison of Taiwan science students' outcomes with inquiry-group versus traditional instruction. *The Journal of Educational Research, 92* (6), 342.

Single Group Interrupted Time-Series Design

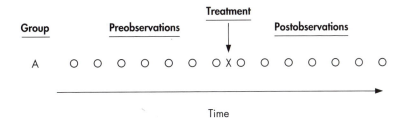

Several conditions should be met in employing this design. First, the observations should be made at equal time intervals and should be conducted with the same procedures in order to reduce the threat of instrumentation. Second, the treatment introduced should be a distinctive, abrupt intervention that is clearly new to the existing environment. Third, there should be some evidence that the subjects involved in each observation are the same (that is, have low subject attrition). A variation of using the same subjects for each measurement is to use different but very similar groups. A new curriculum could be assessed very well in this manner. For example, sixth-grade student achievement could be plotted for several years with the old curriculum, and then achievement scores could be recorded for several years after the new curriculum is introduced. The key element in this design is that the characteristics of the sixth-grade students must be about the same year after year. Obviously, if there is an immigration of brighter students over the years achievement will increase regardless of the curriculum.

Some possible outcomes for the study are indicated in Figure 10.1. If outcome A is achieved, then the researcher may conclude that the curriculum had a positive effect on achievement. Outcome B indicates a steady improvement of scores, so it is difficult to interpret the effect of the curriculum, and outcome C indicates little change over the time span. In interpreting these results, however, the researcher should look for alternate explanations. If there happened to be a change in the student population, such as with migration from the city to suburban schools, then the observations would be expected to change. The testing instrument would need to be the same (there should be no change in the norming group). Perhaps the most serious threat to validity is history. It is possible that events other than the treatment, in this case the curriculum, occurred at about the same time and affected the posttest observations; for example, maybe in the same year the curricula were changed, the teachers also changed. Other threats include seasonal variation (self-concept scores may be lower in winter than in spring) and pretesting (the effect of the pretesting on the treatment).

Control Group Interrupted Time-Series Design In this design a control or comparison group is added to the single group interrupted time series. The addition of a

FIGURE 10.1   Possible Outcome Patterns of Achievement over Time for Time-Series Designs

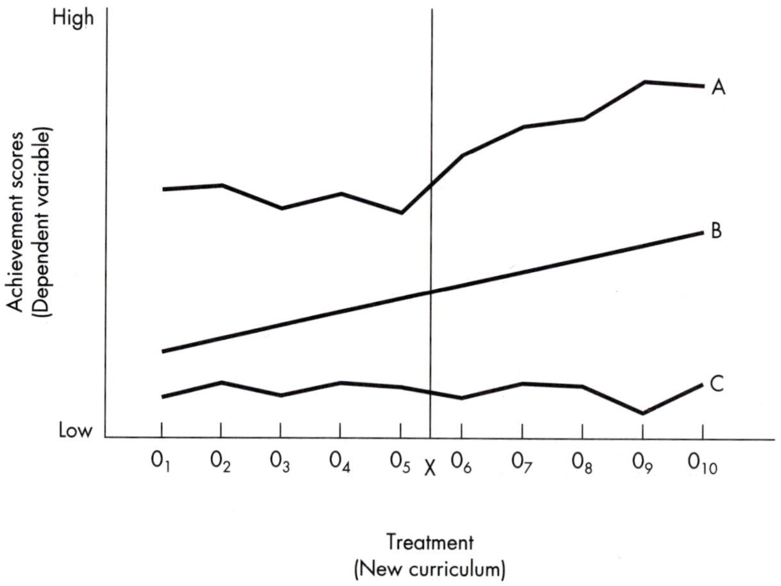

Treatment
(New curriculum)

control group strengthens the design considerably, since the major threat of history is eliminated. Instrumentation is also a less likely explanation, and if random assignment is included then selection is not a threat to validity. Since a control group is present, however, diffusion of treatment becomes a threat. This design is represented below.

Control-Group Interrupted Time-Series Design

Time

There are many variations of the basic time-series design. A treatment can be removed rather than added, for example, and multiple treatments can be compared, either with one group or several groups. Some variations are indicated in the next diagram. In situation 1 three different treatments are compared, using three groups of subjects. In situation 2 only one group of subjects is used and two treatments are compared, and in situation 3 the same treatment is compared in two groups at different points in time.

```
             A   O   O   O   O   O X₁ O   O   O   O   O
Situation 1  B   O   O   O   O   O X₂ O   O   O   O   O
             C   O   O   O   O   O X₃ O   O   O   O   O
_____

Situation 2  A   O   O   O   O X₁ O   O   O   O X₂ O   O   O   O
_____

             A   O   O   O X₁ O   O   O   O   O   O   O
Situation 3  B   O   O   O   O   O   O   O X₁ O   O   O
_____ ►

                              Time
```

The quasi-experimental designs that have been introduced in this chapter are simple, basic designs that are usually expanded in actual studies, and there are several designs that have not been mentioned. The choice of design will depend on the variables studied, the circumstances of the setting in which the research is conducted, and the plausibility of threats to internal validity. The important point is that there are weaknesses in all research designs, and it is necessary for the investigator and reader of research to search out and analyze plausible rival hypotheses that may explain the results. Table 10.5 summarizes threats to internal validity of quasi-experimental designs.

TABLE 10.5

Threats to Internal Validity of Quasi-Experimental Designs

Design	History	Selection	Statistical Regression	Pretesting	Instrumentation	Subject Attrition	Maturation	Diffusion of Treatment	Experimenter Effects	Treatment Replications	Subject Effects	Statistical Conclusion
Nonequivalent groups pretest–posttest design	?	−	?	+	?	?	−	?	?	?	?	?
Single group interrupted time-series	−	?	+	?	?	?	+	NA	+	?	?	?
Control group interrupted time-series	+	?	+	+	?	?	+	?	?	?	?	?

Note: In this table, and in Tables 10.4 and 10.5, a minus sign means a definite weakness, a plus sign means that the factor is controlled, a question mark means a possible source of invalidity, and NA indicates that the threat is not applicable to this design (and is also, then, not a factor).

Single-Subject Designs

The pre-experimental, true experimental, and quasi-experimental designs that have been discussed are based on a traditional research concept that behavior is best investigated by using groups of subjects. We are typically interested, for example, in fourth-grade students' attitudes in general, or whether a particular method of reading is in general best. There are, however, many circumstances in which it is either undesirable or impossible to use groups of subjects, such as when examining instructional strategies to be used with individual students. In these situations **single-subject designs** are often employed to provide rigorous causal inferences for the behavior of one, two, or a few individuals. The term "single-subject" actually refers to the way the results are presented and analyzed, by individual subject, as contrasted with group designs that use average scores. The basic approach is to study individuals in a nontreatment condition and then in a treatment condition, with performance on the dependent variable measured continually in both conditions.

The design characteristics that achieve high internal validity with single-subject designs are somewhat different from those of techniques covered previously in the context of group designs. The most important characteristics of single-subject designs are summarized below:

1. *Reliable measurement.* Single-subject designs usually involve many observations of behavior as the technique for collecting data. It is important that the observation conditions, such as time of day and location, be standardized; that observers be well trained and checked for reliability and bias; and that the observed behavior be defined operationally. Consistency in measurement is especially important as the study moves from one condition to another. Because accurate measurement is crucial to single-subject designs, the researcher typically reports all aspects of data collection so that any threat to validity can be reasonably ruled out.

2. *Repeated measurement.* A distinct characteristic of single-subject designs is that a single aspect of behavior is measured many times, in the same way, throughout the study. This is quite different from measurement in many group studies in which there is a single measure before or after the treatment. Repeated measurement controls for normal variation that would be expected within short time intervals, and provides a clear, reliable description of the behavior.

3. *Description of conditions.* A precise, detailed description of all conditions in which the behavior is observed should be provided. This description allows application of the study to other individuals in order to strengthen both internal and external validity.

4. *Baseline and treatment condition; duration and stability.* The usual procedure is for each condition to last about the same length of time and contain about the same number of observations. If either the length of time or number

of observations varies, then time and number of observations become confounding variables that complicate the interpretation of the results and weaken internal validity. It is also important that the behavior be observed long enough for the establishment of a stable pattern. If there is considerable variation in the behavior, then it will be difficult to determine whether observed changes are due to natural variation or to the treatment. During the first phase of single-subject research, the target behavior is observed under natural conditions until stability is achieved. This period of time is called the **baseline**. The treatment phase occurs with a change in conditions by the researcher and also must be long enough to achieve stability.

5. *Single-variable rule.* It is important to change only one variable during the treatment phase of single-subject research, and the variable that is changed should be described precisely. If two or more variables are changed simultaneously, the researcher cannot be sure which change, or changes, caused the results.

A–B Designs

In order to distinguish single-subject designs from traditional group designs, a unique notational convention is used. In it the letters, instead of representing groups of subjects, stand for conditions: *A* stands for the baseline condition and *B* for the treatment condition.

The **A–B design** is the most simple, and least interpretable, single-subject design. The procedure in using it is to observe target behavior until it occurs at a consistent stable rate. This condition is the baseline, or A condition. A treatment is then introduced into the environment in which baseline data have been collected, and this condition is labeled B. The design can be diagrammed as follows:

A–B Single-Subject Design

The interpretation of the results is based on the premise that if no treatment were introduced, the behavior would continue as recorded in the baseline. If the behavior does change during the treatment condition, it may be attributable to the intervention introduced by the researcher. Other factors, however, such as testing and history, often cannot be ruled out reasonably in this design, so it is relatively weak in internal validity.

A–B–A Designs

A more common design in single-subject research is the **A–B–A design**, also called a **reversal** or **withdrawal design**, in which a second baseline period is added after the treatment. In this design, which is represented below, the researcher establishes a baseline (A), introduces the treatment (B), and then removes the treatment to reestablish the baseline condition (A).

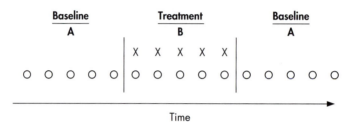

A–B–A Single-Subject Design

This design allows strong causal inference if the pattern of behavior changes during the treatment phase and then returns to about the same pattern as observed in the first baseline after the treatment is removed. As a hypothetical example to illustrate this design, suppose a teacher is interested in trying a new reinforcement technique with John, one of the fifth-graders, in the hope that the new technique will increase the time John spends actually engaged in study (time on task). The teacher first records the average amount of time on task for each day until a stable pattern is achieved. Then the teacher introduces the reinforcement technique as the intervention, and continues to observe time on task. After a given length of time, the teacher stops using the reinforcement technique to see whether the on-task behavior returns to the baseline condition. Figure 10.2 illustrates results of this hypothetical study that provides good evidence of a causal link between the reinforcement technique and greater time on task.

Further evidence of a change in behavior that is caused by the treatment may be obtained if the A–B–A design is extended to reinstitute the treatment, or become A–B–A–B. Not only does the A–B–A–B design provide stronger causal inference than the A–B–A design, it also ends with the treatment condition, which often, for ethical reasons, is more favorable for the subject. If the pattern of results fails to support the effect of the treatment, then the interpretation is less clear. If the behavior is changed during the treatment but fails to return to the baseline condition once the treatment is ended, the researcher does not know whether factors other than the treatment caused the change, or

FIGURE 10.2   Results from a Hypothetical Study Using an A–B–A Design

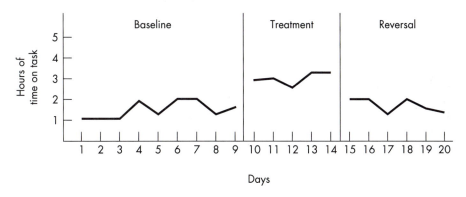

the treatment was so effective that it could be removed and still have an impact on behavior.

The A–B–A–B design is illustrated in Excerpt 10.4. The purpose of this experiment was to investigate the effects of reprimands given to one student on a second student.

EXCERPT 10.4

A–B–A–B SINGLE-SUBJECT DESIGN

EXPERIMENTAL DESIGN

A reversal design was used in this experiment. After stable baseline performance was obtained for both Jeanette and Natalie, reprimands were made contingent upon Jeanette's disruptive behavior according to a variable interval 2-min schedule of punishment. During this condition, Natalie's disruptive behavior was not reprimanded. After a return to baseline conditions, reprimands were again made contingent upon Jeanette's disruptive behavior. The experiment was terminated after this treatment because the school year had come to an end.

Baseline 1 During this condition the teacher was instructed not to praise or reprimand either Jeanette or Natalie and to conduct the class in her usual manner.

Reprimand Jeanette 1 During this condition Jeanette's disruptive behavior was reprimanded by the teacher on a VI 2-min schedule of punishment. The teacher was signaled when to deliver reprimands using the same procedure as in the preceding experiment. As in Experiment 3A, a variety of signals was used.

Baseline 2 This condition was carried out in the same manner as the first baseline condition.

(continued)

(continued)

Reprimand Jeanette 2 This condition was carried out in the same manner as the first reprimand Jeanette condition.

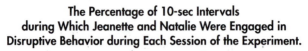

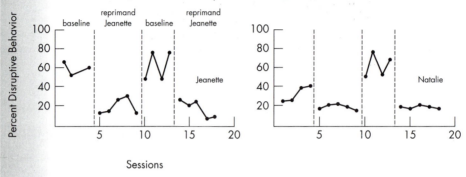

Source: From Van Houton R. et al. (1982). An analysis of some variables influencing the effectiveness of reprimands, Journal of Applied Behavior Analysis, 15, 65–83, Copyright © 1982 by the Society for the Experimental Analysis of Behavior, Inc. Reprinted by permission.

Multiple-Baseline Designs

When it is impossible or undesirable to remove a treatment condition, or when the effects of a treatment condition extend into a second baseline phase, strong causal inference can be made by using **multiple-baseline designs** rather than by a simple A–B design. Multiple-baseline designs employ the A–B logic, but rather than using one subject and one kind of target behavior, the researcher collects data on two or more actions, subjects, or situations, or some combination of actions, situations, and subjects.

Multiple-Baselines Across Behavior In this design baseline measurements are recorded on two or more discrete, independent behaviors for one subject. After a stable baseline is established for all behaviors, the treatment is first applied to one behavior, then, after a constant time interval, applied to the second behavior, and so forth until all have received the treatment.

Strong causal inference can be made of the effect of the treatment if performance shows consistent change only after the treatment is introduced for each type of behavior. To provide a meaningful comparison it is necessary to begin the treatments at different times for each one. In this way, behavior remaining at the baseline condition provides control for that receiving the treatment condition. The most troublesome problem with this design is using two or more behaviors so similar that the first time the treatment is introduced, it affects both.

Multiple-Baselines Across Situations In this design a single type of target behavior of one individual is observed in two or more settings. A teacher might, for example, be interested in investigating whether a student would respond the same way to individualized feedback in math, science, and English. The basic design is the same as in the multiple-baselines across behaviors design except that situation replaces types of behavior as the condition that is varied (such as learning behavior in both a classroom and a grocery store, or classroom and cafeteria).

Multiple-Baselines Across Individuals This design uses two or more individuals and holds the behavior and the situation constant. After a stable baseline is observed for one subject, the treatment is introduced for that subject only. After a given interval, the second subject receives the treatment, and so forth. This design is effective as long as the subjects involved are uninfluenced by one another because one of them has received the treatment (for example, with students in the same class or with siblings). A good use of this type of design would be to have a teacher employ the same treatment procedure with individual students in four different classes.

Many variations of the three multiple-baseline designs are possible. A good source for further detail on these designs is Barlow and Hersen (1984), Kazdin (1982) and Franklin, Allison, & Gorman (1997). The A–B–A and A–B–A–B formats can be combined with multiple-baseline designs. The designs that involve removal, reversal, or reinstatement of the treatment are generally strongest with respect to internal validity. As might well be suspected, the external validity of single-subject designs is quite limited. The generalizability of results of one study is increased primarily by replication with other subjects and different settings.

Standards of Adequacy

In judging the adequacy of the designs that have been presented in this chapter you should focus your attention on a few key criteria. These criteria are listed here in the form of questions that should be asked for each type of design.

True Experimental Designs

1. Was the research design described in sufficient detail to allow for replication of the study?
2. Was it clear how statistical equivalence of the groups was achieved? Was there a full description of the specific manner in which subjects were assigned randomly to groups?
3. Was a true experimental design appropriate for the research problem?
4. Was there manipulation of the independent variable?
5. Was there maximum control over extraneous variables and errors of measurement?

6. Was the treatment condition sufficiently different from the comparison condition for a differential effect on the dependent variable to be expected?
7. Were potential threats to internal validity reasonably ruled out or noted and discussed?
8. Was the time frame of the study described?
9. Did the design avoid being too artificial or restricted for adequate external validity?
10. Was an appropriate balance achieved between control of variables and natural conditions?
11. Were appropriate tests of inferential statistics used?

Quasi-Experimental Designs

1. Was the research design described in sufficient detail to allow for replication of the study?
2. Was a true experiment possible?
3. Was it clear how extraneous variables were controlled or ruled out as plausible rival hypotheses?
4. Were all potential threats to internal validity addressed?
5. Were the explanations ruling out plausible rival hypotheses reasonable?
6. Would a different quasi-design have been better?
7. Did the design approach a true experiment as closely as possible?
8. Was there an appropriate balance between control for internal validity and for external validity?
9. Was every effort made to use groups that were as equivalent as possible?
10. If a time-series design was used, (a) Was there an adequate number of observations to suggest a pattern of results? (b) Was the treatment intervention introduced distinctly at one point in time? (c) Was the measurement of the dependent variable consistent? (d) Was it clear, if a comparison groups was used, how equivalent the groups were?

Single-Subject Designs

1. Was the sample size one?
2. Was a single-subject design most appropriate, or would a group design have been better?
3. Were the observation conditions standardized?
4. Was the behavior that was observed defined operationally?
5. Was the measurement highly reliable?
6. Were sufficient repeated measures made?
7. Were the conditions in which the study was conducted described fully?
8. Was there stability in the baseline condition before the treatment was introduced?
9. Was there a difference between the length of time or number of observations between the baseline and the treatment conditions?

10. Was only one variable changed during the treatment condition?
11. Were threats to internal and external validity addressed?

Summary

The purpose of this chapter has been to introduce designs that permit investigation of the causal effect of one variable on another. The challenge to most researchers is using the design that, given the conditions of the research, is best suited to their goal. The major points of the chapter are summarized below.

1. Experimental research, as defined in the natural sciences, involves manipulating experimental variables and randomization of subjects to groups in order to investigate cause-and-effect relationships.
2. Classic experimental research is characterized by random assignment of subjects to treatment and control groups, manipulation of independent variables, and tight control of extraneous variables.
3. Strict control of extraneous variables in experimental educational research may lead to limited generalizability of results.
4. Planning experimental research involves the creation of experimental and comparison groups, manipulation of the factor of the group to receive the treatment, and assessment of the effect of the treatment on behavior.
5. The key element in interpreting experimental studies is to rule out plausible rival hypotheses.
6. Pre-experimental designs control for very few threats to internal validity.
7. True experimental designs control for most threats to internal validity, but some threats, such as local history and diffusion of treatment, may constitute plausible rival hypotheses.
8. Quasi-experimental designs are often employed because of the difficulties in conducting true experiments.
9. Time-series designs, in which many observations are made before and after the treatment, are especially useful in cases where periodic testing is a natural part of the environment.
10. Single-subject designs provide techniques for making strong causal inferences about the effect of a treatment on a single individual or group.

Self-Instructional Review Exercises

Sample answers are in the back of the book.

Test Items

1. Classic experimental research, as conducted in the natural sciences, involves
   a. manipulation, random assignment, application of results.
   b. random assignment, manipulation, control.

    c. control, manipulation, generalizability.

    d. generalizability, control, independence.

2. A disadvantage of experimental research in educational settings is that

    a. it is difficult to make causal inferences.

    b. internal validity is weak.

    c. it is usually expensive to conduct.

    d. generalizability is often limited.

3. The design that has the weakest internal validity is

    a. one-group posttest only.

    b. one-group pretest–posttest.

    c. A–B–A–B single-subject design.

    d. time-series design.

4. The results of pre-experimental designs usually have many plausible rival hypotheses because of

    a. insufficient planning.

    b. lack of random assignment.

    c. lack of generalizability.

    d. using only one group.

5. True experimental designs control for which of the following sources of internal invalidity?

    a. selection, pretesting

    b. regression, history

    c. selection, maturation

    d. diffusion of treatment, selection

6. The most important advantage of using true experiments, with respect to internal validity, is that _____ is controlled.

    a. selection

    b. history

    c. pretesting

    d. experimenter effects

7. The nonequivalent groups pretest–posttest design controls for which source of invalidity?

    a. regression

    b. history

    c. pretesting

    d. selection

8. The distinguishing characteristic of time-series designs is that

    a. several treatments are compared.

    b. many preobservations and postobservations are made.

    c. history is effectively controlled.

    d. subjects are randomly assigned to groups at different times.

9. The A–B single-subject design is particularly vulnerable to which of the following threats to internal validity?

    a. diffusion of treatment, selection

    b. selection, history

     c. diffusion of treatment, regression
     d. instrumentation, history
10. Which of the following sets of characteristics distinguishes single-subject designs from other experimental designs?
     a. good generalizability, using baseline data
     b. varying only one variable, using multiple methods
     c. using comparison groups, using random assignment
     d. varying only one variable, using random assignment
11. Multiple-baseline designs are especially useful for what type of situation?
     a. when two or more subjects are available
     b. when it is undesirable to use only one baseline
     c. when it is undesirable to remove the treatment
     d. when two or more types of behavior are available for study

Application Exercises

For each of the following cases, state the design that is used, and represent it using the notation system discussed in the chapter.

1. A researcher wants to test the effectiveness of three methods of teaching typing to a group of eleventh-grade students. The researcher locates a school willing to cooperate, and a teacher says that the researcher can use three of his classes. The researcher then administers a pretest to all students, each class receives a different method of teaching for two weeks, and then the researcher gives all students a posttest.

2. A teacher is interested in determining the effect of using a point system with students in order to control misbehavior. The teacher decides to record the amount of misbehavior of two students, a boy and a girl who seem to have more problems than other students. For two weeks the teacher records the misbehavior of the students. At the end of the second week the teacher begins using the point system with the boy and at the same time continues to record misbehavior for another two weeks. The girl does not receive the point treatment until the end of the third week.

3. A researcher is interested in whether the order of questions in a multiple-choice test affects the number of items answered correctly. The researcher makes three forms of the test: one with easy items first, difficult last; another with easy items last, difficult first; and a third with no order at all, easiest and difficult mixed together. The test is given to a class of sixty students. The tests are organized into twenty piles, with each pile containing Forms 1, 2, and 3. The twenty piles are then put together and the tests are passed out to the students. The researcher then compares the average scores of students taking each form of the test.

CHAPTER 11

Inferential Statistics

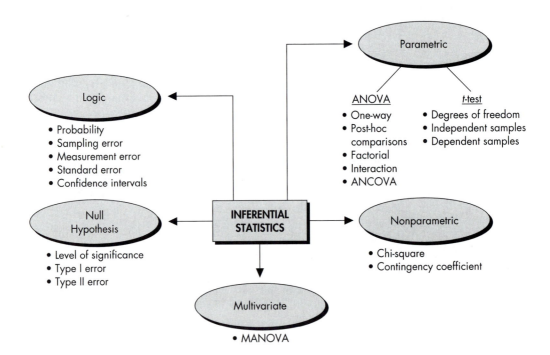

KEY TERMS

probability

sampling distribution

standard error

confidence interval

statistical hypothesis

null hypothesis

level of significance

Type I error

Type II error

alpha level

statistically significant

effect size

t-test

degrees of freedom

independent samples *t*-test

dependent samples *t*-test

analysis of variance (ANOVA)

post hoc comparisons

planned comparisons

factorial ANOVA

interaction

analysis of covariance

(ANCOVA)

parametric

nonparametric

chi-square

independent samples chi-

square test

contingency table

phi coefficient

contingency coefficient

multivariate

This is the part of research books that most readers dread. The words *inferential statistics* send waves of anxiety and fear into students already concerned about the so-called more simple descriptive data analysis procedures! These feelings are based on the mistaken perception that complex and difficult mathematical calculations are necessary to understand inferential statistics. It is true that the actual computations associated with inferential statistics are complicated, but you do not need to learn equations and complete calculations to understand and use the results of these procedures (some calculations are presented in Appendix C). Learning the principles of inferential statistics requires study and application, but it is more a matter of understanding logic than of mathematical calculations.

In this chapter we will present the logic on which inferential statistics are based, the principles of hypothesis testing, and a few commonly used statistical procedures. The emphasis throughout is on presenting the concepts so that you will understand and evaluate the use of these procedures in designing and reading research.

The Logic of Inferential Statistics

In some ways it would be very nice if we could be certain in predicting the outcomes of events. When we go see a movie, how sure are we that we will enjoy it? When a teacher uses a particular grouping procedure, how sure is he or she that it will work? How confident is a patient that an operation will be successful?

Are farmers certain that there will be sufficient rain for their crops? The questions are endless because it is in our nature to try to predict the future, and the degree to which we can be certain about the predictions varies greatly. There are very few things in our world we can be absolutely certain about, and in the social sciences and education there is usually a fair amount of uncertainty. In making statements about investigated phenomena we must therefore use language that reflects the probabilistic nature of the case. The numbers, concepts, and terms used in inferential statistics provide this language. Although there are a great number of inferential statistical procedures, many quite complicated, the purpose is always the same. The goal is to determine in a precise way the probability of something.

Probability

Probability is a scientific way of stating the degree of confidence we have in predicting something. Kerlinger (1979) defines probability theoretically as "the number of 'favorable' cases of the event divided by the total number of (equally possible) cases" (pp. 67–68). (*Favorable* here means favorable to an event whose probability we are assessing.) If the total number of cases is 12, therefore, and the number of favorable cases 6, the probability of the favorable case is 6/12 or .50. Dice rolling is a more concrete example. With one die there is a total of six possible cases. If the favorable case is rolling a four, the probability of actually rolling a four would be 1/6, or .17; that is, if a die is rolled 100 times, about 17 fours will be rolled. If we have two dice, what is the probability of rolling a seven? Since there is a total of 36 different combinations for throwing two dice (1 and 1; 1 and 2; 1 and 3, and so on) and only six of these equal 7 (1 and 6; 2 and 5; 3 and 4; 6 and 1; 5 and 2; and 4 and 3), the probability of rolling a seven is 6/36, or .17. What about throwing boxcars (two sixes)? There is only one combination of numbers that will give you boxcars, so the probability is 1/36, or .03.

This logic is applied to more complicated situations in research. How sure, for example, can pollsters be that their predictions are accurate? What is the probability of being right or wrong? As with the Gallup Poll, how certain can we be that the results from a so-called scientific sample accurately reflect the attitudes of the American public? When teachers use positive reinforcement, how sure are they that the desired behavior will increase in frequency? In these situations the number of total cases may be unknown and the assessment of the events is imperfect. We thus make probability statements that are influenced by the amount of error possible in measuring and sampling events.

Error in Sampling and Measurement

Sampling was discussed in Chapter 6 as a technique for studying a portion from the population of all events or observations under consideration. The population is the larger group to which the researcher intends to generalize the results obtained from the sample. As a subgroup of the population, the sample is used to derive data, and then inferential statistics are used to generalize to the population. Let us assume, for example, that a researcher is interested in assessing the self-concept of fourth-graders in a school district. The researcher could measure the self-concept of every fourth-grader, but that would be time-consuming, expensive, and probably unnecessary. Rather, the researcher takes a *sample* of the fourth-graders and measures their self-concepts. Then the researcher *infers* what the self-concept of all fourth-graders is from the results of the sample chosen. Inferential statistics are used to make such inferences. The group of all fourth-graders is the population, and the researcher uses descriptive statistics (mean and standard deviation) from the sample to estimate the characteristics of the population.

Where does probability enter this process? When a sample is drawn, the resulting statistics represent an imperfect estimate of the population. There is error in drawing the sample, and probability relates to our confidence in the fact that the sample accurately represents the population. Even if the researcher uses a random sample, the mean and variance of the particular sample drawn would be slightly different from those of another sample. A third sample would also be different, as would a fourth, a fifth, and so on. The sample descriptive statistics only estimate the population values, so the inferences made must take into account what possible sample statistics could have been generated.

Consider the following example (Figure 11.1). Let us say that a researcher is interested in determining the reading level of ninth-graders of a school district. A random sample is selected and the mean of the sample is, let us say, 65, with a standard deviation of 2.5 (Figure 11.1a). Now let us say the researcher draws another random sample, and this time the mean is 66. Now there are two means (Figure 11.1b). Which one is correct? He or she decides to take five more samples and gets means of 64, 63.5, 64.5, 65.7, and 65.2 (Figure 11.1c).

FIGURE 11.1   Random Sample with (a) One Mean, (b) Two Means, (c) Several Means, and (d) the Means Showing a Normal Curve

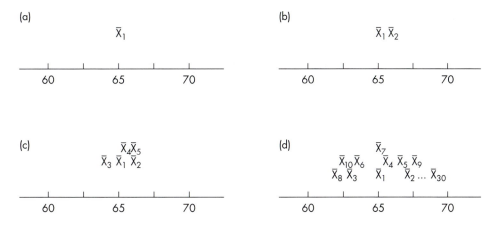

Now which one is correct? The researcher decides to really find out and takes thirty more samples. Surely that will do it! Different sample means are drawn, but when the means are put together they begin to look like something familiar—a normal curve (Figure 11.1d).

In fact, if 100 samples were drawn, the sample means, when put together, would constitute a normal curve, with its own mean and standard deviation. The resulting distribution is called the **sampling distribution**, and the standard deviation is termed a **standard error.** Thus, when we imagine that multiple samples are extracted from the population and scored, the standard error is the standard deviation of this sampling distribution. The *mean of means*, then, and the standard error of the sampling distribution can be calculated, and the researcher can use this information to know not what the population mean is, but the probability of its having a certain value based on the properties of the normal curve. That is, about two-thirds of the means drawn would be within one standard error of the mean of means, and 96 percent of the means would be within two standard errors. The researcher, therefore, can now describe a range of probable means and be fairly certain of the range, even though individual sample means will be slightly different.

In reality, a researcher rarely takes more than one sample, but from the mean and variance of that sample the range of population means that could be drawn, if possible, can be calculated. Here, then, is where probability is integrated with inferential statistics. Inferential statistics are used to estimate the probability of a population mean's being within a range of possible values. The researcher is able to say, to infer, that 68 times out of 100 the population mean will be within one standard error of the mean of means, and that 96 times out of 100 it will be within two standard errors.

A related concept that is being used with increased frequency is *confidence interval.* The **confidence interval** (CI) is a range of numerical values in which the actual value of the population probably lies. The upper and lower boundaries of the confidence interval are called the *confidence limits.* Typically, researchers report a 95 or 99 percent confidence interval, meaning that the probability of the population value is between the confidence limits is 95 or 99 percent, respectively. For example, if it is reported that the 99 percent confidence interval from a statewide poll is .435–.492, this means that the from the sample it can be inferred that there is a 99 percent chance that between 43.5 and 49.2 percent of the population is in favor of a particular proposal. Thus, it is highly likely that the majority of the population is against the proposal. If the 99 percent confidence interval was completely above .50, then a majority probably favors the proposal.

Suppose a researcher is not interested in taking a sample from a population, but rather includes the entire population as the sample. Would this mean that the researcher could ignore the principles of sampling error and inferential statistics in obtaining a result that represents the entire group? While sampling error is not a concern, measurement error is. Recall in Chapter 8 that whenever we assess variables in education the measurement is never perfect—there is always some degree of error, summarized statistically as the standard error of measurement. Thus we *infer* a real or true value on a variable from the imperfect measure. This could be thought of as a type of sampling error in the sense that the one measure obtained is a "sample" estimating the true value. Consequently, in all educational research there is definitely measurement error, and in some research there is also sampling error.

This section of the chapter has explained the logic of inferential statistics in estimating population means from sample means and introduced confidence intervals. In most research, however, we are interested in much more than estimating populations from samples. We usually want to compare population means with each other or with some established value. The next section discusses how these comparisons are made.

Null Hypothesis

Let us assume that a researcher wants to compare the attitudes of sixth-graders toward school to those of fourth-graders. The researcher randomly selects samples of sixth- and fourth-graders and finds the means of each group. The means are 30 for fourth-graders and 37 for sixth-graders. Can the researcher then assume that sixth-graders have more positive attitudes than fourth-graders? Perhaps, but this conclusion must take into account sampling and measurement error. The population means are thus estimated and compared to find the probability that the possible population means of each group are different. The probabilities are formalized by statements that are tested. These statements are referred to as *hypotheses*. Research hypotheses have already been introduced as the research prediction that is tested (in this example, the research hypothesis might be that sixth-graders have more positive attitudes than fourth-graders).

When we refer to probability in terms of sampling and measurement error, the statement used is called the **statistical hypothesis.** Statistical hypotheses are usually stated in what is called the null form. The **null hypothesis,** which is usually implied by the research hypothesis rather than stated explicitly, states that there is no difference between the population means of the two groups. That is, the population means are the same. The researcher employs an inferential statistical test to determine the probability that the null hypothesis is untrue. If the null is false, then there is a high probability that there is a difference between the groups. The null hypothesis in our example would be that attitudes of sixth- and fourth-graders toward school are the same. If we can show that there is a high probability of being correct in rejecting the null, then we have found evidence of a difference in the attitudes.

Theoretically, we know that the population range of means of both groups can be estimated, and if there is little overlap in those ranges then it is likely that the population means are different. This case is diagramed in Figure 11.2. Note that there is virtually no overlap between the two normal curves. This means that we can be confident of being correct in rejecting the null hypothesis.

FIGURE 11.2   Range of Population Means of Two Groups

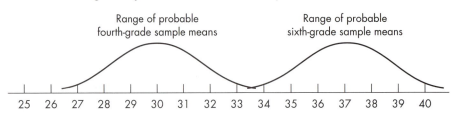

The reason null hypotheses are used with inferential statistics is that we never "prove" anything to be true; we only fail to disprove. Failure to disprove is consistent with the reality of probability in our lives. In other words, if we cannot find compelling evidence that they are different, the most plausible conclusion is that they are the same. For conceiving and designing research the research hypothesis is far more important than the null. The null is a technical necessity in using inferential statistics.

It should also be pointed out that failure to reject the null hypothesis does not necessarily mean that the null is true. It is especially difficult to accept null hypotheses as reality in studies that use a small number of subjects or use instruments with low reliability. The fact that the null hypothesis was not rejected may be a large sampling error or measurement error, or it may be attributable to any of several other factors beyond the scope of this book. In practical terms, be wary of conclusions that are based on unrejected null hypotheses.

Level of Significance

Since the basis of inferential statistics is the probability of estimation, then accepting or rejecting the null hypothesis is also related to probability or chance rather than being a dichotomous decision. That is, because of error in sampling and measurement we can only give the probability of being correct or incorrect in rejecting or not rejecting the null. To put it differently, we can be fairly sure that a certain number of times out of a hundred the sample means we *could* draw would not be the same.

The **level of significance** is used to indicate what the chance is that we are wrong in rejecting the null. Also called level of probability, or *p* level, it is expressed as a decimal and tells us how many times out of a hundred or thousand we would be wrong in rejecting the null assuming the null is true (in other words, how often we would expect no real difference even though we rejected the null). The logic of level of significance is that we assume that the null hypothesis is correct, and then see what the probability is that the sample means we have calculated would be different by chance alone. If we find that

there is a probability of only one time in a hundred that we would find a particular difference in the means by chance or random fluxations, (p = .01), then
we would probably reject the null because it is quite probable that the null is
false. In other words, the level of significance tells us the chance probability of
finding differences between the means. The lower the level of significance,
therefore, the more confidence we have that we are safe in rejecting the null.
After all, for example, if we find a difference of five points between two means
that, through our null hypothesis, we assume to be the same, and our statistics
tell us there is only one chance in a thousand of finding a five-point difference
by chance (p = .001), then it is only logical to assume that the null hypothesis
is false and reject it (or say we are very, very lucky!). We reject the null hypothesis in favor of the research, or alternative, hypothesis.

Some researchers will use a slightly different approach to hypothesis testing, in which a given level of significance is determined prior to data collection
to act as a criteria for accepting or failing to accept the null hypothesis. This
"critical value," is called the alpha level (α), and it determines the conclusion
based on the numbers generated from the results. Using just the alpha level,
however, results in a dichotomous decision, whereas use of significance testing,
with p values, provides more information.

Errors in Hypothesis Testing

The purpose of inferential statistics, null hypotheses, and levels of significance
is to make a decision, based on probability, about the nature of populations and
real values of variables. It is possible that the decision is wrong. When the decision is to reject the null hypothesis when in fact the null hypothesis is true, the
researcher has made what is called a **Type I error.** The probability of making this
type of error is equal to the level of significance: that is, with a significance level
of .05 there is a probability of five times out of 100 that the sample data will lead
the researcher to reject the null hypothesis when it is in fact true. A researcher
consequently avoids a Type I error to the degree that the level of significance is
high (that is, a .001 level is better than .01 for avoiding Type I errors).

Another type of wrong decision occurs when the null hypothesis is not
rejected, when in fact the null hypothesis is actually wrong. This is referred to
as a **Type II error.** While there is no direct relationship between the level of significance and the probability of making a Type II error, as the level of significance increases the likelihood of Type II error decreases. A level of significance
of .10 is thus better for avoiding a Type II error than .05 or .01. Figure 11.3
shows how error type is related to types of decisions.

Interpreting Level of Significance

The interpretation of rejecting or failing to reject a null hypothesis depends on
whether the researcher is interested in avoiding a Type I or Type II error, and in
whether a predetermined alpha level is set. If a predetermined value is stated,

FIGURE 11.3   Relationship of State of Nature, Decisions, and Error in Hypothesis Testing

State of nature

	Null hypothesis is true	Null hypothesis is false
Reject null hypothesis	Type I error	Correct decision
Fail to reject null hypothesis	Correct decision	Type II error

such as .05 or .01 for a Type I error, then the researcher rejects the null by comparing the computed level of significance with the predetermined level. If the calculated significance is less than the predetermined level (for example, .01 < .05) then the null hypothesis is rejected.

In many research studies there is no predetermined alpha level. In these studies statisticians use a general rule for rejecting a null hypothesis. If the p value is the same as or less than .05, then the null is rejected and the statement is made that there is a **"statistically significant"** difference (though more accurately it is always a difference at some level of confidence). A p value between .05 and .10 is usually thought of as *marginally* significant, and anything greater than .10 is labeled a nonsignificant difference. We are saying, then, that if there is more than one chance out of ten of being wrong in rejecting the null (one chance in ten that the means are the same) then that is too much risk to take in saying that the means are different. The results may be due more to error than to a treatment or real difference.

It is best to report the p level for each statistical test because the conventions for rejecting the null hypothesis are general rules of thumb. Individual researchers and consumers, depending on the circumstances, may differ with respect to what constitutes a statistically significant difference. A level of .05, for example, generally agreed to be statistically significant, would probably be unacceptable if the test concerned usage of a drug that might cause death (five times out a hundred, the researcher is wrong in saying no death will occur). In such a situation a level of .000001 may be more appropriately considered statistically significant.

Another important point in interpreting p levels and corresponding conclusions is that while it is common for researchers to fail to reject the null (e.g.,

$p = .20$), the failure to find a statistically significant difference or relationship does not necessarily mean that in *reality* there is no difference or relationship. Only when the circumstances of the research warrant (in which there is what is called "adequate power" in the test) is a nonsignificant finding taken as evidence that there is no relationship. The reason a nonsignificant finding is usually uninterpretable is that many factors, such as low reliability, diffusion of treatment, insufficient number of subjects, and so forth, can cause the nonsignificance. We thus tend to believe a significant finding as indicating that a real relationship exists, but the opposite is not necessarily true. Especially in cases with a small sample size (which makes it more difficult to find a significant difference) a nonsignificant finding should be interpreted to mean that further research is necessary, not that there is no relationship.

One of the most important issues that create confusion in interpreting statistics is the decision whether the results are meaningful. That is, how much will the results make a difference in the real world? Are the results *educationally* significant, not just statistically significant? The statistical test tells only that there is a difference, but the worth or importance of a finding must also be judged. When a finding is reported to be statistically significant, the reader should examine the reported means to see how different they are and the magnitude of the correlations. Meaningfulness is related to the specifics of a situation. For example, there may be a statistically significant difference in reading achievement among first-graders who use curriculum X as opposed to curriculum Y, but that does not mean curriculum X should be purchased. It is possible that the difference represents only one percentile point and that curriculum X costs several thousand dollars more than curriculum Y. Only the reader can judge what is meaningful. Many researchers tend to assume automatically that statistical significance means educational significance, but that is simply untrue.

One of the reasons that statistically significant p values can be misleading is that the value that is calculated is directly related to sample size. Thus, it is possible to have a very large sample, a very small difference or relationship, and still report it as "significant." For example, a correlation of .44 will be statistically significant at the .05 level with a sample as small as 20, and a sample of 5,000 will allow a statistically significant .05 finding with a correlation of only .028, which is, practically speaking, no relationship at all.

The American Psychological Association (1999), and several research journals now strongly recommend or require that investigators report appropriate indicators that illustrate the strength or magnitude of a difference or relationship along with measures of statistical significance. These *effect magnitude measures,* as they are called, are either measures of strength of association or effect size. Measures of association are used to estimate proportions of variance held in common, similar to the coefficient of determination. Effect size is more commonly used. It is typically reported in a generalized form as the ratio of the difference between the group means divided by the estimated standard deviation of the population. According to Cohen (1988), the *effect size index* then

EXCERPT 11.1

REPORTING EFFECT SIZE

On the basis of Cohen's categories of small, medium, and large effect sizes (Buzz, 1995), a power analysis revealed that most of the effect sizes for sex differences in this study were small to medium (see Table 3).

TABLE 3   Summary of Sex Equity Findings

Dependent Measure	Males M	Males SD	Females M	Females SD	F	df	p	Effect Size	Cohen's Category
Instructor calling on students	0.2480	0.2425	0.2034	0.2608	0.71	1, 22	.4131	0.18	Small
Student volunteering	1.1000	1.0615	0.9548	1.3027	0.45	1, 22	.5081	0.12	Small
Instructor interacting with students	1.3274	1.2999	1.5623	1.6247	0.55	1, 22	.5078	0.11	Small
Students raising their hands	0.1835	0.1469	0.1334	0.1155	1.70	1, 22	.2055	0.38	Medium
Staying after class	0.1440	0.0534	0.1066	0.0612	3.18	1, 22	.0885	0.58	Medium
Seat location	1.2496	1.4105	0.3891	0.0571	1.65	1, 28	.2101	1.17	Large

Note: The means presented here are in ratio form. Each female student mean is based on averages on the female response divided by the number of women in the class. Each male student mean is based on averages of the male response divided by the number of men in class. Men and women are compared on the basis of their actual participation rates, taking into consideration the proportion of women to men in class.

Source: Brady, K. L., & Eisler, R. M. (1999). Sex and gender in the college classroom: A quantitative analysis of faculty-study interactions and perceptions, *Journal of Educational Psychology*, 91(1), 127–145.

provides an indication of the practical or meaningful difference. Effect size indexes of about .20 are regarded as small effects, of about .5 as medium or moderate effects, and .8 and above large effects. An example of reporting effect size in a journal is illustrated in Excerpt 11.1. Clearly, measures of effect magnitude, along with confidence intervals, provide much better information than a simple rejection of the null hypothesis.

Excerpt 11.2 gives levels of significance to show which of the results are statistically significant. Remember that various conventions can be used in reporting the level of significance, such as level of significance, p level, and alpha (α). Some researchers may report that the probability (p) is less than ($<$) a specific value (for example, $p < .05$ or $p < .001$) rather than reporting the actual level of significance.

Comparing Two Means: The *t*-Test

There are many research situations in which a mean from one group is compared with a mean from another group to determine the probability that the corresponding population means are different. The most common statistical

EXCERPT 11.2

LEVELS OF SIGNIFICANCE

Adjusted means and standard deviations for the mentions and accuracy scores are presented in Tables 3 and 4. The analysis of mentions scores indicated that across passages (initial and transfer), there is a significant main effect of test-taking training $F(1,68) = 5.32$, $p = .02$. Groups who received test-taking training cooperatively recalled more than those who received individual test-taking training. The main effect of cooperative versus individual study training approached significance, $F(1,68) = 3.31$, $p = .07$. There were no significant interactions.

   The analysis of accuracy scores revealed that across passages, the main effect of cooperative vs. individual study training was significant, $F(1,68) = 4.70$, $p = .03$. The study-training by passage interaction was also significant, $F(1,70) = 5.89$, $p = .01$. Post hoc comparisons revealed that groups who studied Passage 1 cooperatively recalled significantly more accurate information than groups who studied Passage 1 individually ($p < .05$). No other differences between group means were significant.

Source: From Lambiotte, J. G., et al. (1987). Cooperative learning and test taking: Transfer of skills. *Contemporary Educational Psychology, 12*(1). Reprinted by permission of Academic Press, Inc.

procedure for determining the level of significance when two means are compared is the *t*-**test**. The *t*-test is a formula that generates a number, and this number is used to determine the probability level (*p* level) of rejecting the null hypothesis.

   What happens is that the sample means, standard deviations, and size of the samples are used in the *t*-test equation to obtain a *t* value (sometimes called *t* statistic). The formula for calculating the *t* value is

$$t = \frac{\overline{X}_1 - \overline{X}_2}{S_{\overline{X}_1 - \overline{X}_2}}$$

where

$$\overline{X}_1 = \text{mean of group 1}$$
$$\overline{X}_2 = \text{mean of group 2}$$
$$S_{\overline{X}_1 - \overline{X}_2} = \text{standard error of the difference between the means}$$

The standard error of the difference between the means can be conceived of as a measure of the amount of error in estimating the population mean from a sample mean. As the distance between $\overline{X}_1$ and $\overline{X}_2$ gets larger, then, and as the error involved in estimating the means gets smaller, the *t* statistic is greater. The calculated *t* value is a three- or four-digit number with two decimal places, such as

2.30; 3.16; 8.72; 1.85. To determine the level of significance, the researcher compares this number with theoretical t values in a table. The table is called distribution of t, or critical values for the t-test, and is found in Table 11.1. The researcher uses the table by locating two numbers: the **degrees of freedom** (df) and the level of significance desired. The term *degrees of freedom* is a mathematical concept that denotes the number of independent observations that are free to vary. For each statistical test there is a corresponding number of degrees of freedom that is calculated, and then this number is used to estimate the statistical significance of the test. In the distribution of a t-table, the number at the intersection of the degrees of freedom row and the level of significance column is the relevant theoretical value of t. If this critical t is less than the t value calculated by the t-test equation, it means that the observed difference in means is greater than could have been expected under the null hypothesis, so the hypothesis can be rejected at that level of significance.

Notice that at the top of the table there are two rows, the top row for what is called a "one-tailed" and the other for a "two-tailed" test of significance. The "tails" refer to the ends of the normal sampling distribution that are used in the significance test. "One-tail" means that one of the two ends of the distribution is used as the region of rejection, so that if the p value is .05 that 5 percent is all at one end of the distribution. In a two-tailed test the region is divided between both ends of the distribution; for example, for a p value of .05, .025 percent is at each end of the distribution. The one-tailed test is more liberal and should be used only when the researcher is very confident that a result that is opposite the research hypothesis will not be obtained. Unless otherwise stated, significance tests can be assumed to be two-tailed.

The calculated t-statistic and corresponding p level are reported in most studies. In Excerpt 11.3 the results section of a research study is reproduced to show how t-tests are summarized. The number in parentheses following the t is the degrees of freedom.

There are two different forms of the equation used in the t-test, one for independent samples and one for samples that are paired, or dependent. Independent samples are groups of subjects that have no relationship to each other; the two samples have different subjects in each group, and the subjects are usually either assigned randomly from a common population or drawn from two different populations. Therefore, if a researcher is testing the difference between an experimental group and a control group mean in a posttest-only design, the **independent samples t-test** would be appropriate. Comparing attitudes of fourth- and sixth-graders would also utilize an independent samples t-test.

The second form of the t-test can be referred to by several different names, including *paired*, *dependent samples*, *correlated*, or *matched* t-test. This t-test is used in situations in which the subjects from the two groups are paired or matched in some way. A common example of this case is the same group of subjects tested twice, as in a pretest–posttest study. Whether the same or different subjects are in each group, as long as there is a systematic relationship between the groups it is necessary to use the **dependent samples t-test** to calculate the probability of rejecting the null hypothesis.

TABLE 11.1

t Distribution

df	Level of Significance for a One-Tailed Test				
	.05	.025	.01	.005	.0005
	Level of Significance for a Two-Tailed Test				
	.10	.05	.02	.01	.001
1	6.314	12.706	31.821	63.657	636.619
2	2.920	4.303	6.965	9.925	31.598
3	2.353	3.182	4.541	5.841	12.924
4	2.132	2.776	3.747	4.604	8.610
5	2.015	2.571	3.365	4.032	6.869
6	1.943	2.447	3.143	3.707	5.959
7	1.895	2.365	2.998	3.499	5.408
8	1.860	2.306	2.896	3.355	5.041
9	1.833	2.262	2.821	3.250	4.781
10	1.812	2.228	2.764	3.169	4.587
11	1.796	2.201	2.718	3.106	4.437
12	1.782	2.179	2.681	3.055	4.318
13	1.771	2.160	2.650	3.012	4.221
14	1.761	2.145	2.624	2.977	4.140
15	1.753	2.131	2.602	2.947	4.073
16	1.746	2.120	2.583	2.921	4.015
17	1.740	2.110	2.567	2.898	3.965
18	1.734	2.101	2.552	2.878	3.922
19	1.729	2.093	2.539	2.861	3.883
20	1.725	2.086	2.528	2.845	3.850
21	1.721	2.080	2.518	2.831	3.819
22	1.717	2.074	2.508	2.819	3.792
23	1.714	2.069	2.500	2.807	3.767
24	1.711	2.064	2.492	2.797	3.745
25	1.708	2.060	2.485	2.787	3.725
26	1.706	2.056	2.479	2.779	3.707
27	1.703	2.052	2.473	2.771	3.690
28	1.701	2.048	2.467	2.763	3.674
29	1.699	2.045	2.462	2.756	3.659
30	1.697	2.042	2.457	2.750	3.646
40	1.684	2.021	2.423	2.704	3.551
60	1.671	2.000	2.390	2.660	3.460
120	1.658	1.980	2.358	2.617	3.373
∞	1.645	1.960	2.326	2.576	3.291

Source: Fisher and Yates (1974). *Statistical Tables for Biological, Agricultural and Medical Research, Table III.* 6th Ed. London: Longman Group UK Ltd. (previously published by Oliver and Boyd Ltd. Edinburg). Reprinted by permission of the authors and publishers.

Although the formulas and degrees of freedom are different for each form of *t*-test the interpretation and reporting of the results are the same (the *df* for the dependent *t*-test is the number of pairs minus one). Thus, a reader of research need not worry about whether the correct formula has been used.

EXCERPT 11.3

INDEPENDENT SAMPLES *t*-TEST

Means, standard deviations, and obtained *t* statistics for distance education and on-campus course evaluation comparisons are presented in Table 3.

TABLE 3   Means, Standard Deviations, and *t* Statistics for On-Campus and Distance Course Evaluation Comparisons

	SPED 6126			SPED 6127		
	Campus	Distance		Campus	Distance	
Evaluation Area	(*n* = 4)	(*n* = 23)	Obtained *t*	(*n* = 11)	(*n* = 13)	Obtained *t*
Overall rating						
M	3.69	3.94	−0.81	3.69	3.79	−0.48
SD	0.59	0.33		0.28	0.44	
Course						
M	3.56	3.88	−1.82	3.72	3.60	1.14
SD	0.33	0.31		0.29	0.22	
Instructor						
M	3.65	3.88	−0.75	3.65	3.65	0.00
SD	0.59	0.34		0.19	0.43	
Organization						
M	4.15	4.23	−0.44	3.83	4.25	−6.70*
SD	0.34	0.17		0.19	0.10	
Teaching						
M	3.48	3.62	−0.56	3.58	3.42	1.09
SD	0.47	0.44		0.44	0.23	
Communication						
M	3.49	3.79	−1.26	3.56	3.63	−0.54
SD	0.48	0.27		0.13	0.40	

*$p < .01$.

Source: Spooner, F., Jordan, L., Algozzine, B., & Spooner, M. (1999). Student ratings of instruction in distance learning and on-campus courses. *Journal of Educational Research, 92*(3), 132–140.

The *t*-test can be used for purposes other than comparing the means of two samples. The *t*-test is used when a researcher wants to show that a correlation coefficient is significantly different from 0 (no correlation). The mean of a group can be compared with a number rather than another mean, and it is possible to compare variances rather than means. Because there are so many uses for the *t*-test it is frequently encountered in reading research.

A more concrete explanation of using the *t*-test is the following example. Suppose a researcher is interested in finding out whether there is a significant difference between blue-eyed and brown-eyed sixth-graders with respect to reading achievement. The research question would be: Is there a difference in the reading achievement (the dependent variable) of blue-eyed fourth-graders compared with brown-eyed fourth-graders (the independent variable)? The null hypothesis would be: There is no difference between blue-eyed and brown-eyed fourth-graders in reading achievement. To test this hypothesis the researcher would randomly select a sample of brown- and blue-eyed fourth-graders from the population of all fourth-grade students. Let us say that the sample mean of blue-eyed students' reading achievement is 54, and the sample mean for brown-eyed fourth-graders is 48. Since we assume the null hypothesis—that the population means are equal—we use the *t*-test to show how often the difference of scores in the samples would occur if population means are equal. If our degrees of freedom (total sample size minus 1) is 60 and the calculated *t* value 2.00, we can see by referring to Table 11.1 that the probability of attaining this difference in the sample means, for a two-tailed test, is .05, or five times out of a hundred. We reject the null hypothesis and say that there is a statistically significant difference between the reading achievement of blue-eyed and brown-eyed fourth-graders.

Comparing Two or More Means: Analysis of Variance

One-Way Analysis of Variance

If a study is done in which two or more sample means are compared on one independent variable, then to test the null hypothesis the researcher would employ a procedure called one-way analysis of variance (abbreviated ANOVA). ANOVA is simply an extension of the *t*-test. Rather than the researcher's using multiple *t*-tests to compare all possible pairs of means in a study of two or more groups, ANOVA allows the researcher to test the differences between all groups and make more accurate probability statements than when using a series of separate *t*-tests. It is called **analysis of variance** because the statistical formula uses the variances of the groups and not the means to calculate a value that reflects the degree of differences in the means. Instead of a *t* statistic, ANOVA calculates an *F* statistic (or *F* ratio). The *F* is analogous to the *t*. It is a three- or four-digit number that is used in a distribution of *F* table with the degrees of freedom to find the level of significance that the researcher uses to reject or not reject the null. There are two degrees of freedom. The first is the number of groups in the study minus one, and the second is the total number of subjects minus the number of groups. These numbers follow the *F* in reporting the results of ANOVA. For example, in reporting $F_{(4,80)} = 4.25$, the degrees of freedom mean that there are five group means that are being compared and 85 subjects in the analysis.

ANOVA addresses the question: Is there a significant difference between the population means? If the *F* value that is calculated is large enough, then the null hypothesis (meaning there is no difference among the groups) can be rejected with confidence that the researcher is correct in concluding that at least two means are different. Let us assume, for example, that a researcher is comparing the locus of control of three groups—high-, medium-, and low-achieving students. The researcher selects a random sample from each group, administers a locus of control instrument, and calculates the means and variances of each group. Let us further assume that the sample group means are A (low achievement) = 18, B (medium achievement) = 20, and C (high achievement) = 25. The null hypothesis that is tested, then, is that the population means of 18, 20, and 25 are equal, or, more correctly, that these are different only by sampling and measurement error. If the F was 5.12 and $p < .01$, then the researcher can conclude that at least two of the means are different, and that this conclusion will be right 99 times out of 100.

The results of a one-way ANOVA are usually reported by indicating in the results section the groups that are different. A table of means and standard deviations will accompany the written information. In reporting results, occasionally the researcher will write two numbers in front of the ANOVA. This will be a number 1, a multiplication sign, and then another single digit number (for example, 1×3; 1×5; 1×2). This means that there is one independent variable (1) that has the number of groups or levels indicated by the second number. A 1×4 ANOVA is thus a one-way ANOVA that is comparing four group means.

Post Hoc and Planned Comparison Procedures

When a researcher uses ANOVA to test the null hypothesis that three means are the same, the resulting statistically significant F ratio tells the researcher only that two or more of the means are different. Usually the researcher needs to employ further statistical tests that will indicate those means that are different from each other. These tests are called **post hoc comparisons.** Other terms that are synonymous for post hoc comparisons incluse *a posteriori* test, follow up test, and multiple comparison test. Another procedure, called the *Bonferrori technique,* is also used as a post hoc test, though it is more commonly used when researchers are investigating many dependent variables to adjust the level of significance to reduce the chance of finding a significant difference because of multiple statistical tests. They are designed to test each possible pair of means.

There are five common multiple comparison tests: Fisher's LSD: Duncan's new multiple range test, the Newman–Keuls, Tukey's HSD, and the Scheffés test. Each test is used in the same way, but they differ in the ease with which a significant difference is obtained; for some tests, that is, the means need to be farther apart than for other tests for the difference to be statistically significant. Tests that require a greater difference between the means are said to be conservative, while those that permit less difference are said to be liberal. The listing of the tests above is sequential, with Fisher's test considered most liberal and Scheffé's test most conservative. The two most common tests are Tukey (pronounced too-key) and Scheffé, but different conclusions can be reached in a study depending on the multiple comparison technique employed.

You may be wondering why a researcher does not use separate *t*-tests as a follow-up to the significant *F* ratio. The answer is that if multiple *t*-tests were used, the researcher would increase the likelihood of finding a significant difference by chance where none exists. For example, if the research involves computing 100 *t*-tests and the level of significance is 0.05, the researcher can expect that 5 out of 100 *t*-tests would be significant by chance alone. The post hoc tests control this problem by taking into account the number of comparisons being made. In some studies there are no post hoc tests employed even though the *F* ratio is significant. This occurs because a visual examination of the group means obviously shows which means are different. For example, if three group means are 15, 20, and 20.5, and the *F* ratio is significant with a *p* level of .01, it is rather obvious where the differences exist, and there is no need for post hoc tests. A related point should be emphasized here: it is impossible to interpret a *t*-test or analysis of variance without examining the group means; for the inferential statistics to have meaning, it is essential to look at the sample means.

Excerpt 11.4 is an example of using one-way ANOVA and post hoc tests.

EXCERPT 11.4

ANOVA AND POST HOC TESTS

One way analysis of variance was used to analyze the achievement data. Where significant differences were found, SNK tests were used to determine which means differed significantly.

Our second hypothesis stated that the groups taught with the children's book would score significantly higher on the posttest than the group taught with the textbook only. These data supported the hypothesis, $F(2,54) = 10.23$, $p = .0002$. The mean and standard deviation for the group taught with the children's book were 8.79 and 4.66 respectively. The mean and standard deviation for the group taught with the textbook and children's book were 7.17 and 3.40 respectively. The mean and standard deviation for the group taught with the textbook only were 3.80 and 2.07 respectively. Follow-up tests (SNK) indicated that the two groups taught with the children's book differed significantly from the group taught with the textbook only.

TABLE 3   Results of One-Way Analysis of Variance for the Subtest That Measured Content Contained Only in Children's Book

Source	D.F.	Sum of Squares	Mean Square	F Ratio	F Prob
Between	2	253.3526	126.6763	10.2272	.0002
Within	54	668.8579	12.3863		
Total	56	922.2105			

Source: McKinney, C. W., & Jones, H. J. (1993). Effects of a children's book and a traditional textbook on fifth-grade students' achievement and attitudes toward social studies. *Journal of Research and Development in Education, 27* (1), 56–62.

Planned comparisons are similar to post hoc tests in that pairs of means are compared, but the procedure is used with specific comparisons that are identified prior to completing the research. Usually, a few of the possible pairs of means, those that are of particular interest, are included in the analysis. Because the pairs are identified before, rather than after the ANOVA, it may also be referred to as an *a priori test.*

Factorial Analysis of Variance

One-way ANOVA has been introduced as a procedure that is used with one independent variable and two or more levels identified by this variable. It is common, however, to have more than one independent variable in a study. In fact, it is often desirable to have several independent variables because the analysis will provide more information. For example, if a group of researchers investigates the relative effectiveness of three reading curricula, they would probably use a 1 × 3 ANOVA to test the null hypothesis that there is no differ-ence in achievement between any of the three groups (that is, $\bar{X}_1 = \bar{X}_2 = \bar{X}_3$). If the researchers were also interested in whether males or females achieved dif-ferently, gender would become a second independent variable. Now there are six groups, since for each reading group males and females are analyzed sepa-rately. If X is the reading curriculum and M/F is gender, then the six groups are: X_1M; X_1F; X_2M; X_2F; X_3M; and X_3F. This situation is diagrammed below.

Another way to illustrate the study is to put each independent variable on one side of a rectangle, as follows:

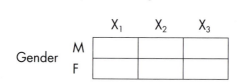

In this hypothetical situation, then, there are two independent variables analyzed simultaneously and one dependent variable (achievement). The statis-tical procedure that would be used to analyze the results would be a two-way ANOVA (*two-way* because of two independent variables). Since *factor* is another word for independent variable, *factorial* means more than one indepen-dent variable. **Factorial ANOVA**, then, is a generic term that means that two or more independent variables are analyzed together. The more specific term, such as *two-way* or *three-way* ANOVA, tells the exact number of independent variables. Researchers can be even more precise in indicating what the analysis is by including the levels of each independent variable. As pointed out earlier, *levels* refers to the subgroups or categories of each independent variable. In the example cited above, *reading curriculum* has three levels and *gender* two levels. The levels can be shown by numbers that precede the ANOVA abbreviation. In our reading example, it is a 2 × 3 ANOVA. (For a three-way ANOVA there would need to be three numbers, such as 2 × 2 × 3 ANOVA. This means that there are two levels in two of the variables and three levels in one variable.) Using this notation, a researcher can concisely communicate a lot of information. The number of factors is usually two or three, and the number of levels can be any number greater than one (though rarely above 10). In the hypothetical example above, if there were four reading curriculums and the researcher was interested in the way each curriculum affected high, low, and medium achievers, then the resulting analysis would be a 3 × 4 ANOVA. It is still a two-way ANOVA, but the number of levels is different. This situation can be illustrated with the following diagram:

Reading curriculum

		X_1	X_2	X_3	X_4
	High				
Ability level	Medium				
	Low				

Excerpt 11.5 is an example of the way researchers refer to two-way factorial designs and how results are reported.

Here is another hypothetical example to clarify the tests of significance that result from a two-way ANOVA: A teacher is interested in whether specific techniques to aid retention are effective in improving the achievement of high-anxiety and low-anxiety students. The teacher has developed two techniques, one with mnemonics and the other with distributed practice in memorizing the material. The teacher also has a control group. Thus there are two independent variables, one with two levels (anxiety: high and low), the other with three levels (treatment techniques: mnemonics, distributed practice, and control group). This would constitute a 2 × 3 ANOVA design, and is illustrated in Figure 11.4.

Within each square in the diagram is a mean for that group. These squares are called *cells*. The number 50 in the upper right hand cell ($\bar{X}_5$) thus refers to the mean of highly anxious subjects who served as the control group. The 2 × 3 ANOVA tests three null hypotheses: that there is no difference between high- and low-anxiety students; that there is no difference between the treatment and

EXCERPT 11.5

FACTORIAL ANOVA

We used a 2 × 2 (Program: Direct Instruction vs. Traditional Instruction x Mobility: Mobile Students vs. Stable Students) analysis of variance to analyze each total score and its component subscores.

For main effects, the direct-instruction students scored significantly higher than did the traditional students on mathematics computation. Also, stable students scored significantly higher than did mobile students on total reading, word attack, vocabulary, comprehension, and total battery. There were no significant differences in the total language scores or two of its components, mechanics and expression, nor was there a significant difference in the total mathematics scores.

There were also three significant interactions related to vocabulary, spelling, and mathematics concepts. A post hoc test using Tukey's HSD procedure revealed that the stable traditional students scored significantly higher than did the mobile traditional students on vocabulary and spelling. On mathematics concepts and applications, the stable traditional students scored significantly higher than did the traditional mobile students and the stable direct-instruction students.

An examination of the means for all groups reveals a similar pattern of significant differences. The pattern shows a similar level of achievement for both direct-instruction stable and mobile students. The stable traditional means are similar to both direct instruction groups. However, the mobile traditional students' means are lower than their stable counterparts and both direct-instruction groups.

Source: From Brent, G., & DiObilda, N. (1993). Effects of curriculum alignment versus direct instruction on urban children. *Journal of Educational Research, 86,* 335. Reprinted by permission.

---

control conditions; and that there is no interaction between the two factors (*interaction* is defined in the next paragraph). The first two hypotheses are similar in interpretation to one-way ANOVAs. They tell the researcher whether any differences occur for each of the factors independent of each other. These are termed *main* or *simple effects* in a factorial ANOVA. There is a main (not neces-

FIGURE 11.4   Hypothetical 2 × 3 ANOVA

		Treatment techniques			
		Mnemonics	Distributed practice	Control	
Anxiety	High	$\bar{X}_1 = 62$	$\bar{X}_3 = 50$	$\bar{X}_5 = 50$	$\bar{X}_7 = 54$
	Low	$\bar{X}_2 = 44$	$\bar{X}_4 = 59$	$\bar{X}_6 = 59$	$\bar{X}_8 = 54$
		$\bar{X}_9 \cong 53$	$\bar{X}_{10} \cong 55$	$\bar{X}_{11} \cong 55$	

sarily significant) effect for anxiety and another main effect for treatment technique. In computing the 2 × 3 ANOVA there will be a separate F ratio for each main effect, with corresponding levels of significance. In our example, the main effect for anxiety is tested by comparing $\bar{X}_7$ with $\bar{X}_8$. These row means disregard the influence of the techniques and address anxiety only. Since X_7 and X_8 both equal 54, the null hypothesis that $\bar{X}_7 = \bar{X}_8$ would not be rejected; examining anxiety alone, that is, there is no difference in achievement between high- and low-anxiety students. For the main effect of technique, $\bar{X}_9$, $\bar{X}_{10}$, $\bar{X}_{11}$ are compared. Again, it appears that there is little difference in achievement between the three technique groups. The first two null hypotheses could have been tested by using separate one-way ANOVAs, but the 2 × 3 ANOVA is more accurate, more powerful in detecting differences, and more parsimonious than using two one-way ANOVAs. In addition, the 2 × 3 ANOVA allows the researcher to test the third null hypothesis. This hypothesis is concerned with what is called an *interaction* between the independent variables.

An **interaction** is the effect of the independent variables together; that is, the impact of one factor on the dependent measure varies with the level of a second factor. Stated differently, it is the joint effect of the independent variables on the dependent variable. An interaction is evident if the differences between levels of one independent variable are inconsistent from one level to another of the other independent variable. In other words, an interaction exists if the effect of one variable differs across different levels of the second variable. In our example, if we look at the difference between $\bar{X}_1$ and $\bar{X}_2$ ($62 - 44 = 18$) and compare that difference with $\bar{X}_3 - \bar{X}_4$ (-9) and $\bar{X}_5 - \bar{X}_6$ (-9), we find that there is a large difference between high and low anxiety as we move across each of the treatment techniques. This is visual evidence of an interaction. Statistically, an F ratio is reported for the interaction with a corresponding level of significance. This statistical test is called the interaction effect.

Now it is clear how a factorial ANOVA can provide more information than one-way ANOVAs. In our example it is evident that treatment techniques do make a difference for high- or low-anxiety students. High-anxiety students do better with mnemonics than distributed practice or with no treatment, while low-anxiety students do better with distributed practice or with no treatment than they do with mnemonics. This finding would be statistically significant even though neither of the main effects by themselves was significant. In Excerpts 11.5 and 11.6, the authors report significant interactions.

It is common to present a graph of an interaction that is significant. The graph shows the nature of the interaction more clearly than cell means do. The graph is constructed by placing values for the dependent variable along the vertical axis (ordinate) and the levels of one independent variable on the horizontal axis (abscissa); all the cell means are located within the graph and identified with the second independent variable. For our hypothetical example the interaction is illustrated in Figure 11.5. In the figure, lines are used to connect the cells means. If the lines are parallel, then there is no interaction. If the lines cross, the interaction is said to be disordinal.

EXCERPT 11.6

ANOVA INTERACTION

The analysis of variance showed a highly significant effect of experimental condition ($F = 10.59$, $p < .01$), a significant effect of school ($F = 3.35$, $p = < .05$), and an interaction between condition and school ($F = 5.01$, $p < .05$). . . . The motivational effect was the same for boys and girls and constant across grade levels, but it differed among schools. Figure 1 shows a very large effect at School A, a large effect at School C, and the control group somewhat higher than the experimental group at School B.

FIGURE 1   Means by Condition and School

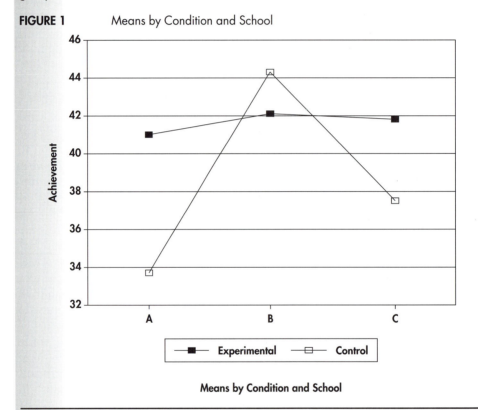

Means by Condition and School

Source: From Brown, S. M., & Walberg, H.J. (1993). Motivational effects of test scores of elementary students. *Journal of Educational Research, 86,* 134, 135.

Analysis of Covariance

Analysis of covariance (ANCOVA) is a statistical procedure used in cases similar to ones in which a one-way or factorial ANOVA is used. ANCOVA has two major purposes: to adjust initial group differences statistically on one or more variables that are related to the dependent variable but uncontrolled, and to increase the likelihood of finding a significant difference between group means.

FIGURE 11.5 **Interaction for Hypothetical Study**

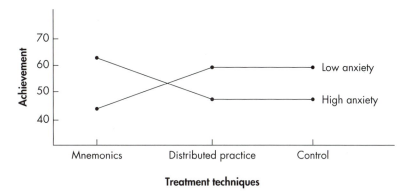

For the first purpose, consider the following example. A researcher uses two classes to investigate whether cooperative or individualized instruction is most effective. On the basis of a pretest the researcher knows that one class has greater knowledge of the dependent variable (achievement in mathematics) than the other group (for example, the cooperative group pretest mean is 12 and the individualized group pretest mean is 10). If a posttest is given and it is found that the cooperative group mean is 24 and the individualized group mean 20, the researcher might be tempted to conclude that the cooperative group achieved more than the individualized. This would be likely to happen if the pretest scores were ignored. An alternative approach would be to look at pretest-posttest gain scores and use a *t*-test to determine whether the gain scores are significantly different. This approach would result in comparing 12 (24 − 12) to 10 (20 − 10). While this approach is theoretically better than not using the pretest scores, for reasons beyond the scope of this book, there are technical problems with comparing gain scores. The best method of analyzing the data in this circumstance is by using ANCOVA. ANCOVA would statistically adjust the posttest scores by the differences that existed between the groups on the pretest. In this example, the posttest score of the cooperative group would be lowered by one point, since this group's mean was higher by one point than the mean of both groups on the pretest. Similarly, because the individualized group pretest mean is one point lower than the mean of the two pretests, the posttest score of 20 would be raised by one point to 21. Instead of comparing 20 to 24, ANCOVA would thus compare 21 to 23.

The variable that is used in ANCOVA to adjust the scores (in the above example the pretest) is called the *covariate* or *concomitant variable*. Covariates are often pretest scores or results from achievement, attitude, or aptitude tests that would be related to the dependent variable. IQ scores and scores on prior standardized achievement tests, for instance, are commonly used as covariates.

The second purpose of covariance analysis is to increase what is called the "power" of the statistical test to find differences between groups. A full explanation of the concept of power is beyond the scope of this book. Briefly, power is

EXCERPT 11.7

USING ANCOVA TO ADJUST FOR GROUP DIFFERENCES

There were 14 ANCOVAs performed that had group (experimental activity-oriented, experimental discussion-oriented, and control) as an independent variable. . . . The pretreatment group scores of school attendance, grade point average, number of disciplinary referrals, total score of the Piers-Harris scale, Behavior cluster of the Piers-Harris scale, and the Happiness and Satisfaction cluster of the Piers-Harris scale were used as the covariates for the 14 ANCOVAs. Using ANCOVAs allowed the researchers to adjust for any pretreatment differences that existed between the experimental groups and the control group.

Source: From Page, R. C., & Chandler, J. (1994). Effects of group counseling on ninth-grade at-risk students. *Journal of Mental Health Counseling, 16,* 346.

the probability of detecting a significant difference. It is useful to increase power when the sample size is low or when the researcher has reason to believe that the differences between the groups will be small.

ANCOVA can be used in several situations: with two groups and one independent variable in place of a *t*-test; with one independent variable that has more than two groups in place of one-way ANOVA; and with factorial analysis of variance. Studies can also use more than one covariate in a single ANCOVA procedure. The reporting of ANCOVA is very similar to the reporting of ANOVA. Excerpt 11.7 shows how covariance analysis was used in an actual study to adjust initial group differences.

Since ANCOVA is used frequently with intact groups, without random assignment, it should be noted that the interpretation of results should weigh the possibility that other uncontrolled and unmeasured variables are also related to the dependent variable and hence may affect the dependent variable. In other words, while statistical adjustment of the effect of the covariate can be achieved, the researcher cannot conclude that the groups are equal in the sense of random assignment.

Nonparametric Tests

In our discussion of statistical tests up to this point we have been concerned with procedures that use sample statistics to estimate characteristics of the population. These characteristics of the population are called parameters, and the statistical procedures are referred to as **parametric** procedures. In addition, parametric statistics are used when the researcher can assume that the population is normally distributed, has homogeneity of variance within different groups, and has data that are interval or ratio in scale.

As long as the assumptions upon which parametric statistics are based are, for the most part, met, the researcher uses a *t*-test, ANOVA, ANCOVA, or some other parametric procedure. If these assumptions are not met—that is, if the data are not interval or ratio or are not distributed normally—the researcher should consider using a **nonparametric** analog to the parametric test. For most parametric procedures there is a corresponding nonparametric test that can be used. The interpretation of the results is similar with both kinds of tests. What differs is the computational equation and tables for determining the significance level of the results. Both procedures test a hypothesis and report a level of significance for rejecting the null. In contrast to parametric tests, however, nonparametric tests do not test hypotheses about the characteristics of a population. Rather, nonparametric procedures test hypotheses about relationships between categorical variables, shapes of distributions, and normality of distribution. While parametric procedures use means, nonparametric techniques are concerned with frequencies, percentages, and proportions. The parametric tests are generally more powerful in detecting significant differences and are used frequently even when all assumptions cannot be met.

Table 11.2 gives the names of nonparametric tests that are analogous to parametric tests we have already discussed.

Chi-square (pronounced kī square) is a common nonparametric procedure that is used when the data are in nominal form. This test is a way of answering questions about association or relationship based on frequencies of observations in categories. The frequencies can be in most any form—people, objects, votes—and are simply counted in each category. The researcher thus forms the categories and then counts the frequency of observations or occurrences in each category. In the single sample chi-square test the researcher has one independent variable that is divided into two or more categories. For example, a college administrator may be interested in the number of freshman, sophomore, junior, and senior students who attended the counseling center, or, in other words, the relationship between year in college and use of counseling services. The independent variable is year in college, with four categories. The researcher might select a random sample of fifty students from each category

TABLE 11.2

Parametric and Nonparametric Procedures[a]

Parametric	Nonparametric
Independent samples *t*-test	Median test Mann-Whitney *U* test
Dependent sample *t*-test	Sign test Wilcoxon matched-pairs signed-ranks test
One-way ANOVA	Median test Kruskal-Wallis one-way ANOVA of ranks

[a]For further information on nonparametric tests, see Siegel (1956), Marascuilo and McSweeney (1977) and Gibbons (1993).

and record the number of students in each category who attended the counseling center. The statistical test compares the reported, or observed, frequencies with some theoretical or expected frequencies. In our example the college administrator might expect that the frequencies in each category would be the same. Then the null hypothesis that is tested is that there is no difference in the number of students attending the counseling center among the four categories. The following table illustrates this example.

	Freshmen	Sophomores	Juniors	Seniors
Observed	30	25	15	30
Expected	25	25	25	25

To obtain the level of significance the researcher computes a formula to obtain a chi-square value ($\chi 2$), uses the appropriate degrees of freedom, and refers to a chi-square table (see Appendix B) in order to determine the level of significance in rejecting the null. In our example it appears that the test would be significant, showing that freshmen and seniors attend the counseling center more than sophomores and juniors and that juniors attend less than any other class.

If the researcher has more than one independent variable, the **independent samples chi-square test**, or **contingency table**, can be used to analyze the data. In our example above, if the administrator was also interested in differences between males and females at each class level, then the analysis is like a factorial ANOVA. In this case it would be a 2 $\times$ 4 contingency table.

There are many uses for the chi-square test. It can be used in attitude research if the researcher categorizes responses to favorable and unfavorable; with high, low, and medium ability students displaying on-task behavior; in special education research with frequencies of appropriate behavior; and many other problems. Researchers may report a generic measure of relationship with the chi-square results. These measures would be termed **phi coefficient** or **contingency coefficient** and would be interpreted in about the same way as a Pearson product-moment correlation coefficient. Excerpt 11.8 is an example of reporting chi-square test results in an actual study.

Multivariate Analyses

Our discussion of inferential statistics would be incomplete if we did not introduce *multivariate* analyses. Social scientists have realized for many years that human behavior in complex situations can be understood best by examining many variables simultaneously, not by dealing with one or two variables in each study. The statistical procedures for analyzing many variables at the same time have been available for many years, but it has only been since computers were available that researchers have been able to utilize these procedures. Today these more complex statistics are commonly reported in journals.

EXCERPT 11.8

CHI-SQUARE

RESULTS

For the question on their general opinion of grade repetition, parents, teachers, and principals were asked to mark one of the following terms: "never," "rarely," "occasionally," "usually," or "always" in response to the question, "Children should _____ be retained if they do not meet the requirements of the grade." When responses of parents, teachers, and principals were examined by *chi*-square analysis, the contrasts attained the .0001 level of significance. As shown in Table 1, the most obvious difference was in the tendency for parents to mark the extreme answers of "never" and "always" more frequently than teachers or principals.

All three groups were also asked to check from the following reasons, (a) chronic nonattendance, (b) parent request, (c) emotional immaturity, (d) academic failure due to reasons other than lack of basic skills, and (e) lack of basic skills, those which the respondent felt were singularly valid grounds for retention. As shown in Table 1, the views of parents, teachers, and principals were significantly different on excessive absences ($p < .0001$), emotional maturity ($p < .0001$), academic failure due to reasons other than lack of basic skills ($p < .0006$), and lack of basic skills ($p < .0001$). The last question common to all three questionnaires asked parents, teachers, and principals who should have the final say on whether a child is retained. A significant difference ($p < .0001$) in opinion was evidenced (see Table 1).

TABLE 1   Comparisons Among Parents, Teachers, and Principals[a]

	Never	Rarely	Occasionally	Usually	Always	N
			Opinions Representative of Their Views **To Be Retained**			
Parents	3.6%	13.0	23.9	37.0	22.6	1,063
Teachers	.7	9.7	24.8	52.4	12.4	145
Principals	.0	8.6	17.1	71.4	2.9	35

($x^2 = 35.474$; $p < .0001$)

	Excessive Absences		Parental Request		Emotional Immaturity	
	Yes	No	Yes	No	Yes	No
			Appropriate Reasons for Retention			
Parents	13.6%	86.3	15.2	84.8	18.6	81.4
Teachers	39.3	60.7	15.9	84.1	53.1	46.9
Principals	68.6	31.4	20.0	80.0	54.3	45.7

($x^2 = 119.109$; $p < .0001$)   ($x^2 = 103.933$; $p < .0001$)

(continued)

(continued)

	Academic Failure		Lack of Basic Skills		Other Reasons	
	Yes	No	Yes	No	Yes	No
Parents	29.6%	70.3	62.6	37.4	5.9	94.1
Teachers	36.6	63.4	85.4	13.9	—	—
Principals	57.1	42.9	94.3	5.7	—	—

$(x^2 = 14.271; p < .0006)$ $(x^2 = 51.451; p < .0001)$

				The Final Say On Retention Decision					
	(T) Teacher	(PR) Principal	(P) Parent	(C) Child	T & PR	T, P, & PR	T & P	PR & P	All Others
Parents	47.8%	14.6	19.6	.4	3.0	3.2	9.2	1.5	.7
Teachers	66.2	11.7	3.4	.0	13.1	3.4	.7	.0	1.4
Principals	22.9	54.3	2.9	.0	11.4	5.7	.0	.0	2.9

$(x^2 = 128.481; p < .0001)$
[a]There were 1063 parents, 145 teachers, and 35 principals in the sample.

Source: From Byrnes, D., & Yamamoto, K. (1986, Fall). Views on grade repetition. *Journal of Research and Development in Education.* Reprinted by permission.

The term **multivariate** refers to methods that investigate patterns among many variables or to studies that involve two or more related dependent variables for each subject. Many researchers will refer to multiple regression as a multivariate procedure, and some researchers use multivariate to describe the analysis in any study of many variables. In contrast, designs that employ *t*-tests, ANOVA, and ANCOVA with a single dependent would clearly be classified as *univariate*.

All of the statistical procedures discussed to this point have had only one dependent variable. Yet there are many instances in which the researcher is interested in more than one dependent variable. For example, if a researcher is studying attitudes toward science, many aspects of a general attitude toward science would be of interest, such as enjoying science as well as valuing science, for chemistry as well as biology, for dissection as well as field trips, and so on. In fact, many attitude instruments have subscales that more specifically and accurately reflect feelings and beliefs than one general score can. The researcher could combine all these different aspects and consider the attitude as a general disposition, but it is better to look at each aspect separately. Why not use a separate univariate analysis for each dependent variable? That is, why not compute as many ANOVAs or *t*-tests as there are dependent variables? The reason is that as long as the dependent variables are correlated, the use of separate univariate analysis will increase the probability of finding a difference simply because so many tests are employed. It is similar to the reason that in ANOVA we use post hoc tests rather than many *t*-tests. Multivariate analyses are also more parsimonious, that is, more direct, quicker, with fewer separate calculations.

TABLE 11.3

Multivariate Analogs

Univariate Test	Multivariate Test
t-test	Hotelling's T^2
ANOVA	MANOVA (Multivariate analysis of variance)
ANCOVA	MANCOVA

Although the computation and interpretation of multivariate tests are quite complex, the basic principle of rejecting null hypotheses at some level of significance is the same as for all inferential statistics. The difference is that all the dependent variables are considered together in one analysis. For most of the procedures previously discussed that have one dependent variable, a multivariate analog can be used when there is the same independent variable or variables but more than one dependent variable. Table 11.3 summarizes some multivariate tests that correspond to procedures used with one dependent variable.

Excerpt 11.9 is an illustration of the way a researcher used a multivariate procedure, MANOVA, to analyze the data.

EXCERPT 11.9

MULTIVARIATE ANOVA

The intercorrelations among the four scale scores from pre- and postquestionnaires are illustrated in Table III. These intercorrelations show that there is a positive but modest relationship between the two RSA subscale scores (positive vs. negative). The affect toward teaching measure is positively related to both RSA subscale scores, but more strongly with the positive score than the negative score. The teaching self-concept measure, however, is negatively related to both RSA subscale scores and to affect toward teaching scores. In addition, the relations are relatively strong. These significant intercorrelations among this set of dependent measures suggest the necessity of multivariate analysis procedures. Thus, to compare differences between the teacher groups, multivariate analyses of variance (MANOVAs) were performed, first on the prequestionnaire measures and then on the postquestionnaire measures. In these analyses teacher group was considered the one independent factor having four levels, and scores from the scales included in the questionnaires were considered four inter-related dependent measures. MANOVA procedures place no restrictions on the number of subjects in the subgroups and, hence, are appropriate even when, as in this case, the numbers are unequal and disproportionate (Finn & Mattsson, 1978, p. 32).

Results from the multivariate analyses of the pre- and postquestionnaires are presented in Table IV. These analyses showed that initially there were no statistically significant differences among the teacher groups. All the groups were comparable in measures of responsibility for positive outcomes, responsibility for negative outcomes, and affect toward teaching. Those teachers who did not use the new strategies appeared to express somewhat greater confidence in their teaching abilities than did any of the other groups of teachers, but this difference was not statistically significant.

Analyses of the postquestionnaire measures indicated that resultant differences among the teacher groups were statistically significant. Follow-up, post hoc comparisons were made by computing .95 Scheffé confidence intervals. These comparisons revealed that those teachers who had experienced a positive change in the learning outcomes of their students felt more responsible for both positive and negative student outcomes and expressed more positive attitudes toward teaching than did the other groups of teachers. Contrary to what had been hypothesized, however, these teachers expressed decreased confidence in their teaching abilities.

Interestingly, the post hoc analyses also showed statistically significant differences for those teachers who did not use the new strategies. Teachers in this group expressed more negative attitudes toward teaching than the other groups of teachers, but also expressed much greater confidence in their teaching abilities.

TABLE III   Intercorrelations Among Measures of Selected Affective Variables

Variable	RSA-positive	RSA-negative	Affect toward teaching	Teaching self-concept
RSA positive		0.233	0.485*	−0.510*
RSA negative	0.341*		0.330*	−0.062
Affect toward teaching	0.427*	0.251*		−0.638*
Teaching self-concept	−0.481*	−0.173	−0.602*	

(diagonal labels: Postmeasures / Premeasures)

Note: N = 17
*$p < 0.01$

TABLE IV   Summary of Multivariate Analyses of Variance

Tests of significance

| | | | | | Univariate F's | |
Sources of variation	df	Multivariate F	R+	R−	Affect toward teaching	Teaching self-concept
Constant	1	—	—	—	—	—
Group (prequestionnaire)	3	0.97	1.08	0.08	0.52	2.52
Group (postquestionnaire)	(3)	15.07*	36.34*	10.92*	18.99*	29.17*

			Univariate Mean Squares			
Total	117	Prequestionnaire	95.88	97.57	34.64	116.01
		Postquestionnaire	77.24	94.37	37.27	82.21

*$p < 0.001$

Source: From Guskey, T. R. (1984). The influence of change in instructional effectiveness upon the affective characteristics of teachers. *American Educational Research Journal, 21,* 250–252.

Summary

This chapter has introduced the logic of inferential statistics and described some of the more common statistical procedures researchers use to analyze data. The following points summarize the concepts presented.

1. Inferential statistics are used to make inferences based on measured aspects of a sample about the characteristics of a population.
2. In conducting research, probability is a concern because of the error involved in sampling and measurement.
3. Sample statistics represent imperfect estimates of the population.
4. Inferential statistics estimate the probability of population characteristics being within a certain range of values. Confidence levels are commonly reported.
5. The null hypothesis is used to test the assumption that there is no difference between population values.
6. Researchers attempt to reject the null hypothesis by using inferential statistics to indicate the probability of being wrong in rejecting the null.
7. The level of significance of the statistical test tells the researcher the probability of making a Type I error in rejecting the null hypothesis.
8. Most researchers use a p level of .05 or less ($<.05$) to indicate statistical significance.
9. Effect magnitude measures, such as effect size, indicates the magnitude of differences and relationships.
10. The t-test is used to compare two means, and, depending on the nature of the research, it uses an independent samples equation or a dependent samples equation to calculate the t value.
11. Analysis of variance is used to compare two or more means, and it reports F statistics with corresponding p levels.
12. One-way ANOVA tests the difference between levels of one independent variable, while factorial ANOVA examines more than one independent variable.
13. Post hoc and planned comparison tests are designed to locate significant differences among pairs of means in ANOVA.
14. An interaction is examined in factorial ANOVA as the unique effect of the independent variables acting together to affect the dependent variable results.
15. Parametric tests assume ratio, interval, or ordinal data, homogeneity of variance, and a normal distribution. Nonparametric tests can be used in cases in which the assumptions are violated and the test is not robust for that violation.
16. Analysis of covariance is used to adjust differences between groups on a covariate variable that is related to the dependent variable.
17. Chi-square is a frequently encountered nonparametric test that is used when the researcher is examining frequencies of occurrences.
18. Multivariate analyses are used in cases in which there are several related dependent variables.

Self-Instructional Review Exercises

Sample answers are in the back of the book.

Test Items

1. Probability statements are made in research because
   a. the total number of expected cases is rarely known.
   b. error exists in sampling.
   c. of the reliability and validity of measurement.
   d. Both b and c are correct.

2. The null hypothesis is a statement that is
   a. the same as the expected result.
   b. necessary because we can only disprove, not prove.
   c. stated in the negative to correspond to statistical tests.
   d. necessary in reporting research.

3. Effect size is helpful in determining
   a. confidence intervals.
   b. standard error.
   c. magnitude.
   d. alpha.

4. Check all of the following statements that are true about level of significance.
   a. .05 <.01.
   b. .05 is better than .01.
   c. .001 is better than .01.
   d. .05 <.10.
   e. .20 is marginally significant.
   f. .01 is statistically significant.
   g. .03 means being wrong in rejecting the null 3 times out of 100.

5. The *t*-test is used to compare
   a. two or more means.
   b. one mean with an established value of interest.
   c. two means.
   d. Both b and c are correct.

6. Another name for the dependent samples *t*-test is
   a. related pairs.
   b. matched pairs.
   c. nondependent.
   d. independent.

7. In one-way analysis of variance the researcher would report
   a. one *F* statistic.
   b. three *F* statistics.
   c. results for all independent variables.
   d. results for all dependent variables.

8. Factorial ANOVA is used when
   a. there are two or more independent variables.
   b. there are two or more dependent variables.

    c. *t*-tests are unfeasible.

    d. Both a and c are correct.

9. Multiple comparison procedures are used because

    a. it is more convenient.

    b. it reduces the chance of making an error in drawing conclusions.

    c. it is the only way to test for all group differences.

    d. other procedures are too conservative.

10. An interaction occurs when

    a. the results of each variable are different.

    b. the effect of each variable is different.

    c. two or more variables combine to result in unique effects.

    d. two or more people talk with each other.

11. A 2×4 ANOVA means

    a. two independent variables and one dependent variable.

    b. one independent variable with two levels and one dependent variable with four levels.

    c. eight independent variables.

    d. one independent variable with two levels and another independent variable with four levels.

12. Examples of nonparametric statistical procedures include

    a. chi-square, ANOVA, MANOVA.

    b. MANOVA, ANCOVA.

    c. chi-square, *t*-test.

    d. chi-square, median test.

13. Multivariate procedures are used when

    a. there are several variables.

    b. there is more than one related dependent variable.

    c. independent variables have more than two levels.

    d. there are multiple tests to be done.

Application Problems

In each of the examples below select a statistical procedure that would best analyze the data.

1. This researcher was interested in the way three different approaches to discipline work with fifth-graders. Student teachers were assigned randomly to one of three groups. Each group received instruction in a different approach to handling discipline problems. Each student teacher was then observed over a three-week period, and the frequency and duration of discipline problems were recorded.

2. A teacher is interested in whether her sixth-graders' attitudes toward sex will change following a four-week sex-education course. To assess the impact of the program, the teacher measures the students' attitudes before and after the course.

3. The teacher in problem 2 now decides to test her program more thoroughly and is able to assign her students randomly to one group that receives a

control condition. The teacher also analyzes the effects on boys and girls.

4. A counselor wants to know if there is a relationship between self-esteem of eleventh-graders and frequency of visits to the counseling center.

5. A doctoral student is interested in studying the attitude differences between high- and low-achieving students who receive different kinds of teacher feedback following performance on tests. Four types of teacher feedback are designed for the study, and there are eight attitudes, such as attitude toward teacher, toward the subject studied, toward learning, and so on.

PART III

Qualitative Research Designs and Methods

Educators frequently ask: How do qualitative researchers design their studies? How do these researcher handle the issues of rigor: validity, subjectivity, and use of the study? When does one employ participant-observation or in-depth interviews? Should one combine different data collection strategies in a single study? How is systematic data analysis done in qualitative research? Are there guidelines for presenting narrative findings? How does a reader judge the credibility of the findings in a qualitative study?

Qualitative research was classified in Chapter 2 as *interactive research* or *noninteractive research,* termed *analytical research.* We address qualitative interactive research in Part III and present analytical research in Part IV.

In Part III, we describe qualitative research design and criteria (Chapter 12), strategies to collect data (Chapter 13), and qualitative data analysis process and techniques (Chapter 14). Interactive data collection strategies are used primarily in the study of current social happenings, social scenes, and processes. Inductive data analysis builds from descriptive data of people's meanings derived from or ascribed to particular events and processes. Qualitative research suggests grounded propositions, provides explanations to extend our understanding of phenomena, or promotes opportunities of informed decisions for social action. Qualitative research contributes to theory, educational practice, policy making, and social consciousness.

Introduction to Designing Qualitative Research

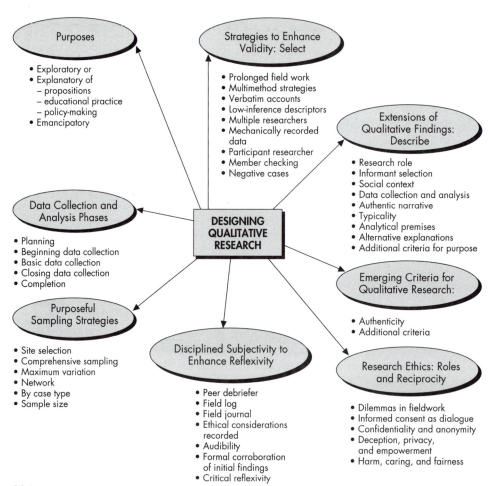

Purposes

- Exploratory or
- Explanatory of
  – propositions
  – educational practice
  – policy-making
- Emancipatory

Strategies to Enhance Validity: Select

- Prolonged field work
- Multimethod strategies
- Verbatim accounts
- Low-inference descriptors
- Multiple researchers
- Mechanically recorded data
- Participant researcher
- Member checking
- Negative cases

Extensions of Qualitative Findings: Describe

- Research role
- Informant selection
- Social context
- Data collection and analysis
- Authentic narrative
- Typicality
- Analytical premises
- Alternative explanations
- Additional criteria for purpose

Data Collection and Analysis Phases

- Planning
- Beginning data collection
- Basic data collection
- Closing data collection
- Completion

DESIGNING QUALITATIVE RESEARCH

Emerging Criteria for Qualitative Research:

- Authenticity
- Additional criteria

Purposeful Sampling Strategies

- Site selection
- Comprehensive sampling
- Maximum variation
- Network
- By case type
- Sample size

Disciplined Subjectivity to Enhance Reflexivity

- Peer debriefer
- Field log
- Field journal
- Ethical considerations recorded
- Audibility
- Formal corroboration of initial findings
- Critical reflexivity

Research Ethics: Roles and Reciprocity

- Dilemmas in fieldwork
- Informed consent as dialogue
- Confidentiality and anonymity
- Deception, privacy, and empowerment
- Harm, caring, and fairness

KEY TERMS

interactive strategies

field research

case study design

emergent design

purposeful sampling

site selection

comprehensive sampling

maximum variation sampling

network sampling (snowball sampling)

validity of qualitative designs

disciplined subjectivity

reflexivity

audibility

positionality

extension of the findings

authenticity

typicality

Interactive qualitative research is inquiry in which researchers collect data in face- to-face situations by interacting with selected persons in their settings (field research). Qualitative research describes and analyzes people's individual and collective social actions, beliefs, thoughts, and perceptions. The researcher interprets phenomena in terms of the meanings people bring to them. Qualitative studies are important for theory generation, policy development, educational practice improvement, illumination of social issues, and action stimulus.

In this chapter we introduce qualitative design and relate the design to the general research question and potential contributions of the study. We explain purposeful sample strategies and the phases of data collection and analysis. A variety of ways to address rigor issues are discussed: strategies to enhance validity, techniques to minimize research bias, and design components to generate extension of results. We also discuss research ethics in field studies, and standards for judging the adequacy of qualitative designs. We point out distinctions between the "traditional" and critical approaches to inquiry.

Purposes, Research Questions, and Case Study Design

Research Approach and Orientation

Before a researcher designs a study, she or he has a general idea of the research problem and has selected a mode of inquiry appropriate for the study. General distinctions between qualitative and quantitative research were summarized in Part 1. Five interactive research approaches (modes of inquiry) discussed in Chapter 2 were ethnographic, phenomenological, case study, grounded theory, and critical studies. Here, we review the research orientation shared among these inquiry modes because it provides a rationale for many design decisions.

Assumptions Qualitative research is based on a constructivist philosophy that assumes reality as multilayer, interactive, and a shared social experience interpreted by individuals. Qualitative researchers believe that reality is a *social construction*, that is, individuals or groups derive or ascribe meanings to specific entities, such as events, persons, processes, or objects. People form constructions in order to make sense of these entities and reorganize these constructions as viewpoints, perceptions, and belief system. In other words, people's perceptions are what they consider "real" to them and what directs their actions, thoughts, and feelings.

Goal Qualitative research is first concerned with understanding the social phenomena from the participants' perspective. Understanding is acquired by analyzing the many contexts of the participants and by narrating participants' meanings for these situations and events. Participants' meanings include their feelings, beliefs, ideas, thoughts, and actions. Learning to read, for example, occurs in the contexts of schools, families, and other situations, and it involves personal and interpersonal histories. All of these influence the learning process and what reading means to a child. Some qualitative research aims to do more than just understanding the phenomena and also generates theory or empowerment.

Multimethod Strategies Qualitative researchers study participants' perspectives with **interactive strategies**, (i.e., participant observation, direct observation, in-depth interviews, artifacts, and supplementary techniques). Research strategies are flexible, using various combinations of techniques to obtain valid data. Most researchers adjust decisions about data collection strategies during the study. The multiple realities are viewed as so complex that one cannot decide *a priori* on a single methodology.

Research Role Qualitative researchers become "immersed" in the situation and the phenomena studied. Researchers assume interactive social roles in which they record observations and interactions with participants. The research role varies with from the more traditional neutral stance to an active participatory role, depending on the selected research approach. Scholars emphasize the importance of collecting data using a skilled, prepared *person* rather than a single instrument.

Context Sensitivity Other features of qualitative research have derived from the belief that human actions are strongly influenced by the settings in which they occur. The study is **field research**, that is, the researcher collects data over a prolonged time at a site or from individuals. The context-bound generalizations are intended to be used by the participants, interested readers, or by other researchers in subsequent research with additional case studies or more structured designs.

Purpose and Research Questions

Historically qualitative researchers cited two major purposes of a study: to *describe and explore* and to *describe and explain*. Similar terms could be to *examine* or *document,* to *understand*, and to *discover* or *generate*. Many qualitative studies are descriptive and exploratory. They add to the literature by building rich descriptions of complex situations and by giving directions for future research. Other qualitative studies are explicitly explanatory. They show relationships between events and meanings, usually as perceived by participants. These studies increase the reader's understanding of the phenomena. Other statements of purpose address action, advocacy, or empowerment which are often the ultimate goals of critical studies (critical, feminist, postmodern, and participatory action research). Although researchers can claim empowerment and taking action as part of the study purpose, realistically they can only note how the inquiry may offer opportunities for informed empowerment (see Table 12.1).

The general research question logically relates to the purpose. Most qualitative questions focus on analytical topics involving the "how" and "why" of a phenomena. To address these concerns, the researcher collects descriptive details about the "who," "what," "where," and "when" of the phenomena. The discussion includes the scope and the case focus for the design. Qualitative researchers usually focus on individuals, groups, processes, or organizations and systems.

TABLE 12.1

Research Purpose and Illustrative Research Questions

Research Purpose	Illustrative Research Questions
Descriptive Exploratory	
To examine "new" or little known phenomena	What is occurring in this social situation?
To discover themes of participant meanings	What are the categories and themes of participants' meanings?
To develop in detail a concept, model, or hypotheses for future research	How are these patterns linked for propositions/ assertions?
Descriptive Explanatory	
To describe and explain the patterns related to the phenomena	What events, beliefs, attitudes, and/or policies impact on this phenomenon?
To identify relationships influencing the phenomena	How do the participants explain the phenomenon?
Emancipatory	
To create opportunities and the will to initiate social action	How do participants describe and explain their problems and take positive action?

Source: Adapted from Marshall & Rossman, 1999, p. 33.

Case Study Design

Qualitative research uses a **case study design** meaning that the data analysis focuses on one phenomenon, which the researcher selects to understand in depth regardless of the number of sites or participants for the study. The "one" may be, for example, one administrator, one group of students, one program, one process, one policy implementation, or one concept.

Qualitative research requires a plan for choosing sites and participants and for beginning data collection. The plan is an **emergent design**, in which each incremental research decision depends on prior information. The emergent design, in reality, may seem circular, as processes of purposeful sampling, data collection, and partial data analysis are simultaneous and interactive rather than discrete sequential steps.[1]

Qualitative researchers investigate in-depth small, distinct groups such as all the faculty in an innovative school, all the students in a selected classroom, one principal's role for an academic year, or one institution. These are single-site studies where there is a natural sociocultural boundary and face-to-face interaction encompassing the person or group. Qualitative researchers also study groups of individuals who have had a similar experience but may not be interacting with each other such as families of children who have been physically abused.

Sometimes the focus is on contrasting sub-units in a program, such as demographic groups (male/female or black/white) or programmatic groups (dropout/graduates or those who do well/those who do poorly), but the purpose is to understand the *one* phonemenon: the entity or process.

Subunits are contrasting groups who are likely to be informative about the research foci.[2] These groups are not viewed as statistically comparative or nor as mutually exclusive; they are often selected to investigate the extent of the phonemenon or the diversity of the phonemenon. The researcher examines the first group thoroughly and then selects another group to contrast or to collaborate the first group. The data collection about the second group requires less time because the researcher has limited the parameters of the study by then. The groups are not done simultaneously because of the complexity and the difficulty of managing the data collection.

In the case study design of Excerpt 12.1 the researcher selected one science teacher, Sarah, for a collaborative study. The purpose was to understand or "make sense" of Sarah's behaviors and the actions of her students, her colleague teachers, and the school administrators in "terms of what she believed and how she constructed the various contexts in which she taught" (Tobin & LaMaster, 1995, p. 227).

---

[1]See Bogdan & Biklen (1998), Giesne & Peshkin (1992), Marshall & Rossman (1999), Strauss & Corbin (1998), Stake (1995), Le Compte & Preissle (1993), and Lincoln and Guba (2000).

[2]Bogdan & Biklen (1998) call a examination of subunits a multi-case study. A multi-case study is *not* a multi-site study which uses a modified analytical induction approach, frequently with multiple researchers.

EXCERPT 12.1

CASE STUDY DESIGN

The research methodology employed in the study was interpretive and endeavored to make sense of the culture of the [two] classes taught by Sarah in terms of the actions of the participants (i.e., Sarah, students, colleague teachers, and school administrators). Accordingly, one rationale of the study was to make sense of Sarah's actions by describing her behaviors, and endeavoring to make sense of them in terms of what she believed and how she constructed the various contexts in which she taught. Our view of collaborative research required that we listen to the voices of Sarah and other participants in the study and also to assign a clear "signature" (Clandinin & Connelly, 1994) to what we learned in terms of interpretation that reflected the perspectives of both authors.

Source: From Tobin, K., and LaMaster, S. U. (1995). Relationships between metaphors, beliefs, and actions in a context of science curriculum change (p. 227). *Journal of Research in Science Teaching, 32*(3), 225–242.

Significance and Justification

To plan a case study design involves not only selecting the general research question, but it also involves incorporating design components which add to the potential contributions and significance of the study. Qualitative research can be designed to contribute to theory, practice, policy, and social issues and action. We describe each of these next in addition to other justifications.

Contributions to Theory Case study design is appropriate for exploratory and discovery-oriented research. *Exploratory studies*, which examine a topic in which there has been little prior research, are designed to lead to further inquiry. The purpose is to elaborate a concept, develop a model with its related subcomponents, or suggest propositions. Some studies provide an understanding of an abstract concept, such as school-based management, from the participants' social experience. Other studies link participants' perceptions to social science and suggests propositions about humans in general rather than linking the findings to an educational concept. The concepts, models, or hypotheses are "grounded theory" because these abstractions are built from observations rather than deduced from prior theories.

Contributions to Practice Qualitative studies can provide a detailed description and analysis of a particular practice, process, or event. Some studies document the happenings while other studies contribute by increasing the participants own understanding of the practice to improve the practice. A series of qualitative studies with similar research foci, conducted *independently* by different researchers in different settings *over a span of years*, may contribute to educational knowledge through the preponderance of evidence accumulated. Specific areas of education for which quantitative designs were inadequate have begun to accumulate case study evidence. One example is a series of case studies on the role of an elementary school principal that indicate the complexities of this administrative position. Until quantitative design difficulties can be resolved, knowledge based on a preponderance of evidence cannot easily be ignored.

Contributions to Policy Qualitative research employing a case study design also contributes to policy formulation, implementation, and modification. Some studies focus on the informal processes of policy formulation or implementation in different settings with diverse cultural values to explain public policy outcomes. Qualitative research can analyze community economic and political influentials' perceptions of an issue, the attitudes of policymakers toward a proposed policy and views of those who implement policy. These studies frequently identify issues that suggest the need to modify statutes or regulations and help policymakers anticipate future issues.

Contributions to Social Issues and Action Critical studies often aim at historical revision and transformation, erosion of ignorance, and empowerment. Some studies focus on the lived experience of racial and ethnic groups, social classes, and gender roles. Researchers place categories such as "race," "ethnic group," "social class," "homosexual," and "female," in a more holistic social context to critique their ideological aspects and the political/economic interests that benefit from the situation. Studies frequently express the "culture of silence" of various groups; others describe forms of resistance and accommodation of groups that develop their own values as a force for cohesion and survival within the dominant culture.

Other Justifications Qualitative research and case study design may be justified for feasibility issues related to obtaining valid data. Qualitative research is typically done when the nature of the situation or the individuals does not permit use of an instrument. Qualitative strategies, for example, are appropriate with persons who are extemely busy or persons who are expressive nonverbally or use a second language. Qualitative research is also done when the topic is controversial or confidential within an institution and only minimal documentation is maintained. In some situations, an experimental study cannot be done for practical or ethical reasons. There many not be sufficient numbers of participants to meet the statistical requirements nor to set up a comparison group.

Purposeful Sampling

Purposeful sampling, in contrast to probabilistic sampling, is "selecting information-rich cases for study in-depth" (Patton, 1990, p. 169) when one wants to understand something about those cases without needing or desiring to generalize to all such cases. Purposeful sampling is done to increase the utility of information obtained from small samples. Purposeful sampling requires that information be obtained about variations among the subunits before the sample is chosen. The researcher then searches for *information-rich* key informants, groups, places, or events to study. In other words, these samples are chosen because they are likely to be knowledgeable and informative about the phenomena the researcher is investigating.

The power and logic of purposeful sampling is that a few cases studied in depth yield many insights about the topic, whereas the logic of probability sampling depends on selecting a random or statistically representative sample for generalization to a larger population. Probability sampling procedures such as simple random or stratified sampling may be inappropriate when (1) generalizability of the findings is not the purpose; (2) only one or two subunits of a population are relevant to the research problem; (3) the researchers have no access to the whole group from which they wish to sample; or (4) statistical sampling is precluded because of logistical and ethical reasons.

Types of purposeful sampling include site selection, comprehensive sampling, maximum variation sampling, network sampling, and sampling by case type (Table 12.2).

Site Selection

Site selection, by which a site is selected to locate people involved in a particular event, is preferred when the research focus is on complex microprocesses. A clear definition of the criteria for site selection is essential. The criteria are related to and appropriate for the research problem and purpose. For example, if the initial problem is phrased to describe and analyze teachers' decision-making regarding learning activities, or students' perspectives and strategies regarding classroom management, or elementary teachers' concept of career, then the site selected should have the likelihood that these viewpoints or actions are present and can be studied.

Comprehensive Sampling

Comprehensive sampling, in which every participant, group, setting, event, or other relevant information is examined, is the preferred sampling strategy. Each subunit is manageable in size and so diverse that one does not want to lose possible variation. For example, a study of mainstreaming autistic children in one school division would probably require observation of all autistic children. Suppose a study of high school student interns in an external learning program had 35 different sites. Each work setting was so diverse—a hospital speech clinic, a community newspaper, a labor union, two legislative offices, an animal shelter, and others—that comprehensive selection would be necessary. Because groups are rarely sufficiently small and resources are seldom plentiful, researchers use other sampling strategies.

TABLE 12.2

Purposeful Sampling Strategies

Sample Strategy	Description
Site selection	Select site where specific events are expected to occur.
Comprehensive sampling	Choose entire group by criteria.
Maximum variation sampling	Select to obtain maximum differences of perceptions about a topic among information-rich informants or group.
Network sampling	Each successive person or group is nominated by a prior person as appropriate for a profile or attribute.
Sampling by case type	
Extreme-case	Choose extreme cases after knowing the typical or average case—e.g., outstanding successes, crisis events.
Intense-case	Select cases that are intense but not extreme illustrations—e.g., below-average students.
Typical-case	Know the typical characteristics of a group and sample by cases—e.g., selection of a typical high school principal would eliminate women, persons too young or too old, single males.
Unique-case	Choose the unusual or rare case of some dimension or event—e.g., the implementation of a new federal policy mandate.
Reputational-case	Obtain the recommendation of knowledgeable experts for the best examples—e.g., principal nominates "competent" teachers or state officials identify "effective" schools.
Critical-case	Identify the case that can illustrate some phenomenon dramatically—e.g., the "real test" case or the "ideal" case.
Concept/theory-based	Select by information-rich persons or situations known to experience the concept or to be attempting to implement the concept/theory—e.g., school implementing site-based management, teacher "burnout."
Combination of purposeful sampling strategies	Choose various sampling strategies as needed or desired for purposes, especially in large-scale studies and lengthy process studies.

Maximum Variation Sampling

Maximum variation sampling, or quota selection, is a strategy to illuminate different aspects of the research problem. For instance, a researcher may divide a population of elementary school teachers by number of years of service into three categories and select key informants in each category to investigate career development. This is *not* a representative sample because the qualitative researcher is merely using this strategy to describe in detail different meanings of teacher career development for individuals with different years of service. See Excerpt 12.2 for a combination of purposeful sampling strategies.

EXCERPT 12.2

PURPOSEFUL SAMPLING: NOMINATION AND MAXIMUM VARIATION

The participants in this study were parents of students who graduated from a medium-size Mid-western city school district's program for individuals with cognitive disabilities between 1989 and 1993. The sample included parents whose children attended three of the four high schools in the city and had mild, moderate and severe cognitive disabilities. Using *purposeful sampling, . . .*participants were selected to represent three schools, presence of socio-economic disadvantage, degree of severity of child's disability and the child's current school status. A sample frame . . . was developed with the assistance of special education administrators in the school district. Parents without phone numbers were eliminated from the sampling frame. Twenty-four names . . . were selected, contacted by the researchers, and asked to participate in the study. The number of participants was based on considerations of time and feasibility. Of the 24 families contacted, 19 agreed to participate.

Source: From Hanley-Maxwell, C., Whitney-Thomas, J., & Pogoloff, S. M. (1995). The second shock: A qualitative study of parents' perspectives and needs during their child's transition from school to adult life (p. 5). JASH: *Journal of the Association for Persons with Severe Handicaps, 20*(1), 3–15.

Network Sampling

Network sampling, also called **snowball sampling,** is a strategy in which each successive participant or group is named by a preceding group or individual. Participant referrals are the basis for choosing a sample. The researcher develops a profile of the attributes or particular trait sought and asks each participant to suggest others who fit the profile or have the attribute. This strategy may be used in situations in which the individuals sought do not form a naturally bounded group but are scattered throughout populations. Network sampling is frequently used for in-depth interview studies rather than participant observation research.

Sampling by Case Type

Other sampling strategies are used when a study requires an examination of a particular type of case. Remember, "case" refers to an in-depth analysis of a phenomenon and not the number of people sampled. Examples of sampling by case type are extreme-case, intensive-case, typical-case, unique-case, reputational-case, critical-case, and concept/theory-based sampling. Each of these sampling strategies is defined in Table 12.2. A researcher may choose combinations of case types as needed or desired, especially in large-scale studies and lengthy process studies.

Purposeful sampling strategies employed in a study are identified from prior information and are reported in the study to enhance data quality. In addition, the persons or groups who actually participated in the study are reported in a manner to protect confidentiality of data. Historical and legal researchers specify the public archives and private collections used and frequently refer to each document or court case in explanatory footnotes. In this manner, researchers using noninteractive techniques to study the past reduce threats to design validity.

Sample Size

Qualitative researchers view sampling processes as *dynamic, ad hoc,* and *phasic* rather than static or *a priori* parameters of populations. While there are statistical rules for probability sample size, there are only guidelines for purposeful sample size. Purposeful samples can range from an $n = 1$ to $n = 40$ or more. Typically a qualitative sample size seems small compared with the sample size needed for representativeness to generalize to a larger population.

The logic of the sample size is related to the purpose of the study, the research problem, the major data collection technique, and the availability of the information-rich cases. The insights generated from qualitative inquiry depend more on the *information-richness of the cases and the analytical capabilities of the researcher* than on the sample size.

The following guidelines are used by qualitative researchers to determine the sample size.

1. What is the purpose of the study? A case study that is descriptive-exploratory may not need as many cases as does a self-contained study that aims at description/explanatory. Further, a phenomenological study usually has fewer informants than the number needed in grounded theory to generate dense concepts.

2. What is the focus of the study? Process-focused studies depend on the natural length of the process and often have fewer participants; whereas an interview study of selected informants depends on the access to the informants.

3. What is the primary data collection strategy? Qualitative researchers frequently discuss the number of days in the field, whether it is for observation or interview. Some studies may have small sample sizes, but the researcher is continually returning to the situation or the same informants seeking confirmation data.

4. What is the availability of informants? Some cases are rare and difficult to locate; other cases are relatively easy to identify and locate.

5. Is the information becoming redundant? Would adding more informants or returning to the field yield any new insights?

6. Researchers submit the obtained sample size to peer review or consensus judgment. Most qualitative researchers propose a *minimum* sample size and then continue to add to the sample as the study progresses.

Phases of Data Collection and Analysis Strategies

Qualitative phases of data collection and analyses are interactive research processes that occur in overlapping cycles. These are not called procedures but *data collection and analysis strategies,* techniques that are flexible and dependent on each prior strategy and the data obtained from that strategy. The research phases are relatively similar for different modes of qualitative inquiry. Figure 12.1 illustrates five research phases: Phase 1 is Planning; Phases 2, 3, and 4 are Beginning, Basic, and Closing Data Collection; and Phase 5 is Completion. The five research phases, explained below, demonstrate the interactive processes of sampling and selecting, data recording, analysis and display, and tentative interpretations during the data collection period.

Phase 1: Planning To plan a qualitative study, researchers analyze the problem statement and the research questions, which focus the data collection efforts. They then describe the kind of setting, sites, or interviewees that would seem logically to yield information about the problem. This description becomes the guideline for purposeful sampling and selection. In Phase 1, a researcher locates and gains permission to use the site or a network of persons.

Phase 2: Beginning Data Collection This phase includes the first days in the field in which the researcher establishes rapport, trust, and reciprocal relations with the individuals and groups to be observed (Wax, 1971). The researcher obtains data primarily to become oriented to the field and to gain a sense of the "totality" of the setting for purposeful sampling.

FIGURE 12.1 Phases of Qualitative Research

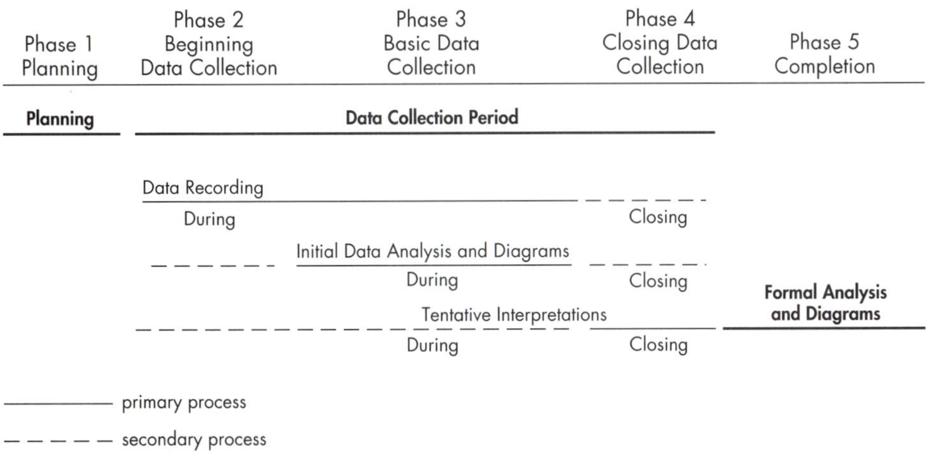

Phase 1 Planning	Phase 2 Beginning Data Collection	Phase 3 Basic Data Collection	Phase 4 Closing Data Collection	Phase 5 Completion
Planning	**Data Collection Period**			
	Data Recording		Closing	
	During			
	Initial Data Analysis and Diagrams		Closing	**Formal Analysis and Diagrams**
		During		
	Tentative Interpretations		Closing	
		During		

———— primary process

— — — — secondary process

The interviewer in Phase 2 interviews the first few persons in a network and begins the snowball sampling technique. Simultaneously the interviewer polishes the interviewing and recording procedures. Adjustments are made in the interviewer's techniques of establishing rapport and trust and in the order and phrasing of questions/statements during the interviews.

Early in the study, the qualitative researcher, regardless of the data collection technique, develops a way to organize, code, and retrieve collected data for formal data analysis (Phase 5). Transcripts of field notes or interviews and the investigator's records of documents often contain thousands of typed pages.

Phase 3: Basic Data Collection The researcher no longer is caught up in adjustments to the newness of the field setting or the idiosyncracies of interviewees. In the basic data collection phase, the inquirer begins to "hear," "see," and "read" what is going on, rather than just listening, looking around, or scanning documents. The researcher continues to make choices of data collection strategies and informants.

Tentative data analysis begins as the researcher mentally processes many ideas and facts while collecting data. Initial working conceptualizations and descriptions are transformed and summarized, often by constructing working integrative diagrams. As initial patterns emerge, the researcher identifies ideas and facts which need corroboration in the closing phase.

Phase 4: Closing Data Collection Data collection draws to a close as the researcher "leaves the field," or conducts the last interview. In qualitative research, there is no *a priori* date for the end of data collection as one might have in quantitative studies, such as when a certain percentage of completed questionnaires is returned. Ending data collection is related to the research problem and the depth and richness of the data collected. In Phase 4, the researcher gives more attention to possible interpretations and verification of the emergent findings with key informants, the remaining interviews, or documents. As Glaser and Strauss (1967) note:

> *The continual intermeshing of data collection and analysis has direct bearing on how the research is brought to a close....[The researcher] believes in his own knowledgeability...not because of an arbitrary judgment but because he has taken very special pains to discover what he thinks he may know, every step of the way from the beginning of his investigation until its publishable conclusions....He has been living with partial analyses for many months, testing them each step of the way, until he has built his theory [interpretations]. What is more, if he has participated [or empathized] in the social life of his subject, then he has been living by his analyses, testing them not only by observation and interview [and reading] but also by daily living (pp. 224–225).*

The researcher senses that further data collection may yield more data but not yield more insights relevant to the research problem.

Phase 5: Completion Completion of the active data collection phase blends into formal data analysis and the construction of meaningful ways to present the data. Data analysis begins with a construction of "the facts" as found in the researcher-recorded data. The researcher reconstructs initial diagrams, time charts, frequency lists, process figures, and others to synthesize a holistic sense of the "totality," the relationship of the parts to the whole. The researcher asks a range of questions of the recorded data as he or she slowly *induces* themes, interpretations, and/or propositions. Data analysis and diagrams are essential before the researcher can make interpretations.

Validity of Qualitative Designs

Validity refers to the degree to which the explanations of phenomena match the realities of the world. Validity in quantitative research includes both internal (causal inferences) and external (generalizability), and issues of objectivity and reliability. Qualitative research employs different assumptions, designs, and methods to develop knowledge. Although there is broad agreement to use different concepts for qualitative research standards, disagreement occurs over the names for specific concepts and the relative importance of each criterion. We use general and well-known terms, that is, validity, disciplined subjectivity, and extension of findings as the most common criteria for qualitative research.

Qualitative Design Validity

Validity addresses these questions: Do researchers actually observe what they think they observe? Do researchers actually hear the meanings that they think they hear? In other words, **validity of qualitative designs** is the degree to which the interpretations and concepts have *mutual meanings* between the participants and the researcher. The researcher and participants agree on the description or composition of events, especially the meanings of these events.

Strategies to Enhance Validity

In qualitative research, claims of validity rest on the data collection and analysis techniques. Qualitative researchers use a *combination* of any of ten possible strategies to enhance validity: prolonged field work, multimethod strategies, participant verbatim language, low-inference descriptors, multiple researchers, mechanically recorded data, participant researcher, member checking, participant review, and negative cases (Table 12.3)

Qualitative researchers typically use as many strategies as possible to insure validity design. The essential strategies are prolonged field work, multiple strategies, verbatim accounts, low-inference descriptors, and negative case search. Other strategies are added as appropriate to maintain the least amount of interference while increasing the quality of the data. Qualitative design validity

TABLE 12.3

Strategies to Enhance Design Validity: Data Collection Strategies to Increase Agreement on the Description or Composition of Phenomena between Researcher and Participants

Strategy	Description
Prolonged and persistent field work	Allows interim data analysis and corroboration to ensure the match between findings and participant reality
Multimethod strategies	Allows triangulation in data collection and data analysis
Participant language; verbatim accounts	Obtain literal statements of participants and quotations from documents
Low-inference descriptors	Record precise, almost literal, and detailed descriptions of people and situations
Multiple researchers	Agreement on descriptive data collected by a research team
Mechanically recorded data	Use of tape recorders, photographs, and videotapes
Participant researcher	Use of participant recorded perceptions in diaries or anecdotal records for corroboration
Member checking	Check informally with participants for accuracy during data collection; frequently done in participant observation studies
Participant review	Ask each participant to review researcher's synthesis of all interviews with the person for accuracy of representation; frequently done in interview studies
Negative cases or discrepant data	Actively search for, record, analyze, and report negative cases or discrepant data that are an exception to patterns or that modify patterns found in the data

also involves issues of ethics and feasibility because of the variety of designs, research questions, and situations.

Prolonged and Persistent Field Work   Participant observation and in-depth interviews are conducted in natural settings to reflect the reality of life experience more accurately than do contrived or laboratory settings. Historical and legal document are records of events that occurred in natural situations. The lengthy data collection period provides opportunities for interim data analyses, preliminary comparisons, and corroboration to refine ideas and to ensure the match between research-based categories and participant reality.

Multimethod Strategies   Most interactive researchers employ several data collection techniques in a study, but usually select one as the central method—either participant observation or in-depth interviews. To some extent participant observation, open observation, interviewing, and documents are an interwoven web of all interactive techniques. How each of these strategies are used varies with the study. In addition, artifact collection and supplementary techniques may be employed (See Chapter 13). Multimethod strategies permits *triangulation* of data across inquiry techniques. Different strategies may yield different insights about the topic of interest and increase the credibility of findings. In its broad sense, *triangulation* also can refer to use of multiple researchers, multiple theories, or perspectives to interpret the data; multiple data sources to corroborate data (see Chapter 14), and multiple disciplines to broaden one's understanding of the method and the phenomenon of interest (Janesick, 1998). For an example of selecting strategies to enhance design validity, see Excerpt 12.3.

Participant Language and Verbatim Accounts Informant interviews, phrased in the participants' language, are less abstract than many instruments used in other designs. To elicit participants' names for events and objects in their daily experiences, one avoids use of the more abstract social science language. Researchers are also sensitive to "cultural translators," that is, informants who translate their words into social science terms or social class language. For example, when tramps were asked "Where is your home? What is your address?" they would translate the question as referring to a typical middle-class residence and respond "I have no home." However, a field researcher found that men called "homeless" by social scientists did, in fact, have "flops," which functioned for them as "homes" did for other social classes (Spradley, 1979).

Verbatim accounts of conversations, transcripts, and direct quotes from documents are highly valued as data. Researchers present in their studies extensive direct quotations from the data to illustrate participants' meanings.

Low-Inference Descriptors Concrete, precise descriptions from field notes and interview elaborations are the hallmarks of qualitative research and the principle method for identifying patterns in the data. *Low-inference* means that the descriptions are almost literal and that any important terms are those used and understood by the participants. Low-inference descriptions are in contrast to the abstract language of a researcher.

EXCERPT 12.3

ENHANCING VALIDITY

The study employed an interpretive design (Erickson, 1986) that followed a hermeneutic cycle whereby what was learned was informed by what was already known, reading of the literature, experience in the field, and continuous data framing, analyses, and interpretations. A number of procedures, such as triangulation, were undertaken to ensure that the study had what Guba and Lincoln (1989) referred to as confirmability [validity]. Triangulation, involving the use of numerous data sources, maximized the probability that the emergent assertions were consistent with a variety of data. Because we were in the field for a prolonged time, the tendency of the participants in the study to exhibit contrived behaviors for the benefit of researchers was minimized. Furthermore, researchers were able to see whether given behaviors were typical or atypical.

Source: From Tobin, K., and LaMaster, S. U. (1995). Relationships between metaphors, beliefs, and actions in a context of science curriculum change (pp. 227–228). *Journal of Research in Science Teaching, 32*(3), 225–242.

Multiple Researchers The use of multiple researchers is one method to enhance validity. The use of more than one researcher is handled in different ways: (1) extensive prior training and discussion during field work to reach agreement on meanings, (2) short-term observations for confirmation at different sites, and (3) more commonly, an arrangement by which each field observer is independently responsible for a research site and periodically meets with the team to share emerging ideas and strategies. Qualitative research based on a large group team approach, however, is infrequently done; most studies involve only two researchers as a team.

Mechanically Recorded Data Tape recorders, photographs, and videotapes may enhance validity by providing an accurate and relatively complete record. However, for the data to be usable, one must note situational aspects that affected the data record and may facilitate data interpretation. Situational aspects may be failure of the equipment, the angles or distance of the taping, the effect of the use of the technical equipment on the social scene and participants, and others.

Participant Researcher Many researchers obtain the aid of an informant to corroborate what has been observed and recorded, interpretations of participant meanings, and explanations of overall processes. Participants may keep diaries or make anecdotal records to share with the researcher.

Member Checking Researchers who establish a field residence frequently confirm observations and participants' meanings with individuals through casual conversations in informal situations. Member checking can also be done within an interview as topics are rephrased and probed to obtain more complete and subtle meanings.

Participant Review Researchers who interview each person in depth or conduct a series of interviews with the same person may ask the person to review a transcript or synthesis of the data obtained from him or her. The participant is asked to modify any information or interpretation of the interview data. Then, the data obtained from each interviewee are analyzed for a comprehensive integration of findings.

Negative Cases and/or Discrepant Data Researchers actively search for, record, analyze, and report negative cases or discrepant data. A negative case is a situation, a social scene, or a participant's view that contradicts the emerging pattern of meanings. Discrepant data present a variant to the emerging pattern. For example, a school ethnographer may find that faculty interact freely among themselves in six situations. No negative cases (situations) are found. Discrepant data, however, may suggest that faculty interactions are "free" in five situations and only "semi-free" in the sixth situation, depending on who is present.

Disciplined Subjectivity in Qualitative Research

Disciplined subjectivity (Erickson, 1973) is the researcher's self-questioning and use of personal experiential empathy in data collection. Disciplined subjectivity facilitates rapport with participants. Self-reflection on one's opinions, personal preferences, and theoretical predispositions can be salutary for any kind of inquiry. Disciplined subjectivity reminds many researchers that the inquirer is part of the setting, context, and social phenomenon that he or she seeks to understand.

Reflexivity is a related, broader concept that includes rigorous examination of one's personal and theoretical commitments to see how they serve as resources for selecting one of several qualitative approaches, framing the research problem, generating particular data, ways of relating to participants, and for developing specific interpretations (Altheide & Johnson, 1998; LeCompte, 1987; Mason, 1996; Marcus, 1998; Schwandt, 1997). In other words, **reflexivity** is rigorous self-scrutiny by the researcher throughout the entire resesrach process. All the data are processed or reconstructed through the researcher's mind as the report is written. Reflexivity is valued as a very important procedure for establishing validity, especially by critical researchers wary that their empirical work will be viewed as an ideological discourse or fearful of duplication of social, racial, ethnic, and gender biases in their studies. In some critical studies reflexivity may require additional strategies for rigor. Qualitative researchers, rather than deny human subjectivity, take into account subjectivity through methodological strategies.

Interpersonal Subjectivity

Interactive research depends to a great extent on the interpersonal skills of the inquirer. These skills involve building trust, keeping good relations, being non-judgmental, respecting the norms of the situation, and having a sensitivity regarding ethical issues. The researcher relates to the participant as a person, not as a lifeless sponge "soaking" up the surroundings. Interpersonal emotions in field work are essential in data collection activities because of the face-to-face interaction. Feelings serve several useful functions throughout the research process (Kleinman & Copp, 1993).

The progress of the study often depends primarily on the relationship the researcher builds with the participants. Essential skills are ones of easily conversing with others—being an active, patient, and thoughtful listener and demonstrating an empathetic understanding of and profound respect for participants' perspectives. Researcher self-monitoring is intimately tied to one's personal ethics. Further, the interactive process is relatively personal; no investigator observes, interviews or relates to others exactly like another. These issues are handled primarily *within* the actual study to enhance reflexivity.

Data obtained from informants are valid even though they may represent a particular view or have been influenced by the researcher's presence. Such data are problematic only if the data are claimed to be representative beyond the context. Potential researcher bias can be minimized if reseachers spend enough time in the field employing multiple data collection strategies to obtain data from different perspectives. Extensive time in data collection allows the researcher to corroborate data and identify misrepresented information. Participant reaction, independent corroboration, and confirmation—done at all stages of the research process—are probably the most effective techiques to identify researcher biases. Providing sufficient details about the design, including selected strategies to enhance *disciplined* subjectivity, is necessary.

Strategies to Enhance Reflexivity

Qualitative researchers combine any of seven possible strategies to monitor and evaluate the impact of their subjectivity and perspective (Table 12.4). The most important strategies are keeping a field log and a field (reflex) journal and documenting for audibility. Other strategies are added as needed or required for valid data.

Peer Debriefer A peer debriefer is a disinterested colleague who engages in discussions of the researcher's preliminary analyses and next methodological strategies in an emergent design. These discussions make more explicit the tacit knowledge that the researcher has acquired. The peer debriefer also poses searching questions to help the researcher understand his own posture and values and their role in the inquiry. In addition, the discussions may reduce the stress that normally accompanies field work.

TABLE 12.4

Strategies to Enhance Reflexivity: Strategies to Monitor and Evaluate Researcher Subjectivity and Perspective

Strategy	Description
Peer debriefer	Select a colleague who facilitates the logical analysis of data and interpretation; frequently done when the topic is emotionally charged or the researcher experiences conflicting values in data collection
Field log	Maintain a log of dates, time, places, persons, and activities to obtain access to informants and for each datum set collected
Field (reflex) journal	Record the decisions made during the emerging design and the rationale; include judgments of data validity
Ethical considerations recorded	Record the ethical dilemmas, decisions, and actions in field journal, and self-reflections
Audibility	Record data management techniques, codes, categories, and decision-rules as a "decision trail"
Formal corroboration of initial findings	Conduct formal confirmation activities such as a survey, focus groups, or interviews
Critical reflexivity	Self-critique by asking difficult questions; positionality

Field Log A field log is a chronological record by date and time spent in the field and in getting access to sites and informants. The field log also contains, for each entry, the places and persons involved. The log documents the persistent field work essential for design validity. A log is frequently an appendix in a study or condensed as tables to illustrate multiple sources and settings.

Field Journal A field reflex journal is a continuous record of decisions made during the emergent design and the rationale at that time. Thus, the researcher can justify, based on the available information, the modifications and reformulations of the research problem and strategies. These records are the basis for reporting changes in a methodology section of a completed study. The field journal may also contain assessments of the trustworthiness of each datum set and of informants. Some field journals, called reflex journals, contain the evolution of the researcher's ideas, personal reactions, possible related literature, and questions for future investigation.

Ethical Considerations Recorded Qualitative researchers frequently face ethical dilemmas and make decisions to resolve these in order to continue the study. A record is maintained of the decisions, the persons involved, the actions taken, and the impact on the study. Researchers make strategy choices in the field; some decisions are based primarily on ethical considerations. Maintaining a record of ethical considerations helps to justify the subsequent choices.

Audibility Audibility is maintaining a record of data management techniques and decision-rules that document the "chain of evidence" or "decision-trail." In qualitative research, the integrity of the findings is rooted in the data themselves. A record is maintained that links the findings to their original sources or data. The record includes the data management techniques and the codes, categories, and themes used to build and interpret the narrative case. The record includes drafts and preliminary integrative diagrams. Thus, the chain of evidence is available for inspection and confirmation by outside reviewers.

Audibility criteria can be met with or without an outside reviewer, that is, an "auditor." Frequently, there is no one available who can serve as the outside reviewer because such a reviewer must be knowledgeable about both the methodology and the topic. An alternative technique is to place a list of files, codes, categories, and decision-rules in an appendix for perusal by the reader. If a formal audit is conducted, the outside reviewer checks the accuracy of the documents that link the findings to the original sources and submits a reviewer's appraisal.

Formal Corroboration of Initial Findings When the findings depend on a few key informants, researchers may conduct formal confirmation data collection activities, such as a survey, focus groups, and in-depth interviews with information-rich individuals not selected originally. Notice that as a corroboration activity, the qualitative data must be completely analyzed first. Confirmation activities assure that the patterns in the data are not unduly contaminated by the researcher's subjectivity. Confirmation activities, if feasible, add to the credibility of the study.

Critical Reflexivity

Reflexivity requires the researcher to do more than self-monitoring and keeping a decision record. Critical reflexivity is the researcher constantly assessing their actions and roles in the entire research process. This heighten self-awareness promotes personal and social transformation. The very act of posing difficult questions to oneself assumes that the researcher cannot be neutral, objective, or detached. For example, one difficult question relates to "voice"—were all the voices allowed to emerge, especially the socially silenced because their perspectives are often counter to the situation.

Another reflex strategy is **positionality** which assumes that only texts where researchers display their own positions (standpoints) and contextual grounds for reasoning could be considered "good" research (Lincoln, 1995; Lather, 1991; J. K. Smith, 1993). Critical researchers often write in the introduction their social, cultural, historical, racial, and sexual location in the study. For example, in the introduction of *I Answer with MY Life: Life Histories of Women Teachers Working for Social Change,* K. Casey (1993) described her own identity as a woman teacher working for social change. This included her life history, theoretical stance, methodological choices, and politics in data discourse and analysis. However, positionality statements can be only a gesture. In participartory action research, the researcher writes into the data his or her own actions. A complicated dual role of researcher and participant requires scrutiny of both the roles and the resulting data. This is not an easy task nor can it be taken lightly.

Extension of Qualitative Findings

Qualitative researchers produce authentic analytical descriptions of phenomena which are informative and useful to research communities, readers, and participants.

Issues of Authenticity and Usefulness

Most qualitative studies employ a case study design in which the single case is not treated as a probability sample of the larger universe. In other words, the researcher does not aim at generalization of results. Instead, the intent is to provide for the **extension of the findings**, which enables others to understand similar situations and apply these findings in subsequent research or practical situations. Knowledge is produced not by replication but by the preponderance of evidence found in separate case studies over time or in more structured quantitative designs.

   Authenticity is the faithful reconstruction of participants' multiple perceptions. To be useful, the research design must be adequately described. Some studies, such as grounded theory, cite the theoretical frameworks and research strategies that are understood by other researchers. Other studies are more contextual and are written for practical implications. A study that is a systematic but idiosyncratic investigation has limited relevance for future inquiry.

Design Components to Generate Extension of Findings

Ten design components affect logical (not statistical) extensions; research role, informant selection, social context, data collection strategies, data analysis strategies, authentic narrative, typicality, analytical premises, alternative explanations, and criteria associated with a particular research purpose (Table 12.5).

TABLE 12.5

Design Components to Generate Use of the Study and Extension of Findings

Strategy	Adequate Description in the Study
Research role	The social relationship of the researcher with the participants
Informant selection	Criteria, rationale, and decision process used in purposeful sampling
Social context	The physical, social, interpersonal, and functional social scenes of data collection
Data collection strategies	The multimethods employed, including participant observation, interview, documents, and others
Data analysis strategies	Data analysis process described
Authentic narrative	Thick description presented as an analytical narrative
Typicality	Distinct characteristics of groups and/or sites presented
Analytical premises	The initial theoretical or political framework that informs the study
Alternative explanations	Retrospective delineation of all plausible or rival explanations for interpretations
Other criteria by research approach (after study completed)	
Ethnography	Comprehensive explanation of complexity of group life
Phenomenology	Understand the essence of lived experience; generates more research questions
Case study	Understand the practice; facilitates informed decision making
Grounded theory	Concepts or propositions relate to social science; generates verification research with more structured designs
Critical traditions	Informs or impowers participants about their situation and opportunities; generates further research; action stimulus

Research Role The importance of the researcher's social relationship with the participants requires that studies identify the researcher's role and status within the group. The preferred research role is that of a person who is unknown at the site or to the participants—in other words, an "outsider." Qualitative researchers also frequently cite personal or professional experiences that enable them to empathize with the participants—that is, they recognize more readily the observed processes and subtle participant meanings than those lacking such experiences. However, participatory action research requires the dual role of participant and researcher.

Informant Selection Informant selection is described with the selection rationale and the decision process. Future research requires that a researcher contact individuals similar to those who were informants in the prior study.

Qualitative researchers view loss of subjects as a normal event. They value each *person*; human informants and participants are *not* interchangeable. If an informant is not cooperative or not available, researchers continue to search for other key informants or use documentary evidence until a pattern emerges. Increasing the number of sites in a case study design does not facilitate extension of findings; the sites are nonprobabilistic samples.

Social Context Social contexts influence data content and are described physically, socially, interpersonally, and functionally. Physical descriptions of people, the time, and the place of the events or of the interviews assist in data analysis. The interpersonal relations among group members and the social relationships among groups may explain individual actions and meanings. The purpose of group meetings such as in-service training, parent conferences, or board meetings require other researchers to find similar social contexts for further study.

Data Collection Strategies Using the study for future research is impossible without precise descriptions of data collection techniques: the varieties of observational and interviewing methods and data recording techniques with the circumstances and processes to assure accurate records. How different strategies were employed is noted. For example, if the primary interest was in observing a group process, then individual interviews and documents would serve as corroborative data collection strategies.

Data Analysis Strategies Simply asserting that formal data analysis was done carefully is insufficient for facilitating extension of findings. The researcher must provide retrospective accounts of how data were synthesized and identify the general strategies of data analysis and interpretation. Frequently, the categories used in data analysis and their decision rules are listed in an appendix.

Authentic Narrative Most qualitative studies contain "thick description" in an analytical narrative interspersed with brief and lengthy quotations representing participants' language. A good narrative is one that may be read and lived vicariously by others. Plausible narratives provide meanings that make sense and shape readers' thinking and practices. A narrative is authentic when readers connect to the story by recognizing particulars, by imagining the scenes, and by reconstructing them from remembered associations with similar events (Connelly & Clandinin, 1990). It is the particular, not the general, that triggers emotions and moves people. Stories stand between the general and particular by mediating the basic demands of research and the personal, practical, concrete demands of living.

Typicality The extent of **typicality** of the phenomenon (Wolcott, 1973)—that is, the degree to which it may be compared or contrasted along relevant dimensions with other phenomena—is reported. Qualitative researchers' "virtual obsession" with describing the distinct characteristics of groups studied demonstrates an appreciation of the importance of this information for extension purposes.

Both qualitative and quantitative attributes of groups and sites are essential. These can include socioeconomic status, educational attainment, age group, racial or ethnic composition, time period, and contextual features of the location. Unique historical experiences of groups and cultures may limit extension, but few group experiences are ethnocentric. Excerpt 12.4 describes the

EXCERPT 12.4

TYPICALITY

The particular school chosen for study was an elementary school operated under the auspices of a conservative Jewish synagogue. This type of Jewish school was desired because it is statistically typical of a large percentage of Jewish schools in America (Lang 1968). As was the case with this school, the largest percentage of students attending Jewish schools nationally (44.4 percent) were enrolled in 2 to 5 day a week afternoon schools (Rockowitz and Lang 1976). Also, the largest number of Jewish schools appear to fall within the range of 100 to 299 students, as did this school with its approximately 250 students (Rockowitz and Lang 1976). Finally, the greatest number of conservative congregations who had such schools had a membership size of 100 to 249 families (Friedman 1979), as was the case in this study in which the congregation had approximately 200 families registered as members. The school met two afternoons (1 1/2 hours each) and one Sunday morning (2 1/2 hours) each week, although one of the afternoon sessions was optional. The curriculum in general conformed with the standard curriculum of the afternoon school.

Source: From David Schoen. (1982). Explaining Jewish Student Failure, *Anthropology & Education Quarterly, 13*(4), Reprinted by permission of the American Anthropological Association.

typicality of a Jewish elementary school on relevant dimensions. Once typicality is established, a basis for extension of understandings is evident, and the findings provide insights across time frames or situations.

Analytical Premises The primary design component that generates further research is an explicit conceptual framework that informs the study and with which findings from prior research can be integrated or contrasted. The selection of a conceptual framework for a study requires that other researchers also begin from similar analytical premises. See Excerpt 12.5 for explicit statements of analytical premises.

Because a major outcome of qualitative research is the generation and refinement of concepts, qualitative researchers must contrast their findings to prior research. When discrepancies are presented, qualitative researchers report the attributes of the group, time period, and settings. This alerts other researchers when they use these findings.

Much qualitative research, however, has a primarily descriptive and explanatory purpose and is not limited to theoretical studies. The choice to focus on narrative and analytic description relates partially to the estent of prior research and to the inquiry purpose. Thus, the concluding paragraph of a study of a bilingual teacher (Excerpt 12.6) states that ideally readers will become more informed about bilingual education based on the realities of their experiences.

Alternative Explanations During data analysis, qualitative researchers search for negative evidence or discrepant data to challenge or modify emerging patterns. Negative or discrepant data are useful for identifying alternative explanations.

EXCERPT 12.5

ANALYTICAL PREMISES

Not surprisingly, then, the girls whose families were *not* like the television families thought the television families were more unrealistic. Following McRobbie's (1991) culturalist approach, the girls were interpreting and assessing media based on their own lived experiences. Greenberg and Reeves (1976) also find that children's personal experiences affect their perceptions of reality on television. Children in general do not have multiple reference points regarding family life, so the girls in this study saw any family deviating from those they know as unrealistic. This data also empirically supports Greenberg and Reeves's prediction that television content is perceived as more like real life if the child's attitudes and behaviors, or in this case, family dynamics, are consistent with the television content.

Source: From Fingerson, L. (1999). Active viewing. Girls' interpretations of family television programs (pp. 398–399). *Journal of Contemporary Ethnography, 28*(4), 389– 418.

EXCERPT 12.6

EXTENSION OF DESCRIPTIVE ANALYTICAL RESEARCH

These strategies carry her (Mrs. S.') implicit, developing perspective on educational processes as they pertain to minority students. An investigation of such perspectives, evolving out of the comparable experiences of teachers in this country (United States), is a dire necessity in the field of educational thought. Such an investigation would, in its turn, lead ideally to a kind of understanding of bilingual education that is more sophisticated, more attentive to the nuances and the diversities of minority communities—above all, more informed by the *realities* of their experience—than is the case at present (p. 189).

Source: Montero-Sieburth, M. & Perez, M. (1987) *Echar Pa'lante,* Moving Onward: The Dilemmas and Strategies of a Bilingual Teacher, *Anthropology & Education Quarterly, 18* (3), 189. Reprinted by permission of the American Anthropological Association.

Ethnographers and interviewers actively search for the informants and social scenes that appear to vary from or disagree with prior data. A major pattern becomes an explanation only when alternative patterns do not offer reasonable explanations central to the research problem. Major and alternative explanations are discussed in the study because both might generate further research.

Other Criteria by Research Approach (after study completed) In addition to providing adequate description of the general components mentioned, specific research approaches may emphasize additional criteria. For example, phenomenology, grounded theory, and critical studies may have slightly different effects on research communities, readers, and participants. An ethnography provides a comprehensive understanding of the complexity of group life, which leads to further case studies. A phenomenological study increases the understanding of lived experience by readers and others. A case study promotes better understanding of the practice or issue and facilitates informed decision making. Grounded theory study, however, usually leads to more structured designs to test the concept or verify a proposition. Some forms of critical traditions not only inform through historical revisionism, but also empower and stimulate action. Thus the researcher frequently has a meeting with the major informants or all participants, reviews the findings, and creates a dialogue. Researchers may also provide additional resource information to foster personal and group empowerment.

When qualitative researchers have appropriately addressed the issues of design validity, disciplined subjectivity, and extension of findings noted above, their work is usually regarded as credible by other qualitative investigators. Many design issues are handled by planning and conducting studies based on the appropriate criteria for research credibility.

Research Ethics: Roles and Reciprocity

Ethical principles in qualitative research are similar to those for quantitative research. Ethical guidelines include, but are not limited to, informed consent, deception, confidentiality, anonymity, harm to subjects, and privacy and others (see Chapter 5). The American Anthropological Association, the American Psychological Association, the American Educational Research Association, and the American Sociological Association have professional ethical guidelines and standards. Field workers, however, must adopt these principles in complex situations.

Ethical Dilemmas in Fieldwork

Qualitative researchers need to be sensitive to ethical principles because of their research topic, face-to-face interactive data collection, an emergent design, and reciprocity with participants. Criteria for a research design involve not only the selection of information-rich informants and efficient research strategies, but also adherence to research ethics.

Some qualitative researchers, for example, have gained the confidence of persons potentially involved in illegal activities to collect data. Other researchers have investigated controversial or politically sensitive topics. When a researcher studies those whose acts are considered criminal or routinely abusive, profound ethical dilemmas arise: "When one decides to attempt to enter their world and to study it, the field worker arrives at a true moral, ethical, and legal existential crisis" (Soloway and Walters, 1977, p. 161). Researchers have faced ethical dilemmas in studying drug addiction, narcotics officers, and caretakers in institutions for the mentally retarded. Because qualitative researchers become involved in the settings and the everyday lives of participants, these researchers are often drawn into morally problematic situations.

Emergent designs require that ethical principles be considered throughout all phases of planning and data collection. Furthermore, some decisions made on the spot have ethical implications (Taylor, 1987). Here are some typical questions: "Do I observe this abuse or do I turn away from it?" "Do I record this 'confession' and, if I do record it, do I put it in a public report?" "If I see 'abuse' or 'neglect,' do I report it to the officials?" "Am I really seeing 'abuse' or 'neglect' or projecting *my* values into the situation?" "If I promised confidentiality when I entered the field as a researcher, am I breaking my 'bargain' if I interfere?" "If I break my 'bargain,' will I be asked to leave the field; if I leave, will the larger research, professional, and public community be uninformed?" These questions suggest that it is difficult to separate research ethics from professional ethics and personal morality.

Most qualitative researchers devise roles that elicit cooperation, trust, openness, and acceptance. At times this means that researchers assume a helping role, dress in a certain manner, or allow themselves to be manipulated.

When people adjust their priorities and routines to help a researcher or even tolerate a researcher's presence, they are giving of themselves. A researcher is indebted to these persons. Some scholars (Marshall & Rossman, 1999) suggest that researchers devise ways, within the constraints of the research and personal ethics, to reciprocate. Reciprocity can be the giving of time, feedback, attention, appropriate token gifts, or specialized services. Some researchers, upon completion of the report, become advocates for a particular group in the larger community, including policy making groups.

Research Ethics in Fieldwork

Most ethical situations require researchers to determine situational priorities, which frequently involve discussions with participants. Below are potential ethical dilemmas in conducting field work and how researchers have resolved them.

Informed Consent as a Dialogue In obtaining permission to enter the field, most researchers give assurances of confidentiality and anonymity and describe the intended use of the data. Because of the research strategies employed, seldom does the issue of physical or psychological harm arise.

Many researchers (L. M. Smith, 1990) view informed consent as a dialogue: each new participant in the study is informed of the purpose and is assured of confidentiality and anonymity. However, there are situations in which a dialogue is impossible, such as a sudden unexpected trauma that brings persons to the scene during the observation, or the observation of public behavior, such as a crowd at a football game. Informing participants is done in a manner to encourage free choice of participation. The time required for participation and the noninterfering, nonjudgmental research role is explained. Usually interview times and places are selected by the informants. Because researchers attempt to establish trusting relationships, they need to plan how to handle the dialogue. Most participants detect and reject insincerity and manipulation.

Confidentiality and Anonymity In general, there is a strong feeling among field workers that settings and participants should not be identifiable in print. Researchers use imaginary locations and disguise features of settings in such a way as to make them appear similar to several possible sites. Researchers routinely code names of people and places. Participant review of the case study of each individual is a means to ensure confidentiality and to protect privacy. In addition, officials can review a report before it is finally released. Researchers have a dual responsibility: protection of the participants' confidences from other persons in the setting whose private information might enable them to identify them, and protection of the informants from the general reading public.

However, the law does *not* protect researchers if the government compels them to disclose matters of confidence. The report, the field notes, and the researcher can be subpoenaed. For example, one researcher had almost completed field work when a school lawyer requested that he be an expert witness in a school desegregation case. The researcher initiated the "ethical principle of dialogue" (L. M. Smith, 1990, p. 271) in presenting the dilemma to several school officials for mutual problem solving. Finally, a top official said the school lawyer would not call the researcher as a witness because it violated the commitments of confidentiality made to the staff, teachers, and administrators of the school. Spradley (1979) stresses the protection of field notes and even suggests that one consider an alternative project if protection of informants is not possible.

Deception, Privacy, and Empowerment Most qualitative researchers view deception as violating informed consent and privacy. However, some well-known ethnographers have posed as hobos, vagrants, and even army recruits to collect data without informing the participants (Punch, 1986). These researchers claim that no harm to the informants resulted from the research. Even informed persons who cooperate may feel a sense of betrayal when they read the findings in print.

Other researchers suggest that field workers negotiate with the participants so that they understand the power that they have in the research process. This power and the decisions that come with it may be an exchange for the privacy lost by participation in a study (Lincoln, 1990). Furthermore, if ethical problems do arise in the field work, mutual problem solving by the researcher and participants can usually lead to alternatives. Such an approach rests on the belief that both the activities of the participants and the inquiry are worth while.

Harm, Caring, and Fairness Although physical harm to informants seldom occurs in qualitative research, some persons can experience personal humiliation and loss of interpersonal trust. Some researchers (Cassell, 1982) state the principle of persons being treated as ends themselves rather than as a means to an end—justifying the possible harm to an individual because it may help others. Other researchers feel that a sense of caring and fairness have to enter into the researcher's thinking and actions. Professional and research ethics for many researchers are intimately related to personal morality.

Many researchers argue for "committed relativism" or "reasonableness" in a particular situation. Although ethical guidelines exist, the difficulty is in the application. Researchers need to identify potential ethical dilemmas and resolve them. Open discussions and negotiation usually promote "fairness" to the persons and to the research inquiry. Knowledge can serve both to empower the participants in their setting and the larger professional community.

Standards of Adequacy

Qualitative designs are judged by several criteria. Below are typical questions that researchers might ask of their designs or that reviewers may use to critique a qualitative design.

1. Is the one phenomenon to be studied clearly articulated and delimited?

2. Are inquiry mode, purpose, research questions, and design presented?

3. Which purposeful sampling technique to identify information-rich cases will be used? Does the sampling strategy seem likely to obtain information-rich groups or cases? (Usually preliminary information is necessary before the sampling strategy can be chosen.)

4. Is the desired minimum sample size stated? Does the sample size seem logical to yield rich data about the phenomenon within a reasonable length of time?

5. Is the design presented in sufficient detail to enhance validity; that is, does it specify essential strategies such as prolonged field work, collection of verbatim accounts with descriptive data, and negative case search?

6. Which multiple data collection strategies are planned to increase the agreement on the description of the phenomenon and its meanings between the researcher and participants? Does the researcher have knowledge and experience with the proposed strategies, or has he or she done a preliminary study?

7. Does the design suggest the emergent nature of the study?

8. Which strategies does the researcher plan to employ to enhance reflexivity?

9. Which design components are included to encourage the usefulness and the logical extension of the findings? Are there others which could be employed, and if so, which ones?

10. Does the researcher specify how informal consent, confidentiality, anonymity, and other ethical principles will be handled in the field?

Qualitative research designs are often difficult to judge because of the flexibility and emergent nature of the design. Designs, if really emergent and for discovery, will be modified as the study progresses. Many of the standards are related to the data collection strategies. (See "Standards of Adequacy for Ethnographic Methodology" in Chapter 13.)

Summary

The following statements summarize the major aspects of qualitative research design.

1. Qualitative researchers study participant's perspectives—feelings, thoughts, beliefs, ideals—and actions in natural situations.

2. Qualitative researchers use interactive strategies to collect data for exploratory, explanatory, or emancipatory studies.

3. Qualitative researchers employ an emergent design.

4. A case study design focuses on one phenomenon to understand in depth, regardless of the number of persons or sites in the study.

5. Case studies are significant for theory practice, policy, and social action development.

6. Purposeful sampling is selecting small samples of information-rich cases to study in depth without desiring to generalize to all such cases.
7. Types of purposeful sampling include site selection, comprehensive sampling, maximum variation sampling, network sampling, and sampling by case type.
8. Sample size depends on the purpose of the study, the data collection strategies, and the availability of information-rich cases.
9. Data collection and analysis are interactive and occur in overlapping cycles.
10. The use of research strategies rather than procedures allows for flexibility to study and corroborate each new idea as it occurs in data collection.
11. The phases of qualitative research are planning, beginning data collection, basic data collection, closing data collection, and formal data analysis and diagrams.
12. Validity of qualitative designs is the degree to which the interpretations and concepts have mutual meanings between the participants and researcher.
13. Qualitative researchers enhance validity by making explicit all aspects of their designs.
14. Data collection strategies to increase validity are a combination of the following strategies: prolonged field work, multimethod, verbatim accounts, low-inference descriptors, multiple researchers, mechanically recorded data, participant researcher, member checking, participant review, and negative case reporting.
15. Qualitative researchers employ interpersonal subjectivity to collect data and reflex strategies to enhance the study..
16. Qualitative studies aim at extension of findings rather than generalization of results. Generalizability is usually *not* the intent of the study.
17. Design components that enhance the extension of findings are specification of the researcher role, informant selection, the social context, data collection and analysis strategies, authentic narrative, typicality, analytical premises, and alternative explanations.
18. Field researchers often employ dialogue and reciprocity while following ethical and legal principles with participants.

Self-Instructional Review Exercises

Sample answers are in the back of the book.

Test Items

1. The purpose of a case study design is to
   a. generalize to all similar cases.
   b. achieve a reliable answer to a problem.
   c. acquire an in-depth understanding of *one* phenomenon.
   d. select a site for observation.
2. Case studies do *not*
   a. develop theory.
   b. statistically compare groups in different experimental conditions.

    c. describe and analyze a practice or process.

    d. identify policy issues.

3. The logic of purposeful sampling is that

    a. a randomly representative sample can generalize to a population.

    b. a few information-rich cases studied in depth yields many insights about a topic.

    c. all cases are included, even though they are not all relevant to the problem.

    d. available cases are used because the researcher has access to them.

4. Which of the following correctly describes the phases of qualitative research?

    a. identifying the research problem, planning, data collection, data analysis, completion.

    b. planning, beginning data collection, basic data collection, closing data collection, completion.

    c. identifying the research hypothesis, data collection, data analysis, conclusions.

    d. planning, identifying the problem, data collection, completion.

5. The following strategies enhance design validity *except*

    a. using low-inference descriptors.

    b. obtaining verbatim accounts.

    c. conducting participant review.

    d. ignoring negative cases.

6. Validity of qualitative design is

    a. increased with a very brief data collection period.

    b. enhanced by the use of abstract social science language rather than participants' language.

    c. enhanced with member checking.

    d. increased by researcher interference in natural events at site.

7. Design validity in qualitative research refers to

    a. consistency of assessments.

    b. how well the descriptions and interpretations have mutual meanings between the researcher and participants.

    c. use of random sampling

    d. use of an experimental variable.

8. Disciplined subjectivity and reflexivity recognize that

    a. emotions in field work are essential in face-to-face interactions but must be monitored and evaluated.

    b. most qualitative researchers are unbiased and objective.

    c. a record of field decisions is unimportant.

    d. establishing audibility is not necessary.

9. Extension of findings in qualitative research

    a. aims at generalization of results to other populations and settings.

    b. depends on exact replications of the case study in other settings.

    c. is enhanced with typicality, authentic narrative, and specification of all design components.

    d. is impossible to achieve with qualitative strategies.

10. Qualitative research ethics include
   a. use of codes and false names for anonymity.
   b. informed consent as a dialogue in which persons have power over the research process.
   c. negotiation with participants and mutual problem-solving of ethical dilemmas occurring in the field.
   d. all of the above.

Application Problems

1. The director of an inner city preschool program wants to obtain parent perspectives of the program. She is especially interested in this year's innovation in one class: a parent education program. Materials are sent home twice a week for a parent or guardian to work with the child, and records of teacher-parent contacts are made. There are twelve children in the preschool class. Four children live with a single parent, six live with both parents, and two children live with one parent and their grandparents.
   a. What type of sampling is appropriate and why? (probability or purposeful)
   b. How should the sampling be done?
   c. Which qualitative methods would be appropriate?
2. A researcher is interested in how principals make decisions about retention of elementary school children. How would you design this study?
3. A researcher wants to understand the concept of site-based school management. He has located a school district that has spent one year in planning and writing guidelines for site-based management at six selected schools. The researcher is primarily interested in how a site-based management team operates and whether this affects the role of the principal and the school's relationship to the district central management. A site-based management team consists of six members from the community and three teachers with the principal as an *ad hoc* member. A central office facilitator frequently attends the monthly meetings after conducting six orientation sessions. How would you design the study?
   a. Which type of sampling is appropriate and why? (probability or purposeful)
   b. How should the sampling be done?
   c. Which qualitative methods would be appropriate?
4. For Problem #1 above, which research strategies could increase design validity, minimize researcher bias, and encourage extension of findings?
5. For Problem #3 above, which research strategies could enhance design validity, decrease researcher bias, and foster extension of findings?

Qualitative Strategies

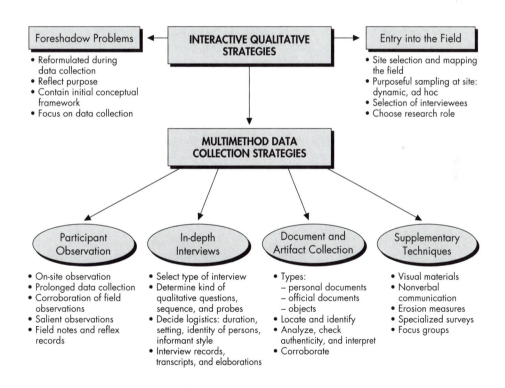

Foreshadow Problems

- Reformulated during data collection
- Reflect purpose
- Contain initial conceptual framework
- Focus on data collection

INTERACTIVE QUALITATIVE STRATEGIES

Entry into the Field

- Site selection and mapping the field
- Purposeful sampling at site: dynamic, ad hoc
- Selection of interviewees
- Choose research role

MULTIMETHOD DATA COLLECTION STRATEGIES

Participant Observation

- On-site observation
- Prolonged data collection
- Corroboration of field observations
- Salient observations
- Field notes and reflex records

In-depth Interviews

- Select type of interview
- Determine kind of qualitative questions, sequence, and probes
- Decide logistics: duration, setting, identity of persons, informant style
- Interview records, transcripts, and elaborations

Document and Artifact Collection

- Types:
  – personal documents
  – official documents
  – objects
- Locate and identify
- Analyze, check authenticity, and interpret
- Corroborate

Supplementary Techniques

- Visual materials
- Nonverbal communication
- Erosion measures
- Specialized surveys
- Focus groups

KEY TERMS

multimethod
strategies
foreshadowed problems
holistic emphasis
mapping the field
research role
participant observation
field residence
field notes
reflex records
in-depth interviews

informal conversation interview
interview guide approach
standardized open-ended interview
key informant interview
career and life history interviews
elite interviews
phenomenlogical interviews
interview probes
interview elaborations
artifact collections

Many of us are familiar with conversations and observations as a way of acquiring useful information about our students, our colleagues, the organizations in which we work, and even our friends and families. We interpret our observations and share with others brief stories about what we learned. Forms of conversations and observations are also the primary data collection strategy in qualitative research.

Qualitative research is *interactive face-to-face* research, which requires relatively extensive time to systematically observe, interview, and record processes as they occur naturally. Data collection strategies focus on what the phenomenon means to participants. Despite considerable variation among qualitative studies, common methodological strategies distinguish this style of inquiry: participant observation, in-depth interviews, and artifact collection. Most qualitative studies are exploratory or explanatory to understand peoples' views of their world. Other studies in the critical traditions employ the same techniques but for an emancipatory purpose. This chapter presents entry into the field, selecting an appropriate research role, interactive research strategies, and standards for appraising qualitative techniques.

Multimethod Strategies

Most qualitative research depends on multimethod strategies to collect data. **Multimethod** is the use of multiple strategies to collect and corroborate the data obtained from any single strategy and/or ways to confirm data within a single strategy of data collection. Qualitative researchers, called field workers, assume that any data can be corroborated during data collection. For example, data from direct observation of elementary classes could be confirmed with casual interviews of teachers and pupils and more formal interviews with the principal and central supervisor. A study of a school system's politics and bureaucracy would corroborate data with interviews, observations of meetings and hearings, press coverage of events, newsletters of interest groups, and reports of the Board of Education.

Qualitative researchers think of participant observation, interviewing, artifact analysis, field observation, and supplementary techniques as strategies. Researchers prefer strategies rather than step-by-step rigid procedures. **Strategies** are sampling and data collection techniques that are continually refined throughout the data collection process to increase data validity. Use of strategies permits the design to emerge or be partially shaped as data are collected and analyzed.

Researchers usually select one primary data collection strategy such as participant observation or interviews and use other strategies to verify the most important findings before completely leaving the field. How each strategy is employed is stated in the final report. Researchers determine the most practical, feasible, efficient, and ethical methods for collecting data as the research progresses. If the research goal is description of processes, events, or concepts, then data collection and purposeful sampling activities are only a means to achieve valid data. Use of multimethod strategies also enhances the credibility of the study. We will discuss each of the following strategies in the chapter: participant observation, in-depth interviews, artifact collection, field observation, and supplementary strategies.

Foreshadowed Problems and Reformulations

Qualitative researchers begin with **foreshadowed problems**—anticipated research problems that will be reformulated in the field during data collection. Foreshadowed problems are typically broadly phrased research questions about the participants (time, place, events); *what* happens, *why* it happens, and *how* it happens. Such problems can focus on the structure and the processes operating in different social scenes and experiences. Below is an example:

> *In order to describe the personnel task of the principal, it is necessary to describe and analyze three sub-topics. First, what were the types of teacher behaviors that principals identified as unsatisfactory? Second, having identified the unsatisfactory behaviors, what actions were then taken by the principals in an attempt to resolve the problems? Third, what are the factors which influenced the principals' decision-making during the identification-resolution process? (Luck, 1985, p. 4)*

Qualitative research problems derive from several possible sources: common, recurring everyday events in education or personal experiences, ideologies and philosophies, theories, prior research, and problems and ideas identified by others in in the setting. In other words, empirical problems lie all around in varying forms and for the most part need only to be recognized for their possibilities. There is almost an intuitive feel for the problems in the form of such questions as, "I wonder what will happen now that . . . ," "What does this event really mean to the participants?," or "How are they going to manage to do that?" Recognizing a possible research problem is an ethnographic skill. Researchers have their curiosity aroused or are puzzled about the whys and hows of what they observe or experience. Qualitative researchers study theory and previous research as much as other researchers do, but they purposely put aside this knowledge until their experience in the field suggests its relevance

The statement of foreshadowed problems indicates that the researcher has tentatively decided the research purpose, research questions, and the focus of the data collection strategies. Most foreshadowed problems have a descriptive emphasis.

Question Reformulations   Discovering participant "meanings" necessitates problem reformulation in the field. Malinowski, a noted anthropologist, emphasized the essential ability of the researcher to recast initial ideas during field work by stating:

> *If a man sets out on an expedition, determined to prove certain hypotheses, if he is incapable of changing his views constantly and casting them off ungrudgingly under the pressure of evidence, needless to say his work will be worthless. But the more problems he brings with him into the field, the more he is in the habit of . . . seeing facts in their bearing upon theory, the better he is equipped for the work, . . . (1922 [Reprint, 1961], pp. 8–9)*

In an exploratory study (Schumacher, 1975) of a planned curriculum diffusion (widespread usage) in one state, for example, the foreshadowed problems were phrased in terms of sequential events planned to result in local school district adoptions of the curriculum. Despite drastic modification of the plans and scheduled events during the year, diffusion of the curriculum occurred. Initial foreshadowed problems were reformulated to focus more on cost-benefit and compromise between the state department of education and the local school systems.

Foreshadowed problems are *not* preconceived ideas but a working knowledge of facts, issues, concepts, and theories that guide the decisions during data collection. Qualitative research has an eclectic approach toward the use of theories in a study. In general, theories can influence research questions in two ways: by generating research questions or provide conceptual frameworks in phrasing initial questions. Scholars trained in certain disciplines and their dominant traditions commonly formulate questions that reflect the concepts and assumptions in that discipline. Whether one enters the field with a sociological, psychological, anthropological, policy, or critical perspective, it is important that this be made explicit. Researchers who enter the field with several conceptual frameworks can recognize more easily the events to expand the latent meanings.

Focus of Data Collection Strategies The foreshadowed problems indicate the focus for data collection. This is particularly important for the selection of the site(s) for participant observation and for the selection of participants for in-depth interviews. Foreshadowed problems do *not*, however, restrict the research, because more research questions evolve during the lengthy field work. Excerpt 13.1 illustrates the selection of an urban elementary school to identify specific educational practices of a successful inclusion model, but reformulation of the initial questions lead to focusing on the entire school culture that was supportive of inclusion.

Entry into the Field

Careful analysis of the foreshadowed problems will suggest criteria for site and/or social scene for participant observation. A similar analysis will suggest the profiles of individuals to be sampled for in-depth interviews. We discuss each of these strategies for entrance into the field. In the negotiations to obtain formal permission to conduct qualitative study, the researcher also makes explicit the research role to be assumed for data collection.

EXCERPT 13.1

FORESHADOWED PROBLEMS REFORMULATED

Inclusion of students with disabilities is one of the major school reform movements of this century . . . researchers on inclusion have focused considerably more attention on identifying specific educational practices that contribute to successful inclusion (Hunt & Goetz, 1997) than on exploring the connection between inclusion and school culture.

    This study began in a similar vein, attempting to identify specific educational practices that contribute to the success of a model inclusion program in an urban elementary school, the Connolly Elementary School (pseudonym) in a culturally diverse community. During the year-long process of participant observations, interviews and document review, it became apparent from our data that educational practices were one aspect of a larger school culture that was wholly supportive of inclusion. By identifying the characteristics of this "inclusive school culture," we hope to inform future efforts to implement inclusion programs.

Source: From Zollers, N. J., Ramanathan, A. K., & Yu, M. (1999). The relationship between school culture and inclusion: How an inclusive culture supports inclusive education. *International Journal of Qualitative Studies in Education, 12*(2), 157–174.

Site Selection and Mapping the Field

Choosing a site is a negotiation process to obtain freedom of access to a site that is *suitable* for the research problems and *feasible* for the researcher's resources of time, mobility, and skills. The field researcher usually obtains information in advance through informal channels. Useful information includes the identities, power alignments, and interests of the principal actors; the general history, routines, and social system of the site; and the activities of the site. Information regarding the site and its potential suitability is obtained from a variety of sources: documents, present and prior associates, and public information. Much depends on the researcher's good judgment, timing, and tact in gathering information informally.

After the researcher identifies a possible site, contact is made with a person who can grant permission for the research. Some researchers make a formal contact after informal confirmation that the research proposal will be positively reviewed. Most prepare a brief written statement that specifies the site, the participants and activities, the length of time for the entire study, and the research role. The statement also provides information about the researcher, the sponsor or organizational affiliation, and the general uses of the data, including the protection of the rights of human subjects. Access to the site and the people are crucial at this time. Schatzman and Strauss suggest that "any restrictions initially accepted by the researcher should be regarded as renegotiable at later, more propitious times" (1973, p. 29). Formal authorization is essential for research ethics and for proceeding to enter the field and establish a research role. Once authorization has been granted, the researcher disengages himself or herself from the leadership of the site to map the field, conduct purposeful sampling, and establish a research role.

Qualitative research describes and interprets any subset of context-bound data within the larger context of the site. This characteristic is often referred to as a **holistic emphasis**: subcases of data are related to the total context of the phenomenon studied. Although all that occurs within a setting is a potential source of data, participant observers *cannot and do not need to observe everything*, but they can obtain sufficient data for a holistic emphasis. By using mapping strategies, the researcher gains a sense of the "totality" and is in a better position to do purposeful sampling of information-rich cases.

Mapping the Field   Gaining entry into the field requires establishing good relations with all individuals at the research site. Research permission comes without a guarantee that the participants will behave naturally before an outsider who takes field notes or that the participants will share their perceptions, thoughts, and feelings with the observer. The inquirer's skill is reflected in whether the participants see the researcher as an interested, respectful, nonjudgmental observer who maintains confidentiality, or whether they view the researcher as a rude, disruptive, critical observer who cannot be trusted. The researcher must attend to maintaining the trust and confidentiality of the participants constantly throughout the data collection period (Schumacher,

1984a). The participants at any time may decline to share their perceptions, feelings, and thoughts with the ethnographer.

Mapping the field is acquiring data of the social, spatial, and temporal relationships in the site to gain a sense of the total context. A *social* map notes the numbers and kinds of people, the organizational structure, and the activities people engage in. A *spatial* map notes the locations, the facilities, and the specialized services provided. A *temporal* map describes the rhythm of organizational life, the schedules, and the unwritten routines.

Purposeful Sampling at Site Once researchers have initially mapped the field, they selectively choose persons, situations, and events most likely to yield fruitful data about the evolving research questions. Initially, the researcher searches for information-rich informants, groups, places, or events from which to select subunits for more in-depth study. Remember, purposeful sampling is a strategy to choose small groups or individuals likely to be knowledgeable and informative about the phenomenon of interest (see Chapter 12). Furthermore, most researchers do not know in advance whether potentially information-rich cases will yield valid data until they have completed an interim data analysis. Thus, usually comprehensive sampling is often planned initially, followed by additional strategies.

As new questions emerge during data collection, participant observers change (through additional purposeful sampling) the observation times and locations in order to collect valid data. Excerpt 13.2 illustrates the relationship between problem statement, site selection, research design, and mapping the field in a study of the admissions process of developmentally delayed children for institutionalization consideration.

Field workers view selection and sampling strategies as *dynamic* and *ad hoc* rather than static or *a priori* parameters of populations for a research design. Thus, purposeful sampling is a process conducted simultaneously as one collects data. The specification of the selection criteria and the purposeful sampling strategies chosen are reported in a study to reduce threats to design validity. In addition, the person or groups who actually participated in the study are reported in a manner to protect confidentiality of data.

Selection of Interviewees

Selection of persons for in-depth interviews begins with a description of the desired attributes or profile of persons who would have knowledge of the topic. An attribute is that each person has had a similar experience, such as voluntary resignation from an administrative position, experience with the death of a child, or former participation in a program.

Locating possible interviewees can be done through use of records, an informal network, or nomination. Examples of records are memberships and required registrations, such as application for a program or a special service. When each person does not interact in face-to-face situations with others

EXCERPT 13.2

PROBLEM STATEMENT, SITE SELECTION, RESEARCH DESIGN, MAPPING THE FIELD

I wanted to learn how the people directly affected by and involved in the process of institutional commitment thought about and defined their experience. . . .

The design of the project was to follow those persons, who were admitted to the Weston Center and/or applied for admission or readmission to the Center between January 1 and December 31, 1981. During this period sixteen applications were filed, of which twelve were admitted and four were turned down. A seventeenth person whose application was approved prior to January 1 was admitted to the Center in March, 1981.

Of the total of seventeen, thirteen are included here. One was not included because the family could not be reached for permission. Two others were not included because the families were unwilling to participate. The fourth was not included because by the time the parent was contacted and had agreed to join the project, the collection of data had been completed. . . .

GAINING ACCESS TO THE WESTON CENTER

I approached the Weston Center in December, 1980. During January and February, 1981, their Research Committee reviewed my proposal and developed the guidelines according to which I was to conduct my research. Parents and staff were required to sign "informed consent" forms before I could include them in the study. I was given complete access to the Center and allowed to attend all meetings which I deemed relevant to my project.

Even with this "carte blanche" from the administration, I realized that my entry into the field was dependent on acceptance by staff at all levels of the organization. Consequently, I spent several weeks introducing myself to staff, discussing the project with them, and answering their questions.

Occasionally, ideas brought out at these meetings would prove instrumental to the later success of the study. For example, it was suggested that I be introduced to parents personally by the social worker in charge of the case rather than making my request over the phone or by mail. While there is no way to compare this approach with what would have happened without a personal introduction, it is significant that only two out of sixteen families contacted refused to participate in the study. In addition, no staff person refused me an interview.

Source: From Foster, S. B. (1987). *The Politics of Caring* (London: Falmer Press Ltd.). Reprinted by permission of Falmer Press Ltd. and the author.

known to have similar experiences, snowball sampling is essential (see Chapter 12). Interviewees may also be nominated by reputation such as the "best" teacher or coach.

Researchers screen each potential interviewee by the attribute or profile developed for the study. Only individuals who meet the criteria are interviewed in depth.

Research Role

Field workers choose a **research role**—relationships acquired by and ascribed to the researcher in interactive data collection—-appropriate for the purpose of the study. Possible roles are complete observer, full participant, participant observer, insider-observer, interviewer, and the dual role of participant-researcher (Table 13.1). These roles vary in terms of the way the researcher's presence affects the social system or persons under study. The role of complete observer is that of one who is essentially physically and psychologically absent. An example is that of an observer looking through a one-way window. The role of full participant is similar to that of living through an experience, recalling the experience, and writing personal insights.

The roles of participant-observer or interviewer are the typical research roles for most forms of qualitative inquiry. The field worker in each instance receives permission to create the role for the sole purpose of data collection. The participant-observer obtains permission from the organization or cultural group; field workers then have to establish their research role with each person or group selected for study. In contrast, the interviewer begins to establish the research role in the first contact with the person when requesting an appointment and explaining the purpose and confidentiality. The interviewee selects the time and place for the interview. In phenomenological studies, interviewers may return three or more times to each person to acquire an understanding of the lived experience.

TABLE 13.1

Possible Interactive Research Roles

Role	Description	Use	Research Approach
Complete observer	Researcher is physically and psychologically absent	Inappropriate	Other types of research
Full participant	Researcher lives through an experience and recollects personal insight	Inappropriate	None
Participant-observer	Researcher creates role for purpose of study	Typical role	Ethnography Case study Some Critical Studies
Insider-observer	Researcher has a formal position in organization	Inappropriate	Extremely rare (depends on topic)
Interviewer	Researcher establishes role with each person interviewed	Typical role	Phenomenological Studies Grounded Theory Some Critical Studies
Participant-researcher	Researcher establishes a dual role for purpose of study	Very difficult to do both roles simultaneously	Critical Studies: participatory action research, action inquiry

More questionable roles are those of the insider-observer and the role of participant-researcher. The insider-observer is a person who already has a role in the site in which he or she intends to study. The role (that is, supervisor, counselor, teacher) exists whether or not the study is conducted. Even studies on highly sensitive topics, which probably could not have been done otherwise, have difficulty being accepted as credible research. Some critical studies employ the dual role of participant-researcher. This role is conducted simultaneously and requires the researcher to have constant self-awareness and to be especially conscious about whose voice is being recorded as data. Because the data contain the researcher reflections on his or her experience as well as those of the "real" participants, the dual role researcher must be exceedingly sensitive regarding which voice is represented in the study.

The research role is really many roles, as the field worker acquires language fluency with the participants, interacts to obtain data, establishes social relationships, and moves from role sets appropriate in one group (or person) to different role sets for other groups (or persons). Some degree of participation is usually necessary to develop trust and acceptance of the outsider and for reciprocity. In addition, the research role may vary with the degree of interaction and intensity. For example, in many ethnographic studies, case studies, and grounded theory approach the interactions are quite widespread but the researcher is less intrusive in collecting data. In phenomenological studies, the interaction is more intrusive, close, and personal. Unlike mechanical recording devices, field workers are able to raise additional questions, check out hunches, and move deeper into the analysis of the phenomenon.

Valid data results when the events unfold naturally and participants act in typical fashion in the researcher's presence. Because the research role affects the type of data collected, the primary role and the various roles assumed in data collection are stated in the study. Excerpt 13.3 is an example of both the roles and types of data collection activities done in an ethnographic study.

EXCERPT 13.3

RESEARCH ROLE

Our year-long ethnography employed participant observation, formal and informal interviewing, and document review. . . . Participant observation in the school milieu allowed us to unobtrusively and systematically obtain data and interact socially with informants. . . . We visited the school at least once a week. On the days of our visits, we participated in the school, shadowing the principal, visiting classroooms, and talking to parents and staff in the halls. We observed teachers, students and staff during the regular course of the school day and during special events.

Source: From Zollers, N. J., Ramanathan, A. K., & Yu, M. (1999). The relationship between school culture and inclusion: How an inclusive culture supports inclusive education. *International Journal of Qualitative Studies in Education, 12*(2), 157–174.

Participant Observation

Participant observation is really a combination of particular data collection strategies: limited participation, field observation, interviewing, and artifact collection. Limited participation is necessary to obtain acceptance of the researcher's presence even though she or he is unobtrusive. Field observation is the researcher's technique of directly observing and recording without interaction. Interviewing may be in the form of casual conversations after an event with others, or a more formal interview with one person. Documents and artifacts are collected when available. Typically the researcher uses multiple strategies to corroborate data. Excerpt 13.4 illustrates multimethod strategies.

Decisions regarding data collection strategies are usually revised after site selection, entry into the field, and initial mapping of the field. Initial plans are reviewed and refined. Information originally planned to be obtained by observation may be available primarily through interviewing; preliminary findings from interview data may have to be substantiated through researcher-constructed questionnaires or artifact analysis. Analysis of documents or unexpected events may suggest new directions for observing or interviewing. Choosing data collection strategies is a process of deciding among available alternatives for collection and corroboration of data and of modifying one's decisions to capture the "reality" of the phenomena.

On-Site Participant Observation The most elementary requirement of the methodology is **field residence**, in which the researcher is present in the field or site for an extensive time. Field work is often viewed as a labor-intensive mode of inquiry. Many field studies focus on processes over time and note change. In Excerpt 13.5: Example A, a study of power and caring, the ethnographer spent one full day per week observing Pam's [the teacher's] class during the academic school year. Qualitative researchers typically report the number of days or hours of field residence as in Excerpt 13.5: Example B.

Prolonged Data Collection Data collection continues until the logical termination of naturalistic event or until the situation changes so dramatically that the site is not relevant for the research focus. The natural boundary for data collection may be the entire three-week period of a state-sponsored summer school arts program. The natural boundary for a study of nursing clinical instruction is the length of the rotation, ten weeks. When the examined situation is no longer relevant to the research foci, the field residence terminates. Data collection might end with the unexpected promotion or resignation of a key person, which, of course, would remove him or her from the site.

Intensive Observing and Listening Participant observation enables the researcher to obtain people's perceptions of events and processes expressed in their actions and expressed as feelings, thoughts, and beliefs. These perceptions or

EXCERPT 13.4

MULTIMETHOD STRATEGIES

COLLECTING DATA

Archival
records

As soon as the project was approved, I began data collection. First, I reviewed the clinical histories of the people included in the study as it was described in their case files, as well as general official documents describing the Weston Center and its activities. Records represent a particular understanding of the individuals concerned, embodied in formal identification and description (Biklen, 1978). The purpose of the review of records was to get at this perspective.

Observation

Second, I spent time as an observer at the Weston Center. I sat in on meetings which were relevant to the intake, evaluation, and placement process at the Center. In several cases, these observations extended to living units and classrooms at the Center. Field notes were written at the end of each observation describing in detail the setting and activities of subjects. . . .

Field notes

Other
observations

However, it was not possible to record field notes while conducting observations in other kinds of settings, such as institution living units and department offices. In order to assure the accuracy and detail of these notes, I had to allow several hours for recording notes after leaving the field.

Summary
observations

Drawings in
field notes

Drawings were an important element of the field notes. . . .

Informal
conservation
interviews

In addition to these observations, I interviewed participants in the institutionalization process, including staff from the Center and other social service agencies, and members of the client's family. These interviews were often more like a conversation than a formal interview and took place in a variety of settings, including offices, living rooms, cars, and hallways. The purpose of these interviews was to allow those involved in the institutionalization process to describe in detail their perceptions and interpretations of the experience.

Interview
guide
approach;
taping and
elaborations

I brought a tape recorder on scheduled interviews and, with the respondent's permission, recorded our conversation. However, observational field notes were also recorded for every interview, describing the setting in which the interview took place, the people, and activities. Often these details would prove as important as the interview itself. . . .

Other
conversations

Sometimes, conversations at the beginning or end of meetings yielded very rich data. Once, a social worker whose client had been denied admission stopped me in the hall afterwards to offer her interpretation of the politics involved in the decision. In cases like this, I would usually take the time to write down notes in my car before driving home in order to insure an accurate and detailed recording of the conversation.

Source: From Foster, S. B. (1987). *The Politics of Caring* (London: Falmer Press Ltd.). Reprinted by permission of Falmer Press Ltd. and the author.

EXCERPT 13.5

PROLONGED DATA COLLECTION

EXAMPLE A

I think you also need to know that Pam's [the teacher's] power extended well beyond the classroom. She was one of the opinion makers in the building, was revered by white and African American parents, and was the teacher who assumed change of the school whenever the principal was out of the building. She was reputed to be the most effective teacher in the building . . . I usually spent one full day a week observing her classroom during the 1989-90 school year. In the course of the year, it finally dawned on me just how powerful Pam really was. I had gone from being a full professor of education a major university to being her "oldest student."

EXAMPLE B

TABLE 1　　Data Collection Time in Hours

| | Interviews | | | | | | Observation | | Document Review | |
| | Formal (taped) | | | Informal | | | | | | |
	Teacher/ Staff	Parents	Mr. Knight	Mr. Knight	Staff & Parents	Campus	Off- Campus	Articles/ Evaluation	Student Essays
Frequency	9	4	5	16	5	16	1	20+	38
Total hours	6	3	5	8	8	96	.5		

Source: Example A—From Nolbit, G. W. (1993). Power and caring. *American Educational Research Journal, 30*(1), 23–38; *Example B*—From Zollers, N. J., Ramanathan, A. K., & Yu, M. (1999). The relationship between school culture and inclusion: How an inclusive culture supports inclusive education. *International Journal of Qualitative Studies in Education, 12*(2), 157–174.

constructions take three forms: verbal, nonverbal, and tacit knowledge. It is crucial that the researcher acquire the particular linguistic patterns and language variations of the individuals observed to record and to interact with them. Field observation is an active process which includes *nonverbal cues*—facial expressions, gestures, tone of voice, body movements, and other unverbalized social interactions that suggest the subtle meanings of language. *Tacit knowledge* is personal, intuitive knowledge that is difficult or impossible for the individual to articulate; instead, the person demonstrates this knowledge by actions or by created objects. Some cultures are called expressive because meanings are conveyed more in the nonverbal and tacit modes than in the verbal mode. Participants' stories, anecdotes, and myths—such as are found in the daily gossip in the teachers' lounge or among student groups in hallways—indicate the content of their world and how they perceive their world.

Listening is also a demanding task; researchers listen with all their senses. Listening involves being able to take on the role of the other person, to see the world as the participant does. The field worker listens for the *ises* and *becauses*. The *is* reveals perceptions of things, people, events, and processes that appear real or factual to a person. The *because* reveals the *whys* and *wherefores,* the beliefs, thoughts, feelings, and values—in essence, the logic about the content of a person's perceptions. To listen intently requires the researcher to put aside his or her own thoughts and seek first those of the participants.

Corroborating Field Observations Although the field worker is noninterfering, he or she actively seeks different views of events from different participants for accuracy and for confirmation. By extended observation of different participants in many contexts, the researchers elicits data that are "nearly impossible with other approaches, and he has access to some unique kinds of information" (Wilson, 1977, p. 256). Ethnographers can, for example, corroborate what a participant says in response to a comment or question, to other people, in different situations, or at different times; what the participant actually does; what the participant implies with nonverbal communication, such as tone of voice and body movements; and what he or she perceives others are feeling, saying, or doing about an activity.

The core of seeking and corroborating different perceptions lies in obtaining data from multiple data sources—different persons in different contexts at various times. Multiple data sources can best be illustrated in a study by listing the strategies, participants, situations, or organizations. Table 13.2 illustrates the multiple data sources in a study of interagency curriculum development.

In seeking to corroborate data, researchers frequently discover discrepancies between what people say and what people do in their observed actions.

TABLE 13.2

Multiple Data Sources

Multiple methods	Observation
	Casual conversations
	Focused interviews
	Documents: project proposals, social studies policy statements, state survey, unit outlines, PERT planning charts, director's journal
Multiple participants	State department officials
	School division central office personnel
	Curriculum specialist
	Director
	Principal and teachers
	Visiting monitoring team
Multiple situations	Project planning council meetings
	Summer workshop
	Teacher writing team meetings
	University curriculum resource center
	State department conferences

Source: Adapted from Schumacher, S. (1979). *Ethnographic inquiry: Theory and application in educational research and evaluation.* (Richmond, VA: Virginia Commonwealth University). (ERIC Document Reproduction Service No. ED 184 108), p. 11.

Participant observation allows corroboration between what individuals think they are doing and what the researcher thinks they are doing based on data.

Salient Field Observations Because the interactive social scene is too complex and too subtle to observe or record everything, the researcher does *not* seek to capture everything that happens. Field workers rely on the prolonged field residences to develop skills in deciding what should be included and what can be excluded. Researchers observe and record the phenomena salient to the foreshadowed problems, their broader conceptual frameworks, and the contextual features of the interactions. These elements explain the diversity of field notes cited in ethnographies despite the commonalities on the methodology.

What do field workers observe? Most record descriptive details about *who, what, where, how,* and *why* an activity or social scene occurred. This information then can be used to obtain more subtle information. See Table 13.3 for a

TABLE 13.3

Participant Observation Grid

Observation	Description
1. *Who* is in the group or scene?	How many people are present; what are their kinds or identities? How is membership in the group or scene acquired?
2. *What* is happening here?	What are the people in the group or scene doing and saying to one another?
a. *What* behaviors are repetitive and irregular?	In what events, activities, or routines are people engaged? How are activities organized, labeled, explained, and justified?
b. *How* do the people in the group behave toward one another?	How do people organize themselves, or relate to one another? What statuses and roles are evident? Who makes what decisions for whom?
c. *What* is the content of their conversations?	What topics are common and rare? What languages do they use for verbal and nonverbal communication? What beliefs do the content of their conversations illustrate? What formats and processes do the conversations follow? Who talks and who listens?
3. *Where* is the group or scene located?	What physical settings form their contexts? What natural resources and technologies are created or used? How does the group allocate and use space and physical objects? What sights, sounds, smells, tastes, and feelings are found in the group contexts?
4. *When* does the group meet and interact?	How often and how long are these meetings? How does the group conceptualize, use, and distribute time? How do participants view their past and future?
5. *How* do the identified elements interrelate—from either the participants' or the researcher's perspective?	How is stability maintained? How does change originate, and how is it managed? What rules, norms, or mores govern this social organization? How is this group related to other groups, organizations, or institutions?
6. *Why* does the group operate as it does?	What meanings do participants attribute to what they do? What symbols, traditions, values, and world views can be found in the group?

participant observation grid. Although no one addresses all these questions at once in studying a group scene, the framework does indicate major areas of observation foci.[1]

Field Notes and Reflex Records

Data are recorded as **field notes**, observations of what occurs while the researcher is in the field. Field notes are dated and the context is identified. The notes are often filled with idiosyncratic abbreviations and are difficult for others to read without editing. Researchers record detailed descriptive fields that are not vague or judgmental. Below are hypothetical examples of vague notes contrasted to the actual field notes in a study of adult beginning readers (Boraks & Schumacher, 1981, pp. 76, 86).

Vague Notes	Descriptive Notes
1. Bea misreads wood for would.	"(OBS: Intensity of Bea is demonstrated by her heavy breathing, even swearing during the reading. There is little doubt she is trying hard.) Sometimes she cues herself, when reading: 'Would you believe I would not do it again,' Bea read would as wood. The tutor says would. Bea tries again to reread, then says, 'Oh, I missed the point, would he.'"
2. June retells few parts of a story and only the parts which relate to herself. She elaborates on these parts.	"June is a tall, thin, talkative woman. A staff member said she was referred by a treatment center and was considered mentally retarded and emotionally disturbed. When asked to tell a story from the text cue, she had to be prompted. For example, her story about an accident:
	June: 'My hair caught on fire.'
	Tutor: 'How did your hair catch fire? Can you tell me more?'
	June: 'I was smoking a cigarette and my lighter went up. I had the lighter close to my ear and it carried to my hair and my whole head was in flames.'
	Tutor: 'Can you tell me anything more?'
	June: 'And they told me I looked like a Christmas tree all lit up.'"

Reflex records, written immediately after leaving the site, synthesize the main interactions and scenes observed and, more important, assess the quality of the data, suggest questions and tentative interpretations. In both the field notes and reflex records, the tentative interpretations, are separated from the actual observations (data). Sometimes these insights have the quality of free associations: they may cite analogies, use metaphors and similes, or note theories and literature that may be useful in subsequent data analysis.

Part of the reflex records typically is the researcher's critical self-monitoring for potential biases. Often stated as "Self in Research" in the study, the researcher reports biographical sources of subjectivity and strategies to minimize the influence on data collection and analysis. (See Excerpt 13.6.)

---

[1]See observation grids of Hall, 1959 and Spradley, 1979.

EXCERPT 13.6

REFLEX NOTES: SELF IN RESEARCH

Like many other qualitatively oriented researchers, we view the research act as one that is far from value free. . . . We view our subjectivity as "a garment that cannot be removed" (Peshkin 1988:17). Rather than make a futile attempt to eliminate this subjectivity, Horvat engaged in a "formal systematic monitoring of self" throughout the course of the data collection which enabled her to manage her own subjectivity. . . . To this end she wrote self-reflective memos, shared manuscripts of analyzed data with study participants, and discussed emerging themes with colleagues familiar with the project.

Moreover we believe that our backgrounds shape our roles as researchers. Horvat is a married white woman in her early thirties who grew up in California in a small city not too far from the area where this research was conducted. She comes from a privileged background similar to that of the two or three of the most economically privileged Hadley students in the study, . . . he attended a private secondary school similar to Hadley. The second author . . . is a Filipino male who was raised by immigrant parents. . . . Socioeconomically, his upbringing is somewhat dissimilar from that of the majority of the informants in the study. . . . As research collaborators, we took advantage of our different backgrounds by actively engaging each other with challenges to possible biases. . . .

Source: From Horvat, E. M., & Antonio, A. (1999). Hey, those shoes are out of uniform: African American girls in an elite high school and the importance of habitus. *Anthropology & Education Quarterly, 30*(3), 317–342.

In-Depth Interviews

In-depth interviews are open-response questions to obtain data of *participant meanings*—how individuals conceive of their world and how they explain or "make sense" of the important events in their lives. Interviews may be the primary data collection strategy or a natural outgrowth of observation strategies. Field interviews vary in formats, specialized applications, question content, question sequence, and the logistics of conducting and recording interviews.

Types of Interviews and Specialized Applications Qualitative interviews may take several forms: the informal conversational interview, the interview guide approach, and the standardized open-ended interview. These forms all vary in their degree of structure and planning and the comparability of responses in data analysis. In the **informal conversation interview**, the questions emerge from the immediate context and are asked in the natural course of events; there is no predetermination of question topics or phrasing. Informal conversations

TABLE 13.4

Types of Interviews

Type of Interview	Description
Informal conversation	Questions emerge from the immediate context. There are no predetermined topics or wording.
Interview guide	Topics are outlined in advance. Researcher decides the sequence and wording during the interview. Interview probes can increase comprehensiveness.
Standardized open-ended	The exact wording and sequence of questions are predetermined. Questions are completely open-ended.

are an integral part of participant observation. In the **interview guide approach**, topics are selected in advance but the researcher decides the sequence and wording of the questions during the interview. Both the informal conversation and the interview guide approach are relatively conversational and situational. In the **standardized open-ended interview**, participants are asked the same questions in the same order, thus reducing interviewer flexibility; however, standardized wording of questions may constrain and limit the naturalness and relevancy of the response (Table 13.4).

Selection of the interview strategy depends on the context and purpose: (1) to obtain the present perceptions of activities, roles, feelings, motivations, concerns, and thoughts; (2) to obtain future expectations or anticipated experiences; (3) to verify and extend information obtained from other sources; and (4) to verify or extend hunches and ideas developed by the participants or researcher.

Specialized applications of the interview strategy are key-informant interviews, career and life-history interviews, elite interviews, and phenomenological interviews. **Key-informant interviews** are in-depth interviews of individuals who have special knowledge, status, or communication skills that they are willing to share with the researcher. They are usually chosen because they have access to observations unavailable to the ethnographer. They are often atypical individuals and must be selected carefully from among possible key informants.[2]

Career and life history interviews, which elicit life narratives of individuals, are used by anthropologists to obtain data about a culture. Educational ethnographers use this interview technique for career histories or narratives of professional lives. For example, when an examination of female elementary school teachers' notion of career differed from the prior research of men's careers, the researcher suggested that the concept of career should be extended to encompass professional women (Biklen, 1985). Career and life history research of educators frequently requires two- to seven-hour interviews and

_____

[2]See J. P. Spradley (1979), *The Ethnographic Interview,* for a detailed discussion of key-informant interviews.

may take considerable time to locate the informants if the shared social experience occurred years ago.

Elite interviews are a special application of interviewing that focus on persons considered to be influential, prominent, and well informed in an organization or a community. Elites are usually familiar with the overall view of the organization, its relations to other organizations, and especially the legal and financial structure of the organization. The researcher must rely on sponsorship, recommendations, and introductions to obtain appointments with elites. Frequently, elites prefer a more active interplay with the interviewer, and much variation will occur in the degree of interview control. Elites respond well to inquiries in broad areas of content and to provocative, intelligent questions that allow them freedom to use their knowledge. Elites often contribute insights and meaning because they are comfortable in the realm of ideas, policies, and generalizations.[3]

Phenomenological interviews are a specific type of in-depth interview used to study the meanings or essence of a lived experience among selected participants. The strategy may be a single long comprehensive interview with each person or three separate interviews with each of the individuals.[4] Phenomenological studies investigate what was experienced, how it was experienced, and finally the meanings that the interviewees assign to the experience. The experience studied is usually something that has affected the individual significantly, such as recalling a teenage pregnancy, childhood incest, or acquiring a physical handicap. Before interviewing, the researcher writes a full description of their own experience with the phenomenon of interest. Phenomenological interviews permit an explicit focus on the researcher's personal experience combined with the experiences of the interviewees. Educators frequently apply phenomenological interviewing in a general manner to obtain the multiple meanings of an experience.

Qualitative Questions, Probes, and Pauses Question content varies because of different research purposes and problems, theoretical frameworks, and the selection of participants. Adopting questions from prior research will probably *not* produce valid interview data; however, the examination of different alternatives is essential in interview script construction.[5] Interview questions can focus on experience or behavior, opinions and values, feelings, knowledge, sensory perceptions, and the individual's background or demographic information (Table 13.5). Each of these question topics can be phrased in a present, past, or future time frame.

---

[3]See L. Dexter (1970), *Elite and specialized interviewing* and R. Gorden (1981), *Interviewing: strategies, techniques, and tactics.*

[4]See Moustakas (1994) and Seidman (1998).

[5]See Denzin, 1978; Lofland & Lofland, 1984; Patton, 1990; Pelto & Pelto, 1978; Schatzman & Strauss, 1973; Spradley, 1979.

TABLE 13.5

*Types of Interview Questions**

Type	Description and Illustration
Experience/behavior	To elicit what a person does or has done—descriptions of experiences, behaviors, actions, activities during the ethnographer's absence: "If I had been here that day, what experiences would I see you having?"
Opinions/values	To elicit what the person thinks about their experiences, which can reveal a person's intentions, goals, and values: "What would you like to see happen or what do you believe about . . . ?"
Feelings	To elicit how the persons reacts emotionally to their experiences: "Do you feel anxious, happy, afraid, intimidated, confident about . . . ?"
Knowledge	To elicit factual information the person has or what the person considers as factual: "Tell me what you know about. . . ."
Sensory	To elicit the person's descriptions of what and how they see, hear, touch, taste, and smell in the world around them: "What does the counselor ask you when you walk into her office? How does she actually greet you?"
Background/demographic	To elicit the person's descriptions of themselves to aid the researcher in identifying and locating the persons in relation to other people: Routine information on age, education, occupation, residence/mobility, and the like.

*May be phrased in past, present, or future tense. See Patton (1990).

Qualitative interviewing requires asking truly open-ended questions. Novice researchers often begin with what data they want to obtain and phrase questions in a manner that enables interviewees to infer the desired responses. These are *dichotomous-response questions,* which elicit a yes/no answer or short phrases as a response. When these occur, the interview assumes an interrogative rather than a conversational tone.

Qualitative in-depth interviews are noted more for their probes and pauses than for their particular question formats. Establishing trust, being genuine, maintaining eye contact, and conveying through phrasing, cadence, and voice tone that the researcher "hears" and connects with the person elicit more valid data than a rigid approach. In Excerpt 13.7, questions 1 through 3 were used to gather information and to establish rapport with inner city mothers in an infant intervention program. Questions 4, 5, and 6 often were collapsed into one topic by some mothers; for other mothers, the different question wording provided a conduit to different information. After a series of interviews, researchers usually feel at ease in adjusting the interview to each person.

Techniques to ensure good qualitative questions are interview script critiques by experienced interviewers, interview guide field-testing, and revision of initial questions for final phraseology. Below are examples of initial phrasing

EXCERPT 13.7

INTERVIEW PROTOCOL WITH ALTERNATIVE QUESTIONS AND PROBES

1. Tell me about how you found out about the _____ infant program.
   Alternative Questions and Probes
   Who told you about the infant program?
   How did you get hooked up with the program?
   Where did you find out about the program?

   . . .

4. What type of services did your son/daughter and your family receive from the infant program?
   How was it decided that your daughter/son and your family would receive those services?
   Alternative Questions and Probes
   What did the infant program do for you (with you)?
   What did the infant program do for your son/daughter?
   What did the infant program do for your family?
   Who decided what the infant program would do for you?
   Were you involved in deciding what the infant program would do?
   Were other members of your family involved in that decision?
   Did you feel like your wants were listened to?

5. What type of control or input did(do) you feel you had(have) about the services you receive(ed)?
   Alternative Questions and Probes
   Who made the decisions about what the infant program would do for you?
   Did you feel like you could make decisions about the services the infant program provided?
   Did what you wanted from the program make a difference? How?/ How not?
   Was your child yours or the infant program's when the staff were working with him/her?

6. What was helpful about the services your child and family received from the _____ infant program?
   Extensions/Probes
   How did the program do these things?
   Who did these things?
   Who decided to do these things?

Note: Often questions #4, #5, and #6 were collapsed into one question from which the same information was collected. However, for some parents, the different wording of the questions provided a conduit to different information.

Source: From Gamel-McCormick, M. T. (1991). *Talking, teaching, and telling.* Unpublished evaluation report. Virginia Commonwealth University: School of Education, Richmond. Appendix B.

with the field-test responses and the final phrasing of an interview guide (Schumacher, Esham, & Bauer, 1985, pp. 150–153).

Initial Dichotomous-Response Questions	Final Qualitative Questions
Q: Did teachers have difficulty in seminars? *R:* Yes.	*Q:* What did you expect teachers to have difficulties with in the seminar?
Q: Did teachers change? *R:* Some of them did.	*Q:* How did participation in the seminar affect the teachers?
Q: Did you learn anything in teaching the seminars? *R:* Yes.	*Q:* What did you learn about the teaching strategies you presented to this group?
Q: Did you identify any problems the Planning Committee should address? *R:* Yes.	*Q:* What would you like to see the Planning Committee do?

Although the above is an extreme example of responses to initial dichotomous-response questions, it is obvious that the qualitative questions would (and did) generate different data, revealing multiple meanings of the seminars.

Dichotomous-response questions can be *leading questions,* which imply a preferred response. Leading questions may frame a "devil's advocate" or a *pre-supposition question,* a query that implies a deliberate assumption designed to provoke a complex or elaborate response. Examples in the left column are dichotomous-response lead-in questions that were rephrased as presupposition lead-in questions in the right column (Schumacher, 1984b, pp. 75–82).

Dichotomous-Response Lead-in Questions	Presupposition Lead-in Questions
Were inservice teachers enthusiastic about taking a class after school hours?	"What were the most difficult aspects [of the program] to implement?" (Presupposition: many difficulties.)
Did you expect the teachers to be different from from having participated in the seminars?	"How did you expect the teachers to be different from having participated in the seminars?" (Presupposition: there was an immediate change.)
Do you know of any unexpected results or spill-effects?	"How did the Planning Committee handle un-anticipated opportunities?" (Presupposition: there were unexpected opportunities.)

Some researchers emphasize the general ineffectiveness of questions preceded with the interrogative *why. Why* questions are usually assumptive, frequently ambiguous, and often too abstract to elicit concrete data. In some situations, however, beginning with the interrogative *why* enables the researcher to elicit cause-and-effect processes or relationships which are potentially informative by revealing assumptions of the person.

Question Sequence Effective interviewing depends on efficient probing and sequencing of questions. Guidelines are suggested below.

1. *Interview probes* elicit elaboration of detail, further explanations, and clarification of responses. Well-designed interview scripts are field tested to

identify the placement and wording of probes necessary to adjust topics to the variation in individuals' responses. Broad questions are often phrased more specifically as probes. An illustration is found in Excerpt 13.7 an interview protocol for parents who had enrolled their child in an early-intervention services program. Researchers should talk less than the respondent; the cues respondents need can usually be reduced to a few words during the interview.

2. *Statements of the researcher's purpose and focus* are usually made at the outset. Assurances of protection of the person's identity and an overview of the possible discussion topics are given at this time. The information communicated is the importance of the data, the reasons for that importance, and the willingness of the interviewer to explain the purpose of the interview in respect for the interviewee. Researchers provide explanations or shifts in the interview focus for informants to adapt their thinking along new areas.

3. *Order of questions* varies, although most researchers make choices to enable them to obtain adequate data for each question from the informant efficiently. Rigid sequencing may ensure comprehensiveness, but it may also produce both informant and interviewer fatigue and boredom. Generally questions are grouped by topic, but in many instances, interviewers ignore the script sequence as people voluntarily elaborate on earlier replies.

4. *Demographic questions* may be spread throughout the interview or presented in the concluding remarks. Some researchers prefer to obtain this data at the beginning of the interview to establish rapport and focus attention.

5. *Complex, controversial, or difficult questions* are usually reserved for the middle or later periods in the interview when the informant's interest has been aroused. Some interviewers prefer to begin interviews with descriptive, present-oriented questions and move to more complex issues of beliefs and explanations.

Interview Logistics Ethnographers choose interview topics and questions while planning the general logistics that influence an interview session. Five contingencies that affect an interview session are (1) *duration*, or length of session; (2) *number*, or how many separate interviews are required to obtain the data; (3) *setting*, or location of the interview; (4) *identity of the individuals* involved and the number present in the session; and (5) *informant styles*, or communication mores of the interviewees. Some research designs plan for periodically scheduled interviews and other designs require interviewing only after important events.

Interviewers vary their interactive styles. Interactive modes can be adversarial, emotionally neutral but cognitively sophisticated, or empathetic. Specific techniques can be used for pacing, keeping control of the interview, and appropriate use of support and recognition. Most qualitative interviewers prefer a conversational tone to indicate empathy and understanding while conveying acceptance to encourage elaboration of subtle and valid data.

Interview Records, Transcripts, and Elaborations The primary data of qualitative interviews are verbatim accounts of what transpires in the interview session.

Tape recording the interview ensures completeness of the verbal interaction and provides material for reliability checks. These advantages are offset by possible respondent distrust and mechanical failure. The use of a tape recorder does *not* eliminate the need for taking notes to help reformulate questions and probes and to record nonverbal communication, which facilitates data analysis. In many situations, handwritten notes may be the best method of recording. Interviewer-recording forces the interviewer to be attentive, can help pace the interview, and legitimizes the writing of research insights (beginning data analysis) during the interview. Neither note-taking nor tape recording, however, should interfere with the researcher's full attention on the person.

Immediately following the interview, the researcher completes and types the handwritten records, or transcribes the tape. Typed drafts will need to be edited for transcriber/typist error and put into final form. The final record contains accurate verbatim data and the interviewer's notation of nonverbal communication with initial insights and comments to enhance the search for meaning. Interviewer notations and comments are usually identified by the interviewer's initials. The final form also includes the date, place, and informant identity or code. Excerpt 13.8 illustrates data obtained from in-depth interviews.

EXCERPT 13.8

INTERVIEW TRANSCRIPTS—SELECTED QUOTATIONS

[Principals' experience with shared governance in their schools]

* *You always wonder if you're really needed. You think, "Well, do they really need me here, or do they even want me here?" A lot of times you start to question, Could this place just run without me? Then a parent calls, one who wouldn't talk with the teacher anymore, and I know I'm needed.*

* *I don't think the teachers always realize how much they need me; sometimes they think that if I was out of the picture, they wouldn't have all these limitations. Now I have more of a community relations role, and I spend more time on community involvement . . .*

* *I'm growing. Learning to become more of a partner, learning to become more democratic. I'm certainly not there yet. You get a lot more accomplished working with a group than trying to work by yourself . . .*

* *Because I'm not controlling everything, the school is actually in better control than it ever was. We talk about all being . . . in this together. There's more power to share, not less . . .*

* *Personally and professionally, [shared governance] has given me a great sense of satisfaction. I like watching people grow. I like to be on the cutting edge, in uncharted territory. When you have shared governance, you move forward on instructional matters and curriculum.*

Source: From Blase, J. & Blase, J. (1999). Shared governance principals: The inner experience (pp. 83, 85). *NASSP Bulletin, 83*(606), 81–90.

Researchers write **interview elaborations** of each interview session—self-reflections on his or her role and rapport, interviewee's reactions, additional information, and extensions of interview meanings. This activity is a critical time for reflection and elaboration to establish quality control for valid data. Many initial ideas developed at this time are subsequently checked out through other data collection activities. As a rule of thumb, for every hour of interviewing, a researcher usually allows four hours of further work to obtain the final record or transcript and the additional elaborations.

Documents and Artifact Collection

Artifact collection is a noninteractive strategy for obtaining qualitative data with little or no reciprocity between the researcher and the participant. Artifact collection is less reactive than interactive strategies in that the researcher does not extract the evidence. During field residence in school settings, for example, ethnographers must interact with individuals—even if only nonverbally—and become, to some degree, participants. This is *not* an impediment if the researcher notes the consequences of this interactive role. In contrast, artifact collection strategies are noninteractive but may require imaginative field work to locate relevant data.

Artifact collections are tangible manifestations that describe peoples' experience, knowledge, actions, and values. Qualitative researchers studying current groups have adopted the techniques of historians who analyze documents (see Chapter 15) and of archaeologists who examine objects created by ancient peoples.

Types of Artifacts

Artifacts of present-day groups and educational institutions may take four forms: personal documents, official documents, objects, and erosion measures (Table 13.6).

Personal Documents Personal documents are any first-person narrative that describes an individuals' actions, experiences, and beliefs. Personal documents include diaries, personal letters, and anecdotal records. These documents are usually discovered by the researcher, but sometimes an ethnographer will ask a participant to make anecdotal records such as a log, a journal, notes on lessons plans, or a parent's development record of a child. Documents can surface during an interview or participant observation.

Official Documents Official documents are abundant in an organization and take many forms. Memos, minutes of meetings, working papers, and drafts of proposals are *informal* documents that provide an internal perspective of the

TABLE 13.6

Documents and Artifact Collections

Type	Examples	Used for
Personal documents	Diaries Personal letters Anecdotal records	Personal perspective
Official documents	Internal papers	Informal or official perspective within the organization
	External communication	Official perspective for the public
	Student records and personnel files	Institutional perspective on child or employee
	Statistical data (enumeration)	Suggests trends, raises questions, corroborates qualitative findings, describes rituals and values
Objects	Symbols	Suggests social meanings and values
	Objects	Suggests social meanings and values

organization. These documents describe functions and values and how various people define the organization. Internal documents can show the official chain of command and provide clues about leadership style and values. Documents used for *external communication* are those produced for public consumption: newsletters, program brochures, school board reports, public statements, and news releases. These documents suggest the official perspective on a topic, issue, or process. School board minutes from 1915 to 1980, for example, were an important source in the study of an innovative school fifteen years after an ethnographic study and the original job applications of the school staff provided demographic clues to locate these persons for interviews.

Existing archival and demographic collections may be located during field residence and are usually readily available to the researcher. Institutions also keep individual records on each student and employee; in order to gain access to these, parental, student, or employee permission is usually required. *Student and personnel files* can become quite elaborate over time and may contain a variety of records and reports. A student's file may have records of testing, attendance, anecdotal comments from teachers, information from other agencies, and a family profile. Researchers use a file not so much for what it tells about the student but rather for what the file suggests about the people who make the records. The file represents different perspectives (psychologists', teachers', counselor's, administrator's) on the student.

Statistical data can be demographic information about a group or population, dropout rates, achievement scores, number of acts of violence and suspension, attendance records, numbers of student handicapping conditions, student eligibility lists for certain federal programs, the number of athletic injuries, and other numerical computations. Qualitative researchers use statistical data several ways: (1) to suggest trends, (2) to propose new questions, or (3) to corroborate qualitative data. Qualitative researchers are more interested in what the statistics tell about the assumptions of the people who use and compile the data—how statistics reveal people's thinking and common-sense understandings. Routinely produced numerical data describe the rituals and social values of an organization. Field workers seldom take statistical data at face value, but question the social process that produced the data and how the data are used.

Objects Objects are created symbols and tangible entities that reveal social processes, meanings, and values. Examples of symbols are logos and mascots of school, teams, and clubs; examples of objects are athletic letters and trophies, diplomas, posters, and award plaques. In a study of institutional collaboration, a symbolic record was a newly created logo that combined parts of the emblems of the university and of the school system to represent a new relationship between the two organizations. Interactive data revealed the difficulties surmounted to obtain official approval to use institutional emblems in a new form. The data obtained the following year described the use of the new logo. Qualitative researchers may investigate teachers' value of student's work by periodically checking bulletin board displays in elementary classrooms and corroborate this finding with other field data.

Analysis and Interpretation of Artifact Collections

Collection and analysis of artifacts requires five strategies:

1. *Location of artifacts* begins with entering the field and continues for the duration of the study. Researchers anticipate the artifacts and proceed to locate and obtain documents and objects. Participants also offer documents and artifacts.
2. *Identification of artifacts* requires placing the artifact in retrievable form and cataloguing for access. Documents are photocopied; objects are photographed, filmed, or taped. Identifications are made by noting the category of artifact, a brief description of the artifact, a history of its use and owners/successors, and data on frequency and representativeness.
3. *Analysis of artifacts* requires descriptive data about the production or acquisition of the artifact by the group. Important questions are who uses it, how is it used, where is it used, and the purpose of its use.
4. *Criticism of artifacts* is the determination of its authenticity and accuracy to identify the meanings of the artifact in the social setting.
5. *Interpretation of artifact meanings* must then be corroborated with observation and interview data. Artifact interpretation for subtle meanings depends on the social context and other data.

Field Observations and Supplementary Techniques

A technique fundamental to all qualitative research is field observation—direct, eye-witness accounts of everyday social action and settings taking the form of field notes. A variety of supplementary techniques are also employed in most studies. Supplementary techniques are those selected to help interpret, elaborate or corroborate data obtained from participant observation, in-depth interview, documents and artifacts.

Field Observation

Qualitative field observations are detailed descriptive recordings as field notes of events, people, actions, and objects in settings. Field observation is an integral part of participant observation and in-depth interviewing. In the former, the researcher relies on careful observation as he or she initially explores several areas of interest at a site, searching for patterns of behavior and relationships. In some social scenes, the participant observer collects the data entirely by observing the scene as it occurs such as a class lesson or a board meeting. The interviewer also makes field records which notes non-verbal interviewee body language and facial expressions to help interpret the verbal data. Field records include descriptions of the context of the interview—in an office, in a restaurant, a home, or other setting.

Supplementary Techniques

Supplementary techniques include visual techniques, analysis of non-verbal communication, erosion measures, special surveys, and focus groups. Each of these are separate, specialized methods with methodological literature. The qualitative researcher, however, selectively uses them as a generalist to corroborate initial findings or to raise additional questions.

Visual techniques   Visual techniques include films and photographs of a current social scene. Film is especially useful for validation. Films document nonverbal behavior and communication and can be a permanent record. Films also can be problematic in interpreting. One must consider the technical intrusion, the selective lens view, and the expense.

Analysis of nonverbal communication   The analysis of nonverbal communication is very important in most qualitative studies. The study of body motion and its messages is called *kinesics*. The recording of facial expressions, gestures, and movements can be triangulated with verbal data. An interviewer would trust the responses more if the body language was congruent with the verbal statements. However, many gestures have different meanings in different cultures.

The study of the people's use of space and its relationship to culture is called *proxemics*.[6] Studies have been conducted on the use of interpersonal space in public places and the identification of territorial customs of certain cultures. Qualitative researchers may note how others react to space and invasion of privacy (personal territory) in assigned classroom seats, crowded work areas, and selecting seats in a formal meeting. Caution must be used in interpreting non-verbal communication because such data should be interpreted with other data.

Erosion measures Erosion measures indicate the degree of selective wear on some material by a group. Examples of erosion measures are the pathways students make across outside grounds or the wear of vinyl tiles in specific hallways as suggestive of frequency of use and possible social gatherings. Although erosion is the measure, the interpretation of the erosion rate derives from a check with the records of ground and building maintenance for grass reseeding and tile replacement during recent years.

Special Surveys Survey instruments may take the form of confirmation-surveys, participant-constructed instruments, and even projective techniques with photographs, drawings, and games. Data on preservice teacher induction activities, obtained through nine months of participant observation, for example, could be corroborated with a questionnaire administered to principals and participant-constructed instruments administered during planning retreats and workshops (Schumacher & Esham, 1986).

Focus Groups A variation of an interview is the *focus group interview* (FGI), a strategy for obtaining a better understanding of a problem or an assessment of a problem, concern, new product, program, or idea by interviewing a purposefully sampled group of people rather than each person individually. By creating a social environment in which group members are stimulated by the perceptions and ideas of each other, one can increase the quality and richness of data through a more efficient strategy than one-on-one interviewing.[7] Participant observers and in-depth interviewers use focus groups as a confirmation techniques. Case study research and critical studies may use focus groups as one of several techniques.

The addition of supplementary techniques to a study can increase the validity of the initial findings and the credibility of the entire study. However, most qualitative researchers are not formally trained in each method and should not use the method exclusively for their data.

---

[6]See E. T. Hall, 1959, 1966, 1974.

[7]FGIs are used primarily in evaluation and policy studies, however sociologists originally developed the approach (Lofland, 1984; Schatzman & Strauss, 1973). FGI is often done in marketing research and to some extent in health care services. See Morgan (1997).

Standards of Adequacy for Qualitative Strategies

Many qualitative studies are published as books or reports rather than as journal articles. With the increasing acceptance of the methodology, more journals are publishing qualitative manuscripts. Studies published in journals are highly synthesized, or only one of the many findings is reported to fit the journal format. The typical journal article may also reduce the methodological procedures that should be explicit in the full study. The following questions will aid a reader:

Entry into the Field

1. Did the foreshadowed research problem provide sufficient selection criteria for the site to be observed or suggest a profile for individuals to be interviewed?
2. Is the research role assumed clearly articulated and appropriate for the research questions?
3. How did the researcher's role affect data collection? How does the researcher address her or his potential influence?

Participant Observation

1. Is the rationale for the purposeful sampling choices made during the field work reasonable?
2. How were the multiple strategies employed in data collection—-what was the primary method and which were employed to corroborate data?
3. Was the length of data collection at the site detailed and reasonable?
4. Are descriptive field notes presented as data? Is there evidence of a reflex record?

In-depth Interviewing

1. Is the purposeful sampling strategies to obtained interviewees described and reasonable?
2. Was each person screened by the attribute or profile developed for the study before proceeding with the interview?
3. Was the type of interview selected appropriate for the research problem?
4. Does the data presented indicate appropriate interview questions and probes?

Supplementary Techniques

1. Were the supplementary techniques employed appropriate for the study and did they yield valid data?

Summary

The following statements summarize the major characteristics of qualitative strategies:

1. Data collection is the use of multimethod strategies, but a primary method, such as participant observation or in-depth interviews, is selected for the study.
2. Foreshadowed problems state the initial focus and conceptual frameworks; they guide the field work but do not limit observations, because other research foci may develop at the site.
3. Foreshadowed problems are reformulated during data collection.
4. Site selection is guided by the criteria implied in the foreshadowed problems and concerns of suitability and feasibility.
5. The participant observer first maps the field to obtain a sense of the total context and to ensure purposeful sampling, thereby gaining a selection of information-rich informants and social scenes.
6. Participant observation is a prolonged field residence that obtains and corroborates salient observations of different perspectives recorded as field notes and reflex records.
7. In-depth interviews vary in format, the kinds of questions posed, question sequence, and interview logistics.
8. Interview records are field notes, tape recordings, transcripts, and interview elaborations.
9. Artifact collections are personal documents, official documents, and objects, and must be corroborated with other evidence.
10. Supplementary techniques are used to verify data collected by participant observation or in-depth interviews; they may be visual techniques, non-verbal communication records, erosion measures, specialized surveys, and focus groups.

Self-Instructional Review Items

Sample answers are in the back of the book.

Test items

1. Selection of qualitative strategies begins with an analysis of
   a. foreshadowed research problems and questions.
   b. a research hypothesis.
   c. a list of variables.
   d. a statistical hypothesis.
2. A statement of foreshadowed problems indicates that the researcher will
   a. adhere rigidly to these preconceived ideas.
   b. observe only those problems anticipated.
   c. reformulate these problems during data collection.
   d. test theories for verification studies.

3. Entry into the field is guided by
   a. probability sampling.
   b. an analysis of the foreshadowed problems.
   c. seeking friends to interview.
   d. the need to obtain a holistic portrayal of the larger social context.
4. Which of the following is an inappropriate research role?
   a. participant observer
   b. interviewer
   c. dual role of participant and researcher
   d. complete observer or full participant
5. Data collection strategies include
   a. participant observation.
   b. in-depth interviews.
   c. documents and artifact collection.
   d. all of the above and supplementary techniques.
6. Participant observation requires descriptions of
   a. who is in the group or social scene.
   b. when and where the social scene occurs.
   c. how the group operates.
   d. all of the above.
7. In-depth interviews are usually
   a. informal conversation interviews.
   b. interview guide interviews.
   c. standardized open-response interviews.
   d. closed response interviews.
8. In-depth interviewers
   a. always tape record the interview sessions.
   b. seldom field test the interview protocol.
   c. avoid alternative questions and probes.
   d. write interview elaborations of each interview.
9. In-depth interviews
   a. are similar to interrogations
   b. encourage interviewee participation with pauses and probes
   c. adhere to rigid question sequence
   d. use dichotomous response questions
10. Documents and artifacts
   a. are useful for verifying other data
   b. is limited to personal documents
   c. are data accepted at face value.
   d. are seldom available.

Application Problems

Answer the questions for each methodological problem.

1. A superintendent asked a researcher to observe how one elementary school implemented a new science curriculum to decide whether other schools

should use the curriculum. The researcher easily established rapport with the science supervisor and the principal and observed the curriculum of five of the six teachers. The sixth teacher, who seemed to oppose the innovation, only related her experiences with the new curriculum. This teacher skillfully managed to avoid teaching the curriculum when the investigator was present. What should the researcher do?

2. A researcher is living in a student dormitory in order to study how high school students attending a state summer school program develop creativity through photography. Although the researcher originally thought observation of the photography classes and the evening program would be sufficient, she found that student social activities during free time and extracurricular activities on the weekends influenced students' photographic productions. Should the researcher observe and record these informal happenings? Would student products—photographs—be a useful source of data?

3. During data collection, an adult education program director overhears the negative remarks made by some adults and sees the researcher recording these remarks. The director explains to the researcher that such remarks, if made public, could create a poor image for the program. The director asks the those particular field notes be destroyed. How should the researcher handle this situation?

4. This is part of a problem statement for a proposed study: There are many studies of the impact of desegregated schools on minority students that focus on the social–psychological dimensions (self-esteem, motivation, racial attitudes, and so on) and on the academic achievement dimensions (grades, standardized achievement test scores, retention and graduation rates, and so on). Most studies, however, have focused on the assessment of quantitative outcomes of either segregated or desegregated schools and not on the qualitative processes in daily schooling. There is a lack of knowledge about classroom processes and the milieu of the school and community in which these processes occur regarding the patterns and dynamics of socialization within desegregated schools. Does the focus of the study seem appropriate for a qualitative study? Justify your answer.

5. Rephrase the following interview guide questions for qualitative questions, and place the questions in an appropriate sequence to elicit teachers' perceptions regarding evaluation by their building principal.

   1. Do you think teachers as professionals should be evaluated by their principals?
   2. Did your principal visit your classroom several times before he did your annual evaluation?
   3. Does your principal hold a conference with you after each visit?
   4. Is the principal's evaluation of your teaching fair?

C H A P T E R   1 4

Qualitative
Data
Analysis

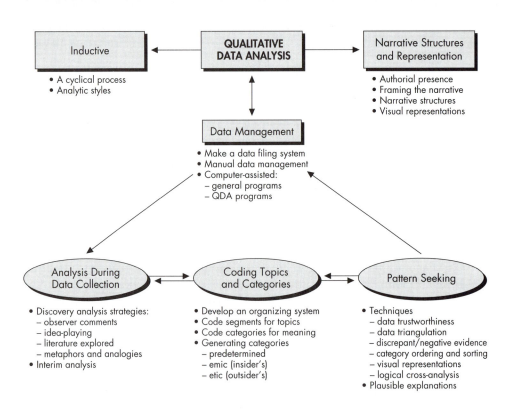

KEY TERMS

inductive analysis	category
crystallization	emic category
metaphor	etic category
interim analysis	pattern
analogy	triangulation
coding	visual representations
constant comparison	data management
segment	data filing system
topic	context
code	

Suppose you had carefully collected a series of field observations of teacher planning meetings in a school, had interviewed a number of children about their notions of a "good" teacher, or had gathered the concerns of principals about a controversial issue. How do you make sense of all of this data, which consists of many pages of field notes and/or interview transcripts and usually documents? Where do you start? How do you organize it so you can locate the important findings? What techniques do researchers use? How can software packages assist in data management and analysis?

Qualitative data analysis is primarily an inductive process of organizing the data into categories and identifying patterns (relationships) among the categories. Most categories and patterns emerge from the data, rather than being imposed on the data prior to data collection. Analytic styles among researchers vary from structured ones to more emergent intuitive ones. There are, However, general processes and some techniques that are common. Most qualitative researchers employ an interpretative/subjectivist style rather than a technical/objectivist style.

This chapter introduces qualitative analysis as a process of interim and discovery analysis, developing coding topics and categories that may initially come from the data or be predetermined, and pattern-seeking for plausible explanations. Techniques that are used by researchers in each phase of data analysis are described. Data are managed by both manual and computer-assisted methods. Word processing programs and specifically designed software packages for qualitative data analysis can assist in organizing numerous data sets (field notes, interview transcripts, and documents) and assembling coded data. Results are presented as a narration. Narrative structures and representations vary moderately with the mode of qualitative inquiry: ethnographic, phenomenological, case study, grounded theory, or critical studies.

Inductive Analysis: An Overview

Data analysis is an ongoing cyclical process integrated into all phases of qualitative research (see Figure 14.1). **Inductive analysis** means that categories and patterns emerge from the data rather than being imposed on data prior to data collection. Inductive processes generate a more abstract descriptive synthesis of the data. Data analysis is not data reduction or a quantitative approach, nor does it depend on computer software programs. Computer programs can assist in the process, but cannot replace the researcher's cognitive activities.

Qualitative analysis is a relatively systematic process of selecting, categorizing, comparing, synthesizing, and interpreting to provide explanations of the single phenomenon of interest. Qualitative data analyses vary widely because of the different research foci, purposes, data collection strategies, and modes of qualitative inquiry.

The Process of Inductive Analysis Data analysis entails several cyclical phases. The general process is represented in Figure 14.1 as four overlapping phases. Notice that as the researcher moves to more abstract levels of data analysis, she or he is constantly returning to the prior level of abstraction, always double-checking and refining her or his own analysis and interpretation. Notice also, that unless certain elements are present in the data, then the analysis does not proceed smoothly. Researchers negotiate permission to return to the field, if necessary, to seek additional data and to validate emerging patterns.

Most qualitative researchers have learned that there is no set of standard procedures for data analysis and for keeping track of analytical strategies. Although the data analysis is inductive, a deductive mode of thinking at appropriate times is used—moving back and forth between analyzing raw data and recasting tentative analyses at each phase of building to more abstract levels of synthesis. "Making sense" of the data depends largely on the researcher's intellectual rigor and a tolerance for tentativeness of interpretation until the entire analysis is completed.

Analytical Styles Qualitative researchers develop analytical styles; they rarely make explicit all of their data analysis strategies. Figure 14. 2 shows a continuum of "idealized" analytic styles from prefigured technical to emergent intuitive (Crabtree & Miller, 1999).

At the extreme objectivist end of the continuum is a *technical and quasi-statistical style*. The researcher decides the categories in advance; categories are predetermined and rigid. One strategy in this style is counting frequencies of specific topics or codes. A *template style* logically applies derived sets of codes and categories to the data, however, these classifications are frequently revised during the data analysis. The initial codes are derived from research questions, topics in the interview guide, or relevant categories from literature. This initial set may or may not be retained in the final analysis. The *editing style* is less prefigured; the interpreter searches the data sets for segments to illustrate cate-

FIGURE 14.1   Process of Inductive Data Analysis

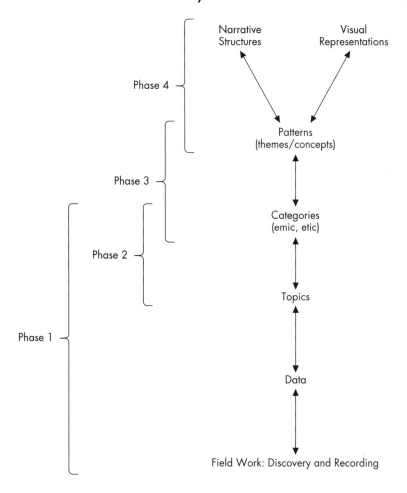

gories of meaning and writes memos during the process. Although there is little or no use of codes, the analyst must group together descriptive memos which illuminate major interpretations to produce abstract generalizations. In the *immersion/crystallization style*, the researcher collapses segmenting, categorizating, and pattern-seeking into an extensive period of intuition-rich immersion within the data. **Crystallization** seeks to open the analyst to maximum experiences within the analytic style. The researcher may conduct intensive reflexive analyses simultaneously. This style often involves reliving each field experience and persistently questioning the data for subtle nuances of meaning. Patterns are identified by iterative reflection.

Most qualitative researchers lean more toward the interpretivist/subjectivist and less toward the technical/objectivist style. Analyzing qualitative data is an eclectic activity—there is no one "right" way and data can be analyzed in

FIGURE 14.2   A Continuum of Analytic Styles

Preferred   Emergent
Technical   Intuitive

Quasi-Statistical   Template Analysis   Editing Analysis   Immersion/
Style   Style   Style   Crystallization Style

Source: Adapted from Marshall & Rossman, 1999, p.151.

more than one way . Most qualitative researchers wish to avoid standardizing the process, because a hallmark of qualitative research is the creative involvement of the researcher. Each analyst must find his or her own *style of intellectual craftsmanship.* Although there are no strict rules that can be followed mindlessly, the researcher is not allowed to be limitlessly inventive. Qualitative analysis should be done artfully, even playfully, but it also demands a great amount of methodological knowledge and intellectual competence.

Analysis begins as soon as the first set of data is gathered and runs parallel to data collection because each activity (data collection and interim analysis) informs and drives the other activities. Data are segmented, that is, divided into relevant parts (units) or chunks of meaning, social scenes, or events. Because it is difficult to process large amounts of diverse content all at once, the analyst concentrates on sets of smaller and similar material at any one time. However, the intensive analysis usually begins with the researcher reading all of the data to gain a sense of the whole, which facilitates the interpretation of smaller units of data.

The main intellectual tool is comparison. The technique of *comparing and contrasting* is used in practically all intellectual tasks during analysis: identifying data segments, naming a topic/category, and classifying. The categories are tentative in the beginning, and they remain flexible, not rigid schemes. The goal is to identify similarities.

Our discussion illustrates a combination of template (use of codes) and editing styles that many researchers use without limiting their subjective analytical processes or "forcing" the data into predispositions. The template style is easily adopted to computer-assisted analysis and may provide an experiential base for a researcher to develop a more interpretative/subjectivist style. We choose to use more general qualitative data analysis terms rather than the terminology of the five qualitative traditions in Chapter 2. Although the data analysis process differs somewhat and the analytic terminology varies by research tradition,[1] several general principles and common practices guide most researchers.

---

[1]For example, phenomenology and grounded theory have the most explicit steps in data analysis. What is termed *open coding* in grounded theory is similar to the first step of classifying phenomenological *statements* or *categorical aggregation* in case study research.

Discovery Analysis in the Field

Discovery analysis and interim analysis occur during data collection. Identifying and synthesizing patterns in the data usually occur after leaving the field. We present strategies as *guidelines* for inductive analysis.

Discovery Analysis

Because researchers, unlike soothsayers, do not know what exactly will unfold in the field, they sequentially select the final foci of a study. Some approaches that facilitate the sequential selection of the research foci are the selection of foreshadowed problems; the choice of conceptual frameworks; the data collection strategies actually used in the study, including purposeful sampling; and interim analysis.

Discovery analysis strategies are used to develop tentative and preliminary ideas during data collection. Some strategies that researchers employ include the following:

1. Write many "observer comments" in the field notes and interview transcripts to identify possible themes, interpretations, and questions. Researcher comments are separated from the actual data, typically enclosed in parentheses. A "rule" is always to separate descriptive data from evolving interpretations; data collection is a descriptive activity, whereas researcher commentary is a reflective activity.

2. Write summaries of observations and of interviews to synthesize and focus the study. Researchers frequently ask themselves after a field visit, "OK, now what did I learn about my topic? How can I briefly describe this to someone who was not present? What are the important details that may relate to a pattern?" By writing summaries, the researcher is forcing his or her mind to selectively pull out the important aspects and rearrange those aspects in a logical order. Because summaries of observation and interviews are one step removed from the actual data, these memos are clearly identified as "summary of..."

3. Play with ideas, an intuitive process, to develop initial topical categories of themes and concepts. Sometimes this takes the form of exploratory diagrams constructed from the data as they are collected. Sometimes it takes the form of a tentative category definition.

4. Begin exploring the literature and write how it helps or contrasts with observations. Some researchers only identify possible literature to read carefully later because the major task in this phase is data collection. Other researchers who collect data periodically scan the literature for what has been written about the topic and for useful concepts to help them understand the data.

5. Play with tentative metaphors and analogies, not to label, but to flush out ideas or capture the essence of what is observed and the dynamics of social situations. A **metaphor** is an implied comparison between things essentially unlike one another to provide a better understanding of the situation. Researchers ask

the question "What does this remind me of?" For example, mainstreaming hand-icapped children in schools could be compared with what is known about racial desegregation in schools to see similarities and differences. An **analogy** is a metaphor made explicit by the word "like" or "as" to compare two seemingly unlike phenomena. For example, teacher roles in a study of student dropout pre-vention were described with analogies of "traffic cop," or a role that keeps stu-dents moving through the system; and of "ostrich," which ignores the situation and hopes someone else will intervene. Metaphors and analogies should be cho-sen with care, especially to avoid possible racist and sexist connotations. However, judiciously used, metaphors and analogies illuminate subtle meanings in a single phrase.

Interim Analysis

Most qualitative researchers do regular, frequent, **interim analysis** during data collection. Interim analysis serves two purposes: (a) to make decisions in data collection and (b) to identify emerging topics and recurring patterns. Researchers do interim analysis as an ongoing activity of data collection, often after each three to five field visits or interviews, using the collected data sets (see Excerpt 14.1).

The following are strategies some researchers use:

1. Scanning all data collected at that point for possible topics the data contain. The emphasis here is not the meaning of the topic but the gaining of a global perspective of the range of data topics.
2. Looking for recurring meanings that may become major themes or pat-terns. Themes come from conversations and language in the social set-tings, recurring activities, feelings, and folk sayings. Researcher commentaries found in the observer comments, interview elabora-tions, and reflex records also suggest themes. Some patterns, that is, regularities and clusters of meaning, are obvious at this time; others are discovered only through later analysis.
3. Refocusing the inquiry for *this* particular data analysis and study. Most qualitative data are so extensive that several studies could be gener-ated. Once again, the researcher narrows the focus for intensive data analysis.

Coding Topics and Categories

It is almost impossible to interpret data unless one organizes them. Qualitative researchers integrate the operations of organizing, analyzing, and interpreting data and call the entire process "data analysis."

Where do researchers obtain ideas for organizing data? More than likely, the researcher has some initial ideas for organizing the data from either field

EXCERPT 14.1

INTERIM ANALYSIS

INSTEAD OF A CONCLUSION

Since I am still in the process of analyzing my data, I feel morally obliged to treat the findings presented herein as what they are: preliminary. There are many questions still unanswered in my research, thus it would be pretentious for me to present conclusions at this point. Instead, I would like these findings to be received by the reader as indicators of larger and far more complex questions that have not yet been seriously tackled in the scholarly discourse. Some of these questions are: To what extent do the young African American women of this rural southern town base their academic decisions on misperceptions as opposed to accurate assessments of their educational, social, and economic situation? Is it possible to make that differentiation in the first place? In what ways do educational myths and lived experiences of education relate to each other among Centerville's African American community? What dynamics were at play between my interviewees and me (as the researcher) during the process of our conversing about and thereby crafting the values of education among this population of students and their mothers. The long and difficult journey into the educational world of rural female African American students, it seems, has just begun.

Source: From Philipsen, M. (1993). Values-spoken and values-lived: Female African Americans' educational experiences in rural North Carolina, *Journal of Negro Education*, 62 (4), 419–426.

experiences or preplanning of the study. There are five sources researchers use for classification systems to organize data:

1. the research question and foreshadowed problems or subquestions
2. the research instrument such as an interview guide
3. themes, concepts, or categories used by other researchers in prior studies
4. prior knowledge of the researcher
5. the data itself

Notice that the first four sources contain predetermined categories and the fifth source produces topics that become part of a more abstract category. All five can be used, but the degree to which each is fruitful will differ, depending on the focus and purpose of the study.

Coding is the process of dividing data into parts by a classification system. Researchers develop a classification system by using one of three strategies:

- segmenting the data into units of content called topics (less than 25–30) and grouping the topics into larger clusters to form categories; or

- starting with predetermined categories of no more than four to six and breaking each category into smaller subcategories; or
- combining the strategies, using some predetermined categories and adding discovered new categories.

The strategies are merely different starting points to create an organizing system. Any starting point begins an inductive, generative, and constructive process because the *final set of categories is not totally predetermined but is carved out of the data according to category meanings*. By dividing the data into topics, researchers rearrange or reorganize the data in order to work with it. Usually any beginning strategy increases the amount of material to process, and only later are the categories grouped for synthesis and interpretation.

This analytical technique is called **constant comparison** (Glaser & Strauss, 1967)—qualitative comparing and contrasting each topic and category to determine the distinctive characteristics of each. Researchers ask "Is this topic the same as or different from another topic?" "How is this topic similar to or different from other topics?" Researchers develop categories from their data by constantly comparing each category with other categories to identify their distinctive attributes. A similar technique is employed in looking for patterns among the categories. We will first describe the process for developing an organizing system from the data, that is, using the fifth strategy.

Developing an Organizing System from Data

Most researchers develop a classification system while collecting data. Some researchers start when they have one fifth or one fourth of the data, or at least three sets. Other researchers begin at a convenient point after obtaining a sense of the whole phenomenon.

Development of an organizing system is dividing the data into segments, that is, smaller parts of data containing a "chunk of meaning." The data parts are called segments, incidents, meaning units, or analysis units. A data **segment** is comprehensible by itself and contains one idea, episode, or piece of information relevant to the study. Segments can be any size—a word, a sentence, a few lines, or several pages containing an entire event or participants' explanations with several shorter units within the segment.

Each segment has two contexts. The first is the data set in which the segment is embedded—the particular field observation or interview. The second context is the "pool of meanings" (Marton, 1986) to which the segment belongs. The researcher eventually has to identify the "pool of meanings," that is, the category, in which each segment belongs. How does a researcher develop an organizing system?

Step 1: Get a Sense of the Whole Read the first data set carefully and continue to read each data set. Write down ideas about the data as you read. This gives you ideas about individual pieces of the data and about the larger phenomenon of interest. When you have read at least three data sets, go to step 2.

Step 2: Generate Topics from the Data Take any data set to begin with and notice the topics as you read the entire field observation or interview. Ask yourself, "What is this about?" "What were these people doing or talking about?" "What was important in this setting at this time about this small piece of data?" A **topic** is the descriptive name for the subject matter of the segment. You are not, at this time, asking "What is said?" which identifies the meaning of the segment. Each topic is written in the margin of a copy of the data set. You do not have to be exhaustive on the topics in each data set at this time. Continue noting topics in the margins of three to five data sets. See Excerpt 14.2 for an illustration of the initial topics in parts of three transcripts. Notice that some topics, such as school goals and retention, are recurring.

Step 3: Compare for Duplication of Topics Make a list of topics on a separate sheet, with one column for each data set. Compare the topics for duplication and overlapping meanings. See Figure 14.3 for a visual image of the process. Draw lines between the columns to connect similar topics, or use colored pens. If you have a topic whose meaning you no longer recognize, reread the original data set and be sure you understand it. On a separate sheet of paper, cluster together similar topics—those connected by lines. With a list of all the topics, group or cluster topics that are similar, returning to the data if necessary. For each cluster of topics, the best-fitting name is stated from among the original topic labels or a new one is created that captures the essence better. At this time some researchers write a provisional description of each topic. Make a new list on a separate sheet containing three columns. The first column contains *major topics* found in the data sets; the second holds *unique topics* that seem important to the research purpose in spite of the rarity of their occurrence; the third column has *leftover topics*. These leftover topics may become important topics or unrelated topics as data collection continues. In Figure 14.3, notice that topics D and E are mentioned only once in the three data sets, but each topic is classified differently according to its importance.

Step 4: Try Out Your Provisional Classification System Using unmarked copies of each data set worked with so far, apply the preliminary classification system, using the topics listed in the first and second columns. Write a **code**, an abbreviation for the topic, next to the appropriate data segment. Some segments may have two or three codes at this point. See Excerpt 14.3 for an illustration of recoded transcripts. Notice that some topics, such as school goal and retention, now have subcomponents and may become categories. School goal has codes G Sk, G SelfC, and G Att; retention has codes R Use, R Alt, and R Ab. The single topic of policy is now two topics, school policy and school board policy, because the content of each differs. This process serves two purposes: it indicates how well the description topic name corresponds with the data, and it

EXCERPT 14.2

INITIAL TOPICS IN TRANSCRIPTS OF ELEMENTARY SCHOOL PRINCIPALS' PRACTICES OF GRADE RETENTION

PRINCIPAL #1

Retention

School goal

Retention

"Well, like I said, retention is failure, and failure is bad for kids. In education it is our job to help kids learn that they are good at things, and that school is a place to develop their skills. School should be a place that helps students develop self confidence and healthy self concepts. Retention doesn't do anything to promote those things, and if I had my way, it would only be used rarely, or maybe not at all!"

PRINCIPAL #2

School goal

Policy

"We're not here to make kids hate school. We're not here to make kids feel like they can't learn. What good does it [retention] do? Our policy is basically that retention is a negative thing, we would rather see other alternatives used to help a child and use retention only as a last resort."

PRINCIPAL #3

Absence

Alternative

Policy

"One thing we have to uphold is, hummmm, when a child has been absent a certain number of days, regardless of the circumstances, we have to consider the possibility of retention simply due to the fact that a lot of material has been missed. . . . hummmm . . . There's nothing we can do about that. So, in those instances, retention becomes something that we are not really in control of, hummmm, and we do what we can, but sometimes we just have to retain a child for that reason. Hummmm . . . there might be a situation where if a parent is willing to work with us, we can still avoid it—attend summer school, use of tutors, possibly even going through a situation where a parent would be willing to hire a tutor, or take the child somewhere for a summer program. Then we would test the child upon the child's return, and possibly we could move him on. . . . hummmm . . . It's not written in stone, but we are required if a certain number of days is missed, according to school board policy, to retain a child, unless we can prove that the child has attained a certain degree of proficiency in school work so that they can successfully move on without being totally frustrated."

TOPICS

retention	absence
school goal	alternative
policy	

Source: From Reed, J. S. (1991). Ethnographic study of the practice of grade retention in elementary schools. Unpublished manuscript.

indicates whether there are other topics in the data that are important but could not be coded with the initial organizing system.

Step 5: Refine Your Organizing System Place the topics that you remember as occurring in all or most of your data sets in one list, then make a list of unique

FIGURE 14.3 Developing a Classification System

Step 1: Identify Segments in a Data Set.

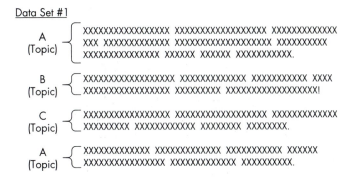

Step 2: List the Topics for each Data Set.

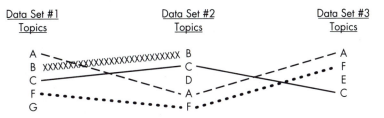

Step 3: Classify Topics as Major, Important, and Leftovers.

Major Topics	Important Topics	Leftover Topics
A	B	E
C	D	G
F		

Step 4: Apply the Classification System and Continue to Refine.

topics that are important for your research purpose. Now look at your topics from different angles. Are some topics closer in content to certain topics than others? Are some of them subtopics of others? Are there other topics in the data that you have not recognized? Refining the topic list continues as the data are collected.

How many topics are essential? When researchers later look for patterns in their data, they have to remember all the codes in their system. It is almost impossible to remember 40 discrete topics. The number of topics depends on the research purpose and the nature of the data. Twenty-five to 35 topics can be manipulated with a little effort; if the topics are grouped as categories with sub-categories it is easier to apply the organizing system.

EXCERPT 14.3

CODED TRANSCRIPTS OF ELEMENTARY SCHOOL
PRINCIPALS' PRACTICES OF GRADE RETENTION

PRINCIPAL #1

RF

G Sk

G SelfC

R Use

"Well, like I said, retention is failure, and failure is bad for kids. In education it is our job to help kids learn that they are good at things, and that school is a place to develop their skills. School should be a place that helps students develop self confidence and healthy self concepts. Retention doesn't do anything to promote those things, and if I had my way, it would only be used rarely, or maybe not at all!"

PRINCIPAL #2

G Att
G SelfC
S Pol
R Alt
R Use

"We're not here to make kids hate school. We're not here to make kids feel like they can't learn. What good does it [retention] do? Our policy is basically that retention is a negative thing, we would rather see other alternatives used to help a child and use retention only as a last resort."

PRINCIPAL #3

R Ab

R Alt

S Alt

S Alt

SB Pol

G SelfC

"One thing we have to uphold is, hummmm, when a child has been absent a certain number of days, regardless of the circumstances, we have to consider the possibility of retention simply due to the fact that a lot of material has been missed . . . hummmm . . . there's nothing we can do about that. So, in those instances, retention becomes something that we are not really in control of, hum-mmm, and we do what we can, but sometimes we just have to retain a child for that reason. Hummmm . . . there might be a situation where if a parent is willing to work with us, we can still avoid it—attend summer school, use of tutors, possibly even going through a situation where a parent would be willing to hire a tutor, or take the child somewhere for a summer program. Then we would test the child upon the child's return, and possibly we could move him on. Hummmm . . . it's not written in stone, but we are required if a certain number of days is missed, according to school board policy, to retain a child, unless we can prove that the child has attained a certain degree of proficiency in school work so that they can successfully move on without being totally frustrated."

CODES

RF	=	Retention as failure
G Sk	=	School goal as skills
G SelfC	=	School goal as self concept
R Use	=	Retention use
G Att	=	School goal as attitudes
S Pol	=	School policy
R Alt	=	Retention alternative
R Ab	=	Retention for absenteeism
S Alt	=	School alternative
P Ch	=	Parent choice
SB Pol	=	School Board policy

Source: From Reed, J. S. (1991). Ethnographic study of the practice of grade retention in elementary schools. Unpublished manuscript.

Developing Topics as Categories

Developing the topics into relatively discrete categories with subcategories forces researchers to think more abstractly. A **category** is an abstract name that represents the *meaning* of similar topics. Topics, however, may be part of more than one category. This is possible because the content of a topic (explicit statements) can have several connotations (implicit meanings).

Developing categories from topics requires researchers to look at the data in different ways. Researchers need to avoid standard ways of thinking about the phenomenon, that is, to debunk assumptions made by the observed people, to search for what people really mean, and to explore all the possible aspects of a category. Below are some strategies that researchers use (Strauss & Corbin, 1998).

1. *Ask basic questions that will lead to more refined questions.* The basic questions are Who? When? Where? What? How? How much? and Why? Giving provisional answers to these questions for each category forces the researchers to think with analytic depth.

2. *Analyze a sentence, a phrase, or sometimes even a single word* that seems significant or of interest. List all of the possible meanings from the most probable to the most improbable. Note that one word can imply many different meanings. These can be validated or refuted in the data. Each different meaning may be a subcategory.

3. *Compare the data to a similar or a far-out situation.* By imagining a very similar situation, researchers can identify the properties in their data and those that might become future subcategories. The same technique can be applied to a far-out situation—a very different situation. This imaginative comparison is merely a technique to avoid "seeing nothing new" in the data and to continue to think in terms of developing category density.

4. *Identify "red flags."* This technique helps researchers see beyond the obvious in data by questioning the assumptions people make. Examples of "red flag" phrases are "Never," "Always," "It couldn't possibly be that way," "Everyone knows that is the way it is done," "There is no need for discussion," and others. These phrases are signals to take a closer look and to ask more questions of the data or in the field. Analytically, researchers never take anything for granted.

Predetermined Categories

Some researchers start with predetermined categories. Remember, sources of predetermined categories are (a) the research questions, (b) the research instrument, such as an interview guide, (c) prior personal experience that becomes relevant from the field work, and (d) categories found in the literature. For example, most qualitative studies contain topics on setting/context, participants' definition of the situation, participants' perspectives, processes, activities, events, consequences, participants' tactics, relationships and social structure, and methodology. Each category would then be divided into subcategories as the data are analyzed. For example, a category "participants' perspectives" could contain subcategories for each different perspective. However, predetermined categories are only starting points. They must be provisionally applied and refined.

Emic and Etic Categories

Researchers use both emic and etic categories. **Emic categories** represent insiders' views such as terms, actions, and explanations that are distinctive to the setting or people. **Etic categories** represent the outsiders' view of the situation—the researcher's concepts and scientific explanations.[2]

Qualitative researchers tend to emphasize emic topics and categories in data collection because the goal is usually to represent the situation from the people's perspective. The preferred name for topics and categories are those that come from the data. Emic categories are explanations of what the phenomenon means to the participants. Excerpt 14.4 illustrates how second-grade children

---

EXCERPT 14.4

EMIC CATEGORIES

RECESS ACTIVITIES

Games	Goofing Around	Tricks
Keepaway	Runnin' around	Getting someone
Hotbox	Making faces on trees	Tripping someone
Relay races	Sucking icicles	Looking under a girl's skirt
Races	Fighting	Splashing someone
Fire red	Talking	Smashing a snowball on
Kick the can	Making fun of people	someone's head
Ditch	Somersaulting into snow	Tapping someone and hiding
Chase	Jumping into piles of snow	Stealing a stocking cap
Frisby	Sliding down the slide into	
Girls catch the boys	snow	
Catch (2)	Sliding down the slide when	
Avalanche	it is covered with ice	
Catch (1)		
Throw sweater at wall		

Source: From Parrott, S. (1972). Games children play: Ethnography of a second-grade recess. In Spradley, J., and McCurdy, D. (Eds.), *The Cultural Experience.* (Chicago: Science Research Associates.)

---

[2]See Pelto & Pelto, 1978, for emic and etic approaches in anthropology.

EXCERPT 14.5

ETIC CATEGORIES

ACTIVITIES OR ACTIONS

A. Working
   1. Doing science
   2. Doing social studies
   3. Doing reading
   4. Doing math
   5. Doing music
   6. Doing spelling
   7. Correcting morning papers
   8. Doing writing
   9. Taking a speed test

B. Doing extra activities
   1. Doing art
   2. Making scrapbooks
   3. Making pictures
   4. Making things for the room
   5. Writing poems
   6. Writing stories

C. Playing games
   1. Playing 7-Up
   2. Playing Eraser-Pass-Back
   3. Playing Eraser-on-the-Head
   4. Playing Hangman
   5. Playing Flying Dutchman
   6. Playing kickball
   7. Playing baseball
   8. Playing Dog Catcher
   9. Playing Changers

D. Having lunch

E. Having lavatory break

F. Having gym

G. Having show and tell

H. Choosing new officers

I. Reading *Reader's Digest*

Source: From Doyle, J. (1972). Helpers, officers and lunchers: Ethnography of a third grade class. In Spradley, J. and McCurdy, D. (Eds.), *The Cultural Experience*. (Chicago: Science Research Associates.)

describe what they do in recess. Notice that the topics "games," "goofing around," and "tricks" are the children's words (language) when they described recess activities to the researcher. "Recess," a term used in the school setting, is a category with three subcategories.

Etic categories represent what the phenomenon means to the researcher. These categories come from the researcher's personal experiences or from his or her academic discipline, or are borrowed from social science literature. Most researchers caution against the use of social science concepts in the early phases of data analysis because such terms often suggest connotations that participants did not mean. However, etic categories in the later phases of data analysis are essential for making a distinctive social situation comprehensible to other researchers for knowledge development. Notice that in Excerpt 14.5 the researcher deliberately used etic categories for the activities of a third-grade classroom. Although children spoke of "doing" different activities and "playing," they did not speak of "working" or "games" per se. These categories were created from the researcher's language. Of the nine categories in this study, three have subcategories.

Patterns

The ultimate goal of qualitative research is to make general statements about relationships among categories by discovering patterns in the data. A **pattern** is a relationship among categories. As researchers develop categories, they look for patterns or relationships among them. *Pattern-seeking means examining the data in as many ways as possible.* In searching for patterns, researchers try to understand the complex links between various aspects of people's situations, mental processes, beliefs, and actions.

Researchers ask themselves how categories affect and are affected by other categories. Qualitative analysis depends on salient, *grounded categories of meanings* held by the participants in the situation.

The Process of Pattern-Seeking

Pattern-seeking starts with the researcher's informed hunches about the relationships in the data. It demands a thorough search through the data, challenging each major hunch by looking for negative evidence and alternative explanations. Researchers now shift to a deductive mode of thinking—moving back and forth among topics, categories, and tentative patterns for confirmation. Part of this phase is to evaluate the data for information adequacy, usefulness, and centrality. Researchers determine how well the data illuminate the research problem and which data are central to the story that is unfolding about the selected phenomenon.

Patterns can take different forms and levels of abstraction depending on the purpose and use of the study. Patterns also relate to the conceptual framework selected for the inquiry. The major pattern(s) serves as the framework for reporting the findings and organizing the reports. The process is schematically represented in Figure 14.4. Notice that the number of segments (the *x*s) that a topic represents varies. Some topics fit into more than one category and other topics are not central to the research problem. Further, a category can fit into more than one pattern. This elasticity of topic and category meanings allows for *patterns of meanings* to emerge. The meanings of topic, categories, and patterns depend on both the content of each and the comparison made with that content—other topics, other categories, or other patterns.

Suppose one identified a topic "pizza." Its description would probably be of the crust, the major ingredients, and the toppings, as distinctive from the topics of "hamburger" and "milk." The topics of pizza and hamburger now are grouped in a category called "fast food," which is distinctive from the categories "four-course dinner" and "snack." One now starts asking additional questions for the study focus—nutritional patterns of family members' eating habits. Part of each category might fit a pattern of nutritional food, and part of each category might fit a pattern of non-nutritional food. Notice, that at each level of abstraction, the meaning is partially derived from the descriptive topic and partially from the category it fits. Of course, one can also search for other patterns among other topics and categories, such as beliefs about food and nutrition,

FIGURE 14.4   Building Patterns of Meaning

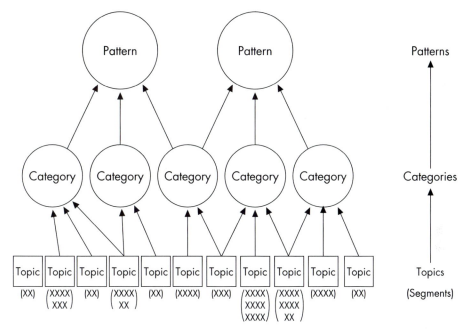

Source: Adapted from A. Vierra & J. Pollock (1992), *Reading educational research* (2nd ed.), Scottsdale, AZ: Gorsuch Scarisbrick Pub. p. 262.

degree of nutritional knowledge, and the social phenomenon of eating. In this way, qualitative researchers build each level of abstraction even though the process is guided by hunches, the research problem, and the selected conceptual framework.

The process is usually a circular one of returning to the data to validate each pattern and then modifying or recasting the idea as part of a larger abstraction. Although some of the process is tedious and time-consuming, it is also a "creative process that requires making carefully considered judgments about what is really significant and meaningful in the data" (Patton, 1990, p. 406).

Techniques of Pattern-Seeking

The following techniques are strategies that facilitate pattern-seeking and are not intended to be exhaustive or prescriptive. Each researcher must select strategies that illuminate the patterns in his or her data. The rigor, duration, and process of data analysis will vary; qualitative researchers are obligated to monitor and report their own analytical techniques and processes as fully as possible.

Gauging Data Trustworthiness   Although gauging the trustworthiness of the data is done at the time of each field experience and in reflex records, it is also important during intensive data analysis. The researcher selects trustworthy evidence for pattern-seeking by qualitatively assessing solicited versus unsolicited data, subtle influences among the people present in the setting, specific versus vague statements, and the accuracy of the sources (an observant person? a thoughtful person? an emotional person? a biased person?). Selecting trustworthy data also involves an awareness of the researcher's assumptions, predispositions, and influence on the social situation.

Using Triangulation   Researchers use **triangulation** (Denzin, 1978), which is the cross-validation among data sources, data collection strategies, time periods, and theoretical schemes. (See Chapter 11.) To find regularities in the data, the researcher compares different sources, situations, and methods to see whether the same pattern keeps recurring. A theme of "institutional collaboration," for example, could be cross-checked by comparing data found in artifact collections (minutes, memos, official brochures, letters), informant interviews (project co-directors, teachers, principals), and field observations of project meetings. Figure 14.5 illustrates cross-method triangulation.

Researchers sense, however, that even though they only directly observed, heard, or recorded one instance, for some types of analysis, a single incident is meaningful.

Evaluating Discrepant or Negative Evidence

Researchers actively search for discrepant or negative evidence that modifies or refutes a pattern (see Chapter 12). A negative case is a situation, a social scene, or a participant's views that contradicts a pattern of meanings. In other words, there are two patterns rather than one pattern. Discrepant data present a variant of a pattern. These exceptions are very useful because they make the original pattern more distinctive and yield insights to modify patterns. For example, a pattern might be that a particular action occurs in most situations except for this type of situation.[3]

FIGURE 14.5   Triangulation

Triangulation for logical pattern

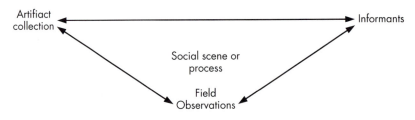

---

[3]See Strauss, A. & Corbin, J. (1998), *Basics of qualitative research: Grounded theory procedures and techniques,* for a conditional matrix.

Ordering Categories for Patterns

Ordering categories can be done several ways to discover patterns. One way is to place the categories in sequence of occurrence. Researchers ask, Which situation or action came first? Did more than one belief accompany the event? What was the consequence or outcome? Arranging the categories in a sequence is useful for a process analysis to identify changes from one time to another time (see Excerpt 14.6).

A second way is to enlarge, combine, subsume, and create new categories that make empirical and logical sense—they "go together" in meaning. The "logical sense" in pattern-seeking is that the meaning of a category is influenced by its relationship to a pattern. In our example of nutritional and non-nutritional food categories, these categories might relate to a pattern of teenager social eating (immediate family, high school friends, grandparents, other adults,

---

EXCERPT 14.6

ORDERING CATEGORIES FOR PATTERNS

IMPLICATIONS

Children's behaviors on the swings developed in a hierarchical fashion. Individual children varied considerably in their demonstration of specific actions or strategies. However, [in] the progression of swinging behaviors, exhibited by the observed children . . . [e]ach stage incorporated what was achieved in the preceding stage as well as what was new in the children's behaviors. Each stage further demonstrated a qualitatively different focus in the children's activities and experiences. . . .

In keeping with this perspective, the developing swinging behaviors observed in this investigation may be represented in two broad phases. During the first phase, children acquired and developed the skills and behaviors needed to swing in standard form. They focused on understanding the movement of the swing, developing the body movements necessary to achieve movement of the swing, and coordinating these body movements to the movement of the swing. The behaviors exhibited during this first phase may be described as developing behaviors on the swings. . . .

During the second phase, children already developed basic behaviors and were able to turn their attention to comparisons with their friends and explorations of their own potential and that of the swing. Refinement, extension, and elaboration of the children's swinging behaviors were evident in the swingers during this phase. These behaviors may be broadly described as developed behaviors on the swings. . . .

CONCLUSIONS

Whether described by phases or stages, swinging behaviors emerge in a predictable sequence. . . .

Source: From Fox, J. E. & Tipps, R. S. (1995). Young children's development of swinging behaviors, *Early Childhood Research Quarterly, 10,* 491–504.

younger children, or self). By creating a new category of nutritional value (balanced meal) which includes nutritional and non-nutritional foods, one might now look for a pattern of food choice—which foods does our teen-ager choose in different social situations?

Sorting Categories for Patterns   Researchers group categories in several ways to identify meanings. In a study of principals and unsatisfactory teachers, the category of unsatisfactory teachers was sorted first by types of unsatisfactory teachers and then by types of resolution (Luck, 1985). Each category was rearranged to see whether there was a pattern between type of unsatisfactory teacher and type of resolution. When no pattern was found, another category—methods of identification of unsatisfactory teachers—was sorted with types of resolution. This sorting led to a pattern that related methods of unsatisfactory teacher identification to types of resolution.

Constructing Visual Representations   Researchers construct **visual representations,** an organized assembly of information, such as figures, matrices, integrative diagrams, and flow charts, which assist in the analysis. There are many forms of visual representation. Examples are Figure 14.6 and Excerpt 14.8. Most researchers using a discovery approach are cautious *not* to reach hasty closure in building integrative diagrams. Descriptive contextual data must accompany diagrams, an abstraction that limits the types of interpretations that can be drawn. Visual representations are *devices* and are not "reality" *per se.* Diagrams assist researchers in moving to a more abstract analysis by allowing them to ask different questions about the data. Researchers attempt to balance a respect for the complexity of reality with the need to simplify for analytical and communication purposes. Integrative diagrams, once finalized, serve as a visual representation of the entire study and are presented in the report.

Doing Logical Cross-Analyses   Usually presented in matrix format, categories are crossed with one another to generate new insights for further data analysis. These cross-categories reveal logical discrepancies in the already-analyzed data and suggest areas in which data and patterns might be logically uncovered. However, the researcher should *not* allow these matrices to lead the analysis but use them to generate hunches for further pattern-seeking. In Figure 14.5 the six categories of teacher roles toward high school dropouts were first developed and then cross-analyzed, which allowed two dimensions of meaning to emerge: behaviors and beliefs.

Plausibility of Explanations

As researchers build their categories and search for patterns they need to search for other plausible explanations for links among categories. Alternative explanations always exist, but they may not be reasonably supported by the data. *A pattern becomes an explanation only when alternative patterns do not offer reasonable explanations central to the research problem.* Plausibility is a matter of judg-

FIGURE 14.6   An Empirical Typology of Teacher Roles with High School Dropouts

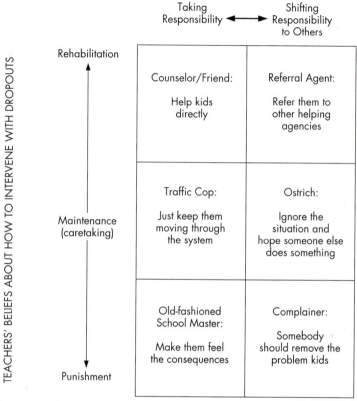

BEHAVIORS TOWARD DROPOUTS

Taking Responsibility ⟷ Shifting Responsibility to Others

TEACHERS' BELIEFS ABOUT HOW TO INTERVENE WITH DROPOUTS

Rehabilitation

Maintenance (caretaking)

Punishment

Counselor/Friend:

Help kids directly

Referral Agent:

Refer them to other helping agencies

Traffic Cop:

Just keep them moving through the system

Ostrich:

Ignore the situation and hope someone else does something

Old-fashioned School Master:

Make them feel the consequences

Complainer:

Somebody should remove the problem kids

Source: From M. Q. Patton (1990), *Qualitative evaluation and research methods.* 2nd ed., Newbury Park, CA: Sage, p. 413.

ment about the quality of the data within the design limitations. Plausibility is demonstrated by the presentation of the data and the rigor of the analysis.

The following analogy illustrates plausibility. If a person were peeling an apple, she or he would first notice the whole apple—its size, shape, and other features. Initially, the skin is encountered; the skin also has distinctive characteristics. Underneath the skin is the flesh. Many people, at this point, stop peeling the apple and are satisfied with their knowledge of the apple. Others are more curious about why there is so much flesh. They continue to probe and finally discover a membrane embedded in the flesh. Some people wonder why there is a membrane. Careful cutting of the membrane yields a seed. At this point, one has understanding—all the pieces "fit" together as a whole. There is an explanation for why the membrane, flesh, and skin surround the core of the apple—the seed. At each phase of cutting the apple, there were alternative explanations for the parts of an apple; however, in the last discovery (the seed), there is no other reasonable explanation for the "real" meaning of the parts of an apple. Notice that to discover the meaning of an apple, one must continue to ask questions and probe each layer to reach the core.

Manual and Computer Techniques in Data Management

Qualitative studies are noted for having "mounds" of data. Researchers have to manage this data for analysis and writing purposes. **Data management** is using a system to retrieve data sets (field notes and interview transcripts) and to assemble coded data in one place. Researchers typically use one of three approaches to data management: manual techniques, general software programs that can be adopted for qualitative research needs, and special software programs designed for qualitative data management. Currently there are many general software programs and over 24 special software programs, several of which have improved versions. Because of the confidentiality of the data, storing qualitative data on a mainframe computer is not recommended. We will first discuss developing a filing system and then manual and computer management of data.

Developing a Data Filing System

Developing a system for filing as data begin to accumulate is essential. A **data filing system** is a procedure to identify and retrieve a particular set of the original field notes or an interview transcript. All pages of each type of record are numbered sequentially to locate information within each data set. In addition, each field note set or transcript set is identified on the first page by date, place, person(s), location, and event or social scene. Because working with data means extensive rearrangement of it either manually or by computer, several copies are made and one is retained as a permanent copy. This permanent copy must be kept in a place where it will not be disturbed, lost, or destroyed.

A data filing system contains each data set either in notebooks, file folders, or on a personal computer (PC). The purpose is the same—to locate field data. The filing system depends partially on the data format and the focus of the study. Researchers have filed data by one or more of the following systems:

- by date of observation or interview, especially if the focus is process analysis;
- by site, especially if the study includes more than one type of physical setting—homes, schools, agencies, offices;
- by person interviewed, frequently numbered as interview #1, interview #2, and so on, with a separate list to identify each number especially if the focus is across cases;

- by type of social scene, especially if many types of social scenes occur for a small number of people, such as classrooms, parent–teacher conferences, faculty meetings, board meetings, and the like.

Planning ahead for color coding, numbering, and use of abbreviations is invaluable in data analysis and writing the final report.

Manual Data Management

There are several ways to manage data manually after topics have been coded on a copy of the data. The final coding of topics also becomes a master copy and is stored in a safe place. Researchers make photocopies of the coded data and work with only the copies for the intensive analysis and report writing.

We will discuss two ways to manage the coded data manually. One technique is the cut-and-file approach; the second technique is the file card system (Bodgan & Biklen, 1998). There are many variations of these techniques.

The cut-and-file technique requires multiple copies of each data set for cutting. Folders are labeled by topic names. As one goes through the data, each data topic (which may vary from one sentence to one paragraph or a series of paragraphs) is first marked to identify the source and the page number. This may be a number or some other system. Be careful that file coding numbers refer to sources, page numbers, and topics and do not refer to interviewees, field sites, or the like. Only after each topic segment has an identification label should pages of data be cut into topic segments and placed in the appropriate folder for each topic. If some data segments contain more than one topic, then copies are needed for each folder.

One variation is to put the whole page of the data set containing the marked topic into the folder. Another variation is to paste or copy the topic data on 3-by–5-inch cards and then put the cards for each topic in a pile. Each card must be marked for topic and source. Either way, the result is a box of file folders or cards that contain all the data segments relevant to each topic. Figure 14.7 graphically represents the process.

At this point, many researchers write up the content of each folder or sets of cards and select illustrative quotable material. It does not matter which folder one selects to read first. By placing all the relevant topic folders together and reading through them, researchers develop topics into categories. If there are many data segments in one folder or many 3-by–5 cards in one pile, the content may be a category that needs to be broken into subcategories.

The file card technique is an indexing system to locate topics within the entire data bank. The researcher has a photocopy of the data with the topics coded on each data set. The researcher also has his or her list of categories for the study. Each data set (source) must be numbered, and both the pages and lines are numbered. Thus, each topic has three methods of identification—the document (or source), the page, and the line(s). Researchers now read their data, select the category for each topic, and write on the index card three identifications: the

FIGURE 14.7   Assembly of Topic Segments into Topics

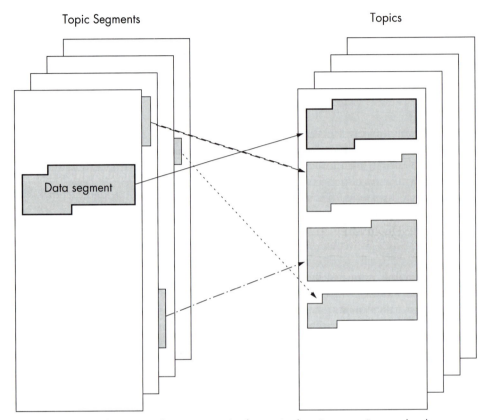

Topic Segments   Topics

Data segment

Source: From R. Tesch (1990), *Choices among Qualitative Analysis Programs*. Presented at the American Evaluation Association Annual Meeting, Washington, D.C.

source number, the page number, and the line number(s). The result of this process is an index of the data relevant to each category.

This method has some advantages. It does not require cutting and bulky folders. Some disadvantages are (1) skimming the entire page to locate the particular topic segment, (2) retrieving all the data to read when they are scattered throughout the entire data bank, and (3) returning each page back to its former place in the filing system to make it accessible for pattern-seeking. However, some researchers, using notebooks to store their data, prefer this technique.

Using Computer Programs

Computer software programs used for qualitative data management range from general programs produced by large software manufacturers to specialized programs, usually developed by qualitative researchers. General programs that have been adopted by researchers to manage the mounds of data range from word processors, text retrievers, and textbase managers to special programs such as code-and-retrievers, code-based theory-builders, and conceptual net-work-builders (Weitzman & Miles, 1995). Furthermore, the use of software programs in qualitative research is a rapidly changing technical innovation. Our discussion is intended to alert you to the possibilities of using computer pro-grams in qualitative data management. Table 14.1 lists uses of computer soft-ware in qualitative research. We will discuss the general programs first and then the special programs.

General programs include word processors, text retrievers, and textbase managers. *Word processors* are designed for the production and revision of text and thus are useful for writing or editing field notes, for transcribing inter-views, for writing memos, for preparing files for coding and analysis, and for writing reports. Most word processing programs will search for character strings, and some will create hypertext links, which connect two points in the text so you can view both simultaneously. *Text retriever* programs are sophisti-cated text search programs that specialize in finding all the instances of words, phrases (or other character strings), and combinations of them in one or more files. *Textbase manager* programs, compared with text retrievers, offer more fea-tures to organize, sort, and make subsets of the text systematically and then provide for search and retrieval. They usually have specialized functions for managing and organizing data and especially for creating different subsets of data for further analysis.

Three types of software packages are specifically intended to assist in qual-itative data analysis (QDA). These programs, although often based on formal

TABLE 14.1

Uses of Computers in Qualitative Research

1. Making notes in the field
2. Writing up or transcribing field notes and interview data
3. Editing—correcting and elaborating field notes and interview transcriptions
4. Coding—placing keywords or symbols to segments of data to permit later retrieval
5. Filing—keeping data in an organized database
6. Search and retrieval—locating relevant segments and chunks of data and making them available for examination
7. Data "linking"—connecting relevant data segments with each other, forming categories and patterns for closer examination
8. Memoing—writing reflective commentaries on some aspect of the data as a basis of deeper analysis
9. Visual representation—placing selected data in a condensed, organized format such as a matrix or network for examination; creating diagrams that depict findings or theories
10. Preparing interim, drafts, and final reports

logic, do not build a researcher's theory or explanatory themes; software programs do not know the meaning of the qualitative data. *Code-and-retrieve programs* specialize in helping the researcher divide text into segments or chunks, and find and display all the chunks with a given code or combination of codes. These programs replace the manual tasks of cut-and-file or forming a file card system. Programs vary in terms of hypertext capability. *Code-based theory-building programs* usually include the same features as the code-and-retrieve programs but also support making connections between codes to develop categories and patterns. *Conceptual network-building programs* also assist in building theory, but the researcher works with systematically built graphic networks. The networks are "semantic networks" developed from the data and the researcher's concepts.

How does computer-assisted data analysis work? The process is similar to the manual data-management techniques we have described. Researchers can attach code symbols, which they have already determined, to segments of data, extract the segments, and assemble those segments in one place. Programs will automatically indicate on each segment where it comes from (page and line of data file). If you prefer to work on hard copy, the program will print all or part of the data. Data can be recoded.

Software programs for qualitative data management are available for MS-DOS, Microsoft Windows, and Macintosh users. Students should decide first what kind of computer user they are, whether they are choosing for one project or the next few years, what kind of database and project it is, what kind of analysis is anticipated, how important "closeness to the data" is, and the cost limit.

Data "closeness" versus "distancing" refers to viewing only small chunks of data at a time compared with the feeling of immersion in the data that comes from flipping through piles of paper or scrolling through pages of data one file at a time. Two other critical issues are user-friendliness and program flexibility—that is, ability to change the initial coding and to customize and adapt the program to the researcher's analytical style and type of database. For example, data from observation and informal conversations are less structured than data from standardized open-response interviews. Some programs require fairly structured data to be efficient.

There are mixed opinions on whether beginning researchers should use specially designed software programs for the mechanical aspects of data analysis. Disagreements center on the time spent in learning a program and the amount of time saved. For persons who are comfortable with computers and who are adept at learning new programs, the time and money invested are worthwhile—particularly for a major study such as a dissertation or to continue a career in research.

Experienced researchers also have preferences. Some want to keep their analytical-cognitive skills separate from data management. Other researchers are advocates of computer data management and software-assisted analysis.

There are significant differences among programs, however, which users should be aware of before selection. Recent books that compare software programs should be consulted before one invests both time and money in a software program.[4] Furthermore, current qualitative data analysis software (QDA) programs can be located through the Internet at Web sites sponsored by individuals at universities and by commercial organizers. QualPage, for example, lists resources for qualitative researchers and includes QDA softwear programs. Other QDA home pages have brief reviews of each program. Some QDA software programs can also be ordered through the Internet. For instance, one such site provides *news* about the current version and release information with examples of how to use the program; a *support page* with a mini-manual and frequently asked questions; a *resource page* with hyperlinks to other sites concerning QDA and social science research; and an *order page* where you can purchase the software.

Variations in Narrative Structure and Representation

A hallmark of most qualitative research is the narrative presentation of data and the diversity of visual representations of data. Data are presented as quotations of participants' language, citing field notes and interview transcripts as sources. Not all data are reported in a single study nor necessarily in the same format to all readers. There are four potential audiences: academic, participants in the study, policymakers, and the general public. The narrative structure depends on the complexities of the phenomenon, the purpose of the research, the research tradition, and the audience.

Qualitative authors recommend an overall structure that does not blindly follow the standard quantitative introduction, methods, results, and discussion format (Richardson, 1998; Van Maanen, 1988). Methods can be called "procedures" or "strategies;" results are called "findings." Sub-headings often use participant's expressive language rather than social science rhetoric. The writing style might be personal, readable, and applicable for a broad audience. The level of detail makes the narrative seem "real" and "alive" carrying the reader directly into the world of the people.

Audience and Authorial Presence

There are a number of issues which a researcher must address in writing a report: encoding for specific audiences, visual representations of findings, and the author's presence (Creswell, 1998). Encoding is the use of literary devices

---

[4]See Fielding, N. G. & Lee, R. M. (1988), *Computer analysis and qualitative research;* Kelle, U. (1995), *Computer-aided qualitative research; Tesch, R. (1993), Personal computers in qualitative research,* in LeCompte, M. D. & Preissle, M. (1993), *Ethnography and qualitative design in educational research* (2nd ed) pp. 279–314; Weitzman, E. A. & Miles, M. B. (1995), *Computer programs for qualitative data analysis.*

to shape a report for a particular audience. For academic audiences and publications, the prominent display of academic credentials of the author, references, footnotes, methodology sections and the use of academic metaphors are appropriate. For moral/political audiences the use of highly connotated "in-group" words (woman, women, feminist in feminist writing), the moral or active "credentials" of the author, and empowerment metaphors are appropriate. For participants and policy-makers, there is less literature and theory, an abbreviated methodological overview, and a detailed description of the practice, addressing practical concerns or issues and use of "lay or common sense" metaphors.

The author's presence is acknowledged through various literary devices. The researcher's role is described. In addition, the author's presence can be acknowledged with reflective footnotes, interpretative commentaries, or an epilogue.[5] In some critical studies, the researcher's political lenses are usually stated in the introductory sections.

Qualitative studies have a variety of narrative structures—descriptive-analytical interpretations, realistic reporting, abstract theoretical discussions and renderings of personal accounts. Despite this variation, usually two aspects of a study are presented as data: the context and quotations of participants' language. The actual statements of the people observed and interviewed represent their constructions of their world, the meanings they give to social situations and experiences. The researcher's task is to arrange these views in a logical manner, making participants' meanings unmistakable to a reader. We first present what is common to most qualitative studies and then discuss the distinguishing features of the narrative structures and representations of five qualitative research approaches (see Chapter 2).

Framing the Narrative and Participants' Language

A study can be framed several ways: the naturalistic context, the phenomenological experience, selected theories relevant to the field data, or a political orientation. The **context** of a study is the situational description of people and events in which the phenomenon of interest occurs. How one frames a study varies within qualitative traditions: ethnography, phenomenology, case study, grounded theory, or critical studies.

In ethnographic studies the context of the cultural-sharing group is the setting, the participants, and the data collection time period. The holistic context in case study research is considered an important finding; the naturalistic setting is described and used to identify contextual elements which influence

---

[5]Some author's presence is located through *signature or discourse,* that is, the text has a rhythm, cadence, and expression that makes the work readily identifiable as the work of a certain author (Clandinin & Connelly, 1998).

the cultural life or the "case." In a study of the first year of operation of an innovative school, for example, the context is the floor plan and details of the new school building, the entire new faculty, and the faculty mandate for the academic year. Part of the context is also how the innovative school fits into larger systems—-school system, community, and state education system.

The frame for a phenomenological study is the type of experience that has happened or is still occurring. The experience is one which both the researcher and each interviewee has had, for example, being a working single parent, a women administrator who voluntarily resigned, or a child who experienced the death of a sibling. The naturalistic situation is used in descriptions of "what" happened and "how" the experience occurred.

Whereas the naturalistic context is very important in ethnographic and case study research, it is less important in grounded theory studies. In grounded theory, the identification of the theories that frame the study is crucial and a brief description of the natural context (i.e., hospital wards, school playgrounds, cancer support groups), is part of the methodology. Because of the different types of critical studies, the narration may be framed by the naturalistic context, a theoretical frame, or a political frame (researcher's political orientation or standpoint). In most studies, framing the narrative to follow is essential for readers to understand the study and for extending the acquired understandings to future research or practices. All proper names are coded for confidentiality

Presentation of participants' language is imperative, because this is *the data*. Data can be presented in several formats: (a) short eye-catching quotations separated from the text, often bulleted or placed in a table; (b) brief embedded quotations within the narrative; and (c) entire paragraphs of field notes and interview transcripts. Brief quotations are integrated into the analytical interpretations throughout the entire study. The longer quotations require guiding the reader "into" the quote and "out of" the quote to focus her or his attention on the controlling idea of the section. An example is Excerpt 2.8 (Chapter 2), in which each interpretation is supported with selected quotations from different teachers. Lengthy quotations are usually set off from the narrative text and cite some identification of the original data set, such as the date or the interviewee number.

Narrative Structures and Visual Representations

The narrative structures and visual representations within each research tradition reflect the analytic process. Diversity within qualitative traditions exist, especially in critical studies. We discuss each tradition with an emphasis on substantive research manuscripts.

Ethnographic studies provide *description, analysis* and *interpretation* of the culture sharing group. The "thick" holistic description is presented in chronological order or narrator order. The analysis may focus on a typical day, a critical event, selected social scenes with dialogue, or tell the "story" from different perspectives. The analysis may also compare and contrast across groups within the culture. Data, transformed as patterns or themes, are summarized and provide a *cultural portrait*, a synthesis of all aspects of the group life illustrating its complexity (Walcott, 1994). The overall interpretation and meaning is discussed with the findings relating to wider scholarly issues or to current issues (see Excerpt 14.7). Visual representations of findings may be tables, charts, and integrative diagrams.

Phenomenological studies of a lived experience emphasize textual descriptions of *what happened* and *how the phenomenon was experienced*. Because the experience is one which is common to the researcher and interviewees, data are drawn from both the researcher's written record of her or his experience and that of the interviewees. The report includes a description of each participant's experience, including the researcher's, followed by a *composite description* and the *essence* of the experience. The *essence* of the experience is a highly synthesized and brief statement of the meaning of the common experience. Visual representations are usually tables of verbatim statements from the interviewees and a figure or table for the essence of the experience.

Case study research, similar to ethnographic studies, contain *description*, *analysis*, and *naturalistic generalizations*. Case studies typically use a report format with vignettes to provide vicarious experiences for the reader (Stake, 1995). Case studies can be 60%/ 40% or 70%/ 30% in favor of description verses analysis and interpretation. There is extensive description of the case and its context based on a wide variety of data sources: documentation, archival records, interviews, field observations, participant-observation, and objects (Yin, 1994). A few key issues are presented so the reader can appreciate the complexity of the case. These issues are drawn from a collection of instances in

EXCERPT 14.7

NARRATIVE PRESENTATION OF FINDINGS

In this vein, the actions of Mack and his classmates transcend simple interpretations of defiance, immaturity, resistance, and reproduction. Rather, these adolescents had. . . . a host of aspirations and intentions that were compatible and incompatible with those of their peers, family, and community. . . . The lives of these black youths . . . tell us how these emergencies are incorporated into personal and public politics; co-opted by mainstream music, language, and fashion marketers; and yet appropriated as negative symbols of racial/ethnic, class, and gender identify for groups such as blacks (Kelley 1997b; Lusane 1993; Rose 1994).

In conclusion, voices and histories like those presented in this article challenge the pejorative and narrow characterizations of black, low-income, working- and middle-class people in public policy debates. . . .

Source: From Cousins, L. H. (1999). "Playing between classes": America's troubles with class, race, and gender in a black high school and community. *Anthropology & Education Quarterly, 30* (3), 294–316.

the data or a close examination of a singe instance to detect issue-relevant meanings. Several of the issues are analyzed further with supporting and negative evidence. Finally, the researcher develops naturalistic generalization (patterns) or "lessons learned" (Lincoln & Guba, 1985) which are useful to the participants or to readers in applying to similar cases. Visual representations include tables, flow charts, figures, and integrative diagrams (see Excerpt 14.8).

Grounded theory studies emphasize an *analytic story* with description kept secondary to the *theoretical scheme or concept density* (elaboration). The analytic story also specifies the variations of the phenomenon and relevant conditions for multiple causes. Visual representations are conditional matrices, integrative diagrams or models with context, causal conditions, intervening conditions, and consequences. A visual representation accompanies the culminating propositions of the grounded theory. Directional arrows indicate the flow of initial events to consequences as in Excerpt 14.8. Because of the emphasis on

EXCERPT 14.8

CONCEPT ANALYSIS: VISUAL REPRESENTATION

DISABILITY DOMINATION

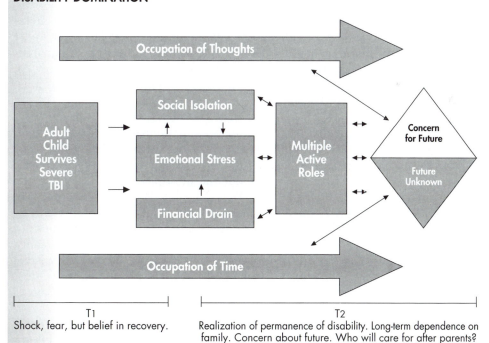

T1
Shock, fear, but belief in recovery.

T2
Realization of permanence of disability. Long-term dependence on family. Concern about future. Who will care for after parents?

Source: From Wood, W. M. (1993). Long-term consequences of severe traumatic brain injury on adults: A qualitative study of families' perceptions of impact and public policy. Unpublished doctoral dissertation, Virginia Commonwealth University, Richmond.

EXCERPT 14.9

GROUNDED THEORY ASSERTIONS

This study was a qualitative investigation of the knowledge and beliefs, roles, and guiding principles of two exemplary high school science teachers. . . .

The findings of the study are summarized in the following assertions.

Assertion 1:   The important knowledge and beliefs of each teacher are best represented as one cluster of teaching principles.

Assertion 2:   Each teacher had multiple teaching roles, with each role described by a different role metaphor.

Assertion 3:   The teaching roles of each teacher are consistent with his or her cluster of teaching principles.

Assertion 4:   Each teacher had guiding principles that are overlying and constant. . . .

Source: From Lloyd, J. M. (1999). Knowledge and beliefs, roles, and guiding principles of two exemplary high school science teachers and model for teacher reflection. Unpublished doctoral dissertation, Virginia Commonwealth University, Richmond.

conceptual discussion and relating the grounded theory to theoretical literature, few readers gain a full appreciation for the entire study. However, some grounded theory studies present a descriptive narrative rather than an analytical narrative which connects the categories and advances the theory or concept density. Theoretical propositions can be presented in narrative form or as a list of assertions (see Excerpt 14.9).

Critical studies include such diverse research as critical ethnography, feminist and ethnic research, narrative analysis, participatory action research, and action research. Most critical ethnographies and many of the feminist and ethnic research adopt substantive research report narrative structures. Authors, however, are particularly concerned about the multiple voices, including the author's, in the discourse.

L. Richardson (1990, 1998) reminds authors that postmodern thinking links language, subjectivity, social organization, and power. Language does not "reflect" social reality, but produces meaning and thus creates social reality. Transforming the field text into a narrative text is the place where the sense of *self* and *personal subjectivity* are constructed. By emphasizing reflexive writing, the author is freed from writing as a single text in which everything is said to everyone at once.

A number of qualitative social scientists are writing experimental forms of *evocative representations.*[6] Some of these writings are narratives of self, ethno-

---

[6]See Richardson, 1998, pp 355-361, for cited examples and journals.

graphic fictional representation, poetic representation, ethnographic drama, and mixed genres. A number of scholarly qualitative journals have published studies employing experimental narrative structures. Many qualitative researchers have been influenced by experimental formats and write more reflexively and self-consciously; they also relate more deeply and complexly to their own texts while nurturing their own voices.

Summary

The following statements summarize the process and techniques of qualitative data analysis:

1. Inductive analysis means that the categories and patterns emerge from the data rather than being imposed on the data prior to data collection.
2. Data analysis involves cyclical phases—discovery analysis in the field, identification of topics that become categories, and synthesis of patterns among categories.
3. Analytic styles of qualitative data analysis include prefigured technical, template, editing, and crystallization styles.
4. Discovery analysis strategies, done during data collection, include writing many "observer comments" and summaries, playing with ideas, exploring the literature, and using metaphors and analogies.
5. Interim analysis assists in making data collection decisions and identifying emerging topics and recurring meanings.
6. Coding is the process of dividing data into parts by a classification system— segmenting the data into topics or using predetermined categories to break into smaller subcategories.
7. The analytical technique is one of constant comparison (comparing and contrasting) to determine the distinctive characteristics of each topic and category.
8. Predetermined categories are derived from the research problem, an interview guide, literature, and the researcher's personal experience.
9. A data segment (a word, sentence, paragraph, or page) is comprehensible by itself and contains one idea, episode, or piece of information relevant to the study.
10. A topic is the descriptive name for the subject matter, not the meaning, of the segment.
11. Researchers refine their provisional classification system of topics throughout the study.
12. A category is an abstract name for the meaning of similar topics.
13. Techniques to develop categories include refining analytic questions, mental comparison of similar and far-out situations, and analysis of "red flags."
14. Emic categories represent the insider's or participants' views; etic categories represent the outsider's or social science views.
15. A pattern is a relationship among categories.

16. Techniques for pattern-seeking include triangulation, ordering and sorting categories, analysis of discrepant or negative evidence, construction of visual representations, and logical cross-analysis.
17. Patterns are plausible explanations when they are supported by the data and alternative patterns are not reasonable.
18. Data management, done both manually and with computer assistance, is a system to retrieve data sets and to assemble coded data in folders or computer files.
19. Qualitative studies encode for different audiences, acknowledge authorial presence and employ narrative structures related to the chosen research tradition.
20. Qualitative studies present the context and the quotations of participant language as the data.

Self-Instructional Review Exercises

Sample answers are in the back of the book.

Test Items

1. Inductive analysis is
   a. imposing categories on the data prior to data collection.
   b. testing hypotheses.
   c. presenting data in statistical tables.
   d. developing categories primarily from the data.
2. Data analysis in qualitative research
   a. is done after all data are collected.
   b. is not done until data are segmented by topics or categories.
   c. is done at regular, frequent intervals during the field experience.
   d. seldom guides the researcher in making data collection decisions.
3. Organizing the data proceeds by
   a. identifying topics and then categories.
   b. starting with predetermined categories and then subcategories.
   c. identifying major patterns and then categories and topics.
   d. Either a or b can be used and can be combined.
4. Which technique does *not* develop topics into categories?
   a. mentally comparing the data to a similar or a far-out situation
   b. asking basic questions—who, what, when, where, how, and why
   c. accepting participants' assumptions and their statements literally
   d. careful analysis of "red flag" statements
5. Sources for predetermined categories to be refined are
   a. the research problem.
   b. the interview or field observation guide.
   c. prior personal experience.
   d. a, b, and c are all possible.
6. In the early phases of data analysis, which type of category is emphasized?
   a. emic categories
   b. categories from social science literature

    c. etic categories

    d. theoretical categories

7. A technique *not* used to identify patterns among categories is

    a. triangulation of data.

    b. discarding negative or discrepant evidence.

    c. constructing tentative visual representations.

    d. doing logical cross-analysis of categories.

8. Data management

    a. is data analysis.

    b. is a manual data filing system.

    c. requires use of computer software programs.

    d. uses a system to retrieve data sets and to assemble coded data in one folder or computer file.

9. Qualitative results are presented by

    a. omission of the context of the phenomenon studied.

    b. analytical memos containing the researcher's language.

    c. quotations of participants' words and statements.

    d. paraphrasing participants' language to change the meaning.

10. An *inaccurate* statement regarding narrative structures is:

    a. Qualitative studies are encoded for different audiences.

    b. The authorial presence is acknowledged by various literary devices.

    c. The research tradition which emphasizes a full descriptive narrative is grounded theory.

    d. Some critical studies adopt a substantive report structure and others employ experimental forms of evocative representations.

Application Problems

1. Below are published paraphrases of teacher beliefs about kindergarten readiness and practices (M. L. Smith & L. S. Shepard, 1988, pp. 316–319). Identify the line numbers for categories of:

    beliefs about child development,

    beliefs about the possibility of "catching up,"

    beliefs about the possibilities of influencing a child's preparation for school,

    beliefs about what teachers can do.

List any other categories you see in the data.

Mrs. Willis:

1 "Because development constitutes physiological unfolding, rates of

2 development are smooth, continuous, with no spurts or discontinuities. The

3 child who is 6 months behind in September will be 6 months behind in

4 June. . . . There is little likelihood that a child who is developmentally behind

5 his agemates would close the gap that separates them . . . . Intervention is

6 futile with a developmentally unready child. Extra help or remediation

7 causes pressure, frustration and compensation. Teachers cannot influence

8 psychomotor abilities, ability to attend, social maturity, and so
9 forth. . . . Teachers can provide the child with more time to mature; place the
10 child in developmental kindergarten or preschool, send him home another
11 year; place the child in a slow group in class; reduce instruction below
12 frustration level, lower expectations, boost self-concept, use
13 manipulatives; retain in kindergarten; providing academic assistance is
14 irrelevant and harmful."

Miss Johnson:
15 "Within broad limits of chronological age, children's readiness is a
16 function of their experience, learning program, and environment. . . . A child
17 who is less prepared than his peers can close the gap given the right
18 educational circumstances; academic assistance is required. . . . The teacher
19 can make a difference as can the parent and other aspects of environment;
20 within a broad range of pupil abilities, what the pupil learns is largely a
21 function of opportunities and experiences....The teacher can provide
22 additional academic help; accommodate differences in achievement; hold high
23 expectations, reinforce and train; work hard and encourage the pupil to work
24 hard."

2. Now, go back and look at the meanings of each category. Do certain beliefs occur with other beliefs, that is, does one category(s) relate to another category(s) to suggest a pattern? State any patterns you see in the data.

PART IV

Analytical
Research

Educators frequently ask: Why is the history of schooling and educational practices important? What does a concept or term mean? How can the knowledge of the past enlighten and inform us in public discussions about education and in decision-making processes?

Qualitative research was classified in Chapter 2 as *interactive research* or *noninteractive research* termed *analytical research*. We address qualitative research that is traditionally non-interactive in Part IV.

Analytical research includes analysis of concepts and historical events and policy-making process. Sources for historical research are documents, oral testimonies, and relics. The researcher uses specialized techniques to search and locate documents in archives, manuscript repositories, libraries, and private collections.

We discuss both the general characteristics of analytical research and the specific procedures employed by concept analysis and historical analysis. We also present the credibility standards for this research tradition and illustrate the value of historical inquiry.

CHAPTER 15

Concept Analysis and Historical Research

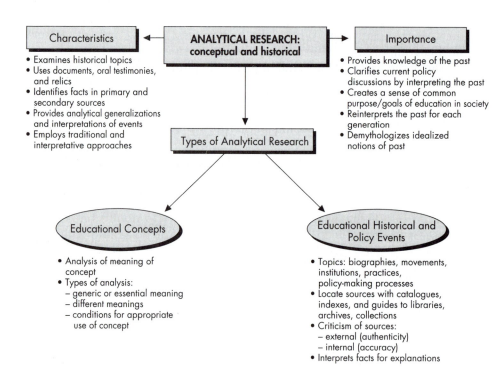

KEY TERMS

historiography

oral history

biography

interpretative biography

documents

oral testimonies

relics

facts

generalizations

analytical interpretation

conceptual analysis

primary source

secondary source

external criticism

internal criticism

One way to understand current educational practices is to know how these practices developed and to clarify the issues concerning them. How often have educators and noneducators made statements or justified decisions on the basis of what they assumed happened in the past? Explanations of past educational ideas or concepts, events, and policies suggest insights about trends, current educational events, and new educational issues (Strickler, 1992; Mason, et. al., 1997)

Analytical research, as a form of qualitative inquiry, draws primarily from the disciplines of philosophy (the meaning of concepts), history, and political science. Concept analysis and historical research are traditionally noninteractive document research. Some forms of historical research, however, such as oral history and interpretative biography, employ interactive techniques supplemented with documents and records. Analytical research describes and interprets the past or recent past from selected sources.

Both interactive and noninteractive forms of qualitative inquiry share commonalities of context-bound generalizations, a discovery orientation, emergent case study design, holistic emphasis (qualities of parts unifies the whole phenomenon), noninterference in the natural setting, and inductive data analysis.[1]

General Characteristics of Analytical Research

Underlying the varieties of analytical research are common methodological characteristics that distinguish analytical studies from other kinds of educational research. These methodological characteristics include a research topic related to past events, primary sources as data, techniques of criticism used in

[1]See Sherman & Webb, 1988, for a comparison of qualitative inquiry traditions such as ethnography, grounded theory, philosophy, history, biography, and others.

searching for facts, and interpretative explanations. Because these characteristics are general, they may be applied in different ways within a particular study.

Historiography is the study of the procedures that different historians use in their research and the changing revisions and interpretations of the past. We limit our discussion of the general characteristics and more specific procedures described later in this chapter to examples drawn from American educational historical and policy events. Many of these studies require the analysis of educational concepts—that is, the meaning of the language used.

Topics of Analysis

Historical Topics   Historical topics include a wide range of new and reoccurring topics of interest. The following topics illustrate the diversity of historical investigation:

1. movements—progressive education, lifelong learning
2. institutions—public education, kindergarten, day care
3. concepts—schooling, the child, literacy, professionalism
4. biographies of influential educators—John Dewey, Phillis Wheatley
5. comparative history of international education—comparison of American education system with those of other nationalities
6. alternative forms of schooling—home instruction, distant education
7. components of education—finance, personnel, accreditation, curriculum, enrollment, organization, administration, instructional methods and materials
8. cultural and minority education—gender, ethic, minority, bilingual education
9. regionalism in American education—geographic regions; state educational systems; urban/rural education
10. other topics—compilation (restoration) of documents with annotations; chronological narration of series of events

More recently, historians have focused on the educational aspects of the following: (a) the family, the church, and professional associations; (b) the urban/rural environment; (c) special institutions such as reform schools, orphanages, and juvenile courts; and (d) popular culture, such as television, songs, and literature (Cohen, 1976).

A continuing trend has been the application of concepts and traditional methods of other disciplines, such as sociology, economics, psychology, and anthropology, to historical inquiry (Kaestle, 1992). The historical past may be a time as recent as the previous year or as distant as centuries in which the historian has no personal experience. Monographs and specialized journals report historical research.

Oral History   A form of historical research is **oral history** which records the spoken words and testimonies of individuals. A study may focus on recording the ballads and stories of a region or a cultural group. Oral interviews of persons who witnessed or participated in important historical events are audio taped and the resulting transcriptions provide a written record. Oral historians collect and preserve the oral history before it is "lost" to future generations.[2]

Biography A study that focuses on *an individual*, especially the pivotal points of their life, as told to the researcher or recorded in documents or archival material, is a **biography**. Biography, as a type of research, can include individual biographies, autobiographies, life histories, and oral history of a life (Smith, 1998). These accounts examine "lesser lives, great lives, thwarted lives, lives cut short, or lives miraculous in their unapplauded achievement" (Creswell, 1998, p. 48).

A researcher may approach his or her topic as a *classical* biography or as an *interpretative* biography. A classical biography is one in which the researcher is concerned about the validity and criticism of primary sources and developing a "factual" base for explanations.[3] An **interpretative biography** is a study in which the researcher's presence is acknowledged in the narrative and with his or her standpoint. Interpretative biographers recognize that in a sense, the writer "creates" the person in the narrative just as the individual created themselves when they told or recorded their life story (Denzin, 1989). In either type of biography, the investigator must be knowledgeable about the historical context of the individual to interpret the person's life within the larger trends in society or in a culture.

Policy Topics Policy topics include two distinct areas:

1. political analysis of the nature and use of power and influence in educational government and
2. policy content and impact of specific governmental actions on education (Mitchell, 1988).[4]

The first topic area seeks to explain school policy by looking at the distribution of power among various stakeholders in the system and following the interactions among these influence groups to reveal the processes of decision making. This research, called "politics-of-education," focuses on the power of professional interest groups, informal social networks that move policy initiatives, the small number of key actors who shape legislative enactments, and the variations of the cultural values among levels of educational governance.

Policy content studies concentrate on a specific policy or issue rather than on power relationships. At a conceptual level, however, policy studies are very diverse. Research on policy content may focus on any of the control mechanisms for shaping the performance of schools, such as school organization and

---

[2]See the annual publication of the *Oral History Review.*

[3]See Angroisino (1989) and Lomask (1986) for the more traditional approach to biographical research.

[4]Policy analysis, a different type of research, is discussed in Chapter 16.

governance, school finance, student testing and assessment, school program definition, personnel training and certification, curriculum materials development and selection, and school buildings and facilities. Policy research also focuses on how policy content changes in distinct policy-making phases, such as articulation of a proposal, aggregation of interest groups and coalition formulation, allocation of power and resources to enact policies, the transformation of laws or rulings into regulations, implementation of the policy into practice, and evaluation of the extent to which policies have been implemented as intended and/or have produced the expected results. Many studies indicate that the content of a policy changes from one phase to another.

Analytical studies provide knowledge and understanding about past educational historical and policy events. Major ideas and concepts are clarified for meaning. Research questions focus on events (who, what, when, where), how an event occurred (descriptive), and why the event happened (interpretative).

Types of Sources

The data for these studies are written sources, many of which have been preserved in archives, manuscript collection repositories, personal collections, or libraries. Sources are documents, oral testimonies, and relics. All of these sources are generally classified as documents. A study may require one or several types of sources.

1. **Documents** are *records of past events*. They are written or printed materials that may be official or unofficial, public or private, published or unpublished, prepared intentionally to preserve a historical record or prepared to serve an immediate practical purpose. Documents may be letters, diaries, wills, receipts, maps, journals, newspapers, court records, official minutes, proclamations, regulations, or laws.

A special type of document is *quantitative records*, which may include enrollment records, staff employment records, membership lists, census records, tax lists, voting records, budgets, test score data, and any compilation of numerical data. The condensing of data, when it is clearly legitimate, makes the information easier to describe and analyze. The difficulty of using quantitative records usually increases with the remoteness of the period studied. As Aydelotte (1986, p. 806) noted, "formal statistical presentations are feasible only for a limited range of historical problems;" however, some political, economic, and demographic data have been handled quantitatively with success.[5]

2. **Oral testimonies** are *records of the spoken word*. The oral testimonies of persons who have witnessed events of educational significance are taped, and verbatim transcripts are made and identified. Oral testimonies are autobiographical or in-depth interviews that are either the primary evidence or are

---

[5]An example is J. Doughtery (1998). Procedures are discussed by J. Aydelotte (1986) and Burton, O. V., & Finnegan, R. (1990).

used to supplement the documentary evidence. Such testimonies may be recorded by participants or witnesses of the establishment of a new institution, the passage of an educational law, or the implementation of a policy.

3. **Relics** are any *objects* that provide information about the past. Although relics may not be intended to convey information directly about the past, the visual and physical properties of the objects can provide evidence of the past. Relics may be textbooks, buildings, equipment, charts, examinations, the physical evidence presented in a court case, or the physical objects in policy making. Table 15.1 illustrates types of sources for historical and policy-making research.

The Search for Evidence

The search for factual evidence begins with the location of sources. While quantitative researchers typically create the data by administering instruments to a sample, the historian depends on sources that have been preserved. These may

TABLE 15.1

Illustrative Types of Sources for Analytical Research

Source	Historical Research	Policy-Making Research
Documents	Letters Diaries Bills and receipts Autobiographies Newspapers Journals, magazines Bulletins Catalogs Films Recordings Personal records Institutional records Budgets Enrollment records Graduation records	Official and unofficial federal, state, local, and school government records • Legislative hearings, debates, reports, publications • Committee prints, minutes, reports • Agency reports • Statistical data, budgets • Regulations, directives • Laws • Voting records Speeches of government officials Proclamations
Oral testimonies	Participants in a historical event Relatives of a deceased person	Participants in policy-making processes: • administrators • school board • members • government • officials • professional staff • special interest groups • professional associations
Relics	Textbooks Buildings Maps Equipment Samples of student work Furniture Teaching materials	Physical objects presented in legislative hearings or other policy-making processes: • charts • diagrams • historical relics

or may not have been catalogued and identified for easy access. Finding and assessing historical sources is an excerise in dectective work. It involves "logic, intuition, persistence, and common sense—the same logic, intuition, persistence, and common sense that one would use to locate contemporary data. . . ." (Tuckman, 1998, p. 258).

The search for evidence requires locating both primary and secondary sources. Primary sources are documents or testimonies of eyewitnesses to an event. Secondary sources are documents or testimonies of individuals who did not actually observe or participate in the event and thus speak from hearsay evidence. Eyewitness accounts are valued more than secondary sources, but both types of sources are subjected to techniques of criticism.

Techniques of criticism assess the authenticity and trustworthiness of the source. Authenticity determines whether the source is a genuine document, forged document, or variant of the original document. Trustworthiness of the source refers to the accuracy of the statements found in the source. The researcher locates the most authentic and trustworthy sources to ascertain the facts. The **facts** are the most accurate parts of the description in the most authentic sources. Interpretations of an event are based on facts.

Analytical Generalizations and Interpretations

Analytical studies suggest **generalizations**, which are summaries of factual data. When inductive logic is applied to a series of generalizations about an event, an explanation is suggested. An **analytical interpretation** is a causal explanation for a specific event. Terms such as *cause, because, since, on account of,* and *for the reason that* connote explanations. Analytical explanations imply causes with such statements as "under the circumstances, it is not surprising that . . .," "naturally at this point, he . . .," and "it was inevitable that . . ." Explanations are suggested with such nouns as *impossibility, necessity, influence, impulse, development, consequence,* and *motives,* and such verbs as *lead to, result in, bring about, stimulate, force,* and *comply.*

Valid analytical interpretations differ from common-sense explanations in the following ways:

1. *An analytical generalization summarizes separate facts that assert that an event took place.* The researcher is interested in the particular circumstances under which an event occurred and recognizes that these circumstances may never be repeated again. Analytical explanations differ from common-sense explanations because they require critical judgement using specialized knowledge about the era in which the event occurred and the connecting circumstances.

2. *Interpretations suggest multiple causes for any single event.* Interpretations of the connections between the generalizations are usually causal. Cause and effect are not treated in an absolute manner and frequently depend on the

chronological order of incidents culminating in a particular event. The more complex the events and the wider their spread in time and space, the greater the need for the historian's interpretation. Usually, an event of any degree of magnitude and complexity needs many generalizations to interpret it.

3. *When analytical interpretations are justified or supported by the facts stated in the study, the explanations are considered valid.* Historians will say, "If you do not believe my explanation, take a closer look at the facts." The specification of details—the who, what, when, where and how—is precisely the feature of the explanation that differentiates it from statistical explanations (Gardiner, 1952). Historians seldom claim, however, that they have all the facts. Instead, a study contains a group of associated facts and ideas which, when clearly presented in a prescribed amount of space, leave no questions unanswered *within* the analysis. However, many questions could be asked about the topic *outside* the analysis in other studies (Barzun and Graff, 1992). See Figure 15.1 for the process of analytical research.

Approaches to Analytical Research

Traditional historical research has focused on investigating the "causes" of past events (Carr, 1967). Most historians argue that historical events are unique and do not repeat themselves. In identifying "causes" of events, historians may rely on the chronology of a series of events, assume the "great man" view of history, refer to compelling ideologies, cite technological and scientific advances, or focus on sociological, psychological, political, or economic influences.

As the noted historian Gottschalk (1969) wrote, the "whole past" can be known to the researcher only "through the surviving record of it…, and most of history-as-record is only the surviving part of the recorded part of the remembered part of the observed part of the whole" (pp. 45–46). It appears that there are no absolute causes waiting to be discovered and offered as explanations by a researcher. Instead, historians write at different levels of abstraction, at different chronological distances from the past event, for different purposes, in different contexts, and from different points of view. Not surprisingly, different studies suggest apparently contradictory but valid explanations of the past.

FIGURE 15.1 The Process of Analytical Research

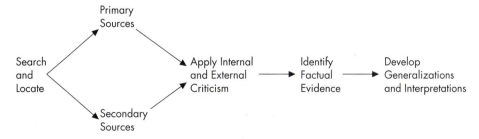

History is often reinterpreted as new interests or concerns become important or as new documents are made available to researchers and the public. Thus,
many historians recognize the fallibility of their interpretations even though
they are reasonable at the time. As *interpretative* historians, they are aware of
their own values, beliefs, and interests in a topic. These frequently surface to
consciousness when they read how other researchers have treated the topic.

During the last few decades, some historians, called *revisionists* or *reconstructionist* historians, have questioned the conventional or popular views of
the past. They suggest schools are a means of political control, social stratifica-
tion, and directly or indirectly promote discrimination against women and ethnic groups. Some revisionist historians are similar to the critical researchers
discussed in Part III.

The next sections of this chapter describe the methodology used in analytical research. We will describe techniques of conceptual analysis and procedures for studying past historical and policy events.

Analysis of Educational Concepts

A **conceptual analysis** is a study that clarifies the meaning of a concept by
describing the essential or generic meaning, the different meanings, and the
appropriate usage for the concept. By presenting an analysis of the concept, the
study helps us understand the way people think about education.3 The focus is
on the meaning of the concept, not on the researcher's personal values or on
factual information. For example, the question "What are the aims of education?" is not answered by collecting data to show that educators have aims or
do not have aims, or by making a value statement that educators should have
aims. Instead, the analyst begins by asking, "Is having an aim an integral and
necessary part of our concept of being an educator?" or "Can a person be an
educator without having an aim?" (Soltis, 1978, p. 15). Asking such questions
allows the analyst to get at the meaning of education by carefully examining
some ideas attached to the concept of aims as an aspect of education. The analyst assumes a neutral position while analyzing a concept before taking a value
position or collecting factual information.

Three strategies may be used to analyze such concepts as *education, literacy, knowledge, teaching, learning, equal opportunity,* and *due process.* Soltis
(1978) illustrates generic, differential, and conditions analyses. Each of these
strategies begins with a different prior question and applies specific techniques
to clarify the concept.

1. *A generic analysis identifies the essential meaning of a concept.* The
analysis isolates the elements that distinguish the concept from other words. To
clarify the concept *academic discipline*, one might, therefore, compare history,
mathematics, and physics as clear standard examples with home economics,
animal husbandry, and water-skiing as counterexamples in order to arrive at the
generic meaning of *academic discipline.*

2. *A differential analysis distinguishes among the basic meanings of the concept and provides a clearer idea of the logical domain covered by the concept.* Differential analysis is used when a concept seems to have more than one standard meaning and the basis for differentiating between meanings is unclear. The prior question is "What are the basic (different) meanings of the concept?" One could, for example, ask the question "What are the different meanings of subject matter?" and analyze the concept of *subject matter* by intuitively classifying the typical uses with concrete examples, such as *Silas Marner,* solar system, school subjects, knowledge, and skills. The distinguishing characteristics of each type of school matter is ascertained to clearly separate the types, and a typology is developed. An example of differential analysis is the distinction between basic, applied, and evaluation research made in Chapter 1, which is intended to provide a clearer understanding of the concept *research.*

3. *A conditions analysis identifies the conditions necessary for proper use of the concept.* The prior question is "Under what context conditions would it be true that the concept is present?" Conditions analysis begins by providing an example that meets the necessary conditions of the concept but can easily be made a noninstance by changing the context. This forces either revision or rejection of the condition and leads to additional conditions with other examples and counterexamples. The purpose of the conditions analysis "is to produce a set of necessary and sufficient conditions for the proper application of a concept to any of its many and varied instances" (Soltis, 1978, p. 65).

Critical to the analysis of educational concepts is the selection of the typical uses of the concept and counterexamples. The analyst uses *purposeful sampling* by choosing examples that demonstrate implicit meanings in the language, which are then analyzed logically. Examples may be drawn from generally accepted common uses of the concepts. Because different sets of examples are used frequently, the analysis of educational concepts may lead to reanalysis and further conceptual clarity.

Analysis of educational concepts is applied in the study of educational concepts and in historical, legal, and policy research. A study of the public school movement, due process in education, or groups that influence the passage of a law must first determine the meaning of *public school, due process,* and *influential groups.*

Analysis of Educational Historical and Policy Events

Analytical research requires systematic application of methodological procedures to phrase a historical problem, locate and criticize sources, and interpret facts for causal explanations. Specialized training is necessary in order to conduct historical and policy research. The historian proceeds in a circular fashion because of the interrelationships of the research problem, sources, criticism, analysis, and explanations.

The Topic and Problem Statement

The researcher begins with an initial subject, such as a historical period, person, idea, practice, institution, or policy. As the analyst obtains background knowledge, the topic is defined more exactly. Simultaneously, the analyst notes possible primary sources relevant to the topic. Statement of the problem delimits and focuses the research study. The problem must be narrow enough to examine the event in detail but broad enough to identify patterns for the interpretation.

In order to phrase the research topic, the historian initially reads widely in secondary sources for background knowledge. Background knowledge suggests the breadth of the subject, previous research on the problem, gaps in knowledge, and possible sources. Background knowledge is obtained from textbooks, monographs, encyclopedias and other reference works, dissertations, and specialized journals. General bibliographies cite secondary sources. Some bibliographies specifically useful to the historian are *A Guide to Historical Literature, The Historian's Handbook: A Descriptive Guide to Reference Works,* and *A Bibliography of American Educational History.* Secondary sources for policy research are located with general historical bibliographies and such specialized bibliographies as *The Study of Politics and Education: A Bibliographic Guide to Research Literature.*

Limiting and phrasing a topic is a continuing effort. The problem statement is expressed most succinctly and clearly at the end of the research, when the sources have been collected, analyzed, and interpreted. Considerations in limiting a topic are the availability and accessibility of primary sources; the analyst's interests, specialized knowledge, and time to complete the study; and the type of analysis to be done.

The statement of a historical problem indicates the particular event, person, institution, or policy. Problems are delimited by the time period, geographic location, and viewpoint of the analysis (see Excerpt 15.1).

Location and Criticism of Sources

Primary sources are essential for analytical research, but secondary sources are used selectively when necessary. Both primary and secondary sources are subjected to techniques of criticism. The sources for a study are cited in the bibliography and frequently footnoted in a study. Criticism of sources may be in the text of a study or in a methodological appendix.

Classification of Sources A **primary source** is the written or oral testimony of an eyewitness or a participant, or a record made by some mechanical device present at the event, such as a tape recorder, a transcript, or a photograph. Primary

EXCERPT 15.1

PROBLEM STATEMENT

Through an examination of the reactions to the GI Bill in the print media, this article seeks to explore not only how a college education increasingly became seemingly more accessible to average Americans—a possibility charged with new meaning, but also what this phenomenon reveals about the underlying cultural values informing this shift in the perception of college. The GI Bill indeed changed the way Americans thought of college education, and these new perceptions dovetailed with and were an intimate aspect of emerging new conceptions of defining oneself in a corporate world and consumer cultural. Nevertheless, these new conceptions also contained traditional notions of the value of college, markers of social class, and gender prescriptions as well, that existed alongside but in contrast with the act's association with democratization. No historians have explored these deeper cultural ramifications involved with the GI Bill. The enormous impact of the GI Bill has been taken as a given. Consequently, I believe, we have not adequately explored the most important result of the GI Bill—its function in reshaping the role of college education in postwar American culture.

Source: From Clark, D. A. (1998). The two Joes meet—Joe College, Joe Veteran: The GI Bill, college education, and postwar American culture (pp.167–169). *History of Education Quarterly, 38* (2), 165–189.

sources for a historical biography are the person's personal and public papers and the relics of his or her life. Primary sources for policy-making research are records of government action and the oral testimonies of eyewitnesses. A primary source is original in the sense that it contains firsthand eyewitness accounts of the events.

A **secondary source** is the record or testimony of anyone not an eyewitness to or participant in the event. A secondary source contains the information from someone else, who may or may not have witnessed the event. Secondary sources contain historical and policy-making research that interprets other primary and secondary sources. These sources provide insights and possibly facts for analysis.

The classification of sources as primary or secondary depends on the research problem. Some sources may be primary in one study and secondary in another. The number of primary sources necessary for a study varies with the topic. To obtain primary sources, the analyst thinks of the sources that would yield information on the topic and then investigates whether the records were preserved and are accessible. A single study may use different kinds of sources, but it is essential that primary sources serve as the basis for documentation. Documentation is the process of proof based upon any kind of source, whether written, oral, or an object.

Location of Sources The credibility of an analytical study is determined partly by the selected primary sources. The problem statement and limitations point to the necessary primary sources. A study of the admissions policies of a university would be seriously flawed without institutional records. A biography of G. Stanley Hall would be questioned if his private papers and writings were ignored. The bibliography cites only those sources actually used for the study.

Documents. Documents are located through specialized guides, catalogues, indexes, and bibliographies or through research centers. Examples of specialized reference works are *A Catalogue of Rare and Valuable Early Schoolbooks, Educational Periodicals During the Nineteenth Century,* and *Selective and Critical Bibliography of Horace Mann.* Researchers may begin with a broader search of documents by using guides to archives and private manuscript collections which often provide annotated lists. *A Guide to Manuscripts and Archives in the United States* describes the holdings of 1300 repositories, and the *Guide to the National Archives of the United States* indexes educational records of government agencies. Other directories are the *National Inventory of Documentary Sources in the United States* and the *Directory of Archives and Manuscript Repositories in the United States.* The *National Union Catalogue of Manuscript Collections,* published annually by the Library of Congress, cites the increasing number of educational collections made available to scholars. Archival research centers devoted to particular historical subjects often contain educational records.[6]

Studies of educational policy-making use government documents and oral testimonies. Federal government documents are indexed in the *Monthly Catalog of United States Government,* the *Publication Reference File (PRF),* the *Congressional Information Service/Index (CIS),* the *American Statistical Index (ASI),* the *Index to Government Documents,* and agencies' publication lists. The *Legislative Research Checklist,* issued monthly by the Council of State Governments, often abstracts the published reports of commissioners or councils that recommend and draft new legislation. Because research tools for state legislative history vary widely from state to state, state law libraries or legislative reference librarians are consulted. Local government documents are not centrally indexed and must be obtained from the agency.

Oral Testimonies. Oral testamonies that are relevant to a topic require pre-planning. The researcher decides which individuals are knowledgeable about the topic, locates these individuals, and collects data through interviews.[7]

---

[6]The archives of Labor History and Urban Affairs at Wayne State University are perhaps the oldest collection. Other topical centers that have documents relevant to education history are the Urban Archives Center at Temple University, the Archives of the Industrial Society at the University of Pittsburgh, the Archives of the History of American Psychology at the University of Akron, the Ohio History of Education Project at the Ohio Historical Society, Social Welfare Archives at the University of Minnesota, and Television News Archives at Vanderbilt University. See Hill, M. R. (1993), *Archival strategies and techniques.*

[7]See W. W. Cutler (1971), Oral history: Its nature and uses for educational history. *History of Education Quarterly, 11,* 184–194; R. Jensen (1981), Oral history, quantification and the new social history. *Oral History Review, 9,* 13–27; and D. Lance (1980), Oral history archives: Perceptions and practices. *Oral History, 8* (2), 59–63.

The selection of informants for oral testimonies is done with purposeful sampling procedures such as snowball sampling or reputational-case selection (see Chapter 12). A panel of experts, for example, nominates individuals on the basis of criteria from the problem statement. Additional considerations are accessibility to the individuals and feasibility (time, finances, number of investigators, and so on). The researcher states the selection criteria.

Oral history is the collection of data through an interview guide approach, similar to certain in-depth interviews. The researcher desires information on the research problem and any other information that may further an understanding of the topic. Oral testimonies are time-consuming to obtain and result in extensive transcripts. The transcripts are subject to internal and external criticism as are other documentary sources frequently used in this methodology. For example, in a case study of the context of policy formation of an Arizona bilingual educational legislation (Excerpt 15.2), seventeen individuals were formally interviewed. These individuals, selected through purposeful sampling strategies, were concentrated among the state's policy "influentials" but spread across four clusters (insiders, near circle, far circle, and often-forgotten players). In addition, the records of the House and Senate, the State Board of Education, administrative regulations, and two newspapers were data sources.

Criticism of Sources Techniques of internal and external criticism are applied to all kinds of sources, such as documents, oral testimonies, and relics. Even sources that are official publications or preserved in archives are subjected to criticism. External criticism determines the authenticity of the source. Internal criticism determines the credibility of the facts stated by the source. Although external and internal criticism ask different questions about the source, the techniques are applied simultaneously. The criticism of sources may be covered in a methodological discussion or in an appendix to a study.

External Criticism. **External criticism** determines whether the source is the original document, a forged document, or a variant of the original document. Typical questions are "Who wrote the document?" and "When, where, and what was the intention?" The more specialized knowledge the analyst has, the easier it is to determine whether a document is genuine. The historian needs knowledge of the way people in the era that produced the document lived and behaved, the things they believed, and the way they managed their institutions. The educational researcher is less likely to deal with forged documents than is a social scientist who studies controversial political, religious, or social movements. Claims to a title or the date of an institution can, however, be forged. Sometimes it is impossible to determine the contribution of an individual for government reports or speeches if there are multiple authors.

The date and place of writing or publication can be established by means of the citation on the document, the date of the manuscript collection, or the contents of the document. However, working papers internal to an institution,

EXCERPT 15.2

SELECTION OF ORAL TESTIMONIES

The conceptual frame adopted in this study was developed by Marshall, Mitchell, and Wirt (1986) for identifying the "power and influence context of policymaking" (pp. 347–348). This study pursued the process leading to the passage of Arizona's 1984 bilingual education law.

The primary data composing this study also were drawn from interviews with "policy elite" (Wirt, Mitchell, & Marshall, 1985). . . . In all, 17 individuals were formally interviewed during the data collection, several more than once. However, both authors were involved in varying degrees throughout the legislative process, attended many meetings, and had numerous informal contacts and conversations regarding the law. In terms of Marshall et al.'s (1986, p. 355) policy group influence rankings and cluster, interviews were concentrated among representatives of Arizona's higher ranking groups, but spread across four clusters (insiders, near circle, far circle and often-forgotten players).

In addition, copies of all legislative proposals and amendments leading to the final, adopted version of the law were analyzed. Arizona has little written legislative history, but a record of all votes is compiled in House and Senate journals, which also include statements by some legislators explaining their final votes. The records of the State Board of Education, including administrative regulations and legislative proposals that involve bilingual education, and back issues of the *Phoenix Republic* and *Tucson Daily Star and Citizen* were reviewed for articles discussing legislative deliberations and actions on bilingual education.

Source: Adapted from Sacken, D. M. & Medina, M., Jr. (1990). Investigating the context of state-level policy formation: A case study of Arizona's bilingual education legislation. *Educational Evaluation and Policy Analysis, 12*(4), 391.

or drafts made by an individual, may contain no dates or be insufficient for use if only the year is stated.

What the educational researcher is more likely to find is variant sources. Variant sources are two or more texts of the same document, or two or more testimonies to the same event. For example, a newspaper account of the results of a state educational testing program may differ from the actual statistical report published by the State Department of Education, and both may differ from the separate drafts of the report. In this situation, the newspaper account, the official report, and the separate drafts are all authentic sources of different texts. Oral testimonies by different individuals may be authentic but variant sources.

Internal Criticism. **Internal criticism** determines the accuracy and trustworthiness of the statements in the source. The historian asks: "Are the statements accurate and the witnesses trustworthy?" Accuracy is related to a witness's chronological and geographical proximity to the event, the competence of the witness, and the witness's attention to the event. Obviously, not all witnesses equally close to the event are equally competent observers and recorders. Competence depends on expertness, state of mental and physical health, educational level, memory, narrative skill, and the like. It is well known that eyewitnesses under traumatic or stressful conditions remember selective parts of an event, yet they are convinced that because they were present, their accounts are accurate. Even though a witness may be competent, he or she may be an interested party or biased. Bias or preconceived prejudice causes a witness to habitually distort, ignore, or overemphasize incidents. The conditions in which the statements were made may influence accuracy. The literary style, the laws of libel, the conventions of good taste, or a desire to please may lead to exaggerated politeness or expressions of esteem.

Several techniques estimate the accuracy and dependability of a statement. Statements by a witness made as a matter of indifference, those injurious to the person stating them, or those contrary to the personal desires of the person stating them are less likely to be biased than others. Statements considered common knowledge or incidental are less likely to be in error. Other credible sources can confirm, modify, or reject statements. In a qualitative analysis; however, the simple agreement of statements from independent witnesses can be misleading, since the research depends only on preserved sources. Agreement with other known facts or circumstantial evidence increases the credibility of a statement. A researcher may cite the source by referring to it: "according to the judge's opinion," "Horace Mann says," or "the Speaker of the House is our authority for the statement that...."

Internal and external criticism requires knowledge about the individuals, events, and behavior of the period under study. "The ability to put oneself in the place of the individuals...to interpret documents, events, and personalities with their eyes, standards, sympathies (without necessarily surrendering one's own standards) has sometimes been called *historical mindedness*" (Gottschalk, 1969, pp. 136–137). Throughout the whole process, the analyst is skeptical and critical of the sources and statements. An analyst is not easily satisfied or convinced that the sources have yielded evidence as close to actual events as possible.

Criticism of Sources. Criticism of sources is treated in several ways within a study. The most obvious citations are the footnotes and the items labeled *Notes, References,* or *Bibliography* following the study. The list is usually extensive. There are, for example, eighty-three footnotes for the twelve-page journal article "A History of Discrimination Against Black Students in Chicago Secondary Schools" (Daniel, 1980); they include official reports of the U.S. Department of Health, Education, and Welfare and other federal departments and agencies, *Laws of Illinois, Board of Education Annual Reports,* the *Census of the United States,* articles from the *Chicago Tribune* and *Chicago Defender,* the *Municipal Code of Chicago,* interviews with participants, reports of the Chicago Commission on Race Relations, the Vice Commission of Chicago, and the Chicago Real Estate Board, and secondary sources.

In methodological discussions in the study or in an appendix, the historian also refers to criticism. The author of Excerpt 15.3 criticized the sources by noting that the long letters, the brief answers on the questionnaires of the 1890s, and the pupil records at Troy must "be interpreted with care." The researcher noted the possible bias of the documents because of the self-selection of those who attended Troy and because those who maintained contact with Troy probably had favorable experiences at the seminary and developed feminist values.

Methodological appendices are written because the study uses sources that are newly collected and analyzed. An appendix, rather than the study *per se*, allows that analyst to expand on the methodological problems of the sources and comment on their scholarly value. Excerpt 15.4 illustrates a reference to methodological problems and the need for a methodological appendix. This study required the identification of all teacher strikes that occurred in 1978–1979. Information gathered by state and national government agencies and by state and national professional associations contained "serious discrepancies" that were due to different definitions of a strike and to information gaps in sources. The method of identifying the 158 strikes was presented in an appendix. The method was made available to other researchers.

EXCERPT 15.3

CRITICISM OF SOURCES

A handful of Troy pupils left some record of what they thought the long-term influence of the institution and its founder upon them had been. A number who replied to the questionnaires sent out in the 1890's responded with long letters, and others, even in brief answers, threw some light on how they recalled the experience. Still others, simply by describing their lives, inadvertently bore witness to the kind of strength of character which Troy reinforced. What stands out in most of these records is the great importance of Willard's own personality in providing her pupils with a new image of what women could be. . . .

Of course such evidence must be interpreted with care. Obviously, a woman who felt very much attached to Troy would be likely to write a detailed response to the questionnaire; children who remembered such attachment would be likely to take the trouble to reply. There was certainly a process of self-selection on the part of the women who chose to go to Troy. These fragments do bear witness, however, to the beginning of a new personality type, the educated woman who was not ashamed of learning and who would inevitably have a wider notion of what the world had to offer than her sisters who had not been encouraged to read widely or to think for themselves. (35)

Source: From "The Ever Widening Circle: The Diffusion of Feminist Values from the Troy Female Seminary, 1822–1872" by Anne Firor Scott, *History of Education Quarterly,* Vol. 19, Spring 1979. Reprinted by permission of the author.

EXCERPT 15.4

CRITICISM OF SOURCES

A major research task was to locate and monitor teacher strikes which occurred during 1978–79. We needed to identify all strike sites so that we could conduct a mailed survey of affected districts, and we needed to locate sites where field studies could be conducted. As it turned out, the task of monitoring strikes was extraordinarily difficult. There is no central national agency which has a reliable system for quickly identifying strike sites. Information gathered by state and national professional associations, and by state and national government agencies, contains serious discrepancies. Some are traceable to differing definitions of what constitutes a strike. Some are traceable to gaps in information sources. The basis for our own calculation that there were 158 strikes is set forth in a technical appendix. . . .

Source: From Colton, D. L., & Graber, E. E. (1980). *Enjoining teacher strikes: The irreparable harm standard.* Grant No. NIE-G-78-0149, 26. Washington, DC: National Institute of Education.

Facts, Generalizations, and Interpretations

Facts are the basis for generalizations that may be interpreted as causal explanations. The process is not this simple, however. Criticism of sources may lead to rephrasing the problem and a further search for sources and facts.

1. *Facts describe the who, what, when, and where of an event.* Most analysts, however, go beyond obtaining descriptive facts and ask the interpretative questions of the ways a historical event occurred and the reasons for it. The analyst thus moves from identifying facts to stating generalizations to inferring causal explanations. The questions asked of the sources are crucial to the entire process.

The researcher's skill in questioning is similar to that of a detective in search of evidence and that of a scientist systematically testing that evidence. Questions may be very specific, such as "When did Henry Barnard die?" or may be abstract, such as "How did the scientific movement influence school administration practices?" Methodological training and experience, both general and specialized knowledge, disciplined intuition, and logic influence the analysis. The researcher operates primarily in an inductive mode of reasoning, going from the specific facts to generalizations. The more questions asked of the sources about the topic, the more comprehensive and complex the analysis is.

When statements and facts conflict, additional information is sought to resolve the apparent differences. Eventually, though, the researcher must decide. Even the sentence "The Troy Female Seminary, officially opened in 1821 but tracing its roots to 1814, was the first permanent institution offering

American women a curriculum similar to that of the contemporary men's colleges" (Scott, 1979, p. 3) required "*decisive* evidence"—evidence that confirms one view and denies alternative views. The decision to accept a statement as fact *rests on possibility and its plausibility* (Barzun & Graff, 1992). In other words, given a set of facts, it is reasonable to assume that the event happened in a certain way, or did not even occur. Facts are weighed and judged by consistency, the accumulation of evidence, and other techniques.

2. *Interpretations of the relationships between facts are generalizations.* As D. M. Potter notes, "generalization in history is inescapable and...the historian cannot avoid it by making limited statements about limited data. For a microcosm is just as cosmic as a macrocosm. Moreover, relationships between the factors in a microcosm are just as subtle and the generalizations involved in stating these relationships are just as broad as the generalizations concerning the relationships between factors in a situation of larger scale" (Potter, 1963, p. 191). Each generalization is subjected to analysis and is usually modified or qualified. Elements that often appear as facts in a study are frequently generalizations of facts for which there is no space for presentation in the study. Excerpt 15.5, for example, taken from the text of a historical study, contains facts (Miss Strachan was president of the Interborough Association of Women Teachers, 1906–1912), generalizations ("when the struggle was over," "chief spokeswoman," "most irritating of gadflies"), and causes of an event (a leader, an organization, unequal pay scales between men and women), and it also implies two theories

EXCERPT 15.5

EXAMPLE OF GENERALIZATIONS

Perhaps the most important reason why the equal pay movement began in New York City can be found in one of those happy accidents of history where a single individual, equipped with the right proportions of character, leadership qualities, ambition, and moral fervor just happens to be at the right place at the right time. Clearly one cannot study the history of the equal pay movement without concluding that it would have been much different, and probably much less effective had not Grace Strachan emerged as its leader and its chief spokeswoman, as well as the most irritating of gadflies to the educational and political establishment. A product of the Buffalo Normal School, Miss Strachan came to the New York City schools as a classroom teacher, probably sometime in the late 1880s. At the time the equal pay movement was at its greatest intensity she was serving as District Superintendent of Districts 33 and 35, containing upwards of 32,000 school children. One of the organizers of the Interborough Association of Women Teachers in 1906, Miss Strachan became its president in 1907 and held that post until 1912 when for all practical purposes the struggle was over.

Source: From "Tempest on the Hudson: The Struggle for 'Equal Pay for Equal Work' in the New York City Schools, 1907–1911" by Robert E. Doherty, *History of Education Quarterly*, Vol. 19, Winter 1979. Reprinted by permission of the author.

of change: accident (an individual with certain qualities "happens to be at the right place at the right time") and the "great leader" ("right proportions of character, leadership qualities, ambition, and moral fervor").

3. *Analytical explanations are abstract syntheses of generalizations, usually stated as conclusions.* Generalizations presented throughout the study are reanalyzed for context, internal consistency, documentation, accumulation of evidence, and logical induction. The process is cyclic, one of constantly returning to the facts and, if necessary, to the documents to derive meaning. A causal explanation stated as an overview in an introduction does not mean the researcher began with this interpretation and set out to prove personal notions. The introductory overview was probably the last section of the study to be written, because the logic of the study must flow from it and the criteria for judging the quality of the study is derived from it.

Conclusions are synthesized generalizations and concepts previously documented in the study. In other words, conclusions are an interpretative summary of the generalizations. Conclusions may be stated in narrative form or as a brief list, followed by statements about the status of knowledge on the topic, identification of policy issues, or suggestions for further research. Excerpt 15.6 illustrates a conclusion that contains three interpretations (paragraph 1) on ways social science is used in legislative policy-making, the reasons it is used, and the effects of its usage. Two policy recommendations (paragraph 2) are made from these findings.

Analytical Research in Perspective

Analytical studies of educational topics aid in the development of knowledge and the improvement of practices. By comprehending educational concepts and events of the past, one can better understand educational policies, trends, and practices of the present. Below are a few of the uses of analytical research.

1. *The analysis of educational concepts can aid in the selection of research problems, designs, and methodology.* The analysis of the concept of teaching as different types of teaching acts, for example, could suggest research questions and aid in designing either quantitative or qualitative research on teaching. A conceptual map of the logical domain of teaching might give a clearer view of the focus of previous research and suggest topics of needed research. An analysis of a concept can provide insights for the selection of a design. Such concepts as *behavioral objectives, alternative schooling,* and *problem solving* are not merely words but part of a language system that constructs a framework for organizing ideas in the researcher's mind. Ascertaining the meaning of the concept before data collection enables the researcher to select more appropriate variables and measures for investigating the concept. In qualitative research, concept analysis is often the entire focus of the study, or the analysis may identify categories for organizing and interpreting the data.

EXCERPT 15.6

ANALYTICAL CONCLUSIONS AND IMPLICATIONS

CONCLUSION

The data analyzed here support three basic conclusions regarding social science utilization within state legislatures: (1) social science is only one of four distinct types of expert authority influencing legislative decisions. The other types of expertise (legal, political and technical) are more prevalent and therefore more frequently utilized. However, social science is frequently utilized by full-time legislators and by fully professional staff consultants. (2) The utilization of social science contributes to both intellectual and social aspects of the decision-making process. Intellectually, scientific expertise orients policy makers to certain aspects of the decisions which they must make. Socially, science utilization alters the processes of collaboration and conflict that control decision outcomes. (3) The contributions of social science shift significantly as legislative proposals move through the four phases of decision making: articulation, aggregation, allocation and oversight. During the earliest phase, science may have both powerful and largely noncontroversial impacts. As legislative issues become more clearly defined and the specifics of who will benefit and who will pay for a proposed policy become identified, social science utilization becomes more partisan and more controversial as it is transformed into a tool or weapon of political conflict.

These findings suggest that social scientists, state legislatures, and science-sponsoring agencies would all be well served if: (a) the development of scientific advocacy for various policy solutions were recognized as a *political* process, requiring the talents of frankly partisan as well as scientifically sophisticated professionals, and (b) systematic efforts were made to bring scientific analysis to bear *earlier* in the legislative process. That is, science utilization should be seen as the mobilization of scientific expertise in support of specific political interests of state legislators who are required to make political rather than scientific decisions. Science utilization serves best to refine and criticize—not to replace—other, more fundamental mechanisms for defining and resolving public policy issues.

NOTE

National Institute of Education Grant No. NIE-G–76–0104 entitled, "Improving Social Science Utilization in Legislative Policy Making for Basic Skills Education." This grant to the University of California, Riverside (Douglas E. Mitchell, principal investigator) was funded in October, 1976.

Source: From "Social Science Impact on Legislative Decision Making: Process & Substance" by Douglas E. Mitchell, *Educational Researcher*, November 1980. Copyright © 1980 American Educational Research Association. Reprinted by permission.

   2. *Analytical research provides knowledge about the so-called roots of educational ideas, institutions, leaders, policies, and practices.* Knowledge of the past informs educational professionals, policymakers, and the general society

about education and its role in American society. Such knowledge often questions educational fables. By examining the fate of past solutions to enduring problems, decision-makers may become more realistic and moderate in their claims and more informed in their choices.

3. *Analytical research can clarify present legal and policy discussions by interpreting the past with disciplined detachment and reasoned historical judgment.* Analytical studies interpret the complexity of past collective educational, social, economic, legal, and political relationships. F. M. Wirt suggests that such research is useful because it is "through the process of removing the unsupportable from discussion of public life that public policy is enriched" (1980, p. 17). Analytical research, however, never claims that it predicts future educational and policy actions.

4. *Historical research may demythologize idealized notions about past events and stimulate action.* Historical research has documented discriminatory practices and policies in education, some of which have been institutionalized since the colonial period and were supported by the social and cultural values at that time. Some revisionist researchers have questioned the stereotyping of specific immigrant and ethnic groups. Other reconstructionist researchers have queried the lack of contributions of women and minorities to the nation displayed in textbooks and other educational materials.

5. *Historical research, in a broader and perhaps more philosophical sense, can create a sense of common purpose.* Historical interpretations typically reflect a fundamental belief that public education in America has served and can serve a common good. Common goals of education and the role of education in the American society are often neglected in fragmented empirical research. Implicit in the purpose of analytical research is a concern that the goals of education and educational practices benefit both the individual and American society.

6. *Historical research is a dynamic area of educational inquiry because each generation reinterprets its past.* Analytical philosophers focus on the changing meanings of educational concepts. Educational historians, especially the revisionists, ask new questions, use a greater variety of sources, analyze the past with a wide range of social science concepts, and apply quantitative procedures when appropriate. Often the conclusions of historical and policy studies are revised. A recent historical event, court case, or a new policy may indicate a basic shift in previous educational principles, policies, or collective educational goals.

Credibility Standards for Historical Studies

Analytical research requires methodological procedures to phrase an analytical topic, locate and critique primary sources, establish facts, and form generalizations for causal explanations or principles. These research processes suggest criteria for judging a historical or policy-making study as credible research. Criteria for judging the adequacy of historical studies is followed by criteria for evaluating legal research.

The reader judges a study in terms of the logical relationship among the problem statement, sources, generalizations, and causal explanations. The logic for the entire study flows from the problem statement. Implicit in the evaluation of a study is the question, "Did the analyst accomplish the stated purpose?" If all the elements of the research are not made explicit, the study can be criticized as biased or containing unjustifiable conclusions.

Problem statements in the introduction delineate the study and are evaluated by the following questions.

1. Is the topic appropriate for analytical research—that is, does it focus on the past or recent past?
2. Does the problem statement indicate clearly the information that will be included in the study and the information that is excluded from the study?
3. Is the analytical framework or viewpoint stated?

Selection and criticism of sources are evaluated in terms of relevance to the problem statement. Sources are listed in the bibliography and footnotes. Criticism of the sources may be discussed in the study, the footnotes, or in a methodological appendix.

1. Does the study use primary sources relevant to the topic?
2. Is the criteria for selection of primary sources stated?
3. Were authentic sources used for documentation?
4. Does the analyst indicate criticism of sources?

Facts and generalizations presented in the text are assessed by asking the following questions:

1. Does the study indicate the application of external criticism to ascertain the facts? If conflicting facts are presented, is a reasonable explanation offered?
2. Are the generalizations reasonable and related logically to the facts?
3. Are the generalizations appropriate for the type of analysis? One would, for example, expect minimal generalization in a study that restores a series of documents to their original text or puts a series of policy statements into chronological order. One would expect some synthesis in a descriptive or comparative analysis.
4. Are the generalizations qualified or stated in a tentative manner?

Interpretations presented as conclusions, are evaluated by the following criteria:

1. Are the interpretations reasonable and logically related to the facts and generalizations presented in the study?
2. Do the explanations suggest multiple causes for complex human events?
3. Does the study address all the questions stated in the introduction— that is, does it fulfill the purpose of the study?

Summary

The following statements summarize the major characteristics of analytical methodology and its application in educational conceptual, historical, policy-making, and legal studies.

1. Analytical research, in contrast to experimental research, describes and interprets the past or recent past from selected sources.
2. Sources are written documents, oral testimonies, and relics.
3. Primary sources are documents or testimonies of an eyewitness of an event. Secondary sources are documents or testimonies of individuals who did not actually observe the event.
4. Analytical studies suggest generalizations of facts (who, what, where, and when), about an event and state interpretations which suggest multiple causes for any single event.
5. A conceptual analysis focuses on the meanings of the language of education by describing the generic meaning, the different meanings, and the appropriate usage of the concept.
6. Historical topics focus on biographies, movements, institutions, and practices. Policy topics include an analysis of the distribution of power among various stakeholders in the system, policy-making processes, and policy content from formulation through implementation.
7. Interpretative biographies recognize the researcher's role within the study.
8. A historical problem is delimited by the time period, the geographic location, the specific event studied, and the viewpoint of the analysis.
9. Specialized bibliographies and indexes locate the primary sources necessary for historical research.
10. Oral testimonies are in-depth qualitative interviews of informants to study past or recent events.
11. External criticism determines whether the source is the original document, a forged document, or a variant of the original document. Internal criticism determines the accuracy and trustworthiness of the statements in the source.
12. Historical research provides knowledge and explanations of the past, clarifies present policy discussions by interpreting the past with disciplined detachment, revises myths of the past, and can create a sense of common purpose about education in American society.

13. Historical studies are not intended to predict future events in an exact manner.
14. Credibility standards for historical research emphasize the logical relationship between the problem statement, selection and criticism of sources, and the facts, generalizations, and explanations.

Self-Instructional Review Exercises

Sample answers are in the back of the book.

Test Items

1. Analytical research differs from experimental research in that it
   a. uses primarily preserved documents.
   b. focuses on past events or on recent events.
   c. uses logical induction to interpret facts.
   d. All of the above are correct.
2. Interpretative explanations
   a. are usually biased generalizations of facts.
   b. suggest single causes for educational events.
   c. are syntheses of generalizations that summarize collaborated facts.
   d. are seldom revised in subsequent studies.
3. A conceptual analysis of an educational concept is done to identify
   a. only the essential meaning of a concept.
   b. examples and counterexamples of the typical uses of the concept by random sampling.
   c. nonstandard meanings of a concept.
   d. the generic meaning, the different meanings, and the appropriate usage for the concept.
4. Which of the following is an example of a historical question?
   a. Is there a relationship between variable x and variable y?
   b. Is there a statistically significant difference between the scores of the experimental and control group?
   c. How did schools become bureaucracies during the 1920s?
   d. What is the cognitive developmental stage of students in an accelerated fifth grade math program?
5. List in order the following steps to conduct a historical study.
   a. identifies facts and obtains collaboration
   b. applies techniques of criticism to sources
   c. uses specialized bibliographies and indexes to locate sources
   d. acquires background knowledge for the problem statement
   e. selects a research topic
6. Criticism of sources requires
   a. questioning the accuracy of each statement in a source.
   b. questioning each source for authenticity.

    c. use of specialized knowledge about the way people lived and behaved in the era.

    d. All of the above are correct.

7–9 Match the following studies with the appropriate types of analytical research:

7. a study of a school board's decision-making processes	a. historical research
8. a biography of the founder of the National Education Association	b. policy research
9. an analysis of the meanings of progressive education	c. analysis of an educational concept

10. Analytical studies serve several functions in educational research. Which functions are analytical studies *least* able to serve?

    a. clarify collective meanings of education that operated in the past and perhaps in present policy discussions

    b. provide knowledge and interpretations of past educational historical and policy events

    c. predict in an exact manner to future events

    d. identify a sense of a common heritage and common purpose in American education

Application Problems

Answer the following questions for each methodological problem.

1. A policy researcher wants to study the decision-making of a local school board.

    a. How could this topic be narrowed and delimited?

    b. List the types of possible sources and examples of sources for this topic.

2. A researcher wants to study student discipline.

    a. How could this research problem be stated if it were a historical study? a legal study? a policy study? an analysis of a concept?

    b. State at least one specialized bibliography or index for each type of study.

3. A researcher is studying the life of Dr. Henry Daniel, who served as the chief state school officer from 1959 to 1979. The following article appeared in a newspaper reporting the remarks of various speakers given at a dinner to honor Dr. Daniel after twenty years of service as the state superintendent of education.

> *More than one hundred educational leaders throughout the state honored Dr. Henry Daniel last evening at the Hotel Johnson in the state capital. Following the remarks of several officials, an engraved plaque was presented to Dr. Daniel in recognition of his outstanding educational leadership to the state.*
>
> *The governor of the state noted that because of the efforts of Dr. Daniel alone, the state established a junior college system which has rapidly grown to meet important state needs in technical-vocational education for the state's industry, provided the only institutions of higher*

education in rural regions, and given a better general education to fresh-man and sophomores than four-year colleges and universities.

The president of the state teachers' organization praised Dr. Daniel for his efforts to raise public school teachers' salaries and to maintain professionalism by expanding the requirements for certification of teachers. However, the president noted that salaries for public school teachers still remained below the national average.

The president of the state association for curriculum development and supervision stated that the efforts of Dr. Daniel alone established the state minimum competency testing program. This innovation has raised standards for all high school subjects and proved to the public that the high school diploma represented a high level of "educational competency."

a. Why would the researcher question the accuracy of the statements reported in this document?

b. How could the researcher corroborate the document's statements?

PART V

Evaluation and Policy Research Designs and Methods

Most educators recognize the increasing emphasis on formal evaluation research and policy analysis. Educators frequently ask how evaluation and policy research can help decision-makers and various policy-making groups improve our schools and make wise educational policies. What are the similarities and differences in evaluating a program and in evaluating a policy? How does one decide which designs and methods are most appropriate to employ in a given situation? Can evaluation research and policy analysis also yield more general educational knowledge about specific practices common to many schools?

In Part V we describe a variety of approaches that are used in the evaluation of educational practices. Different approaches emphasize different questions regarding a specific practice. Some evaluation and policy analyses are primarily quantitative, some are primarily qualitative, and some may combine both quantitative and qualitative methods.

Evaluation Research and Policy Analysis

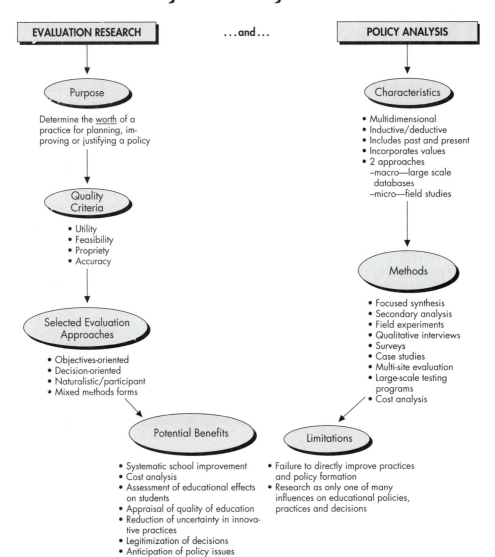

EVALUATION RESEARCH   . . . and . . .   **POLICY ANALYSIS**

Purpose

Determine the <u>worth</u> of a practice for planning, improving or justifying a policy

Quality Criteria

- Utility
- Feasibility
- Propriety
- Accuracy

Selected Evaluation Approaches

- Objectives-oriented
- Decision-oriented
- Naturalistic/participant
- Mixed methods forms

Potential Benefits

- Systematic school improvement
- Cost analysis
- Assessment of educational effects on students
- Appraisal of quality of education
- Reduction of uncertainty in innovative practices
- Legitimization of decisions
- Anticipation of policy issues

Characteristics

- Multidimensional
- Inductive/deductive
- Includes past and present
- Incorporates values
- 2 approaches
  - macro—large scale databases
  - micro—field studies

Methods

- Focused synthesis
- Secondary analysis
- Field experiments
- Qualitative interviews
- Surveys
- Case studies
- Multi-site evaluation
- Large-scale testing programs
- Cost analysis

Limitations

- Failure to directly improve practices and policy formation
- Research as only one of many influences on educational policies, practices and decisions

526

KEY TERMS

evaluation	responsive evaluation
worth	audiences
formative evaluation	mixed methods
summative evaluation	policy analysis
evaluation approach	multisite evaluation
objectives-oriented evaluation	cost–benefit analysis
target group	cost–effectiveness analysis
behavioral objectives	cost–utility analysis
decision-oriented evaluation	cost–feasibility analysis
naturalistic/participant evaluation	

This chapter draws on the previous chapters concerning design, data collection, and data analysis. Evaluators and policy analysts need a breadth of research knowledge sufficient to make informed decisions throughout the empirical process; educators need sufficient research knowledge to commission a study and to interpret an evaluation or policy report.

Evaluation is the application of research skills to determine the *worth* of an educational practice. Evaluation research aids in decision making at a given site(s) and adds to the research-based knowledge about a specific practice that is often relevant to more general audiences. Decisions are those that plan and improve a practice or that justify (or do not justify) widespread adoption of a practice. An evaluator is both a researcher and a concerned educator whose work is essential in the overall functioning of educational organizations.

Policy analysis evaluates government policies to provide policymakers with pragmatic recommendations among policy alternatives. Usually potential economic and/or political effects are considered. Two distinctive approaches in policy analysis are a macro approach, using large databases and a micro approach, which is a field-oriented eclectic research. A program can be viewed as a specific means adopted for carrying out a policy.

In this chapter we summarize the purposes of evaluation research, present an overview of evaluation approaches, and discuss three approaches: objectives-oriented, decision-oriented, and naturalistic/participant-oriented. Policy analysis characteristics and methods, including cost analysis, are summarized. We also cite the standards, potential uses, and limitations of evaluation research and policy analysis.

Purposes and Definition of Evaluation Research

Evaluation activities have always been an integral part of education. Frequently, professional judgments have been made about the placement of students in special programs, the extent of student learning, the selection of materials, and the modification of programs. In the past, these activities were often done unsystematically and informally. The need for formal evaluation increased as society allocated greater responsibilities and resources to education. Evaluation research often was used for accountability purposes. At present, evaluation studies are used to determine the allocation of scarce resources and the effectiveness of alternative educational programs and to make and justify value decisions in many aspects of education.

Purposes and Roles of Evaluation

A brief definition of evaluation research is the determination of the *worth* of an educational program, product, procedure, or objective, or of the potential utility of alternative approaches to attain specific goals. Three major reasons for conducting evaluation research are *planning, improving,* and *justifying* (or not justifying) procedures, programs, and/or products.

Most educators recognize that evaluation can serve a formative purpose (such as to improve a program) or a summative purpose (such as to decide if that program should be continued). More specifically, evaluation can

1. Aid planning for the installation of a program
2. Aid decision making about program modification
3. Aid decision making about program continuation or expansion
4. Obtain evidence to rally support or opposition to a program
5. Contribute to the understanding of psychological, social, and political processes within the program and external influences on the program.

Three reasons most frequently given for conducting an evaluation are 1) to judge the worth of a program; 2) to assist decision-makers; and 3) to serve a political function (Talmage, 1982). In any single report, these purposes will receive different degrees of emphasis.

Evaluation Research Defined

Evaluation requires a formal evaluation design and procedures in order to collect and analyze data systematically for determining the *worth* of a specific educational practice or anticipated practice. To say that a practice or program has **worth** means to examine the program and to judge its value according to standards that are applied relatively or absolutely. Values of an educational practice may be intrinsic to the practice (i.e., reading programs value reading comprehension), or within the site (i.e., community culture and values). Educational practice refers to a program, a curriculum, a policy or administrative regulation, an organizational structure, or a product. Most examples will, however, be drawn from curriculum and program evaluation.

A curriculum or program may be implemented at one site or at multiple sites within a single local government or administrative unit such as a school system of a county or a city. The number of sites in which the educational practice operates influences the evaluation question and the design decisions. Evaluation approaches are applicable to single site or multiple site programs and policies.[1]

Formative and Summative Evaluation

The distinction between formative and summative evaluation has been widely accepted. In **formative evaluation**, researchers collect data to improve a curriculum in a development stage. Typical questions are "What parts of the program are working?" and "What needs to be changed and how?" The evaluation results may lead to a decision to revise the curriculum, to extend the field testing to gather more data, or to abort further development in order not to waste resources on a program that ultimately may be ineffective.

Summative evaluation can be conducted once the program is fully developed—that is, when it functions well or does what the program intended with few detrimental side effects. **Summative evaluation** determines the effectiveness of a program, especially in comparison with other competing programs. A typical question may be "Which of several programs achieves these objectives most effectively and efficiently?" Summative evaluation can aid educators who make purchase or adoption decisions concerning new programs, products, or procedures. Table 16.1 summarizes the distinctions between formative and summative evaluation research.

Note that the audiences and uses for formative and summative evaluation are very different. In formative evaluation, the audience is program personnel; in summative evaluation, the audience is potential users, funding agencies, and other educational officials, as well as program personnel. Both formative and summative evaluations are essential because decisions are needed during the developmental stages of a program to improve it and again, when it is stabilized, to judge its final worth or determine its future. Unfortunately, far too many educational agencies conduct only summative evaluations.

Two important factors that influence the usefulness of formative evaluation are *control* and *timing*. Formative evaluation should collect data on variables over which program administrators have some control. Information that

---

[1]We briefly discuss large scale multisite studies as a policy analysis method.

TABLE 16.1

Differences in Formative and Summative Evaluation

	Formative Evaluation	Summative Evaluation
Purpose	To improve program	To certify program utility
Audience	Program administrators and staff	Potential consumer or funding agency
Who Should Do It	Internal evaluator	External evaluator
Data Collection	Often multimethod, informal	Valid/reliable instruments
Sample	Purposeful and/or probability	Probability
Questions Asked	What is working?	What are the results?
	What needs to be revised?	In what situations?
	How can it be improved?	Requiring what costs, materials, and training?

Source: Adapted from Worthen, B. R., Sanders, J. R., & Fitzpatrick, J. L. (1997). *Program evaluation: Alternative approaches and practical guidelines.* (2nd ed.) New York: Longman, Inc. (p. 17).

reaches administrators too late for use in program improvement is obviously useless.

The distinctions between formative and summative evaluation aid in the selection of an evaluation design. Formative studies are typically conducted by an internal evaluator; summative studies are typically conducted by an external evaluator. An external evaluator, however, may be engaged to conduct either formative and summative evaluations for credibility, a fresh outside perspective, and a neutral attitude toward worth of the practice.

Standards for Judging the Quality of Evaluation Research

The second edition of *The Program Evaluation Standards* (1994) indicates the continued professionalization and specialization of this type of research. The Joint Committee on Standards for Educational Evaluation represented important national associations of school administrators, educational research, evaluation, measurement, teachers, counselors, supervisors, elementary school principles, secondary school principals, school boards, chief state school officers, and the like. The thirty standards were developed to provide a common language, a conceptual framework for evaluation, and a basis for self-regulation by professional evaluators.

The Joint Committee developed four criteria that a good evaluation study satisfies: utility, feasibility, propriety, and accuracy. Each criterion is described further with specific standards. These are summarized below.[2]

---

[2]See Joint Committee on Standards for Educational Evaluation (1994). *The program evaluation standards* (2nd ed.). Thousand Oaks, CA: Sage.

1. *Utility standards* are to ensure that an evaluation will serve the practical and timely information needs of given audiences. These eight standards are audience identification, evaluator credibility, information scope and selection, valuation interpretation, report clarity, report dissemination, report timeliness, and evaluation impact.
2. *Feasibility standards* are to ensure that an evaluation will be realistic, frugal, and diplomatic. These three standards are practical procedures, political viability, and cost effectiveness.
3. *Propriety standards* are to ensure that an evaluation will be conducted legally, ethically, and with due regard for the welfare of those involved in the evaluation and those affected by its findings. These standards are formal obligation, conflict of interest, full and frank disclosure, public's right to know, rights of human subjects, human interactions, balanced reporting, and fiscal responsibility.
4. *Accuracy standards* are to ensure that an evaluation will state and convey technically adequate information about the features of the practice studied that determine its value. These eleven standards are object identification, context analysis, described purposes and procedures, defensible information sources, valid and reliable measurement, systematic data control, analysis of quantitative information, analysis of qualitative information, justified conclusions, and objective reporting.

The standards are not a cookbook of steps to follow but rather a compilation of commonly agreed-on characteristics of good evaluation practice. In any specific formal evaluation situation, choices and trade-offs relating to each standard are within the province of the evaluator. Further, the standards serve as a guide to evaluators, officials who commission studies, and persons who use evaluation reports.

Selected Approaches to Evaluation

Many types of studies are called evaluation research. Evaluation studies are responses to recognized needs by educators and various policy groups. A broad array of educational entities are evaluated. These include

1. Curriculum materials (textbooks, films, software programs, educational television programs, videos)
2. Programs (Head Start, language arts program, talented and gifted programs, preventive dropout programs, distant education)
3. Instructional methods (discussions, lectures, learning centers, discovery)
4. Educators (administrators, preservice teachers, volunteer tutors, inservice teachers)

5. Students (learning disabilities students, elementary students, college students, advanced placement students)
6. Organizations (alternative schools, high schools, vocational–technical schools, higher education)
7. Management, resource utilization, and costs

Crucial to an evaluation is the decision on the entity to be evaluated: a group, a product, a method, an organization, or a management system. Careful delineation of the entity and all of its components helps the evaluator decide which components are the most important for evaluation.

An **evaluation approach** is a strategy to focus the evaluation activities and to produce a useful report. Evaluation is multifaceted and it can be conducted in different phases of a program's development. A number of evaluators have published schema, grouping the approaches. Each approach has prominent theorists, explicit rationales, discussions in the literature, a group of practitioners, actual evaluation studies, and critics. Major evaluation approaches are classified in the list below.

1. *Objectives-oriented approaches,* in which the focus is on specifying goals and objectives and determining the extent to which they have been attained.
2. *Consumer-oriented approaches,* in which the central issue is developing evaluative information on educational "products," broadly defined, for use by educational consumers in choosing among competing curricula, instructional products, and the like.
3. *Expertise-oriented approaches,* which depend primarily on the direct application of professional expertise to judge the quality of educational endeavors, especially the resources and the processes.[3]
4. *Decision-oriented approaches,* in which the emphasis is on describing and assessing an educational change process and resulting outcomes to provide information to a decision-maker.
5. *Adversary-oriented approaches,* in which planned opposition in points of view of different evaluators (pro and con) is the focus of the evaluation.
6. *Naturalistic and participant-oriented approaches,* in which naturalistic inquiry and involvement of participants (stakeholders in the practice that is evaluated) are central in determining the values, criteria, needs, and data for the evaluation.

We discuss the three approaches most frequently used in this chapter. The approaches illustrate the diversity of evaluation research: objectives-oriented

---

[3]Examples are accreditation and informal professional review systems and ad hoc panel reviews such as those by funding agencies or blue-ribbon panels.

evaluation, decision-oriented evaluation, and naturalistic/participant evaluation. These approaches contain diverse approaches to evaluation, especially in the source of the evaluation questions. The source of questions in an objectives-based study is the instructional or program objectives. The source of questions in the decision-making study is the decision-maker, whereas in naturalistic evaluation the source of the questions is the different audiences (that is, stakeholders, including the participants, affected by the practice).

Objectives-Oriented Evaluation

Objectives-Oriented Evaluation determines the degree to which the objectives of a practice are attained by the target group. In other words, the evaluation measures the outcomes of the practice. The discrepancy between the stated objectives and the outcomes is the measure of success of the practice. The practice may be a curriculum, in-service training, an in-school suspension program, parent education, or the like. The **target group**, the group whose behavior is expected to change, may be students, parents, teachers, or others. We will illustrate the steps (see Table 16.2) with curriculum evaluation. Although the approach appears simple, a reader should be aware of the research decisions that affect the usefulness of the results.

Selection of Measurable Objectives An evaluation study measures objectives, not abstract goals, of the practice. Curriculum goals are usually broad, general statements, representing values in the society. Objectives are specific statements that are related logically to the goals and attainable through instruction. A typical social studies goal is that students will become law-abiding citizens. "Law-abiding citizen" refers to an informed adult who pays taxes, votes in elections, serves on juries, and participates in a democracy. This behavior occurs outside the instructional process and is difficult to relate to a specific curriculum. Students can, however, be evaluated on their knowledge of a citizen's duties and rights, their participation in mock elections, and their skills in analyzing current issues.

Only student outcomes stated as **behavioral objectives** are evaluated. *Behavioral objective* is synonymous with performance or measured objective. Behavioral objectives are either the terminal student behaviors or student products (a research paper, clay figurine, oral presentation, and so on), but *not* the process leading to the terminal behavior. The criteria for achievement of the

TABLE 16.2

Steps in Conducting Objectives-Based Evaluation

Step 1	Step 2	Step 3	Step 4	Step 5
Selection of measurable objectives	Selection of instrument(s)	Selection of evaluation design	Data collection and analysis	Interpretation of results

objective may or may not be stated in the objective. Four examples of behavioral objectives that differ in level of generality are these:

> A student, on request, will be able to spell and capitalize his or her name correctly.
>
> A student will be able to compute correctly the answer to any division problems chosen randomly from the review exercises.
>
> A student will produce a drawing that is judged by three raters as creative by the criteria of originality, flexibility, and elaboration developed by the raters.
>
> At least 90 percent of the students will be able to pass 70 percent of a competency test in mathematics.

The last example is a performance objective that states the minimal group performance of 90 percent and the minimal individual student performance. An analysis of the curriculum content coverage and emphasis will suggest the objectives that are the most important.

If the objectives are stated in terms other than behavioral, the evaluator has three choices: reword the objectives in behavioral terms without changing the intent, ignore the nonbehavioral objectives, or communicate to the client the fact that nonbehavioral objectives will not be measured, but that these objectives could be described or appraised with other procedures.

Selection of Instruments and Design Instruments may be tests, questionnaires and self-report devices, rating scales, observation systems, and interview schedules. The typical instrument is a standardized norm-referenced achievement test. Evaluators frequently use data from a routine testing program. Existing test data should be valid for the evaluation. *Content-related* evidence for validity can be determined by a panel of local experts logically by comparing the curriculum content with the test items. The validity and reliability of a subtest may be considerably lower than for the entire test and should be checked in *Mental Measurements Yearbooks*. Other considerations are the appropriateness of the norms for the target group and the type of information sought. Most standardized norm-referenced tests provide only general information about students compared with those in the norm group.

Criterion-referenced instruments may be used to assess student outcomes. Criterion-referenced instruments compare performance to predetermined criteria, standards, or a well-defined behavioral domain: that is, the test developers state the objectives and then develop test items. Criterion-referenced instruments assess both group and individual students. Scores may range from low to high achievement because the reference is to a criterion, not a norm group whose scores are distributed as a normal curve.

Criterion-referenced instruments must meet the requirements of any measurement procedure. If an evaluator or a local school system plans to develop a criterion-referenced instrument, knowledge of measurement and instrument development is necessary. The instrument should be valid and reliable for the evaluation purposes, although the type of validity and reliability may differ from that associated with norm-referenced tests.[4] Field testing is essential.

The most useful design in an objectives-based evaluation is a randomized or matched groups design; however, it may not be feasible. Quasi-experimental designs, such as the one-group pretest and posttest, time series, or counterbalanced designs are used. Because most programs have both cognitive and affective objectives, a comprehensive evaluation would measure different types of objectives if valid and reliable instruments were available or could be developed. Factors in selecting a design are the nature and number of objectives, the target groups, internal and external validity, and the unit of analysis. The unit of analysis is the smallest independent unit of data: a group or an individual.

An evaluation report states the validity and reliability of the scores, which is the only source of data for determining achievement of objectives. Previous validity and reliability studies may be cited. The report also gives a description of the developmental process and field testing results for locally developed instruments. Factors relating to internal and external validity of the design with their possible effects on the results are noted.

Interpretation of Results The evaluation assesses the percentage of the target group that achieved the predetermined objectives, or it assesses which program, compared with others having similar objectives, is more successful in achieving the objectives. When the evaluator looks more closely at the objectives, he or she often finds that they are stated at different levels of specificity and that not all objectives can be evaluated. The means for selecting the objectives for formal evaluation are often inconsistent. Because only terminal outcomes are actually assessed, process evaluation is omitted. The results may suggest modifications of a practice but provide no specific directions for intervention to improve a practice, nor do the results provide complete information necessary for adopting a practice at other sites.

Objectives-based evaluation is probably the most frequently used approach for several reasons. Most educators would agree that successful attainment of objectives does indicate both the merit and worth of a practice. Educators can demonstrate accountability and the productive use of public funds when objectives are attained. Another advantage of the objectives-based approach is its highly definable methodology. The procedures for this approach have been worked out in great detail, a fact that appeals to a number of novice

---

[4]For a minimal competency test required for, say, high school graduation, *curricular validity* is important. It seems unfair to withhold a diploma from someone who did not learn a competency because it was not in the curriculum. The problems of obtaining evidence of curricular validity and *instructional validity*, a more restrictive term, are myriad. See W. A. Mehrens and I. J. Lehmann (1987), *Measurement and evaluation in education and psychology* (4th ed.).

evaluators who must conduct annual evaluations. No other approach has such an elaborate technology and scientific basis. Furthermore, the nonattainment of objectives or some objectives can lead to questioning programmatic components and a closer scrutiny of the practice.

Decision-Oriented Evaluation

Decision-oriented evaluation has a broader scope than the objectives-oriented approach and implies a theory of educational change. In this approach, "evaluation is the process of determining the kinds of decisions that have to be made; selecting, collecting, and analyzing the information needed in making these decisions; and reporting this information to appropriate decision-makers" (Alkin, 1969, p. 2). Decision alternatives are identified by the evaluator and the decision-maker, who determines merit and worth. Decision alternatives can be routine maintenance decisions (staff policies) or incremental decisions leading to system-wide change requiring major resource allocation. **Decision-oriented evaluation** studies may thus be done at any point in a change process: needs assessment, program planning, implementation, or process and outcome evaluation. The types of evaluation studies with their subsequent decisions are summarized in Table 16.3 and below.

1. *Needs assessment* compares the current status and values of an educational system with the desired outcomes. The evaluation identifies the *context*,

TABLE 16.3

Decision-Oriented Evaluation[a]

Needs Assessment	
Evaluation	Current status contrasted with desired status—educational need
Decision	Problem selection
Program Planning and Input Evaluation	
Evaluation	Kinds of programs that fit objectives derived from needs assessment and possible strategies
Decision	Program plan
Implementation Evaluation	
Evaluation	Degree to which the program is implemented as planned
Decision	Program modification
Process Evaluation	
Evaluation	Extent program achieves its objectives and products
Decision	Program modification and improvement
Outcome or Product Evaluation	
Evaluation	Worth of program as reflected by process and outcomes
Decision	Program certification and adoption

[a]Based on Stufflebeam, D. L., et al. (1971). *Educational evaluation and decision-making,* pp. 215–239.

provides base-line data on accomplishments of the site, and identifies unmet needs. Needs can be stated by students, the community, other groups, or the society as a whole in relation to the system. The summary data are primarily historical, descriptive, and comparative. Needs assessment leads to selection of a program to achieve specific objectives.

2. *Program planning and input evaluation* examines alternative strategies, such as adoption of an available program or development of a new program, to achieve the new objectives. Researchers study existing programs for practicality, cost, and the ease of reproducing components to achieve the objectives. They also examine the feasibility of local development of a program. Input evaluation provides information for deciding how to use the resources to meet desired program objectives. The purpose is to assess one or more strategies in terms of how each strategy might affect staffing, time, and budget as well as their potential for meeting the objectives. Program planning evaluation leads to the selection of a plan, including procedures, materials, facilities, equipment, schedule, staffing, and budgets for program development or implementation.

3. *Implementation evaluation* assesses the extent to which a program is developed or implemented as planned, and it identifies any defects in the program. It also provides information with which to anticipate changes necessary for continued program development and implementation. Implementation evaluation monitors and records what happened in program development. The record is useful in retrospective analysis of decisions, strengths, and weaknesses in the plans.

4. *Process evaluation* provides information on the relative success of the various components of a program and the extent to which the objectives and products are achieved. The evaluator collects data that will lead to immediate program improvement. Data collection may require testing procedures and other methods. This kind of evaluation could also focus on the impact of a program on other processes or programs. Process evaluation results in program modification.

5. *Outcome or product evaluation* assesses the extent to which objectives were achieved. The data obtained include objectives-based evaluation and other information from earlier evaluations. Previous information explains why the objectives were or were not achieved, and it helps the decision-maker to eliminate, modify, retain, or expand the program for wider use. The general worth of the program is determined by the way the outcomes it produces relate to the objectives selected from the needs assessment. Outcome evaluation leads to decisions regarding program certification and adoption.

Finally, the decision-oriented approach to evaluation focuses on gathering information by a variety of methods to aid in the decisions made for program development for its wider use. Educational change is a planned activity, and evaluation is an extension of this planning. Possible difficulties in using it lie in conflicting values and goal dissension in a complex educational system and between the educational organization and its constituencies. The decision-oriented approach assumes that the decision-maker is sensitive to possible problems in bringing about educational change and is willing to obtain information regarding these realities. Collaboration rather than cooperation between the evaluator and decision-maker could, however, result in biased data. Furthermore, decisions are not usually expressed as clear alternatives and often change meaning dramatically over time. In other words, with this approach it is more difficult to specify and anticipate decisions to be served than it would first appear. Because the evaluator works closely with the decision-maker, the impact of the evaluation effort depends as much on the skills of the evaluator as it does on the leadership of the decision-maker.

Despite these difficulties, the decision-oriented approach allows for educational and methodological soundness in evaluation. Program evaluation is *not* based on an isolated outcome, since context, input, plans, process, and outcome data are collected and the strengths, weaknesses, and side effects are assessed. The degree of program implementation is addressed before student outcomes are assessed. Participant involvement in evaluation and in communication of useful information is emphasized. The evaluation may affect educational practices informally through the evaluation process or formally through the final evaluation study. The approach is flexible—it may be used for a formative purpose to guide decision-making throughout an educational change process, or it may be used for a summative purpose to demonstrate accountability with a record of prior decisions and the bases for those decisions and a record of the actual process, attainments, and recycling decisions.

Naturalistic/Participant Evaluation

Since 1967, a number of evaluation theorists and users have reacted to what they consider to be the dominance of mechanistic and insensitive approaches to evaluation in education. Several concerns were expressed: (1) technically sophisticated instruments and reports often distracted from what was really happening in education; (2) many large-scale evaluations were conducted without evaluators even once visiting some classrooms; and (3) report recommendations did not reflect an understanding of the phenomena behind the numbers, charts, and tables. Educators further argued that the human element, which was found in the complexities of everyday reality and the different perspectives of those engaged in education, was missing from most evaluation studies. Hence, these approaches are called *naturalistic* and *participant-oriented* by some authors.

Naturalistic/participant evaluation is a holistic approach using multiplicity of data to provide an understanding of the divergent values of a practice from the participants' perspectives. The literature and actual evaluation studies illustrate some commonalities of naturalistic and participant-oriented evaluation:

1. Uses a *holistic approach,* which sees education as a complex human endeavor.
2. Accommodates and protects *value pluralism* by presenting or summarizing disparate preferences about the practice evaluated.

3. Reports *"portrayals"*—as they have come to be called—of a person, classroom, school, district, project, or program that is placed in the broader context in which it functions.

4. Depends on *inductive reasoning,* which emerges from grassroots observation and discovery.

5. Uses *multiplicity of data* from several different sources, usually within a qualitative methodology or combining qualitative and quantitative data.

6. Uses an *emergent design* to give an understanding of one specific practice with its contextual influences, process variations, and life histories.

7. Records *multiple realities* rather than a single reality.

Qualitative strategies have been adopted for evaluation purposes.[5]

Robert Stake noted that many evaluation studies are not used because the report is irrelevant, that is, unresponsive to the client's needs. According to Stake, "an educational evaluation is responsive evaluation if it orients more directly to program activities than to program intents; responds to audience requirements for information; and if the different value-perspectives present are referred to in reporting the success and failure of the programs" (1975, p.14). **Responsive evaluation** is an old alternative based on what people do naturally when they evaluate things: they observe and react. "The responsive evaluation approach tries to respond to the *natural* ways in which people assimilate information and arrive at *understanding*" (Stake, 1973, p. 3). The evaluation design emerges from the issues and concerns expressed at the site.

Prominent Events: Informal Strategies Responsive evaluation is cyclical, including events that recur. To Stake, "any event can follow any event, many events occur simultaneously, and the evaluator returns to each event many times before the evaluation is finished" (1975, p. 18). In Figure 16.1 the prominent events are presented as the face of a clock, emphasizing the cyclic nature of the approach.

The events in responsive evaluation can be expressed as research phases. In phase 1 (noon to 4 o'clock, Figure 16.1) the evaluator talks with clients, program staff, and **audiences**—anyone directly or indirectly connected with the program—to get a sense of the different perspectives and values of the program. The evaluator observes the program in operation. From these activities, the evaluator discovers the meaning of the purposes of the program and conceptualizes the issues and problems. In phase 2 (4 to 7 o'clock, Figure 16.1) the evaluator

---

[5]One example of methodological adoption is the use of focus groups to explore individuals' perceptions about reactions to a particular program, service, or product. The group can be internal staff or a broad range of external stakeholders and consumer groups. The strategy can be employed at the beginning of a program to assess needs, at the mid-point to assess progress and difficulties, or at the end of a program. See Buttram, J. L. (1990). Focus groups: A starting point for needs assessment. *Evaluation Practice, 11* (3), 207–212.

FIGURE 16.1   **Prominent Events in Naturalistic and Participant-Oriented Evaluation**

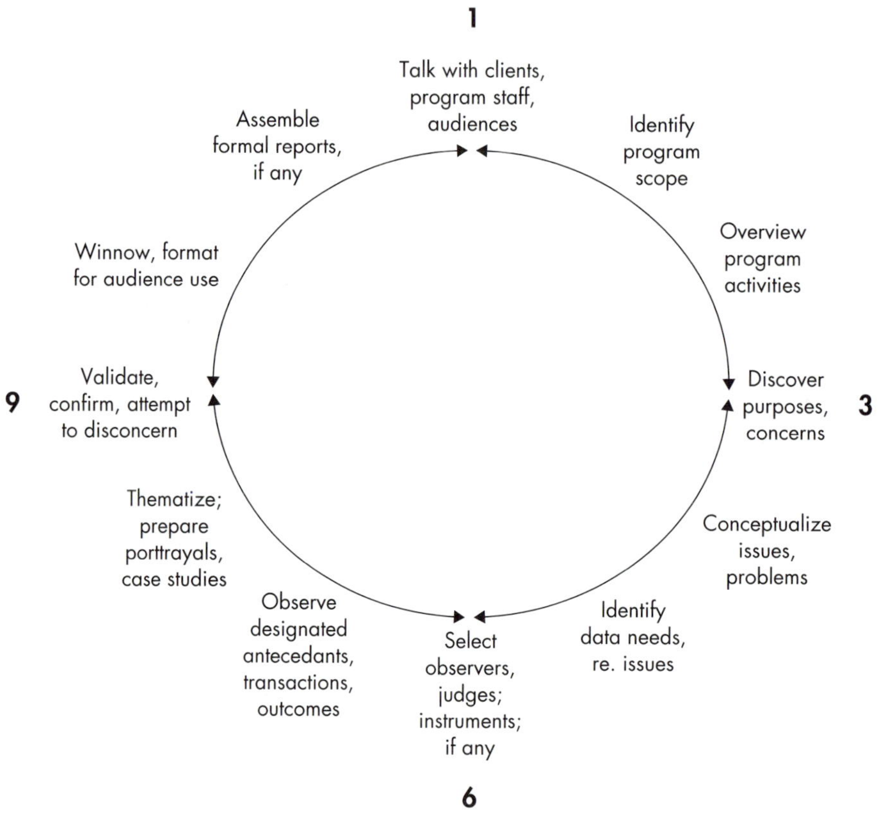

Source: Adopted from Stake, R. E. (1975). *Program evaluation, particularly responsive evaluation.*
Occasional Paper Series, No. 5. Kalamazoo: Western Michigan University Evaluation Center.

ascertains the data needs and selects data collection methods. Although Stake expects observers and judges to be the primary method of data collection, instruments may be appropriate. The data are organized as antecedents, transactions, and outcomes, including both intended and unintended outcomes. In phase 3 (8 to 11 o'clock, Figure 16.1) the evaluator is concerned with communicating the findings in natural ways. Portrayals can be embodied in the conventional research report, but they usually will take the form of descriptive case studies, artifacts, round-table discussions, newspaper articles, graphics, or videotapes, depending on the audience. Only the primary concerns of each audience are reported to that audience. Last, the evaluator assembles formal reports, and other types of reports.

Evaluator's Role   Two aspects of responsive evaluation, the evaluator's role and continuous feedback, distinguish this approach from the prior approaches discussed. The evaluator responds to audience concerns as these change throughout program development and stimulates ideas by trying out data-based insights and findings on the respondents. Negotiation and interaction are part of the method of ensuring accuracy and communication. Communication is a two-stage process in which findings are tried out on different audiences. This may lead to the evaluator's returning to the field for additional data or altering the way findings are stated in order to communicate more effectively. The results presented in the final report should not surprise any audience, because its content has been thoroughly criticized before release.

In summary, the naturalistic evaluator recognizes that the concerns of different audiences about a program represent different values and data needs. The evaluator must select the concerns and issues that, within the limits of time and resources, are important, legitimate, and relevant. The discovery of pluralistic values surrounding a program is made by the evaluator and is independent of the perception of any single decision-maker. The source for the evaluation focus and questions is thus the various audiences. A variety of designs can be used. The flexibility of responsive evaluation assures that the evaluation will be serviceable to the audiences.

Naturalistic/participant evaluation is usually a case study research, and as with other semi-subjective approaches, there is some difficulty in establishing its credibility. Although most case studies differ in matters of emphasis rather than in matters of truth or falsity, different evaluators emphasize different events. Methodological consistency remains a problem with this approach, as does the representation of diverse interests. Some believe that evaluators should balance the interests according to their own sense of justice; other evaluators take a disinterested and neutral position, providing descriptions and analysis but not recommendations. In addition, writing portrayals or case studies requires skill, training, and an ability to handle confidential data. Despite these difficulties, a well-constructed case study is a powerful evaluation, with the potential for being coherent, fair to holders of diverse views in complex situations, and accurate, especially about the inner workings of a program.

Mixed Methods Forms

Evaluators may have questions and situations where it is useful to include both quantitative and qualitative methods in an evaluation. These evaluators tend to be more pragmatic in designing evaluation studies and less rigid in adhering to research inquiry modes. Obviously, some evaluation questions are more appropriately addressed by quantitative methods and others are more suited for qualitative strategies. If only one evaluation question is addressed in a study, then it will require a *single method design*.[6]

---

[6]We discussed multimethod strategies and triangulation in Chapters 12 and 14. Triangulation refers to multimethods to increase validity of findings within one mode of inquiry.

In a comprehensive design where a number of questions are addressed about a practice, a mixed methods approach may be necessary. A **mixed methods** study combines qualitative and quantitative techniques and/or data analysis within different phases of the research process (Tashakkori & Teddlie, 1998). There may be a single application or multiple applications within one evaluation. When combining both quantitative and qualitative methods in one study, the purpose, initiation of different methods, and timing of the data analysis of each method should be carefully planned in advance. Further, the scope (national, state, local), the time frame for study completion (typically up to 5 years), and the fiscal feasibility influence the selection of the type and form of mixed methods. Otherwise, using mixed methods may produce non-interpretable results.

Mixed Methods Types and Purposes

Five types of mixed methods forms and their purposes were identified in a review of 57 mixed methods evaluation studies (Green, et. al., 1989). Because two types are rarely conducted, we concentrate on three types and discuss illustrative forms (see Table 16.4). Heretofore we discussed quantitative and qualitative modes of inquiry as separate approaches; typically the type of sampling, data collection technique, and data analysis are all consistent with one inquiry mode. In mixed methods studies, the data collection, including sampling and instrumentation, and data analysis are separate decisions. Qualitative data, for example, can be analyzed quasi-statistically[7] or random sampling can be applied to selection of participants for in-depth interviews or of participant-observation sites.

TABLE 16.4

Mixed Methods

Type	Purpose	Illustrative Forms
Complementary	To elaborate, enhance, illustrate, clarify the results of one method with that of another method	Simultaneous forms
Developmental	To use the results of one method to develop or inform the sampling or techniques for the second method	Sequential forms
Expansion	To extend the breadth and range of results by using different methods for different program components or questions	Sequential or parallel forms

Source: Adapted from Green, et. al. (1989) and Tashakkori & Teddlie (1998).

---

[7]See Table 14.2 Continuum of Analytic Styles and discussion in Chapter 14.

Three types of mixed methods are complementary, developmental, and expansion. *Complementary mixed methods* forms use the results of one method to elaborate, enhance, illustrate, or clarify the results from another method. Qualitative data can clarify the results of a standardized test or a developmental rating scale of each child can clarify the results of a participant-observation study in a day care center. *Developmental mixed methods* forms apply the results of one method to develop or inform the sampling or data collection technique for the second method. For example, exploratory interviews may be used to develop items for a questionnaire. *Expansion mixed methods* forms extend the breadth of the evaluation results by using different methods for different program components or for multiple questions about the practice. A participant-observation method describes program implementation followed by a standardized test measuring program outcomes.

Mixed Methods Forms

Some forms of mixed methods are *simultaneous* employment of both methods on the same program component, *sequential* ordering of both methods, and *parallel*, that is, using both methods but addressing different components or different questions about the practice. Illustrative examples are provided below.[8]

Illustration 1: Random sampling, qualitative technique , and content analysis. Participants, identified by scores on an administered self-esteem inventory, are randomly assigned to treatment and control groups. In-depth interviews are conducted of all participants in both groups before the program begins and at the end of the program. Content analysis[9] is performed separately on the treatment and the control group; patterns of each group are compared and contrasted. (Mixed Method form: Development and Sequential.)

Illustration 2: Random sampling, qualitative technique, and statistical analysis. At risk students are randomly assigned to treatment and control groups. Interviews, relating to program goals, are conducted of all participants in both groups before and immediately after the program ends. The narrative interview transcripts are given to a panel of independent judges who rate each interview on an eight point scale along several outcome dimensions such as likelihood of success in school, commitment to education, self-esteem, engaging in academic work, and demonstrations of good nutritional and health habits. Inferential statistics were then used to compare the two groups. Ratings were also statistically related to background characteristics of students. (Mixed Method form: Developmental and Sequential.)

---

[8]Illustrations are adapted from Patton (1990); Worthen, Sanders, & Fitzpatrick (1997); and Tashakkori & Teddlie (1998).

[9]We use the term "content analysis" as a generic term for inductive qualitative data analysis in evaluation research (Patton, 1990).

Illustration 3: Purposeful sampling, qualitative and quantitative techniques, statistical and content analysis. Students are selected into the program according to course prerequisites. One observer records the time spent in interactive exercises in each session observed. The second evaluator uses participant-observation to write short narratives of what happened in each session. Two independent readers read both frequency tabulations and narratives and listed what they thought were important events. Both the full descriptions of both the classroom observers and the readers' analyses were reported. (Mixed Method form: Complementary and Simultaneous.)

Illustration 4: Purposeful sampling, qualitative and quantitative techniques, statistical analysis. Students are selected into the program according to educational need. The evaluator has no predetermined categories or variables. The evaluator observes important activities and events in the program, looking for the types of behaviors and interactions that will emerge. For each new type of behavior or interaction, the evaluator creates a category and then uses a time and space sampling design to count the frequency with which those categories of behavior and interactions are exhibited. The frequency of the behaviors and interactions are then statistically related to such characteristics as group size, duration of the activity, teacher-student ratios, and social/physical density. (Mixed Method form: Complementary and Sequential.)

Illustration 5: Purposeful sampling followed by random sampling, qualitative and quantitative techniques, content analysis followed by statistical analysis. Purposeful and random sampling were used to create a sample of men and women across three age categories. Qualitative data consisted of semi-structured interviews; quantitative data consisted of self-report questionnaire. Qualitative analysis generated four themes. Statistical analyses related self-reports to interview themes across age and gender characteristics. (Mixed Method form: Expansion and Sequential.)

Other forms of mixed methods designs are multilevel employment of two methods. Multilevel research is common in both qualitative and qualitative approaches. Statistical data collected at student level can be linked to teacher attributes and school characteristics. Multilevel mixed methods is another way to use both techniques. Other forms of mixed methods designs are those employed in large-scale state, national, and international research. There are usually multiple applications at each stage of the study: sampling, data collection, and data analysis.[10]

Issues in Mixed Methods Studies

Mixed methods studies pose several design issues and concerns. The choice of sampling procedure (probability or purposeful) frames the evaluation and may imply the importance of one method over another. In a sequential mixed

---

[10]See Chapter 8 in Tashakkori & Teddlie (1998).

methods design on the same subjects, the researchers found that the sequence of the two methods affected the result, especially when the questionnaire was administered before the interview (Floyd, 1993). However new questions were identified that would not have been evident from either method.

More recent mixed methods issues focus on methodology with less attention given to problem formulation and inference-making. A few authors, however, have discussed combining the two approaches in most research phases (Patton, 1990; Creswell, 1995; and Sechrest & Sidani, 1995).

Perhaps the most debated issue concerns synthesizing quite different types of data. For example, synthesizing open-ended responses on a questionnaire with statistical analysis of the closed response items is reasonable because the dominate method is deductive inquiry. Most researchers argue that synthesizing the results of different methods is problematic because they serve different purposes: qualitative research is to explore; quantitative research is to confirm (Sechrest & Figueredo, 1993). Both sets of results are reported but may not be synthesized in many studies.

Policy Analysis

Policy analysis evaluates government policies to provide policymakers with pragmatic action-oriented recommendations. Policy is both what is intended to be accomplished by government action and the cumulative effort of actions, assumptions, and decisions of people who implement public policy. Public policy goals are equality, liberty, equity, and efficiency, which are considered just and right in the American cultural, historical, and legal heritage. It is almost impossible to implement these goals to their fullest degree because the exclusive pursuit of one restricts the others. The balance among these goals at any one time is the result of compromises in the political and economic system.

National and especially state policies increasingly influence local school policies. School administrators and teachers, in a real sense, make policy as they carry out their day-to-day jobs. Two features of the educational system allow for diverse policy implementation. First, policy is often a bundle of disparate vague ideas and is vulnerable to different interpretations. Second, even if a policy is coherent and highly specific, the governmental systems through which it passes on the way to schools are fragmented with different advice and multiple priorities. The governance of schooling creates opportunities for administrators and teachers to select implementation procedures and thus modify a policy.

Policy analyses focus on (1) policy formulation, especially deciding which educational problems to address; (2) implementation of programs to carry out policies; (3) policy revision; and (4) evaluation of policy effectiveness and/or efficiency. A program can be analyzed as separate from a policy or it can be defined as a specific means adopted for carrying out a policy.

Characteristics of Policy Analysis

A central concept in policy analysis is choice. *Choice* implies the assessment of *opportunity costs*—the highest-valued course of action is assessed against *tradeoffs*. Tradeoffs are alternative actions that are forsaken when a choice is made. To determine which action to choose, opportunity costs and effects usually are defined in either economic or political terms.

Two distinctive approaches used in policy analysis are (1) a macro approach, which is based on economic models such as cost–benefit analysis and use of large-scale databases, and (2) a micro approach, which is field-based for "getting the facts" and emphasizes qualitative methods. Macro and micro approaches differ in assumptions about policy making, policy values, and guidelines for making policy choices. See Table 16.5 for a summary of the differences.

Many policy studies are eclectic, combining qualitative and quantitative methods. Total dependence on statistical proof is seldom done in policy analysis for major policies. Despite the variations in policy studies, there are certain characteristics of the research that differentiate it from other types of research. A number of these characteristics are shared with evaluation research. Generally, policy analysis tends to 1) be multidimensional in focus; b) use deductive and inductive research orientations; 3) incorporate the future as well as the past; 4) respond to study users; and 5) explicitly incorporate values.

Policy analysis, similar to evaluation research, focuses on variables open to influence and intervention and is responsive to users. Users may be numerous, varying in expectations, values, assumptions, and needs. The values of the users enter into the processes of defining the educational problem; formulating the research questions, design, and policy alternatives; and developing recommendations. Educational values are always embedded in the cultural context. These values often differ at district level and at state level. In addition, the normative values of society at large are considered.

TABLE 16.5

Macro and Micro Approaches to Policy Analysis

	Macro Approaches (Large-Scale Databases)	Micro Approaches (Field Studies)
Assumptions of Policy Making	Scientific Rational	Incremental decisions Highly political Disjointed implementation
Policy Values	Excellence Efficiency Utilitarian	Social justice Common good Decentralization
Policy Choices Guided by	Abstract models Decision trees Mathematical equations	Complex realities of decision-making and implementation

Policy Analysis Methods

Policy analysis incorporates a variety of methodologies in technically analyzing policy problems. These include a focused synthesis, secondary analysis, field experiments, large-scale experimental or quasi-experimental programs, large-scale testing programs, qualitative interviews, surveys, and case study research. Methodologies discussed in prior chapters and others are briefly defined here in the context of policy analysis; cost analysis studies are described in more detail.

Focused synthesis is the selective review of written materials and prior research relevant to the policy question. The synthesis differs from the traditional literature review by discussing information obtained from a variety of sources beyond published articles—interviews with experts and stakeholders, hearings, anecdotal stories, personal experiences of the researcher, unpublished documents, staff memoranda, and published materials. An entire policy analysis study can employ this method.

Secondary analysis is the analysis and reanalysis of existing databases. However, the policy questions or decision models that guide the reanalysis differ from the traditional research question in a meta-analysis study. Rather than examining the databases to determine the state of knowledge about the effect size (see Chapter 4) of a single educational practice, the policy analysis generates different policy models and questions from which to examine the databases.

Field experiments and quasi-experiments investigate the effect or change as a result of policy implementation. Because experimental approaches attempt to explain existing educational conditions, the results may not be useful in projecting into the future. Policy conditions may be so dynamic that the results are confined to that particular period of implementation.

Large-scale experimental or quasi-experimental evaluations of major social or human services programs in areas of health care, education, mental health, or pubic welfare can address several questions about the program and sites. Large scale quasi-experimental policy analysis of projects, usually funded for three to five years, is called **multisite evaluation**. Some reasons for conducting multisite evaluations are

- to determine the overall effect of the program, when effects are aggregated across all sites
- to evaluate the program in a sample of representative sites to estimate the effect of the program across all sites
- to determine if the program works under a variety of implementation conditions
- to study how the program interacts with specific site characteristics
- to compare program performance across sites to identify the most effective and ineffective ways of operating the program
- to facilitate cross-site sharing of "effective practices" and others

---

[11]See Greenberg, Meyer, & Wiseman (1995) and Worthen, Sanders & Fitzpatrick (1997) for a discussion of design issues.

Because these sites are a number of different local administrative units, there is effort to do careful sampling and to standardize program implementation and procedures for collecting and analyzing data.[11] The most widely agreed-upon purposes of multisite evaluations are to increase generalizability of findings, to maximize sample size to increase statistical power, and to respond to a variety of political and social concerns.

Qualitative interviews may be focused groups of individual key informants. Focused groups react to prespecified topics to generate issues and explore potential alternative or causal factors. "Prospective studies," which help policymakers anticipate the implications and consequences of proposed laws or policies, include interviewing key people who are knowledgeable in a field to solicit the latest and best thinking on a proposal and sometimes using existing government reports to identify trends.

Surveys in questionnaire or interview form, with purposeful or probability sampling, yield data on the present educational conditions of selected groups or situations.

Large-scale testing programs at state, national, and international levels in education are policies mandated by governments. These data, collected from multiple sites, can determine the overall effect of a program or policy when outcomes are aggregated. An example is the report to the nation of the status of American education based on the National Assessment of Educational Progress program. Similar studies are also conducted internationally such as The Third International Mathematics and Science Study.

Case study analysis is frequently used for policy research because it can be designed to give a more global analysis of a situation. Case studies provide a more complete understanding of a complex situation, identify unintended consequences, and examine the process of policy implementation, which is useful for future policy choices. For example, in five case studies of the implementation of a state mathematics reform policy, two teachers "missed" the math reform message; two teachers modified their teaching, but also reframed the new policy to prior ideas; and one teacher did not respond at all to the new policy. "Hence the teachers whom we observed produced some remarkable mixtures of old and new mathematics instruction" (Cohen & Ball, 1990, p. 253). Each case study provided different insights about needed support services for policy implementation.

Cost Analysis

Policymakers are concerned with policy effectiveness (Does the policy produce the desired results?) and policy efficiency (Are those results obtained at the least amount of cost?). "Only those alternatives which provide the best results

---

[11]See Greenberg, Meyer, & Wiseman (1995) and Worthern, Sanders, & Fitzpatrick (1997) for a discussion of design issues.

for a given level of resource use or impose the least cost for a given level of results will enable us to maximize the overall effectiveness of programs" (Levin, 1981, p. 17). Cost-effectiveness determines whether the most effective programs are also the most cost-effective. For example, a study determined a cost of $143 (in 1985 dollars) per year to provide one student with computer-assisted instruction (CAI) for 10 minutes per day using a time-shared minicomputer system. Of the instructional alternatives considered, CAI in mathematics was a more favorable cost-effective alternative than either tutoring performed by adults for 20 minutes a day or increasing instructional time by 30 minutes a day. It was less cost-effective than tutoring performed by peers for 20 minutes a day and had about the same cost-effectiveness as reducing the size of mathematics classes (Levin, Glass, & Meister, 1987).

Levin (1981) delineates four cost-analysis modes: cost–benefit, cost–effectiveness, cost–utility, and cost–feasibility. These modes of analysis differ in distinguishing features, strengths, and weaknesses, as noted in Table 16.6.

Cost–benefit analysis (CB) evaluates decision alternatives by comparing the cost and benefits to society. Both costs and benefits are measured in monetary values. The alternative that produced the highest benefits relative to costs should thus be selected. The advantage of CB is that a range of comparisons can

TABLE 16.6

Modes of Cost Analysis

Type of Analysis	Distinguishing Feature	Strengths	Weaknesses
Cost–benefit (CB)	Outcomes measured in monetary values	Compares alternative within service Compares across services Results expressed as internal rate of return, net benefits, or cost–benefit ratios Replicable	Difficulty of converting all outcomes to monetary values
Cost–effective (CE)	Outcomes measured in units of effects	Outcomes can be measured as psychological or physical changes Replicable	Unit of effectiveness must be same among programs with same goals
Cost–utility (CU)	Outcomes measured by subjective judgments	Can integrate multiple outcomes into a single value	Measures are subjective Not replicable
Cost–feasibility (CF)	Estimate possibility of cost within fiscal constraint	Indicates if further consideration of alternative is feasible	Does not deal with outcomes of alternative

Source: From "Cost Analysis" by Henry M. Levin, cited in New Techniques for Evaluation, edited by Nick L. Smith (Beverly Hills, California: Sage Publications, 1981). Reprinted by permission of Henry M. Levin.

be made among alternatives within education (different instructional programs) and among service types (education, health, and transportation). Benefits from three adult literacy programs, for example, could be expressed as improvements in productivity, earnings, and self-provided services in society or could directly assess the changes in earnings, occupational attainments, and self-provided services among the three treatment groups. The advantages of CB in policy formulation are apparent, but all benefits and costs must be expressed in pecuniary terms. Because of the difficulty of converting some educational benefits, such as affective outcomes of learning, to monetary value, CB would be inadequate if those benefits are important. Other modes of cost analysis, however, could be used.

Cost–effectiveness analysis (CE) compares program outcomes (effectiveness) with the costs of alternative programs when the objectives of different programs are similar and when common measures of effectiveness are used. Effectiveness could be measured by standardized achievement tests, psychological tests, or physical tests. Outcome measures need not be converted to monetary values, and the analysis is replicable.

Cost–utility analysis (CU) identifies which alternatives, according to professional judgments, are most likely to produce the most desired outcomes at the lowest cost. Cost–utility analysis may be done for the selection of an alternative or the analysis may be combined with a cost–effectiveness analysis. Often the problem of choosing among alternatives involves more than just the relative effectiveness and cost. The decision may be guided by such issues as equity, social impact, and policy-makers' values. Measurement of utility assigns a numerical value to the desirability each possible outcome has for each decision-maker. When utility measures are combined with cost–effectiveness measures, the resulting decision process more closely reflects the desires of the policy-makers. For example, a study found that in third grade the cost per month of grade placement gain in total mathematics instruction was about $20 per student for CAI and $33 per student for conventional instruction. On the basis of utility ratings by each school board member of the value of student achievement, attitude toward mathematics, and computer literacy, CAI had a greater cost utility (Fletcher, Hawley, & Piele, 1990).

Cost–feasibility analysis (CF) estimates the costs to ascertain whether or not the alternative is realistic, given an existing budget. This is done by inspection of the annual budget after obtaining a cost estimate. If the funds are not available, a number of alternative choices are generated by shifting resources, obtaining lower estimates, seeking additional funds, recommending partial implementation of a policy choice, and the like.

Cost analysis enables policymakers systematically to consider the impact of costs on different alternatives in order to make feasibility decisions, to estimate the probability of several desired outcomes relative to costs, and to compare cost–effectiveness and cost–benefits of alternative programs. However, CB and CE evaluations fail to provide automatic policy choices between alternatives because nonquantifiable outcomes and constraints are not part of the analysis, and small differences between CB and CE ratios among alternatives are not meaningful in decision making. Any form of CE and CU among alternatives will tend to be conservative (Levin, 1988). It is difficult to incorporate multiple outcomes rather than a single outcome into the analysis. Expertise in cost analysis requires formal mastery of the underlying tools of both economic analysis and evaluation.

Educational Evaluation and Policy Analysis: Potential Benefits and Limitations

Evaluation research and policy analysis offer many potential benefits to education, although they are not a panacea for all of the "ills" of education. Education is a complex activity within a larger, changing interdependent social, economic, and political society. In this context, evaluation research and policy analysis bring a rational and empirical perspective to the arenas of educational decisions and policy-making.

Most evaluation and policy studies are intended to be used. A study is utilized if the research is related to a discrete decision or enlightens decision-makers about issues, problem definition, or new ideas for alternative actions.

The later type of research utilization, the psychological processing of a study, does not necessarily direct decisions or dictate action. In a review of 65 studies on the use of evaluation results in education, mental health, and social services, Cousins and Leithwood (1986) found that two factors affected research utilization: (a) the research implementation—the quality and credibility of the study, the relevance and communication quality, the results of the study, and the timeliness; and (b) the decision or policy setting—information needs, current sources of information, users' attitudes toward research in general, flexibility of the decision-making process, and others. Utilization was enhanced when

- the research was appropriate in approach, methodological sophistication, and intensity;
- the decisions to be made were significant to users and of a sort considered appropriate for formally collected data;
- the findings were consistent with the users' beliefs and expectations;
- users were involved in the research process and had a prior commitment to its benefits;
- users considered the data reported to be relevant to their problems; and
- a minimum amount of information from other sources conflicted with the research results.

Some evaluators and analysts, with a realistic understanding of how policy is made, propose types of research most likely to be used. Knowledge using diverse criteria for merit and containing more comprehensive information such as program context and implementation have a greater chance of being used. In addition, systematic, long-term studies are more likely to influence policy-makers, with specifications of the full scope of issues and nontechnical summaries of findings.

Potential Benefits The list of potential benefits increases as more educators gain experience in conducting and using evaluation and policy studies. The most frequently mentioned potential benefits are listed here.

1. *Plan and implement school improvements on a systematic basis.* Identifying needs, selecting the best strategies from known alternatives, monitoring the changes as they occur, and measuring the impact of the changes minimizes the chance of misdirected changes and justifies expenditures. In a similar manner, systematic evaluation can avoid faddism, overreaction to political pressure, and simple lack of effort for letting the public know what is happening in schools or in new programs. Demonstration of what "works" is important in program justification. Demonstration of what does *not* "work" allows decision-makers and policy influentials to recast alternatives considered as solutions.

2. *Test several popular myths about the effects of education on student development.* Professional experience usually dictates most teaching and educational management practices. Systematic and often subtle information to supplant or confirm casual observations generates evaluation studies.

3. *Demonstrate professional responsibility by appraising the quality of educational programs.* Educators continually seek ways to improve the quality of programs, and both evaluation and policy analysis can play a vital role.

4. *Reduce uncertainty about educational practices when experience is limited.* Unanticipated side effects or possible detrimental effects can be identified early.

5. *Satisfy external agencies' requirements for reports to legitimize decisions and improve public images.* Through credible, data-based decision making, images of schooling may become more realistic. As evaluation activities increase, more accreditation groups and agencies expect, if not demand, some form of evaluation research.

6. *Conduct cost–benefit analysis of programs and practices that require large expenditures.* Accountability and the best use of scarce resources can be demonstrated.

7. *Enlighten influentials in decision and policy arenas to enable them to better anticipate program and policy issues.* Even though most actions reflect incremental decision making, a series of decisions made over time can lead to significant programmatic and policy shifts.

Possible Limitations Listed here are the limitations most often cited.

1. *Failure of many studies to improve educational practices and educational policy formulation.* The inadequacies of the conceptualization and the

conduct of many studies partly explains this occurrence. Studies frequently are conducted without understanding factors which affected the use of research information even when the studies are well done.

2. *Lack of appreciation that research is only one of many influences on educational policies, practices, and decisions.* Evaluation and policy analysis cannot *correct* a problem, but it can identify strengths and weaknesses, highlight the accomplishments, expose faulty areas, and focus on realistic policy alternatives. Correcting a problem is a separate step from using research results.

Credibility of Evaluation and Policy Proposals and Reports

Evaluation and policy proposal and reports are submitted to the official or committee who commissioned the study. This may be a local school system or a state or federal agency. An internal evaluator is wise to submit a written proposal to legitimize his or her activities even if there is no additional expenditures or separate contract. Funding agencies at state, national, and international level may issue a Request for a Proposal which contains the guidelines, the amount of funds allocated, and the submission deadline. We briefly summarize general criteria to evaluate proposals and reports.

Standards for Evaluation and Policy Research Proposals

Evaluation and policy research proposals are judged by the focus and design and by other considerations. We use the term evaluation to include policy analysis. The following questions illustrate typical criteria:

1. Is the practice or policy to be evaluated clearly identified?
2. Does the description of the practice or policy include the objectives and expected outcomes? Are the components or scope of the practice or policy briefly and comprehensively described?
3. Are the general purposes of the evaluation effort specified?
4. Are all relevant audiences for the study specified?
5. Are the selected evaluation questions relevant to the audiences for judging worth of the educational practice or policy?
6. Are data collection procedures proposed for each research question? Does the design allow for emergent evaluation questions to be addressed?
7. Are the selected measurement techniques valid and reliable for this study?
8. Does the design call for different kinds of data from different sources to provide a comprehensive and accurate evaluation?

9. Are data collection and analysis feasible for informal feedback and formal reports?

Other elements are considered in accepting an evaluation proposal. Although they may not all be stated in the plan, the evaluator and client need a mutual understanding about them. The next questions illustrate other considerations.

1. Is the release of scheduled reports timely so that audiences can best use the information?
2. Are the method and process of reporting (written, oral, or audiovisual) specified? Does the evaluation plan state editorial control and name the person who will release intermediate and final reports? Are executive reports of the full evaluation report for various audiences specified?
3. Are the rights of human subjects protected?
4. Is the evaluation plan cost-effective? Are fiscal accountability procedures designated?
5. Is the evaluation effort politically feasible for collecting data and presenting a balanced report to all audiences?

Credibility of Evaluation and Policy Reports

A evaluation or policy report is typically long, with several chapters. The report consists of an introduction (focus and design), findings organized by research questions or components of the practice, and a summary with recommendations. The criteria for judging the adequacy of a report emphasize two aspects: the evaluation focus and design, and the findings, conclusions, and recommendations. The following questions illustrate typical criteria.

1. Is the evaluation focus stated, along with the context, objectives, and description of the practice or policy, the general purposes of the study, and the evaluation or policy approaches used?
2. Are the research questions stated, with the data collection and analysis procedures specified? Are the procedures defensible?
3. Are the results reported in a balanced manner, with full and frank disclosure, including the limitations of the study?
4. Is the reporting objective to the extent that the findings are based on verified facts and free from distortion by personal feelings and biases?
5. Are the conclusions and recommendations justified, with sufficient information presented to determine whether these conclusions and recommendations are warranted? Are plausible alternative explanations presented, when appropriate, for findings?

Summary

1. Evaluation research requires a formal design and procedures to determine the worth of a practice. Evaluation research is used to plan, improve, and justify (or not justify) educational practices.
2. The worth of a practice depends on a judgement of its value according to standards applied relatively or absolutely.
3. Formative evaluation helps revise a practice in a developmental cycle.
4. Summative evaluation, conducted when a practice is established, determines the effectiveness of a practice compared with other competing practices.
5. A credible evaluation study satisfies the standards of utility, feasibility, propriety, and accuracy.
6. Major evaluation approaches include objectives-based, consumer- oriented, expertise, decision making, adversary, and naturalistic/participant approaches.
7. Objectives-oriented evaluation focuses on terminal behaviors: the extent to which the measurable objectives of a practice are attained by the target group.
8. Decision-oriented evaluation, such as needs assessment, program planning, implementation, and process and outcome assessment, provides information to decision-makers during program or system change processes.
9. Naturalistic/participant evaluation is based on concerns of various stakeholders. Multiplicity of data, inductive reasoning, and writing portrayals or a series of case studies characterize the approach.
10. A mixed methods study combines qualitative and quantitative techniques and/or data analysis within different phases of the research process.
11. Three types of mixed methods forms are complementary, developmental, and expansion.
12. Policy analysis evaluates government policies to provide policy-makers with pragmatic recommendations. Both macro (large-scale databases) and micro (field studies) approaches are employed.
13. Some policy analysis methods include: focused synthesis, field experiments, large-scale multi-site evaluations, qualitative interviews, surveys, large-scale testing programs, cost-analysis, and case study.
14. Potential benefits of evaluation and policy analysis are systematic school improvements, cost analyses, assessment of educational effects on students, appraisal of the quality of education, reduction of uncertainty in innovative practices, legitimization of decisions and enlightenment of policy influentials to better anticipate program and policy issues.
15. An evaluator, a client, and users can judge the adequacy of an evaluation proposal or report by using a checklist of criteria.

Self-Instructional Review Exercises

Sample answers are in the back of the book.

Test Items

1. Evaluation research
    a. tests theories to develop knowledge in the social sciences.
    b. discovers scientific laws that are generalizable.
    c. determines the value of a specific practice.
    d. lacks a design and procedures to collect information.
2. Formative evaluation, in contrast to summative evaluation
    a. is more time-consuming.
    b. uses quantitative methods more often.
    c. can improve a program; summative evaluation assesses utility.
    d. is more concerned about measurement validity and reliability.
3. Which is an *incorrect* description of objectives-oriented evaluation?
    a. determines which objectives are attained by the target group
    b. evaluates only measurable objectives
    c. requires valid and reliable instruments
    d. provides process evaluation
4. A decision-oriented evaluation
    a. determines the effectiveness of a practice by assessing one outcome.
    b. can focus on needs, program planning, implementation, and process/outcome or a combination.
    c. focuses only on decisions to improve a practice.
    d. is inflexible—that is, it focuses only on system wide changes.
5. In a naturalistic/participant evaluation, an evaluator would
    a. collect data specified only by the decision-maker.
    b. use only one data collection method.
    c. prefer observation and casual interviewing with an emergent design.
    d. ignore the concerns of different stakeholders.
6. Which is an *incorrect* description of mixed methods studies? Mixed methods studies
    a. combine qualitative and quantitative techniques and/or data analysis.
    b. can be used for complimentary, developmental or expansion purposes.
    c. can order the methods sequentially or parallel.
    d. would use probability sampling, measurement instruments, and statistical analysis.
7. Policy analysis
    I. evaluates government policies to provide pragmatic recommendations.
    II. is multidimensional in addressing a number of alternative factors.
    III. explicitly incorporates values.
    IV. may use a macro approach or a micro approach.
        a. I   b. I and II   c. I, II, and III   d. I, II, III, and IV
8. Policy analysis methods include
    a. rigorous literature reviews.
    b. large-scale multisite evaluations.
    c. qualitative interviews.
    d. cost analysis.

9. Evaluation research and policy analysis can
    I.   plan and implement school improvements on a systematic basis.
    II. test popular myths about the effects of education on students.
    III. reduce uncertainty about new educational practices.
    IV. enlighten influentials in decision and policy arenas to enable them to better anticipate program and policy issues.
       a. I   b. II and III   c. I, II, III, and IV   d. I and III
10. An evaluation report would be judged credible if the report
    a. was accurate, but the description of the practice was ambiguous.
    b. was clearly written but biased toward the viewpoint of the decision-maker.
    c. presented justified conclusions, but the information sources were indefensible and instruments were invalid.
    d. presented full disclosure of relevant and valid information with limitations cited.

Application Problems

Analyze the following evaluation situations by identifying the problem and suggesting alternative procedures.

1. A supervisor of instruction wanted an evaluation in order to compare a new independent study approach with the regular instructional approach in high school mathematics. A written formal agreement with the district evaluation staff stated the following arrangements:

   a. The evaluation was to help the high school mathematics department chairpersons decide whether to adopt the independent study approach districtwide.

   b. The procedures were to conduct a districtwide comparison of the two approaches, involving 20 percent of the high school's mathematics teachers and all their students.

   c. Mathematics achievement, student attitude, and teacher enthusiasm would be assessed.

   d. Teachers would be selected randomly and assigned to the two different approaches.

   The supervisor later decided that the evaluation should provide feedback to improve the new approach rather than decide on adoption. She changed the procedure for assigning teachers and students to the project, a change that resulted in their not being assigned randomly.

   The evaluation staff, assuming that the evaluation focus and design, once agreed on, would remain the same, collected and analyzed data as originally planned. The evaluators found that student attitudes toward both approaches were similar, but student achievement and teacher enthusiasm were significantly greater for the independent study approach. The report judged this approach as superior and recommended it for adoption.

   The supervisor was disappointed that the report did not help improve the independent study approach. The department chairpersons complained that the findings were not dependable because many teachers assigned to the independent study approach were biased in favor of it before the study began, and the students in independent study classes were generally high achievers prior to entering the program.

2. Two members of a school district's evaluation office were assigned to the superintendent to help her staff analyze qualitative data on a special crime prevention project. The evaluation data needs were as follows: The superintendent wanted a description of the project activities for a progress report to the funding agency. The funding agency wanted to know whether the contacts between the youngsters in the project and various law enforcement agencies—the police, the courts, and the juvenile officers—had been reduced during the first year.

   The evaluators spent more than a month reading the information that had been collected: staff daily logs, hearings records, newspaper articles, school cumulative files for each enrolled youngster, and official records of police court and juvenile probation officers. The evaluators developed a classification scheme in which every entry could be categorized. They also did a frequency count of the number of times each enrolled youngster had contact with a law enforcement agency during the first project year and in the preceding year. Two things were quickly evident: only a small proportion of the categorized data yielded any insights into the nature of the project activities during the year, and the number of law enforcement agency contacts was almost identical in each of the two years analyzed.

   The evaluators, running out of time, provided only sketchy accounts of activities and informed the superintendent that the project had proved unsuccessful in reducing law enforcement agency contacts. When the superintendent reported these findings to the funding agency, support was withdrawn and the project was ended.

   The project staff was stunned, especially because the number of contacts weighed so heavily in the decision. Its members pointed out that during the preproject year these contacts were arrests and court trial appearances, while during the first project year these contacts were supervisory and counseling sessions with juvenile officers. The juvenile officers said they were pleased with the changes seen in the enrolled youngsters' attitudes and behavior.

3. Units on ecology were introduced in all grades in a middle school. The school's curriculum committee requested that the school district's evaluation department evaluate the effectiveness of these units. Specifically, the committee wanted to know whether students increased their knowledge about environmental issues (preservation of endangered species and conservation of scarce resources) and decreased their practice of littering the school grounds.

   The evaluators used a pretest–posttest design with a test and a questionnaire. The test was the science subtest of a national standardized achievement test, including hygiene, biology, and earth science. The questionnaire was a self-report instrument by which students rated themselves and their classmates on school citizenship (respect for other students, respect for teachers, and respect for school property). The analysis of the data showed there was no change in the pretest–posttest scores on the subtest or on the citizenship questionnaire. The curriculum committee was disappointed in the evaluation and pointed out that it did not really answer their questions.

4. A faculty committee and the principal of a middle school developed materials for role-playing activities to improve school discipline. The materials were then tried out in half the school's social studies classes. After a year of use, the faculty committee requested that the central office's evaluation staff evaluate the materials. The faculty committee wanted to know whether the materials needed revision and whether they should be used in all social studies classes in the school.

   The evaluator interviewed the teachers and students who had used the materials. The evaluator also surveyed the entire faculty with a questionnaire to see whether the teachers believed there had been any changes in school discipline. The evaluator prepared a report that was very favorable to the materials, suggesting few changes in the materials and recommending their use the next year in all social studies classes. The evaluator discussed the report and its findings with the building principal.

   When word got out, two groups strongly protested: the faculty committee responsible for the materials, and the social studies teachers who taught the materials. The committee disavowed the report because it had had no input into the evaluation. The social studies teachers who had used the materials believed they should have been the first to receive the report, since they had used the materials and provided much of the data for the findings.

Answers to Self-Instructional Review Exercises

CHAPTER 1

Answers to Test Items: 1b, 2d, 3a, 4d, 5a, 6c, 7b, 8c, 9d, 10b

Answers for Application Problems

1. A. The teacher is more aware that classroom misbehavior might be related to the home environment.
2. C. A new research question might concern whether the reading comprehension test is also valid for grades 3 and 4.
3. C. A new research problem would be to study the organization of schools since the 1954 Supreme Court rulings.
4. B. The principal decides to send an information letter to parents that explains the new report card and grading system.
5. B. The curriculum developer decides to revise the module to reflect the suggestion from the field-testing of the pilot module.
6 C. The professor proposes a new study to investigate the degree and type of autonomous behavior of superintendents, principals, and teachers.

CHAPTER 2

Answers for Test Items: 1c, 2d, 3c, 4c, 5d, 6d, 7c, 8a, 9c, 10b, 11b, 12b

Answers for Application Problems

1. a. nonexperimental
   b. experimental or nonexperimental

560

   c. nonexperimental or qualitative
   d. experimental
   e. nonexperimental
   f. nonexperimental
   g. nonexperimental
   h. experimental
   i. qualitative

CHAPTER 3

Answers for Test Items: 1d, 2d, 3d, 4d, 5d, 6c, 7c, 8d, 9c, 10d, 11c

Answers for Application Problems

1. a. Need to specify population, "different ways of learning," and "effects." Example: Is there a difference between the SRA social studies achievement scores of eighth graders who had an inquiry approach and those who had a lecture approach?
   b. Need to specify population and measures of two variables. Example: Do the attitudes toward learning of middle school students differ between those in cooperative instruction and those in competitive instruction?
   c. Need to specify which educational opinions of which parents (population). Example: What are the opinions of parents of Fox School pupils toward the proposed athletic eligibility regulations?
   d. Need to specify which family characteristics are to be measured or categorized and measurement for school attendance. Example: Is there a relationship between educational level of parents and number of siblings and their average daily school attendance?
   e. Need to specify type of validity sought, population, and criterion for validity. Example: Is there a relationship between the scores of the WISC and the CAT among primary grade minority children?
2. Directional hypothesis: Low-achieving students reinforced with tangible rewards will demonstrate greater achievement in basic skills than low-achieving students reinforced with intangible rewards. Independent variable is type of reward (categorical) and dependent variable is achievement (continuous or measured).
3. a. High school students in an individualized curriculum will score higher on a social studies test than students in a structured curriculum.
   b. Teacher positive task introduction compared to teacher neutral task introduction statements will produce sustained student engagement in those tasks.
   c. Students who are retained have higher scores on a measure of personal adjustment than comparable students who are promoted.

d. There is a significant difference in the scores of a teacher burnout inventory among teachers of mildly retarded, moderately retarded, and nonretarded children, or, the degree of teacher burnout increases as the students' level of intellectual ability decreases.

4. a. Independent variable: liberal grading
      Dependent variable: faculty evaluations
   b. Variable: classroom behavior
   c. Independent variable: teacher cognitive styles
      Dependent variable: academic achievement gains
   d. no variables
   e. Independent variable: contextual aids
      Dependent variable: intersentence interference
   f. Independent variable: two school-based intervention programs
      Dependent variable: depressive symptoms

5. b and f

6. a. female faculty members of an urban university
   b. the School Board records of a suburban school system, 1920 to 1980
   c. Miss Sue's first year as a teacher in an elementary school
   d. a faculty implementing an innovative middle school program

CHAPTER 4

Answers for Test Items: 1c, 2c, 3e, 4a, 5b, 6e, 7d, 8e, 9b, 10c, 11a, 12e, 13d, 14c, 15b, 16a, 17a, 18c

Answers for Application Problems

1. Search *RIE* by type of document: curriculum guidelines and evaluation studies for Title I ESEA Act mathematics programs and by years desired. By using connecting identifiers with key terms, Chapter 1 (new terminology) can be located.

2. a. For a narrow search:
      A and E and H and J
   b. For a more thorough search:
      Search 1: (A or B) and (E or F) and (H or I) and J
      Search 2: (A or B) and (E or F) and (H or I) and (J or K)
      Search 3: (A or B or C or D) and (E or F or G) and (H or I) and J
      Search 4: (A or B or C or D) and (E or F or G) and (H or I) and (J or K)

3. The order of priority for presenting sources in a literature review is from the least related or most general to the most related literature. The sources would thus be organized as (d) theories, (e) studies on animal behavior, (b) program descriptions, (a) evaluations of instruction, and (c) evaluations of students.

CHAPTER 5

Answers for Test Items: 1b, 2c, 3c, 4d, 5a, 6c, 7d, 8d, 9a, 10d

Answers for Application Problems

1.   Internet Search tools and searches
    a. Search Engine, search for all of the key ideas (Internet, guidelines or policies, Georgia)
    b. Subject Director, search for a category of Internet guidelines or policies, then look for listings by state or by setting. Search for listings of Georgia schools.
    c. Known locations with probable links to policies and/or listings of Web sites for Georgia schools
        a. Georgia Department of Education
        b. Georgia Education Association
        c. American Association of School Administrators
2.   Evaluate each component of the citation, abstract, and bibliography, and address.
    a. Author: Has Catherine Maloney published any other research on this topic? Is there really a Fairfield University? If so, is she listed as a member of the faculty?
    b. Abstract and research methodology: This just sounds ridiculous.
    c. Bibliography: Is there really a journal called Western Musicology Journal?
    d. Address: Located on the University of Louisville's server (uofl.edu), this might look legitimate, but if you shorten the address <http://www.uofl.edu/infoliteracy/>, you find that it is part of an exercise on evaluating Web resources.
3.   Title: Private School Universe Survey, 1997–98
     Internet address: <http://nces.ed.gov/surveys/pss/>
     Summary: Survey data on the characteristics of K–12 private schools. Includes information on school size and religious orientation of school.
     Statistic: The survey reported that 5 million students were enrolled in K–12 private schools in the fall of 1997.

CHAPTER 6

Answers for Test Items: 1b, 2c, 3d, 4a, 5b, 6a, 7b, 8a, 9c, 10b, 11b, 12a, 13a, 14a, 15c, 16b

Answers for Application Problems

1. a. Evidently the instructor knew about the study, and his or her bias could affect the results. Subjects choose the section they will be in; hence, selec-

tion is a major threat. The time of day of the sections may affect selection and is itself a threat to internal validity. There is no assurance that the instructor will treat each section the same. Diffusion of treatment may be a problem if students from different sections interact. Some students may purposely score low on the pretest in order to show significant improvement in the course (instrumentation—the results may be inaccurate). History may also be a threat, depending on the nature of the class groups. The generalizability is limited to the students taking the course in this particular college, the course itself (tennis), the instructor, and the methods used in the class.

b. Instrumentation is a potential threat, since details about the nature of the observations are lacking. Test validity could also be considered, since measuring prosocial behavior in a playground may not reflect the benefits of day care attendance. Compensatory rivalry or resentment might be a factor, because mothers who were chosen as a control group might arrange other experiences for their children that would enhance prosocial behavior. External validity is limited because of the volunteer nature of the sample and the specific programs of the day care institutions utilized. If there are many different day care organizations represented, it would be difficult to generalize about the cause of the difference. Each case would have to be examined individually.

c. The question here is whether the population that votes is the same as the population from which the sample is drawn; after all, those who rent can also vote, so depending on the percentage of renters in the district, sampling property owners alone may be misleading. In addition, not all property owners have children going to school, and only a portion of the population ever votes. The generalizability of the results thus would be suspect. Depending on the nature of the issue at hand, some respondents may provide less than honest information. They may also change their minds within the two weeks before voting.

d. The major threat is selection, since only 60 percent of the poulation returned questionnaires, and teachers could withhold information if they wanted to. Instrumentation may be a threat, depending on the way the questionnaire was designed (validity and reliability, and the standardization of the way it is administered—that is, its directions). There is a chance for scoring error, since each instructor does his or her own scoring. Subject attrition might be a problem. Since the questionnaire was given only once, students who were absent would be excluded. The generalizability of the results would be limited by the nature of the sample that returned questionnaires and the time of year the study was done.

CHAPTER 7

Answers for Test Items: 1a and d, 2c, 3c, 4d, 5a, 6c, 7b, 8d, 9b, 10a

Answers for Application Problems

1. a. mean
   b. Pearson product-moment correlation
   c. standard deviation (the wider the dispersion, the greater the number of groups)
   d. frequencies and percentages
2. a. interval or ordinal
   b. nominal
   c. ordinal

CHAPTER 8

Answers for Test Items: 1b, 2d, 3a, 4d, 5b, 6a, 7d, 8c, 9a, 10c, 11d, 12d, 13d, 14a, 15b, 16b, 17d, 18c, 19a, 20b, 21c

Answers for Application Problems

1. a. questionnaire, to enhance confidentiality of sensitive topics and keep expenses low
   b. observation, since self-report measures would be susceptible to social desirability
   c. phone interview, to ensure representative responses
   d. questionnaire, because the information is simple and easily obtained
   e. observational, to keep the situation as natural as possible
   f. interview, since there would be a need to probe
   g. interview; most small children are honest and are unable to respond to questionnaires
   h. questionnaires or interviews, depending on the specificity of the information needed. An interview is useful for generating specific items that can then be used on a questionnaire.
2. a. ambiguity of the term "open education"
   b. no information about how to rank; is 1 or 10 most important?
   c. use of both senior and junior high teachers creates ambiguity; should ask about either senior or junior high teachers but not both
   d. ambiguity permitting a respondent who thinks "she's not just good, she's great" to answer "strongly disagree"
3. a. alternate individual work sessions and group activities and observe during individual work sessions
   b. teach students to observe themselves (that is, record time taken to complete assignments)
   c. use unobtrusive measures, such as number of requests from students for help, pencil shavings in pencil sharpener, detail and care in assignments, and amount of eraser that is used

CHAPTER 9

Answers for Test Items: 1c, 2d, 3b, 4a, 5b, 6d, 7c, 8d, 9a, 10d, 11b, 12d

Answers for Application Problems

1. Her decision may have been correct, but her inference that the techniques caused the achievement in incorrect because it is possible that other events occurred at the same time as the techniques did to cause greater achievement. This is an example of inferring causation from correlation.
2. a. correlational
   b. comparative
   c. predictive
   d. comparative
   e. descriptive
   f. *ex post facto*

CHAPTER 10

Answers for Test Items: 1b, 2d, 3a, 4b, 5c, 6a, 7c, 8b, 9d, 10b, 11c

Answers for Application Problems

1. Nonequivalent Groups Pretest–Posttest Design

$$A \longrightarrow O \longrightarrow X_1 \longrightarrow O$$
$$B \longrightarrow O \longrightarrow X_2 \longrightarrow O$$
$$C \longrightarrow O \longrightarrow X_3 \longrightarrow O$$

2. Multiple Base Line Across Subjects Design

```
                                   X X X X X X X X X X
Boy    OOOOO   OOOOO   OOOOOOOOOO
Girl   OOOOO   OOOOO   OOOOO X X X X X
                                        OOOOO
```

3. Posttest-Only Comparison Group Design

Randomization	Groups	Treatment	Posttest
60	A	X_1	O
students	B	X_2	O
	C	X_3	O

CHAPTER 11

Answers for Test Items: 1d, 2b, 3c, 4-c-d-f-g, 5d, 6b, 7a, 8a, 9b, 10c, 11d, 12d, 13b

Answers for Application Problems

1. There are three groups in this study. The researcher would hence use one-way ANOVA or an appropriate nonparametric analog, depending on the nature of the dependent variables. Most likely, means would be reported for the groups, and the parametric procedure would be acceptable, followed by post hoc comparisons if necessary.

2. Since the same group of students is assessed twice, a dependent samples *t*-test is the statistical procedure. If there were more than one dependent variable (that is, several facets to sex education), then the teacher should employ a multivariate test.

3. The teacher should now use a 2 × 2 ANOVA (group *x* gender). The analysis will provide a test for each main effect and a test for the interaction between group and gender.

4. There would be two ways to analyze this data: first, a correlation could be computed between self-esteem and frequency of visits and tested by a *t*-test to see whether the correlation is significantly different from zero; or, second, groups of students could be identified (for example, high, low, medium self-esteem), and a 1 × 3 ANOVA computed on the mean frequencies of each group.

5. There are two independent variables and eight related dependent variables, resulting in the need for a 2 × 4 MANOVA, with appropriate post hoc tests if necessary.

CHAPTER 12

Answers for Test Items: 1c, 2b, 3b, 4b, 5d, 6c, 7b, 8a, 9c, 10d

Answers for Application Problems

1. a. Purposeful sampling is appropriate because the interest is only with *these* parents and *this* program. There is no interest in generalizability.

  b. Comprehensive sampling is appropriate because there is only a Director, one teacher of the class, and twelve households. The twelve households are also maximum variation sampling because there are three types of households. The researcher needs to locate within each household who is actually attending the child and his schooling in the parent education program.

  c. Interview, documents of the program, records of parent–teacher contracts, and materials sent to the parent.

2.   Elementary school principals are the key informants. The research question focuses on "how," which suggests obtaining information on the process of decision-making, who is consulted, which records are used, and copies of school and/district guidelines for retention. The design would require use of in-depth interviews and documents analysis. A purposeful sample is used, but the sample size depends on locating principals who have had experience with making retention decisions.

3. a.   Purposeful sampling, because the focus is on understanding a concept and a process.

   b.   Reputational-sampling. Knowledgeable central office personnel who planned, selected the six schools, and did the orientation sessions could select the school where a team is operating on a regular basis. Other cases could be added—such as a negative case or typical case—depending on the information obtained from this site.

   c.   Field observations of the monthly team meetings, in-depth interviews with the principal and the facilitator, and documents (records of all meetings, district guidelines, and others).

4. a.   Extension of findings can be enhanced by specifying the researcher role, informant selection, the multimethods employed, and the data analysis strategies in the report. Data collection strategies, which could increase extension are obtaining verbatim accounts, using low-inference descriptors, having the teacher keep records (participant-researcher), and participant review.

   b.   Strategies to minimize threats to validity are use of participant language, visiting the households and the program, and techniques to enhance critical reflexivity.

   c.   The researcher needs to specify how typical are these households and the common and contrasting features of this parent education program to other programs.

5. a.   Validity can be enhanced by specifying in the study the researcher role, site selection, and the social context of the team meetings, the data collection and analysis strategies and the analytical premises—concept of site-based school management. Data collection strategies to increase validity are verbatim accounts, low-inference descriptors, mechanically recording data, and member checking with team members and others.

   b.   To minimize threats to validity, the researcher can collect data on team meetings for a year, use the language of the site, do all data collection in the field, and keep a reflex journal. Obtaining baseline data is important in a process study.

   c.   The researcher needs to describe typicality of the school and the contrasting dimensions of site-based management with that of other management approaches. Of interest is this district's definition of site-based management contrasted to that of other districts and to the theory of site-based school management. Because prior research has been done on site-based school management, the results of this study can be contrasted to prior research.

CHAPTER 13

Answers for Test Items: 1a, 2c, 3b, 4d, 5d, 6d, 7b, 8d, 9b, 10a

Answers for Application Problems

1.   The researcher can collect data by observations and casual conversations with other teachers and school personnel. Rapport is maintained with the sixth teacher by indicating interest without demanding the teacher to use the curriculum in the researcher's presence. Sufficient data about the curriculum can be obtained from other sources. Further, the ethnographer, for confidentiality of the data, should not tell other district officials of the teacher's reluctance.

2.   A researcher tries to observe all the happenings, formal and informal, in the setting although the major foci may be on the processes within the photography class and the evening programs. Thus, social activities, meals, and extracurricular activities are potential sources of data. Student photographs are sources of data. Field notes of all observations and conversations are made because the ethnographer does not know what is important at the time it occurs.

3.   The researcher can remind the director of the agreement established at entry into the field—all data are confidential and all names and places will be coded. Second, the ethnographer does not know what the remarks mean or if the remarks will be reported in the findings, which reflect only patterns established through cross-checking with other sources. Third, the ethnographer could use the occasion to encourage the director to talk more about these adults so the researcher could assess the trustworthiness of the adult testimony. The ethnographer could also use the occasion to have the director talk about her concerns regarding the public image of the adult education program.

4.   Yes. The proposed study focuses on the dynamic processes of socialization in desegregated schools. Other justifications for the use of ethnography are (1) an interest in the school and community milieu in which the classroom dynamics occur, (2) previous studies have not addressed this research question, and (3) previous research has not used on-site observation as a methodology.

5.   A sample qualitative interview guide is
   a. How do you feel when your principal visits your class?
      Probe: Could you tell me why?
   b. Principals usually have a conference with the teacher after observing their instruction. Can you tell me what these conferences are like?
   c. Do you think that your principal's evaluation of your teaching is fair?
      Probe: Why fair or unfair?
   d. How do you think evaluation relates to your idea of being a professional teacher?

CHAPTER 14

Answers for Test Items: 1d, 2c, 3d, 4c, 5d, 6a, 7b, 8d, 9c, 10a, 11d, 12c, 13b

Answers to Application Problems

1. a. beliefs about child development: lines 1–3, 15–16.
   b. beliefs about the possibility of "catching up": lines 4–5, 17–18.
   c. beliefs about the possibility of influencing a child's preparation for school: lines 6–9, 19–21.
   d. beliefs about what teachers can do: lines 10–14, 22–24.
2.   Some patterns that need confirmation are
   a. Teacher beliefs about child development relate to beliefs about the possibility of "catching up."
   b. Teacher beliefs about the possibility of influencing a child's preparation for school relate to beliefs about what teachers can do.
   c. Teacher beliefs about the possibility of "catching up" relate to beliefs about what teachers can do.

CHAPTER 15

Answers for Test Items: 1d, 2c, 3d, 4c, 5e-d-c-b-a, 6d, 7b, 8a, 9c, 10c

Answers for Application Problems

1. a. This topic could be delimited by which local school board, the years to be included in the study, and by the type of decision—personnel, fiscal, curriculum decisions.
   b. Sources for the study could be (1) documents, (2) oral testimonies, and (3) relics. Documents may be the official board minutes, reports submitted to the school board and released by them, budgets, local newspapers, and newsletters by the school system. Oral testimonies include extended interviews with the incumbents and past members of the school board, the incumbent and past superintendent, the incumbent and past president of the teachers organization, and other living witnesses who appeared before the school board. Examples of relics are charts and diagrams used in presentations before the school board.
2. a. The research problem could be stated as follows:
   1) for a historical study: The research problem is to analyze the concept of the student in the past 50 years with references to moral development.
   2) for a policy study: The research problem is to analyze the implementation of the legislative mandate that "each school division shall develop standards of student conduct and attendance and shall have

implemented a plan conducive to learning and good citizenship in an atmosphere free of disruption."

   3) for an analysis of a concept: The research problem is to identify the essential meaning of "student discipline," the different meanings of "student discipline," and the necessary conditions for the appropriate usage of the concept "student discipline."

  b. Specialized bibliographies for history include *The Historian's Handbook: A Descriptive Guide to Reference Works* and *A Bibliography of American Educational History.* Specialized digests for legal research are the National Reporter System and the American Digest System. Because the policy study focuses on the implementation of a state mandate, the researcher will probably have to obtain assistance from the state law library or legislative reference library and freports from state agencies.

3. a. An analyst questions the accuracy of statements made at a testimonial dinner. Considerations of good taste probably influenced statements that (1) "due solely to," (2) the junior college system meets state needs and provides a better general education, (3) "alone establihsed" minimum competency testing, and (4) the innovation raised students and proved to the public. . . .

  b. Other documents about the junior college system, teacher salaries and certification requirements, and the minimum competency testing program from 1959 to 1979 would confirm, reject, or modify the newspaper account. The private oral testimonies of the dinner speakers and members of the educational agencies and associations might vary from the public statements.

CHAPTER 16

Answers for Test Items: 1d, 2c, 3d, 4d, 5d, 6d, 7d, 8a, 9c, 10d

Answers for Application Problems

1. The evaluators should have monitored and noted the changes in purpose and procedures as they occurred. The evaluators could have met periodically with the supervisor to review purposes or data needs and check on the procedures that were not directly under their control. Near the end of the evaluation, the evaluation staff could have met with the supervisor and department chairpersons to consider the changed purpose and procedures in preparation for forming recommendations.

2. Two errors were made by the evaluators. First, they failed to recognize the need to plan their evaluation in terms of evaluation questions and the time frame for the evaluation. Qualitative analysis must be focused around questions, just like quantitative analysis. Second, they allowed frequency counts to substitute for an adequate analysis of the nature of the contacts between

enrolled youngsters and law enforcement agencies. The evaluators should have entered only the records most likely to furnish the information they sought, such as staff logs. The evaluators should have been less hasty to convert contact records to numbers that failed to reflect differences in kinds of contacts. Even cursory thought about the kinds of contact being recorded should have led the evaluators to question the data and eventually question the project staff. Had they done this, they could have drawn a different conclusion about the project's effectiveness.

3. The evaluators should have chosen or developed instruments and procedures that focused directly on the curriculum committee's questions. The evaluators could have (1) checked the validity of these instruments against the content and objectives of the ecology units and/or (2) asked the curriculum committee and the middle school teachers to judge the validity of the instruments for their questions. The evaluators could have observed the ecology units in operation and the students in and out of the classroom to discover unintended effects of the units on their behavior. The evaluators could have used unobtrusive measures to collect data on the amount of wastepaper, bottles, and cans found in specific locations around the school, the extent to which students used both sides of the notebook paper, and so on.

4. The evaluator erred in not meeting earlier (when planning the evaluation) with the faculty committee and principal to develop a dissemination plan and to identify all of the audiences for the report. When the report was completed, he should have discussed the findings with the principal and given copies of the report to the committee. He should have provided an executive summary of the report for the entire faculty. He should have at least suggested to the principal that the report and its findings be discussed with those social studies teachers who had used the materials.

Guidelines for Research Proposals

W riting a research proposal can be the most difficult yet exciting step in the research process. In this phase, the entire project is synthesized into a specific form. In a proposal, researchers demonstrate that they know what they are seeking, how they will seek and recognize it, and explain why the research is worthwhile. Quantitative proposals reflect a deductive approach to educational research. The format may be a relatively informal outline offered by a professor to satisfy a course requirement, a formal thesis or dissertation proposal presented to a committee, or a structured funding proposal requested by a foundation or government agency.

In Appendix A we describe a general proposal format with guidelines for quantitative proposals and then for qualitative proposals. Although many of the elements of a proposal are similar for quantitative and qualitative research, there are methodological variations. We also describe the preparation and criticism of a proposal.

Quantitative Research Proposals

Writing a proposal for quantitative research requires many design decisions once the specific research questions or hypotheses are formalized. Decisions regarding subjects and instrumentation are as important as the statement of the problem.

General Format

Quantitative research proposals generally follow the format presented here. The outline contains all the steps necessary for formulating and proposing a quantitative research study. Quantitative proposals reflect a deductive approach to educational research.

   I. Introduction
       A. General Statement of the Problem
       B. Review of the Literature
       C. Specific Research Questions and/or Hypotheses
       D. Significance of the Proposed Study
  II. Design and Methodology
       A. Subjects
       B. Instrumentation
       C. Procedures
       D. Data Analysis and Presentation
       E. Limitations of the Design
 III. References
 IV. Appendices

Guidelines for Quantitative Research Proposals

I. Introduction The *general problem statement* is a clear, precise statement of the research problem, which helps the reader recognize the importance of the problem and the area of education in which it lies. The problem statement is then linked to the related literature, to the specific research questions and/or hypotheses, and finally to the significance of the proposed study. A concise and direct statement of the problem is made very early in the introduction, ideally in the first paragraph, followed by a description of the background of the problem. It is crucial to phrase the problem in intelligible terms for someone who is generally sophisticated but who may be relatively uninformed in the area of the problem.

The *literature review* presents what is known about the problem from theoretical discussions and prior research, thus providing the background and need for the study. The literature review concludes with a discussion of the knowledge to date on the problem and the researcher's insights, such as criticisms of designs of prior research and identification of gaps in the literature. The review of the literature, although thorough at this time, frequently is expanded as the research progresses.

Specific research questions and/or hypotheses are stated, sometimes followed by definitions of key terms and variables. Question format is appropriate for survey research. Question or hypothesis format is appropriate for experimental and non-experimental design studies. The statement of the specific questions and/or hypotheses should clearly indicate the empirical nature of the investigation, such as a specific type of research design. Definitions—preferably operational definitions—of variables follow the statement of specific research questions and/or hypotheses.

The *potential significance of the proposed study* notes the importance of the study in terms of (1) the development of knowledge and (2) implications of further research and educational practices. The researcher discusses how the results of the study could add to theory and knowledge in the area identified in the general problem statement. Implications for further research are stated. Finally, the researcher tentatively states potential implications for educational practices. Implications for educational practices are not detailed recommendations for specific problems but general statements for educational practitioners.

Some researchers prefer and some formats require that the significance of the proposed study be placed after the research design is described. Most researchers write and rewrite this part of a proposal because it is a major criterion in obtaining proposal approval.

II. Design and Methodology The design and methodology in quantitative research include the subjects, instrumentation, procedures for obtaining the data, data analysis and presentation, and design limitations.

The researcher identifies the type of design to be used—survey, correlational, experimental, quasi-experimental, and the like. This orients the reader to expect certain design components to be discussed in the proposal.

The *subjects* are identified by describing the population of interest—and how the probability sample will be drawn from this population. The sample size is stated. A rationale for the sampling procedure and the sample size is given.

Most proposals state how the protection of the rights of human subjects will be accomplished. The minimum procedures include how informed consent will be obtained and how confidentiality of the data of individual subjects will be established. The form for consent to participate in the study is usually in an appendix.

The *instrumentation* for the proposed study identifies the instrument(s) to be used and explains why the instrument(s) was selected as the most appropriate operational definition of the variable(s) in research question(s) and/or hypotheses. If the instrument is already established, the reported evidence of its reliability and also its validity for the purpose of the study is given. If the instrument(s) must be developed, then the steps to obtain validity and reliability data for the instrument are outlined. The more technical details of these procedures are often discussed in an appendix to the proposal.

The *procedures* describe the way in which the study will be conducted so that the relationships between variables can be investigated. In survey research this includes preparing the questionnaire or interview schedule, training the interviewer or providing directions for those who administer questionnaires or tests, and the like. In experimental and quasi-experimental research, the procedures may be more complex—identification of the groups, specification of the experimental treatment, and procedures to minimize confounding variables. Procedures for replacement of subjects are noted.

The *data analysis and presentation* states the statistical techniques to be used in data analysis and specifies how the data will be presented. The researcher states the statistical test for *each* research question and/or hypothesis and, if necessary, the rationale for the choice of the test. The rationale may be in terms of purpose of the study, sample size, and type of scales used in the instrument. A statistical technique is selected on the basis of appropriateness for investigating the research question and/or hypothesis; nothing is gained by using a complicated technique when a simple one will suffice.

A researcher often states the forms of data presentation—the kinds of tables, figures, and charts to be used to organize and summarize each set of data. The forms selected are usually linked to each research question and/or hypotheses. Guidelines to the expression of numbers and statistical symbols and for tables and figures are presented in the *Publication Manual of the American Psychological Association* (4th ed.).

The *limitations of the design* section cites the limitations that the researcher can identify at this time: scope of the study, the design, and/or the methodology. The researcher recognizes that the proposed study focuses on only one delineated aspect of a larger research problem, such as the effects of labeling elementary school exceptional children rather than the effects of labeling all students. Stating the design limitations illustrates the researcher's knowledge of the threats to internal and external validity in the proposed design. It is better for the researcher to recognize the limitations rather than claim he or she has a "perfect" design. Methodological limitations relate specifically to validity and reliability of the proposed instrumentation or the instrument(s) that have been developed. Limitations are tempered with reasonableness and should not be so extensive that the study is unimportant. Sometimes researchers prefer to state research assumptions made in order to conduct the study rather than pointing out the limitations.

III. References The references list the sources that the researcher actually used to develop the proposal *and* are cited in the text of the proposal. References are those cited primarily in the literature review, but any sources cited in the general problem statement, significance of the study, and in some instances, in the methodological section, are also listed. Every source cited in the proposal *must* be included in the references and every entry listed in the references *must* appear in the proposal.

An ethical researcher does not cite abstracts of dissertations or of journal articles as references. Part of a study that is quoted in another source is not cited, but the source containing that quotation is cited, and therefore it is listed in the references. The *Publication Manual of the American Psychological Association* (4th ed.) provides guidelines for quotations, reference citations, and reference lists.

IV. Appendices The appendices provide supplementary materials for clarity and economical presentation and are keyed to appropriate references in the text. When placed in the appendices, these materials become options available to the reader as needed, rather than distractions to the logical flow of a proposal. Included in the appendices may be such items as the following:

   a. instructions to subjects
   b. informed subject consent forms
   c. letters of permission to conduct the study in an educational agency or organization
   d. pilot studies
   e. copies of instruments–questionnaires, interview schedules, observation schedules
   f. instructions for and training of data collectors
   g. credentials of experts, judges, or other specialized personnel to be used in the study
   h. diagrammatic models of research design or statistical analysis
   i. chapter outline for the final report
   j. proposed time schedule for completing the study

Qualitative Research Proposals

Writing a qualitative research proposal, similar to writing one for quantitative research, can be the most difficult yet exciting step in the research process. Proposals for qualitative research usually are tentative and open-ended allowing for an emergent design. Qualitative research proposals reflect an inductive approach to research. Qualitative researchers and scholars recognize that the degree of specificity in a written proposal *depends on the extent of preliminary work*. In ethnographic research, preliminary work may be site or network selection or identification of particular cases for investigation. A proposal, however, can be sufficiently specific to indicate systematic research to yield valid data without being so specific that the initial focus and design cannot be reformulated as the data are collected.

General Format

The general format for a qualitative research proposal loosely resembles a quantitative research proposal with methodological variations for an interactive mode of data collection. The outline given here contains the elements of an ethnographic proposal.

   I. Introduction
      A. General Problem Statement
      B. Preliminary Literature Review
      C. Foreshadowed Problems
      D. Significance of Proposed Study
   II. Design and Methodology
      A. Site or Social Network Selection
      B. Research Role
      C. Purposeful Sampling Strategies

   D. Data Collection Strategies
   E. Inductive Data Analysis
   F. Limitations of the Design
 III. References or Bibliography
 IV. Appendices

The general format varies somewhat for the particular ethnographic research.

Guidelines for Qualitative Research Proposals

I. Introduction The introduction consists of the general problem statement, literature review, foreshadowed problems, and the potential significance of the proposed study. Each of these is briefly explained below.

The *general problem statement* is a clear, succinct statement of the research problem that enables the reader to recognize the importance of the problem and the area of education in which it lies. A direct statement of the problem is made very early in the introduction, followed by a description of the background of the problem. Typically the general problem statement is phrased as "to describe and analyze" an ongoing event or a process in a discovery orientation.

The *preliminary literature review* presents the *initial* conceptual frameworks used in phrasing foreshadowed problems/questions and a need for the study by identifying gaps in our knowledge. The literature review frequently cites broad areas of scholarly thinking—sociological, psychological, anthropological, or political—with representative scholars. The literature review is *not* exhaustive, but it is a preliminary review that makes explicit the initial conceptual frameworks on which the researcher enters the field to focus the beginning observations and interviewing. The literature review clearly justifies the need for an in-depth descriptive study using a qualitative approach. For example, prior studies did not examine the phenomena in depth or as a process, related research was conducted with quantitative procedures, or the number of participants is too small to meet statistical requirements of a quantitative design.

The *foreshadowed problems* are stated as broad, anticipated research questions to be reformulated. To state the foreshadowed problems, researchers have usually selected the site or participants and have obtained tentative or formal permission to conduct the study. In other words, the researcher already has preliminary information.

The *potential significance of the study* describes how the study can add to (1) the development of knowledge and (2) implications for further research and educational practices. Qualitative studies frequently add to our knowledge by providing detailed descriptions of a naturalistic event that has not been described fully in the literature. Qualitative studies also may develop concepts or a theoretical explanation for what was observed. Most proposals in a discovery orientation state the intent to suggest further research with similar designs to extend the findings or with other designs and methodologies to verify the findings.

II. Design and Methodology The design and methodology in a qualitative research proposal includes the site or social network selected, the research role, purposeful sampling strategies, data collection strategies, inductive data analysis, and design limitations.

The researcher identifies the proposal as a *case study design,* using qualitative techniques. This orients the reader to expect certain design components to be discussed in the proposal.

The *site selected* is described in terms that illustrate its suitability to investigate the phenomena and processes stated in the foreshadowed problems. For example, if the foreshadowed problems focus on instructional processes, then the site should contain courses or classes—social scenes—which have instructional processes. A description of the site characteristics is essential—public or private school, type of educational agency, and its purpose or role in society, typical activities and processes, the kinds of participants, and the like. The description helps identify how typical the site is to other institutions to allow for extension of findings.

The *selected social network* is described to justify that the group members are likely to be informed about the foreshadowed problems. For example, if the social network is made up of members of a professional association or parents of a sponsored support group for children in a program, then the functions of the network and its organization are described. There should be a logical relationship between the potential information to be elicited through personal contact and the foreshadowed problems.

The researcher states the *research role* to be assumed for data collection. The researcher, at this time, can describe the role only in general terms, for example, participant-observer, or primarily an interviewer. Because the research role affects the relationships in interactive data collection, the role must be delineated as much as possible in terms of the expected social relationships and role sets during data collection. Further, the research role must be appropriate for the foreshadowed problems.

Purposeful sampling strategies are stated in a proposal. The researcher recognizes that strategies will be selected in the field as the research progresses. The intent of purposeful sampling is to obtain small samples of information-rich cases of individuals, social scenes, or processes.

Most proposals state how the protection of the rights of human subjects will be accomplished. The minimum procedures include how informed consent will be obtained and how confidentiality of the data of individual subjects will be established. The form for consent to participate, including assurances of anonymity in regard to data about the site, organization, or social network and to individuals, is usually in an appendix.

Data collection strategies are stated. Although specific data collection strategies will emerge in the field, the intent to use multiple methods should be explicit, to enable corroboration of the data. The researcher specifies which strategies will be used: participant observations, the form(s) of in-depth interviews and artifacts expected to be collected in the field. Some ethnographers specify certain data collection strategies for each research focus in the foreshadowed problems. The researcher also states the expected *length of field work,* the natural time boundary of the event to be observed, such as a semester, the entire program, and the like.

The forms that the data will take, such as field notes, summary observations, and interview records, transcripts, and elaborations are stated. Because the collected data can become "mounds" of information, researchers sometimes state how they will catalogue, store, and retrieve data either manually or with a microcomputer. Although data collection strategies in a proposal are written as planned strategies, they do indicate that the researcher is aware of the need to make choices in the field to obtain valid data as the foreshadowed problems are reformulated.

The description of *inductive data analysis* includes strategies to facilitate discovery in the field with interim analysis, coding topics and developing categories, and techniques of pattern-seeking and establishing the plausibility of patterns. Sometimes a diagram of the inductive process is given in an appendix. Frequently a few pages of a coded transcript or field notes are placed in an appendix. Sometimes researchers cite software programs to be used for data management.

The *limitations of the design,* similar to quantitative research, cites the limitations that the researcher can identify at this time: the scope of the study, methodology, and the design. The limitation of scope relates to the problem statement. The foreshadowed problems usually focus on one aspect of possible research foci at the selected site, such as to describe instructional processes but not to evaluate the teacher or the effectiveness of these processes for student learning. Methodological limitations refer to possible difficulties in assuming the research role, purposeful sampling, and naturalistic events that the ethnographer cannot interrupt legitimately.

Qualitative proposals also address design limitations: validity, reflexivity, and extension of findings. Findings from a case study design are not generalizable, but without a case study design, other research purposes could not be achieved. Researchers discuss the strategies they intend to use to minimize threats to validity and to extension of results.

III. References or Bibliography References for a qualitative study are similar to that for a quantitative study if one uses the APA style manual. Some researchers prefer to use the CMS with its bibliographic format.

IV. Appendices The appendices in a qualitative proposal provide supplementary materials for economical presentation as in quantitative proposals. The items in the appendices, however, are appropriate for the proposal. Included in the appendices for an ethnographic proposal may be such items as the following:

a. letters of permission granting access to the site or social network
b. agreements of informed rights of human subjects from key participants
c. protocols for obtaining informed consent in a social network
d. brief hypothetical examples of field notes and summary observations, interview records, and transcripts
e. description of persons who will nominate participants for reputational-case sampling
f. a few pages of a coded transcript or field notes from a pilot study
g. list of records and artifacts known to be available at the site or through the social network
h. proposed time schedule for completing the study

Preparation and Criticism of a Proposal

Preparation of a proposal involves two additional tasks: conforming to the format and style required for the proposal and obtaining criticisms of a draft proposal before it is typed in finished form. Beginning researchers often consult books on proposal writing.[1]

Preparation of a Proposal

Most colleges and universities either have developed their own format and style manual or have selected a style manual to be followed, such as the *Publication Manual of the American Psychological Association (1994) (4th ed.)* [APA style manual] or *The Chicago Manual of Style: Fourteenth edition, Revised and Expanded (1993)* [CMS]. *Format* refers to the general pattern of organization and arrangement of the proposal. *Style* refers to the rules of spelling, capitalization, punctuation, and typing followed in preparing a proposal. Although neither of these published manuals refers specifically to research proposals, many universities and colleges follow a general format and the style adopted from one of these authoritative manuals. Reference or bibliographic style and format, the headings and sections, and the writing style differ from one manual to the other. Whereas APA style practically eliminates the use of footnotes, the CMS provides for extensive use of explanatory footnotes to cite specific sources for facts presented, methodological insights, comments, and additional information for a greater understanding of the text. Further, a reference list in APA style contains only those that are cited in the text; CMS style can include references that provided background knowledge for the problem or researcher.

---

[1]See, for example, Lock. L. F., Spirduso, W. W., & Silverman, S. J. (1999). *Proposals that work: A guide for planning dissertations and grant proposals* (4th ed.).

Correct spelling, grammar construction, and punctuation are expected in a research proposal, and the use of abbreviations and contractions is generally discouraged. Experienced researchers know that "to write means to rewrite, and rewrite and rewrite and. . . . " Personal pronouns such as *I, my, we,* and *our* should generally be avoided by beginning researchers. If the first word of a sentence is a number, or if the number is nine or less, it is usually expressed as a word. Otherwise, numbers are usually expressed as Arabic numerals.

Format also includes the preliminary pages. In a proposal this usually refers to the title page and perhaps a table of contents if the proposal is over fifteen pages. The title page contains the title of the proposal, the author's name, and the date for a course-required proposal. The title page for a thesis or dissertation proposal may include the title, the author's name, the degree requirement being fulfilled, the name and location of the college or university awarding the degree, the date of submission, and space for the signatures of the committee. The title should be brief (fifteen words or less) yet should describe the purpose of the proposal study. The table of contents is basically the outline of the proposal with the page number of each major section, the references or bibliography, and any appendices.

All proposals are typed, and the same standards of scholarship are applied to the typing of the proposal as to the writing of the proposal. The final typing should be proofread carefully by the author. Word processing software has greatly facilitated scholarly writing. Common features include automatic page numbering and head centering; the ability to edit "on-screen" words, sentences, and paragraphs; spelling checkers; outlining features; and automatically placed footnotes or endnotes. Proofreading is essential because spell checkers do *not* proof for grammar or for word meaning in a sentence.

Criticism of a Proposal

After completing a draft of a proposal, authors read it critically in terms of research criteria appropriate for the purpose and design of the study. Many of these criteria were suggested in prior chapters. In addition to self-criticism, researchers give a draft to colleagues for feedback. Below are some common weaknesses of proposals.

1. *The problem is trivial.* Problems that are of only peripheral interest to educators or show little likelihood of adding to knowledge in education are seldom approved enthusiastically. The problem should be related to one of the mainstreams of educational knowledge, scholarly thinking, research, and educational practices.
2. *The problem is not delimited.* A problem must be focused for both research and practical reasons. Designs cannot yield valid data for every possible variable, nor can qualitative researchers encompass extremely broad questions in a single study. Experienced researchers know how time-consuming research processes are, from the initial

conceptualization of an idea through the final report. Researchers rationally, but reluctantly, delimit the problem. The specific research questions and/or hypothesis or the qualitative foreshadowed problems are stated in such a way that the delineation of the focus is apparent.

3. *The objectives of the proposal are too general.* Sometimes hypotheses are stated in such broad, general terms that only the research design really conveys what the study is about. If the research design does not logically match the specific research questions and/or hypothesis or the qualitative research questions, then the planned study is not capable of meeting proposal objectives. Failure to consider extraneous or confounding variables is a serious error in a quantitative proposal. Qualitative proposals are also focused. Although generally the phrasing of research questions is in broader terms, the particular viewpoint or purpose narrows the focus.

4. *The methodology is lacking in detail appropriate for the proposed study.* Quantitative proposals should be detailed sufficiently in subjects, instrumentation, and data analysis to allow for replication. Qualitative proposals, by their inductive nature, are less specific in certain aspects. A qualitative proposal, however, can be sufficiently specific to connote *possible* purposeful sampling, planned data collection strategies, and inductive data analysis techniques. This specification ensures a review committee that the researcher is aware of subsequent decisions to be made. Much of the specificity for either quantitative or qualitative proposals depends on the extent of the researcher's preliminary work.

5. *The design limitations are addressed insufficiently.* No design is "perfect;" every design represents a series of choices to balance design requirements and standards with feasibility concerns of fiscal, logistical, and time constraints. Experienced researchers are aware of their decisions and cite the major design limitations with their rationale and procedures to minimize their effect on the study.

APPENDIX B

Glossary

A–B design: A single-subject design that compares frequency of behavior during the baseline (A) with treatment (B) conditions.

A–B–A design: A single-subject design that compares the baseline (A) with treatment (B) and then baseline (A).

achievement tests: Tests that measure knowledge, skills, or behavior.

action research: Teachers using research methods to study classroom problems.

agreement: A type of reliability based on the consistency of ratings or observations among two or more persons.

alpha level: Predetermined level of probability to reject null hypothesis.

alternative assessment: Procedures to measure performance through constructed- response answers unlike traditional paper-and-pencil tests.

analogy: A metaphor, made explicit by the word "like" or "as;" compares two unlike phenomenon.

analysis of covariance (ANCOVA): An inferential statistical test used to adjust statistically the effect of a variable related to the dependent variable.

analysis of variance (ANOVA): An inferential statistical procedure for determining the level of probability of rejecting the null hypothesis with two or more means.

analytical interpretation: In historical research, a causal explanation for a specific event.

analytical research: An analysis of documents to investigate historical concepts and events.

applied research: Research that is conducted in a field of common practice and is concerned with the application and development of research-based knowledge.

aptitude test: A test used to predict behavior.

artifacts/artifact collections: Material objects of a current or past event, group, person, or organization which reveal social processes, meanings, and values.

assessment: Measuring a variable and using the results—for example, testing students and reporting scores.

assigned variables: *See* attribute variables.

attenuation: The lowering of a measure of relationship between two variables because of the unreliability of the instruments.

attribute variables: *Also* assigned variables. Independent variables that cannot be manipulated.

audibility: A record of data management techniques and decision rules that documents the "chain of evidence" or "decision trail."

audiences (in evaluation research): Persons who will be guided by the evaluation in making decisions; anyone directly or indirectly connected to the program.

authenticity: The faithful reconstruction of participants' multiple perceptions.

bar graph: Graphical presentation of frequency of nominal variables.

baseline: The first phase of single-subject research, in which behavior is recorded before any changes are introduced.

basic research: Research that tests or refines theory; not designed to be applied immediately to practice.

behavioral objectives: *Also* performance objectives, measured objectives. Objectives of a practice stated in terms of observable terminal performances that can be measured.

beta weight: Standardized regression coefficient.

biography: As a type of research, can include individual biographies, autobiographies, life histories, and oral history of a life.

bivariate: correlation among two variables.

box-and-whisker plot: graphic illustration of variability of a set of scores.

career and life history interviews: Interviews that elicit life narratives of individuals or career histories of professional lives.

case: A particular situation selected by the researcher in which some phenomena will be described by participants' meanings of events and processes.

case study: Qualitative research which examines a "bounded system" or a case over time in detail, employing multiple sources of data found in the setting.

case study design: The one phenomenon the researcher selects to understand in depth regardless of the number of settings, social scenes, or participants in a study.

categorical variable: A variable used to divide subjects, objects, or entities into two or more groups.

category: An abstract term that represents the meaning of related topics.

checklist: A type of questionnaire item in which subjects check appropriate responses that are provided.

chi-square: *Also* goodness of fit. A nonparametric statistical procedure used with nominal data to test relationships between frequency of observations in categories of independent variables.

closed form: A type of questionnaire item in which the subject chooses between or among predetermined options.

cluster sampling: A form of probability sampling in which subjects are first grouped according to naturally occurring units.

code: An abbreviation for a topic or category.

coding: The process of dividing data according to a classification system.

coefficient of determination: Squared correlation coefficient that indicates the percentage of variance accounted for in a relationship.

coefficient of multiple correlation: An indicator of the combined relationship of several variables to another variable.

comparison group: One of the groups whose performance in behavior is compared in an experiment.

comparative: See comparative research.

comparative research: Type of nonexperimental quantitative research that examines differences between groups.

complete observer: An observer who remains completely detached from the group or process of interest.

comprehensive sampling: The type of sampling in qualitative research in which every participant, group, setting, event, or other information is examined.

concept analysis: A study that clarifies the meaning of a concept by describing the generic meaning, the different meanings, and the appropriate usage for the concept (philosophical research).

confidence interval: Range that describes probable population values.

constant comparison: A qualitative technique to identify the distinctive characteristics between topics, categories, or patterns by noting similarities and differences.

construct: A complex abstraction that is not directly observable, such as anxiety, intelligence, self-concept; a meaningful combination of concepts.

construct irrelevant variance: The extent to which an assessment measures facets not related to the purpose of the assessment.

construct underrepresentation: Assessment that fails to incorporate important facets of what is being measured.

construct validity: A type of external validity that refers to the extent to which the study represents the underlying construct.

contamination: In quantitative research, a type of observer bias that results from observer knowledge of the study.

content-related evidence: A type of evidence for validity in which the content of a test is judged to be representative of a larger domain of content.

context: Description of site and selected settings, social scenes, participants, and time period of data collection.

contingency coefficient: *Also* phi coefficient. A single index that shows the degree of relationship in a contingency table.

contingency questions: Questions that when answered in a certain way provide directions to subsequent questions.

contingency table: *Also* independent samples chi-square test. A chi-square test with two or more independent variables.

continuous observation: An observational data-gathering technique in which the observer records all important behaviors.

continuous variable: *Also* measured variable. A variable in which the property or attribute of an object, subject, or entity is measured numerically and can assume an infinite number of values within a range.

control: Efforts to remove or otherwise take account of factors or variables other than the independent variable that might affect the dependent variable.

control group: The subjects in an experiment who receive no treatment.

control group interrupted time-series design: A quasi-experimental time-series study that compares the treatment group to a control group.

controlled vocabulary: Systematic and consistent subject and term definitions to describe entries in a database.

convenience sampling: A nonprobability method of selecting subjects who are accessible or available.

correlation: A measure of relationship that uses a correlation coefficient.

correlation coefficient: A number that is calculated to indicate the size and direction of the degree of relationship between two variables.

correlational research: Research in which information on at least two variables is collected for each subject in order to investigate the relationship between the variables.

cost–benefit analysis: Evaluates decision alternatives by comparing the costs and benefits to society.

cost-effectiveness analysis: Compares the outcomes of similar practices in relation to their costs, when the different programs have the same objectives and measures.

cost–feasibility analysis: Estimates the cost of a practice to determine whether the practice is a realistic consideration within an existing budget.

cost–utility analysis: Compares alternative practices to determine the practice that is most likely to produce the most desired outcomes at least cost.

credibility: The extent to which the results approximate reality and are judged to be trustworthy and reasonable.

criterion variable: In a prediction study, the variable that is predicted.

criterion-referenced: Instruments whose scores are interpreted by referral to specific criteria or standards rather than to the performance of others.

criterion-related evidence: A type of evidence for test validity in which the test scores are correlated with scores from a meaningful criterion.

critical studies: Qualitative research in which the researcher is committed to expose social manipulation, change oppressive social structures, and may have emancipatory goals.

Cronbach Alpha: A type of internal consistency reliability for items with scaled responses.

cross-sectional: A research strategy in which several different groups of subjects are assessed at the same time.

crystallization: An analytical style whereby the researcher collapses segmenting, categorizing, and pattern-seeking into an extensive period of intuition-rich immersion within the data

data: Results obtained by research from which interpretations and conclusions are drawn.

database (in computer searches): Sources indexed by a particular reference service.

datasets: Large collections of available data from primary sources archived for research purposes.

data filing system: A procedure to identify and retrieve a particular set of field notes or interview transcript.

data management: Using a system to retrieve data sets and to assemble coded data in one place.

decision-oriented evaluation: An evaluation that supplies information for pre-specified decisions, such as needs assessment, program planning, program implementation, or outcomes.

deductive reasoning: A reasoning that assumes that if the premises are correct, the conclusion is automatically correct.

degrees of freedom: A mathematical concept that indicates the number of observations that are free to vary.

demand characteristics: A possible source of bias when any aspect of a study reveals the purpose of the research and subjects respond differently because of their knowledge of purpose.

dependent samples *t*-test: *Also* correlated samples *t*-test. An inferential statistical procedure for determining the probability level of rejecting the null hypothesis with two samples of subjects that are matched or related.

dependent variable: A measured variable that is the consequence of or depends on antecedent variables.

descriptive: Research that describes an existing or past phenomenon quantitatively.

descriptive research: Research that describes the current status of something.

descriptive statistics: Statistical procedures that describe something.

developmental studies: Research that investigates change of subjects over time.

diffusion of treatment: A threat to internal validity in which subjects are aware of other conditions of the independent variable.

disciplined inquiry: Research conducted in such a way that the argument can be painstakingly examined.

disciplined subjectivity: Rigorous self-monitoring by the researcher; that is, continuous self-questioning and reevaluation of all phases of the research process.

documents: Records of past events in the form of letters, diaries, anecdotal notes, and documents usually preserved in collections.

domain-referenced tests: *See* criterion-referenced tests.

double-barrelled questions: Single questions that contain two or more ideas to which the subject must make one response.

duration recording: A type of observer recording procedure in which the duration of behavior is recorded.

ecological external validity: Refers to the extent to which results of research can be generalized to other conditions or situations.

effect size: Statistical index of the practical or meaningful difference between groups.

electronic resources: Literature "published" on computer databases.

elite interviews: A special application of in-depth interviews of persons considered to be influential, prominent, and well informed in an organization or a community.

emergent design: A research plan in which each step depends on the results of the previous field data.

emic categories: Insider's views—such as terms, actions, and explanations—that are distinctive to the setting or people.

empirical: Guided by evidence, data, or sources.

equivalence: A type of test reliability in which scores from equivalent or parallel forms of the same instrument, given at about the same time, are correlated.

ERIC (Educational Resources Information Service): Comprehensive database and index of education literature.

ERIC digest: Short reports that synthesize education literature on a topic.

ethnography: A description and interpretation of a culture or social group or system.

etic categories: Outsider's views of the situation—such as the researcher's concepts and scientific explanations.

evaluation: A study which requires a formal design to collect and analyze data to determine the worth of practice or an anticipated practice; see evaluation research.

evaluation approach: A strategy to focus the evaluation activities and to produce a useful report.

evaluation research: Designed to assess the worth of a specific practice in terms of the values operating at the site(s).

evidence based on test content: A type of evidence for validity in which scores represent an underlying meaning, interpretation, trait, or theory.

evidence based on internal structure: Validity evidence showing appropriate intercorrelations among items.

evidence based on relations to other variables: Validity evidence showing appropriate correlations with other measures.

evidence based on response processes: Validity evidence showing consistency between intended and actual response processes.

exhaustive literature search: A literature search on a narrowly focused problem for ten or more years using the most relevant reference services.

experimental design: Research in which the independent variable is manipulated to investigate cause-and-effect relationships between the independent and dependent variable.

experimental group: The subjects who receive the condition that the experimenter hypothesizes will change behavior.

experimental research: *See* experimental design.

experimental variable: The variable in experimental or quasi-experimental design that is manipulated or changed by the researcher to see the effect on (relationship to) the dependent variable.

experimenter effects: *Also* experimenter contamination. A threat to internal validity in which the researcher's differential treatment of subjects affects results.

explanation: A theory or analytical generalization that states cause-and-effect relationships in simple statements.

ex post facto design: *See ex post facto* research.

ex post facto **research:** Research that investigates events that have already occurred and implies cause-and-effect relationships from the results.

extension of the findings: Qualitative studies which enable others to understand similar situations and apply the findings in subsequent research.

external criticism: Analytical procedures carried out to determine the authenticity of the source, that is, whether the source is the original document, a forged document, or a variant of the original document.

external validity: Refers to the extent to which results of a study can be generalized to other subjects, conditions, or situations.

factorial analysis of variance: An analysis of variance statistical procedure with two or more independent variables that permits testing each independent variable and the interaction of the variables.

facts: In analytical research, descriptions of who, what, when, and where an event occurred, obtained from decisive evidence.

field notes: Data obtained by participant observation in the setting while the researcher is in the field.

field observations: A fundamental technique to all qualitative research in the form of detailed descriptive field notes of events, people, actions, and objects in settings.

field research: Research that views the setting as a natural situation in which the researcher collects data over a prolonged time.

field residence (in ethnography): Being present in the field or site for an extensive time to collect data.

field test: A preliminary study of a program or materials, or a test in a setting like those where it is to be used.

historical analysis: A systematic collection and criticism of documents to describe and interpret past events.

foreshadowed problems: Anticipated research problems that will be reformulated during data collection.

formative evaluation: Evaluation used to improve an ongoing practice or program.

frequency-count recording: A type of observer recording procedure in which the frequency of behavior is recorded.

frequency distribution: A display of a set of scores by the number of times each score was obtained.

frequency polygon: A graphic representation of a frequency distribution formed by connecting in a line the highest frequency of each score.

generalizability: The extent to which the findings of one study can be used as knowledge about other populations and situations.

generalization: In analytical research, interpretation of facts that focus on the way or the reason an event occurred.

grounded theory: Qualitative procedures to develop detailed concepts or conditional propositions for substantive theory.

Hawthorne effect: The tendency of people to act differently because they realize they are subjects in a study.

high inference: Type of observation in which observer records judgements about what has occurred.

histogram: Graphic illustration of a frequency distribution, using bars to represent the frequency of each score.

historical analysis: Application of analytical methodology to the study of the past, as in biographies and studies of movements, institutions, and concepts.

history: A threat to internal validity in which incidents or events that occur during the research affect results.

historiography: A study of the procedures that different historians use in their research; also a study of the changing revisions and interpretations of the past.

holistic emphasis (in ethnography): Subcases of data are related to the total context of the phenomenon studied.

hyperlink: Automated connection to other Internet Web sites or parts of the same Web site.

independent samples chi-square test: *See* contingency table.

independent samples *t*-test: An inferential statistical procedure for determining the probability level of rejecting the null hypothesis with two samples of subjects that have no relation to each other.

independent variable: A variable antecedent to or preceding the dependent variable; also called, in experimental design, the experimental or manipulated variable.

in-depth interview: Use of a general interview guide with a few selected topics and probes (not a set of standardized questions); a conversation with a goal for at least an hour.

inductive analysis: Categories and patterns emerge from the data rather than being imposed on the data prior to data collection.

inductive reasoning: A reasoning by which observation of particular cases is generalized to the whole class.

inferential statistics: Procedures that indicate probabilities associated with saying something about populations based on data from samples.

informal conversational interview: Questions that emerge from the immediate context and are asked in the natural course of events; there is no predetermination of question topics or phrasing.

informed consent: Obtaining permission from individuals to participate in research before the research begins.

instrumentation: A threat to internal validity in which changes in the instruments and unreliability affect the results.

interaction: The unique effect of different levels of independent variables on the dependent variable.

interactive strategies: Ethnographic observation or ethnographic interview as a data collection strategy.

intercorrelation matrix: A table that presents intercorrelations among many variables.

Interim analysis: Regular, frequent qualitative data analysis to help make data collection decisions and to identify emerging topics.

internal consistency: A type of test reliability in which the homogeneity of the items of an instrument is assessed after one administration of the instrument.

internal criticism: Analytical procedures to determine the credibility of the statements in a source; the accuracy and trustworthiness of the facts.

internal validity: The degree to which extraneous variables are controlled.

Internet: interconnected computers that share information worldwide.

interpretative biography: A study in which the researcher's presence is acknowledged in the narrative and with his or her standpoint.

interval recording: A type of observer recording procedure in which behavior that occurs during a given time interval is recorded.

interval: A type of measurement scale in which numbers are rank-ordered with equal intervals between ranks.

interview elaborations: Reflections by interviewers on their role and rapport, interviewees' reactions, additional information, and extensions of interview meanings.

interview guide approach: Topics are selected in advance, but the researcher decides the sequence and wording of the questions during the interview.

interview probes: Brief questions or phrases that elicit elaboration of detail, further explanations, and clarifications of responses.

interview schedule: *See* standardized interviews.

ipsative: A type of measurement response format in which answers to one question or category determine what the answers can be in remaining questions or categories.

key-informant interview: In-depth interview of an individual who has special knowledge, status, or communication skills.

Kuder–Richardson: A type of internal-consistency reliability for items scored right or wrong.

leading question: In qualitative interviews, a question in which the wording encourages certain responses.

level of significance: *Also* level of probability, level of confidence. A value selected to indicate the chance that it is wrong to reject the null hypothesis.

Likert scale: A type of scale in which subjects express degrees of agreement or disagreement with a statement.

literature review: A compressed critique of the status of knowledge on a carefully defined educational topic; a section of a study or proposal the provides the rationale for the research problem.

longitudinal: A research strategy in which quantitative data are collected on subjects over a period of time.

low inference: Type of observation in which observer records occurance of specific behaviors.

mailing list: (listserv) Shared list to communicate through email on specific topics.

manipulated variable: The independent variable in experiments that is determined by the researcher.

mapping the field: In qualitative research, acquiring data of the social, spatial, and temporal relationships in the site to gain a sense of the total context.

maximum variation sampling (quota sampling): In qualitative inquiry, a strategy to sample anticipated different meanings of the research phenomenon or concept.

maturation: A threat to internal validity in which maturational changes in subjects such as growing older or more tired, or becoming hungry, affect the results in quantitative research.

mean: A measure of central tendency, the arithmetical average of the scores.

measured variable: *See* continuous variable.

measurement scales: Properties that describe the relationships between numbers.

measures of central tendency: Summary indices of a set of scores that represent the typical score in a distribution.

measures of variability: Numerical indices that indicate the degree of dispersion of scores from the mean.

median: A measure of central tendency, the point or score in a distribution that is the midpoint.

meta-analysis: A research procedure that uses statistical techniques to synthesize the results of prior independently conducted studies.

metaphor: An implied comparison between things essentially unlike one another.

metasearch engines: Search engines that search multiple Internet search engines at one time.

mixed methods: A study which combines qualitative and quantitative techniques and/or data analysis within different phases of the research process.

mode: A measure of central tendency; the most frequently occurring score.

mode of inquiry: A collection of eclectic research practices based on a general set of methodological preferences, philosophical and ideological beliefs, research questions, and feasibility issues; also called a research tradition.

multimethod: In qualitative research, the use of multiple strategies to corroborate the data obtained from any single strategy and/or ways to confirm data within a single strategy of data collection.

multiple-baseline designs: A type of single-subject design that uses several subjects, types of behavior, or situations simultaneously.

multiple comparisons: *See* post hoc comparison.

multiple regression prediction equation: A statistical procedure for using several variables to predict something.

multisite evaluation: Qualitative research designed to report the practices at each site and to make generalizations across sites.

multivariate: A family of statistics used when there is more than one independent variable and/or more than one dependent variable.

narrative descriptions: Detailed narrations of people, incidents, and processes.

naturalistic/participant evaluation: A holistic evaluation using multimethod to provide an understanding of the divergent values of a practice from the participants' perspectives.

negative relationship: A relationship in which increases of one variable correspond to decreases of another variable.

negatively skewed: A distribution of scores that has a disproportionately large number of high scores.

network sampling (snowball sampling): A qualitative strategy in which each successive participant or group is named by a preceding group or individual.

newsgroup: Electronic forum where information, messages and questions on shared interests are communicated.

nominal: A type of measurement scale in which objects or people are named, classified, or numbered.

noncognitive: Areas other than mental processes, such as affect and emotions.

nonequivalent group posttest-only design: A pre-experimental design in which one or more groups of subjects, not randomly assigned, receives a treatment and a posttest, and one group of subjects receives only a posttest.

nonequivalent groups pretest–posttest design: A quasi-experimental design in which groups that have not been randomly assigned to treatments are compared.

nonexperimental: Research that requires no direct manipulation of variables, such as descriptive and correlational research.

nonparametric: Types of statistical procedures used when the assumptions necessary to use parametric procedures are violated.

nonprobability sampling: A sampling procedure in which the probability of selecting elements from the population is not known.

nonproportional sampling: Stratified sampling in which the number of subjects selected from each stratum is not based on the percentage of the population represented by each stratum.

nonreactive: *See* unobtrusive measures.

norm-referenced: An interpretation of test results in which a score or group of scores is compared with the typical performance of a given (norm) group.

normal distribution: A symmetrical bell-shaped distribution of scores with the same mean, median, and mode.

null hypothesis: A formal statistical statement that usually is a statement of no relationship between two or more variables.

objectives-oriented evaluation: An evaluation that determines the degree to which the objectives of a practice are attained by a target group.

objectivity: Data collection and analysis procedures from which only one meaning or interpretation can be made.

observation schedule: *See* structured observations.

observational research: Field research in which observational data are collected through noninterfering procedures.

one-group posttest-only design: A pre-experimental design in which a single group of subjects receives a treatment and a posttest.

one-group pretest–posttest design: A preexperimental design in which a single group of subjects receives a pretest, a treatment, and then a posttest.

open form: A type of questionnaire item in which subjects write in a response to a question.

operational definition: A definition of a variable achieved by assigning meaning to a variable by specifying the activities or operations necessary to measure, categorize, or manipulate the variable.

oral history: A form of historical research which records spoken words and testimonies of individuals about the past.

oral testimonies: Records or interview transcripts of witnesses of or participants in a past event studied.

ordinal: A type of measurement scale in which objects or persons are rank-ordered from lowest to highest.

paper-and-pencil tests: Instruments that have a structured set of questions that measure cognitive knowledge and skills.

parametric: Types of statistical procedures that assume normality in the population distributions, homogeneity of variance, and interval or ratio scale data.

participant observation: An interactive data collection of researchers who experience the daily activities of participants over an extended time and record descriptive field notes.

path analysis: A statistical procedure that uses correlations among a set of variables that are logically ordered to reflect causal relationships.

pattern: A relationship among categories.

percentile rank: The point in a distribution at or below which a given percentage of scores is found.

performance-based assessment: A type of test in which student proficiency is assessed by observing performance in an original, authentic context.

phenomenological interviews: A specific type of in-depth interview to examine the meanings or essence of a lived experience.

phenomenological study: Research that describes the meanings and "essence" of a lived experience.

phi coefficient: *See* contingency coefficient.

planned comparison: predetermined statistical testing of selected pairs of means.

plausible rival hypotheses: Possible explanations, other than the effect of the independent variable, for cause-and-effect relationships.

policy analysis: Evaluates government policies to provide policymakers with practical recommendations.

population: A group of individuals or events from which a sample is drawn.

population external validity: Refers to the extent to which the results of research can be generalized to other people.

portfolio: Alternative assessment in which materials demonstrating student performance are purposefully collected, organized, and evaluated.

positionality: Qualitative researchers may display their own positions or standpoints by describing their own social, cultural, historical, racial, and sexual location in the study.

positive relationship: A relationship in which increases of scores of one variable correspond to increases of scores of another variable.

positively skewed: A distribution of scores that has a disproportionately large number of low scores.

post hoc comparison: *Also* multiple comparison. Statistical tests that are used with pairs of means, usually conducted after a statistical test of all means together.

posttest-only control-group design: A true experimental design in which one or more randomly assigned groups of subjects receives a treatment and a posttest, and one randomly assigned group of subjects receives only a posttest.

prediction studies: Research in which behaviors or skills are predicted by one or several variables.

predictor variable: The antecedent variable in a prediction study.

pre-experimental designs: A type of experimental design that generally has weak internal validity.

preliminary search: A search limited by use of one or two reference services, number of years to be reviewed, or number of sources desired; usually to select a research problem.

pretest: An assessment of performance given before a treatment is administered.

pretesting: A threat to internal validity in which taking a pretest can affect the results.

pretest–posttest control-group design: A true experimental design in which one or more randomly assigned groups of subjects receives a pretest, a treatment, and a posttest, and one randomly assigned group of subjects receives only the pretest and posttest.

primary literature: Original research studies or writings by researchers and theorists.

primary source: In analytical research, a document or testimony of an eyewitness to an event.

probability: A scientific way of stating the degree of confidence in predicting something.

probability sampling: Subjects drawn from a population in known probabilities.

probing: *See* interview probes.

proportional sampling: A type of stratified sampling in which the numbers of subjects selected from each stratum is based on the percentage of subjects in the population of each stratum.

purposeful sampling: A strategy to choose small groups or individuals likely to be knowledgeable and informative about the phenomenon of interest; selection of cases without needing or desiring to generalize to all such cases.

qualitative descriptions: Detailed narrations of people, incidents, and processes.

qualitative field records: Data recorded as participant observation field notes, in-depth interview records, or researcher notes of historical documents.

qualitative inquiry: An in-depth study using face-to-face techniques to collect data from people in their natural settings.

qualitative research: Research that presents facts in a narration with words; also see qualitative inquiry.

qualitative techniques: Data collection strategies that acquire data in the form of words rather than numbers.

quantitative research: Research that presents results with numbers.

quantitative techniques: Data collection techniques that use numbers to describe or measure the results.

quasi-experimental: Research that has no random assignment of subjects, but investigates cause-and-effect relationships by manipulating the independent variable.

questionnaire: A written set of questions or statements that assesses attitudes, opinions, beliefs, and biographical information.

questionnaire research: Research in which information is collected by subjects' responses to written questions.

quota sampling: A nonprobability method of sampling in which subjects are selected in proportion to characteristics reflected in the population.

random assignment: A procedure used to assign subjects to different groups so that every subject being assigned has an equal chance of being in every group.

random sampling: Selecting subjects from a population in such a way that every member of the population has an equal chance of being selected.

range: A measure of variability; the difference between the highest and lowest scores in a distribution.

ratio: A type of measurement scale in which numbers are expressed meaningfully as ratios.

real time: (synchronous communication) Immediate communication via technology.

reflexivity: Rigorous researcher self-scrutiny throughout the entire qualitative research process.

reflex records: Records made immediately after leaving the field; contains summary of observations, addresses quality of data, suggests next steps, and self-monitoring notes.

regression coefficient: A factor used in multiple regression to weight the contribution of each variable in the equation.

related literature: Literature that is relevant to the problem or is related in some essential way to the design.

reliability: The extent to which measures from a test are consistent.

relics: In historical research, any object that provides information about the past.

replication: A study that duplicates a prior study but uses different settings or techniques.

report literature: Documents other than journals that are in the ERIC Document Microfiche Collection and indexed by *Resources in Education;* that is, presentations, final reports of projects, or evaluation studies.

research: A systematic process of collecting and logically analyzing data for some purpose.

research design: The plan that describes the conditions and procedures for collecting and analyzing data.

research hypothesis: A tentative statement of the expected relationship between two or more variables.

research methods: Procedures used to collect and analyze data.

research problem: A formal statement of question or hypothesis that implies empirical investigation.

research role: The relationships acquired by and ascribed to the researcher in interactive data collection, appropriate for the purpose of the study.

research synthesis: A procedure that systematically evaluates and narratively or statistically summarizes comparable studies.

responsive evaluation: An evaluation designed to supply information about the issues and concerns of the audiences; uses an emerging design to provide an understanding of the program.

restriction in range: A set of scores that represents only a part of the total distribution.

retrieval alogrithms: Determines the number of pages and organization of an Internet search.

reversal designs: *Also* withdrawal designs. In single-subject research, refers to ending a treatment condition and reinstituting the baseline condition.

sample: The group of subjects from which data are collected; often represents a population.

sampling distribution: Frequency distribution of possible samples from a population.

scale: Questionnaire items that consist of gradations, levels, or values describing various degrees of something.

scatterplot: A graphic representation of relationship made by forming a visual array of the intersections of subjects' scores on two variables.

science: The generation and verification of theory through research.

scientific inquiry: The search for knowledge by using recognized procedures in data collection, analysis, and interpretation.

scientific method: A sequential research process of defining a problem, stating a hypothesis, collecting and analyzing data, and interpreting results.

search engine: A service that catalogs and retrieves Internet information.

secondary literature: A synthesis of previous literature: theoretical or empirical or both.

secondary sources: In historical research, documents or testimonies of individuals who did not actually observe or participate in the event.

segment: A part of a data set that is comprehensible by itself and contains one idea, episode, or piece of information relevant to the study.

selection: A threat to internal validity in which differences between groups of subjects affect results.

semantic differential: A type of scale in which subjects make a response between adjective pairs in relation to a concept or object.

semistructured questions: A type of interview question that allows individual, open- ended responses to questions that are fairly specific.

significance level: *Also* alpha level. *See* level of significance.

significance of the problem: The rationale for a problem or importance of a study as it relates to developing educational theory, knowledge, and/or practice.

simple random sampling: *See* random sampling.

single-group interrupted time-series design: A quasi-experimental design in which multiple observations of the dependent variable are made before and after the treatment.

single-subject: Research done with individual subjects in order to study the changes in behavior associated with the intervention or removal of a treatment.

site selection: The specification of site criteria implied in the foreshadowed problems and for obtaining a suitable and feasible research site.

skewed: *See* positively skewed *or* negatively skewed.

social desirability: The tendency of subjects to respond to items in a manner that will appear desirable to others.

sources of variability: systematic, error, and extraneous influences related to research design.

split-half: A type of internal-consistency reliability in which equal halves of a test are correlated.

spurious correlation: A correlation that over represents or under represents the true relationship.

stability: A type of test reliability in which scores from the same instrument taken on two occasions are correlated.

standard: A level of performance commonly agreed on by experts.

standard deviation: A measure of variability; a numerical index that indicates average dispersion or spread of scores around the mean.

standard error: Standard deviation of sampling distribution.

standard scores: Converted numbers from raw distributions with constant means and standard deviations.

standardized open-ended interview: A form of qualitative interview in which participants are asked the same questions in the same order to obtain data of participant meanings; see in-depth interview.

standardized tests: Tests that are administered and scored according to highly structured, prescribed directions.

statistical conclusion: A threat to the internal validity of a study because of inappropriate uses of statistical procedures.

statistical hypothesis: Hypotheses stated in terms of statistical results.

statistical regression: The tendency for extreme scores to become closer to the mean score on a second testing.

statistically significant: A term used in evaluating results of inferential statistics that indicates that the differences noted are very probably not due to chance.

statistics: Procedures for organizing and analyzing quantitative data.

strategies: Qualitative sampling and data collection techniques that are continually refined throughout the data collection process to increase data validity.

stratified random sampling: A form of random sampling in which a population is first divided into subgroups or strata and subjects are selected from each subgroup.

structured interviews: Systematic interviews that employ the same questions and response categories.

structured observations: Systematic observations of behavior according to specific categories.

structured questions: *Also* limited-response questions. A type of interview question that is followed by a predetermined set of responses.

subject attrition: A threat to internal validity in which loss of subjects affects the results.

subject directory: Lists of cataloged Internet resources.

subject effects: Changes in subject behavior in response to being in a study.

subjects: The person or persons from whom data are collected in a study.

summative evaluation: Evaluation designed to determine the merit, the worth, or both of a developed practice and to make recommendations regarding its adoption and widespread use.

supplementary techniques: Selected qualitative techniques to help interpret, elaborate or corroborate data obtained from participant observation, in-depth interviews, documents, and artifacts.

survey research: The assessment of the current status of opinions, beliefs, and attitudes by questionnaires or interviews from a known population.

synthesized abstractions: Summary generalizations and explanations of the major research findings of a study; format varies with the selected qualitative tradition.

systematic sampling: A form of sampling in which subjects are selected from a continuous list by choosing every *n*th subject.

***T*-scores:** A type of standard score with a mean of fifty and a standard deviation of ten.

***t*-test:** An inferential statistical procedure for determining the probability level of rejecting the null hypothesis that two means are the same.

target group: The group whose behavior is expected to change as a result of a practice.

test reliability: An indication of the consistency of measurement.

test research: Research in which test scores of subjects are used as data.

test validity: The extent to which inferences made on the basis of test scores are appropriate.

theory: The prediction and explanation of natural phenomena.

thesaurus: A publication that lists and cross-references key terms or descriptors used in an index for a reference service (database) such as ERIC or *Psychological Abstracts*.

time sampling: A type of observer recording procedure in which specific time periods are used in order to observe behavior.

time-series designs: Research designs in which one group of subjects is measured repeatedly before and after a treatment.

topic: Descriptive name for the subject matter of a segment.

treatment group: *See* experimental group.

treatment replications: A threat to internal validity in which the number of replications of the treatment does not equal the number of subjects.

triangulation: Qualitative cross-validation among multiple data sources, data collection strategies, time periods, and theoretical schemes.

true experimental: Research in which subjects are randomly assigned to groups, at least one independent variable is manipulated, and extraneous variables are controlled to investigate the cause of one or more independent variables on the dependent variable or variables.

Type I error: Rejecting a null hypothesis when it is in fact true.

Type II error: Failing to reject a null hypothesis when it is in fact false.

typicality: The degree to which a phenomenon may be compared with or contrasted to other phenomena along relevant dimensions.

unobtrusive measures: *Also* nonreactive. Use of methods to collect information so that the subject is unaware of being a participant in the research.

unstructured questions: A type of interview question that is broad and allows open- ended responses.

validity: The degree to which scientific explanations of phenomena match the realities of the world.

validity of qualitative designs: The degree to which the interpretations and concepts have mutual meanings between the participants and researcher.

variability: *See* measures of variability.

variable: An event, category, behavior, or an attribute that expresses a construct and has different values, depending on how it is used in a study.

variance: Generically, the degree of spread or dispersion of scores; mathematically, the square of the standard deviation.

verification: Research results that can be or are confirmed or modified in subsequent research.

visual representation: An organized assembly of information such as figures, matrices, integrative diagrams and flow charts which assist in qualitative data analysis.

withdrawal design: *See* reversal design.

worth: The value of a practice in relationship to the values, standards, and practical constraints of a potential adopting site.

z-score: A type of standard score with a mean of zero and a standard deviation of one.

APPENDIX C

Calculations for Selected Descriptive and Inferential Statistics

In this appendix we will present a step-by-step guide for performing calculations for several simple statistical procedures.[1] Our intent is not to derive formulas, but to show how the statistics are calculated. We believe that being able to apply these formulas assists greatly in understanding the meaning of the statistics.

Measures of Central Tendency

Measures of central tendency are descriptive statistics that measure the central location or value of sets of scores. They are used widely to summarize and simplify large quantities of data.

The Mean

The mean is the arithmetical average of a set of scores. It is obtained by adding all the scores in a distribution and dividing the sum by the number of scores. The formula for calculating the mean is

$$\overline{X} = \frac{\Sigma X}{n}$$

---

[1]Statistical tables are located at the end of the appendix.

where

$\overline{X}$ is the mean score
ΣX is the sum of the X_s (i.e., $X_1 + X_2 + X_3 \ldots X_n$)
   n is the total number of scores

Example: Calculation of Mean If we have obtained the sample of eight scores—17, 14, 14, 13, 10, 8, 7, 7—the mean of this set of scores is calculated as

$$\Sigma X = 17 + 14 + 14 + \ldots + 7 = 90$$
$$n = 8$$

Therefore,

$$\overline{X} = \frac{90}{8} = 11.25$$

The Median

The median is the score in a distribution below which half the scores fall. In other words, half the scores are above the median and half are below the median. The median is at the 50th percentile.

To calculate the median, the scores are rank-ordered from highest to lowest; then one simply counts, from one end, one half the scores. In distributions with an odd number of scores the median is the middle score, as illustrated below:

50% of scores above $\left\{ \begin{array}{l} 25 \\ 23 \\ 23 \\ 22 \\ 19 \end{array} \right.$

Median $\longrightarrow$ 18

50% of scores $\left\{ \begin{array}{l} 16 \\ 16 \\ 15 \\ 10 \\ 9 \end{array} \right.$

If the distribution has an even number of scores, the median is the average of the two middle scores. In this case the median is a new score or point in the distribution, as shown below:

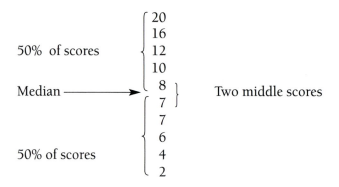

Thus, the median in this example is

$$7 + \frac{8}{2} = \frac{15}{2} = 7.5$$

The median is relatively easy to find in studies with a small number of subjects. As the number of scores increases, the calculation is done either by a formula or by placing the scores into intervals of scores and using the interval to make the calculations. The computer is able to apply these more complicated calculations easily, quickly, and reliably.

The Mode

The mode is simply the most frequently occurring score in a distribution, and it is found by counting the number of times each score was received. The mode in the distribution below, for example, is 22.

23
22
22
22
20
18
18
17
16

Measures of Variability

Measures of variability are used to show the differences among the scores in a distribution. We use the term *variability* or *dispersion* because the statistics provide an indication of how different, or dispersed, the scores are from one another. We will discuss three measures of variability: range, variance, and standard deviation.

The Range

The range is the simplest; but also least useful, measure of variability. The range is defined as the distance between the smallest and the largest scores, and is calculated by simply subtracting the bottom, or lowest, score from the top, or highest, score:

$$\text{Range} = X_H - X_L$$

where

X_H = the highest score
X_L = the lowest score

For the following scores, then, the range is $26 - 6 = 20$.

$$6 \quad 8 \quad 10 \quad 11 \quad 15 \quad 20 \quad 26$$

The range is a crude measure of variability and is unstable. Because the range can be biased, it is rarely used as the only measure of variability.

Variance

The variance (s^2 or σ^2) is a measure of dispersion that indicates the degree to which scores cluster around the mean. The variance provides the researcher with one number to indicate, in a sense, the average dispersion of scores from the mean. Computationally, the variance is the sum of the squared deviation scores about the mean divided by the total number of scores.

$$s^2 = \frac{\Sigma(X - \bar{X})^2}{N}$$

where

s^2 is the variance
$\Sigma(X - \bar{X})^2$ is the sum of the squared deviation scores
$(X - \bar{X})$ is the deviation score
N is the total number of scores

For any distribution of scores the variance can be determined by following five steps:

1. Calculate the mean: ($\Sigma X/N$).
2. Calculate the deviation scores: ($X - \bar{X}$).
3. Square each deviation score: $(X - \bar{X})^2$.
4. Sum all the deviation scores: $\Sigma(X - \bar{X})^2$
5. Divide the sum by N: $\Sigma(X - \bar{X})^2/N$.

These steps are illustrated with actual numbers as follows:

(1) Raw Scores	(2) $(X - \overline{X})$	(3) $(X - \overline{X})^2$	(4)	(5)
20	7	49		
15	2	4		
15	2	4		
14	1	1		
14	1	1	$\Sigma(X - \overline{X})^2 = 120$	$\frac{\Sigma(X - \overline{X})^2}{N} = 12$
14	1	1		
12	-1	1		
10	-3	9		
8	-5	25		
8	-5	25		

$\Sigma X = 130$
$N = 10$
$\overline{X} = 13$

Substituting directly in the formula

$$s^2 = \frac{120}{10} = 12$$

Another formula that can be used to calculate the variance, which is computationally more simple, is

$$s^2 = \frac{\Sigma \overline{X}^2 - N\overline{X}^2}{N}$$

Because the variance is expressed as the square of the raw scores, not the original units, it is not usually reported in research. To return to units that are consistent with the raw score distribution, we need to take the square root of the variance. Taking the square root of the variance yields the standard deviation.

Standard Deviation

The standard deviation (s, σ, or SD) is the square root of the variance. It is a measure of dispersion that uses deviation scores expressed in standard units about the mean; hence the name standard deviation. The standard deviation is equal to the square root of the sum of the squared deviation scores about the mean divided by the total number of scores. The formula is

$$s = \sqrt{\frac{\Sigma(X - \overline{X})^2}{N}}$$

where

s is the standard deviation
$\sqrt{}$ is the square root
$\Sigma(X - \bar{X})^2$ is the sum of the squared deviation scores
$(X - \bar{X})$ is the deviation score
N is the total number of scores

To calculate the standard deviation, simply add one step to the formula for variance: take the square root. In our example for variance, for instance, the standard deviation would be

$$s = \sqrt{\frac{\Sigma(X - \bar{X})^2}{N}} = \sqrt{\frac{120}{10}} = \sqrt{12} = 3.46$$

The standard deviation is commonly reported in research and, with the mean, is the most important statistic in research. It tells the number of scores (that is, the percentage of scores) that are within given units of the standard deviation around the mean. This property of standard deviation is explained in the section called "Normal Distribution," which follows.

Standard Scores

Standard scores are numbers that are transformed from raw scores to provide consistent information about the location of a score within a total distribution. They are numbers that are related to the normal distribution.

Normal Distribution

The normal distribution is a set of scores that, when plotted in a frequency distribution, result in a symmetrical, bell-shaped curve with precise mathematical properties. The mathematical properties provide the basis for making standardized interpretations. These properties include possessing one mode, a mean, and median that are the same; having a mean that divides the curve into two identical halves; and having measures of standard deviation that fall at predictable places on the normal curve, with the same percentage of scores between the mean and points equidistant from the mean. This third characteristic is very important. We know, for example, that at $+1s$, we will always be at about the 84th percentile in the distribution (percentile score is the percentage of scores at or below the designated score). This is because the median is at the 50th percentile, and $+1s$ contains an additional 34 percent of the scores ($50 + 34 = 84$). Similarly, the percentage of scores between $+1s$ and $+2s$ is about 14 percent, which means that $+2s$ is at the 98th percentile. These characteristics are illustrated in Figure C.1, the graph of the standard normal distribution.

FIGURE C.1   Graph of the Standard Normal Distribution or Normal Curve

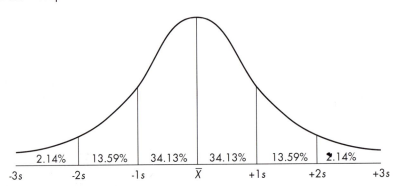

2.14%	13.59%	34.13%	34.13%	13.59%	2.14%

| -3s | -2s | -1s | $\overline{X}$ | +1s | +2s | +3s |

The pleasing aspect of this property is that, for any raw score distribution with unique units, such as 1 or 2 as s, the interpretation is always the same. If one distribution has a mean of 10, therefore, and a standard deviation of 3, and a second distribution a mean of 50 and a standard deviation of 7, a score of 4 in the first case is at about the same percentile (the second) as a score of 36 on the second distribution.

z-Scores

The most basic standard score is called a z-score, and it is expressed as a deviation from the mean in standard deviation units. A z-score of 1 is thus at one standard deviation, -1 is at minus one standard deviation, $+2$ at two standard deviations, and so forth.

After the mean and standard deviation are calculated for a set of scores, it is easy to convert each raw score to a z-score, which then indicates exactly where each score lies in the normal distribution.

The formula for calculating a z-score is

$$z = \frac{X - \overline{X}}{s}$$

where

z is the z-score value
X is any particular score
$\overline{X}$ is the arithmetic mean of a distribution of scores
s is the standard deviation of that same distribution

Taking the scores used to illustrate variance and standard deviation, the z-scores would be found as follows:

For the raw score of 20: $z = \dfrac{20 - 13}{3.46} = 2.02$

For the raw score of 14: $z = \dfrac{14 - 13}{3.46} = 0.29$

For the raw score of 10: $z = \dfrac{1 - 13}{3.46} = -0.87$

Once the z-score has been calculated, it is easy to refer to conversion tables to find the percentile rank corresponding to each z-score.

T-Scores

One limitation of using z-scores is the necessity for being careful with the negative sign and with the decimal point. To avoid these problems, other standard scores are used by converting the z-scores algebraically to different units. The general formula for converting z-scores is

$$A = \overline{X}_A + s_A(z)$$

where

A is the new standard score equivalent to z
$\overline{X}_A$ is the mean for the new standard-score scale
s_A is the standard deviation for the new standard-score scale
z is the z-score for any observation

For T-scores, $\overline{X}_A = 50$ and $s_A = 10$. The equation for converting z-scores to T-scores is thus

$$T = 50 + 10(z)$$

For example, the T-scores for our earlier illustration would be as follows:

For the raw score of 20: $T = 50 + 10(2.02) = 70.2$
For the raw score of 14: $T = 50 + 10(0.29) = 52.9$
For the raw score of 10: $T = 50 + 10(-0.87) = 41.3$

Other Standard Scores

Other common standard scores include the following:

1. Normal Curve Equivalent (NCE) has a mean of 50 and s of 21.06. Thus NCE $= 50 + 21.06$ (z-score).
2. IQ score has a mean of 100 and s of 15 or 16. Thus IQ $= 100 + 15$ (z-score).
3. College Entrance Examination Boards (CEEB, such as SAT) uses a mean of 500 and an s of 100. Thus, CEEB $= 500 + 100$ (z-score).
4. ACT (American College Testing Program) uses a mean of 20 and an s of 5. Thus, ACT $= 20 + 5$ (z-score).

5. Stanine. The stanine is also commonly reported. Stanines are standardized on a mean of 5 and s of 2, but unlike other standard scores, the numbers refer to intervals rather than to specific points on the normal distribution. Stanine 5 is located in the center of the distribution and includes the middle 20 percent of scores; stanines 4 and 6 include 17 percent of the scores; 3 and 7, 12 percent; 2 and 8, 7 percent; and 1 and 9, 4 percent. Stanines are illustrated in Figure 6.11, the normal curve.

Measures of Relationship

Measures of relationship are used to indicate the degree to which two sets of scores are related, or covary. We intuitively seek relationships by such statements as: "If high scores on variable X tend to be associated with high scores on variable Y, then the variables are related," or "If high scores on variable X tend to be associated with low scores on variable Y, then the variables are related." As we have indicated in Chapter 6, the relationship can be either positive or negative and either strong or weak.

We use correlation coefficients as a statistical summary of the nature of the relationship between two variables. They provide us with an estimate of the quantitative degree of relationship. The numbers are almost always between -1.00 and $+1.00$. We will show how to calculate two common correlation coefficients, the Pearson product-moment and the Spearman rho correlations.

Pearson Product-Moment (Pearson *r*)

The Pearson product-moment correlation coefficient is the most widely used measure of relationship. The Pearson r is calculated to show the linear relationship between two variables. To compute the Pearson r, two measures on each subject are needed. Suppose, for example, we have a group of ten subjects, and for each subject we have measures of self-concept and achievement. We can then calculate the Pearson r between self-concept and achievement for these ten subjects, using the following formula:

$$\text{Pearson } r = \frac{N\Sigma XY - (\Sigma X)(\Sigma Y)}{\sqrt{N\Sigma X^2 - (\Sigma X)^2} \cdot \sqrt{N\Sigma Y^2 - (\Sigma Y)^2}}$$

where

ΣXY is the sum of the XY cross products
ΣX is the sum of the X scores
ΣY is the sum of the Y scores
ΣX^2 is the sum of the squared X scores
ΣY^2 is the sum of the squared Y scores
N is the number of pairs of scores

This formula may appear complex but is actually quite easy to calculate. The scores can be listed in a table, as shown below; to use it, one simply finds the values for each summation in the formula, substitutes where appropriate, and performs the math indicated.

Subject	Self-concept Score X	X^2	Achievement Score Y	Y^2	$X \cdot Y$
1	25	625	85	7225	2125
2	20	400	90	8100	1800
3	21	441	80	6400	1680
4	18	324	70	4900	1260
5	15	225	75	5625	1125
6	17	289	80	6400	1360
7	14	196	75	5625	1050
8	15	225	70	4900	1050
9	12	144	75	5625	900
10	13	169	60	3600	780
	$\Sigma X = 170$	$\Sigma X^2 = 3038$	$\Sigma Y = 760$	$\Sigma Y^2 = 58400$	$\Sigma X \cdot Y = 13130$
	$(\Sigma X)^2 = 28900$		$(\Sigma Y)^2 = 577600$		

Step 1: Pair each set of scores; one set becomes X, the other Y.
Step 2: Calculate ΣX and ΣY.
Step 3: Calculate X^2 and Y^2.
Step 4: Calculate ΣX^2 and ΣY^2.
Step 5: Calculate $(\Sigma X)^2$ and $(\Sigma Y)^2$.
Step 6: Calculate $X \times Y$.
Step 7: Calculate $\Sigma X \times Y$.
Step 8: Substitute calculated values into formula.

$$\text{Pearson } r = \frac{10(13130) - (170)(760)}{\sqrt{10(3038) - 28900} \cdot \sqrt{10(58400) - 577600}}$$

$$= \frac{13130 - 129200}{\sqrt{3038 - 28900} \cdot \sqrt{58400 - 577600}}$$

$$= \frac{2100}{\sqrt{1480} \cdot \sqrt{6400}}$$

$$= \frac{2100}{(38.47) \cdot (80)}$$

$$= \frac{2100}{3078}$$

$$= 0.68$$

The value of 0.68 shows a moderate positive relationship between self-concept and achievement for this set of scores. The level of significance of correlation coefficients are indicated in Table C.2 at the end of this appendix.

Spearman Rank (*r* ranks or Spearman rho)

The Spearman rho is used when ranks are available on each of two variables for all subjects. Ranks are simply listings of scores from highest to lowest. The Spearman rho correlation shows the degree to which subjects maintain the same relative position on two measures. In other words, the Spearman rho indicates how much agreement there is between the ranks of each variable.

The calculation of the Spearman ranks is more simple than calculating the Pearson *r*. The necessary steps are

Step 1: Rank the Xs and Ys.
Step 2: Pair the ranked Xs and Ys.
Step 3: Calculate the difference in ranks for each pair.
Step 4: Square each difference.
Step 5: Sum the squared differences.
Step 6: Substitute calculated values into formula.

The formula is:

$$\text{Spearman rho} = 1 - \frac{6\Sigma D^2}{n(n^2 - 1)}$$

For the data used in calculating the Pearson *r*, the Spearman rho would be found as follows:

Subject	Self-concept Rank X	Achievement Rank Y	Difference D	D^2
1	1	2	−1	1
2	3	1	2	4
3	2	3.5	−1.5	2.25
4	4	5.5	−1.5	2.25
5	6.5	8	−1.5	2.25
6	5	3.5	1.5	2.25
7	8	8	0	0
8	6.5	5.5	1	1
9	10	8	2	4
10	9	10	−1	1
				$\Sigma D^2 = 20$

Note: When ties in the ranking occur, all scores that are tied receive the average of the ranks involved.

$$r \text{ ranks} = 1 - \frac{6(20)}{10(100 - 1)}$$

$$= 1 - \frac{120}{990}$$

$$= 1 - 0.12$$

$$= 0.88$$

In most data sets with more than fifty subjects, the Pearson r and Spearman rank will give almost identical correlations. In the example used here the Spearman is higher because of the low n and the manner in which the ties in rankings resulted in low difference scores.

Chi-Square

Chi-square (χ^2) is a statistical procedure that is used as an infererential statistic with nominal data, such as frequency counts, and ordinal data, such as percentages and proportions. In the simplest case, the data are organized into two categories, such as yes and no, high and low, for and against. If, for example, a researcher is interested in the opinions of college professors about tenure and asks the question "Should tenure be abolished?" then all responses could be categorized as either *yes* or *no*. The total frequency in each category (observed frequencies) is then compared to the expected frequency, which in most cases is chance. This means that with two categories, half the responses should be *yes* and half *no*. Assume the following results:

Should tenure be abolished?

	Yes	No
Observed	40	60
Expected	50	50

These values are then used in the following formula to calculate the chi-square statistic:

$$\chi^2 = \Sigma \frac{(f_o - f_e)^2}{f_e}$$

where

χ^2 is the chi-square statistic
Σ is the sum of
f_o is the observed frequency
f_e is the expected frequency

Inserting the values from the table, the result is

$$\chi^2 = \frac{(40 - 50)^2}{50} + \frac{(60 - 50)^2}{50}$$

$$= \frac{100}{50} + \frac{100}{50}$$

$$= 2 + 2$$

$$= 4.0$$

The obtained value, in this case 4, is then used with the degrees of freedom in the problem ($df = k - 1$, where k equals the number of categories; in our example $df = 2 - 1$, or 1) to find the value of the chi-square in the critical values of chi-square table (Table C.3 at the end of this appendix) to determine the level of significance of the results. By referring to the table and locating 4.00 within the table with 1 df, the result is significant at just less than a p value of 0.05. Consequently, it would be appropriate to say that there is a significant difference in the number of professors responding *yes* as compared to the number responding *no*.

Suppose the researcher wanted to go a step further with this problem and learn whether administrators and professors differ in their responses to the question about abolishing tenure. The researcher would then have what is called a contingency table, which is a cross-tabulation of the frequencies for the combinations of categories of the two variables. A hypothetical contingency table is shown below for administrators and professors.

Should tenure be abolished?

	Professors	Administrators	Raw Totals
Yes	$40(p = 0.40)$	$40(p = 0.80)$	$80(p_e = 0.53)$
No	$60(p = 0.60)$	$10(p = 0.20)$	$70(p_e = 0.47)$
	$n = 100$	$n = 50$	$n = 150$

Notice in the table that the proportion of responses in each response category (*yes* and *no*) is shown for both professors and administrators, and the total proportions are shown in the last column. These proportions are used in the following equation:

$$\chi^2 = \frac{\Sigma n(P - P_e)2}{P_e}$$

where

χ^2 is the chi-square statistic
Σ is the sum of all cells in the problem (in our example there are four cells)
n is the number of total observations in each column
P is the proportion of observed frequencies in each cell
P_e is the expected proportion for each row

For our example, therefore, the result would be

$$\chi^2 = 100\frac{(0.4 - 0.53)^2}{0.53} + 100\frac{(0.06 - 0.47)^2}{0.47}$$

$$= 50\frac{(0.80 - 0.53)^2}{0.53} + 100\frac{(0.20 - 0.47)}{0.47}$$

$$= 100\frac{0.20}{0.53} + 100\frac{0.20}{0.47} + 50\frac{0.07}{0.53} + 50\frac{0.07}{0.47}$$

$$= 3.77 + 4.26 + 6.60 + 7.45$$

$$= 22.08$$

In contingency tables the degrees of freedom are equal to $(r - 1)(c - 1)$, where r is the number of rows and c is the number of columns. In our example the $df = (2 - 1)(2 - 1) = 1$. By locating 22.08 with 1 degree of freedom in the critical values of chi-square table (Table C.3) we note that the result is highly significant, $p < 0.001$. This result indicates that there is a significant association or relationship between the two variables (professors and administrators, and yes and no).

t-Test

The *t*-test is used to indicate the probability that the means of two groups are different. We will present two common forms of the *t*-test, one used with independent samples, the other with dependent samples.

Independent Samples *t*-test

The independent samples *t*-test, or *t*-test for independent groups, is used to determine whether the mean values of a variable on one group of subjects is different from a mean value on the same variable with a different group of subjects. It is important to meet three statistical assumptions: that the frequency distributions of scores for both the populations of each group are normal, that the variances in each population are equal, and that the observation of scores in one group is independent from the other group. If the sample size is greater than 30, violating the assumption of normality is not serious; and as long as the sample sizes are equal, violation of the assumption of homogeneity of variance is not a problem. It is crucial, however, that the observations for each group are independent.

The formula for calculating the *t*-test statistic is

$$t = \frac{\bar{X}_1 - \bar{X}_2}{s_{\bar{X}_1 - \bar{X}_2}}$$

where

> t is the t test statistic
> $\overline{X}_1$ is the mean of one group
> $\overline{X}_2$ is the mean of the second group
> $s_{\overline{X}_1-\overline{X}_2}$ is the standard error of the difference in means

The standard error of the difference in means is estimated from the variances of each distribution. This part of the formula is calculated by pooling the variances of each distribution to result in s. This is done by the following formula:

$$s = \sqrt{\frac{\Sigma x_1^2 + \Sigma x_2^2}{df_1 + df_2}}$$

Then,

$$s_{\overline{X}_1-\overline{X}_2} = s\sqrt{\frac{1}{n_1} + \frac{1}{n_2}}$$

As an example, consider the data we present below:

Group x_1	Group x_2
$\overline{X}_1 = \overline{X}_1 18$	$\overline{X}_2 = 25$
$n_1 = 20$	$n_2 = 20$
$\Sigma X_1^2 = 348$	$\Sigma X_2^2 = 425$

From this point we can calculate the t test statistic in the following steps:

1. Calculate s:

$$s = \sqrt{\frac{348 + 425}{19 + 19}}$$

$$= \sqrt{20.34}$$

$$= 4.51$$

2. Calculate $s_{\overline{X}_1-\overline{X}_2}$:

$$s_{\overline{X}_1-\overline{X}_2} = 4.51\sqrt{\frac{1}{20} + \frac{1}{20}}$$

$$= 4.51\sqrt{\frac{1}{10}}$$

$$= 4.51(0.32)$$

$$= 1.44$$

Substitute into *t*-test formula:

$$t = \frac{18 - 25}{1.44}$$

$$= \frac{7}{1.44}$$

$$= 4.86$$

Once the *t*-test statistic is calculated, it is found in the critical values for *t*-table (Table 11.1) with corresponding degrees of freedom (which for the independent samples *t*-test is $n_1 + n_2 - 2$, or in our example $20 + 20 - 2 = 38$) to determine the significance level of the results. In this example the *t*-test statistic of 4.86, with 38 *df*, is significant at $p < 0.001$.

Here is another example of a computation with the *t*-test, beginning with raw data:

Group 1		Group 2	
x^1	x_1^2	x_2	x_2^2
		7	49
8	64	7	49
8	64	8	64
6	36	6	36
5	25	6	36
5	25	4	16
6	36	4	16
6	36	3	9
9	81	5	25
8	64	5	25
$\Sigma x_1 = 68$	$\Sigma x_1^2 = 480$	$\Sigma x_2 = 55$	$\Sigma x_2^2 = 325$
$n = 10$	$n = 10$	$\overline{X}_2 = 5.5$	
$\overline{X}_1 = 6.8$			

Step 1: $s = \sqrt{\dfrac{480 + 325}{9 + 9}} = \sqrt{44.72} = 6.69$

Step 2: $s_{\overline{X}_1 - \overline{X}_2} = 6.69\sqrt{\dfrac{1}{10} + \dfrac{1}{10}} = 6.69\sqrt{\dfrac{1}{5}} = (6.69)(0.45) = 2.99$

Step 3: $t = \dfrac{6.8 - 5.5}{2.99} = \dfrac{1.3}{2.99} = 0.43$

In this case the *t*-test statistic of 0.43, with 18 *df*, is not statistically significant. Even though the means for the groups are different, therefore, there is a good possibility that they could be different by chance alone.

Dependent Samples *t*-Test

When two groups that have been matched are being compared, as in a pretest–posttest design, the *t*-test formula must take into account the interrelationship between the groups: that is, the groups are not independent; rather, they are related. The formula for this type of *t* test is easier to calculate than for the independent samples *t*-test:

$$t = \frac{\overline{D}}{\sqrt{\dfrac{\Sigma D^2 - \dfrac{(\Sigma D)^2}{N}}{N(N-1)}}}$$

where

$\overline{D}$ is the mean difference for all pairs of scores,
ΣD^2 is the sum of the squares of the differences,
$(\Sigma D)^2$ is the square of the sum of the differences,
N is the number of pairs of scores, and
$N-1$ is the degrees of freedom (one less than the number of pairs of scores).

Consider the following example and steps:

Subjects	Posttest Scores x_1	Pretest Scores x_2	$\overline{D}$	D_2
1	22	15	7	49
2	21	16	5	25
3	20	17	7	49
4	23	16	7	49
5	19	14	5	25
6	21	15	6	36
7	18	12	6	36
8	22	18	4	16
			$\Sigma D = 47$	$\Sigma D^2 = 285$

Step 1: $\overline{D} = \dfrac{\Sigma D}{N} = \dfrac{47}{8} = 5.9$

Step 2: $(\Sigma D)^2 = 47^2 = 2209$

Step 3: Substitute into formula

$$t = \frac{5.9}{\sqrt{285 - \dfrac{\dfrac{2209}{8}}{8(8-1)}}}$$

$$= \frac{5.9}{\sqrt{\dfrac{285 - 276}{56}}}$$

$$= \frac{5.9}{\sqrt{\dfrac{9}{56}}}$$

$$= \frac{5.9}{0.40}$$

$$= 14.75$$

The calculated *t*-test statistic (14.75) is located in the critical values of the *t* table, with the degrees of freedom ($N - 1$, or in this example $8 - 1 = 7$). The result from the table is that the group means are clearly different from each other, statistically significant at $p < 0.001$.

TABLE C.1

Random Numbers

03 47 43 73 86	36 96 47 36 61	46 98 64 71 62	33 26 16 80 45	60 11 14 10 95
97 74 24 67 62	42 81 14 57 20	42 53 32 37 32	27 07 36 07 51	24 51 79 89 73
16 76 62 27 66	56 50 26 71 07	32 90 79 78 53	13 55 38 58 59	88 97 54 14 10
12 56 85 99 26	96 96 68 27 31	05 03 72 93 15	57 12 10 14 21	88 26 49 81 76
55 59 56 35 64	38 54 82 46 22	31 62 43 09 90	06 18 44 32 53	23 83 01 30 30
16 22 77 94 39	49 54 43 54 82	17 37 93 23 78	87 35 20 96 43	84 26 34 91 64
84 42 17 53 31	57 24 55 06 88	77 04 74 47 67	21 76 33 50 25	83 92 12 06 76
63 01 63 78 59	16 95 55 67 19	98 10 50 71 75	12 86 73 58 07	44 39 52 38 79
33 21 12 34 29	78 64 56 07 82	52 42 07 44 38	15 51 00 13 42	99 66 02 79 54
57 60 86 32 44	09 47 27 96 54	49 17 46 09 62	90 52 84 77 27	08 02 73 43 28
18 18 07 92 46	44 17 16 58 09	79 83 86 19 62	06 76 50 03 10	55 23 64 05 05
26 62 38 97 75	84 16 07 44 99	83 11 46 32 24	20 14 85 88 45	10 93 72 88 71
23 42 40 64 74	82 97 77 77 81	07 45 32 14 08	32 98 94 07 72	93 85 79 10 75
52 36 28 19 95	50 92 26 11 97	00 56 76 31 38	80 22 02 53 53	86 60 42 04 53
37 85 84 35 12	83 39 50 08 30	42 34 07 96 88	54 42 06 87 98	35 85 29 48 39
70 29 17 12 13	40 33 20 38 26	13 89 51 03 74	17 76 37 13 04	07 74 21 19 30
56 62 18 37 35	96 83 50 87 75	97 12 25 93 47	70 33 24 03 54	97 77 46 44 80
99 59 57 22 77	88 42 95 45 72	16 64 36 16 00	04 43 18 66 79	94 77 24 21 90
16 08 15 04 72	33 27 14 34 09	45 59 34 68 49	12 72 07 34 45	99 27 72 95 14
31 16 93 32 43	50 27 89 87 19	20 15 37 00 49	52 85 66 60 44	38 68 88 11 80
68 34 30 13 70	55 74 30 77 40	44 22 78 84 26	04 33 46 09 52	68 07 97 06 57
74 57 25 65 76	59 29 97 68 60	71 91 38 67 54	13 58 18 24 76	15 54 55 95 52
27 42 37 86 53	48 55 90 65 72	96 57 69 36 10	96 46 92 42 45	97 60 49 04 91
00 39 68 29 61	66 37 32 20 30	77 84 57 03 29	10 45 65 04 26	11 04 96 67 24
29 94 98 94 24	68 49 69 10 82	53 75 91 93 30	34 25 20 57 27	40 48 73 51 92
16 90 82 66 59	83 62 64 11 12	67 19 00 71 74	60 47 21 29 68	02 02 37 03 31
11 27 94 75 06	06 09 19 74 66	02 94 37 34 02	76 70 90 30 86	38 45 94 30 38
35 24 10 16 20	33 32 51 26 38	79 78 45 04 91	16 92 53 56 16	02 75 50 95 98
38 23 16 86 38	42 38 97 01 50	87 75 66 81 41	40 01 74 91 62	48 51 84 08 32
31 96 25 91 47	96 44 33 49 13	34 86 82 53 92	00 52 43 48 85	27 55 26 89 62
66 67 40 67 14	64 05 71 95 86	11 05 65 09 68	76 83 20 37 90	57 16 00 11 66
14 90 84 45 11	75 73 88 05 90	52 27 41 14 86	22 98 12 22 08	07 52 74 95 80
68 05 51 18 00	33 96 02 75 19	07 60 62 93 55	59 33 82 43 90	49 37 38 44 59
20 46 78 73 90	97 51 40 14 02	04 02 33 31 08	39 54 16 49 36	47 95 93 13 30
64 19 58 97 79	15 06 15 93 20	01 90 10 75 06	40 78 78 89 62	02 67 74 17 33
05 26 93 70 60	22 35 85 15 13	92 03 51 59 77	59 56 78 06 83	52 91 05 70 74
07 97 10 88 23	09 98 42 99 64	61 71 62 99 15	06 51 29 16 93	58 05 77 09 51
68 71 86 85 85	54 87 66 47 54	73 32 08 11 12	44 95 92 63 16	29 56 24 29 48
26 99 61 65 53	58 37 78 80 70	43 10 50 67 42	32 17 55 85 74	94 44 67 16 94
14 65 52 68 75	87 59 36 22 41	26 78 63 06 55	13 08 27 01 50	15 29 39 39 43
17 53 77 58 71	71 41 61 50 72	12 41 94 96 26	44 95 27 36 99	02 96 74 30 83
90 26 59 21 19	23 52 23 33 12	96 93 02 18 39	07 02 18 36 07	25 99 32 70 23
41 23 52 55 99	31 04 49 69 96	10 47 48 45 88	13 41 43 89 20	97 17 14 49 17
60 20 50 81 69	31 99 73 68 68	35 81 33 03 76	24 30 12 48 60	18 99 10 72 34
91 25 38 05 90	94 58 28 41 36	45 37 59 03 09	90 35 57 29 12	82 62 54 65 60
34 50 57 74 37	98 80 33 00 91	09 77 93 19 82	74 94 80 04 04	45 07 31 66 49
85 22 04 39 43	73 81 53 94 79	33 62 46 86 28	08 31 54 46 31	53 94 13 38 47
09 79 13 77 48	73 82 97 22 21	05 03 27 24 83	72 89 44 05 60	35 80 39 94 88
88 75 80 18 14	22 95 75 42 49	39 32 82 22 49	02 48 07 70 37	16 04 61 67 87
90 96 23 70 00	39 00 03 06 90	55 85 78 38 36	94 37 30 69 32	90 89 00 76 33

Source: Taken from Table XXXII of Fisher and Yates': *Statistical Tables for Biological, Agricultural and Medical Research* (6th Edition 1974) published by Longman Group UK Ltd. London (previously published by Oliver and Boyd Ltd, Edinburgh) and is reprinted by permission of the authors and publishers.

TABLE C.2

Critical Values for the Pearson Correlation Coefficient

	Level of Significance for a One-Tail Test				
	.05	.025	.01	.005	.0005
	Level of Significance for a Two-Tail Test				
df	.10	.05	.02	.01	.001
1	.9877	.9969	.9995	.9999	1.0000
2	.9000	.9500	.9800	.9900	.9990
3	.8054	.8783	.9343	.9587	.9912
4	.7293	.8114	.8822	.9172	.9741
5	.6694	.7545	.8329	.8745	.9507
6	.6215	.7067	.7887	.8343	.9249
7	.5822	.6664	.7498	.7977	.8982
8	.5494	.6319	.7155	.7646	.8721
9	.5214	.6021	.6851	.7348	.8471
10	.4973	.5760	.6581	.7079	.8233
11	.4762	.5529	.6339	.6835	.8010
12	.4575	.5324	.6120	.6614	.7800
13	.4409	.5139	.5923	.6411	.7603
14	.4259	.4973	.5742	.6226	.7420
15	.4124	.4821	.5577	.6055	.7246
16	.4000	.4683	.5425	.5897	.7084
17	.3887	.4555	.5285	.5751	.6932
18	.3783	.4438	.5155	.5614	.6787
19	.3687	.4329	.5034	.5487	.6652
20	.3598	.4227	.4921	.5368	.6524
25	.3223	.3809	.4451	.4869	.5974
30	.2960	.3494	.4093	.4487	.5541
35	.2746	.3246	.3810	.4182	.5189
40	.2573	.3044	.3578	.3932	.4896
45	.2428	.2875	.3384	.3721	.4648
50	.2306	.2732	.3218	.3541	.4433
60	.2108	.2500	.2948	.3248	.4078
70	.1954	.2319	.2737	.3017	.3799
80	.1829	.2172	.2565	.2830	.3568
90	.1726	.2050	.2422	.2673	.3375
100	.1638	.1946	.2301	.2540	.3211

Source: Taken from Table VII of Fisher and Yates: *Statistical Tables for Biological, Agricultural and Medical Research* (6th Edition, 1974) published by Longman Group UK Ltd. London (previously published by Oliver and Boyd Ltd, Edinburgh) and is reprinted by permission of the authors and publishers.

TABLE C.3

Critical Values of Chi-Square

df	.99	.98	.95	.90	.80	.70	.50	.30	.20	.10	.05	.02	.01	.001
1	.0002	.0006	.0039	.016	.064	.15	.46	1.07	1.64	2.71	3.84	5.41	6.64	10.83
2	.02	.04	.10	.21	.45	.71	1.39	1.41	3.22	4.60	5.99	7.82	9.21	13.82
3	.12	.18	.35	.58	1.00	1.42	2.37	3.66	4.64	6.25	7.82	9.84	11.34	16.27
4	.30	.43	.71	1.06	1.65	2.20	3.36	4.88	5.99	7.78	9.49	11.67	13.28	18.47
5	.55	.75	1.14	1.61	2.34	3.00	4.35	6.06	7.29	9.24	11.07	13.39	15.09	20.52
6	.87	1.13	1.64	2.20	3.07	3.83	5.35	7.23	8.56	10.64	12.59	15.03	16.81	22.46
7	1.24	1.56	2.17	2.83	3.82	4.67	6.35	8.38	9.80	12.02	14.07	16.62	18.48	24.32
8	1.65	2.03	2.73	3.49	4.59	5.53	7.34	9.52	11.03	13.36	15.51	18.17	20.09	26.12
9	2.09	2.53	3.32	4.17	5.38	6.39	8.34	10.66	12.24	14.68	16.92	19.68	21.67	27.88
10	2.56	3.06	3.94	4.86	6.18	7.27	9.34	11.78	13.44	15.99	18.31	21.16	23.21	29.59
11	3.05	3.61	4.58	5.58	6.99	8.15	10.34	12.90	14.63	17.28	19.68	22.62	24.72	31.26
12	3.57	4.18	5.23	6.30	7.81	9.03	11.34	14.01	15.81	18.55	21.03	24.05	26.22	32.91
13	4.11	4.76	5.89	7.04	8.63	9.93	12.34	15.12	16.98	19.81	22.36	25.47	27.69	34.53
14	4.66	5.37	6.57	7.79	9.47	10.82	13.34	16.22	18.15	21.06	34.68	26.87	29.14	36.12
15	5.23	5.98	7.26	8.55	10.31	11.72	14.34	17.32	19.31	22.31	25.00	28.26	30.58	37.70
16	5.81	6.61	7.96	9.31	11.15	12.62	15.34	18.42	20.46	23.54	26.30	29.63	32.00	39.25
17	6.41	7.26	8.67	10.08	12.00	13.53	16.34	19.51	22.62	24.77	27.59	31.00	33.41	40.79
18	7.02	7.91	9.39	10.86	12.86	14.44	17.34	20.60	22.76	25.99	28.87	32.35	34.80	42.31
19	7.63	8.57	10.12	11.65	13.72	15.35	18.34	21.69	23.90	27.20	30.14	33.69	36.19	43.82
20	8.26	9.24	10.85	12.44	14.58	16.27	19.34	22.78	25.04	28.41	31.41	35.02	37.57	45.32
21	8.90	9.92	11.59	13.24	15.44	17.18	20.34	23.86	26.17	29.62	32.67	36.34	38.93	46.80
22	9.54	10.60	12.34	14.04	16.31	18.10	21.34	24.94	27.30	30.81	33.92	37.66	40.29	48.27
23	10.20	11.29	13.09	14.85	17.19	19.02	22.34	26.02	28.43	32.01	35.17	38.97	41.64	49.73
24	10.86	11.99	13.85	15.66	18.06	19.94	23.34	27.10	29.55	33.20	36.42	40.27	42.98	51.18
25	11.52	12.70	14.61	16.47	18.94	20.87	24.34	28.17	30.68	34.48	37.65	41.57	44.31	52.62
26	12.20	13.41	15.38	17.29	19.82	21.79	25.34	29.25	31.80	35.56	38.88	42.86	45.64	54.05
27	12.88	14.12	16.15	18.11	20.70	22.72	26.34	30.32	32.91	36.74	40.11	44.14	46.96	55.48
28	13.56	14.85	16.93	18.94	21.59	23.65	27.34	31.39	34.03	37.92	41.34	45.42	48.28	56.89
29	14.26	15.57	17.71	19.77	22.48	24.58	28.45	32.46	35.14	39.09	42.56	46.69	49.59	58.30
30	14.95	16.31	18.49	20.60	23.36	25.51	29.34	33.53	36.25	40.26	43.77	47.96	50.89	59.70

Source: Taken from Table IV of Fisher and Yates': *Statistical Tables for Biological, Agricultural and Medical Research* (6th Edition 1974) published by Longman Group UK Ltd. London (previously published by Oliver and Boyd Ltd, Edinburgh) and is reprinted by permission of the authors and publishers.

References

Airasian, P. W. (1991). *Classroom assessment*. New York: McGraw-Hill, Inc.

Alkin, M. C. (1969). Evaluation theory development. *Evaluation Comment, 2,* 2–7.

Altheide, D. L., & Johnson, J. M. (1998). Criteria for assessing interpretative validity in qualitative research. In N. K. Denzin & Y. S. Lincoln (Eds.), *Collecting and Interpreting Qualitative Materials* (pp 283–312). Thousand Oaks, CA: Sage Publications, Inc.

American Psychological Association. (1994). *Publication manual of the American Psychological Association* (4th ed.). Washington, DC: Author.

American Psychological Association. (1999). Statistical methods in psychology journals. *American Psychologist, 54* (8), 594–604.

American Psychological Association. (2000). *Standards for educational and psychological tests*. Washington, DC: Author.

Angroisino, M. V. (1989). *Documents of interactions: Biography, autobiography, and life history in social science perspective*. Gainsville: University of Florida Press.

Aydelotte, W. O. (1986). Quantification in history. *American Historical Review, 71,* 803– 825.

Babbie, E. R. (1973). *Survey research methods*. Belmont, CA: Wadsworth, Inc.

Babbie, E. R. (1998). *The practice of social research*. (8th ed.). Belmont, CA: Wadsworth, Inc.

Barlow, D. H., & Hersen, M. (1984). *Single case experimental designs: Strategies for studying behavior change*. New York: Pergamon.

Barzun, J., & Graff, H. G. (1992). *The modern researcher* (5th ed.). New York: Harcourt Brace Janovovich.

Betts, J. R., & Shkilnik, J. L. (1999). The behavioral effects of variations in class size: The case of math teachers. *Educational Evaluation and Policy Analysis, 21* (2), 193–213.

Biddle, B. J. (1996). Better ideas: Expanding funding for educational research. *Educational Researcher, 25* (9), 12–14.

Biklen, S. K. (1985). Can elementary school teaching be a career? A search for new ways of understanding women's work. *Issues in Education, 3* (3), 215– 231.

Blase, J. & Blase, J. (1999). Shared governance principals: The inner experience. *NASSP Bulletin, 83* (606), 81–90.

Bogdan, R., & Biklen, S. K. (1998). *Qualitative research for education* (3rd ed.). Boston: Allyn & Bacon, Inc.

Boraks, N., & Schumacher, S. (1981). *Ethnographic research on word recognition strategies of adult beginning readers: Technical Report.* Richmond: Virginia Commonwealth University, School of Education. (ERIC Document Reproduction Services ED No. 207 007.)

Boruch, R. F., & Cecil, J. S. (1979). *Assuring the confidentiality of social research data.* Philadelphia: University of Pennsylvania Press.

Boss, M. W., & Taylor, M. C. (1989). The relationship between locus of control and academic level and sex of secondary students. *Contemporary Educational Psychology, 14,* 315– 322.

Brickhous, N., & Bodner, G. M. (1992). The beginning science teacher: Classroom narratives of convictions and constraints. *Journal of Research in Science Teaching, 29,* 471–485.

Burton, O. V., & Finnegan, R. (1990). Teaching historians to use technology: Databases and computers. *International Journal of Social Education, 5,* 23–35.

Buttram, J. L. (1990). Focus groups: A starting point for needs assessment. *Evaluation Practice, 11* (3), 207– 212.

Campbell, D. T. (1984). Can we be scientific in applied social science? In R. F. Conner, D. G. Altman, & C. Jackson (Eds.), *Evaluation studies review annual* (Vol. 9). Beverly Hills, CA: Sage Publications, Inc.

Campbell, D. T., & Stanley, J. C. (1963). *Experimental and quasi-experimental designs for research.* Chicago: Rand, McNally & Co.

Carnoy, M. (1995, Winter). Why aren't more African Americans going to college? *Journal of Blacks in Higher Education,* 66–69.

Carr, E. H. (1967). *What is history?* New York: Random House.

Carspecken, P. F. (1996). *Critical ethnography in educational research: A theoretical and practical guide.* New York: Routledge.

Cassell, J. (1982). Harm, benefits, wrongs, and rights in fieldwork. In J. Seiber (Ed.), *The ethics of social research* (pp. 7– 32). New York: Springer-Verlag.

Cassell, J., & Wax, M. (Eds.). (1980). Ethical problems in fieldwork. Special issue of *Social Problems, 27.*

Chicago manual of style: Fourteenth edition, revised and expanded. (1993). Chicago: The University of Chicago Press.

Chun, K. T., Cobb, S., French, J. R. P., Jr. (1974). *Measures for psychological assessment: A guide to 3,000 original sources and their applications.* Ann Arbor: Institute for Social Research, University of Michigan.

Clandinin, D. J. & Connelly, F. M. (1998). Personal experience methods. In N. K. Denzin & Y. S. Lincoln (Eds.), *Collecting and interpreting qualitative reseach* (pp. 150–178). Thousand Oaks, CA: Sage Publishers.

Cohen, J. (1988). *Statistical power analysis for the behavioral sciences*. Hillsdale, NJ: Erlbaum.

Cohen, S. (1976). The history of the history of American education, 1900–1976: The uses of the past. *Harvard Educational Review, 46* (3), 298–330.

Cohen, D. K., & Ball, D. L. (1990). Relations between policy and practice: A commentary. *Educational Evaluation and Policy Analysis, 12* (3), 249–256.

Committee on Scientific and Professional Ethics and Conduct (1977). Ethical standards of psychologists, *APA Monitor, 8*, 22–23.

Comrey, A. L., Backer, T. E., & Glaser, E. M. (1973). *A sourcebook for mental health measures*. Los Angeles: Human Interaction Research Institute.

Connelly, F. M., & Clandinin, D. J. (1990). Stories of experience and narrative inquiry. *Educational researcher, 19* (5), 2–14.

Conoley, J. C., & Kramer, J. J. (Eds.). (1989). *The tenth mental measurements yearbook*. Lincoln: University of Nebraska Press.

Cook, T. D., & Campbell, D. T. (1979). *Quasi-experimentation: Design and analysis issues for field settings*. Chicago: Rand-McNally & Co.

Cooley, V. & Shen, J. (1999) Who will lead? The top 10 factors that influence teachers moving into administration. *NASSP Bulletin, 83* (606), 75–80.

Cooper, H. (1998). *Synthesizing Research*. Thousand Oaks, CA: Sage Publications, Inc.

Cousins, J. B., & Leithwood, K. A. (1986). Current empirical research on evaluation utilization. *Review of Educational Research, 56* (3), 331–364.

Cousins, L. H. (1999). 'Playing between classes': America's troubles with class, race, and gender in a black high school and community. *Anthropology and Education, 30* (30), 294–316.

Crabtree, B. F., & Miller, W. L. (Eds.) (1999). *Doing qualitative research* (2nd ed.). Thousand Oaks, CA: Sage Publishers.

Creswell, J. W. (1995). *Research design: Qualitative and quantitative approaches*. Thousand Oaks, CA: Sage Publications, Inc.

Creswell, J. W. (1998). *Qualitative inquiry and research design: Choosing among five traditions*. Thousand Oaks, CA: Sage Publications, Inc.

Cronbach, L. J. (1982). *Designing evaluations of educational and social programs*. San Francisco: Jossey-Bass, Inc., Publishers.

Cronbach, L. J., & Suppes, P. (Eds.). (1969). *Research for tomorrow's schools: Disciplined inquiry for education*. New York: Macmillan Publishing Co.

Cusick, P. A. (1973). *Inside high school: The student's world*. New York: Holt, Rinehart & Winston.

Cutler, W. W. (1971). Oral history: Its nature and uses for educational history. *History of Education Quarterly, 11,* 184– 194.

Daniel, L. G. (1999). A history of perceptions of the quality of educational research: issues and trends with implications for the teaching of educational research. Paper presented at the annual meeting of the American Educational Research Association, San Diego, CA.

Daniel, P. T. (1980), A history of discrimination against Black students in Chicago secondary schools, *History of Education Quarterly, 20* (2), 140–155.

Denzin, N. K. (2000). *Interpretative biography* (2nd ed.). Newbury Park, CA: Sage.

Denzin, N. K., & Lincoln, Y. S., (Eds.) (2000). *Handbook of qualitative research 2/e.* Thousand Oaks, CA: Sage Publications, Inc.

Dexter, L. (1970). *Elite and specialized interviewing.* New York: Basic Books.

Doughtery, J. (1998). "Thats when we were marching for jobs": Black Teachers and the Early Civil Rights Movement in Milwaukee, *History of Education Quarterly, 38* (2), 121–142.

Ebmeier, H., & Good, T. L. (1979). The effects of instructing teachers about good teaching on the mathematics achievement of fourth grade students. *American Educational Research Journal, 16* (1), 1– 16.

Erickson, F. (1973). What makes school ethnography "ethnographic?" *Anthropology and Education Quarterly, 9,* 58– 69.

Erickson, F. (1986). Qualitative methods in research on teaching. In M. D. Wittrock (Ed.), *Handbook of research on teaching* (3rd ed.)(pp. 119–161). New York: Mcmillan.

The ETS test collection. Volume 1: Achievement tests and measurement devices (2nd Edition). (1993). Phoenix, AZ: Oryx Press.

The ETS test collection. Volume 2: Vocational tests and measurement devices. (1988). Phoenix, AZ: Oryx Press.

The ETS test collection. Volume 3: Tests for special populations. (1989). Phoenix, AZ: Oryx Press.

The ETS test collection. Volume 4: Cognitive aptitude and intelligence tests. (1990). Phoenix, AZ: Oryx Press.

The ETS test collection. Volume 5: Attitude tests. (1991). Phoenix, AZ: Oryx Press.

The ETS test collection. Volume 6: Affective measures and personality tests. (1992). Phoenix, AZ: Oryx Press.

Fabiano, E. (1989). *Index to tests used in educational dissertations.* Phoenix, AZ: Oryx Press.

Fielding, N. G., & Lee, R. M. (1998). *Computer analysis and qualitative research.* London: Sage Publishers.

Fine, M. (1998). Working the hyphens: Reinventing self and other in qualitative research. In N. Denzin & Y. Lincoln (Eds.), *The landscape of qualitative research* (pp. 130–155). Thousand Oaks, CA: Sage Publications, Inc.

Fletcher, J. D., Hawley, D. E., & Piele, P. K. (1990). Cost, effects, and utility of micro computer assisted instruction in the classroom. *American Educational Research Journal, 27* (4), 783– 806.

Floud, R. (1979). *An introduction to quantitative method for historians.* London: Methuen, Inc.

Floyd, J. A. (1993). The use of cross-method triangulation in the study of sleep concerns in healthy older adults. *Advances-in-Nursing-Science,* 16 (2), 70–80.

Fontana, A., & Frey, J. H. (1998). Interviewing: The art of science. In N. K. Denzin & Y. S. Lincoln (Eds.), *Collecting and interpreting qualitative reseach* (pp. 47–78). Thousand Oaks, CA: Sage Publications, Inc.

Franklin, R. D., Allison, D. B., & Gorman, B. S. (1997). *Design and analysis of single case research.* Mahwah, NJ: Lawrence Erlbaum Associates.

Garard, D. L., Hund, S. K., Lippert, L., & Paynton, S. T. (1998). Alternatives to traditional instruction: Using games and simulations to increase student learning and motivation. *Communication Research Reports,15* (1), 36–44.

Gibbons, J. D. (1993). *Nonparametric statistics: An introduction.* Newbury Park, CA: Sage Publications, Inc.

Giesne, C., & Peshkin, A. (1992). *Becoming qualitative researchers: An introduction.* New York: Longman, Inc.

Giordano, F. G., Schwiebert, V. L., & Brotherton, W. D. (1997). School counselor's perceptions of the usefulness of standardized tests, frequency of their use, and assessment training needs. *The School Counselor, 44* (3), 198–205.

Glaser, B. G., & Strauss, L. L. (1967). *The discovery of grounded theory: Strategies for qualitative research.* Chicago: Aldine.

Goldman, B., & Mitchell, D. (1995). *Directory of unpublished experimental mental measures.* (Vol. 6). Washington, DC: American Psychological Assoc.

Goodwin, W. L., & Driscoll, L. A. (1980). *Handbook for measurement and evaluation in early childhood education.* San Francisco: Jossey-Bass, Inc., Publishers.

Gorden, R. (1981). *Interviewing: Strategies, techniques, and tactics.* Homewood, IL: Dorsey.

Gottschalk, L. (1969). *Understanding history: A primer of historical method* (2nd ed.). New York: Alfred A. Knopf, Inc.

Green, J. C., Caracelli, V. J., & Graham, W. F. (1989). Toward a conceptual framework for mixed-method evaluation designs. *Educational Evaluation and Policy Analysis, 11,* 255–274.

Greenberg, D., Meyer, R. H., & Wiseman, M. (1995). Multisite employment and training program evaluations: A tale of three studies. *Industrial and Labor Relations Review, 47,* 679–691.

Guba, E. G., & Lincoln, Y. S. (1989). *Fourth generation evaluation.* Beverly Hills, CA: Sage Publications, Inc.

Gulino, J. & Valentin, J. S. (1999). Middle school programmatic practices and student satisfaction with school. *NASSP Bulletin,83* (608), 90–99.

Gutowski, T. W. (1988). Student initiative and the origins of the high school extracurriculum: Chicago, 1880– 1915. *History of Education Quarterly, 28* (1), 49– 72.

Hall, E. T. (1959). *The silent language.* New York: Doubleday & Co.

Hall, E. T. (1966). *The hidden dimension.* New York: Doubleday & Co.

Hall, E. T. (1974). *Handbook for proxemic research.* Washington, DC: Society for the Anthropology of Visual Communication.

Halperin, S. (1978, March). *Teaching the limitations of the correlation coefficient.* Paper presented at the annual meeting of the American Educational Research Association, Toronto.

Hambrick, R. S. (1987). *Analysis for decision-making: Using non-quantitative group methods. Commonwealth papers, 1987.* Richmond: Virginia Commonwealth University, Center for Public Affairs.

Harding, S. (Ed.). (1987). *Feminism and methodology.* Bloomington: Indiana University Press.

Hedges, L. V., & Olkin, I. (1985). *Statistical methods for meta-analysis.* New York: Academic Press, Inc.

Hedges, L. V., & Olkin, I. (1986). Meta-analysis: A review and a new view. *Educational Researcher, 15* (8), 14– 21.

Henry, G. T. (1990). *Practical sampling.* Newbury Park, CA: Sage Publications, Inc.

Hersen, M., & Bellack, A. (1988). *Dictionary of behavioral assessment techniques.* New York: Pergamon Press.

Hertz, R., & Imber, J. B. (1995). *Studying elites using qualitative methods.* Thousand Oaks, CA: Sage Publications, Inc.

Hill, M. R. (1993). *Archival strategies and techniques.* Thousand Oaks, CA: Sage Publications, Inc.

Hoepfner, R., et al. (Eds.) (1972). *CSE-RBS test evaluation: Tests of higher order cognitive, affective, and interpersonal skills.* Los Angeles: Center for the Study of Evaluation, UCLA Graduate School of Education.

Hopkins, K. D., & Anderson, B. L. (1973). Multiple comparisons guide. *Journal of Special Education, 7,* 319– 328.

Hopkins, K. D., & Gullickson, A. R. (1992). Response rates in survey research: A meta-analysis of the effects of monetary gratuities, *Journal of Experimental Education, 61,* 52– 62.

Hopkins, K. D., & Glass, G. V. (1996). *Basic statistics for the behavioral sciences* (3rd ed.). Englewood Cliffs, NJ: Prentice-Hall, Inc.

Hopkins, K. D., & Stanley, J. C. (1981). *Educational and Psychological Measurement* (6th ed.). Englewood, NJ: Prentice-Hall.

Horvat, E. M., & Antonia, A. L. (1999). 'Hey, those shoes are out of uniform:' African American girls in an elite high school and the importance of habitus. *Anthropology & Education Quarterly, 30* (3), 317–342.

Interviewer's Manual (1999). Ann Arbor, MI: University of Michigan Survey Research Center.

Jaeger, R. M. (Ed.). (1984). *Sampling in education and the social sciences.* New York: Longman, Inc.

Jaeger, R. M. (Ed.). (1988). *Complementary methods for research in education.* Washington, DC: American Educational Research Association.

Janesick, V. J. (1998). The dance of qualitative research design: Metaphore, methodolatry, and meaning. In N. K. Denzin & Y. S. Lincoln (Eds.) *Strategies of qualitative inquiry* (pp 35–55). Thousand Oaks, CA: Sage Publications, Inc.

Jensen, R. (1981). Oral history, quantification, and the new social history. *Oral History Review, 9,* 13– 27.

Johnson, O. G. (1976). *Tests and measurements in child development: Handbook II.* San Francisco: Jossey-Bass, Inc., Publishers.

Joint Committee on Standards for Educational Evaluation (1994). *The program evaluation standards* (2nd ed.). Thousand Oaks, CA: Sage Publications, Inc.

Joyce, B. (1987). A rigorous yet delicate touch: A response to Slavin's proposal for "best-evidence" reviews. *Educational Researcher, 16* (4), 12– 16.

Kaestle, G. F. (1992). Standards of evidence in historical research. *History of Educational Quarterly, 32* (3), 361–366.

Katz, M. B. (1968). *The irony of early school reform: Educational innovation in mid-nineteenth century Massachusetts.* Cambridge, MA: Harvard University Press.

Kazdin, A. E. (1982). *Single case research designs: Methods for clinical and applied settings.* New York: Oxford University Press.

Kelle, U. (Ed.) (1995). *Computer-aided qualitative research.* Thousand Oaks, CA: Sage Publications, Inc.

Kerlinger, F. N. (1979). *Behavioral research: A conceptual approach.* New York: Holt, Rinehart & Winston.

Kerlinger, F. N. (1986). *Foundations of behavioral research* (3rd ed.). New York: Holt, Rinehart & Winston.

Keyser, D. J., & Sweetland, R. C. (Eds.) (1984– 94). *Test critiques, Volumes 1– 10.* Kansas City, MO: Test Corporation of America.

Kimmel, A. J. (1981). *Ethics of human subject research.* San Francisco: Jossey-Bass.

Kirby, S. N., Berends, M., & Naftel, S. (1999). Supply and demand of minority teachers in Texas: Problems and prospects. *Education Evaluation and Policy Analysis, 21* (1), 47–66.

Kleinman, S., & Copp, M. A. (1993). *Emotions and fieldwork*. Newbury Park, CA: Sage Publications, Inc.

Kraemer, H. C., & Thielman, S. (1987). *How many subjects? Statistical power analysis in research*. Newbury Park, CA: Sage Publications, Inc.

Kramer, J. J., & Conoley, J. C. (Eds.) (1991). *Supplement to the tenth mental measurements yearbook*. Lincoln, Nebraska: Buros Institute of Mental Measurement.

Krueger, R. A. (1994). *Focus groups: A practical guide for applied research* (2nd ed.). Thousand Oaks, CA: Sage Publications, Inc.

Lance, D. (1980). Oral history archives: Perceptions and practices. *Oral History, 8* (2), 59– 63.

Lather, P. (1991). *Getting smart: Feminist research and pedagogy with/in the postmodern*. New York: Routledge.

Lawrence, S., & Giles, C. L. (1999). Accessibility of information on the Web. *Nature, 400*, 107–109

LeCompte, M. D. (1987). Bias in biography: Bias and subjectivity in ethnography research. *Anthropology and Education Quarterly, 18* (1), 43– 52.

LeCompte, M. D., Millroy, W. L., & Preissle, J. (Eds.) (1992). *The handbook of qualitative research in education*. San Diego: Academic Press, Inc.

LeCompte, M. D., & Preissle, J. (1993). *Ethnography and qualitative design in educational research*. (2nd ed.) San Diego, CA: Academic Press, Inc.

Lehmann, J. P., Bassett, D. S., Sands, D. J., Spencer, K., & Gliner, J. A. (1999). Research translated into practices for increasing student involvement in transition-related activities. *Career Development for Exceptional Individuals, 22* (1), 3–20.

Lesko, N. (1986). Individualism and community: Ritual discourse in a parochial high school. *Anthropology and Education Quarterly, 17* (1), 25– 39.

Levin, H. M. (1981). Cost analysis. In N. Smith (Ed.), *New techniques for evaluation*. Beverly Hills, CA: Sage Publications, Inc.

Levin, H. M. (1988). Cost-effectiveness and educational policy. *Educational Evaluation and Policy Analysis, 10* (1), 51– 69.

Levin, H. M., Glass, G. V., & Meister, G. R. (1987). A cost-effectiveness analysis of computer-assisted instruction. *Evaluation Review, 11* (1), 50– 72.

Lincoln, Y. S. (1990). Toward a categorical imperative for qualitative research. In E. W. Eisner & A. Peshkin (Eds.), *Qualitative inquiry in education* (pp. 277– 295). New York: Teachers College Press.

Lincoln, Y. S. (1995). *Emerging criteria for quality in qualitative and interpretive research*. Paper presented at the annual meeting of the American Education Research Association, San Francisco.

Lincoln, Y. S., & Guba, E. G. (1985). *Naturalistic inquiry*. Beverly Hills, CA: Sage Publications, Inc.

Locke, L. F., Spirduso, W. W., & Silverman, J. J. (1999). *Proposals that work: A guide for planning dissertations and grant proposals* (4th ed.). Thousand Oaks, CA: Sage Publications, Inc.

Lofland, J., & Lofland, L. H. (1984). *Analyzing social settings: A guide to qualitative observation and analysis* (2nd ed.). Belmont, CA: Wadsworth, Inc.

Lomask, M. (1986). *The biographer's craft.* New York: Harper & Row.

Luck, J. S. (1985). *The principal and the unsatisfactory teacher: A field study.* Unpublished doctoral dissertation. Virginia Polytechnic Institute and State University, Blacksburg, VA.

Lustberg, R. S., Molta, R., & Naccari, N. (1990). A model using the WISC-R to predict success in programs for gifted students. *Psychology in the Schools, 27,* 126–131.

Maddox, J. (Ed.) (1996). *Tests: A comprehensive reference for assessments in psychology, education, and business* (4th ed.). Kansas City, MO: Test Corporation of America.

Malinowski, B. (1922). *Argonauts of the western Pacific.* New York: E. P. Dutton. (Reprint, 1961).

Marascuilo, L. A., & McSweeney, M. (1977). *Nonparametric and distribution-free methods for the social sciences.* Monterey, CA: Brooks/Cole Publishing Co.

Marcus, G. E. (1998), What comes (just) after "post"?: The case of ethnography. In N. K. Denzin & Y. S. Lincoln (Eds.), *The landscape of qualitative research: Theories and issues.* Thousand Oaks, CA: Sage Publications, Inc. (pp. 383–406).

Marshall, C. (1990). Goodness criteria: Are they objective or judgement calls? In Guba, E. G. (Ed.), *The paradigm dialog,* (pp. 188–197). Newbury Park, CA: Sage Publications, Inc.

Marshall, C., & Rossman, G. R. (1999). *Designing qualitative research* (3rd ed.). Newbury Park, CA: Sage Publications, Inc.

Martens, M. L. (1992). Inhibitors in implementing a problem-solving approach to teaching elementary science: Case study of a teacher in change. *Social Science and Mathematics, 93,* 150–156.

Marton, F. (1986). Phenomenography—a research approach to investigating different understandings of reality. *Journal of Thought, 2* (3), 28–48.

Mason, J. (1996). *Qualitative Researching.* Thousand Oaks, CA: Sage Publications, Inc.

Mason, R. O., McKenny, J. L., & Copeland, D. G. (1997, September). An historial method for MIS research: Steps and assumptions. *MIS Quarterly,* 307–319.

Maxwell, D. M. (1999). Teachers embracing the magic: How do effective teachers make use of thier intuitive knowledge? *The Journal of the Association of Teacher Educators, XX* (1) 88–97.

McMillan, J. H. (2000). *Educational research. Fundamentals for the consumer* (3rd ed.). New York: Longman.

Mehrens, W. A., & Lehmann, I. J. (1987). *Measurement and evaluation in education and psychology* (4th ed.). New York: Holt, Rinehart & Winston.

Messick, S. (1989). Validity. In R. L. Linn (Ed.), *Educational measurement.* (3rd Edition) (pp. 13– 103) Washington, DC: American Council on Education and the National Council on Measurement in Education.

Messick, S. (1989). Validity of psychological assessment: Validation of inferences from person's responses and performances as scientific inquiry into score meaning. Keynote address presented at the Conference on Contemporary Psychological Assessment, Stockholm, Sweden.

Miles, M. B., & Huberman, A. M. (1994). *Qualitative data analysis: An expanded sourcebook.* Thousand Oaks, CA: Sage Publications, Inc.

Miller, D. C. (1991). *Handbook of research design and social measurement.* (5th ed.). Newbury Park, CA: Sage Publications, Inc.

Miller, W. L., & Crabtree, B. F. (1994), Clinical research. In N. K. Denzin & Y. S. Lincoln (Eds.), *Handbook of qualitative research* (pp. 340– 352). Thousand Oaks, CA: Sage Publications, Inc.

Mitchell, D. E. (1988). Educational politics and policy: The state level. In N. J. Boyan (Ed.), *Handbook on research in educational administration* (pp. 453–466). New York: Longman, Inc.

Montero-Sieburth, M., & Perez, M. (1987). Echar pa'lante, moving onward: The dilemmas and strategies of a bilingual teacher. *Anthropology and Education Quarterly, 18* (3), 181– 189.

Morgan, D. L. (1997). *Focus groups as qualitative research* (2nd ed.). Thousand Oaks, CA: Sage Publications, Inc.

Moss, P. A. (1995). Themes and variations in validity theory. *Educational measurement: Issues and Practice, 14,* 5– 13.

Moustakas, C. (1994). *Phenomenological research methods.* Thousand Oaks, CA: Sage Publications, Inc.

Oja, S. N., & Smulyan, L. (1989). *Collaborative action research: A developmental approach.* London: The Falmer Press.

Patton, M. Q. (1990). *Qualitative evaluation and research methods* (2nd ed.). Newbury Park, CA: Sage Publications, Inc.

Pelto, P. J., & Pelto, G. H. (1978). *Anthropological research: The structure of inquiry* (2nd ed.). Cambridge, England: Cambridge University Press.

Peshkin, A. (1993). The goodness of qualitative resesarch. *Educational Researcher, 22* (2), 23–29.

Popham, W. J. (1981). *Educational measurement.* Englewood Cliffs: Prentice Hall.

Popper, K. R. (1959). *The logic of scientific discovery.* New York: Basic Books, Inc., Publishers.

Potter, D. M. (1963). Explicit data and implicit assumptions in historical study. In L. Gottschalk (Ed.), *Generalizations in the writing of history.* Chicago: The University of Chicago Press.

Punch, M. (1986). *The politics and ethnics of fieldwork.* Beverly Hills, CA: Sage Publications, Inc.

Quantz, R. A. (1985). The complex visions of female teachers and the failure of unionization in the 1930s: An oral history. *History of Education Quarterly, 25* (4), 439– 458.

Rachal, J. R. (1998). We'll never turn back: Adult education and the struggle for citizenship in Mississippi's Freedom Summer. *American Educational Research Journal, 35* (2), 167–198.

Reynolds, P. (1982). *Ethnics and social research.* Englewood Cliffs, NJ: Prentice-Hall, Inc.

Rice, J. K., (1999). Impact of class size on instructional strategies and the use of time in high school mathematics and science courses. *Educational Evaluation and Policy Analysis, 21* (2), 215–229.

Richardson, L. (1990). *Writing strategies: Reaching diverse audiences.* Newbury Park, CA: Sage Publications, Inc.

Riemer, J. W. (1977). Varieties of opportunistic research. *Urban Life, 5,* 467– 477.

Rist, R. C. (1982). Beyond the quantitative cul-de-sac: A qualitative perspective on youth employment programs. *Policy Studies Journal, 10* (3), 522– 538.

Robinson, J. P., & Shaver, P. (1973). *Measures of social psychological attitudes* (rev. ed.). Ann Arbor: University of Michigan.

Romano, J. L. (1997). Stress and coping: A qualitative study of 45th and 5th graders. *Elementary School Guidance and Counseling, 31* (4), 273–282.

Rosenthal, R., & Jacobson, L. (1968). *Pygmalion in the classroom: Teacher expectation and pupil's intellectual development.* New York: Holt, Rinehart & Winston.

Rosenthal, R., & Rosnow, R. L. (1975). *The volunteer subject.* New York: John Wiley & Sons, Inc.

Rossman, G. B., & Rallis, S. F. (1998). *Learning in the field: An introduction to qualitative research.* Thousand Oaks, CA: Sage Publications, Inc.

Rowntree, J. S. (1941). *Poverty and progress: A second social survey of York.* London: Longman, Green.

Samson, G. E., Strykowski, B., Weinstein, T., & Walberg, H. J. (1987). The effects of teacher question levels on student achievement: A quantitative synthesis. *Journal of Educational Research, 80* (5), 290– 295.

Sax, G. (1979). *Foundations of educational research.* Englewood Cliffs, NJ: Prentice-Hall, Inc.

Sax, G. (1980). *Principles of educational and psychological measurement and evaluation* (2nd ed.). Belmont, CA: Wadsworth, Inc.

Schatzman, L., & Strauss, A. L. (1973). *Field research: Strategies for a natural sociology.* Englewood Cliffs, NJ: Prentice-Hall, Inc.

Schumacher, S. (1975). Political processes of an interagency project renewal policy: A case study of a federal agency's negotiations to influence state and local policies. Paper presented at the AERA Annual Meeting, Washington, DC (ERIC Document Reproduction Service No. 111-024.

Schumacher, S. (1984a). *Ethnographic methodology in a study of word recognition strategies of adult beginning readers.* Paper presented at the Adult Education Research Conference, Raleigh, NC. (ERIC Document Reproduction Services No. ED 246 272)

Schumacher, S. (1984b). *Evaluation of CoTEEP field-testing of workshop-seminar series and principles for summative evaluation.* Richmond: Virginia Commonwealth University, School of Education. (ERIC Document Reproduction Service No. ED 252 499)

Schumacher, S., & Boraks, N. (1981). *1980 cultural shock: Evolving ethnographic procedures to study adult learning-to-read behaviors.* Paper presented at the Second Annual Ethnography in Education Research Forum, University of Pennsylvania. (ERIC Document Reproduction Service No. ED 207 007)

Schumacher, S., Esham, K., & Bauer, D. (1985). *Evaluation of a collaborative teacher education program: Planning, development and implementation, Phase III.* Richmond: Virginia Commonwealth University, School of Education. (ERIC Document Reproduction Service No. ED 278 659)

Schuman, H., & Presser, S. (1996). *Questions and answers: Experiments in the form, wording and context of survey questions.* Thousand Oaks, CA: Sage Publications, Inc.

Schutt, R. K. (1996). Investigating the social world: The process and practice of research. Thousand Oaks, CA: Pine Forge Press.

Schwandt, T. A. (1997). *Qualitative inquiry: A dictionary of terms.* Thousand Oaks, CA: Sage Publications, Inc.

Sechrest, L., & Figueredo, A. J. (1993). Program evaluation. *Annual Review of Psychology, 44,* 645–674.

Sechrest, L. & Sidani, L. (1995). Quantitative and qualitative methods: Is there an alternative? *Evaluation and Program Planning, 18* (1), 77–87.

Seidman, I. E. (1998). Interviewing as qualitative research: A guide for researchers in education and the social sciences (2nd ed.). New York: Teachers College Press.

Shepard, L. A. (1993). Evaluating test validity. In L. Darling-Hammond (ed.), *Review of Research in Education, 19, 405– 450.*

Sherman, R. R., & Webb, R. B. (1988). Qualitative reserch in education: A focus. In R. R. Sherman & R. B. Webb (Eds.), *Qualitative research in education: Focus and methods* (pp. 2–21). New York: The Falmer Press.

Shulman, L. S. (1981). Disciplines of inquiry in education: An overview. *Educational Researcher, 10* (6), 5–23.

Shulman, L. S. (1986). Paradigms and research programs in the study of teaching: A contemporary perspective. In M. Wittrock (Ed.), *Handbook of research on teaching,* (3rd ed.) (pp. 3– 36). New York: Macmillan Publishing Co.

Siegel, S. (1956). *Nonparametric statistics for the behavioral sciences.* New York: McGraw-Hill Publishing Co.

Slavin, R. E. (1984). Meta-analysis in education: How has it been used? *Educational Researcher, 13* (8), 6– 15.

Slavin, R. E. (1986). Best-evidence synthesis: An alternative to meta-analytic and traditional reviews. *Educational Researcher, 15* (9), 5– 11.

Smith, J. K. (1993). *After the demise of empiricism: The problem of judging social and education inquiry.* Norwood, NJ: Ablex.

Smith, L. M. (1990). Ethics in qualitative field research: An individual perspective. In E. W. Eisner & A. Peshkin (Eds.), *Qualitative inquiry in education: The continuing debate* (pp. 258– 276). New York: Teachers College Press.

Smith, L. M. (1998). Biographical method. In N. K. Denzin & Y. S. Lincoln (Eds.), *Strategies of qualitative inquiry* (pp. 184–224). Thousand Oaks, CA: Sage Publications, Inc.

Soloway, I., & Walters, J. (1977). Workin' the corner: The ethics and legality of ethnographic fieldwork among active heroin addicts. In R. S. Weppner (Ed.), *Street ethnography* (pp. 159– 178). Beverly Hills, CA: Sage Publications, Inc.

Soltis, J. F. (1978). *An introduction to the analysis of educational concepts* (2nd ed.). Reading, MA: Addison-Wesley Publishers, Inc.

Spradley, J. P. (1979). *The ethnographic interview.* New York: Holt, Rinehart & Winston.

Spradley, J. P. (1980). *Participant observation.* New York: Holt, Rinehart & Winston.

Stake, R. E. (1973). Measuring what learners learn. In E. R. House (Ed.), *School evaluation.* Berkeley, CA: McCutchon.

Stake, R. E. (1975). *Program evaluation, particularly responsive evaluation.* Occasional Paper Series, No. 5. Kalamazoo, MI, Evaluation Center, Western Michigan University.

Stake, R. E. (1995). *The art of case study research.* Thousand Oaks, CA: Sage Publications, Inc.

Stake, R. E. (1998). Case studies. In N. K. Denzin & Y. S. Lincoln (Eds.), *Strategies of qualitative inquiry* (pp 86–109). Thousand Oaks, CA: Sage Publications, Inc.

Stinger, E. T. (1996). *Action research: A handbook for practitioners.* Thousand Oaks, CA: Sage Publications, Inc.

Stock, W. A., Okun, M. A., Haring, M. J., Miller, W., Kenney, C., & Ceurvorst, R. W. (1982). Rigor in data synthesis: A case study of reliability in meta-analysis. *Educational Researcher, 11* (6), 10–14.

Strauss & Corbin (1998). *Basics of qualitative research* (2nd ed.). Thousand Oaks, CA: Sage Publications, Inc.

Strauss, A., & Corbin, J. (1998). *Basics of qualitative research: Grounded theory procedures and techniques* (2nd ed.). Thousand Oaks, CA: Sage Publications, Inc.

Strickler, F. (1992). Why history? Thinking about the uses of the past. *History Teacher, 25* (3), 293–312.

Stufflebeam, D. L.,& Shinkfield, A. J. (1985). *Systematic evaluation.* Boston: Kluwer-Nijhoff.

Stufflebeam, D. L., Foley, W. J., Gepart, W. J., Guba, E. E., Hammond, R. L., Merriman, H. O., & Provus, M. (1971). *Educational evaluation and decision-making.* Itasca, IL: F. E. Peacock.

Sweetland, R. C., & Keyser, D. J. (Eds.) (1991). *Tests: A comprehensive reference for assessments in psychology, education, and business* (3rd ed.). Kansas City, MO: Test Corporation of America.

Talmage, H. (1982). Evaluation of programs. In H. E. Mitzel (Ed.), *Encyclopedia of educational research* (5th ed.) (pp. 595–610). New York: John Wiley & Sons, Inc.

Tashakkori, A., & Teddlie, C. (1998). *Mixed methodology: Combining qualitative and quantitative approaches.* Applied Social Research Methods Series, *46.* Thousand Oaks, CA: Sage Publications, Inc.

Taylor, S. J. (1987). Observing abuse: Professional ethics and personal morality in field research. *Qualitative Sociology, 10* (3), 288–300.

Tesch, R. (1993). Personal computers in qualitative research, in M. D. LeCompte & M. Preissle, *Ethnography and qualitative design in educational research* (2nd ed.)(pp. 279–314). San Diego: Academic Press.

Thompson, B. (1996). AERA editoral policies regarding statistical significance testing: Three sugested reforms. *Educational Researcher, 25* (2), 26–30.

Tobin, K., & LaMaster, L. U. (1995). Relationships between metaphors, beliefs, and actions in a context of science curriculum change, *Journal of research in science teaching, 32* (3), 225–242.

Tuckman, G. (1998). Historical social science: methodologies, methods, and meanings. In N. K. Denzin & Y. S. Lincoln (Eds.), *Strategies of qualitative inquiry* (pp. 225–260). Thousand Oaks, CA: Sage Publications, Inc.

Tyack, D. B. (1979). The high school as a social service agency: Historical perspectives of current policy issues. *Educational Evaluation and Policy Analysis, 1* (5), 45– 57.

Van Maanen, J. (1988). *Tales of the field: On writing ethnography.* Chicago: The University of Chicago Press.

Van Manen, M. (1990). *Researching lived experience.* New York: State of New York Press.

Viadero, D. (1999a, June 23), New priorities, focus sought for research. *Education Week, XVIII* (41), 1, 36,37.

Viadero, D. (1999b, June 23), What is (and isn't) research? *Education Week, XVIII* (41), pp. 33, 34, 36.

Vierra, A., & Pollock, J. (1992). *Reading educational research* (2nd ed.). Scottsdale, AZ: Gorsuch Scarisbrick Publishers.

Walberg, H. J. (1986). Synthesis of research on teaching. In M. Wittrock (Ed.). *Handbook of research on teaching* (3rd ed.)(pp. 214– 229). New York: Macmillan.

Walker, D. K. (1973). *Sociomotional measures for preschool and kindergarten children.* San Francisco: Jossey-Bass, Inc., Publishers.

Wax, R. H. (1971). *Doing fieldwork: Warnings and advice.* Chicago: The University of Chicago Press.

Webb, E. J., Campbell, D. T., Schwartz, R. D., & Sechrest, L. (2000). *Unobtrusive measures* (Revised Edition). Thousand Oaks, CA: Sage Publications, Inc.

Weitzman, E. A., & Miles, M. B. (1995). *Computer programs for qualitative data analysis: A softwear sourcebook.* Thousand Oaks, CA: Sage Publications, Inc.

Wiersma, W. (2000). *Research methods in education: An introduction* (7th ed.). Boston: Allyn & Bacon, Inc.

Wijnberg, M. H., & Weinger, S. (1998), When dreams wither and resources fail: the social support systems of poor single mothers. *The Journal of Contemporary Human Services, 79* (2), 212–223.

Wilson, S. (1977). The use of ethnographic techniques in educational research. *Review of Educational Research, 47,* 245–265.

Wirt, F. M. (1980). Neoconservatism and national school policy. *Educational Evaluation and Policy Analysis, 2* (6), 5– 18.

Wolcott, H. F. (1973). *The man in the principal's office: An ethnography.* New York: Holt, Rinehart & Winston.

Wolcott, H. F. (1990). *Writing up qualitative research.* Newbury Park, CA: Sage Publications, Inc.

Wolcott, H. F. (1994). *Transforming qualitative data: Description, analysis, and interpretation*. Thousand Oaks, CA: Sage Publications, Inc.

Wolcott, H. F. (1995). *The art of fieldwork*. Walnut Creek, CA: AltaMira.

Worthen, B. R., Sanders, J. R., & Fitzpatrick, J. L. (1997). *Program evaluation: Alternative approaches and practical guidelines* (2nd ed.). New York: Longman.

Yin, R. K. (1994). *Case study research* (2nd ed.) Thousand Oaks, CA: Sage Publications, Inc.

Ysseldyke, J. E., Thurlow, M. L., Christenson, S. L., & Weiss, J. (1987). Time allocated to instruction of mentally retarded, learning disabled, emotionally disturbed, and nonhandicapped students. *The Journal of Special Education, 21*, 43–55.

Author Index

Ahlgren, A., 263, 264
Algozzine, B., 224, 225, 372
Alkin, M. C., 536
Allison, D. B., 353
Altheide, D. L., 411
American Educational Research Association, 195n, 196, 196n
American Psychological Association, 53, 195n, 196, 196n, 367, 576
Anderson, D., 195
Angroisino, M. V., 501n
Antonio, A. L., 4, 443
Aydelotte, W. O., 502, 502n

Babbie, E. R., 258, 270
Backer, T. E., 184
Ball, D. L., 548
Barlow, D. H., 353
Barzun, J., 505, 516
Battistich, V., 242
Bauer, D., 448
Bellack, A., 185
Betts, J. R., 5
Biddle, B. J., 22
Biklen, S. K., 56–69, 398n, 444, 483
Blase, J., 4, 450
Blase, J., 4, 450
Bodner, G. M., 4
Bogdan, R., 37, 135, 398n, 483
Bond, H. M., 98–99
Boraks, N., 442
Boruch, R. F., 198
Boss, M. W., 45–51
Brady, K. L., 368
Brent, G., 378

Brickhous, N., 4
Brown, S. M., 380
Buros, O., 183
Buros Institute of Mental Measures, 184
Burton, O. V., 502n
Buttram, J. L., 539n

Campbell, D. T., 166n, 167, 186, 192, 194, 321, 329, 342, 344
Carnoy, M., 4
Carr, E. H., 505
Carspecken, P. F., 38
Caruso, C., 157n
Casey, K., 414
Cassell, J., 422
Cauley, K. M., 290
Cecil, J. S., 198
Chandler, J., 382
Chang, C., 344
Chaudhry, L. N., 4
Cheong, Y. F., 176
Christenson, S. L., 288, 289
Chun, K. T., 184
Clandinin, D. J., 417, 487n
Clark, D. A., 509
Cobb, S., 184
Cogan, S., 308
Cohen, D. K., 548
Cohen, J., 367
Cohen, S., 500
Colton, D. L., 515
Comrey, A. L., 184
Connelly, F. M., 417, 487n
Cook, T. D., 186, 192, 194, 329, 342, 344
Cooley, V., 5, 78, 79
Cooper, H., 137, 296
Copp, M. A., 411

Corbin, J., 37, 398n, 473, 478n
Cousins, J. B., 551
Cousins, L. H., 5, 489
Crabtree, B. F., 462, 542
Creswell, J. W., 38, 487, 501, 545
Cronbach, L. J., 10
Cross, G. M., 340
Cross, L. H., 340
Cutler, W. W., 510n

Daniel, L. G., 22, 24
Daniel, P. T., 513
Day, M., 98
Dayton, C. M., 173, 174
Delucchi, K. L., 242
Denzin, N. K., 15, 35n, 445n, 478, 501
Dewey, J., 500
Dexter, L., 445n
DiObilda, N., 378
Doherty, R. E., 516n
Doughtery, J., 502n
Doyle, J., 475
Draper, K., 91, 92, 95, 96–97
Driscoll, L. A., 185

Edelsky, C., 91, 92, 95, 96–97
Educational Testing Service (ETS), 183–184
Ehri, L. C., 214
Eisler, R. M., 368
Erickson, F., 16, 36, 411
Esham, K., 448, 455

Fabiano, E., 183
Feldhusen, J. F., 87n
Fielding, N. G., 486n
Figueredo, A. J., 545
Fingerson, L., 418

Finken, L. L., 182, 292
Finnegan, R., 502n
Fisher, R. A. 371, 622–624
Fitzpatrick, J. L., 530, 543n, 547n
Fletcher, J. D., 550
Floyd, J. A., 545
Foster, S. B., 434, 438
Fox, J. E., 479
Franklin, R. D., 353
French, J. R. P., Jr., 184
Frieze, I. H., 272–273

Gamel-McCormick, M. T., 447
Garard, D. L., 4, 88n
Gardiner, P., 505
Gibbons, J. D., 383
Giesne, C., 398n
Giles, C. L., 150
Giordano, F. G., 4
Glaser, B. G., 37, 406, 468
Glaser, E. M., 184
Glass, G. V., 209n, 549
Goldman, B., 183
Goodwin, W. L., 185
Gorden, R., 445n
Gorman, B. S., 353
Gottschalk, L., 505, 513
Graber, E. E., 515
Graff, H. G., 505, 516
Green, J. C., 542
Green, K. E., 172
Greenberg, D., 547n
Griffin, N. L., 182, 292
Guba, E. G., 37, 398n, 490
Gulino, J., 4
Gullickson, A. R., 309
Guskey, T. R., 388
Gutowski, T. W., 92

Hall, E. T., 442n, 455n
Hall, G. S., 510
Halperin, S., 298
Hanley-Maxwell, C., 403
Harding, S., 37n
Harry, B., 98
Hawley, D. E., 550
Hedges, L. V., 137
Henry, G. T., 170n
Hersen, M., 185, 353
Hill, M. R., 510n
Homan, R., 195n
Hopkins, K. D., 209n, 309

Horvat, E. M., 4, 443
Howe, K. R., 195n
Huffman, D., 290
Hunt, S. K., 88n

Iran-Nejad, A., 195n

Jackson, S. E., 297
Jacobs, J. E., 182, 292
Jacobson, J. W., 158
Jacobson, L., 197
Jaeger, R. M., 22, 170n, 177n
Janesick, V. J., 409
Jensen, R., 510n
Johnson, D. T., 195
Johnson, J., 195
Johnson, J. M., 411
Johnson, O. G., 184
Johnson, R. T., 195
Joint Committee on Standards for Educational Evaluation, 530–531, 530n
Jones, H. J., 375
Jordan, L., 224, 225, 372

Kaestle, G. F., 500
Kazdin, A. E., 353
Kelle, U., 486n
Kerlinger, F. N., 8, 13
Keyser, D. J., 184
Kirby, S. N., 4
Kitsantas, A., 341
Kleinman, S., 411
Kraemer, H. C., 177n

LaMaster, L. U., 12, 398, 399, 409
Lambiotte, J. G., 369
Lance, D., 510n
Lather, P., 37, 414
Lawrence, S., 150
Lawrenz, F., 290
LeCompte, M. D., 36, 398n, 411, 486
Lee, R. M., 486n
Lehmann, I. J., 53n, 303, 535n
Lehmann, J. P., 4
Leithwood, K. A., 551
Lesko, N., 95
Levin, H. M., 549, 551
Lincoln, Y. S., 15, 35n, 37, 398n, 414, 422, 490
Lippert, L., 88n

Lloyd, J. M., 492
Locke, L. F., 581n
Lofland, J., 445n, 455n
Lofland, L. H., 445n, 455n
Lomask, M., 501n
Luck, J. S., 429, 480
Lustberg, R. S., 294

Maddox, J., 184
Malinowski, B., 94, 430
Mao, S., 344
Marascuilo, L. A., 383
Marcus, G. E., 411
Marshall, C., 37, 397, 398n, 421, 464
Martens, M. L., 4
Marton, F., 468
Mason, R. O., 16, 411, 489
Maxwell, D. M., 4
McAdoo, H. P., 217
McCurdy, D., 474, 475
McKinney, C. W., 375
McMillan, J. H., 186, 248, 287, 288
McSweeney, M., 383
Medina, M., Jr., 512
Mehrens, W. A., 53n, 303, 535n
Meister, G. R., 549
Messick, S., 240
Meyer, R. H., 547n
Miles, M. B., 484, 486n
Miller, D. C., 183
Miller, W. L., 462, 542
Millroy, W. L.
Minger, M., 290
Mitchell, D., 183
Mitchell, D. E., 501, 518
Montero-Sieburth, M., 419
Morgan, D. L., 455n
Moses, M. S., 195n
Motta, R., 294
Mounts, N. S., 313
Moustakas, C., 36, 445n
Mulick, J. A., 158
Murdock, T. B., 233
Murray, F. B., 290

Naccari, N., 294
National Center for Education Statistics, 215

Nolbit, G. W., 439
Nye, B., 296

Oja, S. N., 20
Olkin, I., 137

Page, R. C., 382
Parrott, S., 474
Patton, M. Q., 400, 445n, 446, 477, 481, 543n
Paynton, S. T., 88n
Pearson, P. D., 195n
Pelto, G. H., 445n, 474n
Pelto, P. J., 445n, 474n
Perez, M., 419
Peshkin, A., 24, 398n
Philipsen, M., 467
Piele, P. K., 550
Pogoloff, S. M., 403
Pollock, J., 477
Popham, W. J., 205
Popper, K. R., 9
Potter, D. M., 516
Pounder, D. G., 289
Preissle, J., 36, 398n
Preissle, M., 486n
Presser, S., 309
Punch, M., 422

Quantz, R. A., 93, 94
Quist, F., 98

Rachal, J. R., 4
Rallis, S. F., 38
Ramanathan, A. K., 431, 436, 439
Raudenbusch, S. W., 176
Reed, J. S., 470, 472
Resnick, L. B., 5
Reyes, P., 289
Reynolds, P., 195n
Rice, J. K., 4
Richardson, L., 487, 490, 491n
Riemer, J. W., 91
Robinson, J. P., 184
Roeser, T. D., 87n
Romano, J. L., 5
Roopnarine, J. L., 313
Rosenthal, R., 177, 197
Rosnow, R. L., 177
Rossman, G. B., 38, 397, 398n
Rossman, G. R., 37, 421, 462

Rowan, B., 176
Rowntree, J. S., 177, 179

Sacken, D. M., 512
Samson, G. E., 139n
Sanders, J. R., 530, 543n, 547n
Saracho, O. N., 173, 174
Sarmiento, R. F., 133
Sax, G., 269
Schaps, E., 242
Schatzman, L., 432, 445n, 455n
Schoen, David, 417
Schuler, R. S., 297
Schumacher, S., 430, 432–433, 440, 442, 448, 455
Schuman, H., 309
Schutt, R. K., 305
Schwab, R. L., 297
Schwandt, T. A., 42, 411
Schwartz, A. A., 158
Scott, A. F., 514, 516
Seashore, H. G., 227
Sechrest, L., 545
Seidman, I. E., 36, 445n
Shaver, P., 184
Shen, J., 5, 78, 79
Shepard, L. A., 240
Sherman, R. R., 499n
Shkolnik, J. L., 5
Shulman, L. S., 10
Sidani, L., 545
Siegel, S., 383
Silverman, J. J., 581n
Slavin, R. E., 138, 139, 216
Smith, H. G., 133
Smith, J. K., 414
Smith, K., 91, 92, 95, 96–97
Smith, L. M., 421, 422, 501
Smith, N. L., 549
Smulyan, L., 20
Snyder, H. M., 272–273
Soderstrom, I., 232
Solomon, D., 242
Soloway, I., 420
Soltis, J. F., 506, 507
Spirduso, W. W., 581n
Spooner, F., 224, 225, 372
Spooner, M., 224, 225, 372
Spradley, J. P., 409, 422, 442n, 444n, 445n, 474, 475
Stake, R. E., 36, 398n, 490, 539–540

Stanley, J. C., 166n, 167, 186, 321, 329
Stevens, J., 302
Stinger, E. T., 20
Strachan, G., 516
Strauss, A. L., 37, 398n, 432, 445n, 455n, 473, 478n
Strauss, L. L., 37, 406, 468
Strickler, F., 499
Strykowski, B., 139n
Stufflebeam, D. L., 536
Suppes, P., 10
Sutton, A., 232
Sweetland, R. C., 184

Talmage, H., 582
Tashakkori, A., 16, 542, 543n, 544n
Taylor, M. C., 45–51
Taylor, S., 135
Taylor, S. J., 420
Teddlie, C., 16, 542, 543n, 544n
Tesch, R., 486n
Thielman, S., 177n
Thompson, B., 24
Thurlow, M. L., 288, 289
Thurston, J. R., 87n
Tipps, R. S., 479
Tobin, K., 12, 398, 399, 409
Tuckman, G., 504
Tyack, D. B., 79

Urban, Wayne J., 98, 99
Valentin, J. S., 4
Valentine, J. C., 296
Van Houton, R., 352
Van Maanen, J., 487
Van Manen, M., 36
Vasta, R., 133
Viadero, D., 5, 22
Vierra, A., 477

Walberg, H. J., 6, 7, 139n, 380
Walker, D. K., 184
Walters, J., 420
Watson, M. S., 242
Wax, R. H., 405
Webb, R. B., 499n
Weinger, S., 80
Weinstein, T., 139n
Weiss, J., 288, 289
Weitzman, E. A., 484,

486*n*
Westbury, I., 226
Wheatley, P., 500
Whitney-Thomas, J., 403
Wijnberg, M. H., 80
Wilce, L. S., 214
Wilson, S., 440
Wirt, F. M., 519
Wiseman, M., 547*n*

Wolcott, H. F., 36, 417
Wood, W. M., 491
Worthen, B. R., 530, 543*n*,
    547*n*
Wright, J. D., 182, 292

Yates, F., 371, 622–624
Yin, R. K., 36, 490
Ysseldyke, J. E., 288, 289

Yu, M., 431, 436, 439

Zimmerman, B. J., 341
Zollers, N. J., 431, 436, 439

Subject Index

A-B-A-B single-subject
 design, 351–352
A-B-A designs, 350–352
A-B designs, 349–350
Ability grouping, 91
Ability tests, 252
Abstracting, 130–131
Abstractions, synthesized,
 94
Abstracts, 44
 education-related,
 116–117
Academic discipline, 506
Accuracy standards, 531
Achievement tests, 254
ACT (American College
 Testing Program), 612
Action research, 20
Adequacy standards, in
 literature reviews,
 139–140
Adversary-oriented evalua-
 tion approaches, 532
Affective instruments,
 256
Agreement, coefficient of,
 247
Alpha level, 365
AltaVista, 148
Alternative assessments, 41,
 254–256
American Educational
 Research Association,
 196
American Psychological
 Association (APA), 116,
 196, 367
 publication manual of, 576
American Statistics Index,
 118
Analogy, 466

Analysis
 of data, 138
 discovery, 465–466
 inductive, 462–464
 interim, 466, 467
 of nonverbal communica-
 tion, 454–455
 policy, 20
 topics of, 500–502
Analysis of covariance
 (ANCOVA), 380–382
Analysis of variance
 (ANOVA), 373–382. *See
 also* ANOVA interaction;
 Factorial analysis of
 variance (ANOVA);
 Multivariate analysis of
 variance (MANOVA)
Analytical conclusions,
 518
Analytical explanations,
 517
Analytical generalizations,
 504
Analytical interpretations,
 504–505
Analytical premises, 418
Analytical research, 38,
 499–507
 approaches to,
 505–506
 types of sources for, 503
 uses of, 517–519
Analytical styles, 462–464
Annual reviews, 113
Anonymity, in fieldwork,
 421–422
ANOVA interaction, 380
APA Web page, 158
A posteriori test, 374
Appearance, interviewer, 270

Appendices
 methodological, 514
 in research proposals,
 576–577, 580–581
Applied research, 19
A priori tests, 376
Aptitude tests, 252–254
Artifact collections, 451–453
 analysis and interpretation
 of, 453
Artifacts, 43
 types of, 451–453
AskERIC, 114
Assessments
 performance-based, 255
 portfolio, 255–256
Assigned (attribute) vari-
 ables, 322
Attenuation, 300
Attitude inventories,
 256–257
Attrition, internal validity
 and, 334
Audibility, 413
Audience presence, 487
Audiences, 539
Audio conferencing, 153
Authentic alternative assess-
 ments, 41
Authenticity, 415
 in qualitative research
 design, 414–415
Authentic narrative,
 416–417
Authorial presence, 487
Average, 214

Bar graphs, 211–212
Baseline, 348–349. *See also*
 Multiple-baseline
 designs

Basic research, 17–18
Behavioral objectives, 533–534
Beta weights, 294
Bias, 170
    controlling, 186
    in interviews, 268
    in observational research, 275
    researcher, 412
    in survey responses, 309
    of witnesses, 513
Biased questionnaire items, 259–260
Bibliographies, historical, 508
Bibliography of American Educational History, 508
Bimodal distribution, 217
Biography, 501
Bivariate correlational studies, 291–292
Bond, Horace Mann, 98, 99
Bond Papers, 98, 99
Bonferrori technique, 374
Box-and-whisker plot, 224, 226
BRS database, 127
Buckley Amendment, 199
Business Education Index, 117

Career and life history interviews, 444–445
Caring, in fieldwork, 422
Case studies, 36–37, 419
Case study analysis, 548
Case study design, 38, 330
    in qualitative research design, 398–399
Case study research, 490
Case type, sampling by, 403–404
Categorical (classificatory) measurement, 208
Categorical variable, 82
Categories
    developing topics as, 473
    emic and etic, 474–475
    ordering for patterns, 479–480
    predetermined, 473–474
Causal-comparative design, 310
Causal explanations, 517

Causal observations, 77
Causation, correlation and, 298–299
CD-ROMs, 113
Ceiling effect, 252
Cells, 377
Center for Education Reform, 158
Central tendency
    measures of, 214–219, 604–606
    relationships among measures of, 218–219
"Chain of evidence," 413
Charter School Research Project, 158
Checklist questionnaire items, 264–265
Chicago Manual of Style, 581
Child Development Abstracts and Bibliography, 117
Chi-square, 383, 385, 615–617
    critical values of, 624
Citation, of Internet sources, 158
Citation indexes, 118
Classification, of references, 131
Closed form questionnaire items, 260–261
Cluster sampling, 173
Code, writing, 469
Code-and-retrieve programs, 484–485
Code-based theory-building programs, 485
Code transcripts, 472
Coding, 466–468
Coefficient of determination, 301
Coefficient of multiple correlation, 295
Coercion, in research, 198
Cohort studies, 284
College Entrance Examination Boards (CEEB), 611
"Committed relativism," 422
Communication, external, 452
Comparative inquiry, 33–34

Comparative research, 287–291
    standards of adequacy in, 314
Comparison group, 325
Compensatory rivalry, 192
Complementary mixed methods, 543
Completed Research in Health, Physical Education and Recreation Including International Sources, 117
Complete observers, 273, 435
Comprehensive Dissertation Index, 118
Comprehensive sampling, 401
Computer data management techniques, 484–486
Computer searches, 110
    conducting, 124–129
    steps for conducting, 119–131
Computer search plan, 125, 126
Concept analysis, 38, 499
Conceptual analysis, 506
Conceptual network-building programs, 485
Conclusions
    in educational research, 13
    framework for reporting, 79–80
Concomitant variable, 381
Concurrent evidence, 242
Condensed problem statement, 95
Conditions analysis, 507
Conferencing, Internet, 153
Confidence, level of, 301
Confidence interval (CI), 362
Confidence limits, 362
Confidentiality
    in fieldwork, 421–422
    in interviews, 268
    in research, 198
Confirmation activities, 413–414
Constant comparison, 468
Constructionism, 15

Construct irrelevant variance, 240
Constructivist philosophy, 396
Constructs, in deductive logic, 82
Construct underrepresentation, 240
Construct validity, 194
Consumer-oriented evaluation approaches, 532
Content-related evidence, 534
Context-bound generalizations, 16
Context of a study, 488
Context sensitivity, 396–397
Contingency coefficient, 384
Contingency questions, 265–266
Contingency table, 384
Continuous (measured) variable, 82
Continuous observation, 274
Control (comparison) group, 325
Control group design, 336–337, 341
Control group interrupted time-series design, 345–347
Controlled vocabulary, 147
Controversial questions, 449
Convenience sampling, 169, 172, 175
Convergent evidence, 242
Conversation interviews, informal, 443
Correlation, causation and, 298–299
Correlational designs, 15
Correlational research, 34, 177, 291–304
interpreting, 296–304
standards of adequacy in, 314
Correlation coefficients, 230–233
size of, 301–304
Correlation matrix, 233
Correlations
spurious, 299–301
strength and direction of, 231

Corroboration activities, 413–414
Cost analysis, 548–551
Cost-benefit (CB) analysis, 549–550
Cost-effectiveness (CE) analysis, 550
Cost-feasibility (CF) analysis, 550–551
Cost-utility (CU) analysis, 550
Counterbalancing of instruments, 250
Covariate (concomitant) variable, 381
Credibility, defined, 166
Credibility standards, of historical studies, 519–521
Criterion-referenced instruments, 534
Criterion-referenced interpretation, 252
Criterion-related evidence, 242
Criterion variable, 83, 293
Critical reflexivity, 414
Critical studies, 37–38, 419, 490
Criticism
external, 511–512
internal, 512–513
of literature, 140
methodological, 133
Cronbach Alpha, 247
Cross-analyses, logical, 480
Cross-sectional studies, 284
Crystallization, 463
Cultural portraits, 489–490
Culture. *See* Ethnography
Current Index to Journals in Education (CIJE), 115, 121
Current issues, 100
Curvilinear relationships, 230
Cut-and-file technique, 483

Data
discrepant, 410, 418–419
as evidence, 12
gauging trustworthiness of, 477–478

graphic portrayals of, 210–214
mechanically recorded, 410
organizing system for, 468–472
topic generation from, 469
Data analysis, 14, 138, 575–576. *See also* Qualitative data analysis
Data analysis strategies, 416
Database selection, 110, 121
Database services, 130
Data collection, 14, 138. *See also* Data collection techniques; Prolonged data collection
prolonged, 437, 439
in qualitative research design, 406
via surveys, 306
Data collection and analysis strategies, 405–407
Data collection methods, 180
Data collection strategies, 416, 579–580
focus of, 431
primary, 428
Data collection techniques, 39–43, 180–185, 285. *See also* Qualitative data collection techniques; Quantitative data collection techniques
quantitative, 237–281
strengths and weaknesses of, 276
Data evaluation, 138
Data filing system, developing, 482–483
Data management, techniques of, 482–486
Data organization, coding topics in, 466–468
Data scanning, 466
Data segments, 468
Datasets, 155, 157
Data sources, 52
multiple, 440
Deception
in fieldwork, 422
in research, 197

Decision-oriented evaluation, 532, 536–538
"Decision-trail," 413
Decisive evidence, 516
Deductions from theory, 77
Deductive logic
    constructs and, 82
    operational definitions and, 84
    variables and, 82–84
Deductive reasoning, 12
Degrees of freedom, 370
Delimiting variables, 169
Demand characteristics, 192
Demographic questions, 449
Dependent samples *t*-test, 370, 620–621
Dependent variables, 83, 225
Descriptions, narrative, 93–94
Descriptive inquiry, 33
Descriptive research, 283–286, 289
    standards of adequacy in, 314
Descriptive research questions, 87
Descriptive statistics, 204–236
    calculations for, 604–621
    defined, 206
    graphic portrayals of data in, 210–214
    measures of central tendency in, 214–219
    measures of relationship in, 227–233
Descriptors, low-inference, 409
Design limitations, 576, 580
Design validity, 167–169
Development, of instruments, 185
Developmental mixed methods, 543
Developmental studies, 284
Diagrams, integrative, 480
DIALOG database, 127
Dichotomous-response questions, 446, 448
Dictionary of Behavioral Assessment Techniques, 185

Difference questions, 87–88, 287
Differential analysis, 507
Diffusion of treatment, 190–191, 346
    validity and, 338
Digest of Educational Statistics, 118
Directories of membership, 130
Directory of Unpublished Experimental Mental Measures, 183
Discipline, 17
Disciplined inquiry, 10–11
Disciplined subjectivity, 16
Discovery analysis, 465–466
Discrepant data, 418–419
Discrepant evidence, evaluating, 478
Discriminant evidence, 242
Disproportionate sampling, 172
Dissertation Abstracts International, 118
Documentary research style, 36
Documents, 42–43, 451–453
    historical, 502–503
    location of, 510
Dogpile, 150
Domain-referenced tests, 252
Double-barrelled questions, 259
Duncan's new multiple range test, 374
Duration recording, 274

Ecological external validity, 193–195
Ecological threats to validity, 328–329
Editing analytical style, 462
Education
    as a field of inquiry, 21–25
    public nature of, 23
Education Abstracts Information, 115
Educational Administration Abstracts, 117
Educational concepts, analysis of, 506–507, 517–518
Educational context, 78–79

Educational evaluation, benefits and limitations of, 551–553
Educational events, analysis of, 507–517
Educational ideas, roots of, 518–519
Educational Index, 116
Educational practice, 529
Educational programs, appraising, 552
Educational Psychology Review, 113
Educational research, 2–28. *See also* Research
    characteristics of, 11–14
    as disciplined inquiry, 10–11
    importance of, 5–7
    on the Internet, 145–162
    limitations of, 22–24
    relevance of, 24–25
    in the twenty-first century, 3–11
Educational significance, 367
Educational Testing Service (ETS), 183
Educational theories, 19
Educational web sites, 153–155
Education Week, 3
Educators, research influences on, 24
Effect magnitude measures, 367
Effect size (ES), 137
    reporting of, 368
Effect size index, 367–368
Electronic resources, 108–109
Elite interviews, 445
Email, 152
Emergent design, 15, 398, 420, 539
Emic categories, 474–475
Empiricism, in educational research, 12
Empowerment, in fieldwork, 422
Encoding, 487
Encyclopedias, 113–114

Enduring educational practice, knowledge of, 99–100

Equivalence, coefficient of, 246

Equivalence and stability, reliability coefficient of, 246

ERIC (Educational Resources Information Center), 114, 115–116

ERIC access points, 128

ERIC Clearinghouses, 127, 155, 156, 184

ERIC database, 146–147

ERIC descriptors and terms, 124

ERIC Digests, 114

ERIC Document Microfiche Collection, 116

ERIC Educational Listserv Archive, 152

ERIC *Thesaurus*, 129

Erosion measures, 455

Error, 244. *See also* Sampling error; Standard error
in hypothesis testing, 365
Type I and Type II, 365

Ethical decisions, recording of, 413

Ethics
in qualitative research design, 420–422
in quantitative research design, 195–200

Ethnographic interviews, 135

Ethnographic literature review, 135

Ethnographic problem statements/questions, 98

Ethnographic studies, 436, 489

Ethnography, 16, 35–36

Etic categories, 474–475

ETS Test Collection, 183–184

Evaluating Web Sites for Educational Uses: Bibliography and Checklist, 157

Evaluation. *See also* Evaluation research
decision-oriented, 536–538
formative and summative, 529–530
of instruments, 183–185
of Internet sources, 155–157
naturalistic/participant, 538–541
objectives-oriented, 533–536
purposes and roles of, 528
of qualitative research, 69–70
of quantitative research, 53–55

Evaluation approach, defined, 532

Evaluation instruments, selecting, 534–535

Evaluation proposals, credibility of, 553–554

Evaluation research, 19–21, 527, 528–531
approaches to evaluation, 531–541
benefits and limitations of, 551–553
credibility in, 553–554
defined, 528–529
judging the quality of, 530–531
mixed methods evaluations, 541–545
policy analysis, 545–551

Evaluation results, interpreting, 535–536

Evaluators
naturalistic, 541
role of, 540–541

Evidence
based on internal structure, 241
based on relations to other variables, 241–242
based on response processes, 241
based on test content, 240–241

evaluating negative or discrepant, 478
searching for factual, 503–504

Evocative representation, 491

Exceptional Child Education Resources (ECER), 117

Exhaustive searches, 120

Expansion mixed methods, 543

Experimental (treatment) group, 325

Experimental designs. *See* Pre-experimental design; Quasi-experimental designs; True experimental designs

Experimental modes of inquiry, 32–33

Experimental research, 320–347
characteristics of, 321–323
planning, 324–326
strengths and limitations of, 323–324

Experimental treatments, organization by, 133–134

Experimental variable, 83

Experimenter effects, 191, 338
internal validity and, 334

Experiments
defined, 320–321
external validity of, 327–329
internal validity of, 326–327

Expertise-oriented evaluation approaches, 532

Explanations
analytical, 517
in educational research, 12
plausibility of, 480–482

Exploratory research, 101

Exploratory studies, 399

Ex post facto designs, 88, 187

Ex post facto inquiry, 34–35

Ex post facto research, 310–313
standards of adequacy in, 315

Extension of findings, in qualitative research design, 414–419
External communication, 452
External criticism, 511–512
External validity, 167, 193–195
    of experiments, 327–329
    threats to, 328
Extraneous variables, 168
Eyewitness accounts, 504

Face-to-face research, 428
Face validity, 241
Factorial analysis of variance (ANOVA), 376–380
Facts, 504
    assessment of, 520
    as the basis for generalizations, 515
Factual evidence, search for, 503–504
Fairness, in fieldwork, 422
Family Educational Rights and Privacy Act of 1974, 199
Feasibility standards, 531
FedStats, 158
Field, discovery analysis in, 465–466. *See also* Fieldwork
Field entry
    as a qualitative strategy, 431–436
    standards of adequacy for, 456
Field experiments, 547
Field journal, 413
Field log, 413
Field mapping, for qualitative research, 432–433
Field notes, 442
    confidentiality of, 421–422
Field observations, 42, 454
    corroborating, 440–441
    salient, 441–442
Field records, qualitative, 92–93
Field research, 396
Field residence, 437

Fieldwork
    ethical dilemmas in, 420–421
    formal authorization for, 432
    in qualitative research design, 408
    research ethics in, 421–422
Field workers, 428
File card technique, 483–484
Film ethnography, 43
Financial constraints, 179
Findings
    formal corroboration of, 413–414
    interpreting, 14
FirstSearch, 115
Fisher's LSD test, 374
Flow charts, 480
Focused synthesis, 547
Focus group interviews (FGIs), 455
Follow-up, on surveys, 307–309
Follow-up test, 374
Foreshadowed problems, 94–95, 429–431, 578
Formal evaluation, 19
Formal problem statements, 78–80
Format, of a research proposal, 581–582
Formative evaluation, 529
Frequency-count recording, 274
Frequency distribution, 210–211
Frequency polygons, 212–214
F statistic (ratio), 373, 375, 379
Full participant role, 435
Fundamental (pure) research, 17

Generalizability, 17, 100
Generalizations, 515–517
    analytical, 504
    assessment of, 520
    context-free and context-bound, 16

Generalizing across a population, 194
Generic analysis, 506–507
Goals, of qualitative research, 396
Government documents, 510
Government documents indexes, 117–118
Government web sites, 153
Graphs
    bar, 211–212
    interpreting, 291
"Grounded theory," 37, 399, 492
Grounded theory studies, 419, 490
Group differences, using analysis of covariance (ANCOVA) to adjust for, 382
Guide to Historical Literature, A, 508

Handbook for Measurement and Evaluation in Early Childhood Education, 185
Handbook of Research Design and Social Measurement, 183
Handbooks, 114
Hawthorne effect, 192, 193, 194, 199
High-inference observations, 273
Histograms, 211–212, 214
Historian's Handbook: A Descriptive Guide to Reference Works, 508
Historical analysis, 38–39, 507–517
Historical mindedness, 513
Historical problem statements/questions, 98, 99
Historical research, 499, 519
    traditional, 505
Historical researchers, 135
Historical studies, credibility standards of, 519–521
Historical topics, analysis of, 500
Historiography, 500
History, internal validity and, 186–187

Holistic approach, 538
Holistic context, 488
Holistic emphasis, 432
Home pages, qualitative data analysis, 486
HotBot, 151
Human subjects, in educational research, 22–23. *See also* Subjects
Hyperlinks, 150
Hypotheses, 54. *See also* Research hypotheses
 defined, 363
 standards for, 89–90
Hypothesis testing, errors in, 365

If-then logic, 89
Immersion/crystallization analytical style, 463
Implementation evaluation, 537
Independent samples, 370
Independent samples chi-square test, 384
Independent samples *t*-test, 370, 372, 617–619
Independent variables, 83, 225
In-depth interviews, 42
 standards of adequacy for, 456
Indexes, education-related, 116–117
Index to Tests Used in Educational Dissertations, 183
Inductive analysis, 462–464, 580
Inductive logic
 of narrative descriptions, 93–94
 of qualitative field records, 92–93
 of synthesized abstractions, 94
Inductive reasoning, 12–13, 91, 539
Inferences, types of, 240
Inferential statistics, 207, 358–392
 analysis of variance in, 373–382

calculations for, 604–621
level of significance in, 364–368
logic of, 359–363
multivariate analyses in, 384–388
nonparametric tests in, 382–384
null hypothesis in, 363–364
t-test in, 368–373
Informal conversation interviews, 443
Informal documents, 451
Informants, information-rich, 401
Informant selection, 416
Informed consent, 197–198
 as a dialogue, 421
Input evaluation, 537
Inquiry. *See also* Modes of inquiry
 disciplined, 7–8, 10–11
 education as a field of, 21–25
 interactive, 35–38
 noninteractive, 38–39
 scientific, 7–9
Insider-observer role, 435, 436
Institutional records, 452
Instructions, for surveys, 306
Instrumentation, 189–190, 575
Instruments, 52. *See also* Evaluation instruments
 appropriateness of, 249
 counterbalancing of, 250
 developing, 185
 noncognitive, 256, 257
 sources for locating and evaluating, 183–185
Instruments sections of studies, 182
Integrative diagrams, 480
Intellectual craftsmanship, 464
Intelligence tests, 252
Interaction, 379
Interactive inquiry, 35–38
Interactive mixed methods, 543

Interactive modes of inquiry, 35
Interactive qualitative research, 395
Interactive research roles, 435
Interactive strategies, 396
Intercorrelation matrix, 231
Interdisciplinary field of inquiry, 21–22
Interest inventories, 256–257
Interim analysis, 466, 467
Internal consistency, 246–247
Internal criticism, 512–513
Internal structure, evidence based on, 241
Internal validity, 167
 of design, 186–193
 of experiments, 326–327
 of pre-experimental designs, 331
 of quasi-experimental designs, 347
 threats to, 327, 327
 of true experimental designs, 337
Internet, 113
 defined, 146
 educational research on, 145–162
 research strategy for, 148–153
 scholarly communication via, 152–153
 strengths and weaknesses of, 146–148
Internet datasets, 155, 157
Internet research, known locations for, 153
Internet searches, 127, 158–159
 choosing tools for, 148–152
Internet sources, evaluating and citing, 155–158
Internet subject directories, 148–149
Interpersonal subjectivity, in qualitative research, 411–412
Interpretations
 analytical, 504–505
 of data, 138, 140

Interpretative biography, 501
Interpretative historians, 506
Interquartile range, 221
Inter-rater reliability, 247
Inter-university Consortium
    for Political and Social
    Research (ICPSR), 155
Interval measurement, 208
Interval recording, 274
Interviewees, selecting,
    433–434
Interview elaborations, 451
Interviewer characteristics,
    effect of, 269–270
Interviewer's Manual (Babbie),
    270
Interviewers
    interactive styles of,
        449
    role of, 435
    training of, 272
Interview guide approach,
    444
Interview guide field-testing,
    446
Interview logistics, 449
Interview probes, 448–449
Interview procedure,
    272–273
Interview questions
    order of, 449
    types of, 268–269, 446
Interviews
    in-depth, 42, 93,
        443–451
    oral, 500–501
    participant language in,
        409
    protocol for, 447
    qualitative, 548
    structured, 40
    types of, 443–445
Interview schedules,
    267–271
    interview protocol and,
        270–271
    preparing the interview
        and, 268–270
Interview summaries, 465
Interview transcripts,
    449–451
Inverse relationships, 229
Investigator responsibility,
    198

IQ scores, 611
IQ tests, 227

John Henry effect, 192
Joint Committee on
    Standards for
    Educational Evaluation,
    530
Journal articles, 131
Judgmental sampling,
    175–176
Justification, of qualitative
    research design,
    399–400

Key-informant interviews,
    444
Key informants, information-
    rich, 401
Keyword searching, 115
Kinesics, 454
Kuder-Richardson (K-R)
    formula, 247

Large-scale experimental
    evaluations, 547–548
Large-scale testing programs,
    548
Latent variable modeling,
    296
Leading questions, 269,
    448
Legal considerations, in
    quantitative research
    design, 199–200
Legal researchers, 136
Letter of transmittal, 307,
    308
Level of confidence, 301
Level of significance, 369
    in inferential statistics,
        364–368
    interpreting, 365–368
Libweb, 153
Life histories. *See* Career
    and life history inter-
    views
Likert scale, 262–263
Limited response questions,
    268–269
LISREL modeling, 296
Listening
    in fieldwork, 439–440
    intensive, 437–440

Literature
    abstracting, 130–131
    alternative presentations
        of, 136–137
    criticism of, 132–134
    related, 77–78
Literature reviews, 14,
    51–52, 54, 107–144,
    574, 578. *See also*
    Computer searches;
    Primary literature;
    Secondary literature
    abstracting and organizing
        references in, 130–131
    continuous, 136
    functions of, 108–112
    meta-analysis, 137–139
    organizing, 132
    in qualitative research,
        134–137
    quantitative research and,
        132–134
    sources for, 111–119
    standards of adequacy in,
        139–140
    steps in, 110–112
Literature selection,
    139–140
Logic. *See also* Deductive
    logic; Inductive logic;
    Inferential statistics
Logical cross-analyses, 480
Logical positivism, 15
Logical reasoning, 12
Longitudinal studies, 284
Low-inference descriptors,
    409
Low-inference observations,
    273

Macro approach to policy
    analysis, 546
Mailing lists, Internet, 152
Main (simple) effects, 378
Manipulated variables, 83,
    322
Manual data management
    techniques, 483–484
Maturation, 190
    internal validity and, 333,
        334, 343–344
Maturation effects, 344
Maximum variation sam-
    pling, 402–403

Meaning. *See also* "Pool of meanings"
  building patterns of, 477
  mutual, 407
  participant, 430, 443
  patterns of, 476
  recurring, 466
Mean of means, 362
Means, 215–216. *See also* Analysis of variance (ANOVA); *t*-test
  calculating, 604–605
Measurable objectives, selecting, 533–534
Measured variable, 82
Measurement. *See also* Effect magnitude measures
  of central tendency, 214–219, 604–606
  of relationship, 227–233
  of variability, 219–227
Measurement error
  in inferential statistics, 360–363
  sources of, 244
Measurement reliability, in single-subject designs, 348
Measurement scales, 207–209
Measures for Psychological Assessment, 184
Measures of association, 367
Measures of Social Psychological Attitudes, 184
Median, 216–217
  calculating, 605–606
Median-split technique, 217
Mediated on-line searches, 127
Member checking, 410
Mental Measurements Yearbooks, 181, 184, 534
Meta-analysis literature reviews, 137–139
Metacrawler, 150
Metaphor, 465
Metasearch engines, 148, 149, 150–151
Methodological advancement, 100
Methodological criticism, 132–133

Methodological difficulties, 23–24
Methodology, 52, 54
Micro approach to policy analysis, 546
Microsoft Internet Explorer, 152
Mirrors for Behavior III: An Anthology of Observation Instruments, 184
Mixed methods studies, 541–545
  issues in, 544–545
Mode, 217
  calculating, 606
Modes of inquiry, 30–31. *See also* Inquiry
  experimental, 32–33
  nonexperimental, 33–35
  qualitative, 35–39
  quantitative, 31–35
Multifactor aptitude tests, 253
Multimethod strategies, 428–429, 438
  in qualitative research design, 408–409
Multiple-baseline designs, 352–353
Multiple-baselines across behavior design, 352
Multiple-baselines across individuals design, 353
Multiple-baselines across situations design, 353
Multiple comparison tests, 374
Multiple correlation research, 297
Multiple data sources, 440
Multiple realities, 539
Multiple regression, 294
Multiple regression analysis, 296
Multiple treatment inference, 328
Multiplicity of data, 539
Multisite evaluation, 547
Multivariate analogs, 387
Multivariate analyses, 384–388

Multivariate analysis of variance (MANOVA), 387–388

Narrative
  authentic, 416–417
  framing, 488–489
Narrative descriptions, 93–94
Narrative reviews, 139
Narrative structure, 489–492
  variations in, 486–487
National Assessment of Educational Progress program, 548
National Research Act of 1974, 199
National Science Foundation, 6
Naturalistic context, 488
Naturalistic generalizations, 490
Naturalistic/participant evaluation, 532, 538–541
Needs assessment, 536–537
Negative (inverse) relationships, 229
Negative cases, 410
Negative correlation, 34
Negative data, 418–419
Negative evidence, evaluating, 478
Negatively skewed distributions, 218
Negative questionnaire items, 259
Netscape Navigator, 152
Network (snowball) sampling, 403
Newman-Keuls test, 374
Newsgroups, Internet, 152
News readers, 152
Nominal (categorical) measurement, 208
Noncognitive instruments, 256, 257
Noneducational policy groups, 5
Nonequivalent groups posttest-only design, 333–335
Nonequivalent groups pretest-posttest design, 342–344

Nonexperimental modes of inquiry, 33–35
Nonexperimental research, relationships in, 286–287
Nonexperimental research design, 282–318
Noninteractive inquiry, 38–39
Nonparametric tests, 382–384
Nonprobability sampling, 173–177
Nonproportional sampling, 172
Nonreactive techniques, 41
Nonresponse, to surveys, 309
Nonverbal communication, analysis of, 454–455
Nonverbal cues, 439
Normal curve, 213, 227
Normal Curve Equivalent (NCE), 611
Normal distribution, 218
calculating, 609–610
Norm group, 250, 252
Norm-referenced interpretation, 251–252
Notation system, for pre-experimental designs, 329
Notes
interview, 450
organizing, 110
Note taking, during interviews, 271
Novelty effect, 192
NSSE Yearbooks, 114
Null hypothesis, 363–364

Objectives
defining for questionnaires, 258
of surveys, 305–306
Objectives-oriented evaluation, 532, 533–536
Objectives-oriented evaluation approaches, 532
Objectivity, in educational research, 11
Objects, 453
Observational units, defining, 274

Observations, 84. *See also* Participant observation
casual, 77
field, 42
intensive, 437–440
recording, 274–275
structured, 40
Observation schedules, 271–275
Observation summaries, 465
"Observer comments," 465
Observers
role of, 273
training of, 275
Official documents, 451–453
One-group posttest-only design, 330
One-group pretest-posttest design, 330–333
One-tailed test of significance, 370
One-way analysis of variance, 373–374
On-line searches, mediated, 127
On-site participant observation, 437
Open-ended interviews, standardized, 444
Open-form questionnaire items, 260–261
Operational definitions, in deductive logic, 84
Opportunity costs, 546
Oral history, 500–501
Oral testimonies, 502–503, 511, 512
Ordinal measurement, 208
Organization, of references, 131
Outcome evaluation, 537
"Outlier" data, 301, 302

Panel studies, 284
Paper-and-pencil tests, 40, 250–256
Parametric procedures, 382, 383
Parent Teacher Associations, 5
Participant language
in interviews, 409
presentation of, 488–489

Participant meanings, 94, 443
discovering, 430
Participant observation, 41–42, 437–443
standards of adequacy for, 456
Participant observation grid, 441
Participant observer role, 435
Participant researchers, 410
role of, 435, 436
Participant review, 410, 421
Path analysis, 296
Patterns, 137
ordering categories for, 479–480
in qualitative data analysis, 476–482
Pattern-seeking, 476–477
techniques of, 477–478
Pearson correlation coefficient
critical values for, 623
Pearson product-moment correlation coefficient (Pearson *r*), 230–232, 612–614
critical values for, 623
Peer debriefer, 412
Percentile rank, 222
Percentiles, 227
Performance-based assessments, 255
Periodicity, 171
Personal documents, 451
Personal experiences/insights, 78
Personality tests, 256
Personnel files, 452
Phenomenological interviews, 445
Phenomenological studies, 36, 419, 489–490
Phi coefficient, 384
Physical Education Index, 117
Pilot testing, 307
of an instrument, 185
Planned comparison procedures, 376
Plausibility of explanations, 480–482
Plausible rival hypotheses, 167

Policy analysis, 20, 527, 545–551
  benefits and limitations of, 551–553
  cost analysis, 548–551
  macro and micro approaches to, 546
  methods in, 547–548
Policy evaluation, 100–101
Policy events, analysis of, 507–517
Policy formulation, qualitative research and, 400
Policy proposals, credibility of, 553–554
Policy topics, 501–502
Political issues, 78
"Politics-of-education" research, 501
"Pool of meanings," 468
Population
  in qualitative research design, 169
  size of, 180
Population external validity, 193
Portfolio assessments, 255–256
"Portrayals," 539, 540
Positionality, 414
Positive correlation, 34
Positively skewed distributions, 218
Positive relationships, 228
Post hoc comparisons, 374–375
Posttest-only control group design, 339–342, 341
"Power" of a statistical test, 381–382
Precision, in educational research, 11
Predetermined categories, 473–474
Prediction studies, 292–296
Predictive evidence, 242
Predictor variable, 293
Pre-experimental design, 329–335
Preliminary literature review, 134–136
Preliminary searches, 120
Presupposition questions, 448

Pretesting, 189, 307, 332, 334
  of questionnaires, 267
Pretest-posttest control group design, 331, 335–339, 340
Pretest sensitization, 328
Primary data collection strategies, 428
Primary literature, 112–113. *See also* Secondary literature
  indexes for, 112
  index selection for, 120–122
  reading, 110
  sources for, 115–119
Primary sources, 504, 508–509
Printouts, of computer searches, 129–130
Privacy, in fieldwork, 422
Probability, in inferential statistics, 360
Probability sampling, 170–173. *See also* Nonprobability sampling
Probing, 271
Problem focus, 78–79
Problem formulation, 137–138. *See also* Problem reformulations
  in qualitative research, 90–99
  in quantitative research, 80–90
Problem reformulations, 94–95
  emergent design and, 96–97
Problem selection, significance of, 99–101
Problem statement, 578
  adequacy standards for, 101–102
  in analytical research, 508, 509
  analyzing, 110
  condensed, 95
  ethnographic, 98
  evaluating, 520
  general, 574
  historical, 98

Process evaluation, 537
Product evaluation, 537
Professional books, 113
Program Evaluation Standards, 530
Program planning evaluation, 537
Prolonged data collection, 437. *See also* Data collection
Prominent events, 539–540
Proportional sampling, 172
Proposals. *See* Research proposals
Propriety standards, 531
Prototypical studies, 15–16
Proxemics, 455
Psychological Abstracts, 116–117
Psychology, educational research and, 21
PsycINFO, 116
PsycLIT, 116
Publication Manual of the American Psychological Association, 576, 581
Public policy, 545
Public presentation, of meta-analysis, 138
Pure (fundamental) research, 17
Purposeful sampling, 175–176, 400–404, 507, 544
  at site, 433
  strategies for, 402
Purpose statements, in qualitative research, 95–99

Qualitative data analysis, 460–495
  coding topics and categories in, 466–475
  data management techniques in, 482–486
  discovery analysis in the field, 465–466
  inductive analysis, 462–464
  narrative structure and representation in, 486–492
  patterns in, 476–482

Qualitative data analysis (QDA) software, 484–486
Qualitative data collection techniques, 41–43
Qualitative field records, 92–93
Qualitative interviews, 548
Qualitative modes of inquiry, 35–39
Qualitative probability, 516
Qualitative questions, 445–448
Qualitative research, 14–16
    guidelines for evaluating, 69–70
    literature reviews in, 134–137
    phases of, 405
    problem formulation in, 90–99
    purpose and question statements in, 95–99
    reading, 55–69
    use of computers in, 485
Qualitative research design, 394–426
    case study design in, 398–399
    critical reflexivity in, 414
    data collection and analysis strategies in, 405–407
    disciplined subjectivity in, 411–414
    ethics in, 420–422
    extension of findings in, 414–419
    purpose and research questions in, 397
    purposeful sampling in, 400–404
    standards of adequacy in, 422–423
    subjects of, 169–180
    validity of, 407–410
Qualitative research problems, 76–77
Qualitative research proposals, guidelines for, 577–581
Qualitative research report, 56–69

Qualitative strategies, 427–459
    documents and artifact collection, 451–453
    entry into the field, 431–436
    field observations and supplementary techniques, 454–455
    foreshadowed problems and reformulations in, 429–431
    in-depth interviews, 443–451
    multimethod, 428–429
    participant observation, 437–443
    standards of adequacy for, 456
QualPage, 486
Quantitative data collection techniques, 40–41, 237–281
    interview schedules in, 267–271
    observation schedules in, 271–275
    paper-and-pencil tests, 250–256
    technical adequacy in, 239–250
    unobtrusive measures in, 275–277
Quantitative modes of inquiry, 31–35
Quantitative records, 502
Quantitative research, 14–16. *See also* Quantitative research design
    guidelines for evaluating, 53–55
    literature reviews and, 132–134
    problem formulation in, 80–90
    reading, 44–53
Quantitative research design, 164–203
    data collection techniques in, 180–185
    ethical and legal considerations in, 195–200
    external validity of, 193–195

    internal validity of, 186–193
    procedures in, 186
    purpose of, 166–169
Quantitative research proposals, guidelines for, 573–577
Quantitative research report, 45–51
Quarterly reviews, 113
Quasi-experimental designs, 342–347
    standards of adequacy for, 354
Quasi-experimental evaluations, 547–548
Quasi-experimental mode of inquiry, 32–33
Quasi-experimental pretest-posttest comparison group design, 344
Question matrix, 266
Questionnaires, 40, 257–267
    general format for, 266–267
    item format for, 265–266
    pilot testing of, 267
    steps in developing, 258
    types of items for, 260–265
    writing questions and statements for, 258–260
Question reformulations, 430–431
Questions. *See also* Interview questions; Questionnaires
    qualitative, 445–448
    relevance of, 259
Question sequence, 448–449
Question statements, in qualitative research, 95–99
Quota sampling, 176–177

Random assignment, 32
Randomization, 168
Random sampling, 169, 170, 170–171, 543, 544. *See also* Stratified random sampling
Range, 220–221
    calculation of, 607
Ranked questionnaire items, 264
Rank-order assessments, 264

Rank-order distribution, 210
Ratio scale measurement, 209
Reasoning, inductive, 91
Recording. *See also* Records
  of ethical decisions, 413
  of observations, 274–275
Records
  institutional, 452
  interview, 449–451
  quantitative, 502
  reflex, 442–443
"Red flags," identifying, 473
Reference group, 252
References, 53
  abstracting and organizing
    references, 130–131
  locating, 130
  in research proposals, 576,
    580
  specialized, 114
Reference works, specialized,
  510
Reflexivity, 16, 411. *See also*
    Critical reflexivity
  enhancing, 412–414
Reflex records, 442–443
Regression
  internal validity and, 334
  multiple, 294, 296
  statistical, 188–189
Regression coefficient, 294
Related literature, 108–109
Relationship, calculating
    measures of, 612–615
Relationship questions, 87
Relations to other variables,
    evidence based on,
    241–242
Reliability, 244–250. *See also*
    Test reliability
  effect on research, 248–250
  procedures for estimating,
    248
  types of, 245–247
Reliability coefficients, 245
  interpretation of, 247–248
Reliability estimates, types of,
  245
Relics, 503
Replication, 7
  avoiding, 109
Reporting. *See also* Reports
  of effect size, 368
  of reliability, 249

Report literature, 116
Reports, credibility of,
    553–554
Request for Proposal, 553
Research. *See also*
    Analytical research;
    Correlational research;
    Descriptive research;
    Educational research;
    Evaluation research;
    Experimental research;
    Historical research;
    Qualitative research;
    Quantitative research
  defined, 9–10
  effect of reliability on,
    248–250
  effect of validity on, 243
  ethics of, 196–199
  functions of, 16–21
  methodological criticisms
    of, 132–133
  observational, 271–275
  quantitative and qualitative
    approaches to, 14–16
  reading, 43–70
  as scientific and disci-
    plined inquiry, 7–8
  survey, 304–309
Research design, 30–31. *See
    also* Qualitative research
    design; Quantitative
    research design
  nonexperimental, 282–318
  pre-experimental, 329–335
Researcher bias, 412
Researcher purpose/focus,
    statements of, 449
Researcher responsibility, 198
Researchers
  multiple, 410
  participant, 410
  role of, 16, 416
Research ethics. *See* Ethics
Research hypotheses, 52,
    88–90, 179
  developing, 110
Research methods, 9, 15
Research problems, 14, 51,
    54, 74–106
  analyzing, 119
  complexity of, 23
  formulating in qualitative
    research, 90–99

formulating in quantitative
    research, 80–90
  nature of, 75–80
Research process, 13–14
  in literature reviews,
    137–138
Research proposals
  criticism of, 582–583
  guidelines for, 573–583
  preparation and criticism
    of, 581–583
Research purpose, 15
Research questions, 86–88,
    574. *See also*
    Questionnaires
  in qualitative research
    design, 397
Research Related to Children,
  117
Research role, 435–436, 579
  in qualitative research,
    396
Research subjects. *See*
    Subjects
Research synthesis, 7
Research topics, coding,
    466–468. *See also* Topics
Research traditions, 30
Resentful demoralization,
    192
Resources in Education (RIE),
    115–116, 122. *See also*
    RIE Document Resume
*Resources in Vocational
    Education*, 117
Respondents, competence of,
    259
Response processes, evidence
    based on, 241
Response sets, 256
Responsive evaluation, 539
Restriction in range, 300
Results (findings) section of a
    report, 52–53
Retrieval algorithms,
    151–152
Reversal (withdrawal)
    design, 350
Review exercises, answers to,
    560–572
*Review of Educational
    Research*, 113
Revisionist (reconstruction-
    ist) historians, 506

RIE Document Resume, 123
Rigorous research reviews, 137–139
Rival hypotheses, 167, 312
"Robots," 150
r ranks, 614. *See also* Pearson product-moment correlation coefficient (Pearson *r*)

Sample participants, 52
Samples, 169
    volunteer, 176–177
Sample size, 177–180
    in qualitative research design, 404
Sampling. *See also* Purposeful sampling
    by case type, 403–404
    in surveys, 306–307
Sampling bias, 300
Sampling distribution, 362
Sampling error, in inferential statistics, 360–363
Sampling frame, 169
Sampling methods, strengths and weaknesses of, 178–179
Sampling strategies, 579
Scaled questionnaire items, 261–264
Scatterplots, 228–230, 303
Scheffé's test, 374
Scholastic Assessment Test (SAT), 225–226
    trend analysis of scores in, 284
School improvements, 552
Science Citation Index (SCI), 118
Scientific inquiry, 8–9
    research as, 7–8
Scientific method, 9
Scorer agreement, 247
Scores, standard, 225–227
Script critiques, 446
Search engines, 115, 148, 149, 150. *See also* Metasearch engines
Search language, 110, 151–152
Search Wizard, 129
Secondary analysis, 547

Secondary literature, 112–113. *See also* Primary literature
    searching and reading, 110
    sources for reviews of, 111, 113–115
Secondary sources, 504, 509
    searching for, 114–115
Selected response questions, 261, 268–269
Selection, 187–188
    internal validity and, 332, 343
"Self in research," 442
Self-monitoring, researcher, 411
Semantic differential scales, 263–264
Semistructured questions, 269
Shotgun approach, 292
Significance
    of qualitative research design, 399–400
    statistical, 301
Significance of the problem, 99–101
"Significant differences," 249
"Significant" relationships, 180
Single group interrupted time-series design, 344–345
Single method design, 541
Single-subject designs, 348–353
    standards of adequacy for, 354–355
Single-subject modes of inquiry, 33
Single-variable rule, 349
Site, purposeful sampling at, 433
Site selection, 434, 579
    in qualitative research, 401, 432–433
Skewed distributions, 218
Smithsonian Science Information Exchange (SSIE), 118–119
Snowball sampling, 403, 434, 511
Social construction, 396

Social context, 416
Social desirability, 256
Social issues, 78
    qualitative research and, 400
Social map, 433
Social network, 579
Social Science Citation Index (SSCI), 118
Socioemotional Measures for Pre-School and Kindergarten Children, 184
Sociological Abstracts, 117
Software, qualitative data analysis (QDA), 484–485
Solomon four-group design, 342
Sorting, of categories for patterns, 480
Sourcebook of Mental Health Measures, 184
Sources
    evaluation of, 520
    for historical studies, 502–503
    location and criticism of, 508–515
Sources of variability, 166–167
Spatial map, 433
Spearman-Brown formula, 247
Spearman rank (rho), 614–615
Special surveys, 455
"Spiders," 150
Split-half reliability, 246–247
Spurious correlations, 299–301
Stability, coefficient of, 246
Standard deviation, 221–224, 225, 227
    calculation of, 608–609
Standard error, 362
Standardized open-ended interview, 444
Standardized tests, 250–251
    examples of, 253
Standards-based interpretation, 252
Standard scores, 225–227
    calculating, 609–612

Standards for Educational and Psychological Testing, 239

Standards of adequacy, 313–315
  for experimental designs, 353–355
  in qualitative research design, 422–423
  for qualitative strategies, 456

Stanine scores, 612

State Education Journal Index, 117

Statistical analysis, 543, 544

Statistical conclusions, 192–193

Statistical data, 452–453

Statistical hypothesis, 363

Statistical regression, 188–189, 332
  internal validity and, 343–344

Statistical significance, 301, 366

Statistics. *See also* Descriptive statistics; Inferential statistics
  calculations for, 604–621
  types of, 206–207

Stem-and-leaf display, 210

Strategies, 429

Stratified random sampling, 172–173

Stratified sampling, 169

Structured equation modeling, 296

Structured interviews, 40

Structured observations, 40

Structured questions, 261, 268–269

Student development, effects of education on, 552

Student files, 452

Studies
  financial constraints on, 179
  historical perspective on, 109
  instruments section of, 182

Study context, 488

Style manuals, 581

Subject attrition (mortality), 190, 332

Subject directories, 148–149

Subject effects, 192, 338

Subjectivity, in qualitative research, 411–414

Subjects, 169, 575

Summaries, writing, 465

Summary statistics, 206

Summative evaluation, 529–530

Supplementary techniques, 43, 454–455
  standards of adequacy for, 456

Survey batteries, 254

Survey instruments, 455

Survey Kit, The, 309

Survey population, 169

Survey research, 34, 304–309
  standards of adequacy in, 314–315

Surveys, 548
  special, 455

Synthesized abstractions, 94

Systematic sampling, 171–172

Tacit knowledge, 439

Taped interviews, 270–271

Target group, 533

Target population, 169
  for surveys, 306

t distribution, 371

Technical/quasi-statistical analytical style, 462

Telecommunications, Internet, 153

Template analytical style, 462

Temporal map, 433

Test content, evidence based on, 240–241

Test-criterion relationships, 242

Test Critiques, 184

Testimonies, oral, 502–503, 511

Testing programs, large-scale, 548

Test reliability, 181–182

Test-retest procedure, 246

Tests, 41. *See also* Instruments

Tests: A Comprehensive Reference for Assessments in Psychology, Education, and Business, 184

Tests and Measurements in Child Development, 184

Tests in Print, 183

Test validity, 181
  components of, 243

Textbase manager programs, 484

Text retriever programs, 484

Theory
  deductions from, 77
  defined, 8
  testing, 100

Thesaurus, 122

Thesaurus of ERIC Descriptors, 122

Theses indexes, 118

Three-way analysis of variance, 377

Time sampling, 274–275

Time-series designs, 344–347

Topic organization, refining, 470–471

Topics. *See also* Research topics
  in analytical research, 508
  developing as categories, 473
  generating from data, 469
  in quantitative research, 80–81

Tracking, 91

Tradeoffs, 546

Training
  interviewer, 272
  observer, 275

Trait causal modeling, 296

Transcripts, interview, 449–451

Treatment group, 325

Treatment replications, 191–192, 338

Trend studies, 284

Triangulation, 408, 478, 541

Trimodal distribution, 217

True (universe) score, 244

True experimental designs, 321, 335–342
  standards of adequacy for, 353–354

True experimental mode of inquiry, 32
T-scores, calculating, 611
t-test, 368–373, 617–621
Tukey's HSD test, 374
Two-tailed test of significance, 370
Two-way analysis of variance, 377
Type I error, 365
Type II error, 365
Typicality, 417–418

Understanding, extensions of, 100
Universe (target population), 169
Universe (true) score, 244
Unobtrusive measures, 41, 275–277
Unstructured questions, 269
Usefulness, in qualitative research design, 414–415
Utility standards, 531

Validity. *See also* Test validity
    design, 167–169
    effect on research, 243
    of qualitative designs, 407–410
    in quantitative data collection, 239–250
Value inventories, 256–257
Value pluralism, 538
Variability. *See also* Sources of variability
    calculations of, 606–609
    measures of, 219–227
    sources of, 166–167
Variables
    control of, 323–324
    in deductive logic, 82–84
    delimiting, 169
    in interpreting correlations, 298
    manipulation of, 322
Variance
    calculation of, 607–608
    of a distribution, 223
Variant sources, 512

Verbatim interviews, 409
Verification, in educational research, 11–12
Video conferencing, 153
Visual representations, 480, 489–492
Visual techniques, 43, 454
Volunteer samples, 176–177

Web pages, publishing, 147
Web sites, educational, 153–155
Whole language classroom, 92, 95
Withdrawal design, 350
Word processors, 484
World Wide Web, 146

Yahoo!, 148, 149
Yearbooks, 114

Zero-order studies, 291–292
z-scores, 226
    calculating, 610–611